MI5, the Cold War, and the Rule of Law

MI5, the Cold War, and the Rule of Law

K. D. EWING
JOAN MAHONEY
ANDREW MORETTA

OXFORD
UNIVERSITY PRESS

OXFORD
UNIVERSITY PRESS

Great Clarendon Street, Oxford, OX2 6DP,
United Kingdom

Oxford University Press is a department of the University of Oxford.
It furthers the University's objective of excellence in research, scholarship,
and education by publishing worldwide. Oxford is a registered trade mark of
Oxford University Press in the UK and in certain other countries

First Edition published in 2020

Impression: 1

Published in the United States of America by Oxford University Press
198 Madison Avenue, New York, NY 10016, United States of America

British Library Cataloguing in Publication Data
Data available

Library of Congress Control Number: 2019946269

ISBN 978–0–19–881862–5

Printed and bound by
CPI Group (UK) Ltd, Croydon, CR0 4YY

Preface

This book started as a general survey of civil liberties during the Cold War. As we dug into the material, it was clear that everything led back to the Communist Party and related bodies. Although no longer criminalized, as it had been in 1921 and 1925, and as it was in the United States, the treatment of the Communist Party nevertheless gave rise to serious questions of freedom of association.

This in turn led back to MI5 and it became even clearer that an understanding of civil liberties could not be secured without a deeper understanding of the role of the Security Service. Here we were fortunate to be writing shortly after the publication of MI5's authorized history, which revealed much about the Service, but fortunate also that important information about MI5 is now available in the National Archives. This is information that has been unavailable to previous generations of civil liberties scholars.

There are, however, serious limitations about the information released to the National Archives, which we discuss in the text that follows. But even in relation to that which is available, a major constraint is the time, energy, and awareness required when examining the material. So far as awareness is required, the files require forensic examination to identify redactions, to assess the importance and purpose of redactions, and to interpret the significance of what has been preserved.

The book began as a joint project between Ewing and Mahoney, and indeed before then in Mahoney's Ph.D. work completed in 1989. But it was radically transformed when Moretta joined the team in 2012. His skill, attention to detail, and drafting of complex material led to a major refocusing of the project, and a greater understanding of the issues to be confronted in the study as a whole. This is work that neither Ewing nor Mahoney could have undertaken either alone or together; Moretta's contribution has been immense.

In the course of this research we gradually realized that the volume of material is such that it is impossible to provide a sensible account of civil liberties during the Cold War in a single volume. This is in effect volume one, dealing with the State agency directly responsible for restraints. The publication of a second volume dealing with wider questions of freedom of association, freedom of assembly, and freedom of expression will thus have to wait, though much of it has been written.

In this volume, we are thus concerned with the powers, activities, and accountability of MI5, principally in the period from 1945 to 1964. It was a body without statutory authority, with no statutory powers, and with no obvious forms of statutory accountability. It was established as a counter-espionage agency, yet in the period of the study was beset by espionage scandals on a frequency that suggested if not high levels of incompetence, then high levels of distraction and the squandering of resources.

The scandals in question included those involving scientists Alan Nunn-May, Klaus Fuchs, and Bruno Pontecorvo, as a result of which the most sensitive weapons information was passed to the Russians. But they also included the disappearance of Burgess and Maclean (and later Philby), and subsequently the prosecutions of Blake, the Portland spy ring, and Christopher Vassall. The Russians had penetrated the highest levels of British government, and indeed could claim a contribution to the collapse of the Tory administration in 1964.

While all this was going on, MI5 was worried about the membership lists of the Communist Party, monitoring inane conversations between Party officials and their spouses, finding out who was supplying cars to Communist Party electoral candidates, infiltrating organizations such as the Haldane Society of Socialist Lawyers, and following a lawyer with historic Communist Party connections to a restaurant rendezvous with a mistress. Easy work plodding around after people at public expense, but pointless and ineffective.

As suggested, in the pages that follow we address four questions:

- the evolution of MI5's mandate, which set out its role and functions and to a limited extent the lines of accountability (chapters 2 and 3);
- the surveillance targets of MI5 and the surveillance methods that it used for this purpose, with a focus in two chapters on MPs and lawyers, respectively (chapters 4–8);
- the purposes for which this information was used, principally to exclude people from certain forms of employment (chapters 9–12); and
- the accountability of MI5 or the lack thereof for the way in which it discharged its responsibilities under the mandate (chapters 13 and 14).

As the title of the book suggests, as lawyers our concern is to consider these questions within the context of the Rule of Law, one of the core principles of the British constitution, the values of which it was the duty of the Security Service to uphold. One concern has been to question whether there is evidence that MI5 operated without legal authority or exceeded the legal authority that did exist, though we are mindful that material is carefully weeded and redacted before being released to the National Archives.

In writing this book we have acquired debts to large numbers of people, none of whom is responsible for anything that follows. It would, however, be remiss on our part not to acknowledge (i) our intellectual debt to Tony Bradley and John Hendy, the late Paul O'Higgins, and David Whyte; (ii) the support we have received from our families and academic institutions; and (iii) the access we have had to the National Archives and various libraries which hold the private papers of a number of figures and organizations featured in the text that follows.

The libraries include the British Library of Political and Economic Science (LSE) (which holds the papers of several figures referred to in the text); Cambridge University Library; the Hull History Centre (which holds the National Council for Civil Liberties (NCCL) archive); the Peoples' History Museum, Manchester (which holds Labour Party and the Communist Party archives, respectively); the Squire Law Library, Cambridge; and the University of Sussex Library (which holds the papers of Benn Levy).

We also record that this work has not enjoyed the dubious benefit of any grants or funding by external agencies, the curse of modern academia which, in the long term, will make it more difficult for work of this kind to be undertaken. Small parts of what follows were published in T. Campbell, K. D. Ewing, and A. Tomkins (eds), *The Legal Protection of Human Rights: Sceptical Essays* (Oxford: OUP, 2011), the *Modern Law Review*, the *Socialist Lawyer*, and the *Morning Star*, and we are grateful for permission to reproduce that material here.

We are grateful to Jamie Berezin and Eve Ryle-Hodges at OUP for their initial enthusiastic support for the project, and particularly to Catherine Rogers for her patience and encouragement thereafter.

KDE, JM, AM

13 February 2019

Contents

List of Abbreviations

ACPO	Association of Chief Police Officers
AEU	Amalgamated Engineering Union
AUEW	Amalgamated Union of Engineering Workers
AUT	Association of University Teachers
BBC	British Broadcasting Corporation
BCP	British Communist Party
BEA	British European Airways
BOAC	British Overseas Airways Corporation
BPC	British Peace Committee
CIA	Central Intelligence Agency
CND	Campaign for Nuclear Disarmament
CPGB	Communist Party of Great Britain
CPLG	Communist Party Lawyers' Group
CPP	Convention People's Party
CPS	Criminal Prosecution Service
CSCA	Civil Service Clerical Association
DG	Director General
DDG	Deputy Director General
DPP	Director of Public Prosecutions
DSS	Director Security Service
ECtHR	European Court of Human Rights
ETU	Electrical Trades' Union
FBI	Federal Bureau of Investigation
GC&CS	Government Code and Cypher School
GCHQ	Government Communications Headquarters
GPO	General Post Office
GRU	Russian Military Intelligence
HMSO	Her Majesty's Stationery Office
HOW	Home Office Warrant
IADL	International Association of Democratic Lawyers
ICI	Imperial Chemical Industries
ILO	International Labour Organization
ILP	Independent Labour Party
IRD	Information Research Department
IRIS	Industrial Research and Information Services Ltd
IUS	International Union of Students
JTUDC	Joint Trade Union Defence Committee
LCC	London County Council
LRD	Labour Research Department

LSE	London School of Economics
LSIC	London Signals Intelligence Centre
NAAFI	Navy, Army and Air Force Institutes
NCCL	National Council for Civil Liberties
NEC	National Executive Committee
NGO	non-governmental organization
NJAC	National Joint Advisory Council
NRC	National Research Council (Canada)
NUM	National Union of Mineworkers
NUS	National Union of Students
NUVB	National Union of Vehicle Builders
PF	Personal File
PLP	Parliamentary Labour Party
PPU	Peace Pledge Union
PUS	Permanent Under-Secretary
PV	positive vetting
PWC	Port Workers' Committee
RAE	Royal Aircraft Establishment
SF	Special Facilities
SIS	Secret Intelligence Service
SLO	Security Liaison Officer
SOE	Special Operations Executive
TGWU	Transport and General Worker's Union
TUC	Trades Union Congress
WFTU	World Federation of Trade Unions
WPC	World Peace Council
YCL	Young Communist League

1
Introduction

I.

The Security Service was created in 1909, initially to deal with the problems of German espionage.[1] Although its existence was acknowledged by government and its head sometimes referred to in the press, the Official Secrets Act 1911 ensured that the activities of MI5 were protected from unwelcome public attention for much of the twentieth century. During this time, however, the great bulk of its activity was devoted to the Communist Party, its members and related organizations, and during the Cold War this was MI5's principal pre-occupation.[2] Working with the Metropolitan Police Special Branch and provincial police forces, MI5's interests expanded to include the wider Communist 'orbit',[3] and then to cover a wider constellation still.

But while our concern is mainly with MI5, it was of course one of only a number of security agencies, the others being the SIS or MI6 and GCHQ.[4] Both were responsible mainly for overseas activity, though in the case of GCHQ, its responsibilities included the monitoring of signals between London and the USSR.[5] Unlike MI5, however, the policy of successive governments was to refuse even to acknowledge the existence of SIS, a policy expressly acknowledged in a Cabinet minute as late as 1962. Such was the secrecy of GCHQ in contrast, that its existence was unknown even to senior ministers, with documents referring to GCHQ being censored before circulation to the Cabinet.[6]

That said, a great deal has already been written about the Security and Intelligence Services, particularly by historians. This includes a sympathetic and

[1] See C. Andrew, *Secret Service: The Making of the British Intelligence Community* (London, 1985) for an engaging historical account.

[2] For legal developments between 1920 and 1945, see K. D. Ewing and C. A. Gearty, *The Struggle for Civil Liberties: Political Freedom and the Rule of Law in Britain, 1918–1945* (Oxford, 2001).

[3] See Industrial Relations and Research Services (IRIS), *The Communist Solar System* (London, 1957).

[4] Known variously as the GC&CS, the LSIC, 'Eastcote', and during the early 1950s, and thereafter, as 'Cheltenham'. See R. J. Aldrich, *GCHQ—The Uncensored Story of Britain's Most Secret Intelligence Agency* (London, 2010), pp. 85–6. The GC&CS became better known as GCHQ in the immediate aftermath of the war and moved from the west London suburbs (Eastcote) to Cheltenham between 1952 and 1954 (ibid., p. 103). The GC&CS had famously been based at Bletchley Park in Buckinghamshire earlier in the war.

[5] See ibid., Ch. 4, and TNA, HW 15 series (Government Code and Cypher School and Government Communications Headquarters: Venona Project: Records).

[6] TNA, PREM 11/1587 (Minute from Home Secretary to Anthony Eden, 1 March 1956).

MI5, the Cold War, and the Rule of Law. K. D. Ewing, Joan Mahoney, and Andrew Moretta, Oxford University Press (2020). © K. D. Ewing, Joan Mahoney, and Andrew Moretta. DOI: 10.1093/oso/9780198818625.001.0001

well-received authorized history of MI5 by a leading academic expert specializing in intelligence and security studies.[7] A valuable resource providing great insight, this latter work comprehensively covers the ground, with benefits that only privileged and exclusive access to information can provide. Yet the questions asked by the political historian are nevertheless not necessarily the questions that would be asked by a lawyer, though there will inevitably be important overlaps between the two. But for the lawyer the central questions are about power and its accountability.

The lawyer is thus typically concerned with three questions. The first is the source of the legal authority of a security and intelligence agency, in this case MI5. How was it established and by whom? Second, for what purposes was it established, and how were these purposes defined? And third, what powers were given to the organization to carry out its purposes? Alongside these three central questions are a number of others, which are perhaps just as important. Thus, what forms of control were in place to ensure that MI5 did not overstep the mark and exceed the scope of its purpose or authority? This in turn leads to other questions, relating to the accountability of the Service generally, and its accountability in relation to specific operations.

II.

But although this is a field dominated by scholars from security and intelligence studies, lawyers have also made a mark. The great pioneer was Professor Sir David Williams, whose *Not in the Public Interest* was written more than fifty years before we put fingers to keyboard.[8] Although Professor E. C. S. Wade at the University of Cambridge had previously covered the Security Service and related matters in his textbook on *Constitutional Law*,[9] Williams' account is the first systematic legal study to cover MI5, its purpose, and its powers. And while there have been important articles by other scholars, it was some thirty years before Williams' book could claim to have a peer, with Lustgarten and Leigh's *In from the Cold* taking legal scholarship in this field to heights that have not been scaled since.[10]

Lustgarten and Leigh started with the assumption that 'all states are entitled to protect their territory from invasion or attempts to detach portions of it by insurrection', and that 'efforts to gain access to certain narrow and specific categories of information ought to be prevented to protect any nation's immediate or

[7] C. Andrew, *The Defence of the Realm—The Authorised History of MI5* (London, 2009).

[8] D. G. T. Williams, *Not in the Public Interest—The Problem of Security in Democracy* (London, 1965).

[9] E. C. S. Wade and G. G. Phillips, *Constitutional Law* (6th edn by E. C. S. Wade, London, 1960), ch. 40. There is also discussion of security matters in H. Street, *Freedom, the Individual and the Law* (Harmondsworth, 1963), a pioneering work of a different kind.

[10] L. Lustgarten and I. Leigh, *In from the Cold: National Security and Parliamentary Democracy* (Oxford, 1994).

longer-term defence needs'.[11] We do not start with that assumption, nor do we begin with the objective that underpins Lustgarten and Leigh, which is to develop a 'democratic conception of national security' as a justification for 'extraordinary measures' in the interests of the defence of the realm or national security,[12] though we see that their approach shares many of the questions relating to power and accountability with which we are concerned.

We write in contrast from a more sceptical tradition, perhaps less willing to be dismissive of 'organisations engaging in fanciful conspiracies and elaborate deceptions'.[13] We write also in a civil liberties tradition, and as such we write from a position of distrust of State power and State agencies engaged principally in the practice of political discrimination. In the post-war era this meant the discriminatory treatment of a growing body of people on the Left of the political spectrum, and with it surveillance practices which by our endeavours we now know to have been operating on an industrial scale. In writing in this tradition, we acknowledge the benefits of access to security files now on deposit at the National Archives, benefits not available to civil liberties and other legal scholars who have gone before us.

These files—which are being deep mined by security and intelligence scholars—cast new light on the operation of MI5 and the police: their authority, influence, powers, practices, and accountability. That said, the files are not without their limitations, to which we return later in this chapter. In the meantime, however, our aim, in contrast to that of Lustgarten and Leigh, is to assess the extent to which—if at all—MI5's violations of civil liberties were sanctioned by the law, and by the human rights obligations then emerging. We present an account in which MI5 operated under a mandate with doubtful legal provenance; engaged in activities with no legal authority, sometimes in violation of the rights of others; and without any effective legal or political accountability.

III.

The lawyer's questions referred to in Part I are asked against a background of constitutional principle. The first and most significant of these principles is the Rule of Law, now recognized by the Constitutional Reform Act 2005 (s. 1). In recognizing the principle, the latter nevertheless fails to define it, though an elegant attempt to provide a working definition was provided by Lord Bingham in a well-received lecture at Cambridge University shortly after the 2005 Act was passed.[14] But it is

11 ibid., p. 35.
12 ibid.
13 ibid., p. vii.
14 Lord Bingham, 'The Rule of Law' [2007] 66 *CLJ* 67.

equally important to acknowledge as well that the principle is 'recognized' but not 'created' by statute: the Rule of Law does not exist because of the Constitutional Reform Act 2005. On the contrary, it is an established principle of the British constitution, despite the chronic uncertainty and vigorous academic disputes over many years in the United Kingdom and beyond about its meaning. These disputes are no less important for being often hair splitting and sometimes pinhead dancing.

The starting point for any discussion of the Rule of Law is still the work of A. V. Dicey, whose influence it has proved impossible for contemporary scholars to shake off. E. C. S. Wade, writing during the Cold War, highlighted in particular Dicey's exposition of the Rule of Law as the aspect of Dicey's work which 'had most influence and at the same time has received most modern criticism'.[15] According to Dicey, the Rule of Law had three meanings, the first of which was 'the absolute supremacy or pre-dominance of regular law as opposed to the influence of arbitrary power', excluding 'the existence of arbitrariness, or prerogative, or even of wide discretionary authority on the part of government'.[16] In this sense, 'the rule of law is contrasted with every system of government based on the exercise by persons in authority of wide, arbitrary, or discretionary powers of restraint',[17] and as such was 'peculiar to England, or to those countries . . . that had inherited "English institutions"'.[18]

Dicey's second principle also continues to have a contemporary resonance, though perhaps not as intended. This is the principle of equality before the law in the sense of the 'equal subjection of all classes to ordinary law of the land administered by the ordinary courts',[19] said to convey the idea that 'no man is above the law; that officials like private citizens are under a duty to obey the same law; and . . . that there are no administrative courts to which are referred claims by citizens against the State'.[20] That principle was to be seen at work in the great decision in *Entick v Carrington*,[21] a decision which illustrates all three of Dicey's principles. In that case, a Home Office official was held to have no right to enter and search the premises of John Entick without clear legal authority, a warrant issued by the Home Secretary being insufficient in circumstances where there was no legislation authorizing the Home Secretary to issue such a warrant. No one was above the law, not even government officials; State necessity was no defence.[22]

[15] Wade and Phillips (n 9), p. 59. Wade had in fact just edited the tenth (and the last) edition of Dicey's seminal text.

[16] A. V. Dicey, *Introduction to the Study of the Law of the Constitution* (10th edn by E. C. S. Wade, London, 1959), p. 202.

[17] ibid., p. 188.

[18] ibid.

[19] ibid., p. 202.

[20] Wade and Phillips (n 9), p. 60.

[21] (1765) 19 St Tr 1030.

[22] ibid. But compare *Council of Civil Service Unions v Minister of State for Civil Service* [1985] AC 374.

This emphasis on (i) regular law; and (ii) equality before the law led inexorably to Dicey's third principle, which was a celebration of the constitutional importance of the common law as the basis for the protection of fundamental freedoms:

> [W]ith us the law of the constitution, the rules which in foreign countries naturally form part of a constitutional code, are not the source but the consequence of the rights of individuals, as defined and enforced by the Courts; that, in short, the principles of private law have with us been by the action of the Courts and Parliament so extended as to determine the position of the Crown and of its servants; thus the constitution is the result of the ordinary law of the land.[23]

Although elliptically expressed, this and accompanying passages are usually taken to mean that the Rule of Law embraces ideas about the protection of the rights of individuals. But as in *Entick v Carrington*,[24] for Dicey such protection is a consequence of the common law and a sovereign Parliament, which offer guarantees equal to, if not greater than, those to be found in the constitutional codes of foreign countries.

IV.

As suggested by E. C. S. Wade, Dicey's formulation of the Rule of Law has been the subject of powerful criticism, not least by the young Ivor Jennings, who was to write generally in an excoriating account that Dicey's classic text was no more than an expression of (Whig) political prejudice masquerading as legal principle.[25] Not only did Dicey fail to understand the true nature of the constitution, his account of the Rule of Law was said to be based on a 'partial presentation of the facts', and to represent no more than 'his own subjective notions', presented as 'the firm and unalterable principles of English constitutional law'.[26] Jennings' most biting criticism, however, is addressed to Dicey's suggestion that the Rule of Law was a sufficient basis for the protection of civil liberties. Turning Dicey on his head, in the first edition of his book Jennings claimed that:

[23] Dicey (n 16), p. 203. This last passage was taken to mean that the 'legal rights of the subject, e.g. his freedom of action and speech, are secured not by guaranteed rights proclaimed in a formal code but by the operation of the ordinary remedies of private law available against those who unlawfully interfere with his liberty of action, whether they be private citizens or officials' (ibid., p. 61).

[24] (1765) 19 St Tr 1030.

[25] W. I. Jennings, *The Law and the Constitution* (5th edn, London, 1959), p. 308. On Jennings, and *The Law and the Constitution* in particular, see K. D. Ewing, '*The Law and the Constitution*: Manifesto of the Progressive Party' (2004) 67 MLR 716.

[26] Jennings (n 25), p. 54.

> The immunities which the people of many other countries possess as fundamental rights protected by their constitution are with us merely liberties left to us by the ordinary law. They may be less or greater in England than in other countries, for it depends entirely on the law in force for the time being. Since they are given by the law, they may be taken away by the law. An ordinary Act of Parliament is sufficient to extinguish them. A Government with a majority in both Houses of Parliament can thus abolish any or all of the personal liberties, no matter how 'fundamental' they may be considered to be by the minority.[27]

The young Ivor Jennings had a point which he embellished with the claim that while Britain 'has the reputation of being one of the freest of all countries', that was beginning to change:

> The old law is being revived not to enable the constitutional parties to interfere with each other, but to enable any of them to put down the small but growing Communist Party. For that party not only believes that a radical reorganisation of society is not possible without revolution, but actually preaches revolution. Once more, therefore, the musty weapons have been taken from the legal armoury. *It has been shown that the citizen has no right of free speech, of free association, and of free assembly, according to law.*[28]

Yet for all his criticism of Dicey, Jennings was to relent in subsequent editions of his book, in which he abandoned notions of the 'reign of law', in favour of a model of the 'rule of law', which seemed remarkably similar in its core aspects to Dicey.[29] Writing during the Cold War, Jennings defined the Rule of Law to mean (i) that 'all governmental powers, save those of the representative legislature, shall be distributed and determined by reasonably precise laws'; (ii) a notion of equality whereby 'among equals the laws should be equal and should be equally administered, that like should be treated alike'; and (iii) in the sphere of the criminal law a requirement that 'the limits of police powers should be rigidly defined'. The only point of potentially continuing disagreement was in relation to Dicey's third principle, about which Jennings was silent, on whether the protection of Dicey's rights of the individual was an essential element of the Rule of Law.

Jennings' apparent conversion thus reflected what was in the 1950s an emerging liberal consensus around the Rule of Law, or what Wade described as a 'universal discussion and endeavour' to formulate the basic elements of the principle, 'now considered as a basic idea which can serve to unite lawyers of many differing

[27] W. I. Jennings, *The Law and the Constitution* (1st edn, London, 1933), p. 246.

[28] ibid. Emphasis added. Jennings is referring to *Elias v Pasmore* [1934] 2 KB 164; *Thomas v Sawkins* [1935] 2 KB 249; and *Duncan v Jones* [1936] 1 KB 218.

[29] See Ewing (n 25), pp. 739–80.

systems'.[30] But whatever the importance of the Rule of Law as a constitutional principle, Jennings had been right to emphasize that it was a deeply ideological tool that had at best a limited effect in protecting liberty. That openly ideological purpose was to serve a different end during the Cold War, with the Rule of Law being deployed not in Dicey-esque terms to defend the principles of economic liberalism over advancing social liberalism, but to defend capitalism against socialism, or at least the version of the latter practised in Soviet Russia. This is quite explicit in the work of E. C. S. Wade, who, drawing on Dicey and others, outlines the core elements of the Rule of Law ('as the mark of a free society'),[31] before claiming that:

> it is only necessary to contrast the state of affairs in the totalitarian states, with their apparatus of secret police and people's courts administering not law, but the orders of those who can dictate what is the people's will.[32]

Yet we too had a secret police, which indeed is the focus of this study. In light of the foregoing it would be expected that MI5 would be both empowered and constrained by the Rule of Law. But it was neither. The Security Service operated in secret, it did so without a statutory mandate, and it cut across personal liberty without legal authority. This was done to defend the values which its own operations and activities compromised. Apart from the hypocrisy, at a doctrinal level this tells us much about the nature of the Rule of Law as a constitutional principle, reflected in Wade's important insight that the Rule of Law is not a 'fixed principle of law from which there can be no departure'.[33] In the same way—as Jennings points out—that the Rule of Law can adapt to empower the police to quell Communist dissent in the 1930s, so in the 1970s and 1980s it can adapt retrospectively to authorize the behaviour of government and the Security Service in the entire post-war era. By judicial sleight of hand, the Rule of Law no longer required State agencies to have legal authority for their actions, but simply required them not to act unlawfully.[34] The difference is fundamental, though the judicial licence extended in 1979, would not have been known to or predicted by MI5 and its advisers in the period covered by this book, even though it would draw a veil of legality over much of what is discussed in the pages that follow.

[30] Wade and Phillips (n 9), p. 70.

[31] ibid., p. 72.

[32] ibid. On political vetting of jurors and justice behind closed doors, see Chapter 14.

[33] See Chapter 14; ibid., p. 72. Wade also claims that: 'the rule of law may be explained not merely in terms of positive law and legal institutions but also as meaning a climate of legality in which the citizens of Western Europe and North America live and value so highly that they wish to preserve it' (ibid., p. 73).

[34] *Malone v Metropolitan Police Commissioner* [1979] Ch 344.

V.

The Rule of Law is perhaps a preoccupation of lawyers, though it is nevertheless important in underpinning the suspicion of arbitrary powers and the defence of liberty. There is, however, a different tradition to acknowledge which promotes respect for civil liberties not simply as a feature of the Rule of Law, but as an autonomous constitutional principle, fully recognized by a generation of progressive British public lawyers even before the Human Rights Act 1998 enabled the bulk of the European Convention on Human Rights to be enforced in the domestic courts.[35] It was also an autonomous constitutional principle recognized by the post-war Labour government, which was anxious to restore the liberties that had been lost in war time. Famously committing to restoration in *Let us Face the Future*, the Labour Party's seminal general election manifesto announced that:

> The Labour Party stands for freedom—for freedom of worship, freedom of speech, freedom of the Press. The Labour Party will see to it that we keep and enlarge these freedoms, and that we enjoy again the personal civil liberties we have, of our own free will, sacrificed to win the war.[36]

This commitment to civil liberties was expressed in a remarkable lecture delivered by the then Home Secretary on 16 October 1948.[37] Not remarkable in the sense that it was likely to stop the traffic, or even to make it to the BBC News. But remarkable in the sense of the glimpse it provided of the constitution, and those who were empowered and constrained by it. Remarkable too in the sense that it is inconceivable that the same tone would be struck by a Home Secretary in public (or private) today, such is the change that has taken place in the Home Office since. The Home Secretary in question was James Chuter Ede, who occupied the position for the whole period of the Attlee government, briefly combining the office with the position of Leader of the House in 1951.[38] Addressing the theme of 'Parliament and the Liberty of the Subject', Chuter Ede spoke to his audience about 'the balance between civil liberty and orderly government which is the main concern of our complex system of government to preserve'.[39]

[35] Well-known leading exponents of this legal scholarly tradition in the Cold War era include Professors Paul O'Higgins (Cambridge and KCL), Harry Street (Manchester), and D. G. T. Williams (Cambridge). On the contemporary significance of the ECHR, see Wade and Phillips (n 9), p. 70. It was ratified by the United Kingdom on 8 March 1951.

[36] Labour Party, *Let us Face the Future* (London, 1945), p. 3.

[37] J. Chuter Ede, 'Parliament and the Liberty of the Subject' (1947) 1 *Parliamentary Affairs* 10.

[38] Chuter Ede retired from the House of Commons in 1964, and was appointed to the House of Lords. He died in 1965.

[39] Chuter Ede (n 37), p. 10.

Reminding those present that it is 'on the wisdom and vigilance of Parliament that the preservation of this system depends', Chuter Ede added that 'in most periods of history' no attempt has been made to preserve the balance to which he referred. The scales had 'fallen heavily on the side of order, and this has generally been regarded as right and proper'. In the process 'we sometimes fail to realise how precarious is the belief in liberty and how recent is the development of the civil liberties we enjoy, and too often take for granted'.[40] Clearly affected by the memory of fascism and war—time controls, Chuter Ede reflected on the 'long ages in the history of every country, our own included, in which authority has prevailed and its stereotyped ideas have been docilely accepted from generation to generation'. With an urgency of tone, Chuter Ede was to debunk Magna Carta as the 'palladium of our liberties', on the ground that 'we cannot attribute to the autocratic nobles and prelates assembled at Runnymede any conception of civil liberty as we now understand it'.[41]

Indeed, it is possible to find a trace in Magna Carta of only one of the four great civil liberties. The latter is the freedom from arrest and imprisonment, those missing according to Chuter Ede being freedom of speech, freedom of association, and freedom of assembly. These are said to have been relatively modern creations, having been established only within the previous 150 years, though that may be an optimistic assessment, given the propensity in Britain too for these liberties to be 'abandoned in a crisis in favour of authoritarianism'.[42] Nevertheless, in a simple but brilliant insight, Chuter Ede went on to assert that:

> The essence of liberty is freedom to criticise the authorities, to persuade others that the Government is wrong and that the laws ought to be amended, and to be in a position, if one can persuade enough people, to bring about changes in the law or in methods of administration.[43]

There is no equivocation or exception, in a lecture that draws freely on Mill and Tocqueville, while dismissing not only Magna Carta but also Milton. The latter's *Areopagitica* was not 'stating generally recognised principles but appealing against the habit of that fiercely ideological age of demanding liberty for one's own group in order to deny it to others'.[44] That is not a criticism that could be made of Chuter Ede in what is probably the strongest and most thoughtful defence of civil liberties ever articulated by a British Home Secretary.

[40] ibid., p. 11.
[41] ibid.
[42] ibid., p. 12.
[43] ibid.
[44] ibid., p. 11.

VI.

The commitment to constitutional principle that the foregoing represented ought not to be under-estimated. But—as with the Rule of Law—nor should it be exaggerated, for as Chuter Ede pointed out the challenge for government was one of constantly balancing liberty with order: the former could never be absolute. And although Chuter Ede won his spurs for stoutly defending liberty in the early years of the Attlee government, these were to lose their shine shortly after he delivered his impressive speech, with his lengthy bans on marches in London,[45] his advocacy for statutory restrictions on Communist activity during the Korean War,[46] and his use of immigration powers to exclude Communists.[47] As Home Secretary, it is also the case that at the time, Chuter Ede had no responsibility for defence or security, matters that were to be transferred to his successor. Here too a balance is to be struck, but here too we find that even as Chuter Ede was delivering his lecture, the platform on which he was standing was beginning to give way beneath him. That balance was to tilt even more under Chuter Ede's successor, a man with a much-exaggerated reputation as a defender of liberty.

The period after the Second World War was one of ambitious restoration of civil liberties, and in some respects it parallels the early years of the Blair government, when the same innocence produced the Human Rights Act 1998. But despite the claims about liberty, such periods were exceptional in a century where liberty was easily sacrificed in the interests of public order and national security, civil liberties at best providing the framework within which controls were imposed and a basis against which these controls were to be justified. Chuter Ede was either naïve or disingenuous, for even at the time of his speech there was a legacy of restraint and control that a lecture alone would not dispel. There was, of course, the war, during which Fascists and Fascist sympathizers were famously interned (as had been foreign nationals during the First World War).[48] But although members of the Communist Party avoided the same fate, and although the Party was not proscribed during the period of its neutrality, in the early stages of the war the *Daily Worker* and a number of other Communist publications were controversially banned in 1941.[49]

Like the Rule of Law scholars writing in a different genre, Chuter Ede underestimated the role and impact of the courts in restricting liberty (and he had curiously

[45] D. Renton, *Fascism, Anti-Fascism and Britain in the 1940s* (London, 2000), p. 76.

[46] K. D. Ewing, J. Mahoney, and A. Moretta, 'Civil Liberties and the Korean War' (2018) 81 *MLR* 395.

[47] TNA, CAB 129/38 ('Naturalisation Policy', Memorandum by the Home Secretary, 16 March 1950). This step was taken in the aftermath of Klaus Fuchs' conviction. Hitherto Communist Party membership or association had not been regarded as a reason for refusal, 'provided the applicant was of good character and not engaged in any activity detrimental to [the] country' (ibid.).

[48] *Liversidge v Anderson* [1942] AC 206.

[49] HC Debs, 22 January 1941, col. 185. For details, see W. Rust, *The Story of the Daily Worker* (London, 2010 edn). See pp. 55–6 below.

little to say about their role in protecting it). Although it is true that Parliament introduced the Public Order Act 1936 to authorize the Home Secretary to ban marches (mainly by the British Union of Fascists),[50] it was the courts that convicted leading Communists for seditious conspiracy in 1925.[51] And it was the judges who authorized the entry, search, and seizure of property belonging to the progressive National Unemployed Workers Movement, authorized police infiltration at a meeting of the Communist Party about the Incitement to Disaffection Bill, and authorized the police effectively to prohibit the right of public meeting on the part of a Communist Party activist.[52] In the first of these cases, it was held expressly by the court in a manner implied in the other two that the actions of the police otherwise unlawful could be justified on the grounds of State necessity. That is a dangerous concept that had been repudiated by the judges in 1765,[53] yet which was to reappear during another judicial crackdown on liberty some fifty years later.[54]

But just as the 1910s (First World War), the 1920s (the Communist Party and the General Strike), the 1930s (the rise of fascism and the Communist resistance to it), and the 1940s (the Second World War) were decades of civil liberties restraint,[55] so were the 1950s (Cold War). This is represented randomly by the banning of the Sheffield Peace Congress (despite the acknowledged absence of any legal authority to ban meetings),[56] the prosecution and conviction of unofficial strikers by a Labour government,[57] and the brutal treatment of protestors against the Suez War under a Conservative government.[58] It is also represented in the minutes of the Official Committee on Communism in 1950 unearthed by Maguire, where it is recorded that senior civil servants were now advising that:

> 'If there is one thing more certain than another', the Cabinet Committee concluded, 'it is that the English Channel is no defence against [fifth-column] penetration'. Consequently, the British Government could not 'treat Communism in the United Kingdom as a democratic political issue detached from the main Soviet threat to our existence'. It was a national security concern, not just a domestic policy issue. Was it not, therefore, 'quixotic to insist on extending to the

50 Ewing and Gearty (n 2), ch. 6.

51 ibid., ch. 4.

52 *Elias v Pasmore* [1934] 2 KB 164; *Thomas v Sawkins* [1935] 2 KB 249; and *Duncan v Jones* [1936] 1 KB 218.

53 *Entick v Carrington* (1765) 19 St Tr 1030.

54 *Attorney General v Guardian Newspapers Ltd (No. 2)* [1990] 1 AC 109, at p. 190 (Lord Donaldson).

55 Ewing and Gearty (n 2), chs 2–6.

56 P. Deery, 'The Dove Flies East: Whitehall, Warsaw and the 1950 World Peace Congress' (2002) 48 *Australian Journal of Politics and History* 449.

57 See pp. 77–9 below.

58 J. Mahoney, *British Civil Liberties and the Cold War: 1945–1956* (Ph.D. dissertation, University of Cambridge, 1990, Cambridge University Library), ch. 9.

Communists the protection afforded by a nice respect for the rules of that democratic system which they themselves aim to destroy?' [59]

VII.

Before concluding this introduction, we return by way of critical explanation to the files on which much of the account that follows is based. The amount of information collected and stored in each file varies, and the nature of the contents depends on whether it is a personal or organizational file, or a file on a particular subject—a 'special' file. In most cases, the files run to multiple volumes, and in some cases each individual volume may be very thick. In the case of Phil Piratin, for example, one of the volumes is several inches thick (covering the period he was an MP).[60] The files would generally contain background information about the organization or individual; observation notes by police officers who may have attended meetings or other events; information about intercepted phone calls in or out; typed extracts from intercepted documents; copies of intercepted telegrams; correspondence with external third parties (such as chief constables) relating to the subject; and internal memos exchanged between individual officers.[61]

In the case of files on individuals, there might be a photograph and copies of newspaper articles or leaflets relating to the individual in question. It all seems rather random. In some cases, there is also a photograph of the subject's Communist Party card (obtained either by interception, from a source inside, or by unlawful entry to premises), and where appropriate copies of bugged conversations from inside Party headquarters. The files of someone like the well-known MP and lawyer, D. N. Pritt KC, who was never an official member but who nevertheless visited the Party's King Street headquarters, would include transcripts of conversations in which he participated, and transcripts of those in which he was mentioned. There is a striking amount of cross-referencing to other files, indicating that the same information is contained in more than one location, and also a striking amount of marginal notation indicating, along with the dates stamped on them registering

[59] T. J. Maguire, 'Counter-Subversion in Early Cold War Britain: The Official Committee on Communism (Home), the Information Research Department, and State-Private Networks' (2015) 30 *Intelligence and National Security* 637, at p. 648. In the British system the tilt to security would be difficult to restrain, particularly as it was not announced publicly and could be effected administratively without the need for legislation. The role of the Committee was 'To focus all available intelligence about Communist activities in the United Kingdom, and to recommend to Ministers what activities can properly be taken to counter such activities' (TNA, CAB 21/4371). Chaired by Norman Brook, members were drawn from the Treasury, the Foreign Office, the Home Office, the Ministry of Defence, and the Ministry of Labour, as well as MI5 (ibid.).

[60] TNA, KV 2/2033 (1935–50).

[61] See also *Hewitt and Harman v United Kingdom* (1992) 14 EHRR 657 for an account of the files.

each occasion that they were removed from the Registry, that many of these files were in active use.[62]

The files are interesting not just for the insight they provide into the lives of others, but also because of the insight they provide into the working methods of the Security Service. So far as the former is concerned, however, there is an issue here about the releasing of some of this information into the public domain after people have died and are unable to protect their reputations. Although we do not claim to have inspected all the personal files released, we have seen enough to know that they contain thinly veiled suggestions of treachery by clearly identifiable individuals, abusive and insulting remarks about family members of individuals under surveillance, and allegations of marital affairs (which may have been unknown to the surviving family of the individuals in question) by an individual found to have been wrongly suspected of subversion. It is clear that MI5 control over the files to be released and the redactions are such that historians are being required to write a victor's vindication of the Security Service during the Cold War.

So far as the working methods of MI5 are concerned, the files reveal administrative practices containing an element of procedural formality indicative of a large-scale operation. The significant formalization of the process finds expression in what appears to have been (i) an annual register of Communist Party members; (ii) the Suspect Book held at each port and airport to facilitate the monitoring of the movement of Communists; and (iii) the Security Service and Special Branch surveillance report forms, the latter for reporting on meetings and rallies. The level of formality is not to be underestimated, revealing a bureaucracy governed by rules and procedures (albeit self-generating and self-regulating), and also a bureaucratic operation of some significance, in terms of the breadth of those subject to surveillance and the depth of that surveillance. That said, when a file is opened, no one has the right to see it except on the terms dictated by the State,[63] which usually means after censorship by weeding and redaction. In the era of freedom of information, the British State remains curiously circumspect about MI5's secret past. MI5's lack of accountability during the Cold War continues to this day.

VIII.

Although our focus is different, we share with Lustgarten and Leigh a concern to explore 'the recurring themes of constitutionalism to the realm of security and

[62] The covers of the original files have columns rather like old-style library books, where the dates were recorded.

[63] See Public Records Act 1958, s. 3(4): 'any records may be retained' if 'in the opinion of the person who is responsible for them, they are required for administrative purposes or ought to be retained for any other special reason'. See also Freedom of Information Act 2000, ss 23, 24.

intelligence'.[64] Which brings us back to the lawyers' concern with the Rule of Law as a constitutional principle. As suggested by E. C. S. Wade, Dicey's formulation of the Rule of Law has been the subject of powerful criticism, notably by Jennings, who ended up nevertheless following the master's lead. Others have since tried to produce a better account, with no conspicuous success, Rule of Law scholarship dividing between those who favour what Goldsworthy later referred to as thick and thin conceptions or what others have referred to as procedural and substantive conceptions.[65] This tension is to be seen in the work of Dicey (and in Wade's claim that the Rule of Law 'has come to be identified with the rights of man') on the one hand,[66] and Jennings on the other, the latter's early work appearing to eschew any meaningful substantive content to the Rule of Law.

As we will explain, the British constitution in the Cold War period would have struggled to satisfy even the most minimalist requirements of the Rule of Law. Based on the discussion in this Introduction and drawing freely on Dicey, Jennings, and Wade (and informed by Kafka),[67] these minimum requirements would include:

(i) no secret laws;
(ii) no secret powers;
(iii) no arbitrary powers, whether secret or not;
(iv) reasonably precise laws, with discretionary power at a minimum;
(v) no legal privileges or immunities for State officials;
(vi) police powers of various kinds rigidly defined;
(vii) *nulla poena sine lege*;
(viii) no secret courts or judicial processes;
(ix) an independent judiciary; and
(x) respect for civil liberties and fundamental rights.

MI5 revealed the Rule of Law to be a deception, an ideological tool that did not exist in practice, undermined by conduct that violated what ought to have been its core provisions. This would be true in relation to MI5's legal authority, the purposes for which was it established, and the powers it acquired.

The foregoing catalogue of the essential features of the Rule of Law includes respect for fundamental rights. We include it because this was accepted at the time by leading scholars—notably Wade relying on Dicey—as axiomatic.[68] But independently of the Rule of Law, there was a constitutional tradition in the United

[64] Lustgarten and Leigh (n 10), p. vii.
[65] J. Goldsworthy, 'Legislative Sovereignty and the Rule of Law', in T. Campbell, K. D. Ewing, and A. Tomkins (eds), *Sceptical Essays on Human Rights* (Oxford, 2010), ch. 4,
[66] Wade and Phillips (n 9), p. 70.
[67] See F. Kafka, *The Trial* (Harmondsworth, 1975 edn, first published 1925).
[68] Compare J. Raz, 'The Rule of Law and its Virtue' (1977) 93 *LQR* 195, with which we broadly agree.

Kingdom long before the Human Rights Act 1998 which included respect for civil liberties. It is in this tradition that Chuter Ede was speaking, and in fairness one in which he was a sometime exponent. Although he has been rightly criticized for his actions towards the end of the Attlee government in particular, Chuter Ede nevertheless resisted attempts to ban Fascist parties after the war,[69] as well as proposals to discredit the Communist Party on the ground that 'from the constitutional point of view, it would be very difficult for the Government to take official action of this kind against a political party which had not been declared to be an illegal organisation and was in fact represented in the House of Commons'.[70]

As we will see, however, disregard for the Rule of Law was inevitably accompanied by disrespect for civil liberties and human rights. Although purportedly a counter-espionage agency, MI5 was heavily engaged in counter-subversion, which compromised a number of the liberties which Chuter Ede had celebrated. This was particularly true of the right to freedom of association, to the extent that much of MI5's focus was directed initially against the Communist Party and related organizations, including the peace movement, trade unions, and what would now be said to be NGOs, such as NCCL and the Haldane Society of Socialist Lawyers. These were lawful bodies, the interference with which by State agents could be justified—if at all—on only the most compelling grounds. There was no such justification. On the contrary, the violation of liberty was compounded by methods which not only violated civil liberties on multiple grounds, but also revealed little understanding of the constitutional principles MI5 had been mandated to defend.

Sali populi suprema lex was no longer the governing principle of the British constitution.[71] But it continued to be the governing principle of the Security Service.

[69] See Renton (n 45), p. 99. Also D. N. Pritt, *Autobiography of DN Pritt, Part Two, Brasshats and Bureaucrats* (London, 1966), pp. 52–7.

[70] Mahoney (n 58), p. 107, citing a 'general agreement' to this effect at a Cabinet meeting on 19 December 1949.

[71] See *Michaels v Block* (1918) 34 TLR 438.

2
The Stewart Report

I. Introduction

We begin our analysis of the compatibility of government practice with constitutional principle by examining the report of Sir Samuel Findlater Stewart, which had been commissioned in 1944 by Anthony Eden (at that time Foreign Secretary), and presented to the Prime Minister in 1945.[1] Stewart was a career diplomat, who until 1941 had been PUS in the India Office, and thereafter Chairman of the Home Defence Executive. Said shortly after its completion to be 'the document from which the present constitution of the Security Service springs',[2] the Stewart Report is the new starting point for an understanding of the modern Security Service. The contents of the document have received little publicity, having been released only in 2013, and even then, not without significant redactions to censor information that would apparently embarrass MI5 today.[3] Despite Stewart's significant contribution to accountability, full accountability is still incomplete some seventy years after the event.

Stewart's inquiry was undertaken at a time of relative calm. The Germans had been defeated, and the Russians were not yet an enemy in the immediate aftermath of war. But with spectacular bad luck, the report was submitted shortly after (i) Igor Gouzenko's defection from the Soviet Embassy in Ottawa on 5 September 1945; and (ii) the attempted defection of Konstantin Volkov from the Soviet Embassy in Ankara. Gouzenko was to provide information implicating British scientist Alan Nunn May in what was apparently a very widespread Soviet espionage network in Canada, while Volkov had offered information on a substantial number of Soviet spies operating against the United Kingdom, and in particular on agents in the British Intelligence and Security Services. The little information Volkov had provided had made it apparent to Harold 'Kim' Philby that the Russian was likely to

[1] TNA, CAB 301/31 (Findlater Stewart, Report on the Security Services), 'Stewart Report'.

[2] 'The present' being 4 December 1948: TNA, CAB 21/2734 ('Ministerial Responsibility for the Security Service', Mr Hewison to Mr Johnston, 4 December 1948). Only six copies of the report were issued.

[3] See D. W. B. Lomas, '" . . . the Defence of the Realm and Nothing Else": Sir Findlater Stewart, Labour Ministers and the Security Service' (2015) 30 *Intelligence and National Security* 793, and subsequently D. W. B. Lomas, *An Uneasy Relationship? Intelligence, Security and the Attlee Governments, 1945–1951* (Manchester, 2016).

MI5, the Cold War, and the Rule of Law. K. D. Ewing, Joan Mahoney, and Andrew Moretta, Oxford University Press (2020). © K. D. Ewing, Joan Mahoney, and Andrew Moretta. DOI: 10.1093/oso/9780198818625.001.0001

identify him as a Soviet spy. Thanks to Philby's intervention during September and October 1945, the Russians were able to deal with Volkov.[4]

That there was a longstanding and wide-ranging Soviet espionage campaign being conducted against the West was thus becoming evident to the very few who were aware of these events. Guy Liddell—then head of MI5's counter-espionage division—recorded in his very full Diary that Stewart was a regular visitor to MI5 during 1945 while he was conducting his inquiries, and although Stewart clearly enjoyed the trust of senior Security Service staff, it is unknown just how much he was told about the very secret and sensitive Gouzenko and Volkov cases. Given his access to MI5 officials, it is most likely that Stewart would have been fed as much information as was necessary to enable him to write in a way that would best suit MI5's interests. There were nevertheless aspects of the report that were not to MI5's liking, and it seems possible that Stewart was not made fully aware of the scale of the espionage operations.

The report was submitted to Clement Attlee in November 1945, Labour having won its famous 'landslide' victory earlier that year. Stewart was writing at a time when many institutions were in a state of transition in the immediate post-war era. In the case of MI5, it was not simply the transition from one enemy to another, but a transition to a different kind of challenge for surveillance activity. The nature of that challenge was set out in great detail a year later in MI5's Civil Security Review for the Prime Minister, which mainstreamed the Communist Party.[5] That said, our view is that knowledge that the Soviets were engaging in numerous intelligence operations against their wartime allies ought not to have made any difference to the questions Stewart had undertaken to consider or the way in which the questions were addressed. These are the timeless and fundamental questions related not only to MI5's role and functions in the post-war era, but also to the legality and accountability of the Security Service and its operations in the post-war democracy.

II. Questions of Survival

Towards the end of the Second World War, three questions were being asked about the future role of MI5. First, should it continue to exist; second, if so what would it do; and third, on what terms? Churchill, of all people, had expressed serious doubts as to the first, commenting that:

> Every department which has waxed during the war is now considering how it can quarter its officials on the public indefinitely when peace returns. The less we

[4] TNA, KV 4/466 (Liddell Diary, 5 October 1945). See also K. Philby, *My Silent War* (London, 1968), pp. 143–54 for Philby's version of events.

[5] TNA, PREM 8/1353 ('Civil Security Review', No. XVIII, November 1946).

> encourage these illusions the better. It will be quite easy to find the necessary personnel for such Security or Secret Services as we may require.[6]

The war had drained the nation's resources, and money could not be wasted monitoring those who did not pose a threat to national security. At the very least, the Security Service was facing the prospect of deep budget cuts.

Budget cuts aside, however, there was probably never any serious doubt about the survival of the Security Service, though victory in war brought other challenges for MI5, with the temper of the time leading to anxiety about 'the idea of an internal *Gestapo*',[7] for reasons that hardly need to be explained. There were already concerns about what would be referred to today as 'mission creep' on the part of the Service, with Norman Kendal, then Director of Special Branch informing Cabinet Secretary Sir Edward Bridges in 1943:

> Recently I have had cases connected with Inland Revenue frauds, so called Black Market, and attempts to leave the country carrying away banknotes or portable property, in which MI5 have moved heaven and earth to be kept in the picture, although in no instance was security affected except in the sense that every anti-social act can be said to affect security. The cases were all either matters for the police or the Inland Revenue or both. It comes to this that they are beginning to try to overlap in and take charge of ordinary criminal investigation. I have also had a case in which Hinchley-Cooke [an MI5 officer] made an arrest in the street himself and conducted certain enquiries before passing the matter on to the police.[8]

But although there were issues to address, the question whether MI5 should continue to operate in the post-war era was considered only cursorily by Stewart, who thought it unnecessary 'to argue at length the need in these times for the kind of work done by MI5', claiming that its record in the inter-war years and during the Second World War, should be a 'sufficient answer to any doubts about the need for secret means to counter underground attempts to penetrate our military secrets'.[9] Although the end of the war was the right time to review the organization and the scope of its work, Stewart thus:

> started from the basic assumption that some organization must remain in being adequate in experience and numbers to detect and counter attempts during the peace to penetrate our Defence organization and to re-establish any hostile espionage system; and with the capacity to expand rapidly upon any threat of war.[10]

6 TNA, CAB 301/11 ('Future of Secret Services', Prime Minister's Personal Minute M231/3, 4 April 1943).

7 TNA, CAB 301/31 (Peter Loxley to Edward Bridges, 27 June 1944).

8 TNA, CAB 301/11 (Norman Kendal to Edward Bridges, 27 July 1943).

9 Stewart Report (n 1), para. 3.

10 ibid.

This seems unexceptional, particularly when combined with Stewart's more principled focus on the way in which MI5 should go about its business. That said, it is nevertheless unclear whether Stewart's analysis relating to espionage was informed by looking backwards at the prosecution of Communist Party activists Percy Glading and Douglas 'Dave' Springhall in 1938 and 1943 respectively for offences under the Official Secrets Act 1911,[11] or whether he was now engaged with the new challenges presented by Gouzenko and Volkov of Soviet spy-rings independently of any domestic Communist Party involvement. The preoccupation with subversion and the Communist Party in the report points strongly in favour of the former, and that MI5 had persuaded Stewart wrongly that the real threat to security continued to be presented by political activists such as the trio immortalized by litigation in the 1930s, and known as a result to successive generations of law students.[12]

III. Questions of Legality

Before turning to working practices and supervision, there was a logically prior question. Thus, what would be the legal foundations of the Service, an issue fudged but not overlooked, Stewart making it clear in the first paragraph of his report that he had been advised on legal questions by Sir Thomas Barnes, the Treasury Solicitor.[13] Stewart rightly insisted that MI5 should operate within the law, though it is notable that he did not consider whether there was legal authority for the creation of a body such as MI5 in the first place. So far as we can tell, it was not until the legal challenges in Strasbourg under the European Convention on Human Rights in the mid-to-late 1980s that these matters were first formally addressed. The latter are dealt with in the pages that follow.[14] At this stage it is to be noted that although the Service had been established in 1909 for purposes related to war,[15] that alone would not provide legal authority for its continued operation, any more than would subsequent extravagant claims that it was part of the defence forces of the country.

[11] Glading was a prominent member of the Communist Party who had organized a spy ring at Woolwich Arsenal to secure secret designs of guns, which he planned to pass on to Soviet Russia. The operation was thwarted when Glading unwittingly recruited Olga Gray, an MI5 agent who had worked as Harry Pollitt's secretary, to find a safe house. He was arrested and convicted under the Official Secrets Act 1911 for his espionage activities. See below, pp. 57–8. Springhall was a senior member of the Party who was convicted of espionage in 1943 for handing over the Russians classified information provided by an Air Ministry contact (also a Party member). The affair was an acute embarrassment to the Party, from which Springhall was expelled: F. Beckett and J. Murray, *Enemy Within—The Rise and Fall of the British Communist Party* (London, 1995), p. 86. These cases were ever after cited as examples of Party officials who were willing to spy for the Soviets, and justification for monitoring of the Party.

[12] *Elias v Pasmore* [1934] 2 KB 164; *Thomas v Sawkins* [1935] 2 KB 249; and *Duncan v Jones* [1936] 1 KB 218.

[13] Stewart Report (n 1), para. 1.

[14] *Hewitt and Harman v United Kingdom* (1992) 14 EHRR 657.

[15] Stewart Report (n 1), para. 4.

It is widely thought—by lawyers,[16] politicians,[17] and the Security Service itself—that MI5's legal authority was derived from the common law powers of the Crown in the form of the royal prerogative. But a note of caution is required: assumption is one thing, authority another. There is no general prerogative power allowing the government to do whatever it likes for the defence of the realm, or specifically to create and maintain a secret service, however much Locke may claim that '*Prerogative is nothing but the Power of doing publick good without a Rule*'.[18] The great authorities emphasize the relatively precise nature of the prerogative powers, Blackstone writing that 'one of the principal bulwarks of civil liberty, or (in other words) of the British constitution, was the limitation of the King's prerogative by bounds so certain and notorious that it is impossible he should ever exceed them'.[19] This sense of certainty about the substance of the prerogative is reflected also in Chitty's attempt to 'present a comprehensive and connected, yet compressed and logical, view of every prerogative and corresponding right of the subject'.[20]

So if we are to find support for the view that MI5 is a prerogative creation, we must look elsewhere than a general authority that does not exist, mindful in doing so of Chitty's observation that the prerogative 'is not the iron tie of unbridled power'.[21] An examination of the specific measures identified by Chitty suggests that the most relevant would be the war power on the one hand and those relating to foreign affairs on the other. There are nevertheless problems in constructing a power to create a domestic security service from these foundations. So far as the war power is concerned, Chitty is clear that: 'In all these cases the emergency is the avowed cause, and the act done is as temporary as the occasion. The King cannot change by his prerogative of war, either the law of nations or the law of the land, by general and unlimited regulations.'[22] Equally, although the foreign affairs power is celebrated on the ground that 'the rapidity and secrecy which are generally necessary to the due execution of [foreign transactions], will never be found in large assemblies',[23] the activities of MI5 extended well beyond external enemies.

[16] See L. Lustgarten and I. Leigh, *In from the Cold, National Security and Parliamentary Democracy* (Oxford, 1994), p. 374.

[17] HC Debs, 15 December 1988, col. 1151: 'Since its inception in 1909, members of the Security Service have been told that their work is covered not by statute but by the royal prerogative' (Rupert Allason). Also, HC Debs, 15 December 1989, col. 1159 (Mr William Powell), and HL Debs, 27 February 1990, col. 871 (Lord Dacre). And see HC 422 (2003–4), para. 10.

[18] J. Locke, *Two Treaties of Government (A Critical Edition with an Introduction by P Laslett), Book II*, para. 166 (Cambridge, 1960 edn) (emphasis in original).

[19] Sir W. Blackstone, *Commentaries on the Laws of England*, Vol. 1 (Oxford, 1753), p. 161.

[20] J. Chitty, *Treatise on the Law of the Prerogatives of the Crown* (London, 1822), p. iv.

[21] ibid., p. iii.

[22] ibid., p. 50.

[23] ibid., p. 39.

The failure of Stewart to address the question of MI5's legal foundations is important, even if understandable. Despite showing some concern for civil liberties and constitutional propriety, he showed no concern for the most fundamental of all questions of legality. This was perhaps a symptom of the times, when legal questions did not always loom large in government decision-making. Any criticism is perhaps thus unfair, being delivered from the lofty heights of hindsight in a very different legal and political environment. But whether intended or not, the result nevertheless was to lead to the continuation of a secret organization with a mandate of untested legal authority, and an uncertain legal status as a result. Although MI5's 'charter' was eventually published, the government appeared to claim subsequently that it did not have 'the force of law', and that its contents did not 'constitute legally enforceable rules concerning the operation of the Security Service'.[24] That being the case, on what legal basis did Stewart recommend the continued operation of MI5?

IV. Questions of Function

Apart from the question whether (i) MI5 should continue to operate; and if so (ii) on what legal basis, a third question relates to its role and function. What would it do? Here Stewart gave prominence to the attention MI5 paid to the German Auslands organization,[25] and the British Union of Fascists between 1929 and 1931. But he accepted that the Service had been primarily interested in left-wing subversion during the 1920s and 30s, and acknowledged long-standing interest in monitoring the activities of those associated with the Communist Party. In the inter-war years the Service had focused its energies on monitoring the Party and its associates, and in 1945 MI5 was set to continue with its pre-war work.[26] According to Stewart:

> In MI5's view, close study of the Communist Party in this country and its membership is justified on two counts, (a) apart from remnants of extreme Right Wing movements and such people as the Anarchists and the IRA, most of the *persons concerned with the promotion of political aims by unconstitutional methods* are members of the Communist Party, and (b) many of its members are exposed to,

24 *Hewitt and Harman v United Kingdom* (n 14), para. 40.

25 The branch of the Nazi Party for expatriate Germans: 'By 1935 it had 288 members' in the United Kingdom, 'and some 1,500 contacts and these numbers had grown to 300 and 2,000 by 1937': F. H. Hinsley and C. A. G. Simkins, *British Intelligence in the Second World War: Vol 4—Security and Counter Intelligence* (London, 1990), p. 14.

26 Dick White (later MI5 DG) visited Guy Liddell (later Deputy Director General, DDG) at his home on 12 August 1945 and the next day Liddell recorded in his Diary: 'I talked to him about the CP and the difference of view about keeping a close watch on all Party members. We came to the conclusion that it would probably be necessary to continue this work on as detailed a basis as manpower would allow': TNA, KV 4/466 (Liddell Diary, 13 August 1945).

and some succumb to, pressure to engage in espionage on behalf of international Communism, and, at one remove, the Soviet Union.[27]

In endorsing the continued operation of MI5, Stewart thus appeared to endorse its role in relation to those engaged in espionage on the one hand, and subversion by the *promotion of political aims by unconstitutional methods* on the other. Unlike espionage, however, the *promotion of political aims by unconstitutional methods* has no obvious legal meaning, and appeared to support the release of MI5 from any obligation to adhere to any objective legal standard in the pursuit of its functions. In contrast, until 1931 MI5's responsibility was ostensibly limited to the 'Detection of Espionage and of Seditious Movements directed against or arising within the Armed Forces of the Crown'.[28] The role of MI5 was thus formally linked to a legal standard, however opaque that standard might have been, in the sense that it was watching organizations that were seditious and therefore potentially unlawful, perhaps with a view to a prosecution being brought.

The Communist Party had been regarded as a 'seditious organization' and unlawful since its foundations, its leading members famously convicted in 1921, and again in 1925,[29] while the *Daily Worker* had been proscribed under emergency powers for a short period during the Second World War.[30] The latter step was under wartime regulations, which authorized action to be taken against newspapers (and others) engaged in the 'systematic publication of matter calculated to foment opposition to the prosecution of the war to a successful issue'. [31] The problem with sedition by the 1940s, however, was that 'prosecutions for sedition have been so few that the ingredients of the offence cannot be stated with assurance'.[32] This is because the law on sedition was very old, rooted in the political struggles in the eighteenth and nineteenth centuries, emphasizing the need for an 'intent to incite to violence against the institutions and laws of the State or a section of the community'.[33]

27 Stewart Report (n 1), para. 31. Stewart acknowledges that by 1945 agents were restricted to the CPGB and 'the remnants of the British Union of Fascists'—MI5 were evidently short of target organizations (para. 27).

28 TNA, CAB 301/11 (Secret Report of the Cabinet Secret Service Committee, 1 December 1925, quoted by Kendal in a letter to Bridges, 27 July 1943). According to Kendal, the report was signed by the eponymous Fisher, as well as John Anderson and Maurice Hankey. Sir Norman Brook was unable to locate the original conclusions and recommendations of the committee.

29 See K. D. Ewing and C. A. Gearty, *The Struggle for Civil Liberties: Political Freedom and the Rule of Law 1914–1945* (Oxford, 2001), ch. 3.

30 See HC Debs, 28 January 1941, col. 523. The ban had been imposed on 21 January 1941 and was not revoked until 26 August 1942, despite the Communist Party's support for the war since July 1941. See W. Rust, *The Story of the Daily Worker* (London, 2010).

31 According to the Home Secretary (Herbert Morrison), who imposed the ban, the 'object of this propaganda' was 'to bring about the downfall of democratic and constitutional government', though the prospects of such propaganda making headway were 'small': HC Debs, 21 January 1941, col. 187. The government was strongly condemned by Aneurin Bevan for what was said to be an 'extraordinary deterioration in democratic standards in Great Britain' (HC Debs, 22 January 1941, col. 465).

32 S. A. de Smith, *Constitutional and Administrative Law* (2nd edn, Harmondsworth, 1973), p. 483.

33 ibid.

The 'very tendency of sedition' was said to be incitement of 'the people to insurrection and rebellion',[34] which is not where the Communist Party was in the 1940s, the Party now marching on the parliamentary road to socialism. Other formulations of the law had indicated a need for 'violence or defiance for the purpose of disturbing public authority',[35] but even the advocacy of violence would not necessarily secure a conviction, as revealed in an infamous sedition case in 1947. In *R v Caunt*, the editor of the *Morecambe and Heysham Visitor* was acquitted, after being prosecuted for carrying an article that appeared to advocate violence against British Jews following atrocities against British troops in Israel.[36] It was presumably not expedient to limit the role of MI5 to the surveillance of seditious organizations, not least because reliance on a common law standard would restrict the Security Service to (contracting) legal definitions beyond its control.

V. Questions of Methods

So far as the methods used to contain Communist activists are concerned, the Stewart Report considered the various forms of surveillance used by MI5, as well as its 'Registry' (its central card index and 'Special Purpose Index' devoted to the Party), and files of information on individuals, organizations, and particular matters. So far as surveillance is concerned, Stewart noted that:

> In the work of investigation and study of the Party organisation all of the methods detailed [mail interception, phone taps, covert microphones] are used, but, in addition, considerable reliance is placed on police reports for routine matters. The use of the police for this work is a long standing arrangement dating from the period in which the study of subversive organisations was the responsibility of Scotland Yard . . . the reports rendered generally concern such matters as the speeches made at public meetings . . . changes in ranks of local officials and, where they become known to the police, the names of new members. These contacts are maintained with the knowledge and approval of the Home Office.[37]

Crucially, however, Stewart also observed in relation to surveillance methods that apart from intelligence bearing on security obtained from the SIS (or MI6 as it is sometimes referred to):

[34] *R v Sullivan* (1868) 11 Cox CC 44.

[35] Law Commission, Codification of the Criminal Law: Treason, Sedition and Allied Offences (Working Paper 72, 1977), pp. 42–3. Sedition has since been abolished.

[36] The case is unreported. For an account of this affair, see E. C. S. Wade, 'Seditious Libel and the Press' (1948) 64 *LQR* 203. For a brief account, see E. C. S. Wade and G. G. Phillips, *Constitutional Law* (6th edn, London, by E. C. S. Wade), p. 495.

[37] Stewart Report (n 1), para. 32.

> there are three secret sources of information available to the two divisions ['B' Division (Counter-Espionage) and 'F' Division (Counter-Subversion)], viz, (a) agents and watchers, (b) the interception of letters and telephone conversations and (c) the installation of microphones.[38]

Remarkably, however, paragraph 20 of the Stewart Report—dealing with the use of hidden microphones—has been redacted, and it looks very likely that the censors have taken a sizable portion of paragraph 19—on telephone interception—along with it. This is the only part of the report to have been censored, a step reflecting Edward Bridges' concern in a note to Attlee about the report that it refers to 'certain matters (see in particular paragraph 20) which ought to be known to the smallest number of people'.[39] Nevertheless, Stewart's 'Summary and Conclusions' has been left unscathed and refers back to paragraph 20. Point (v) gives the game away by recommending that 'Specific authority should be obtained from the Home Secretary or in certain cases from the Foreign Secretary [for domestic SIS operations presumably], whenever it is proposed to install a microphone (para 20).'[40] Essentially, Stewart proposed putting bugging on the same footing as mail interception and telephone tapping.[41]

This, of course, is to be highly commended, though any suggestion that bugging was taking place without any authority would be a matter of grave concern. Nevertheless, also to be commended are Stewart's reservations about the Registry, Stewart suggesting that there was too much unnecessary information on file about too many individuals, even if the information was not used improperly. He proposed as a result that the contents of files should be 'rigorously restricted', and that they should be cleared of any matter that was inconsistent with the defence of the realm.[42] And further to be commended was Stewart's insistence that no inquiry should take place unless it had a bearing on defence, with obvious implications for the scope of surveillance measures. If nothing else, it was an endorsement of the then DG's decision in 1944 that only 'important' Communists should be 'carded',[43] a decision which, as we will discuss in Chapter 3, was resisted by senior MI5 officials.

[38] ibid., para. 17. In view of the treatment meted out to paras 19 and 20 it is remarkable that mention of microphones remains in the text.

[39] TNA PREM 8/1520 (Note from Bridges, 28 November 1946, initialled by Attlee, 29 November 1946).

[40] Stewart Report (n 1), para. (v) of Summary and Conclusions (p. 27).

[41] ibid., para. 21.

[42] Stewart Report (n 1), paras 42–43. In a Diary entry on 2 July 1946, Liddell recorded that he had been told that Stewart's recommendation that the Registry be 'cleared periodically' was the result of Stewart looking up records on three people whose names he was familiar with during his research, including the tennis player Gillian Bennett and the tank expert General Martell. Stewart was apparently unimpressed to find information about their private lives on file. Liddell took the view that MI5 was quite correct to retain the information, as Bennett's husband had been a SOE man believed to have talked openly about secret matters, and Martell had been accused of similarly 'careless talk'.

[43] Confusingly to 'card', depending on the context, could mean either to open a file on an individual or to place a name in the card index.

Stewart had thus exposed potential lawlessness and arbitrariness, and was proposing significant changes on two major issues (surveillance methods and the number of people subject to surveillance). While Stewart accepted that MI5's surveillance activity (in terms of targets and methods) was justified subject to a number of safeguards,[44] he nevertheless thus recommended that this activity should take place within clear boundaries. Stewart was emphatic that the Service should be 'politically neutral', and made his now long-famous primary recommendation very clear:

> Let me say first, and it is the foundation of my recommendations, that not only the index and the special powers, but the whole of the operations of MI5 are used for one purpose, and one purpose only—'the Defence of the Realm'.[45]

Moreover, unlike many associated with government and security, Stewart was prepared to offer a relatively succinct definition of what amounted to subversion for the foregoing purposes, and to differentiate this peacetime definition from the wartime use of the term.[46] In peacetime, when civil liberties could no longer be 'tempered by patriotism', Stewart acknowledged that the electorate were likely to find MI5 investigations on wide terms of reference to be unacceptable:

> Sir Findlater Stewart's constitutional principle was this: There are obviously serious objections to a secret Security Service operating in a democratic state, and such a Service can only be justified on the basis of an appeal to the paramount interests of national defence.[47]

[44] Stewart Report (n 1), para. 37.

[45] But note ibid., Summary and Conclusions, para. (iv):

> The Records should be cleared as quickly as possible of any matter which is inconsistent with the above purpose; and, except under specific authority of the responsible Minister (see (vi) below), no enquiry should be carried out by MI5 on behalf of any Department *unless an important public interest, with at least an indirect bearing on defence, is at stake* (paras 40, 42, and 43).

The words we have italicized appear to stretch the authority of the Service, and reflects the fact that MI5 did not always act in the defence of the realm. During the war, in addition to the work outlined above, F Division also kept observation on the activities of such organizations as the Shop Stewards' Movement, the PPU and Jehovah's Witnesses, the first because it was closely connected with the Communist Party and the second and third on the ground that, although neither of these bodies was subversive in the strict sense of the word, their activities were prejudicial to the war effort: Stewart Report (n 1), paras 31–33. See also, Appendix, below, pp. 475–6.

[46] Stewart Report (n 1), para. 33.

[47] TNA, CAB 301/18 ('Enquiry by Sir Norman Brook into the Secret Intelligence and Security Service; correspondence and general papers', P. Sillitoe, Comments on Sir Norman Brook's Report on the Secret Intelligence and Security Services, para. 42). The Liddell Diary reveals that Dick White was the author of Sillitoe's memo (TNA, KV 4/473, Liddell Diary, 19 and 30 March 1951), although Sillitoe

VI. Questions of Legal Authority

Stewart thus revealed a wide range of surveillance methods used by MI5. However, the use of these methods was vulnerable to criticism on two grounds. The first is that there was an absence of legal authority, with the exception of mail checks, which had the authority of statute. But what was the legal base on which telephone tapping and the use of bugging devices stood? Stewart's failure to consider these matters was wholly unsatisfactory, for the legality of neither could be assumed. Indeed, the uncertain legal status of phone tapping was exposed by the Birkett Report some ten years later,[48] which reinforced these doubts by producing a legal justification so cryptic that few could understand it. The issue for Stewart was not whether any rights were violated, but the more basic requirement identified by Jennings that 'all governmental powers, save those of the representative legislature, shall be distributed and determined by reasonably precise laws'.[49]

The use of bugging devices or special facilities (SF) as they were referred to was different.These could be installed only by the illicit entry of private property, the consent of the property owner (even if given) making the whole procedure pointless. Yet the illicit entry into private premises in this way—whether to search the premises or install hidden microphones to monitor conversations—was clearly unlawful, even if authorized by senior MI5 officials, Home Office civil servants, and/or the Home Secretary himself. As we consider in Chapter 8 below,[50] any such entry would be a trespass, for which 'State necessity' would be no excuse, quite apart from any question of criminal liability. That said, there would never be a prosecution, and we should not minimize the difficulties likely to be encountered in bringing a civil claim. A civil case would never get off the ground; even if it did, the applicant would face formidable procedural barriers, in the form of Crown privilege which would prevent the disclosure of evidence which might be necessary to have a fighting chance of success.[51]

(who disliked White) claimed to have made considerable changes to it before it was presented to Attlee (TNA, KV 4/473, Liddell Diary, 9 April 1951). The Brook Report (March 1951), although generally complimentary about MI5, infuriated senior officers by recommending that ministerial responsibility for the Service be shifted from the Prime Minister to the Home Secretary (TNA, CAB 301/17). (See Chapter 3). The memorable phrase 'tempered by patriotism' is taken from the Director of Special Branch's 1943 letter to Edward Bridges condemning MI5 (n 8 above).

[48] Cmnd 283, 1957. See Chapter 5.

[49] W. I. Jennings, *The Law and the Constitution* (5th edn, London, 1959), p. 48.

[50] See pp. 207–10.

[51] See *Duncan v Cammell Laird & Co.* [1942] AC 624. See also *Attorney General v Guardian Newspapers (No. 2)* [1988] 2 WLR 805, where breaking and entry by MI5 was condoned as being equivalent to the emergency services speeding through a red traffic light.

The best that we can say then is that the procedures for authorising these activities were administrative rather than statutory and that—mail interception apart—they had no legal basis. But these defects were compounded by the fact that (i) the procedures were not always followed in practice; (ii) there was no one to ensure that they were followed; and (iii) there was no remedy or sanction if they were breached. So far as phone tapping is concerned, initially the agencies were permitted to self-authorize, despite assurances that had been given at least since 1922 that it would take place in 'the interests of justice' only with the authority of the Postmaster General.[52] These assurances seem to have been worthless, at least if they were meant to convey the impression that all telephone surveillance was subject to such approval. The rules were changed in 1937, with one internal memorandum referring to the need for 'an additional safeguard against a too free use of this procedure',[53] suggesting that self-authorization was out of control.

The procedures introduced in 1937 were described by Stewart,[54] with a Home Office Warrant (HOW) signed by the Secretary of State required before telephone tapping could take place, an administrative procedure that appears to be based on the statutory procedure for mail checks. It is clear, however, that the laxity of the pre-war years continued thereafter, with evidence that the same personnel on both the MI5 and GPO sides were in post before and after the war. A circular issued in 1940 stated that:

> As regards the Telephone Check, Col Allan was most insistent that, although he is prepared to co-operate in every way, and without a warrant, for a 'snap' Telephone Check, if you want to have systematic listening on a private line, you must telephone him and myself, so that we can get a Home Office Warrant from the under Secretary of State at the Home Office.[55]

A subsequent circular asked officers and secretaries not to contact the GPO for telechecks without obtaining permission from either Colonel 'Jasper' Harker or Guy Liddell,[56] while a 1941 memo on telecheck procedure itemized the internal paperwork that had to be completed before the officer could 'ring up the GPO and tell them that the check may now be operated (the warrant itself may take

[52] HC Debs, 4 April 1922, col. 2025 (Postmaster General, at that time a Cabinet Minister).

[53] TNA, HO 144/20619 (Memorandum by C. R., 29 April 1937).

[54] The Stewart Report (n 1), at para. 19, states that a HOW is required for a telephone interception. See below, pp. 103–4.

[55] TNA, KV 4/222 (MI5 Circular to all RSLOs (Regional Security Liaison Officers), 23 June 1940). See also TNA, KV 4/222 (Circular by Petrie on Mail and Telephone Interceptions, 15 August 1941).

[56] TNA, KV 4/222 (Miss G. H. Johnson, 20 August 1940). Harker had recently been appointed Director of MI5. He was replaced by Donald Petrie in 1941 (Petrie was appointed DG). Harker became DDG, and retained responsibility for approving HOW applications.

anything up to 10 days before it reaches the GPO)'.[57] Though obviously a time of national emergency, the slackness that pervaded this approach is to be seen also in the post-war period, revealing a failure by Stewart to report on what was happening in practice.

VII. Questions of Accountability

Apart from the role of and means used by the Service, Stewart also addressed questions of accountability, which he thought to be 'constitutionally' important,[58] recognizing that the 'special powers of enquiry' available to the Service had the potential to cause political problems: 'The possibility of public criticism of the special methods of MI5 raises one of the major matters with which this report is concerned—the Ministerial responsibility for the Service.'[59] Stewart noted that during the war, while the Home Office had sanctioned the interceptions, and the Treasury had governed the funding, the Home Defence (Security) Executive had co-ordinated MI5's activities, first under Lord Swinton, then under Duff Cooper (both of whom had executive control of MI5 in addition to their Security Executive role), and finally under Anthony Eden.[60] Post war, with the Security Executive disbanded, and in accord with his central contention that the Service's sole purpose was the defence of the realm, Stewart

[57] TNA, KV 4/222 (Undated 1941 memo). A later set of procedures (21 May 1942) look more rigorous (Allan was supposed to receive paperwork 'to enable preparations to be made to operate the HOW [for mail checks] when it is signed by the Home Secretary'), but substantial redactions have been made to the section relating to telephone checks, arguably indicative of the retention of the permissive approach—and, perhaps, mention of 'Special Facilities'.

[58] Stewart Report (n 1), para. 45. On this aspect of the Stewart Report, see the especially lucid account by Lomas, '. . . the Defence of the Realm and Nothing Else' (n 3).

[59] Stewart Report (n 1), para. 44.

[60] Eden's work as chair of the Security Executive was in addition to his responsibilities as Foreign Secretary. During 1940–2, Lord Swinton, not a Minister, but Chair of the Home Defence (Security) Executive [not to be confused with the Home Defence Executive headed by Findlater Stewart during 1940–5] had immediate responsibility for the Security Service, while John Anderson, Lord President of the Council, was said by Alfred Duff Cooper to have 'supervisory authority over its activities': TNA, CAB 301/11 (The Future of the Secret Service, 23 March 1943). Cabinet Secretary Edward Bridges described this as a 'general, somewhat ill-defined responsibility' (ibid., note to Codrington, 12 April 1943), but in a February 1941 Note to the Prime Minister on the question of David Petrie's review of MI5 (the Service was failing to meet the challenges of war posed during 1940–1), and of Petrie being appointed head of the Service, Bridges suggested that Churchill might 'wish to speak to the Lord President, who exercises Ministerial responsibility therefor, and also to the Home Secretary, as the Minister in charge of the Department which has a vital interest in MI5': TNA, CAB 301/25, 11 February 1941. This subtle hierarchy is perhaps better grasped when it is understood that the first four copies of the Petrie Report went to Churchill, Anderson, Swinton, and Bridges—in that order (TNA, CAB 301/25, Harris to Armstrong, 17 February 1943). Duff Cooper, in the Cabinet as Chancellor of the Duchy of Lancaster and without departmental brief, succeeded Swinton as Chair of the Security Executive during 1942–4, with Anderson retaining his supervisory authority until (the domestic threat much reduced after the Normandy landings), Eden became responsible Minister in July 1944, a role unrelated to his work as Foreign Secretary.

recommended that the Minister of Defence (or in the absence of a Minister of Defence, the Prime Minister) should be the minister responsible for MI5.[61] This was a point on which Stewart was quite emphatic: 'The Service should have a responsible Ministerial head. He should be the Prime Minister.' [62]

In making this recommendation, Stewart addressed concerns about the 'undue burden' that would be placed on the responsible minister (whether the Prime Minister or the Minister of Defence), and the corresponding burden that would be placed on the Cabinet Secretariat. But unwilling to be deflected by these concerns, Stewart made clear that ministerial responsibility did not mean ministerial control of operational matters, and that the only contact that would be required with the Service would be through the Director General (DG) who, because of the nature of the work, would need direction only on the 'broadest lines'.[63] The real challenge for the responsible minister would be to recruit the right person for the job as DG; but having done so there would be 'no alternative to giving him the widest discretion in the means he uses and the direction in which he applies them—always provided he does not step outside the law'.[64]

Despite the burden, Attlee (it seems enthusiastically) accepted Stewart's recommendation, and took personal charge in 1946 at a time when he was both Prime Minister and Minister of Defence. However, Attlee subsequently retained responsibility for MI5, even after off-loading defence responsibilities to the little-known Albert Alexander later that year.[65] As Chairman of the Committee of Imperial Defence, and with the overall constitutional responsibility for national security that goes with the office of Prime Minister, Attlee's assumption of the role can be seen to have had some constitutional logic. With the benefit of hindsight, however, it made sense only to the extent that MI5 had a function genuinely related to the defence of the realm, and it has since been claimed that Stewart exaggerated the extent to which MI5 was part of the nation's defence forces.[66] That link was certainly strained by MI5's focus on subversion as well as espionage,[67] straining too any claim that MI5's legal foundations could be said to derive from the prerogative powers of the Crown.

On the 11 March 1946, the Cabinet unsurprisingly expressed 'general agreement with the view that the Service should have a responsible Ministerial head and that he should be the Prime Minister', and 'took note that the Prime Minister would

61 Stewart Report (n 1), para. 45.

62 ibid., Summary and Conclusions, para. (vi). According to Liddell, 'The new DG, and the department, are to come directly under the PM in his capacity as Minister of Defence, and the DG is to see the PM once a fortnight. This part of the recommendation is satisfactory': TNA, KV 4/467 (Liddell Diary, 25 April 1946).

63 Stewart Report (n 1), para. 46.

64 ibid.

65 For a fuller account, see Lomas, '. . . the Defence of the Realm and Nothing Else' (n 3).

66 See TNA CAB 301/17 (Sir Norman Brook, 'The Secret Intelligence and Security Services, Report of Enquiry', March 1951, para. 42 (the 'Brook Report')). See Chapter 3 below.

67 And strained also by de facto duties of MI5 unrelated to the Defence of the Realm—see below, Chapter 3.

issue a Directive to the new Director General of the Security Service'.[68] Attlee's assumption of responsibility for MI5 could be seen less as an attempt to concentrate knowledge and power in the office of Prime Minister, and more as a step towards ensuring the better political protection against MI5 excess—'the buck' could be seen to stop with the Prime Minister, as Sillitoe was later to acknowledge.[69] But while there would be responsibility to the Prime Minister, it goes without saying that the Stewart Report was not tabled in either the House of Commons or the House of Lords, Parliament kept completely in the dark about Stewart and just about everything else where MI5 was concerned (including its budget).[70]

VIII. Conclusion

We set out in this chapter our intent to examine questions of legality, power, and accountability in relation to MI5 and government. That examination has been located at this stage in the Stewart Report, in which Sir Findlater Stewart looked at MI5's targets, methods, and boundaries, and intentionally or otherwise revealed that MI5 was:

(i) created and continued by a secret process, with secret functions, and using secret methods;
(ii) established on the basis of unquestioned but questionable legal authority;
(iii) performing functions relating to 'subversion' and 'unconstitutional methods', terms which had no legal grounding, but which nevertheless authorized the surveillance of people not acting unlawfully;

[68] TNA, CAB 301/31 (Cabinet Conclusions, 11 March 1946).

[69] According to Percy Sillitoe, Stewart had favoured the Prime Minister as responsible Minister 'because in the last resort, he believed that the country might expect an assurance from no less a person than the Prime Minister himself that the "special powers of enquiry" vested in the Security Service are not being abused': TNA, CAB 301/18 (P. Sillitoe, Comments on Sir Norman Brook's Report (n 47)). The 'special powers of inquiry' referred to are mail interception, telephone tapping, and the use of hidden microphones, as well as the Registry.

[70] This is not to say that there would be no ministerial responsibility to Parliament when security lapses were revealed, as when Attlee defended MI5 in the wake of the arrest and conviction of 'atom bomb spy' Klaus Fuchs in March 1950. The press had been shocked that MI5 had cleared a man with known communist antecedents to work on the nuclear project. The explosion of the first Soviet atom bomb in September 1949 had come as something of an unpleasant surprise to many—the Soviets were considered years away from becoming a nuclear power. Fuchs' information had enabled the Russians to build their own bomb. Attlee, addressing the Commons in the immediate wake of the affair, made a very robust defence of the Service, perhaps unaware that crucial information had been withheld from him (on which, see M. S. Goodman and C. Pincher, 'Clement Attlee, Percy Sillitoe and the Security Aspects of the Fuchs' Case' (2005) 19 *Contemporary British History* 67). According to Attlee:

> there is a great deal of loose talk in the press suggesting inefficiency on the part of the security services. I entirely deny that . . . I take full responsibility for the efficiency of the Security Services . . . I do not think there is anything that can cast the slightest slur on the Security Services (HC Debs, 6 March 1950, cols 71–72).

(iv) engaged in activity which was either (a) unlawful, or (b) had no legal authority, or both;
(v) governed by procedures which were secret and which were not always followed in practice;
(vi) engaged in activity in excess of the purposes for which it was established, and in breach of the extra-legal procedures by which it was governed;
(vii) not subject to any external scrutiny or supervision to check excess of power or methods in the pursuit of its functions;
(viii) not subject to any meaningful parliamentary supervision as to its funding or activities.

Not all of these defects were addressed directly by Stewart: some are a consequence of his findings, or the necessary implications thereof. Nevertheless, the foregoing was the very antithesis of the Rule of Law, which contemporary scholars celebrated not just as an essential normative requirement of liberal democracy, but also as an example of the superiority of the British constitution over the practices operating elsewhere, and particularly the Soviet Union. Whatever else it might mean, the Rule of Law must mean (i) no secret laws; (ii) no secret powers; and (iii) no arbitrary powers whether secret or not. Otherwise the doctrine is diminished to absurdity. This is not to say, of course, that Stewart was content with the position, procedures, and practices he encountered, the report being impressive for its recommendations that there should be greater scrutiny and better accountability. That said, the recommendation for a greater role for the Prime Minister was not without its obvious dangers, despite Stewart's apparently benign intentions.

For all that, the Stewart Report was seriously wanting in some respects, particularly around questions of legality. It is all very well to have greater supervision and accountability, but greater supervision and accountability relating to what? As we have seen, Stewart seemed prepared to permit MI5 to (i) operate without establishing the legal foundations for doing so (important because these foundations contain what may or may not be done); (ii) pursue objectives for the defence of the realm in relation to conduct (subversion) which had no legal foundation and went well beyond any relevant legal standard (sedition); and (iii) permit activities (such as the surreptitious breaking into people's homes) on the authority of a government minister which, if undertaken by the police in the investigation of crime, would at least formally require a magistrate's warrant—that is to say the authority of a judicial officer not a politician, or more likely an administrative official acting on the latter's behalf.[71]

[71] See Wade and Phillips (n 36), p. 470.

Yet the Stewart Report was to be the high-water mark, the beginning and the end of concerns about the need to contain and supervise the work of MI5. As the Cold War began to heat up in earnest shortly after the report was submitted to Attlee, priorities clearly began to change: the funding and resources of MI5 quickly returned to, and eventually exceeded, wartime levels; scrutiny and supervision initially tightened following the Stewart Report were greatly relaxed; and the 'dogs were let off the leash' to fight the Soviets with no questions asked, to politically disastrous effect. This was a mistake: scrutiny and accountability are important not only to contain those who are subject to scrutiny, but also—as Stewart recognized—to protect those to whom they are accountable, as Macmillan was eventually to discover at great personal cost.[72] In Chapter 3, we examine the steps taken to implement Stewart's recommendations, along with steps taken very soon thereafter to shred them.

[72] See Chapters 13 and 14 below.

3

The Security Service Mandate

I. Introduction

In 1931, MI5 had slipped free of the War Office to acquire what Professor Andrew has described as 'an enhanced but ill-defined status within Whitehall as an inter-departmental intelligence service'.[1] As suggested in Chapter 1, such casual references to the status of a security service are likely to raise the hackles of the impertinent lawyer. What was its previous status? In what sense was the new status ill-defined? In what way was the new status enhanced? And in what sense was it inter-departmental? Acting on behalf of or at the behest of several departments? Subject to oversight and supervision by more than one department, in which case which departments? Accountable to more than one department, in which case which departments? These are questions to which answers might prove elusive, particularly in view of the claim that 'even MI5 had no accurate written record of the changes'.[2]

The lawyer is thus put on notice for the similar questions that arise after the Second World War when further re-organization of MI5 took place in response to the Stewart Report. Concerned with questions of authority, power, and accountability, in this chapter we trace the steps taken to implement the Stewart Report, and the fresh mandate for the Security Service which it produced. This was the Attlee Directive, a bowdlerized version of which adopted in 1952 became known as the Maxwell Fyfe Directive, diluting the political supervision of the Service which the Attlee Directive had embraced. The Attlee Directive was never published and was released to the National Archives only in 2009,[3] while the Maxwell Fyfe Directive was revealed in 1963.[4] What has not been revealed until now, however, is the expansion of MI5's mandate by means of secret Supplementary Directives, in response to the clear failure of MI5 to operate within the boundaries of its authority.

[1] C. Andrew, *The Defence of the Realm—The Authorised History of MI5* (London, 2009), p. 130. In his Report on the Security Service on 13 February 1941, Petrie argued that 'the placing of the Service under the care and direction of a centrally placed Minister without Departmental responsibility is a step which should prove entirely beneficial . . . much may be lost by placing the Service under a single Department. Moreover, since the Service acts for so many Departments, it is doubtful whether the rest would be satisfied for control to be handed over to any one of them. Security is essentially an inter-departmental matter. The Service should be the agent of all departments, and it should be able to do the work far better than if each one were to undertake it for itself' (TNA, CAB 301/25), para. 47.

[2] Andrew, ibid.

[3] TNA, PREM 8/1520 ('Attlee Directive').

[4] Lord Denning's Report, Cmnd 2152, 1963 ('Denning Report'). See Chapter 14 below.

MI5, the Cold War, and the Rule of Law. K. D. Ewing, Joan Mahoney, and Andrew Moretta, Oxford University Press (2020). © K. D. Ewing, Joan Mahoney, and Andrew Moretta. DOI: 10.1093/oso/9780198818625.001.0001

The new Directive was initialled by the Prime Minister and issued to Percy Sillitoe on 20 April 1946, shortly before he became DG. With the mandate came a tight Prime Ministerial grip, reflecting the Labour leader's intention to bring MI5 'under the direct control of the Prime Minister'.[5] Far from affording the DG 'virtual autonomy',[6] the Attlee Directive to the DG gave the Prime Minister a well-defined supervisory role. The Liddell Diary reveals that Attlee and Sillitoe agreed to meet at least once a fortnight,[7] with Liddell (Sillitoe's DDG) and occasionally Dick White (Director B Division, who succeeded Sillitoe in 1953) also paying visits to Number 10 to discuss security matters. As we will see, as well as his close interest in the activities of MI5, Attlee was also to take a keen interest in the information MI5 held about some of Atlee's parliamentary colleagues,[8] information which may well have had some influence during 1946–7 in persuading him to stop urging Sillitoe to follow Stewart's advice and purge MI5's records of all matters not immediately relevant to the defence of the realm.[9]

In this chapter we draw out the broader significance of the Attlee Directive, which was first brought to public notice by the important scholarship of Dan Lomas, writing in a tradition of political history rather than constitutional law.[10] Apart from emphasizing the broader constitutional significance of the Attlee Directive, our aim in this chapter is to consider, with the help provided by the Liddell Diary and other sources, the pressures to change MI5's lines of accountability, leading to the Maxwell Fyfe Directive in 1952. We examine the two texts and seek to provide an explanation for the differences between them, while also revealing the extent to which the Maxwell Fyfe Directive had formally to be expanded on several occasions to deal with activity in which MI5 was engaged but for which neither Directive appeared to provide any authority. We begin with an outline of the eponymous Attlee Directive.

[5] P. Sillitoe, *Cloak without Dagger* (London, 1955), from the 'Foreword by the Rt Hon. C. R. Attlee, FC, OM, CH, MP': 'MI5, though technically a branch of the War Office, is under the direct control of the Prime Minister'. Shortly before Attlee addressed the House of Commons on the Fuchs case to announce that he took full responsibility for the *efficiency* of the Service (see pp. 29–30, especially n. 70 above), his private secretary spoke to Liddell about the speech, and Liddell wrote that: 'There is really only one point, namely should he say positively that the Security Service was responsible directly to him and not to the Minister of War [who was assumed to be the responsible minister, and was being criticized in the press] or whether he should confine himself to a statement to the effect that he accepted full responsibility for the work of the Security Service.' Sillitoe and Liddell agreed to advise Attlee to take the latter course, which arguably understated his real role: TNA, KV 4/472 (Liddell Diary, 6 March 1950).

[6] L. Lustgarten and I. Leigh, *In from the Cold: National Security and Parliamentary Democracy* (Oxford, 1994) took the view that the Maxwell Fyfe Directive replaced 'The arrangement which had emerged from the war' which, in their view 'had given the Director General of the Service virtual autonomy, for the Prime Minister who was left in nominal charge, had little day to day (or even month to month) contact' (p. 375).

[7] See TNA, KV 4/467 (Liddell Diary, 26 February and 25 April 1946).

[8] See esp. Chapter 6 below.

[9] See p. 24, esp. note 42 above.

[10] D. W. B. Lomas, 'Labour Ministers, Intelligence and Domestic Anti-Communism 1945–1951' (2013) 12 *Journal of Intelligence History* 113, and D. W. B. Lomas, *An Uneasy Relationship? Intelligence, Security and the Attlee Governments, 1945–1951* (Manchester, 2016).

II. The Attlee Directive

The Atlee Directive began by making it clear that the DG of the Security Service was 'responsible to the Prime Minister', to whom he had the right of direct access. It was also made clear that it was the responsibility of the DG 'to keep the Prime Minister constantly informed of subversive activities likely to endanger the security of the State' (para. 1). In terms of the functions of the Service, the latter was said to be part of the defence forces of the country, with no concern with the enforcement of the criminal law. Otherwise:

> Its task is the Defence of the Realm as a whole, from external and internal dangers arising from attempts at espionage and sabotage, or from actions of persons and organisations, whether directed from within or without the country, which may be judged to be subversive of the security of the State. In consultation with the Colonial Office you will be responsible for similar work in Colonial and other British territories overseas (para. 2).

In accordance with the recommendations of the Stewart Report,[11] the principle of necessity was written into the text, in the sense that special care was to be taken 'to ensure that the work of the Security Service is strictly limited to what is necessary for the purposes of this task' (para. 3). Moreover, the DG should by a process of regular weeding of files 'aim to clear, as soon as possible, the records of the Security Service of any matter which is not required for the fulfilment of its responsibilities' as defined (ibid.). Reflecting an important principle of the Stewart Report, the Directive expressly stated that it was:

> essential that the Security Service should be kept absolutely free from any political bias or influence and nothing should be done which might lend colour to any suggestion that it is concerned with the interests of any particular section of the community, or with any other matter than the Defence of the Realm as a whole (para. 4).

In addition, the DG was to impress on his staff that they had 'no connection whatsoever with any matters of *a Party political character* and that they must be scrupulous to avoid any action which could be so misconstrued' (para. 4). The passage in italics appears to have been redrafted in the immediate aftermath of a ministerial meeting on 7 March 1946, with J. A. Drew (the Cabinet Office civil servant with special responsibility for MI5) making the point in a hand-written note to Sir Edward Bridges (the Cabinet Secretary) that:

> MI5 personnel are, oddly enough, legalistic in attitude and they may *haggle at the ham* on matters of 'a Party or Party political nature' since the Communist Party is

[11] TNA, CAB 301/31 (Findlater Stewart, Report on the Security Services) ('Stewart Report').

> after all an accepted political party.? [sic.] leave out the words 'Party or'. Party political conveys the real point.[12]

Drew was clearly keen to ensure that the Service should not be discouraged from monitoring Communists. The suggestion was accepted.

No enquiry was to be carried out on behalf of any government department unless the Director was satisfied that 'an important public interest bearing on the Defence of the Realm, as defined in paragraph 2 is at stake' (para. 5). In case of doubt, the DG was to refer to the Prime Minister. In addition, the Service was to 'maintain the well-established convention whereby Ministers do not concern themselves with the detailed information which may be obtained by the Security Service in particular cases, but are furnished with such information only as may be necessary for the determination of any issue on which their guidance is sought' (para. 6). More enigmatic were the provisions of paragraph 7, to which we return in Chapter 8. For the moment, it is to be noted that paragraph 7 stated:

> You will be subject to the Directions of the Secretary of State for the Home Department in all questions concerning the use of 'special facilities' in the discharge of your responsibilities, and you will report to him in cases where your investigations show that action should be taken.

III. Proposals for Change

In the summer of 1950, both Edward Bridges (who had been made Permanent Secretary at the Treasury and Head of the Civil Service in 1946), and Norman Brook (who had replaced Bridges as Cabinet Secretary), pressed for ministerial responsibility for MI5 to be shifted to the Home Secretary. A secret internal report to this effect was produced by Brook in 1951,[13] Brook having previously proposed to Bridges the transfer responsibility to the Minister of Defence.[14] MI5 was apparently horrified, not least by the prospect of interference ('departmentalization') from the likes of Sir Frank Newsam (the Home Office PUS), and took issue with Brook's claim that Stewart had exaggerated the national defence aspect of MI5's work—ostensibly the main reason it had become the responsibility of the Prime Minister. MI5 was also unimpressed with Brook's apparent belief that the Prime Minister's role as

[12] TNA, CAB 301/31 (Note from Drew to Bridges, 11 March 1946).

[13] TNA, CAB 301/17 (The Secret Intelligence and Security Services, Report of Enquiry by Sir Norman Brook, March 1951) ('Brook Report').

[14] See TNA, CAB 21/2734 ('Ministerial Responsibility for the Security Service', Brook to Bridges, 15 December 1948). Brook had been discouraged by Bridges: ibid. (Bridges to Brook, 30 December 1948). Remarkably, Brook had not seen or even heard of either the Stewart Report or the Attlee Directive, and he had been unaware of the arrangements for ministerial responsibility, one of his staff unearthing Bridge's copy of the Stewart Report, and a copy of the Attlee Directive, at the end of 1948.

responsible minister was 'justified mainly by the fact that it enhances the status of the Service', Brook unable to see 'why this Service should enhance its prestige at the expense of the Prime Minister'.[15] The principal reason for a departmental shift, however, related to the Service's capacity for causing political embarrassment. Although it appears that this was not an aspect of their case that Brook and Bridges felt able to emphasize, at least not on the official record, it was clearly enough expressed in private communications between them. Edward Bridges, in a note to Brook that remains in a Cabinet Office file, confirmed that this was the case:

> The determining argument in my view was that we wanted to protect the PM from having to accept departmental responsibility for MI5's *laches*.[16]

This was a real concern: in February 1950, the Fuchs' case had revealed that MI5 failures had enabled a Soviet spy to work on the nuclear programme in the UK and in the USA. Bluntly, Fuchs had given the Soviets the atom bomb,[17] the Americans identifying him from decrypted diplomatic messages sent between Moscow and the USA. Other MI5 errors became apparent in the months after Fuchs' conviction. From his prison cell, the latter had identified Oxfordshire 'housewife' Ursula Beurton as having been one of his 'handlers'. Beurton was German born, and known by MI5 to have run a successful pre-war espionage ring in Switzerland—the 'Rote Drei'. Codenamed 'Sonya', Beurton was an officer in the GRU, and by 1950 had a rank equivalent to that of a Colonel in the Red Army.[18] Together with her family, Beurton had been subject to a long and fruitless Security Service investigation—involving all of the 'special powers of enquiry'—which was closed after Beurton and her husband were interrogated in 1947.[19] In the course of the investigation, Beurton had refused to discuss her intelligence work, and the two interrogating officers, 'Jim' Skardon and Michael

[15] Brook Report (n 13), para. 42. This aggressively worded and rather empty attack smacks of an attempt to bolster a weak argument. See also TNA, KV 4/473 (Liddell Diary, 16 February and 19 March 1951) for MI5's thoughts on Brook's comments.

[16] TNA, CAB 301/18. Bridges' note is dated 11 April 1951, following a discussion with Brook about Sillitoe's objection to ministerial responsibility moving from the Prime Minister to the Home Secretary. He was politely suggesting that the Service was prone to make mistakes, using an archaic French term for slackness or negligence.

[17] TNA, KV 4/473 (Liddell Diary, 24 January 1950):

> FUCHS has confessed that from 1942 to February 1949 he was active as a Soviet agent and had given the Russians everything he could, including details of the manufacture of the atomic bomb. Dick and I discussed the matter with the DG and came to the conclusion that there was nothing we could do tonight.

Tom Bower's book, written with the co-operation of Dick White, quotes White as acknowledging that Fuchs gave the Soviets 'Nothing less than the full design of the atom bomb' (T. Bower, *The Perfect English Spy: Sir Dick White and the Secret War 1935–90* (London,1995), p. 96).

[18] See Ruth Werner, (Beurton's 'pen name'), *Sonya's Report* (London, 1991), p. 187 for details of her rank, and more widely for her lack of respect for British counter-intelligence. See TNA, KV 6/41–5 for MI5's side of the story.

[19] See pp. 217–20 below.

Serpell, drew their own, erroneous, conclusions. Beurton escaped to East Berlin in February 1950, on the day before Fuchs' trial.[20]

A Revealing Conversation

Guy Liddell met Sir Frank Newsam to discuss the Brook Report in March 1951, Liddell concerned to prevent the transfer of political responsibility from the Prime Minister to the Home Secretary. To this end, Liddell told Newsam that almost everything MI5 did was 'in the interests of defence', and claimed that the Service's interest in the Communist Party was rooted only in defence—'we wished to prevent Communists from getting government secrets. The revolutionary aspect of the Communist Party was much more a matter for the Home Secretary and the Police', although MI5, with its knowledge of the Party, 'could make a contribution. *Nobody, however, would suggest that we were on the brink of a revolution in this country*' (emphasis added). As discussed later in this chapter, this was to be confounded by a preoccupation with the Communist Party which could not readily be justified on espionage grounds alone.

Also prescient was Newsam's thinking about the nature of political supervision under the proposed new arrangements. Liddell asked whether the Home Secretary would take responsibility for MI5's work for the defence committees and the chiefs of staff. Newsam told him that 'the Home Secretary would do nothing of the kind'. MI5 should be returned to its old status 'more or less responsible to everybody and nobody . . . there was too much publicity given to MI5 . . . if questions were asked the affairs of the Department could not be discussed in Parliament'. According to Liddell, 'The Home Secretary would deny knowledge of our activities and suggest that if we had infringed the law in any way the appropriate remedy was to bring an action against us.' Understandably, Liddell was unhappy with this and said that MI5 needed someone prepared to stand up for it in Parliament. Without that protection, staff would play safe and fail to get the required information.[21]

Just as seriously—although it was perhaps more of a public relations disaster—the Service had let Donald Maclean and Guy Burgess escape to the Soviet Union in 1951, a few weeks after Brook's report was circulated.[22] Maclean had been identified by the same means as Fuchs. Yet these damaging and humiliating affairs were

[20] Werner (n 18), p. 289.

[21] TNA, KV 4/473 (Liddell Diary, 21 March 1951).

[22] The Government subsequently published a white paper on the 'disappearance' of the pair, which did little to improve public perceptions of the Security Service (Cmd 9577, 1955): 'The Burgess–Maclean White Paper has served only to confirm the impression that the Foreign Office and the security authorities between them have made egregious asses of themselves' (*The Spectator*, 29 September 1955).

by no means isolated,[23] while there were other risks of a more routine nature presented by the Service's use of intrusive surveillance and the interception of communications. Russian KGB officer Harold 'Kim' Philby reflected in 1968 on the dangers of certain forms of covert surveillance:

> MI5 operates on British territory, and is therefore sensitive to the law of the land. It can, and often does, press for specific breaches of the law, but each one requires the explicit sanction of the government, *usually* in the form of a Home Office Warrant. Armed with such warrants, MI5 can arrange, for instance, to tap the telephones of private citizens or of institutions such as foreign embassies and the headquarters of the Communist Party. But it must watch its step. If MI5 makes a mistake, questions are asked in Parliament, the press launches campaigns, and all manner of public consequences ensue, of a kind distasteful to a shy and furtive organisation.[24]

Although Philby perhaps exaggerates the parliamentary consequences, they were nevertheless real enough, while it is also the case that this was an era in which many regarded the existence of the domestic telephone as an invasion of privacy. The revelation that the government was permitting Crown servants to listen to telephone calls would have been serious, but public knowledge that the installation of 'special facilities' *allowed them to listen to whatever was being said or done in the room when the handset had been replaced in the cradle*, was potentially explosive.

Norman Brook suggested to Attlee, in English rather than medieval French, but with all the delicacy expected of a senior civil servant, that Prime Ministerial responsibility 'draws special attention to the failures and mistakes of the service which are bound to occur from time to time: it is a disadvantage that the Prime Minister should be drawn, directly and immediately, into Parliamentary discussion of these'.[25] Paradoxically, it fell to Bridges and Brook to draft Attlee's rejection of their proposals for ministerial responsibility, though the reasons offered make little sense, reflecting as they do Attlee's own careful approach to discussing such matters on the record. There is no mention of (i) the Fuchs, Burgess and Maclean, or other fiascos; (ii) Security Service incursions into civil liberties; or (iii) the role of the Home Secretary in sanctioning the interception of communications and electronic eavesdropping:

> As regards the argument that it is a disadvantage that the Prime Minister should be drawn directly and immediately into Parliamentary discussion of the failures

[23] Also notable is the defection in 1950 of Bruno Pontecorvo, a British-based Italian physicist. See HC Debs, 23 October 1950, col. 2488; 6 November 1950, col. 567. See also F. Close, *Half-Life: The Divided Life of Bruno Pontecorvo* (New York, 2015).

[24] K. Philby, *My Silent War: The Autobiography of a Spy* (London, 1968), p. 92 (emphasis added).

[25] From Brook Report (n 13), para. 42.

and mistakes of the Security Service, *it is fair to point out that such failures and mistakes are likely to arise mainly in regard to what may be called questions of liberty of the subject. But action taken against the liberty of the subject is always taken by the police authorities of the country on information supplied to them by the Security Service and any question of the exercise of these powers would therefore, under the existing arrangements, fall to be defended by the Home Secretary.* The suggestion that the Home Secretary should be the Minister responsible for the Security Service seems to rest mainly on the argument that most of the work of the Security Service is now concerned with the study of Communism as a subversive movement in this country . . . It seems doubtful whether on balance advantage would be gained by placing the Security Service under the Home Secretary.[26]

IV. The Maxwell Fyfe Directive

The October 1951 election saw a Conservative victory, the Conservatives winning fewer votes but more seats than Labour. Churchill became Prime Minister, and David Maxwell Fyfe was appointed Home Secretary. Seizing the moment, Brook wrote to Churchill, giving a very brief account of the disagreement over ministerial responsibility, advising him that 'with all your other pre-occupations, you should not retain responsibility for this service', and that the Home Secretary should take the burden instead.[27] In February 1952, Churchill informed Maxwell Fyfe of his new role, suggesting that before he saw Sillitoe, he 'should have a talk with Sir Norman Brook, who knows my views and is familiar with all the details'.[28] The public justification—when it emerged in 1963 that the move had taken place—was not the need to 'protect the PM from having to accept departmental responsibility for MI5's *laches*', but the more contestable claim that the 'functions of the Security Service are much more closely allied to those of the Home Office'.[29] Subsequent events nevertheless support the view that change was made primarily to protect the Prime Minister should things go wrong.

[26] Emphasis added. Brook and Bridges swallow their words and record Attlee's opinion. The document is undated, but Brook's annotations are dated 2 May 1951. Brook had evidently been under the impression that Attlee had agreed to the shift to the Home Office following an interim report he had submitted on 25 October 1950. Brook wrote to Attlee on 11 May pointing this out. Attlee's handwritten comments indicate that he had thought the idea was 'that a Junior Minister should assist me by keeping a check on the (?) progress and general scope of MI5's work': (initialled) C R A 12 5 51 (TNA, CAB 301/18).

[27] TNA, CAB 301/128 (Brook to Churchill, 9 November 1952). Brook told the Prime Minister that 'Bridges supports the recommendation' and that should he wish to look into his arguments in more detail he should read para. 42 of his 1951 report.

[28] TNA, CAB 301/128 (Churchill to Maxwell Fyfe, 20 February 1952, Prime Minister's Personal Minute M66/52).

[29] Brook Report (n 13), para. 42. This paragraph is reproduced in the Denning Report (n 4), para. 237. It was the only paragraph quoted by Denning.

Following the switch of responsibility, Sillitoe had a meeting with Maxwell Fyfe on 3 March 1952, which appeared to put the Service concerns about Home Office interference to rest; Liddell seemed particularly impressed by the Home Secretary's assurance that he would merely be deputizing for the Prime Minister, and would take responsibility for the Service in the House. It seems that the Service was so grateful that a cocktail party was held in the Home Secretary's honour at MI5's HQ Leconfield House a fortnight later.[30] Shortly thereafter, Liddell recorded an MI5 internal agreement that 'no suggestion should be made on our part for the revision of the Prime Minister's Directive in consequence of the delegation of supervision to the Home Secretary'.[31] Nevertheless, in July 1952, Sillitoe wrote to E. J. Whittick at the Home Office confirming that when they had last met they had 'discussed whether the late Prime Minister's Directive to the Director General of the Security Service required revision'.[32] Having re-examined the document, Sillitoe attached for the Home Secretary's consideration 'a draft of a new directive', which he said 'conforms more accurately to my present responsibilities'.[33] Sillitoe's letter had been drafted by Liddell, whose Diary records that:

> We discussed the revision of the Charter at the DG's meeting today on the basis of a draft which we had prepared. With some slight amendments, the draft was agreed and the DG asked me to write a covering letter to the Home Secretary.[34]

The entire document submitted by Sillitoe proved acceptable to Bridges—the sources indicating that he was advised by a Treasury civil servant called J. Podmore—and to Brook. Initially, Sillitoe had omitted from the new draft paragraph 9 of the Attlee Directive governing relations between MI5 and SIS (not referred to above), on the ground that 'it relates to internal arrangements between the secret departments which are well understood and seem unsuitable for a charter of this kind'.[35] Perhaps having second thoughts after their revisions had been accepted so readily, MI5 submitted a draft paper covering relations with SIS,

[30] TNA, KV 4/474 (Liddell Diary, 3 March 1952).

[31] TNA, KV 4/474 (Liddell Diary, 17 April 1952). The 1952 Diary has been heavily censored, and it is very likely that material relating to discussions with the Home Office during that spring and summer has been removed.

[32] TNA, CAB 301/128 (Churchill to Maxwell Fyfe, 20 February 1953, Prime Minister's Personal Minute).

[33] ibid.

[34] TNA, KV 4/474 (Liddell Diary, 15 July 1952). Any amendments made on 15 July must have been very minor indeed, because the draft that accompanied the letter of 13 July (albeit without the annex) is identical to the Maxwell Fyfe Directive, dated 24 September 1952 (TNA CAB 301/128).

[35] TNA, CAB 301/128 (Churchill to Maxwell Fyfe, 20 February 1953, Prime Minister's Personal Minute, Sillitoe to Whittick) .

and the delineation of responsibilities in the Commonwealth and colonies, which for our purposes are essentially summarized in paragraph 4 of the draft paper, which provided that, 'In the field of subversive movements and counter espionage, there should be the closest co-operation in the collection, collation and dissemination of all information.'[36] After being cleared with 'C' (the head of SIS), MI5's four-paragraph paper was also accepted in its entirety by Bridges and his colleagues, and subsequently adopted as an annex to the Maxwell Fyfe Directive, albeit not reproduced by Lord Denning in 1963.

The real significance of the Maxwell Fyfe Directive is thus not the reheating of a number of core provisions of the Attlee Directive so much as the transfer of Prime Ministerial responsibility to the Home Secretary. That significance is reinforced by the fact that the new mandate was not even signed off by the Prime Minister (as it had been in 1946) but by the Home Secretary. The victory was complete: it was the Maxwell Fyfe Directive, not the Churchill Directive; the Home Secretary's document, not the Prime Minister's. The Maxwell Fyfe Directive, rather than the original 'governing instrument' which sought to define the constitutional status of the Service, was no more than a diluted version of the Service's original charter, and compelling documentary evidence of the surrender of effective ministerial supervision. Cue the critical passage from Norman Brook's report formally proposing the change:

> I recommend that the Security Service should in future be responsible to the Home Secretary . . . I believe that it would be helpful to the Director-General of the Security Service to be able to turn to a senior Permanent Secretary for advice and assistance on the policy aspects of his work and on his relations with other Government Departments; and that he would receive from the Permanent Head of the Home Office support and guidance which the Prime Minister's secretariat is not in a position to give.[37]

Despite mentioning the Home Secretary, at no point does Brook indicate what his or her role would be, the clear implication being that it would be purely nominal (unlike Attlee's), in what reads like the offloading of responsibility from one senior civil servant to another less senior civil servant. For MI5 the loss of status would be more than compensated by the lack of political scrutiny to which it would be subjected under the new regime.

[36] TNA, CAB 301/1128 (Sillitoe to Bridges, 29 July 1952, draft attached).

[37] Brook Report (n 13), para. 42 (Recommendation XXIV in para. 48). Paradoxically Brook's own role in relation to the Security Service expanded later in the 1950s, while the involvement of the Home Secretary was reduced. By the time of the Profumo affair, Brook was dealing with MI5 DG Roger Hollis on behalf of the Prime Minister, while Home Secretary Henry Brooke appeared not to know that he was the minister responsible for the Security Service (see below pp. 422–5).

V. The Differences

The Maxwell Fyfe Directive was issued in September 1952. Reflecting the decision about the transfer of responsibility, paragraph 1 provided that the DG would be 'responsible personally to the Home Secretary', while making it clear that the Security Service was not part of the Home Office. In contrast to the Attlee Directive, which required the Prime Minister to be 'constantly informed of subversive activities likely to endanger the security of the State' (para. 1), the Maxwell Fyfe Directive provided that on 'appropriate occasion' the DG would have the 'right of direct access to the Prime Minister' (para. 1). The core of the new Directive, however, was paragraph 2, setting out the functions of the Service in a way virtually identical to paragraph 2 of the Attlee Directive, as set out above. Thereafter both directives contain virtually the same phrase relating to the need for 'special care to see that the work of the Security Service is strictly limited to what is necessary for the purposes of this task',[38] although the Attlee Directive went further and dictated that the DG had to be 'fully aware' of the extent of its activities (para. 3).

Reproducing paragraph 4 of the Attlee Directive, the corresponding paragraph 4 of the Maxwell Fyfe Directive repeated the strong guidance:

> It is essential that the Security Service should be kept absolutely free from any political bias or influence and nothing should be done that might lend colour to any suggestion that it is concerned with the interests of any particular section of the community or with any other matter than the Defence of the Realm as a whole.

Crucially, however, the Maxwell Fyfe Directive omitted a second sentence that had appeared in the Attlee Directive at Attlee's instruction: '*You will impress on your staff that they have no connection whatever with any matters of a Party political character and that they must be scrupulous to avoid any action which could be so misconstrued*.' Only the Attlee Directive addressed the issue of 'special facilities' (para. 7), the Maxwell Fyfe Directive removing the stipulation that bugging operations were to be undertaken under the direction of the Home Secretary, apparently on the unpersuasive ground that it was unnecessary because the sanction of the Home Secretary was already acknowledged even before the implementation of the Attlee Directive.[39]

Also notable is that the Maxwell Fyfe Directive removed the provisions requiring the Service to weed the Registry on a regular basis. This was a significant victory for MI5, which had winced at the Stewart recommendation and the corresponding provision in paragraph 3 of the Attlee Directive that MI5 should 'aim to

[38] The Maxwell Fyfe Directive alters the phrase slightly: 'necessary for the task'.

[39] TNA, CAB 301/128 (Churchill to Maxwell Fyfe, 20 February 1953, Prime Minister's Personal Minute, Sillitoe to Whittick).

clear, as soon as possible, the records of the Security Service of any matter which is not required for the fulfilment of its responsibilities'.[40] It is clear from the files and from Liddell's Diary that MI5 had strongly resisted this obligation and fought hard to persuade Attlee not to enforce it. They were emboldened in their opposition by the claim that 'we are misleading the departments for whom we vet if we do not at least card all industrial workers who are members of the CP'.[41] And because of concerns about a potential fifth column in war time, it was thought essential to 'card as much as we can about industrial workers, in addition, of course, to the intellectual groups', though it was expressly thought not necessary to include 'housewives'.[42]

No doubt it suited (and now suits) both the Home Office and Security Service to characterize the Maxwell Fyfe Directive as a step towards effective regulation of the Service, rather than a step back from supervision and oversight. Yet it is implausible to argue that the Maxwell Fyfe Directive was anything other than

- a loosening of the accountability of MI5 by the Churchill government; and
- a gutting of the Directive of some of the main recommendations of the Stewart Report.

Attlee's requirements to keep the Prime Minister 'constantly informed' of subversive threats, and to consult the Prime Minister in any cases where there were doubts about whether a proposed operation was legitimate were important. They ensured that the discretion afforded the Service to judge whether a matter was 'subversive of the State' was not only contained, but also that its exercise had to be explained.[43] Much better for MI5 to be freed from Attlee's constraints, and for Roger Hollis (later to be DG) to be able to claim in evidence to a judge-led inquiry in April 1961 that:

> I am answerable ministerially to the Home Secretary. I have on occasion direct access to the Prime Minister, which I have never exercised [Hollis had been DG since 1956] . . . But to some extent we enjoy, as you say, glorious independence.[44]

[40] Stewart Report (n 11). See also paras 42–43 and (iv) of his Summary and Conclusions in the same file.

[41] TNA, KV 4/468 (Liddell Diary, 30 October 1946). One incidental point here is the open acknowledgement that vetting was taking place long before it was officially announced. A few weeks later, Liddell and Hollis told the DG's meeting much the same thing, arguing that 'the present ruling' on monitoring only important Communists was stopping them fulfilling their responsibilities to the Joint Intelligence Committee and the Chiefs of Staff: TNA, KV 4/468 (Liddell Diary, 11 November 1946).

[42] TNA, KV 4/468 (Liddell Diary, 11, 14 November 1946).

[43] Moreover, had para. 7 been retained, and had it been published along with the rest of the Maxwell Fyfe Directive in 1963, the use of 'special facilities' would draw attention to MI5, civil service, and political involvement in law-breaking activities, with which the government would obviously not wish to be directly involved, and which the Service would very likely now prefer us to forget.

[44] TNA, CAB 301/252 (Romer Committee, Transcripts, vol. I, Roger Hollis, Tuesday, 11 April 1961).

VI. Supplementary Directives

We have seen so far that MI5 emerged after the war with the purpose of defence of the realm, with specific reference to espionage, sabotage, and subversion. We have also seen that both the Attlee and the Maxwell Fyfe Directives provided that 'No enquiry was to be carried out on behalf of any Government Department unless "an important public interest bearing on the Defence of the Realm" was at stake',[45] suggesting that the activities of MI5 were confined to acting on behalf of government departments, and no one else. Yet an organization chart drafted by Dick White in 1947 reveals the existence of an MI5 section headed by Guy Poston responsible for 'Commercial, Banking and Lloyds Shipping, BOAC and BEA enquiries'.[46] Moreover, the Loeffler file discussed below revealed Poston providing information to a third party ostensibly (but feebly) to protect the Bank of England, doing so on his own initiative, and without a request from a government department or anyone else.[47] The ink was thus barely dry on the Attlee Directive when it was already clear that the shoe was pinching too tightly, and that MI5 was already operating well beyond its limits.

The government response was formally to extend the powers of the Service, with a Supplementary Directive being issued to the Service in 1959 by 'Rab' Butler, then Home Secretary. The latter included an extension of the role of MI5, which has neither ever been officially acknowledged, nor as far as we are aware, ever discussed in print. Although the numbering of the paragraphs suggests that there might well have been more to it,[48] the 1959 text simply states that:

> 1(1) I am satisfied that it is necessary for the Security Service, in carrying out its task as part of the Defence forces of the country, from time to time to make enquiries and provide information and reports to the public authorities listed below for the purposes of countering threats of subversive activity and sabotage and for the purposes of preventing the improper disclosure of classified information in the possession of these authorities. This Directive is

[45] Attlee and Maxwell Fyfe Directives, para. 5.

[46] The word 'banking' had been written by hand above a hole in the paper where it appears an MI5 officer had done some in-house censorship with a razor blade: TNA, KV 4/162 (Memo on Section Responsibilities in B4 by Dick White, 17 January 1947).

[47] In Loeffler's file it was recorded that having eavesdropped on Loeffler and his wife discussing his job interview at the Institute of Chartered Accountants, MI5 intervened as follows: 'In view of the fact that we know Francis Loeffler is a member of the Communist Party, Poston "felt that it would be *kind* to inform Mr. McIvor [Secretary of the ICA who had worked with MI5 during the war] of this unofficially"' (TNA KV2/2928, Minute sheet entry 16 May 1951).

[48] Possibly related to MI5 'surveillance of colonial delegations' in independence negotiations referred to by Andrew (n 1), p. 466, where it is reported that Hollis had—using the traditional Security Service phrase reserved for such occasions—'confessed' to the Home Secretary that the London eavesdropping operations meant 'we were moving a little outside the strict terms of my Directive'.

issued to confirm that you are authorized to take such action as may be necessary for these purposes.

(2) The public authorities referred to above are the following, that is to say –
The British Overseas Airways Corporation;
The British European Airways Corporation;
The British Broadcasting Corporation;
The Bank of England;
The Royal Aeronautical College;
The Medical Research Council;
NAAFI.[49]

The Supplementary Directive was re-issued by Frank Soskice, who became Home Secretary in the Labour government elected in 1964.[50] Soskice had served briefly as Attorney General in the dying days of the Attlee government when as a young and inexperienced incumbent he revealed himself to be very insecure, and in need of Prime Ministerial approval (in direct contrast to the over-confident Hartley Shawcross who had preceded him).[51] He had also revealed himself willing to use his position and the legal process as instruments of intimidation of those who criticized the government, showing insufficient concern for civil liberties.[52] On becoming Harold Wilson's first Home Secretary in 1964, we can only presume that Soskice was a soft touch for MI5,[53] the revised Supplementary Directive issued in 1965 stating in paragraph 1 that:

> *In extension of the general directive* given to the Director General of the Security Service on the 24th September 1952 you are hereby authorized to make inquiries for, and provide information to, such public authorities as the Secretary of State may from time to time specify, for the purpose of countering threats of subversive activity and sabotage and for the protection of classified information in their possession.[54]

In a text annexed to the 1965 Supplementary Directive, there is express reference to the 'Supplementary Directive to the Director-General of the Security Service dated 13th December 1965'. There can be no doubt that MI5's role had been extended in

49 TNA, CAB 301/230. Butler's signature is not on the copy in the National Archives, but the documented is dated 30 July 1959.
50 TNA, PREM 13/3471 (Supplementary Directive to Director General Security Service). The text is signed and dated 13 December 1965.
51 See K. D. Ewing, J. Mahoney, and A. Moretta, 'Civil Liberties and the Korean War' (2018) 81 *MLR* 395.
52 ibid.
53 See also Andrew (n 1), pp. 524–5.
54 TNA, PREM 13/3471 (Supplementary Directive to Director General Security Service), para. 1 (emphasis added).

1959 and 1965, the latter being a substantial reproduction of the former (which was expressly revoked by the 1965 Directive), with a number of minor changes. So, although the public authorities continued to include BOAC, BEA, the BBC, the NAAFI, and the Bank of England, they now also included the UK Atomic Energy Authority, while the Royal Aeronautical College and the Medical Research Council were omitted.

The Supplementary Directive in both of its iterations was concerned principally with legitimizing activity already being undertaken outside the scope of the mandate in relation to domestic public authorities. But this was not the only purpose. Paragraph 2(a) of the Soskice Supplementary Directive also formally acknowledged MI5's powers in relation to international affairs, the Home Secretary, now expressly permitting MI5:

> To make such inquires and provide such information and advice, at the request of the appropriate department of Her Majesty's Government in the United Kingdom, as is necessary to meet the obligations and requirements of Her Majesty's Government in connection with the security needs of
> (a) the United Nations Organisation and its agencies and of other International Organisations and their dependent military formations and civilian agencies
> (b) Commonwealth and friendly foreign powers.

In addition, by paragraph 2(b) of the Soskice Supplementary Directive, MI5's mandate was extended to enable it to provide work for and information to SIS and GCHQ (still not officially acknowledged), to assist them in carrying out their lawful functions.[55] Notably, it is not expressly provided that the extended reach of MI5 as set out in both paragraphs 1 and 2 of the Supplementary Directive are to be exercised only for the defence of the realm, and as we shall see, this was not inadvertent, and cannot be implied.

VII. Regularizing Excess of Power

What this suggests, of course, is that someone suddenly discovered that MI5 had been acting in breach of its mandate (on two counts—public authorities supported and information shared), and that steps should be taken to regularize the position. As pointed out in Part VI above, paragraph 5 of both the Attlee and Maxwell Fyfe Directives made it clear in terms apparently accepted by MI5's lawyers that MI5

[55] In relation to SIS and GCHQ, however, a rider was added to the effect that the 'new' powers were to be exercised subject to the proviso that 'no injury to the primary purpose of the Security Service is likely to result and subject to prior consultation with the Home Office in cases in which consultation would be required if the activity were being undertaken for the purposes of the Security Service itself' (para. 2).

had no authority to act on behalf of anyone other than a government department, and that it had no authority to act except in the case of an important public interest bearing on the defence of the realm. Yet it is also clear that in practice MI5 had been for some time exceeding the scope of this authority. This is evident in correspondence between Soskice and the Prime Minister (Harold Wilson), in which the former sought to justify his Supplementary Directive:

> Apart from its main work, the Security Service has to give security assistance to certain public authorities in the United Kingdom; to provide a service of vetting and security advice for the benefit of international bodies with which the United Kingdom government is associated, and of some Commonwealth and friendly foreign countries; and to give certain forms of help to MI6 and GCHQ. The existing documents covering those tasks are not altogether suitable in form or content. For example, they do not in terms cover work that has to be done for the United Nations, NATO and other international bodies with which we are associated; *nor is all the work which the Security Service has to do strictly (as the main directive of 1952 requires) for 'the defence of the realm'* (emphasis added).[56]

It seems that no one thought it appropriate to challenge this excess of authority, and that MI5 was now to be rewarded for acting in excess of its power by having its mandate expanded. For that reason alone, the Supplementary Directives were significant developments, though they were significant also for the fact that it was the Home Secretary who on his own gave the political authority to extend the reach of MI5 (para. 1), and the use of its powers for the benefit of other 'International Organisations and their dependent military formations and civilian agencies', as well as other friendly foreign powers (para. 2). The 'other international organisations' would include NATO, and the 'other friendly powers' would, of course, apply to the United States, while dependent military formations and civilian agencies would cover the CIA and the FBI, and no doubt much else besides.[57] The fact that this was done by the hand of the Home Secretary alone provoked a row in Whitehall, to which we return below. The row related to the exclusion of the Prime Minister from important decisions of this kind, not such a problem for Butler as it was for Soskice, Butler serving under a Prime Minister who was shortly to be revealed by the Profumo affair as clueless on security matters.[58]

56 TNA, PREM 13/3471 (Note from Soskice to Wilson, 13 December 1965) (emphasis added).

57 All this was clear in the accompanying note from Soskice to the Prime Minister of 3 December 1965 (ibid., with copies going to Wigg and Sir Burke Trend (Cabinet Secretary)) informing him of the Supplementary Directive, expressing the hope that the latter 'will satisfactorily cover the activities of MI5 outside the ambit of their main Directive for some time to come'. The note is in both TNA, PREM 13/3471 and TNA, CAB 301/230.

58 See Chapters 13 and 14 below.

Despite the significance of the Supplementary Directive, an attempt was made to play down what Soskice and his MI5 handlers had done. Although the Soskice Supplementary Directive made clear that it was 'an extension' of the 1952 Directive (para. 1), a Home Office official nevertheless defended it on the ground that 'it made no change in the existing instructions to the Service—its purpose was to codify them and tidy it up'.[59] This echoed the endorsement of Sir Charles Cunningham, Newsam's successor as Home Office PUS, who wrote to the Cabinet Secretary (Sir Burke Trend) telling him that the Supplementary Directive had been issued *at the request of Roger Hollis*, 'consolidating and tidying up various documents (other than the main directive of 1952)'.[60] Of course, it was a 'tidying up' exercise: as Soskice made clear in his correspondence with the Prime Minister, MI5 was already providing several agencies specified by Butler and Soskice with information, and as we will see when we discuss the files of lawyers such as D. N. Pritt and Neil Lawson, it was already providing intelligence information about British citizens to the governments of Commonwealth and other 'friendly' powers, including the United States.[61]

But why would this suddenly cause a problem in 1959 and 1965, when MI5 had been exceeding its mandate for the best part of fifteen or twenty years? The answer may lie in another passage in the correspondence from Soskice to Wilson, referred to above. According to Soskice, the existing mandate was not 'in a convenient form for production—if necessary—to a court or tribunal'.[62] This is perhaps surprising because there was little prospect of MI5 having to account to a court or tribunal at the time, protected as it was by a battery of substantive and procedural rules from having to appear in legal proceedings. So this was either a lie in what was a blatant attempt by MI5 to consolidate its expansion of power and the loosening of the defence of the realm constraint, or it was true in what was a nervous reaction to the new climate since the Profumo affair.[63] Although there was little chance of judicial scrutiny in a court or tribunal, Lord Denning had blown the lid from the mandate, which was now in the public domain,[64] with the risk of continuing judicial scrutiny

[59] TNA, PREM 13/3471 (Minute from R. Shuffrey to D. J. Mitchell, 24 January 1966) (emphasis added).

[60] TNA, CAB 301/230 (Cunningham to Trend, 14 December 1965).

[61] Amendments were made to the list of organizations in Supplementary Directives in 1967 and again in 1970, using the powers under para. 1 of the Soskice Directive, thereby bringing in a number of other public authorities: the Post Office ('following its change of status'), the National Research Development Corporation, the British Council, the British Airports Authority, and the Crown Agents for Overseas Governments and Administrations. See correspondence in TNA, PREM 13/3471, particularly letters on 8 May 1967 and 4 May 1970 from Phillip Allen to the Prime Minister's Office seeking clearance from the Prime Minister. It was acknowledged that there had been no amendment of the actual Directive to the DG.

[62] TNA, PREM 13/3471 (Minute from R. Shuffrey to D. J. Mitchell, 24 January 1966).

[63] On which see Chapter 14 below.

[64] Denning Report (n 4).

enhanced by the creation of the judge-led Security Commission in 1964.[65] That, however, would not explain the Butler Supplementary Directive in 1959.

VIII. Conclusion

We set out in this chapter to examine the scope and evolution of MI5's mandate, a mandate which formed the foundations for its work throughout the Cold War and beyond. In the course of our inquiries we were surprised by the intensity of the secrecy that we encountered: it appears that not even the Cabinet Secretary knew about either the Stewart Report or the Attlee Directive. We were also surprised to find that despite received wisdom to the contrary, the Maxwell Fyfe Directive was not MI5's foundation text after all, but in fact a diluted version thereof, and surprised further to discover the role of MI5 in drafting the Maxwell Fyfe Directive. Also unknown was the extent to which MI5 appeared to be congenitally incapable of abiding by the procedures which its senior officials had drafted, procedures which as a result had to be expanded on several occasions to accommodate the Service's constantly expanding de facto mandate. It was in essence a shadowy organization with (i) secret powers; (ii) the terms of which MI5 itself drafted; yet (iii) with which it was unable or unwilling to comply; for which (iv) the response was formally to extend the powers at its own request; rather than (v) to hold the organization to account for its excess of zeal and/or authority.

The other finding revealed in this chapter has been the slackening if not off-loading of political responsibility for the Service, from the Prime Minister to the Home Office, with successive Tory Home Secretaries leaving MI5 to define its own powers and rules of engagement. It was not until the election of the Labour government in 1964 that steps were taken to re-assert greater Prime Ministerial authority, though, as we will see when we return to this matter below, this was a formal assertion of constitutional propriety and political power, rather than a re-creation of the operational accountability associated with the Attlee years. Secret and unaccountable power of this nature enabling the Prime Minister to give directions to the Security Service is one with obvious risks, particularly in an era of heightened counter-subversion activity so extensive that the working definition of subversion also had to be expanded. Although it has been claimed that 'for the first half of the Cold War, the balance was arguably tilted too far in favour of counter espionage',[66] the evidence we have seen suggests that MI5 found counter-intelligence very difficult, and that its efforts were concentrated mainly on counter-subversion as a result.

[65] HC Debs, 23 January 1964, col. 1271. The first Chairman of the Security Commission was Lord Justice Winn.

[66] Andrew (n 1), p. 916.

This is hardly surprising, given that MI5's role in counter-subversion was one of the justifications for the transfer of responsibility to the Home Office. In the light of this preoccupation, it is striking that there was no definition or subversion in either the Attlee of Maxwell Fyfe Directives, the term variously defined internally to mean '*threaten[ing] the overthrow of the constitution by violent means*' (Stewart Report),[67] to be replaced at some point by '*the overthrow of the Government by unlawful means*' (Lord Denning's Report).[68] Quite how this was wide enough to catch the Communist Party is a matter to which we return in Chapter 4. The latter nevertheless gave way to a further diluted version (at a time when the revolutionary threat of the CPGB was zero), underlining even more heavily the fiction that MI5 was concerned only with the defence of the realm. The new definition was announced to Parliament by Lord Harris (a junior Home Office Minister in the second Wilson administration), not in a government statement, nor even in a written answer, but slipped out in a speech, albeit in an important debate on security initiated by Lord Chalfont, shortly after his resignation from the Labour Party in 1974:

> Subversive activities are generally regarded as those which *threaten* the safety or well being of the State, and which are *intended* to undermine or overthrow Parliamentary democracy by *political, industrial or violent means*. Militancy in the pursuit of trade union or other disputes with employers is obviously not necessarily subversive. We might define terrorism, for the purposes of this debate, as the use of violence for political ends. Not all subversive organisations are terrorist organisations. Terrorist groups generally have subversive aims, but not all the groups which have operated against British interests have the aim of subverting Parliamentary democracy in this country.[69]

Quite apart from the form of words used, further evidence that MI5 was being authorized to act as a secret political police force rather than a counter-espionage agency is to be found in the claim that this definition was based on the ACPO/Home Office Special Branch Guidelines, as amended in 1970.[70] Henceforward, action that was both lawful and constitutional could nevertheless be subversive, if the aim was to undermine parliamentary democracy by political means. It was subversive to use parliamentary democracy to replace parliamentary democracy, though subversion would also cover much else besides. It seems that the aim was to set in stone a particular form of government (even within the liberal democratic tradition), and to regard anyone who would challenge it as being beyond the pale. In

[67] Stewart Report (n 11), para. 31.
[68] Denning Report (n 4), para. 230.
[69] HL Debs, 26 February 1975, col. 947.
[70] See D. Campbell and S. Connor, *On the Record: Surveillance, Computers and Privacy—The Inside Story* (London, 1988), pp. 259–60. See also Home Affairs Committee, *Special Branch*, HC 71 (1984–5), p. 4.

this sense, the new definition was redolent of the early sedition cases in which radicals were charged for proposing a republic rather than a monarchy, as well as universal suffrage and the reform of the House of Lords.[71] It was great news of course for MI5, the lid now officially lifted to allow what they had been doing in any case for the past seventy years, and for 'files [to be] opened on people who were not actively threatening the State'.[72]

[71] See, e.g., *R v Tooke* (1794) St. Tr. 1; *R v Collins* [1839] 9 C&P 461. More recently, *Boucher v R* [1951] 2 DLR 369. See also Law Commission, Codification of the Criminal Law: Treason, Sedition and Allied Offences (Working Paper 72, 1977).

[72] S. Rimington, Interview with Richard Taylor Norton and Alan Rusbridger, *The Guardian*, 8 September 2001.

4
Surveillance Targets

I. Introduction

In this chapter we consider the targets of surveillance. It has been known that it was the public policy of the State formally to discriminate against Communists since 1948, and to this end it has been stated policy that it is necessary to know the identity of Communists.[1] It has also been known that the Security Service existed to help identify Communists, the mandate of the Security Service having been formally acknowledged in 1963, and informally for some time before. And it has been known too and formally acknowledged at least since 1957 that the Security Service employed various techniques for this purpose, including the interception of communications.[2] There have also been reports from former members of the Security Service, in addition to a great deal of well-informed speculation, about the targets of Security Service interest, along with the surveillance methods used by the Service.

Some added colour has now been provided by the opening in recent years of Security Service files, catalogued in the KV series at the National Archives. We referred to some of the unsatisfactory aspects of the manner of the release of these files in Chapter 1. That said, each individual who was under surveillance has a PF number, though by no means all personal files have been released. Those that have been released include not only members of the Communist Party or people associated with Communism, but also Russian diplomats and intelligence agents. They also include a small number of Fascists (such as the Mosleys) and Fascist sympathizers (including G. K. Chesterton), as well as Irish nationalists and other activists of various stripes, along with German and Japanese intelligence agents working in the United Kingdom before and during both world wars.

So far as Communists are concerned, the files are far from complete. First, they are limited by time, with the bulk of the files relating to the 1930s, 1940s, and 1950s, with fewer from the 1960s onwards. Second, they are limited in terms of the number of files released, the number probably not exceeding 1,000. And third, they are limited in terms of the subjects whose files have been released, which tend to be the high-profile figures associated with the Communist

[1] HC Debs, 15 March 1948, col. 1703. It had been going on informally for years beforehand, of course. See Chapters 9–11 below.

[2] Report of the Committee of Privy Councillors appointed to inquire into the Interception of Communications (Chair: Lord Birkett), Cmnd 293, 1957.

MI5, the Cold War, and the Rule of Law. K. D. Ewing, Joan Mahoney, and Andrew Moretta, Oxford University Press (2020). © K. D. Ewing, Joan Mahoney, and Andrew Moretta. DOI: 10.1093/oso/9780198818625.001.0001

Party, but not usually the foot-soldiers. So apart from senior Party officials and leading activists, the files opened otherwise include those of George Orwell, Sam Wanamaker, and Paul Robeson, designed no doubt to stimulate interest in the National Archives. An important figure for whom there appears to have been files which have not been opened include the one-time MP and prominent barrister, John Platts-Mills.[3]

In this chapter, we examine four groups that were subject to surveillance during the Cold War: the CPGB, the peace movement, the trade union movement, and the NCCL, which might be described today as an NGO. It is important to stress that the organizations and individuals subject to surveillance were involved in lawful activity and that the Security Service had no statutory authority to engage in the surveillance in question. It is also important to emphasize that these were not the only organizations to be the subject of surveillance, the Haldane Society of Socialist Lawyers being another notable example, in addition to those already mentioned. And it is important finally to be reminded that the organizations considered in this chapter were under surveillance by virtue of a mandate that gave MI5 authority to defend the realm, particularly in relation to threats from espionage, sabotage, and subversion.

II. The Communist Party

The Communist Party was a lawful organization in Great Britain, with open membership and parliamentary and local authority representation. But although it may have been a lawful party, its lawful status was to some extent formal only, with the Party operating in what might be described as a legal twilight zone. The intense government effort to contain the Party was no less real for the fact that the response was more sophisticated than the vulgar example of the United States, where the Party was proscribed.[4] As the Cold War developed, that containment was co-ordinated in part by a Ministerial Committee on Communism, appointed in 1949 to examine 'existing policy and machinery for offensive and defensive action against the Soviet and Communist menace at home and abroad'. The latter was reinforced by an Official Committee on Communism established by Attlee in 1951 to 'focus all available intelligence about Communist activities in the United Kingdom' and to recommend to ministers 'how such activities should be countered'. The Official Committee survived until 1962.

[3] Files on other lawyers have been released, including those on Kenneth Brown (and his firm, Kenneth Brown, Baker, Baker (Solicitors)), Neil Lawson QC, Jack Gaster, and Harry Thompson. See Chapter 7 below.

[4] See *Dennis v United States*, 341 US 394 (1951)—ban upheld by the Supreme Court. In contrast, legislation banning the Communist Party of Australia was held to be unconstitutional: *Australian Communist Party v Commonwealth* (1951) 83 CLR 1.

1. Resisting Prohibition

Arguments in favour of banning the Communist Party were to grow in intensity after the end of the Second World War, especially from the Tory Right. In 1947, Sir Waldron Smithers—the 'organ-playing, right wing Conservative MP for Orpington'—sent the Prime Minister a report published by the House Un-American Activities Committee in Washington.[5] This was to inform Attlee that Smithers intended to table a question as to whether the Prime Minister would be willing to set up a Committee of Un-British Activities, comparable to the United States Committee. When the question was asked, Herbert Morrison (standing in for Attlee) replied for the government with a one liner: 'No Sir'.[6] Smithers followed up with a supplementary: 'if, in view of the rapidly increasing menace of Communist infiltration, he will come out into the open and introduce a Bill to outlaw Communists and sequestrate their funds; and have a showdown before it is too late'. The answer was still no, Morrison taking the view that 'the other political parties can take care of Communists'.[7]

Rounding on Smithers, Morrison, as Leader of the House made it clear that he was not 'afraid' of the Communists, and that he could not understand why Smithers in contrast should be so fearful, or 'why he should exclude other subversive influences from consideration'.[8] On 24 February 1949, the indefatigable Sir Waldron Smithers tried another line of attack, asking the Prime Minister if he would introduce legislation to enable the government to take action against Communist agitation on the lines of the action that had been taken recently by the governments of India and France. Predictably disappointing Sir Waldron, Mr Attlee responded by saying that 'the government did not consider that any amendment of the law for this purpose is either necessary or desirable', the Prime Minister reflecting harshly on the 'somewhat drastic measures that are being taken by Provincial Governments in India', which were said to include 'the power to detain without trial on suspicion of subversive activities, and a number of other things which are generally regarded as rather dangerous here'.[9]

So although the Communist Party was banned in the United States and briefly in Australia, as well as a number of other countries, there is thus no evidence that this was ever contemplated by a British government. There were genuinely held views about political liberty that would not be easy to overcome, while the experience during the Second World War suggested that any such step would be

[5] P. Hennessey and G. Brownfeld, 'Britain's Cold War Security Purge: The Origins of Positive Vetting' (1982) 25 *Historical Journal* 965.
[6] HC Debs, 27 October 1947, col. 503, as cited by Hennessey and Brownfeld (n 5).
[7] HC Debs, 27 October 1947, col. 504.
[8] HC Debs, 24 February 1949, col. 2019.
[9] ibid.

impossible politically because of the strength of the Party itself. According to A. W. B. Simpson, Churchill had written bitterly to Herbert Morrison the war-time Home Secretary, 'grousing at the immunity' of the Communists, who, unlike Mosley and the Fascists, avoided detention without trial.[10] Citing the principled reason why the Communists were not detained like the Fascists under Regulation 18B (the country was not at war with Russia), Simpson claimed that the predominant reason may have been that the Party was 'too powerful': 'Bevin feared industrial unrest', while there would also be concern about 'trouble from the left-wing of the Labour Party'.[11]

That said, the Communist Party did not escape war-time controls completely, with the *Daily Worker* banned for a short period. This gave rise to stinging parliamentary criticism of the Home Secretary (Herbert Morrison), the charge against him led by Aneurin Bevan. Referring to an 'extraordinary deterioration in democratic standards in Great Britain',[12] and acknowledging that while 'in time of war restrictions upon liberty must be greater than they are in times of peace', Bevan nevertheless insisted that 'it was not expedient to suppress the *Daily Worker* because we could still afford the amount of liberty which the newspaper was enjoying'.[13] He continued:

> What influence did the *Daily Worker* exercise? It would have had to exercise such influence as to be undermining the war effort, before the right hon. Gentleman would have been justified in taking away its liberty. What evidence is there that the war effort of the country and the morale of the population were being affected? We have stood up against the worst bombardment that any civil population has ever had, and we have been called upon to bear trials which no other population has been called upon to bear. We have sustained them to the admiration of the world. In fact so negligible, so unimportant, so uninfluential was the circulation of the *Daily Worker* that it was unable to undermine the morale of the country when it was exposed to the greatest bombardment in its history.[14]

These arguments would apply even more forcefully in the immediate post-war period. It is inconceivable a political party with two MPs and multiple local authority representatives could be proscribed. The Party also had a strong presence in a number of trade unions, which could not be expected to respond with equanimity to any attempts at proscription on the American or Australian models.

[10] A. W. B. Simpson, *In the Highest Degree Odious* (Oxford, 1992), p. 197.
[11] ibid.
[12] HC Debs, 28 January 1941, col. 465.
[13] ibid., col. 466.
[14] ibid., col. 467.

2. Questions of Espionage

Although the Communist Party was not banned, there were nevertheless concerns about the role of Party members in espionage activity on behalf of Russia. Perhaps unwisely, Willie Gallacher had written about the Soviet Union being in the 'vanguard of the world's workers in the fight to establish International Brotherhood', and that the British Communist Party was 'ready at all times to give it our support against International Capitalism'.[15] Unwise, because in 1938 Percy Glading was convicted under the Official Secrets Act 1911, having organized a spy ring at Woolwich Arsenal for the transmission of military secrets to Russia, in a case that to our knowledge has curiously attracted no attention from legal scholars working in this field. Although the plot was foiled when Glading unwittingly recruited a former MI5 officer as an assistant, in a review of the case after the war the Security Service concluded that:

> The British subjects employed in GLADING's espionage organisation appear to have been exclusively members of the Communist Party of Great Britain. GLADING himself was, of course, one of the most prominent members. These persons all appeared to have dropped open Communist Party work, and in some cases to have resigned from the Party as soon as they were recruited for espionage work. It is clear that [Glading's accomplices] were perfectly aware that they were working for the Russian Intelligence Service and were not under any impression that they were simply providing information for the Communist Party. Miss 'X' [the former MI5 agent] was also left in no doubt as to who the real masters of the organisation were.[16]

Glading's imprisonment did little to convince the Security Service that he was no longer an espionage threat, and shortly after his release in 1942 it was brought to the attention of the Security Service by a 'top secret' source that one of his former espionage colleagues had tried to contact him. According to a note on Glading's Security Service file, 'it appeared that the matter about which this [unnamed] communist wished to see GLADING related to undercover, if not to actually espionage, activity'. The concern was that it therefore 'seemed possible that GLADING might have retained in November 1943 and as far as the Security Service knew might still be retaining, some authority over his former espionage assistants'.[17] But a period of intense surveillance under the guidance of MI5's indefatigable Miss

[15] W. Gallacher, *The Case for Communism* (Harmondsworth, 1949), p. 204.

[16] TNA, KV 2/1023 (Percy Glading, Note on the Woolwich Arsenal Case). For an official assessment of the prosecutions, see TNA, KV 3/234–5. See also TNA, KV 4/227 (Maxwell Knight, History of the Operations of MS during the War 1939–1945). Despite the title, Knight included a section on 'The Case of Percy Glading' (p. 32).

[17] TNA, KV 2/1023 (Note on Percy Glading, 6 November 1946).

Diana Mumford in 1946 proved these concerns to be unfounded, the surveillance involving the interception of his correspondence, the tapping of his phone, and the observation of his movements (that is to say, he was followed everywhere he went).[18] Although Glading continued to play an important part in Communist Party industrial activity, and that there were some 'facts' that might suggest he was involved in some undercover work, the investigation failed to establish that he was engaged in espionage.

A more serious example of espionage exposed after the war was the case of Alan Nunn May, a British scientist convicted under the Official Secrets Act 1911 for having passed 'small amounts of enriched Uranium-233 and Uranium-235 to his Soviet handler'.[19] Nunn May—who had been educated at Trinity Hall, Cambridge and was later employed as a Lecturer in Physics at King's College London—had been invited in 1942 to join a team of Cambridge scientists who were 'trying to find out if German plans to use heavy water as the basis for an atomic reactor were feasible'.[20] While at King's, Nunn May had been a member of the Communist Party and an active member of the Association of Scientific Workers. It was after his transfer to Montreal in 1943 to work on the Manhatten Project, however, that he was recruited by the Russians. As was so often the case, Nunn May was exposed by a Russian defector, on this occasion Igor Gouzenko. Sentenced to ten years, Nunn May was unrepentant, claiming that he passed on the information at a time when the Soviet Union was an ally, that what he did was 'morally right' in the interests of humanity, and not for reasons of personal interest.

Gouzenko's defection also helped to expose Klaus Fuchs, an even bigger fish than Alan Nunn May. Fuchs had left Germany in 1933 and settled in this country, but was initially interned during the war. He was, however, a distinguished scientist, and following his release in 1942 Fuchs worked on a number of important projects, spending time during the war years in the United States. A member of the Communist Party in Germany, at an early stage in his working life Fuchs had initiated contact with the Russian intelligence services and passed on information throughout a career in the course of which he become senior principal scientific officer at the Harwell Atomic Research Establishment. Like Nunn May, Fuchs was prosecuted under the Official Secrets Act 1911, where at his trial it was said by the Attorney General (Sir Hartley Shawcross) that he was motivated by an 'unswerving devotion to Communism'. Although he pleaded guilty, Fuchs suffered as a foreigner, being given a maximum sentence of fourteen years, sent down with the condemnation of Lord Chief Justice Goddard ringing in his ears: 'You have

18 Copies of detailed Observation Reports are on his file, as is a record of the mail he received (as a result of a letter check), while a phone check revealed nothing of interest. See TNA, KV 2/1921 (Percy Glading).

19 *Daily Telegraph*, 24 March 2003 (Obituary).

20 ibid.

betrayed the hospitality and protection given to you by this country with the grossest treachery.'[21]

3. Questions of Subversion

In light of the foregoing, it would be hard to deny that Communist Party members had been engaged in espionage, though it was wrong to conclude for that reason that *all* Communist Party members were an espionage risk. It is also the case that the espionage threat changed, and that as MI5 was to acknowledge in 1955 the risk was not now from the Communist Party but from other sources.[22] But this was not the only concern, the government fixated by the capacity of the Communist Party to channel industrial discontent, as revealed by the Home Secretary in a secret memorandum to ministers during the war.[23] Based on leaked minutes of the Communist Party's Central Committee, the Party was said to exploit existing grievances, with one 'Party leader' claiming that 'there was not a factory in which there was no grievance, and there was not a grievance which could be turned into a strike'.[24] However, although it was possible 'to quote very many instances in which Communists took a leading part in pressing for strike action', it could 'not be said that the strikes themselves had no industrial basis'. The best that could be said was that, 'given goodwill, a settlement could have been reached without a stoppage'.[25]

Nevertheless, this perception of the Communist Party as being responsible for strikes persisted after the war, an early indication of this revealed at a Cabinet meeting on 17 November 1947, where the Home Secretary and the Minister of Labour reported on a strike at the Savoy Hotel, a dispute it was claimed was being exploited by unnamed people acting under the directions of the Communist Party. It was thought that one of the objects of the Communist Party was to cause inconvenience 'by continuing this strike throughout the week of the Royal Wedding'.[26] Some sixteen months later, a recent sudden stoppage of work at Barking Power Station was said by the Minister of Labour to have 'not been justified by the ostensible grounds of dispute', as well as being 'in breach of the men's contract of service'.[27] Stoppages had been threatened at other power stations on 'equally trivial and unjustified grounds', the Communists getting the blame as being 'responsible for these occurrences'.[28] In the course of Cabinet discussion it was suggested that:

[21] *BBC News*, 26 January 2011. See *R v Fuchs*, *The Times*, 2 March 1950.
[22] TNA, CAB 134/1325 (Security Conference of Privy Counsellors [sic.], Memorandum on 'Communism as a Security Problem').
[23] TNA, CAB 66/35/9 (Communist Party of Great Britain, Memorandum by the Home Secretary, 13 March 1943).
[24] ibid., p. 4.
[25] ibid.
[26] TNA, CAB 128/10 (Cabinet Conclusions, 17 November 1947).
[27] TNA, CAB 128/49 (Cabinet Conclusions, 21 March 1949).
[28] ibid.

> If there were signs that Communists were likely to try to stage lightning strikes in electricity undertakings with a view to paralyzing the community, a survey would have to be conducted of the extent to which Communists were employed in the electricity supply industry and steps would have to be taken to weed them out.[29]

Continuing government concerns were revealed at a Cabinet meeting on 14 September 1950, at which the first item was 'Industrial Disputes—Communist Incitement'.[30] According to George Isaacs (Minister of Labour), the Communist Party was by unofficial industrial action attempting to disrupt the transport network, while 'evidence' was emerging of Communist-led preparations for unofficial action in the docks. Concern was also expressed about information received that an attempt 'might be made to interfere with the sailing of two ships which were loaded with goods for Korea'. Finally, Isaacs suggested that 'early discussions should be held with the TUC General Council on the steps that could be taken 'to counter the Communist campaign', while noting that the General Secretary of the TGWU was 'pressing for action' to be taken against the Communist Party. In the course of discussion, the Cabinet concluded that:

> The Communists had evidently embarked upon a campaign of political warfare, which they would intensify as the Government's defence programme got under way. Hitherto they had tried to obtain representation in Parliament and to secure control of the trade unions: they had now abandoned parliamentary action and were concentrating on fomenting industrial troubles. They would doubtless continue their efforts to capture control of the key unions.

Informed more by hysteria and suspicion rather than fact and evidence, here was a welcome opportunity for the government to take action, with a wide-ranging discussion about legal controls and steps to be taken 'to counter Communist endeavours to cause industrial unrest'. As an immediate step, Isaacs was authorized to make a parliamentary statement about Communist intrigues on 15 September, to be followed up by a BBC broadcast:

> This should give any reliable evidence of foreign intervention in the industrial affairs of this country, since the workers would not tolerate any suggestion that they were to be used for furthering international Communist policies. Charges of foreign intervention should not, however, be made unless they could be fully substantiated. It might also be desirable to refer by name to individual Communists in this country who were prominent in fomenting industrial strife for political

29 ibid.

30 TNA, CAB128/18/18 (Cabinet Conclusions, 14 September 1950).

> purposes; but here again no statement or allegation should be made that could not be fully substantiated.[31]

In addressing the House of Commons as agreed, in a short statement Isaacs claimed that recent newspaper reports about 'attempts to be made to cause serious industrial unrest in this country' were 'not without foundation'. He continued by saying that evidence was accumulating that 'an organisation is being created chiefly by men prominent in previous unofficial strikes, including some who were expelled from their union because of their anti-union activities and others who have just returned from a meeting with their Cominform friends in Warsaw'.[32]

4. Containment and Surveillance

As time past, the case against the Communist Party based on espionage and subversion was to become steadily even weaker. The policy of containment nevertheless demanded a surveillance operation as big as a policy based on prohibition to identify Communists and their friends in order to exclude them from sensitive employment and to monitor their activities. That said, as already pointed out in Part I above, there has not been a full release of files either of individual members or those relating to the activities of the Party, so we do not yet know the full extent to which the Party was subject to surveillance. Since 2010, it has been possible to consult the material that was removed from the Communist Party during Special Branch raids in 1921 and 1925,[33] and it is possible to inspect more recent surveillance material.[34] But the released files on the CPGB itself stop around 1946, though it is obviously the case that the Party was the subject of intense surveillance after that date. We know this from the files of the Young Communist League, which cover the period until 1949,[35] and also from the files of leading Party officials such as Harry Pollitt, whose personal file of fourteen thick volumes covers the period until 1953.[36]

The surveillance of the Party also included a close scrutiny of Party leaders, along with other influential individuals close to the Party. That surveillance was

[31] At the same meeting, the Lord President, in consultation with the Home Secretary and the Minister of Labour was asked to consider 'what further steps could be taken to counter Communist endeavours to cause industrial unrest'.

[32] HC Debs, 15 September 1950, col. 1405. Although the 'instigators are the same people and the technique is always the same', this activity was said to be a matter of particular concern 'at a time when our men are facing serious risks in Korea and when it is essential that there should be no danger of interference with their supplies and their supports'.

[33] On the latter, see TNA, KV 3/1833.

[34] For an account of the 1921 and 1925 raids, see K. D. Ewing and C. A. Gearty, *The Struggle for Civil Liberties: Political Freedom and the Rule of Law in Britain, 1918–1945* (Oxford, 2001), ch. 3.

[35] TNA, KV 5/90 (YCL). The CPGB I TNA, KV3/388–402.

[36] TNA, KV 2/1034–47.

as wide as it was deep. This is revealed by John Gollan's file,[37] Gollan being Pollitt's successor as General Secretary, a position which he held from 1956 for twenty years. Like other files, Gollan's file includes a reference on the front to the names of all the other people related to the file subject about whom the Security Service also had files, along with their PF numbers: in this case Gollan's father, his wife, his brother, and his three sisters. But it also includes his niece, Ruth Taylor, whose file appears either to have been destroyed or withheld, along with the files of Gollan's other relatives. It is unclear to what extent these people were the subject of surveillance, or why: were they Party members or were they targets simply because of their connection to Gollan? Equally notable is Ruth Taylor's PF number—PF 815,946—suggesting that by the mid-1960s there were at least close to a million people who were or who had been the subject of Security Service surveillance. That number was likely to have risen exponentially in the late 1960s, as Northern Ireland burst onto the agenda, along with greater militancy by trade unions, peace campaigners, and others.

The Pollitt files reveal the existence of a specific Security Service form, for 'carding' purposes. This would include details of name, address, occupation, employer, Party branch, trade union, and year of joining the Party. As pointed out in Chapter 1, the files would otherwise contain copies of intercepted correspondence and transcripts of intercepted telephone calls. They would also contain transcripts of meetings at Party headquarters, picked up by surveillance devices installed there by MI5. This and other carefully filed information would be cross-referenced to the files of other subjects in what was an impressive administrative exercise in the days before computers. And as also pointed out above, all this would be kept alongside newspaper clippings, as well as Special Branch reports of any meetings which the individual in question may have addressed. It is presumed that much of the same stuff would have been included in the Party's dedicated organizational files, though it is not known what else would have been included in the latter or why they have not been released. The failure to release files is presumably designed to protect the reputation of politicians and MI5 officials, and the identity of sources as well as people who may still be alive.

A stunning feature of the files that have been opened is the amount of tedium that is retained, and the amount of material that does not appear to have any subversive content consistent with the mandate of the Security Service. Take as an example one volume of Pollitt's file (which begins in 1921 and provides enough material for a decent biography). The volume in question contains a mixture of political and personal content,[38] with one notable anonymous minute—dated 24 May 1951—acknowledging that:

[37] TNA, KV 2/1772–8.

[38] This and other PFs confirm that there were separate files containing political, as opposed to personal intelligence. Thus, there is evidence of interception of minutes of Executive Meetings (with decisions relating to individuals being copied to their personal files).

> It would be a mistake to regard POLLITT and his immediate followers as 'agents of Moscow', in the sense that they would take orders from abroad in any circumstances. The extreme care so far taken by foreign Communists in their dealings with POLLITT and the very considerable freedom of action given to him indicates nothing of the sort. POLLITT'S own repeated statements about the superiority of the British race (which is, in fact, what many of them amount to), would hardly be just amusing to the foreign Communists.[39]

Notable too are the minutes giving an account of the disagreements in the Party leadership and a significant extract from a conversation explaining Pollitt's decision not to stand at the forthcoming general election. Otherwise, this particular volume contains reports about Pollitt's international travel (intercepted phone calls between his office and the travel agency about his tickets to Prague), an inquiry about the fitting of a Motorolo car radio, and the arrangements for delivering a cupboard that had been given as a birthday present. It is not clear that the retention of any of this could easily be justified as being necessary in the defence of the realm.

III. The Peace Movement

The Government and the Security Service were concerned not only with the Communist Party, but also more widely with 'the Communist Solar System'. This included a number of 'international front organisations', said to be 'little more than instruments of Soviet policy and sounding-boards for Communist propaganda'.[40] They embraced the World Peace Council (WPC), the World Federation of Trade Unions (WFTU), and the International Association of Democratic Lawyers (IADL).[41] So far as the WPC is concerned, it was founded in 1949 following a Communist Information Bureau (Cominform) resolution to co-ordinate national peace movements. According to the IRIS, an anti-Communist operation, the WPC generally had 'two main functions, which it performed in the "Cominform interest"'. Thus:

> (a) under the guise of general peace propaganda it seeks to enlist support for 'peace' on Soviet terms, and
> (b) it aims at incitement to subversion and sabotage of the rearmament efforts of the NATO powers, and obstructing the movement and supply of arms to Europe for the USA.[42]

[39] TNA, KV 2/1046.
[40] IRIS, *The Communist Solar System* (London, 1957), p. 12.
[41] ibid., pp. 12–13.
[42] TNA, FO 1110/349 (Aims of the World Peace Movement), probably drafted by the IRD.

1. The British Peace Committee

The British government regarded the BPC as a 'front organisation'.[43] Formed initially as the British Cultural Committee for Peace by James Crowther in 1948, it changed its name and became the British affiliate to the WPC in 1949. Well known to Special Branch and MI5, Crowther was also General Secretary of the World Federation of Scientific Workers, and head of the science department at the British Council. Previously a science correspondent with the *Daily Worker* and the *Manchester Guardian*, Crowther was the subject of close surveillance, as were other prominent members of the British Peace Committee (BPC).[44] These included Vincent Duncan-Jones, PF 55,907, who replaced Joyce Smith as Secretary in October 1950. The son of a senior cleric in the Church of England, Duncan-Jones had been a member of the Communist Party since 1937, and had previously been the editor of *Soviet Weekly*.[45]

Crowther and Duncan-Jones were not the only leading Communists actively associated with the BPC, as MI5 files clearly reveal. But although the BPC thus enjoyed close links to the Communist Party, it is unlikely that all of its celebrity members were Communists, though it is equally likely that some would have been. As revealed by its headed notepaper recorded in MI5 files, the celebrity members included Fellows of the Royal Society (Professor J. D. Bernal and Professor J. B. S. Haldane) and the British Academy (Professor Gordon Childe), as well as actors (Dame Sybil Thorndike), authors (Sean O'Casey), and poets (Hugh McDiarmid). Other prominent members included the General Secretary of the NCCL, Elizabeth Allen, and the MPs (and barristers), John Platts-Mills and D. N. Pritt.[46] Despite the uncertain politics of all of its members, links with the CPGB were nevertheless strengthened by Phil Piratin's appointment by the Party to a prominent role in the BPC following his defeat at the general election in 1950.

The British government was very well informed about the BPC, the Prime Minister claiming in a speech in November 1950 that 'more than 90% of the members of its permanent committee are known to be Communists or fellow travellers'.[47] How would he know that? Although information is not given about the number of members, IRIS counter-propaganda on behalf of the government reported that the BPC worked through 'a widespread network of regional and local peace committees, of which there were between 300 and 400 altogether'.[48] It seems

[43] IRIS (n 40), p. 27.
[44] TNA, KV 2/3341–4. These files cover the period 1929–59.
[45] TNA, KV 2/2922–6. These files cover the period 1936–57.
[46] There are open files on Childe ('a left wing peace campaigner', under surveillance since 1917, but not known to be a member of the Communist Party until 1947), Professor J. D. Bernal, McDiarmid, and Pritt. There is an open file on one of Bernal's assistants (Francis Aprahamian, CPGB member and a member of Science for Peace). The files on Allen, Platts-Mills and J. B. S. Haldane have not been released.
[47] The speech is reproduced in part in IRIS (n 40), p. 27.
[48] ibid.

to have been a movement with an extraordinary wide coverage, for apart from national and regional organizations such as the Scottish Peace Committee, the Welsh Peace Council, and the London Peace Federation, at a 'humbler level', there were 'numerous local committees, of varying consequence, organised on an urban, village or factory basis'.[49] All this was supplemented by peace organizations in various professions (notably Artists for Peace, and the Architects' Society for Peace), and bodies such as the Ex-Service Movement for Peace and the Christian Peace Group.[50]

The very helpful 1957 IRIS publication *The Communist Solar System*—the author, or authors preferred to remain anonymous—included the addresses, and the names of office-holders of these organizations. It is one thing to publish the address of the BPC in City Road, London, but another altogether to identify in an official counter-propaganda document Miss Christian Hamp, the Secretary of the Architects' Society for Peace, who was then said to run the society 'from home address at 37, Newton Road, London, W2'.[51] Charming, particularly in view of the claim that the Architects' Society was 'perhaps the least in importance of these professional peace societies'.[52] The anonymous IRIS authors claimed that 'genuine pacifists and other British peace-lovers' had tended to give the BPC and its activities a 'very wide berth', on the ground of the BPC's overwhelmingly Communist complexion.[53] According to IRIS:

> It has been calculated that, of the sixty leading officials of the BPC, at least ten are open members of the Communist Party, a further five have been expelled from the Labour Party for pro-Communist activities and about forty are prominently associated with other Communist front organisations.[54]

Calculated by whom? And how would a body like IRIS have access to so much information?

2. The Sheffield Peace Congress

On 3 August 1950, Mrs Joyce Smith, the then Secretary of the BPC, wrote to the Prime Minister to say that the World Peace Committee intended to hold its second World Peace Congress in Britain later that year. The first Congress having been held in Paris in 1949, Smith thought it an 'honour to the British people that this

[49] ibid.
[50] ibid., pp. 27–36.
[51] ibid., p. 30.
[52] ibid., p. 29.
[53] ibid.
[54] ibid.

great international event' was to be held in 'our country', and sought an assurance that 'no obstacles will be put in the way by government departments or other authorities to the holding of this event and the reception of the hundreds of distinguished persons who will visit our shores'.[55] The government was, of course, well aware that the WPC had planned to hold their meeting in the United Kingdom, though it seems that the original plan had been to hold it in London (a plan apparently thwarted by the inability to secure an appropriate venue). The BPC was presumably also well aware that the government knew, though perhaps it was not fully aware of the depth to which it had been infiltrated.

Thus, KV files make clear that MI5 was receiving (presumably from the inside)—among other things—detailed reports of the BPC's Conference Committee from as early as 24 May 1950 with details of all the arrangements for the event. Indeed, a copy of one important report is to be found in at least five KV files, suggesting that it was circulating widely within government. Coincidentally, also on 24 May 1950 we find a note from E. W. Battersby to G. F. Saffery of the Post Office Special Investigations Unit requesting a telephone interception, explaining that:

> PIRATIN, as the official in charge at Communist Party headquarters of the Party's peace campaign, will have some responsibility for the arrangements for the meeting of the World Bureau of the Partisans of Peace in London on 31 May [1950].[56]

This and other surveillance would clearly inform MI5 about the operational capacity as well as the operational activities of the BPC. One notable piece of intelligence was found in an anonymous minute, it having been 'learnt' (presumably by MI5) that in October 1950 the BPC had been promised £30,000 to cover the expenses of the World Peace Congress, the Committee at the time being virtually bankrupt.[57]

That said, by 20 October 1950 the money had not arrived, and there was a fear that 'because of grave financial difficulties', the World Peace Congress would have to be abandoned.[58] Over the following weekend, however, £7,000 was transferred to the Committee's bank account from the WPC in Paris. At the same time, the BPC knew that it could rely on another £20,000 from the Russians:

> In July of this year [1950] the British Peace Committee was almost without funds but now thousands of pounds are at their disposal for the hire of a great hall in

55 TNA, PREM 8/1150 (Letter to Attlee from Joyce M. Smith, Secretary of the British Peace Committee, 3 August 1950).

56 TNA, KV 2/2033 (Letter to G. F. Saffery from E. W. Battersby, Applying for a Telephone Home Office Warrant on Ealing 8575, 24 May 1950). An extract of the warrant appears in the same file.

57 TNA, PREM 8/1150 (Finances of the Second World Peace Congress).

58 ibid.

> Sheffield and for the reception and entertainment of the thousands of foreign delegates. These funds are being supplied from overseas. There is no doubt in my mind that they come from Cominform sources.[59]

MI5 came close to making an intervention, Guy Liddell recording in his Diary on 3 October 1950 that a man called Grey from the CPGB 'finance department' had smuggled a large amount in dollars into the United Kingdom, observing that 'if this money is for the World Peace Congress the prosecution of Grey might be valuable from the propaganda point of view'.[60] By 12 October 1950, however, Liddell was of the view that even if a prosecution of Grey was feasible, it 'would drive the whole funding operation underground'.[61]

The presence of the Second World Peace Congress in England was the last thing the government would have wanted, and indeed it would have been a major diplomatic embarrassment. When an official eventually got around to replying to Mrs Smith on 13 September, after much prompting from Smith herself, it was nevertheless to report that:

> The Prime Minister has asked me to say that in this free country there is no power to prohibit the proposed Congress provided that it is conducted in such a way as not to infringe the law regarding the holding of public meetings. Applications from foreigners to attend the Congress will be dealt with on their individual merits and His Majesty's Government must reserve the right to refuse admission to any foreigner who is persona non grata. His Majesty's Government are however not prepared in any event to allow foreigners to come to the United Kingdom for the purpose of organizing the Congress.[62]

In fact, there was already in train a strategy to disrupt the meeting. Although there was no power to ban it,[63] Liddell and Graham Mitchell decided to 'go on with our preparations in Sheffield to cover the Congress, which are in effect considerable'.[64] Technical surveillance appears to have been the mainstay of the proposed operation.[65] But all this was to prove unnecessary, for although legally there was no power to ban the meeting, nevertheless it was effectively prohibited.[66]

59 ibid.

60 TNA, KV 4/472 (Liddell Diary, 3 October 1950). The DPP was consulted, but considered the case not strong enough, and as Liddell noted, MI5 might well not be able to 'find the dollars'.

61 ibid. Liddell was referring to the funding of the CPGB rather than the WPC.

62 TNA, PREM 8/1150.

63 Indeed, the Home Office felt there was no need to ban it, Liddell recording that as there was no real threat to security, freedom of speech must be upheld: TNA, KV 2/472 (Liddell Diary, 18 October 1950).

64 TNA, KV 2/472 (Liddell Diary, 31 October 1950).

65 Redactions in certain entries in the Liddell Diary relating to meetings with Newsam about the WPC suggest the use of special facilities.

66 For further details, see S. Deery, 'The Dove Flies East: Whitehall, Warsaw and the 1950 World Peace Congress' (2002) 48 *Australian Journal of Politics and History* 449.

3. The Warsaw Peace Congress

Thus, when delegates began to arrive 'in considerable numbers' on 11 November 1950, many were turned back, even though they had visas.[67] According to an MI5 assessment, the refusals to enter took place only after 'careful interrogations by immigration officers', MI5 also claiming that 'most' of those refused entry were 'executives of the World Peace Committee, persons with a Communist record or those thought likely to combine activities of a directly subversive character with their visit to Sheffield'.[68] MI5 commented further that the number of delegates refused leave to land in this way 'caused consternation' at BPC HQ,[69] with 'vigorous protests being made to the Home Office and the immigration authorities especially by lawyers sympathetic with the Communist Party'.[70] These protests were likely to have fallen on deaf ears, British peace activists gathering in Sheffield now subject to highly provocative MI5 surveillance, leading to Graham Mitchell being ejected from a protest meeting.[71] Why a senior MI5 officer was blundering around in Sheffield was never explained.

The Sheffield Peace Congress reduced to a 'farce',[72] the BPC announced on 11 November that 'the repressive measures used by the British government to prevent the arrival of delegates to the Congress had resulted in a decision to hold the Congress in Warsaw instead'.[73] But how were people going to get there, and get there at such short notice? While the British government turned hundreds of people away, it also permitted some to enter, even if they were in Pritt's terms 'rank-and-file' delegates. Also pertinent for our purposes was the question of the British delegates, who never expected that they would be going to Warsaw, and certainly not so soon. Travel arrangements would have to be made for them; but this would not be straightforward. Not only would they have to be booked onto planes, boats, and trains, but not all of them would have passports, without which the journey would be impossible. Here was another opportunity for disruption by the IRD and

[67] We should be careful, nevertheless, to avoid exaggeration. It is not the case that admissions were 'only few in number', though it is the case that admissions were largely confined to the 'rank and file': D. N. Pritt, *Autobiography of DN Pritt, Part Three, The Defence Accuses* (London, 1966), p. 138. Following another Cabinet decision, capping the number of delegates at 500, Liddell had complained on 9 November that:

> It is therefore necessary to work on a percentage basis . . . some of those who received visas will be turned back . . . we had made it clear that we can no longer accept any responsibility with regard to those who are let in or let out. It is clear that if the Home Secretary is asked in the House why he let X in and kept out Y he will have no answer (TNA, KV2/472, Liddell Diary, 9 November 1950).

[68] TNA, FO 1110/370 (Second World Peace Congress Sheffield/Warsaw 1950, 15 January 1951, para. 19). The paper was sent by Millicent Bagot, B1B, to J. H. Peck of the IRD, 30 January 1951.

[69] ibid., para. 20.

[70] ibid.

[71] TNA, KV 2/472 (Liddell Diary, 15 November 1950).

[72] HC Debs, 14 November 1950, col. 1649 (Sydney Silverman).

[73] ibid.

chums in the Foreign Office. Sure enough, in a minute by a senior Foreign Office official (Sir Andrew Noble) on 13 November 1950, it was suggested that 'we should continue the passive obstruction that has so successfully prevented [the] meeting in Sheffield'.[74]

With little assistance from the British government, the Second World Peace Congress nevertheless duly opened in Warsaw on 16 November 1950, attended by some 2,000 people from eighty countries. This too was the subject of intense surveillance by the British security and intelligence machinery at every stage of the operation. A despatch from the British Embassy in Warsaw to Foreign Secretary Ernest Bevin on 1 December 1950, ostensibly written by the British ambassador, Sir Charles Bateman, but obviously heavily reliant on intelligence and security sources, gave a very full account of the Congress and the activities of the delegates generally.[75] Sir Charles was, however, nothing if not partisan, scornful, and cynical in equal measure about the kindness and hospitality of the Polish hosts. This was matched only by the scorn and cynicism about the 'calibre and gullibility of the delegates', who in his view had not been 'chosen by responsible organisations'.[76] It was nevertheless acknowledged that 'those from Sheffield set the tone of the Congress even before they left the railway station, by publicly comparing the "freedom of democratic Poland" with the chicanery rampant in England'.[77]

The 250 British delegates in particular were watched closely in Warsaw. They were said by the same British Embassy source referred to above, Sir Charles Bateman, as having been led by James Crowther, 'with Professor John Bernal, Dr Ivor Montagu and Dean Hewlett Johnson in the van',[78] no mention being made of Vincent Duncan-Jones or Phil Piratin, who were also present. Other members of the delegation were said to include 'an active and intent nucleus of Communists and fellow-travellers', who kept a watchful eye on 'the hotch-potch of middle-aged women, workers and semi-intellectuals gathered together through the various British peace committees'.[79] The same source also reported on the opening speech of Ivor Montagu,[80] while the plenary speech of Professor Bernal was highlighted and derided for advocating that 'every sort of organization should be brought into the peace movement, and that freedom of movement and assembly should be guaranteed in every country'.[81] But the surveillance did not stop there, MI5 having

74 TNA, FO 1110/349.

75 ibid.

76 TNA, FO 1110/349 (Bateman to Bevin, December 1950, paras 5 and 9).

77 ibid., para. 1.

78 ibid., para. 5.

79 ibid., para. 5.

80 Montagu read greetings from South Wales Labour MP, Stephen Davies, 'on behalf of all honest people in Great Britain' (ibid., para. 6).

81 ibid. This appeared to have caused some alarm:

> Apart from the implied reference to the Sheffield interlude, this was clearly an attempt to infiltrate the Peace Movement into every conceivable collective activity and ostensibly to

obviously infiltrated the delegation, with accounts of meetings on M/S Batory (a Polish ocean liner) on the journey home, making their way to MI5.

4. 'Genuine Pacifists and other British Peace-Lovers'

As we saw in section 1 above, IRIS claimed that 'genuine pacifists and other British peace-lovers' had nothing to do with the BPC.[82] This, however, did not excuse them from MI5 and Special Branch surveillance. Take the Peace Pledge Union (PPU), which claims to be the oldest non-sectarian pacifist organization in the United Kingdom, having been established in 1934.[83] Although very much non-aligned, it did not require much evidence to justify the surveillance of the organization and its officers during the period of the Cold War, with a Special Branch Report claiming that:

> The PPU has in the recent past taken a very active part alongside the communists in the Peace Campaign, but on occasions they have been at pains to state that they do not associate with the communists. *There may be something in the view that some of PPU members have accepted some of the views of the communists on peace, and for that reason they can be regarded as fellow travellers*; to put it briefly in the event of war with Russia the communists would oppose the efforts of this country and so *might* PPU members.[84]

Canon Stuart Morris PF 51,277—the Secretary of the PPU—was said in the same report to be 'well known to Special Branch'.[85] Morris had been appointed as Secretary of the PPU in 1946,[86] and his Security Service file reveals that he had been a German sympathizer who resigned from the priesthood in 1939 because of the Church's attitude to the war.[87]

Morris, it seems, could be 'discreetly' approached on behalf of Special Branch to determine whether other members of the PPU were fellow travellers, in one case (that of Eric Tucker) helpfully pointing out that Tucker was not a 'Moscow

dissociate it from Communism. In furtherance of these aims, doctors who were present at the Conference have formed 'International Union of Doctors for Peace'. Judging from the composition of the British delegation it is likely that the co-operative women's guild is considered ripe for similar action (ibid., para. 10).

[82] IRIS (n 40), p. 29.

[83] www.ppu.org.uk.

[84] TNA, KV 2/1088 (Extract from Special Branch Report, re TUCKER, Eric Stanley, 4 September 1951).

[85] ibid.

[86] *Peace News*, 12 July 1946.

[87] Note on Stuart Morris, prepared for Intelligence Division, British Army of the Rhine (BAOR), 10 August 1951.

communist' but a 'Christian communist', 'well thought of in pacifist quarters'.[88] But although acknowledged in a secret telegram not to be 'of current security interest',[89] Morris was closely monitored, it being noted that despite his politics, he was 'prepared to co-operate with the Communists in so far as they are able to stop the approach of another war, although he is not in sympathy with the ultimate aim of the communists'.[90] Morris' file reveals that he was watched at the ports when he left to attend international peace conferences;[91] that his press statements were clipped and retained; and that the offices he held in various peace organizations (such as War Resisters' International) were recorded.[92] The police also attended and reported on the public meetings at which he spoke, including a branch meeting of the PPU held at the Friends' Meeting House, Northampton on 23 November 1950, attended by thirty people, Detective Sergeant Hodson of the Northampton police being amongst them.[93]

The PPU was not the only peace organization operating outside the Communist Party orbit. The other notable organization at the time was the Union of Democratic Control (UDC), which had been formed during the First World War, and which had gradually adopted a pacifist position in the years shortly thereafter.[94] Although of declining influence after the Second World War, the UDC offered a home mainly to those on the social democratic left. But what if these people were Communists? They needed to be watched just in case, as revealed by the file of Kingsley Martin (PF 41,632), a leading pacifist and editor of the *New Statesman*.[95] According to a Special Branch report, Mr Martin addressed a meeting in London on 27 March 1952 organized by the London Anarchist Group. In the presence of 650 people, Mr Martin said that:

> There was a creeping plague of injustice and tyranny evident in the world today . . . The Middle Ages were almost kindly in comparison with Europe today, There were however a few patches of freedom left. He spoke of the methods adopted in Spain of making prisoners confess through cruelty . . . and said that

[88] TNA, KV 2/1088 (Extract from Special Branch Report, re TUCKER, Eric Stanley, 4 September 1951).

[89] TNA, KV 2/1088 (Secret Telegram for Despatch in Cipher, 26 May 1948 (from Security Service to BAOR)).

[90] TNA, KV 2/1088 (Note on Stuart Morris, prepared for Intelligence Division, British Army of the Rhine (BAOR), 10 August 1951).

[91] TNA, KV 2/1088 (Metropolitan Police Special Branch, Report from Port of Harwich on Canon Stuart White, 12 June 1952)—Morris leaving for a week to attend conference in Denmark. Discrete search of baggage by H. M. Customs found nothing of special interest.

[92] TNA, KV 2/1088 (Extract from *Peace News* dated 24 August 1951 headed 'New WRI Council').

[93] TNA, KV 2/1088 (County Borough of Northampton Police, Meeting of Peace Pledge Union on 23 November 1950, Copy of Report, 27 November 1950).

[94] On the origins of the UDC, see M. Swartz, *The Union of Democratic Control in British Politics during the First World War* (Oxford, 1971). A surveillance file had been kept on the UDC Secretary, Dorothy Woodman, alias Dorothy Kingsley-Martin, since 1932.

[95] TNA, KV 2/2093. MI5 had opened a file on Martin in 1932.

> such confessions were accepted at the trials. It was the law in Spain that people must adapt themselves to the existing regime . . . A steady policy is needed of encouraging resistance in Spain, Franco is now sensitive to criticism as he wants to join the Western Community. We must force the Government to say to the Spanish government 'As you are today, the British People will not take you as allies and friends.'[96]

That was enough to justify surveillance and the retention of information. It seems the authorities were willing Martin to be a Communist. Like countless others, Martin's foreign travel was monitored—not only at the airport, where surreptitious Special Branch baggage searches took place, but also on arrival. His visit to Kenya in November 1952 caused some concern for the diplomatic corps there, a British official contacting London to say that Mr Martin's 'outspoken views on racial discrimination [to which he was opposed] and remarks that terrorism cannot be attributed to Mau Mau have naturally irritated local authorities'.[97] A security check was requested, following which the reply came that Martin was 'not known to be a member of the Communist Party', but that he was a pacifist who had for a long time been an active member for the Union of Democratic Control and was probably still a member of the NCCL.[98] His non-membership of the Party was not enough to protect him from prying eyes. But it ought to be a matter of concern that the editor of a magazine as innocuous as the *New Statesman* was a surveillance target.

IV. Trade Unions

MI5 was never required publicly to justify its targeting of either the Communist Party or the various strands of the peace movement, or to explain why the scale of the operation was necessary for the defence of the realm. Perhaps just as well, for as we have seen there were serious doubts about whether all or any of it could be justified on the grounds of counter-espionage or counter-subversion. But if that was true of a political party and pacifist groups, it was even more true of trade unions, which were also the subject of intense surveillance, purportedly to determine the extent of their infiltration by a lawful political party. It is difficult to tell on what basis this could be justified, it being reported at a Cabinet meeting in 1949 that there was no Communist Party member on the TUC General Council, which typically included the most senior figures in the movement.[99]

96 TNA, KV 2/2093 (Extract from SB Report re London Anarchist Group Meeting, 27 March 1952).
97 TNA, KV 2/2093 (Telegram Received, 6 November 1952).
98 TNA, KV 2/2093 (Telegram for Despatch, 12 November 1952).
99 TNA, CAB 128/18/18 (Cabinet Conclusions, 14 September 1950).

1. Surveillance of Trade Unions

A striking feature of the KV files is the absence of evidence of the systematic surveillance of trade unions. This is despite MI5's assessment of the industrial strategy of the Party, much of which was devoted to the 'penetration of the Trade Union movement', a process that was said to have been going on 'steadily for nearly thirty years'.[100] It simply does not seem credible that there were not organizational files on individual unions (as well as PFs on trade unionists), just as there were files on law firms, as well as individual lawyers. Snatches of misplaced information make it quite clear, nevertheless, that trade unions were under active surveillance. Thus, the personal file of Labour MP Wilfred Vernon includes the following minute:

> **Association of Scientific Workers**
> I have passed over our records the names of the Officers, Executive Committee, TUC Delegates and the Standing Orders Committee of the AScW for the year 1950–51. The following list . . . gives an indication of the degree of Communist domination in this body. You will see that I have quoted our file reference numbers and have used the abbreviations NT for 'no trace' and NRA for 'nothing recorded against', and the expression 'Party member' meaning member of the British Communist Party.[101]

In addition, as we will see below in section 4, Bert Edwards' file reveals not only that trade union activists were kept under close surveillance, but that so too was the TUC, which would no doubt have been greatly affronted had it known.

Whatever the extent of direct surveillance of trade unions, there is clear evidence of collateral surveillance through penetration of the Communist Party. The importance of this source is provided by Frank Haxell's file, Haxell a leading figure in the ETU and one of the few trade unionists whose files have been opened.[102] A member of the Party's NEC, Haxell's file provides a tantalizing insight into one way MI5 found out about the internal affairs of the trade union movement, with an entry from 7 May 1952 reporting a Communist Party departmental meeting in which disagreements between comrades on the ETU executive were discussed, the disagreements between Les Cannon and the others requiring intervention by the Communist Party's industrial organizer (Peter Kerrigan). This resolved that:

> 1) there was a collective leadership operating in the Union, 2) that everybody had full confidence in Haxell's leadership, 3) that although criticism was

100 ibid.
101 TNA, KV 2/996 (24 July 1950).
102 TNA, KV 2/1845–6. The Haxell file was opened in 1941. Nothing in the file dating from after 1954 has been released to the National Archives.

> important in the collective leadership, they should demand that Cannon stop this continuous campaign of his, 4) that the comrades present should work together in a constructive way. Cannon was not satisfied and demanded to see Pollitt. Pollitt could not see him and Kerrigan had another discussion with him and after 1½ hours Cannon accepted all the points and agreed to co-operate on the leadership.[103]

But that is all that there is. Although there is a lot of personal detail about Haxell in a file that has been edited, neither Haxell's file nor any other file we encountered contains anything on the difficult period leading up the ETU trial in 1961. As a result of the latter, a number of senior ETU officials were found to have been party to a conspiracy to 'rig' elections for key posts in the union.[104]

We do know, however, that in 1957, when public allegations began to emerge about electoral irregularity in the ETU, the Minister of Labour briefed the Cabinet on the situation. Apart from writing that there was 'little or no evidence of the truth of the various allegations', and that he was 'fairly confident that everything done has been within the rules', the Minister (Ian McLeod), wrote that:

> The best solution of course is for the members of the union (if they will and if they can) to rally against the Communist leadership. There is a chance that they will. I feel in present circumstances we should do nothing and say nothing that will hinder them from doing this.

We also know that some help was provided to ensure that the 'best solution' was the solution reached: Christopher Andrew records that 'from 1957 onwards, the [Security] Service provided much of the material which was covertly used by Whitehall to orchestrate publicity campaigns against Communist influence in the union movement'.[105] 'By far the most successful of these campaigns' he continues, 'was against Communist ballot rigging in the ETU', referring to a minute from Roger Hollis to the Home Office, in which Hollis said that:

> We know from our coverage of Party Headquarters and of two or three of the private meeting places chosen by it that 12 meetings were held in 1959 of the Party's advisory committee for the ETU. This committee consists of 9 communist members of the union, including the President, General Secretary and Assistant General Secretary, and is chaired by [Peter] Kerrigan, the Party's National Industrial Organiser. On one or two recent occasions [John]

103 TNA, KV 2/1846 (Source North—Top Secret).
104 *Byrne v Foulkes*, *The Times*, 29 June 1961. See further Chapter 12 below.
105 C. Andrew, *The Defence of the Realm—The Authorised History of MI5* (London, 2009), p. 409.

> Gollan himself has attended. This information has been made available to the Ministry of Labour.[106]

The foregoing tends to support the view that trade union surveillance was not always systematically undertaken and that in some cases MI5 relied on secondary sources for intelligence. But, however obtained, that information could then be shared, as confirmed by Christopher Mayhew, sometime Labour MP and founding father of the IRD, the 'black propaganda unit' loosely associated with the Foreign Office and SIS. Mayhew writes (in a passage brimming with information):

> At a critical moment, an important meeting was held between Cabinet Secretary Norman Brook, Pat Dean representing the Foreign Office, the director of MI5, Mr (later Sir) Roger Hollis, and Norman Reddaway representing IRD. At the end of it, Brook instructed Hollis to make available to the Foreign Office, with security collateral, intelligence about communist malpractices in the unions that could be used by the IRD. This led, among other things, to the ousting of Foulkes and Haxell from the leadership of the Electrical Trades' Union.[107]

What is unknown is whether any information obtained by MI5 was passed onto the plaintiffs' legal team in the subsequent 'ETU trial', which was led by Gerald Gardiner QC, an ardent anti-Communist and formerly a member of the Haldane Society of Socialist Lawyers, until it split in 1948.[108]

2. Surveillance and Industrial Action (1)

Surveillance of trade unions for evidence of Communist penetration is one thing; surveillance of industrial action something different altogether. Nevertheless, the files reveal not only that there was intermittent but intense monitoring of industrial disputes, but also that this was done on the pretext that the disputes were instances of Communist subversion, rather than to establish whether the disputes were or were not manifestations of subversive influences. This surveillance involved liaison between MI5 and the Special Branch, but also between the Home Office and the Ministry of Labour. Despite the existence of Order 1305 (a wartime regulation prohibiting strikes, which was still in force and not revoked until 1951), there had been a rash of unofficial strikes in vital industries during the summer and autumn of 1949.[109] The reaction of the Cabinet to these events provides us with a rare glimpse

[106] ibid., pp. 409–10.
[107] C. Mayhew, *A War of Words: A Cold War Witness* (London, 1998), p. 46.
[108] See Chapter 7 below.
[109] According to *The Times*, 19 August 1949, there were in the region of 1,700 strikes every year between 1946 and 1949.

of the monitoring by MI5 and others of workers engaged in industrial action, with the central role of the Home Office in the affair revealed in a Whitehall file full of Special Branch reports on workers' meetings, as well as letters confirming the involvement of section B1D of the Security Service.[110]

The dock workers had been engaging in sporadic unofficial action since 1945, an unofficial Port Workers' Committee (PWC) regarded by the government as the leaders of a Communist conspiracy. To the annoyance of their union leadership (TGWU), dockers had established 'PWCs' in London and Merseyside, and were represented on the Road Haulage and Allied Trade Committee—another thorn in the side of the TGWU. At a Cabinet meeting on 29 June 1950, ministers essentially resolved in the words of Hugh Dalton to 'Go for [the] Port Committee and get them in jail'.[111] To this end, MI5 and Special Branch were already under pressure from the Attorney General (Hartley Shawcross) to look into subversive activities in the dock yards with a view to mounting a prosecution,[112] efforts which were renewed in early July 1950, when the head of Special Branch was directed by Shawcross to gather evidence on the related unofficial Smithfield Market disputes.[113] By September the London bus drivers, the Smithfield drivers and porters, and the general road haulage lorry drivers were either out on strike or threatening to take action, and all were questioning whether the TGWU—its leadership very 'tight' with the government—was capable of representing their interests.

However, it was the report in the *Daily Herald* on the return of PWC members from a visit to Poland, alleging that the dockers were receiving orders to strike direct from the Comintern, that appeared to provoke ministers into action. The rather excitable Hugh Dalton (a man of notoriously poor judgement) is reported again in the Cabinet Secretary's Notebook as ranting rhetorically: 'Are these men capable of being arrested for conspiracy? Jail them. Plus full publicity'.[114] Cabinet Conclusions reveal, however, that:

> The criminal law could not be invoked effectively against these efforts to cause industrial strife. The promotion of a series of strikes was not in itself an offence; and, when it came to proof of seditious intention in any charge of conspiracy, it would

[110] TNA HO 45/25546 (Disturbances: Strikes in industry: Communist-instigated subversion).

[111] TNA, CAB 195/8/14 (Cabinet Secretary's Notebook, 29 June 1950).

[112] On 7 July 1949, Liddell recorded that 'Paling of the DPP's office called to see me. He has been asked by Shawcross for an assurance that Special Branch and the Security Service were doing all they could in connection with the dock strikes. I explained to Paling the situation as we saw it.' Liddell and Paling agreed that 'there was not likely to be any evidence upon which to stage a prosecution' (TNA, KV 2/471, Liddell Diary, 7 July 1949).

[113] TNA, KV 2/472 (Liddell Diary, 5 July 1950). On 7 July 1950, Cabinet Secretary Norman Brook had visited MI5 to prepare material for his report to the Prime Minister on MI5 and SIS and in the margins of one of the documents he took with him to Leconfield House, he had written, 'Who is behind the docks strikes?'

[114] TNA, CAB 195-8-29 (Cabinet Secretary's Notebook, 14 September 1950).

> be difficult to establish that an accused person had not been moved by a desire to improve the conditions of the workers who were being asked to strike.[115]

Although wiser counsel appears to have trumped Dalton for the time being, the temperature was raised by Attlee's instruction that Isaacs as Minister of Labour should warn Parliament of the danger posed by the plotters, and the decision that Isaacs would also make a BBC broadcast urging workers not to be drawn into unofficial strike action.

As pointed out above, Isaacs duly addressed the Commons the next day—a Friday.[116] On the same day, a telephoned request was made by the Ministry of Labour to F3 Division of the Police Department at the Home Office, to arrange for Special Branch coverage of the meat and haulage workers' meetings planned for that Sunday.[117] On Saturday 16 September the newspapers were full of stories reporting that Special Branch had infiltrated the inner circle of the plotters and that the police were poised to make arrests. It is very likely that the Ministry of Labour had briefed Fleet Street, and that Isaacs was effectively warning the strikers to 'back off'. However, Special Branch had long had the PWC under very close surveillance, and concern was expressed that these operations could have been compromised by the Minister of Labour's intervention. Guy Liddell, who, let it not be forgotten, was DDG of MI5, was particularly unimpressed by the Minister of Labour's antics, recording in his Diary that:

> Isaacs, the Minister of Labour, has made a stupid speech about Communist plots. It is likely to recoil on our heads. He had little or no evidence on which to base his statement.[118]

3. Surveillance and Industrial Action (2)

The story so far provides us with several glimpses of MI5's role in industrial action: being charged actively to find out what was going on; inactively to engage in doleful hand-wringing from the touchline. It also confirms that it is much easier to collect information than for the government to use it wisely. Thereafter, however, the events were to reveal that MI5 was part of a complex surveillance operation and that industrial action provided an opportunity to keep the registry up to date and the files refreshed. Picking up the story, Isaacs had an ally in the Home Secretary (Chuter Ede), and meetings were convened at the Home Office on 19 and 26 September

115 TNA, CAB 128/18 (Cabinet Conclusions, 14 September 1950).
116 HC Debs, 15 September 1950, col. 1405.
117 Recorded in TNA, HO 45/25546, the origin, unless specified otherwise, of all subsequent material referred to in this section.
118 TNA, KV 4/472 (Liddell Diary, 18 September 1950).

1950. The 'top men' from Special Branch and MI5 were assembled with the Chief Constables of various port-side police authorities and representatives from the Home Office's F3 Division. The PUS at the Home Office (Sir Frank Newsam) and the DPP (Sir Theobald Mathew) also present, gave instructions for intelligence and evidence on Communist activity in the docks to be gathered, Sillitoe agreeing to make any MI5 intelligence available to Special Branch. Of primary interest was evidence that would stand up in court. All information was to be fed back to Scotland Yard.

The best evidence would be obtained by Special Branch officers' comprehensive notes of what was said at dock workers' meetings. Where this was not possible, informants were used, as on occasions were hidden microphones. Reports of these meetings were sent to the Home Office and to MI5. Meanwhile, an unofficial London Gas Workers' strike was starting to bite, and Special Branch looked for evidence of a Communist conspiracy there as well. Although unable to find any such evidence,[119] ten men thought to be 'ringleaders' were nevertheless selected from the 1,500 strikers for prosecution under the penal provisions of Order 1305.[120] On 5 October the men were convicted at Bow Street Magistrates' Court, and each given a month's jail sentence, but granted bail pending appeal.[121] Within days, a Joint Trade Union Defence Committee (JTUDC) had been established. Although dominated by the ETU and the AEU, the London PWC also played a prominent role on the Committee, the aims of which were the acquittal of the ten gas workers, the revocation of Order 1305, and 'the disbanding of all police organisations set up to spy on trade unionists'.[122]

At the appeal on 21 November 1950, the prison sentences were substituted by £50 fines for each of the ten men. The JTUDC continued its fight, and the publicity given to the Special Branch monitoring of trade unionists meant that Special Branch—and their informers—were now attending meetings where those assembled were protesting against Special Branch spies attending their meetings.[123] Meanwhile, Special Branch continued to monitor the dock leaders, and early in February 1951 dockers in Birkenhead, believing that the TGWU again had let them down in pay negotiations, walked out in protest. Strikes at Liverpool and Manchester followed. Three of the Merseyside dock leaders visited London to discuss the situation, and evidently taking the view that this was their best chance of obtaining evidence of a conspiracy, Special Branch arrested the men, along with four of the leading lights of the London PWC, when they met in a pub in Stepney on 8 February. Commander Burt of Special Branch visited MI5 a few days later, telling Liddell of various unspecified 'exploits' in pursuit of evidence against the dockers,

[119] Special Branch Report, 21 September 1950. The unions concerned were primarily the AEU, the ETU, and the Boilermakers' Union.

[120] TNA, HO 45/25546 (Letter to Phillip Noel—Baker from Hartley Shawcross, 25 September 1950).

[121] After the prison sentences had been handed down, the Minister of Labour told his colleagues that they 'Need prosecution. Press for penalty, on appeal.' He was upbraided by Bevin: 'Don't discuss that in Cabinet': TNA, CAB 195/8/33 (Cabinet Secretary's Notebook, 9 October 1950).

[122] *The Daily Worker*, 13 November 1950.

[123] Special Branch Report, 12 November 1950.

Liddell's account revealing that Burt 'had run considerable risks in obtaining information', including the use of covert listening devices.[124]

Charged with breaching Order 1305 as well as with conspiracy to induce breach of contract and conspiracy to damage the economic interests of their employer 'otherwise than in relation to a trade dispute', prospects looked bleak for the seven men. The file reveals, however, that when during the trial it had seemed that convictions were assured, Shawcross (who led for the prosecution) had spoken privately to the trial judge (Lord Chief Justice Goddard) in a bid to persuade him not to be too severe when sentencing.[125] Perhaps fearing lengthy jail sentences for trade unionists at a time of political instability, the case collapsed with Shawcross compelled to enter 'a *nolle prosequi* to the whole indictment'.[126] But although the dockers were thus acquitted, the suffocating level of surveillance continued. Indeed, Special Branch reported on the trial from within the court room, and officers outside the court recorded the jubilant scenes when the seven dockers walked out of the Old Bailey. But there was no report to Cabinet, which had been consulted about the gas workers' prosecution,[127] and no formal discussion thereafter by the Attlee Cabinet of the role of the Communist Party in industrial disputes.[128]

Surveillance and the South Wales Miners

In 1951, South Wales miners, evidently undeterred by the Attlee government's 'hard line', took unofficial action against pit closures. The Glamorgan police liaised with F3 (Home Office), MI5, and the DPP, and some of the paperwork generated was placed with the material on the gas and dock strikes released to the National Archives, revealing that the police had a considerable knowledge of local Communists.[129] The reports sent to London provided names, addresses, and car registration numbers for the MI5 Registry, and make it obvious that the local police had informants in the NUM Lodges. The Chief Constable, Joseph

[124] TNA, KV 4/473 (Liddell Diary, 15 February 1951). See also T. Bunyan, *The History and Practice of the Political Police in Britain* (London, 1977), pp. 124–5, and C. J. Davis, *Waterfront Revolts, New York and London Dock Workers 1946–61* (Urbano and Chicago, IL, 2003), p. 196. Both refer to an audio recording of a meeting in Canning Town.

[125] TNA, HO 45/25546 (Shawcross to Chuter Ede, 14 April 1951).

[126] The words of Shawcross reported by Special Branch, 20 April 1951 (TNA, HO 45/25546).

[127] See, e.g., TNA, CAB 195/8/31 (Cabinet Secretary's Notebook, 26 September 1950). The decision to prosecute was subsequently approved by the Ministerial Emergencies Committee and then by the Cabinet.

[128] Order 1305 was revoked in 1951 and replaced by SI 1951 No. 1376, which removed the criminal liability for industrial action. See TNA, CAB 129/46 (Memorandum by the Minister of Labour, 20 July 1951). This was done ostensibly because 'the prohibition could not be effectively enforced': Cmnd 3623, 1968, para. 237.

[129] TNA, HO 827723/346 ('Disturbances. The Chief Constable of Glamorgan. Unofficial Colliery Strikes'). It is apparent that a number of documents were removed from this file before it was submitted to the National Archive.

Jones, ready and willing to crack down on Communists if required, had sought clarification on whether his men were required to make arrests and assemble evidence for prosecutions.

However, the political embarrassment generated by the gas and docks cases now meant that Order 1305 was on the verge of being rescinded, and if it had not yet become apparent to the government that workplace grievances rather than Communist plots and criminal conspiracies were what had been provoking workers into taking unofficial strike action, by now they at least had an appreciation of the difficulties such cases presented. Ultimately, it was the DPP who advised the Chief Constable that no prosecutions would be brought, and MI5's stance was that while they were:

> not directly concerned with what advice is given to Mr Jones, the investigations into subversive activities, however, are of the greatest value to us, and we are anxious that the investigation into the South Wales coal strike, from this point of view, should be continued. I have already written to Mr Jones thanking him for the results of his investigations so far, and stating that we shall look forward to the receipt of further material of this nature.[130]

4. Surveillance of Trade Union Activists

The release of Frank Haxell's file (discussed above in section 1 above) is unusual. But it is important because it confirms and reveals clearly that leading trade unionists were under MI5 surveillance. Because of the censorship of the official records, however, we know little about which other trade union officials were subject to such surveillance. The same is true in relation to trade union activists, where great care appears to have been taken to remove any evidence of surveillance, though the industrial action files referred to above make it clear that disputes were used as an opportunity for gathering as well as using intelligence. So far as individuals are concerned, sometimes what look like mistakes are made, the release of Bert Edwards' file being a case in point.[131] Edwards was London District Secretary of the NUVB who came to the notice of Special Branch in the 1930s, being mentioned in correspondence between Special Branch and MI5, on account of his 'Communistic views'. A Labour councillor after the war, Edwards was not a national figure, he was not especially well known, and he was not an especially significant trade unionist.

Edwards' file contains a lot of biographical detail about Edwards himself (born in 1896), as well as his wife and son. The descriptions of his appearance are as

[130] TNA, HO 827723/346 (R. E. C. Broadbent B1D to Mr Oakley F3, 21 June 1951).
[131] TNA, KV 2/3062.

unflattering as some of those penned more recently by the Consulting Association to describe construction workers.[132] Otherwise, we learn that Edwards was born in Liverpool, it being reported in later entries on the file that he was the son-in-law of the great James Connolly, a point that curiously attracts little interest or emphasis. We also learn about the identity of his various employers in the London region, and his work as a shop steward. In addition to speaking with a 'slurred north country accent', the following facts were noted:

- 'Motor cycle Index Number RX6147, a Norton, is still owned by Edwards but he intends shortly to exchange it for a Rudge Whitworth.'
- 'Edwards expects to visit Manchester frequently during the summer months, the object undoubtedly being to attend Union Conferences.'

How would they know all this? Only by the most pointed inquiries, which also generated information about his family. He had two adult children: Special Branch 'enquiries show that while there is little doubt that these persons share the same views as their father they do not appear to have been openly active in extremist matters up to the present'. Of whom were enquiries made? How many other trade unionists were treated in this way?

This file is a rare find, making it very clear that trade union activists were under surveillance by both MI5 and the Special Branch. Some of the surveillance is direct, in the sense that Special Branch had a physical presence at meetings. These include workplace gatherings, such as the lunchtime meeting of 150 workers employed at Briggs Motors, the meeting held at the rear of the Princess Cinema, Dagenham under the auspices of the NUVB. Where Special Branch officers were unable to watch or attend particular meetings (such as a strike meeting of 300 Park Royal Vehicle employees at Acton Town Hall, restricted to union members only), they brazenly report that 'they kept observation outside'. These events would be attended or watched to gather information on all those present, and would help to nourish several files. The same would be true of other sources of information that appeared on the files, including informants (presumably employers), as well as the interception of letters and phone calls. But because so much of the Edwards' file has been censored to save MI5 embarrassment and conceal even greater abuses, it is impossible to say just how extensive was the letter and phone surveillance. It looks like any surveillance of his Labour Party activities has been carefully removed from the file, for obvious reasons.

This surveillance of multiple activities by multiple means allowed the State to build up a profile of Edwards, which at various points in the file is summarized by State officials. What is notable about this file, however, is the extent to which the

[132] See K. D. Ewing, *Ruined Lives: Blacklisting in the UK Construction Industry* (Liverpool, 2010).

surveillance penetrated the official structures of the trade union movement. It is perhaps predictable that the State would have its spies and narks close to radical individuals and groups, and that organizations believed to be Soviet dominated (such as the WFTU) would be closely watched (in the last case revealing an interesting criticism of the NUVB from Walter Reuther for working so closely with the WFTU). What is less predictable is the surveillance of the TUC, with Edwards' role as delegate to the TUC Annual Congresses of 1948 and 1952 deemed to be worthy of note. The latter generated particular interest in Edwards as he rose to defend the London Trades Council and to oppose its expulsion from the TUC on account of its 'subversive' influence. This led to a renewed interest in Edwards by MI5, and an inquiry by them to the Commander of Special Branch for information about where Edwards was now employed and whether he had come to their notice since 1941. There was no need for his address—this had been supplied by the TUC list of delegates, *held by MI5 department B1D*.[133]

V. The NCCL

Quite what meddling in trade union activity has to do with the defence of the realm is, of course, an obvious question to which there is no clear answer. And quite how MI5 involvement in the gathering of evidence to prosecute unofficial strikers could be justified as being for the defence of the realm is even more difficult to answer. Yet the distance between what MI5 was authorized to do and what it did in practice grew even further with its monitoring of NGOs, of which the best that can be said is that they were at the extreme outer limits of any possible Communist orbit. One of these NGOs was the NCCL, formed in 1934 in response to the rise of fascism, and which quickly came to the attention of the authorities. Many of its activists were members of the Communist Party, and many were arrested in their opposition to Mosley. As such, the NCCL was subject to intense surveillance, though initially by the Special Branch rather than the Security Service. Although there are released Metropolitan Police files on the NCCL from the pre-war era, the files suggest that it was not until after the war that the organization was the subject of systematic MI5 surveillance.[134]

[133] It was an article in the *Daily Worker* about the London Trades Council resolution that had aroused MI5 interest, and it is no doubt reassuring that MI5 should presume that Special Branch would have seen this latter report. The concern, it seems, was that the 'reference back' of a General Council motion was a 'Communist resolution', and the fact that Edwards had moved it indicated that he 'continues to be either a Party member, or a sympathiser'. It looks like MI5 had been slack, though it is not clear whether Special Branch were any better able to confirm his Party status. The best they could do was to insist that Edwards was an 'ardent communist', now employed by a firm in north London.

[134] See TNA, MEPO 3/553 for police interest in Ronald Kidd, and the reinvigorated NCCL (almost all of the relevant Special Branch files remain unreleased).

1. Post War

As we saw in Part II, the United Kingdom did not follow the US example of either banning the Communist Party or even banning all Communists from government employment. The position adopted by the Attlee government was to ban Communists from some but not all civil service employment, leading to a purge of these posts. The Prime Minister made an announcement to this effect in a statement to Parliament on 15 March 1948,[135] though notably the statement was made without consulting the civil service unions in advance, notwithstanding the potential impact of the purge on union members. Although no one seemed to question the legal authority for the government's actions,[136] the failure to consult appears to have been bitterly resented, with one civil service union leader writing to complain that the civil service unions had not been invited to express an opinion on the safeguards which might be provided against the possibility of a wrong or unduly harsh decision.

In announcing the new security procedures on 15 March 1948, Attlee nevertheless made clear the government's view that 'there are certain duties of such secrecy that the State is not justified in employing in connection with them anyone whose reliability is in doubt'. This was said to be because 'experience, both in this country and elsewhere', has shown that 'membership of, and other forms of continuing association with, the Communist Party may involve the acceptance by the individual of a loyalty, which in certain circumstances can be inimical to the State'.[137] While not suggesting that 'all those who adhere to the Communist Party would allow themselves thus to forget their primary loyalty to the State', there were those who 'would be prepared to endanger the security of the State in the interests of another Power', but there was no way of distinguishing between the two. Thus:

> The Government have, therefore, reached the conclusion that the only prudent course to adopt is to ensure that no one who is known to be a member of the Communist Party, or to be associated with it in such a way as to raise legitimate doubts about his or her reliability, is employed in connection with work, the nature of which is vital to the security of the State.[138]

135 HC Debs, 15 March 1948, col. 1703–8.

136 The legal position relating to civil service employment was stated by the Prime Minister on 25 March 1948 with chilling frankness:

> The civil servant holds office at the pleasure of the Crown. He can he dismissed. There is no remedy at law if he is dismissed if his conduct and efficiency do not come up to standard. Further, he has no right to occupy a particular office and to be in a particular Department. Even promotion does not come of right. A man can be transferred from any part of the Civil Service (HC Debs, 25 March 1948, cols 3418–19).

137 HC Debs, 15 March 1948, col. 1703.

138 ibid., col. 1704.

There was no ambiguity in the NCCL's response to the Prime Minister's statement. At their Annual General Meeting, conveniently held on 20 March 1948, the following resolution was passed:

> The National Council for Civil Liberties expresses unqualified condemnation of the Prime Minister's pronouncement of political discrimination which imperils the freedom not only of civil servants but of all other employed persons. It calls for its complete withdrawal as entirely alien and repugnant to the British tradition of civil liberties for 250 years.[139]

A pamphlet issued by the civil service branch of the NCCL described the 'real reason' for the purge in the following terms:

> In the USA anything bordering on socialism is anathema. The British Government being a Labour Government with a socialist programme is gravely suspect. How then can the British Government, dependent on American goodwill for American aid placate American public opinion? How better than by a violent campaign against the 'Reds' commencing with the public removal of Civil Servants, and developing in the press, on the radio and at public meetings of all kinds, a violent tirade against everything Russian and leading to—what![140]

One notable, and presumably unanticipated, consequence of the NCCL resolution was that it led to the resignation of E. M. Forster, the former president of the organization. According to his biographer, Forster had not been active in the NCCL for a number of years, and friends such as Leonard Woolf had continually warned him about its Communist leanings.[141] After the foregoing resolution had been passed, Forster wrote a letter to the *New Statesman*, on 15 May 1948, resigning from the NCCL on the ground that its action in response to the civil service purge had been political rather than concerned with civil liberties.[142] While it is true that the NCCL had acted immediately after the Prime Minister's statement, it should have been obvious by May 1948 that the procedure raised due process problems as well as questions of political discrimination, suggesting that Forster's use of this incident was pretextual, representing an attempt to disassociate himself from an organization that was increasingly being red-baited.

139 NCCL, *Political Discrimination in the Civil Service* (London, 1948).
140 NCCL (Civil Service Branch), *The Purge* (London, 1948), p. 3.
141 P. N. Furbank, *E. M. Forster: A Life* (London, 1977, repr. 2008), pp. 280–1.
142 ibid.

2. Renewed Interest

It was, however, Forster's resignation that brought the NCCL back to the attention of the intelligence community, with Murray, of the Foreign Office's IRD,[143] having been led to believe that the NCCL was 'breaking up' and was now effectively moribund. His interest having been aroused by Forster, in July 1948 Murray sought information about just what was happening to the NCCL, and 'what its political colour is at the moment'.[144] Murray was still expressing surprise a few weeks later that he had not received a report from MI5 about Forster's resignation, given that developments following his announcement 'are or might be really interesting'.[145] It is clear that in view of the press reports following the resignation, Murray was sniffing around to find out the extent if any to which there was a Communist presence within the NCCL, particularly struck by 'condemnation' of the NCCL by the *Manchester Guardian*, one loose press story enough to provoke heightened security interest.

It is clear that MI5's section B1A knew exactly what was going on at the NCCL but that it did not consider there to be a major issue with an organization that seemed to be dormant. A largely understated report provided a succinct but well-informed account of the origins of the NCCL, which professed to be 'a non-political organization existing to defend the civil liberties of the individual and to work for the establishment of further civil liberties for the broadening and development of democracy'. The report went on to claim, however, that since its inception, NCCL 'has been of great interest to the British Communists, who succeeded at an early stage in effecting penetration and have for some considerable time been the dominant element in all its activities'. But unlike other organizations that had been 'Communist penetrated', the NCCL continued to be supported by people of other political persuasions.

Given the criticism of the purge, MI5 nevertheless seemed remarkably relaxed, noting that NCCL campaigns have 'in general been such as might legitimately have been sponsored by a body dealing with civil liberties', even if it had 'supported issues which have been matters of interest to the Communist Party'.[146] According to MI5, there was only one occasion where political considerations were allowed to override the NCCL's commitment to civil liberties, this being its protest against the release of Mosley from detention under wartime regulations. It was noted, however, that the Chairman of the Executive Committee was L. C. White, who had been General Secretary of the CSCA until his removal following a right-wing coup in the union. As a Communist Party member and *Daily Worker* editorial board

[143] See TNA, FO 1110/145 (IRD file, Activities of National Council for Civil Liberties). On the work of the IRD, see p. 75 above, and pp. 86–8, 456–8 below.

[144] TNA, FO 1110/145 (Murray to MI5, minute sheet entry, 26 July 1948).

[145] TNA, FO 1110/145 (Murray to MI5, minute sheet entry, 16 August 1948).

[146] TNA, FO 1110/145 (Unsigned letter from MI5 to M. G. R. Joy of the Foreign Office, 10 August 1948).

member, White was well known. Elizabeth Allen, the General Secretary of the NCCL had 'less blatant Communist associations'.[147] There was, however, no evidence that the NCCL was 'breaking up'.

Further inquiries by MI5 were able to provide more detail of the AGM of 20 March—the resolution condemning the government being moved by White himself. MI5 sources were able to report that the resolution was not unanimously approved, and that some members thought the NCCL was being used to support the political ends of the Communist Party, though it would surely have been surprising if a civil liberties organization were not to take a firm stand on a matter of political discrimination, which would be unlikely to stop at government employment. MI5 was also able to provide a full list of the executive committee elected at the meeting on 20 March, a list that included some of the usual suspects. Fifteen of the twenty-three named individuals were said to have or to have had Communist affiliations, suggesting that none of the NCCL's activities could be regarded as 'strictly non-political'.[148] The fact that members of the Haldane Society featured heavily on the Committee was noted by the IRD, and it is notable that D. N. Pritt featured alongside future Attorney General and Home Secretary Frank Soskice—both Vice Presidents of the NCCL.

3. Collaboration with the TUC

Although clearly being watched by MI5, IRD, and Special Branch, the question was what to do about the NCCL. Here the files suggest that the agencies were not passive collectors of information for their political masters, but that they would happily engage in black propaganda to disrupt and undermine organizations they disliked, presumably to produce desired political outcomes. In the case of the NCCL, there was clearly frustration that there was not yet sufficient cause for such intervention, the organization being small and in low water financially, which was curtailing its activities. That frustration is revealed in a hand-written note in the file, in which the NCCL is condemned as 'another fellow-travelling organization which has drawn a number of useful innocents such as E. M. Forster into its toils'.[149] According to the same official,

> Ultimately the only effective measure we can take would seem to be a really well documented and publicized exposure of aims and activities, showing how they follow the Russian line, and every change in it.[150]

[147] ibid.

[148] TNA, FO 1110/145 (IRD file: 'Further Information on the National Council for Civil Liberties', letter from H. M. Gee, MI5, 30 September 1949).

[149] TNA, FO 1110/145 (Minute sheet note by Mrs E. Illingworth, 31 January 1949).

[150] TNA, FO 1110/145 (Note by Mrs Illingworth). Another minute sheet note, a response to a complaint by Murray that the information on the NCCL was not being passed on to his department, states

It has to be said that there was little evidence of the NCCL following the 'Russian line', but of course that would not be allowed to get in the way of a good story. In the meantime, the NCCL was to be punished for its opposition to the purge, with an approach to be made to the TUC to discourage affiliation to the NCCL by individual trade unions, presumably to further diminish income and opportunities for action. The proposal that unions should disaffiliate 'with a good deal of publicity' was presumably designed to encourage others to do the same, thereby reinforcing the attack on income. What is fascinating about this proposal is that it revealed the existence of clear channels of communication between MI5 and the TUC. Thus, we have Murray of IRD writing to the aptly named H. M. Gee of MI5's B1A section to say that:

> The idea has occurred to us that the idea [sic.] might be acceptable to the TUC that Trade Unions should be made aware of the activities of the [NCCL] and should, where possible, be persuaded to withdraw their support, affiliation or connection with the Council . . . If this idea commends itself to you, would it be possible for you to raise it informally with the TUC or do you think it should be dealt with at political level?[151]

Gee did in fact raise the matter with the TUC, replying to Murray a fortnight later that the TUC were under no illusions about the NCCL, and was advising affiliates not to link up with it. Although this advice was not binding, 'in the great majority of cases unions would follow the TUC's clear-cut lead in a case of this kind'.[152] Gee asked his contact at the TUC—a man called Bell—whether the TUC would be opening an offensive against bodies like the NCCL as part of its general 'anti-Communist drive',[153] to be told that the 'essential objective' of the TUC was to 'educate their members into taking action for themselves', experience suggesting that a 'directive from above' would be likely to end in failure.[154] Gee signed off in his letter to Murray by saying that:

> The man in charge of this in the TUC is Mr Feather, whom you know, and we might arrange to get together with him some time, if you wish.[155]

that it had come to their notice that the NCCL was organizing the London 'International Conference on Human Rights', which D. N. Pritt was closely involved with. As a consequence, Mrs Illingworth had been asked 'to look into the affairs of the Council to see if we could not nobble anyone there', and a subsequent note, dated 1 February, suggested that the matter 'would be worth taking up with Mr Gee'.

151 TNA, FO 1110/261 (Murray to Gee, 3 February 1949).
152 TNA, FO 1110/261 (Gee to Murray, 18 February 1949).
153 ibid.
154 ibid.
155 ibid. According to a handwritten note on the file by Murray, 'This is now going quite well, as regards the TUC' (25 April 1949).

Mr Feather was then an Assistant Secretary at the TUC and, of course, became General Secretary of the TUC in 1969, in time for the bloody battles with the Heath government over the Industrial Relations Act 1971.

TUC 'education' would cut little ice with those unions said to have a 'powerful Communist element', such as the AEU (engineers), ETU (electricians), construction workers, tobacco workers, firefighters, and the CSCA.[156] But it seems to have been all that was possible, Murray scribbling that if he saw a chance, it might be possible to take unspecified action of the kind that 'seems to be now becoming effective in the Haldane Society and which may result in the exclusion of the Communists'.[157] It is not clear how good a comparison this was, for the strategy in relation to Haldane appears to have been to split the Society, with the Labour Party members breaking away to form the Society of Labour Lawyers. There seemed little prospect of that happening in the case of the NCCL, which was now 'making such little fuss when compared with its prominence in the 30s, that we may as well let sleeping dogs lie'.[158] In the meantime, Special Branch continued to hoover up intelligence.

4. Surveillance of Officers

The involvement of Communists in its activities gave MI5 an opportunity to find out a great deal of what the NCCL was up to through the surveillance of key personnel. These were people such as Kenelm Digby, who did not appear to be particularly significant national figures, but who were Communist Party members and as a result were deemed worthy of interest.[159] Digby had been under surveillance from his student days at Oxford where he participated in a debate that 'this House has no confidence in H M Government' at the student union in 1932, following which he was reported in *Isis*, the Oxford student newspaper, in the following terms:

> Mr K H Digby (St Johns), an inveterate hand-pocketer, rose up like a hurricane and let loose a disorderly whirlwind of words. His republican sentiments sent the Conservatives white with fury.[160]

This intervention led to a request from Vernon Kell (then DG of MI5) to the Chief Constable of Oxfordshire to have Digby checked out, the file revealing that MI5

156 ibid.

157 TNA, FO 1110/145 (IRD file: Return of papers regarding the National Council of Civil Liberties, 28 January 1949).

158 ibid.

159 TNA, KV 2/3809 (Kenelm Hubert Digby).

160 A copy of the newspaper is not included, this extract being provided for the file by D. C. Driver, whose identity is unknown.

had snouts in both the Labour and Communist clubs at Oxford at the time, Digby appearing as a member of both.[161]

Interest in Digby was renewed when he joined the NCCL as their legal adviser in 1939, also becoming a member of the executive committee. His file reveals that he had become a barrister (like his father), and that he had been a pupil of Neil Lawson, also a Communist Party member. As the legal adviser to the NCCL, it fell to Digby to conduct defence work in the petty sessions in and around London, and there are several Special Branch reports on his file about his work on behalf of anti-war activists arrested under the Metropolitan Police Act for minor offences relating to what in all probability is the distribution of pacifist literature, and the making of anti-war speeches. There is a suggestion that the NCCL's clients included Fascists as well as the PPU. In 1940, however, Digby moved to an official position in Sarawak, North Borneo, a move that caused MI5 some anxiety. This anxiety was fuelled in part by the fact that Digby had joined the secret Communist Party Lawyers' Group (CPLG), the concern made clear by Roger Hollis in correspondence with a Colonial Office official:

> The Legal Group of the Communist [sic.] is a section which we view with considerable suspicion as it is made up of men of education and intellectual power. Membership of this, unlike most sections of the Party is secret, and the main vocation of members is to advise the Party on their legal position and at times on questions of tactics.[162]

Digby appears to have worked for the Sarawak government in an administrative capacity, before being appointed to judicial office, positions that were a cause of some anxiety in the Colonial Office, where officials seem to have made it their business to destabilize him. Surveillance continued, it being noted that Digby still received *Liberty* (presumably the magazine of the NCCL); while his *Daily Worker* subscription probably consumed more of the time of officials than it strictly deserved. Colonial Office officials also made it their business to make it known locally what Digby had been up to before the war, leading one blimpish colleague based in Singapore to respond as follows:

> It is believed that he is an official member of the Communist Party which means that he must have formally renounced the Christian faith and all it stands for including the principles upon which the British Empire is based. Had this been known beforehand, I do not think that the Sarawak

161 TNA, KV 2/3809 (Kenelm Hubert Digby) (Kell to Fox, 24 November 1953). The Communist Club was known as the 'October Club'.

162 TNA, KV 2/3809 (Letter to Poynton of the Colonial Office, 4 July 1940).

> government would have asked for him to come out again. I should certainly have advised against it.[163]

A reorganization of the judiciary in 1951 provided an opportunity to get rid of Digby, the Governor unwilling to offer him one of the newly created judgeships. Although thought by one source to be a 'good citizen and a conscientious officer',[164] Digby made little effort to conceal his political views, and no one will have been surprised by his departure.

Back in England, Digby appears to have reconnected with the NCCL and other friends, his file being amended in 1953 to record that he was now again a member of the NCCL's executive, this being deemed relevant 'security information'.[165] Digby's file also provides some insight into the continuing surveillance of the NCCL, with extracts recording his re-election to the NCCL executive also revealing that there was a separate file for the NCCL to which we have not had access.[166] Extracts from intercepted mail further indicates that in 1953 letters sent *from* the NCCL were intercepted,[167] which means that there may have been a HOW in place for reasons that seem unfathomable in view of the largely unobtrusive nature of the organization at the time.[168] Even more bizarre is that information from the intercepted correspondence that was thought worth copying, circulating, and filing. By way of illustration, one entry on Digby's file was a minute of the NCCL's British Overseas sub-committee meeting, at which it was agreed that Digby would assist in the preparation of a memorandum on the use of collective punishment on British territory. The surveillance was nothing if not methodical.[169]

VI. Conclusion

The organizations considered above form only part of the surveillance interest of MI5. It is very clear that there were many other organizations which were also

163 TNA, KV 2/3809 (Letter by E. W. Pepys to the Private Secretary of His Excellency the OAG, Singapore, 30 August 1940).

164 TNA, KV 2/3809 (Abell (Office of Governor Sarawak) to Morton (SIFE), June 1950).

165 As was his appearance as 'large, corpulent and choleric': from a 'source' report of the NCCL AGM, 8 May 1954.

166 This appears to be TNA, OF 89/1. It is impossible to say how many volumes of NCCL material there are. It is notable that the legal challenge to MI5's activities under the European Convention on Human Rights was brought by two NCCL officers: *Hewitt and Harman v United Kingdom* (1992) 14 EHRR 657. See Chapter 15 below.

167 This is the procedure known as RATCATCHER. See below, p. 102 and p. 180 . Quite why it was necessary to use this exceptional procedure against the NCCL is unknown.

168 TNA, KV2/3810 (Kenelm Hubert Digby) (Extract from Intercept Letter to Miss Marie CUTBUSH, 13 Whitehall Park, London, N 19 from E. A. Allen, General Secretary of the National Council of Civil Liberties, 46 Westbourne Grove, London, W2, 19 November 1953).

169 This had been intercepted as NCCL correspondence to Marie Cutbush. The only Marie Cutbush we have been able to identify is a celebrated, Australian-born, London-based scientist working in the field of blood transfusion, who subsequently married and settled in Canada, where she died in 2009.

very closely monitored, including 'friendship' groups, such as the British Soviet Friendship Society, the British–Hungarian Friendship Society, and the British–Polish Friendship Society, about all of which IRIS appeared to be spectacularly well informed. But there were others, of which the Labour Research Department (LRD) and the National Assembly of Women were said to 'deserve some investigation',[170] and others still, such as the Society of Socialist Clergy, which were of 'only marginal interest'.[171] According to IRIS, the LRD was 'one of the very first Socialist organisations in this country to be captured by the Communists', having been founded by the Webbs in 1912 to 'serve as an information and statistical unit for the use of the Fabian Society'.[172]

The National Archives reveal that the LRD file was opened in 1925, 'with the first indications that the LRD was controlled from Moscow or was acting as a front for Communist activities'. The file is described to include 'LRD publications, intercepted correspondence to and from LRD officials', with 'the first Home Office Warrant to intercept mail [being] taken out in 1932'. The mail interceptions operated continuously until 1939, though once discontinued, the mail checks were replaced with a phone tap, the files being reported by the National Archives to include the reports of intercepted conversations. These were for the most part of very little interest. This material continues after the war, and is said to include 'a summary note identifying LRD's focus on uncovering discreditable facts about the government of the day', which seems to provide a poor justification for surveillance: contemporary think-tanks take note.

There are, however, flashes of light even in the LRD file, which reveal the extent of penetration of the Labour Movement and the co-operation of the TUC into the efforts of the State, even during periods of Conservative government. To this end, a particularly revealing minute from MI5's R. E. C. Broadbent reports on a meeting he had at Scotland Yard earlier in the day (17 January 1952). Broadbent had attended to hand over a paper (presumably an MI5 paper) on 'Communist Penetration of Trade Unions'. The minute continues:

> In the course of general conversation about Communist penetration, Chief Superintendent Jones said that Sir Vincent Tewson of the Trades Union Congress was taking drastic steps to purge the trade unions of Communist penetration, and had even been heard to say that he hoped to purge the Electrical Trades' Union within two years. In addition, CYNOG-JONES was a TUC agent in the Labour Research Department and there was a TUC agent in the ETU also. Mr Jones gave the name of this agent and I believe it was FISHER, but the opportunity did not arise to confirm this. There is no person of that name in the published leadership

170 IRIS (n 40), p. 58.
171 ibid.
172 ibid, p. 59.

> of the ETU. [MI5] information is that CYNOG-JONES has been a member of the Executive Committee of the LRD since 1948 and is also Treasurer.[173]

Unless the British government opens up *all* of the MI5 archive to everyone and not just a privileged few—in the same way that STASI archives have been opened—we will never know the full extent of such co-operation,[174] or indeed the full extent of MI5 surveillance. But the foregoing pages provide indication enough of the extent to which the Labour movement was deeply penetrated. Although there were no statutory boundaries on the extent of MI5 surveillance, it should not be forgotten that MI5 operated within a framework of powers in a directive issued by government. That directive made clear that the function of MI5 was the defence of the realm, relating in particular to attempts at espionage, sabotage, and subversion. The Directive did not give powers to deal with the awkward, the malcontent, or the malevolent, using the democratic process and democratic rights to fight the class war, however inconvenient that might be. It is clear, nevertheless, that at this stage MI5 was over-concerned with dissidents and not enough with spies, using methods to which we now turn.

[173] TNA, KV 5/77 (Note by R. E. C. Broadbent, B1D, 17 January 1952).

[174] Note too TNA, KV 4/475 (Liddell Diary, 27 January 1953), where Liddell made the following remarkable entry:

> some little time ago the TUC expressed a desire to have some contact with ourselves in an unofficial way. We had made it clear that while we were always ready to receive information, it would be quite impossible for us to enter into any kind of exchange which might facilitate the task of the TUC in getting rid of their communists.

The entry continues by saying that 'TU leaders could not be trusted where their own interests were concerned and they would be almost certain to misuse any information that was given to them, with possibly disastrous results.'

5
Surveillance Methods

I. Introduction

Having identified *who* did the surveillance of *whom*, the third question is *by what means*? How did the Security Service obtain information about individuals and organizations? Then there are fourth and fifth questions: *what did it do* with the information it obtained, and *with whom* was it shared? It is a curious feature of MI5's mandate that it included nothing about the methods to be used for the purposes of the defence of the realm, which was its core task. This is with the exception of an enigmatic reference to 'special facilities' in the Attlee Directive, to which we return in Chapter 8. It is to be noted here, however, that the removal of any reference to SF in the Maxwell Fyfe Directive did not mean that this particular form of surveillance was discontinued in 1952; far from it.

The Security Service would obtain information about individuals and organizations in a number of ways, through (i) volunteers who spontaneously reported fellow citizens; (ii) monitoring by Special Branch; (iii) infiltration and the use of informers; (iv) watching and following; (v) interrogation and questioning; and (vi) the interception of communications (mail, telegrams, and telephones); as well as (vii) the use of secret microphones hidden in various locations; and (viii) foreign security and intelligence agencies. By modern standards, this may seem rather primitive, but it is to be recalled that this was a time when very few people had telephones at home and when methods of communication were very different from today. It is also the case, of course, that there were no computers and no internet communications.

In this chapter, we touch on all of these various forms of surveillance, returning to SF or secret microphones in some detail in Chapter 8. Reading the files, we are struck by the different circumstances in which these different forms of surveillance were used: a contrast between routine and intense surveillance; between passive and active surveillance; and between constant and periodic surveillance. In some cases, organizations and individuals were the subject of what might be referred to as constant, but passive, yet routine surveillance, in the sense that information from various sources was simply collected and stored for no obvious purpose other than the collection and storage of information. In some cases, however, an event would trigger a much more targeted investigation, perhaps to find out where an individual lived and worked, or to find out who he or she socialized with or visited.[1]

[1] Such investigations might be made by a local police force, the Metropolitan Police Special Branch, or, where an individual was of particular interest, by MI5 itself.

MI5, the Cold War, and the Rule of Law. K. D. Ewing, Joan Mahoney, and Andrew Moretta, Oxford University Press (2020). © K. D. Ewing, Joan Mahoney, and Andrew Moretta. DOI: 10.1093/oso/9780198818625.001.0001

In these latter cases, the scrutiny would be intense (using various forms of surveillance), it would be active (in the sense that strenuous efforts would be made to find the information sought), and it would be periodic (in the sense that it would be discontinued when there was no reason to continue). But whatever the intensity of the surveillance, lurking in the background again is the lawyer's question. That is to say, what was the authority for this activity? Here there are two issues, one being the legal authority of MI5 to operate a surveillance operation against an identified target; and the second being the legal authority for the means used. The 1946 and 1952 Directives would provide administrative authority but not legal power in relation to the former, while the common law and legislation would potentially provide legal authority in relation to the latter.

II. Sources of Information

As suggested in Part I, one of the ways by which MI5 obtained information was through the reporting of suspicious persons to the local police. It is unknown how often this was done, or how the police reacted when public-spirited individuals approached the desk sergeant with such information. But that it did happen is revealed by the file of the celebrated musician Professor Alan Bush, which records a detailed complaint by the father of one of his students about his teaching methods and his politics.[2] Professor Bush was under surveillance from 1935 until at least 1960 (when the released file stops), and he is described by the National Archives as having:

> successfully combined work as an internationally known musician (pianist), lecturer, composer and organizer of musical events, with a long career as an influential Communist Party member. He was active in numerous Communist-controlled or affiliated organisations, particularly those with a musical or cultural bias, a generous contributor to Party funds and a frequent visitor to Soviet Bloc countries, notably Russia and East Germany.

1. Special Branch

Apart from targeting people about whom they were suspicious and building up volumes of personal information as a result, there was also an extensive programme of routine monitoring of Communist Party members by Special Branch. According to

[2] TNA, KV 2/3515–22 (eight volumes).

the Metropolitan Police Commissioner (Sir Harold Scott), addressing the Cabinet Committee on Communism in 1949:

> the police were the ultimate source of information for MI5. The task of guarding against subversive activities fell within the province of the Special Branch at Scotland Yard. The Special Branch had its own sources of information, apart from any reports which might be received from police forces outside London. The Special Branch kept under observation the Communist Party and all its branches in London, as well as such bodies as the Young Communist League . . . information was duly passed on to MI5, with whom they maintained the closest daily contact.[3]

This observation took a number of forms, including the attendance of Special Branch officers at public meetings (for which lawful authority was conveniently provided by the decision in *Thomas v Sawkins*).[4] There are dozens, if not hundreds, of police reports that appear in the personal files of surveillance targets, these reports typically outlining in some detail what was said at the meeting and by whom, and identifying known Communists (along with their PF numbers) who were in attendance.[5]

Some of these meetings must have been fascinating, such as the 'Brains Trust' at Hammersmith Town Hall, organized by the Pritt Supporters' Committee, attracting over 1,000 people, and 'admirably managed' by Gilbert Harding of the famous BBC radio programme 'The Brains Trust'.[6] But others must have been spectacularly dull, such as the meeting and film show held at the Unity Theatre, organized by the YCL in support of the World Federation of Democratic Youth. According to the report of Sergeant Copping, the proceedings were orderly, commenced at 7.45 p.m. and finished at 9.50 p.m., admission was by ticket, and a collection was taken during the

[3] TNA, CAB 134/53, Minutes of the Cabinet Committee on Communism, 1 July 1949. Mr Cornish of the Home Office's F3 division told the Committee that outside London local police forces were:

> responsible to Watch Committees or other Local Authorities [in contrast to the Met, who were responsible directly to the Home Secretary]. Each force . . . had at least one officer charged with duties corresponding to those of the Special Branch at Scotland Yard. The Watch Committees were political bodies, and the Chief Constables would have to be very circumspect in undertaking action against any political party such as the Communists. The Chief Constables did, however, co-operate unostentatiously with MI5 and it was their assistance that the MI5 list of all members of the Communist Party was being checked and brought up to date. Chief Constables also received circular directives from MI5 indicating in what aspects of Communism they were particularly interested in from time to time (ibid., 1 July 1949).

[4] [1935] 2 KB 249.

[5] Where there were people present at the meeting who were unknown but about whom there was some suspicion (perhaps because they had played a prominent part), a full personal description would often be provided for the purposes of further investigation. Reports were sent in from all over the country, in the case of Communist MP William Gallacher from places as far apart as Lochgelly, Fife (11 September 1950) to Pontllanfraith, Monmouthshire (14 January 1951). See TNA, KV 2/1754.

[6] TNA, KV 2/1065 (Metropolitan Police (Special Branch) Report, 11 July 1950).

evening, but the amount was not disclosed. And so it goes on, with an account of speeches made and films shown (namely 'The Bridge' (about the reconstruction of a railway bridge in Yugoslavia), and 'Spanish Earth' (about the Spanish Civil War, showing peasants working in the fields just behind the front line)).

Apart from attending meetings and rallies, the other role of Special Branch was to track the movements of individuals within the United Kingdom. The personal file of William Gallacher contains an entry headed 'Movement of Communists', again providing clear evidence that individuals were closely watched.[7] There is abundant evidence in the files that as a matter of routine Communists were watched at ports and airports, with Special Branch surveillance reports revealing the existence of a 'Special Branch Port Suspect Book'. Those who were known to be members or supporters of the Communist Party would be recorded when leaving the country, the surveillance reports also recording the identity of any travelling companion, and the destination, where known. There would usually be a report of the 'discreet' search of the target's bags, which would usually find nothing of security interest, the police here working hand in glove with the customs' authorities.

The pantomime was repeated on re-entry, on this occasion a close inspection of the passport allowing Special Branch to find out where the individual in question had been, rather than where they were going. When Harry Pollitt returned to the United Kingdom from Prague on 25 July 1950, it was reported that he had addressed a Communist congress in the Soviet Zone of Germany, having visited Berlin as well as Prague. The search of his baggage revealed that he was in possession of the scripts of the various speeches he was believed to have given, together with a number of gifts, including pictures of Stalin.[8] And when barrister D. N. Pritt returned to Northolt airport on 12 January 1952, it was recorded that Monica Felton (PF 76,286) accompanied him.[9] According to the report, Felton was subject to an extensive search by H. M. Customs, at the request of the Immigration Officer, but nothing of interest was found, before she was collected by an unknown man.[10]

2. Infiltration and Informers

In addition to the above, the Security Service also relied on insiders to provide information about meetings and their personnel. This is abundantly clear from the surveillance harvest stored in the Security Service files. Whether it be the CPGB, YCL, trade unions, the Haldane Society of Socialist Lawyers, the BPC, the NCCL,

[7] TNA, KV 2/1754 (Movement of Communists, 21 August 1951).

[8] TNA, KV 2/1045 (Metropolitan Police (Special Branch), Northolt Airport, 25 July 1950).

[9] TNA, KV 2/1065 (Metropolitan Police (Special Branch), Northolt Airport, 12 January 1952). On Monica Felton, see K. D. Ewing, J. Mahoney, and A. Moretta, 'Civil Liberties and the Korean War' (2018) 81 MLR 395.

[10] TNA, KV 2/1065 (Metropolitan Police (Special Branch), Northolt Airport, 12 January 1952).

the MacDonald Discussion Group,[11] or the Workers' Music Society,[12] it is inconceivable that there was not a State presence in the meetings, either a member who had been recruited as an informer, or an agent of the Security Service embedded in the organization. Although the identity of the informer would rarely be revealed in the files (though oversights sometimes occurred, as we discuss in Chapter 7 below), there has been no reluctance on MI5's part about revealing the sources on whom the narks relied.

In the case of the Communist Party, for example, it is clear that MI5 had a source close to the well-placed Percy Glading, a founding member of the Party, who had been jailed in 1938 for offences under the Official Secrets Act 1911 relating to the supply of information to Soviet Russia.[13] Glading is mentioned in an entry of 18 September 1950 in Harry Pollitt's file in the following terms:

> According to Percy GLADING, Secretary of the North London District of the Amalgamated Engineering Union, who is a close friend of Harry POLLITT whom he meets socially twice a week, POLLITT is now completely ostracised by the other members of the Executive Committee, who are unwilling to stage a purge, knowing that many of their friends and even of themselves might be affected. This ostracism is in the nature of a silent conspiracy. No one ever comes out openly against him, but they just will not help in anything. They offer no constructive suggestions and use a kind of delaying tactics.[14]

Glading's mission it seems was to support and strengthen the hand of Pollitt, who was a 'notoriously bad psychologist', and who 'from a sense of fairness was most unwilling to take steps against anyone he dislikes'.[15]

Glading is also reported as stating that Stalin had sent Pollitt a greeting on his last birthday but that the Executive Committee had blocked its publication.[16] The same file entry also refers to E. Tuckfield (who 'supplied Glading with information on "the bad ones"').[17] Both Glading and Tuckfield are referred to in a later note of 12 October 1950 about a fight-back initiated by Pollitt,[18] and again in a file entry

[11] On the MacDonald Discussion Group, an informal left-leaning group with a membership drawn mainly from the film and arts worlds, see TNA KV 5/80 (MI5 Organization File 'OF'), and J. Smith, 'The MacDonald Discussion Group: A Communist Conspiracy in Britain's Cold War Film and Theatre Industry—or MI5's Honey-Pot?' (2015) 35 *History Journal of Film, Radio and Television* 454. Smith suggests that actor and member Ferdie Mayne may have been MI5's man inside the group.

[12] On surveillance of the Workers' Music Society, see TNA, KV 3/475-80 drawn from the 'Special Files' on 'Communist Activities among Musicians (and Actors)'.

[13] See also pp. 57–8 below.

[14] TNA, KV 2/1045 (Minute dated 18 September 1950)—clearly very sensitive, stamped in red with 'WARNING REFER TO APPROPRIATE OFFICER BEFORE USING'. Glading was said to be a friend of Pollitt's, whom he met socially twice a week.

[15] ibid.

[16] ibid.

[17] ibid.

[18] TNA, KV 2/1045 (British Communist Party)—one-page minute stamped with the same warning notice as the Minute of 18 September referred to in n 14.

dated 26 February 1951. Glading is reported in the latter note as saying that Pollitt had given up on Reg Birch (PF 62,201) and Fred Elms (PF 96,802), and saw 'no other way of dealing with them than by expulsion', proposing 'a revolt against the present industrial leadership of the Party'.[19] There is a further reference to Glading in a note date 15 May 1951 in which a report is provided of Pollitt's health:

> According to Percy GLADING, who is on close contact with POLLITT, the main reason for POLLITT'S 'depression' is simply that the numerous promises made by him to the Cominform about twelve months ago are still far from being fulfilled and are unlikely to be for a long time. GLADING is obviously worried and inclined to believe that POLLITT has developed some kind of megalomania.[20]

There are many similar examples in Security Service files where it is apparent that trusted 'insiders' were unwittingly providing intelligence—or gossip—such as reports of closed meetings.[21] While it is possible for Special Branch officers to be present at large public meetings of 800–1,000 people, their presence as uninvited guests at private events such as the *Daily Worker* dinner would not be easy to conceal.[22] In any event, it is openly acknowledged in the personal files that there were 'well placed source(s) at 16 King Street',[23] with one such anonymous source being reported in the Arthur Horner file as saying that the proposed visit to Russia by the miner's leader had been on the instruction of the Party (backed by Moscow) to help deal with his chronic alcoholism.[24] Also in relation to Horner, there is information—this time from a named unwitting source (Sam Henderson)—that Horner had regained some of his lost prestige at Party HQ, having done 'some very concentrated work with the other leaders of the NUM', reporting that 'the miners

[19] TNA, KV 2/1046 (R Birch and Fred Elms, 26 February 1951)—one-page minute stamped with the same warning notice as the Minute of 18 September referred to in n 14.

[20] TNA, KV 2/1046 (Untitled Minute, 15 May 1951).

[21] TNA, KV 2/1046 (B1H Source Report Re *Daily Worker* dinner held on 22 March 1951, at the Bridge House Hotel, London).

[22] See, e.g., the Special Branch report of a public meeting at Stratford Town Hall, attended by 800 people, to hear Harry Pollitt give a talk on the 'British Road to Socialism': TNA, KV 2/1046 (Metropolitan Police (Special Branch), 18 March 1951). It appears, however, that Pollitt's sixtieth birthday celebrations were attended by both MI5 informers and the Special Branch, a notable distinction for a man whose influence was waning. The MI5 account reports on the event, the gifts, and speeches (TNA, KV 2/1045 (Harry Pollitt's 60th Birthday, 28 November 1950)). They would have followed him to the toilet had propriety permitted. According to the report, 'the Bakers' group gave Pollitt a huge cake decorated with a sugar plaque bearing the hammer and sickle, and around the edges of the cake little doves were perched in the act of flying away. On the sides of the cake were little pictures depicting scenes in the 'working-class struggle'. It sounds delicious, but it was no doubt the source of some mirth at MI5 HQ (Leconfield House), where it seems that agents were engaged in what had become little more than unemployment relief for frustrated police officers and out-of-work typists. The five-page Special Branch report of the same event by Chief Inspector Francis Cohen reveals that he was accompanied by a detective sergeant and two detective constables. Apparently, there were 1,200 people present.

[23] TNA, KV 2/1529 (Report, 25 April 1953). The author is MK; the source is said to be 'usually reliable'. MK is Maxwell Knight, erstwhile Fascist.

[24] ibid.

are prepared to take action re Saturday morning work as from April'. The Party was said to be 'very pleased'.[25]

3. Watching and Watchers

Monitoring by Special Branch and the infiltration of organizations is what we would refer to as the routine or soft surveillance that was going on all the time, sometimes targeted on particular events or issues relating to the organization concerned. However, there would be a gear-shift when the surveillance would become much more intense and directed, and when the individual in question was under suspicion of specific misdeeds (which may not necessarily have been unlawful). In these cases, the intensification could lead to various forms of surveillance—telephone intercepts and mail checks, where not already in place, and 'watching' by MI5's team of watchers. As the Neil Lawson file reveals, not a great deal would be required to arouse suspicion for this purpose, Lawson being a distinguished barrister with a history of Communist Party activity, who had been taken on as a constitutional adviser to the Malay Rulers, and who had developed an international practice taking him to Ghana and Ceylon.

The release of Lawson's file in 2011 attracted some interest in North London where he had lived, the *Camden New Journal* revealing that 'spies trailed Sir Neil Lawson suspected of communist sympathies', also providing some information from the released files about the methods employed.[26] In this case, the process yielded information of no consequence whatsoever, except perhaps that he regularly visited a Mme Juliana de Beaujeu, amusing but no business of the State. It also involved the observation of his movements each day, which meant that he was followed all day and every day, with a watch being placed on his house at 30a Heath Drive, Hampstead, and on his Chambers at 1 Harcourt Buildings, Temple, London. This activity was undertaken without any express legal authority (which presumably was not needed, because no actionable wrong was being committed by the Security Service staff who did the watching). It was undertaken with the authorization of a senior officer within the Security Service itself, following a bid by the case officer (in this case D. R. Johnston-Jones) for 'A4 services [surveillance] at a priorities meeting'.[27]

In this case, the authorization was requested for 'about a fortnight as from the time of his return to England in order to see if he makes contact with CP officials

[25] TNA, KV 2/1529 (Report, 21 January 1953). The author is MK.

[26] *Camden New Journal*, 1 September 2011.

[27] A4 was then the designation of the technical and physical surveillance section, made famous by P. Wright, *Spycatcher—The Candid Autobiography of a Senior Intelligence Officer* (Toronto, 1987) (see Appendix).

or shows in any other way that he is still in touch with the Communists'.[28] As the existence of pro-forma 'A4 Surveillance Reports' makes clear, observation of this kind was by no means unusual. In this case, the observation—code named 'Old Boots'—started on Monday 16 September 1957 and finished on 27 September 1957,[29] with a daily surveillance report showing that he was followed to the Underground, being picked up at the other end by a different team, and followed to his chambers, which were watched all day, though they were acknowledged to be a difficult place to watch because of 'all the entrances and exits' to and from the building. He was followed when he left the office during the day, and followed home again at night. The Security Service learned that he went for lunch at a Chinese restaurant on Charing Cross Road on Tuesday 17 September, with two Security Service officers at a neighbouring table to keep an eye on him.[30]

There were two particularly notable aspects of Lawson's surveillance at this time, the first being its scope, and the second its nastiness. A 'Loose Minute' in the file dated 18 September 1957 from D. R. Johnston-Jones gave guidance to colleagues about what was being sought. Thus, they were told to look out for seven categories of information in particular, such as any donations by Lawson to the CPGB, as well as any information about the political views of any member of his family, and any views of family members on current affairs (such as the New Year's Honours list, Cyprus, Indonesia, or America). They were also instructed to look for 'revealing items of information about the private life of Mr *or* Mrs Lawson; for example, information regarding his affair with Mrs Juliana de Beaujeu' (emphasis added).[31] The snooping on the family (and others) is staggering and frankly disgusting; the hunt for compromising personal information explicable perhaps by the opportunity it would provide for blackmail of both Lawson and Beaujeu, with Lawson's file entries about his professional success possibly indicating the blackmailer's potential leverage.

[28] TNA, KV 2/3593 (Observation Briefing Sheet, issued 11 September 57 following Priorities Meeting 3 September 57).

[29] The daily surveillance reports are to be found in TNA, KV 2/3593, and TNA, KV 2/3594 (Neil Lawson), but mainly the latter.

[30] While in the restaurant, Lawson's female companion made a telephone call, after which they resumed their lunch 'in quiet tones'. Two days later, Lawson was followed into a bank, where he cashed a cheque and asked for a bank statement, and then onto a bus, before being observed buying sweets outside Hampstead tube station, where he was joined by his wife, with whom he entered the Everyman Cinema. We do not know what film they saw, but on the following day Lawson was followed to Queen's Gardens, London W2, where again his wife joined him, the couple staying till late. On the following day (a Saturday), the observation commenced at 7.45 a.m. in the vicinity of Heath Drive. At 8.45 a.m., Lawson appeared 'wearing an old white sweater'. Not only that: 'he had a dachshund with him'. But there was more: 'he exercised this dog as far as West End Lane Post Office where he made a purchase at the stamp counter'. There is no record of the dog having stopped to relieve itself. But there is more still: on his return walk, Lawson 'purchased a copy of the *Radio Times*' and finally reached home at 9.15 a.m. And so it goes on.

[31] TNA, KV 2/3594 (Loose Minute, 18 September 1957).

4. Interrogation and Questioning

Another indication of a gear-shift in the intensity of surveillance would be the deployment of staff to question and/or interrogate suspects or witnesses, usually where major espionage activity was suspected. For much of this time, William 'Jim' Skardon would lead the questioning and interrogation where required. According to Victor Davis (who was refused permission by MI5 to write Skardon's biography), 'Jim' 'was MI5's gentleman interrogator, a secret agent with the soft touch'.[32] In a remarkable hagiography, Davis continues by contrasting Skardon favourably with more contemporary intelligence personnel, alleged at the time Davis was writing to be complicit in torture:

> Tall, thin, moustachioed and pipe-smoking, with a polite, unassuming demeanour . . . [Skardon] blended in. You couldn't mistake him for anything but an old-school gent in a raincoat and a trilby hat. And if he came calling, you'd be only too happy to let him in. He'd ask how you and your wife were, and how your runner beans were coming along. He wouldn't say no to a cup of tea. And he'd just love to pet your dog while you put the kettle on. A visit from Jim Skardon was like having a warm wallow in benevolence. He would not, of course, mention that the room in which you sat exchanging pleasantries was bugged. Nor that your mail was being examined for secret messages. And he certainly wouldn't let slip that you were being followed everywhere you went while he prepared to put you behind bars.[33]

All very British, but this fails to give a full sense of the questioning and interrogation that was undertaken. Following Burgess' flight to Moscow, it was Skardon who visited Burgess' mother and his step-father, to find 'a very stupid woman'.[34] It seems that Skardon was there by invitation. He also interviewed Jack Hewitt (Burgess' friend), after asking him to attend the Foreign Office, where he encountered 'a loathsome creature'.[35] This was for the purposes of information-gathering rather than prosecution, as presumably were the interviews with Duncan Macrae Taylor,[36] as part of the investigation into Ursula Buerton, the Russian Military Intelligence GRU officer ('Sonya') who was Klaus Fuchs' handler in the United Kingdom, Skardon letting 'Sonya' slip through his fingers.[37] Although the

[32] *Daily Mail*, 12 February 2010.
[33] ibid.
[34] TNA, KV 2/4102 (Interview by Skardon, 7 June 1951).
[35] ibid.
[36] The file records information on Taylor and his wife Barbara (Beurton's sister). The surname was Taylor, but confusingly Duncan Burnett Taylor, son of William Macrae Taylor was sometimes known as Duncan Burnett Macrae Taylor while his wife Barbara Taylor (née Kuczynski) was usually known as Barbara Macrae Taylor, giving the impression of a 'double barrelled' surname.
[37] See Chapter 6 below.

investigation of Buerton's extended family was too late (she had already gone to the German Democratic Republic), Skardon did put pressure on her brother-in-law (Duncan Macrae Taylor), and was not above implying that his job at the BBC would be at risk if he did not cooperate.[38]

Skardon's activities tend to contradict Lord Denning's remarks in his report on the Profumo affair in 1963, where he wrote about the members of the Security Service being in the eye of the law 'ordinary citizens with no power greater than anyone else'.[39] As Denning continued, they have 'no special powers of arrest such as the police have', and no 'special powers of search are given to them'.[40] But it seems that they did have the power in practice to question and interrogate, including those suspected of committing serious violations of the Official Secrets Acts 1911–39, presumably in some cases with a view to securing evidence for the purposes of prosecution. Skardon interrogated Alan Nunn May (whom he is said to have befriended),[41] and Klaus Fuchs, both of whom were convicted of espionage offences under the Official Secrets Act 1911, s. 1. It is unknown whether any evidence obtained in this way was ever relied on, as the trials were held in secret.[42]

Skardon of course was not the only person involved in questioning and interrogation by MI5. Another well-known character was Buster Milmo, an Irish-born barrister who served in MI5 during the Second World War and shortly thereafter. Milmo is said to have worked with Kim Philby during the war, and was given the responsibility of interrogating him in 1950, when Philby came under suspicion as a spy.[43] But Milmo, who was later to become a High Court judge (appointed in 1964), failed to match the achievements of Skardon. Returning to Skardon's frustrated biographer writing in 2010, Milmo's 'bullying court room manner' was counter-productive in a four-hour interview, though for all his guile Skardon was to fare no better when his turn came to interrogate Philby. The most interesting feature of the Milmo story, however, is not his failure with Philby, but the promiscuity of a constitution in which it is thought appropriate for a Security Service officer to become a High Court judge.[44]

[38] TNA, KV 2/2937 ('Barbara Macrae Taylor and Duncan Burnett Taylor', by W. J. Skardon, 27 March 1952). See Chapter 8 below.

[39] Lord Denning's Report, Cmnd 2152, 1963, para. 273. See Chapter 14 below.

[40] Denning Report, para. 273.

[41] According to Victor Davis, above, Skardon's 'non-violent interrogation techniques were based on those of Dostoyevsky's Inspector Porfiry [Petrovich] in *Crime and Punishment* who befriends the murderer before pouncing': *Daily Mail*, 12 February 2010.

[42] See Official Secrets Act 1920, s. 8(4)—this applied where 'the publication of any evidence to be given or of any statement to be made in the course of the proceedings would be prejudicial to the national safety'—Skardon's shield.

[43] It seems clear that this was done in order to obtain evidence with a view to prosecution: Cmd 9577, 1955, para. 11.

[44] Milmo sat in the Queen's Bench Division of the High Court from 1964 to 1982. His *Who was Who* entry records that he was part of the civilian staff of the War Office between 1940 and 1945. Before appointment to the High Court, he was Deputy Chairman of the West Sussex Quarter Sessions, these being local courts responsible for administering criminal justice.

III. Telephone Tapping and Mail Checks

There was of course no legal regulation of these forms of surveillance. The position was different, however, in relation to surveillance by means of mail, telegraph, and telephone interception. So far as mail checks are concerned, the Post Office Act 1908 provided that it was a criminal offence for a Post Office employee 'contrary to his duty' to open, or wilfully detain or delay a postal packet, unless one of a number of defences applied, as where the employee in question acted 'in obedience to an express warrant in writing under the hand of a Secretary of State'.[45] Note the mandatory nature of the language used, but note also that warrants would be issued not only to intercept mail *to* a particular address but occasionally also *from* a particular individual or address usually requiring the invocation of a procedure known as RATCATCHER.[46] There was, however, no provision regulating the practice of phone tapping, the legality of which was not fully examined until 1957.[47]

1. Home Office Warrants

In the absence of comprehensive statutory regulation, the Home Office Warrant (HOW) procedure for the interception of communications by MI5 developed by way of administrative practice. The matter was examined by Sir Findlater Stewart in 1945, who reported that there was a degree of procedural formality in the sense that:

> Formal application to the Home Secretary for a warrant is made in each case by MI5 accompanied by a statement of the reasons for it and it is the practice for the Home Secretary to satisfy himself personally of the need for the warrant.[48]

This would apply to both mail and telephone interceptions, even though there was no legal obligation to do so in the latter case. Other sources confirm the existence of a formal procedure,[49] which required (i) an application to be made by an MI5 officer

[45] These provisions were replaced in due course by the identical provisions of the Post Office Act 1953, s. 58.

[46] A related if less clandestine practice dating from the 19th Century which involved letters being intercepted, read and then returned to the sender was acknowledged by the Birkett Committee, Cmnd 283, 1957. This approach was said to be used now 'somewhat more frequently but still on a very small scale' with twenty-eight cases between 1946 and 1957 (para. 88). The Committee thought that 'no one suffers any damage if a sender's own letter is returned to him' (para. 89). The extension of postal HOWs to permit 'emanating interceptions' was negotiated between Liddell and Newsam in 1949 (see KV 4/471 (Liddell Diary 8 and 29 June 1949). See pp. 90 and 180 below.

[47] Cmnd 283, 1957. See below, Part V.

[48] TNA, CAB 301/31 (Findlater Stewart, Report on the Security Services, 'Stewart Report') para. 18.

[49] See Birkett Report, Cmnd 283, 1957, paras 53–90, and Part V below.

to the DDG; (ii) an application to the Home Office; (iii) the approval or otherwise of the Home Secretary; and (iv) a subsequent application to the Post Office.

The Communist Party was obviously the subject of surveillance by phone tapping, along with a number of organizations thought to be under its influence (such as the BPC). As we have seen, however, many of the Party files have not been released, in contrast to the files of some of its prominent members. It is known, nevertheless, that the Party phone (Temple Bar 2151) was tapped as a result of the hundreds, if not thousands, of transcripts of conversations on this number that appear in the personal files of Communist Party members and others. The reason for what appears to be the constant routine and passive surveillance of the Communist Party HQ has not been formally explained, though it would have to be based on 'major', 'subversive', 'sabotage', or 'espionage' activity. It remains to be seen whether any evidence that would have justified this surveillance is ever produced.

So far as Party members are concerned, it is likely that senior officials such as Harry Pollitt were subject to constant surveillance, with one warrant issued in the distant past allowing for indefinite monitoring. In addition, however, warrants would be issued from time to time to tap the phones of other prominent Party members. Examples of the reasons for surveillance in these cases (from warrants in the public domain) are given below.

> The subscriber to TUDOR 2648 is reported to have acted as link between Russia and the Communist Party of India on his recent visit to India. It is therefore desired to learn more of his activities and contacts.
>
> (Palme Dutt, 17 December 1946).[50]

> The subscriber to PRIMROSE 4162, an important Communist official and editor of the *Daily Worker*, who is taking a leading part in the Communist Party's forthcoming National Congress and Empire Conference. It is desired to learn as much as possible in this connection.
>
> (William Rust, 19 February 1947).[51]

> The subscriber to [the] number [referred to in the warrant], and long-standing member of the Communist Party, is in charge, at Party headquarters, of the peace campaign. It is desired to investigate his activities more closely.
>
> (Phil Piratin, former MP).[52]

In these cases, the interception was undertaken mainly for the purposes of gathering information about prominent people. At other times, however, it would be

[50] TNA, KV 2/2505.
[51] TNA, KV 2/1050.
[52] TNA, KV 2/2033.

done as part of a specific investigation, as in the case of Neil Lawson, the HOW for whom explains that:

> Neil LAWSON is the subscriber to this number and is a former member of the British Communist Party. He remains in sympathy with the Party, is in touch with officials of it and from time to time contributes to Party funds. LAWSON has been employed by the Malayan Rulers to advise them on constitutional problems. It is desired to investigate more closely the nature and extent of his connexion with the British Communist Party.[53]

In the latter types of case, steps sometimes moved remarkably speedily, and it seems that the procedures explained in the Stewart Report were by-passed, as suggested by Peter Wright in his back-handed compliment to Major Denham of the Post Office Special Investigations Unit, responsible for executing the warrants. According to Wright, Denham was very particular about warrants: 'He was prepared to install a tap or intercept an address without a warrant only on the strict understanding that one was obtained as soon as possible.'[54] Denham was in charge for most of the 1950s, assisted principally by Colonel Allan and G. F. Saffery. Later, a Mr Harlow became the most prominent of the men described by MI5 as 'our link at the GPO'.[55] All appear to have been GPO employees, but they worked very closely with MI5 and Special Branch. They were men entrusted with very secret information, and appear at times to have been as loyal to MI5 as to the Post Office.[56]

2. Irregular Mail Checks

It is evident that the legal and administrative procedures described above did not apply in all cases, and that they did not apply in cases of urgency. Formalism was not permitted to stand in the way of an investigation. This is made abundantly clear by the intense surveillance of Guy Burgess and Donald Maclean around the time of their disappearance on 25 May 1951.[57] Health warning: the detail of what follows is complex, and we can cover here only some of the complexity revealed. Beginning with mail checks, Donald Maclean's file contains a HOW dated 29 May 1950 recording the authorization required for the detention, opening, and production of

[53] TNA, KV 2/3593 (Neil Lawson).

[54] P. Wright, *Spycatcher—The Candid Autobiography of a Senior Intelligence Officer* (Toronto, 1987), p. 46.

[55] TNA, KV 4/222 (Letter to Col. Francis from an unnamed MI5 officer, 10 April 1940).

[56] C. Andrew, *The Defence of the Realm—The Authorised History of MI5* (London, 2009), p. 336, describes Major Denman's Special Investigations Unit (AKA Investigation Department) as having been an 'outstation' of MI5.

[57] See Report Concerning the Disappearance of Two Former Foreign Office Officials, Cmd 9577, 1955, para. 1.

all mail addressed to '*and emanating from*' *Donald Maclean and his wife* at their home in Tatsfield, Surrey.[58] A partially redacted note by an MI5 officer tells Colonel Allan that, 'I have today [29 May] applied for authority to operate a letter check, both incoming and outgoing, on Donald Maclean [REDACTION] provides the reason for emanating part of the warrant.'[59] This warrant was put into immediate effect and was not approved by the Home Secretary until 10 June, some two weeks later.

Maclean's file also contains:

- A note by MI5 officer R. T. Reed dated *31 May 1950* stating that he had asked 'Mr Harlow, GPO, today to impose two letter checks *in anticipation* of the HOWs'.[60] Applying to 'Any Name', the addresses in question were *Lady Maclean*, 87 Iverna Court, London, and *Burgess*' home address. Lady Maclean was Donald Maclean's mother. Mail checks were to take place *before* the warrant was signed and issued. *Note what was being authorized here by the HOW: all mail to any person, not just at a particular address but in the building where Lady Maclean's flat was located, which conceivably could be several dozen homes.*[61]
- A copy of a HOW dated a week later (*7 June 1951*), ostensibly authorizing the detention, opening, and production of all mail addressed to 'Any name' at Lady Maclean's block of flats, Iverna Court, in Kensington, West London. A revealing handwritten note by an MI5 officer on 7 June added to the minute sheet entry stated that he and B4 (Colonel Malcolm Cumming) considered that—because they assumed that the Home Secretary was aware of the circumstances of Lady Maclean's mail check—they had in effect authority under the HOW.[62] Indeed, at a meeting with Guy Liddell as early as 19 April,[63] Frank Newsam (PUS at the Home Office) had evidently approved the Lady Maclean HOW.

On *10 June*, however, although authorizing the mail check on Maclean, the Home Secretary (James Chuter Ede) declined to authorize the check on Lady Maclean, Reed receiving a note from Dick White on the 11th informing him that White had spoken to Miss Turner, the private secretary to Newsam. Running to keep up with events, the Home Secretary had baulked at ordering the interception of Lady

58 TNA, KV 2/4140 (Donald Maclean).

59 ibid. *Note what was being authorized here: the 'emanating part of the warrant' was an application for authority to implement the so-called* RATCATCHER procedure.

60 Reed had sent White the required 'letter to Col. Allan GPO and the necessary forms [for the HOW application]' on 1 June 1951.

61 TNA, KV 2/4141 (Donald Maclean).

62 TNA, KV 2/4141.

63 TNA, KV2/4140. However, at the height of the crisis Dick White was MI5's link with the Home Office. Liddell was in Wales between 3 and 11 June.

Maclean's mail for reasons unknown, though her title was likely to have been an issue. So too was the fact that her husband had been a Cabinet minister in inter-war Liberal and National governments. Chuter Ede's refusal did not, however, make a lot of difference in practice, as Reed at MI5 had received photostats of all the Iverna Court mail from 1 June to 11 June, before Newsam's secretary returned to MI5 the warrants Chuter Ede had been expected to sign. Those interfering with Lady Maclean's mail, and that of the residents in the block of flats where she lived, were thus denied even the unconvincing defence that their actions had been retrospectively sanctioned by the Home Secretary.

Apart from revealing interception to have taken place before warrants were issued and that a single warrant could apply to multiple persons at the same address, the warrant applied for in the Burgess case referred to above revealed yet another abuse. This was the adding of multiple addresses to a single warrant,[64] with the HOW in Burgess' file apparently authorizing both an '*Any name*' mail check at Burgess' address, *and* at the flats where his mother lived.[65] Burgess' mother was now married to a Colonel Bassett, and lived at Arlington House apartments in central London. Rather than seek a separate warrant, as in the case of Lady Maclean, the Bassetts' address had merely been added to the Burgess postal warrant, with both mail interceptions justified because they related to addresses 'used by Guy BURGESS'. No specific mention was made either of the Bassetts, or of course the other residents in the block of flats. This application to include the Bassetts was stopped by Newsam without being presented to the Home Secretary, though again not without MI5 enjoying the benefit of the interception in the meantime.

3. Irregular Phone Tapping

Turning from mail checks to phone taps, as already pointed out the major difference between the two is that the latter, unlike the former, did not as a matter of law require the Secretary of State's signed approval before the interceptions took place. But internal procedures identified and approved by the Stewart Report did, nevertheless, require a formal application to the Home Secretary 'in each case', this to be 'accompanied by a statement of the reasons' for the warrant, it being 'the practice for the Home Secretary to satisfy himself personally of the need for the warrant'. If

[64] As Colonel Allan noted in 1941, it was 'the number of addresses that matters here—rather than the number of HOWs'. He was referring to the approximately 600 mail HOWs which authorized the interception of mail going to 924 addresses then currently active: TNA, KV 4/222 (Letter and memo Allan to Abbot of MI5, 2 April 1941). The memo was a very secret Home Office/GPO document which broke down the interceptions into categories ('Communism' and 'Subversion' were separate). In their covering letters, both Abbott and Saffery warned that this was not a matter to be referred to in communications with either the GPO or the Home Office.

[65] TNA, KV 2/4102 (Guy Burgess). In this case, however, Reed asked Allan to confine interceptions to letters addressed to Bassett at 14 Arlington House on 5 June 1951.

these formal procedures were not followed in the case of mail checks, where there was an admittedly imperfect legal obligation underpinning the practice, it is not surprising that the evidence tends to suggest that they were not followed in the case of phone tapping either, given that there was no such legal obligation.

As might be expected, there is a good deal of traffic in the Burgess and Maclean files about phone taps, both before and after their disappearance. The ubiquitous R. T. Reed had asked Saffery to impose a telephone check on Maclean as early as 18 April 1951, also the date of the relevant HOW. As with mail checks, the date on the HOW is the date of the application, when the warrants ready for signature are sent to the Home Office. They do not record when the Home Secretary signed the documents. In this case, however, Liddell sought and received verbal assurances from Newsam as early as 20 April that the phone tap '*will* be be approved'[66] On 25 May 1951, Reed had asked Saffery to add Lady Maclean's phone number to 'CURZON's [Maclean's] telephone check'. Although he had only required arrangements to be in place by 'early next week', the tap was operating on 26 May 1951.[67] After MI5 had acknowledged that the men had disappeared, the Burgess file records that Malcolm Cumming, at 6 p.m. on 29 May 1951, 'had requested Saffery to arrange the urgent imposition of telephone checks' on Burgess' flat, as well as Maclean's psychiatrist's consulting rooms and house. They were in operation by 7.30 p.m.,[68] without the sanction of either Frank Newsam or the Home Secretary.

Similarly, we find an entry in Maclean's file credited to the ever ubiquitous R. T. Reed, with a note of action taken on 2 June 1951:

> B2 [Robertson] suggested that we should impose a telephone check on Philip Toynbee. I asked Mr Hackney to check the Food Office particulars for this man. Later during the morning he confirmed that Philip Toynbee was still registered as living at 25 Sussex Place, and I therefore telephoned Mr Saffery at 1200 hours and asked him to impose a telephone check on Paddington 4841 installed at the address in the name of Robert Kee.[69]

An *Observer* correspondent, Toynbee was an acquaintance of Maclean. Phone tapping could begin almost immediately on MI5 informing Saffery, who would do what was required in anticipation of the HOW being issued. Other relatives, friends, and acquaintances of Burgess and Maclean were targeted in the same way by MI5's panic-stricken officers. Some, as we will see in Chapter 8, had their houses bugged. By 4 June 1951, a minute sheet in the Maclean file noted that 'during the past week', seven telephone checks had been put into operation, which

66 ibid. (emphasis added).

67 TNA, KV 2/4101 ('Concordance of events immediately before and after the disappearance of Burgess and Maclean on 25 May 1951').

68 TNA, KV 2/4101 ('B4 note on events of night of 29-5-51').

69 TNA, KV 2/4141. Kee was a writer and journalist.

were being 'monitored continuously'.[70] These were phones belonging to Jack Hewitt (Burgess' friend); Erna Rosenbaum (Maclean's psychiatrist); Maclean's home; Lady Maclean; Colonel and Mrs Bassett; Philip Toynbee; and Peter Floud. Others associated with the Foreign Office men were subject to less intensive phone monitoring.

At this stage, there is no evidence of any written ministerial approval (though the existence of such evidence in so far unreleased sources should not be completely discounted). Nor—subject to the same caveat—is there any written evidence of ministerial approval for the request in yet another minute from R. T. Reed on 7 June that Saffery 'add' the Bassetts' number to HOW 1238 (which at that point referred only to Burgess' and Hewitt's phone). Given that the Bassetts were already under telephone surveillance, this appears to be a request that the GPO alter their copies of the pending Burgess/Hewitt HOW 1238 (dated 30 May) in anticipation of the Home Secretary approving the revised version of that warrant, which was submitted to the Home Office on 7 June along with other HOWs, including the ill-fated Bassett and Lady Maclean mail HOWs. A subsequent entry in the Burgess file, on 9 June, following White's discussions with Newsam, records that the telephone check on the Bassetts was to be cancelled,[71] a second casualty of Newsam's evident disapproval of MI5's interest in the Bassetts. The tapping had nevertheless been taking place for well over a week, and as was the case with the mail check, it had never been revealed to the Home Secretary, let alone sanctioned, or—to consider the wording of a warrant—*ordered* by him.

4. Procedures in Practice

The Burgess and Maclean files—released only in 2015—give a glimpse of how the interception procedures really operated. But while the decisions to invoke the power to intercept in these cases may have been hard to contest, the reasons given for using the power were both brief and poorly expressed, and do less than justice to the circumstances:

- in Maclean's letter check HOW: 'he has been reported to be a Communist, and it is desired to learn more about his activities and the associates of himself and his wife';[72]
- in Burgess' letter check HOW: 'he was said 'to have Communist sympathies and associates and whose activities it is desired to investigate';[73]

[70] ibid.
[71] TNA, KV 2/4102.
[72] TNA, KV 2/4101.
[73] TNA, KV 2/4102.

- in Burgess' telephone HOW: 'Guy Burgess the user of this telephone is employed in the Foreign Office where he has access to secret information. He has been reported to be a Communist and it is desired to learn about his associates and activities'.[74]

It is to be noted that while the pair had been suspected of conduct that would have been a serious criminal offence in breach of the Official Secrets Act 1911, s 1 (espionage), this does not form the basis of the HOWs, while it is also notable that the investigations as to their whereabouts were conducted by MI5 rather than the police.

More significant perhaps is the procedural irregularity exposed by the files, displaying a casual relationship between the procedures explained by the Stewart Report and the procedures as they operated in practice.[75] Moreover, there is a clear sense from the documentation that those involved—Saffery, Reed, and Allan; MI5's DDG (Liddell) and Dick White; Newsam and his personal secretary; and the Home Secretary—were all following a well-established pattern of behaviour. There was on the one hand a public insistence on formality, while on the other a private acceptance of informality. As we have seen, this is a pattern that appears to have been established during the Second World War, some ten years earlier.[76] It is thus clear that whatever may have been said in the Stewart Report, something along the lines of these war-time procedures continued to operate during the Cold War. It is true that the Burgess and Maclean files reveal that in practice interception requests were almost invariably made on the understanding that a HOW would be sought. They also reveal, however, that the interceptions would begin as soon as they had been authorized by MI5 internally and a request made to the Post Office. This meant that MI5 had days, if not weeks, in which to decide whether to process a warrant or to discontinue the surveillance.[77]

So despite the intensity of the surveillance of a host of people immediately after the 'disappearances' of Burgess and Maclean, there is no record of any formal ministerial involvement until 10 June 1951, when the Home Secretary was informed

[74] TNA, KV 2/4101.

[75] On Stewart, see p. 27 above.

[76] See pp. 27–8 above.

[77] Quite unrelated to Burgess and Maclean, further evidence that interception took place on the say-so of MI5 without a warrant in advance is provided by the following entry from Liddell's Diary:

> Money told me that Inspector Cooper of the Gold Coast Police, accompanied by a Special Branch Inspector, had just returned from a visit to the house of BOWMAN, a Communist, where three Nigerians were housed. The object was to interrogate these Nigerians about the falsity of their passports and about a proposed visit to a University in Eastern Germany. BOWMAN had refused SB entry to the house and, unfortunately, the Inspector had made it clear that he wanted to interrogate the Nigerians about their passports. It seemed likely, therefore, that the Nigerians would move to another house or even leave the country. Would I authorize B6 observation? I said that I did not think we should profitably use B6, since to be of any value the watch would have to be a 24 hour one and might go on for some time. It seemed to me better to put a TC on BOWMAN. I rang up Saffery and got this done (TNA, KV 4/473 (Liddell Diary, 2 July 1951)).

of only two telephone checks, these being HOW 1238 (Burgess), and HOW 1224 (Maclean).[78] In other words, it appears that Dick White informed Chuter Ede (through Newsam's secretary) of only two telephone checks, these relating to Burgess and Maclean directly.

Given the large numbers of checks on friends and relatives aimed at establishing the whereabouts of the men, this is surprising. Of particular interest was the Maclean telephone warrant which, as we have seen, had his mother's number added in the same way that the Bassetts' number was added to the Burgess phone warrant, and their address added to the Burgess mail warrant—with only the primary targets mentioned. We also saw that Newsam had approved the mail check on Lady Maclean, but was overruled by the Home Secretary.[79] That Chuter Ede refused to sanction the mail warrant but was nevertheless apparently willing to sign the phone warrant (which had Lady Maclean's number on it but not her name) at the very least gives rise to speculation about whether this was one that White got past the PUS, or that the latter had connived with White to get Chuter Ede's signature. That said, given Newsam's apparent squeamishness about Lady Maclean's mail, it is not clear why he would be any more sanguine about the interception of her phone.

While Newsam could say 'no' without consulting the Home Secretary, he also knew how to get the Home Secretary to say 'yes', a point illustrated by the case of Kenneth de Courcy, the right-wing editor of *Intelligence Digest*, which routinely published embarrassing inside information on government, security, and intelligence matters. According to Liddell again, Newsam advised that:

> unless we could satisfy the Secretary of State that the action we proposed was necessary from the point of view of the Defence of the Realm or the security of the state, he felt that he would be in difficulties if he asked him to sign the warrant. I said that we would review the position and see whether we could justify the warrants on these grounds.[80]

Two weeks later Newsam '*still felt nervous about the case and was reluctant to go forward with it until he knew whether there was going to be a change of Home Secretary* . . . de Courcy had done nothing against the law, and from the evidence available, had no intentions in that direction'. Nevertheless,

> Newsam agreed to the following formula for the warrant on de Courcy: I hereby authorize and require you to detain open and produce for my inspection all postal

[78] This is not to discount the likelihood that Ministers may have been kept informed informally of the investigation and methods adopted.

[79] See above, pp. 106–7.

[80] TNA, KV 2/472 (Liddell Diary, 3 February 1950).

> packets and telegrams addressed to or emanating from . . . believed to be intended for or sent by agents of a foreign power. This in fact means that we will have to open everything.[81]

IV. The Birkett Whitewash

In light of the foregoing, it was timely that the question of phone tapping in particular should have erupted in 1956 when it was revealed that intercepted communications of a notorious criminal (Billy Hill) were passed on to the Chairman of the Bar Council, which was investigating professional misconduct complaints against a barrister (Patrick Marrinan).[82] The matter caused a row, at a time when there was great anxiety about the 'secret police' generally, and phone tapping in particular. The government responded in June 1957 by appointing Lord Birkett (a seventy-three-year-old judge, who had just stood down from the Court of Appeal) to chair a committee:

> to consider and report upon the exercise by the Secretary of State of the executive power to intercept communications and, in particular, under what authority, to what extent and for what purposes this power has been exercised and to what use information so obtained has been put; and to recommend whether, how and subject to what safeguards, this power should be exercised and in what circumstances information obtained by such means should be properly used or disclosed.[83]

1. Legality

The first question for Birkett related to the legality of phone tapping—there was no equivalent to what was by now the Post Office Act 1953 for telephones. The legal authority for phone tapping was by no means straightforward, with a number of witnesses presenting a powerful case contesting its legality, not dissimilar to those encountered in Chapter 3 in relation to the legal foundations of MI5 itself. The Home Office clearly took the view that the power of interception was a prerogative power, the Home Secretary telling the House of Commons in the debates about the Marrinan affair that this prerogative power could be used 'only by the personal

[81] ibid., 17 February 1950 (emphasis added).

[82] For details, see Report of the Committee of Privy Councillors Appointed to Inquire into the Interception of Communications, Cmnd 283, 1957, paras 91–101.

[83] ibid., para. 1.

authority of the Secretary of State', and was used 'solely in cases involving the security of the State, or for the purpose of detecting serious crime'.[84]

Birkett acknowledged the problem in the sanitized and understated way often found in British judicial inquiries: 'It is a singular circumstance that the source of the power [to tap phones] has never been the subject of judicial pronouncement, and the text-book writers have not discussed it with any fullness.'[85] Apparently, Anson claimed that the Home Secretary had the 'right and the duty, if occasion requires, of detaining and opening letters in the Post Office'.[86] But this does not mention telephones (invented after Anson's time), though it does include telegrams. Those denying any such power referred to Chitty, who in 1822—as we saw in Chapter 2—purported authoritatively to catalogue all prerogative powers. But apart from the fact that the telephone had yet to be invented, 'nowhere is any reference made to a prerogative power of detaining and opening communications'.[87]

Those (unnamed) witnesses contesting the prerogative as a source of authority referred also to the powerful judgment of Lord Camden in *Entick v Carrington*,[88] where the Home Secretary (the Earl of Halifax) had issued a warrant authorizing his messengers to search and seize John Entick, 'together with his books and papers'. In proceedings at the suit of the latter, Lord Camden held that general warrants of this kind were 'illegal and unconstitutional',[89] critics arguing that the same was true of warrants to tap phones. Particularly notable in relation to the claimed power to 'search, seize and carry away all the papers of the subject', Lord Camden said in a passage which resonated very loudly in the ears of the government's critics:

> . . . that such a right should have existed from the time where the memory of man runneth not to the contrary, and never yet found a place in any book of law; is incredible. But if so strange a thing could be supposed, I do not see how we could declare the law upon such evidence.[90]

It would, of course, have been hugely embarrassing if Birkett had concluded that the entire foundations of telephone tapping were illegal, which was never likely to happen. But in the absence of clear authority, Birkett fudged the outcome in what was a less-than-convincing performance in relation to a matter that at the time was a hugely controversial practice. Thus in refusing to rule on the claims of the

[84] HC Debs, 7 June 1957, col. 1765. See also Herbert Morrison, 'The Phone Talks I Would Tap', *Empire News and Chronicle*, 30 June 1957.
[85] Cmnd 283, 1957 (n 82), para. 10.
[86] W. R. Anson, *Law and Custom of the Constitution*, Vol. II, Part II, quoted in ibid., para. 10.
[87] Cmnd 283, 1957 (n.82), para. 23.
[88] (1765) 19 St Tr 1030.
[89] ibid.
[90] ibid. Reference was also made to the famous passage in that case that, 'If it is the law it will be found in our books. If it is not to be found there it is not law (Cmnd 283, 1957 (n 82), para. 24).

rival camps (the Home Office and its critics), Birkett came up with the most extraordinary legal justification for the practice, which is that phone tapping must be lawful because the power has been used for a long time and because Home Office officials believe it to be lawful. Acknowledging that the origins of the power to intercept communications 'can only be surmised', the 'power has been exercised from very early times; and has been recognised as a lawful power by a succession of statutes covering the last 200 years or more'.[91] But although none of these statutes applied to phones, Birkett nevertheless concluded in a most unconvincing way that if there is a lawful power to intercept communications in the form of letters and telegrams, then it is wide enough to cover telephone communications.

2. Grounds

Birkett thus gave the government a crucial free pass on the legal authority for phone tapping. But although it fluffed its lines on the legal question, the Birkett Report was nevertheless invaluable for shedding some light on contemporary practice, or at least in providing some transparency about the grounds for which warrants might be issued, and the procedures that should be followed before a warrant was granted. Birkett explained that since 1937 it had been the practice to intercept telecommunications only with the authority of a HOW, explaining further that the practice was for warrants to be issued by either the Home Secretary or the Secretary of State for Scotland. Warrants could be issued on one of two grounds, the detection of serious crime (to the police and customs), or safeguarding the security of the State (to the Security Service).[92] Our concern here is with warrants issued for the latter reason to the Security Service, but we do not diminish the possibility of concerns relating to the former, or overlook the possibility that the two may overlap, as in the Burgess and Maclean case.[93]

So far as issuing warrants to safeguard the security of the State is concerned, Birkett reported that these would be issued where first, there was a major subversive

[91] Cmnd 283, 1957 (n 82), para. 8.

[92] Cmnd 283, 1957 (n 82), para. 57.

[93] So far as warrants on the former ground are concerned, three conditions had to be met before a warrant was issued: the offence being investigated must have been really serious; normal methods of investigation must have been tried and failed (or must from the nature of things have been unlikely to succeed); and there must have been good reason to believe that interception would result in a conviction. 'Serious' crime for these purposes was defined to mean an offence 'for which a man with no previous record could reasonably expect to be sentenced to three years' imprisonment, or offences of lesser gravity in which a large number of people were involved (ibid., para. 64). In practice, it seems that most warrants for the detection of crime were issued mainly to the Metropolitan police, principally for one of three purposes: to deal with organized crime; to catch 'men on the run'; and to detect receivers of stolen property (ibid., para. 103). So far as customs were concerned, interception was used mainly to frustrate the violation of exchange controls, and in particular the illicit export of capital usually in the form of diamonds (ibid., para. 104).

or espionage activity that was likely to injure the national interest; and second, the material likely to be obtained from the interception would be of direct use to the Security Service in compiling information which is necessary to the carrying out of its tasks. But unlike in the case of warrants for the detection of crime, where the term 'serious crime' was at least defined (albeit in the widest terms), there was no definition of 'major', 'subversive', or 'espionage' activity. In view of the constitutional position of the Security Service as set out in the Maxwell Fyfe Directive in 1952, these presumably would be matters for the Service itself to determine, subject to the Home Secretary's right to give direction and guidance, subject in turn to the overriding consideration that everything must be done only for the purpose of the 'Defence of the Realm'.[94]

The requirement that applied to criminal investigation warrants about the normal means of detection having tried and failed applied also in the case of Security Service warrants, though there was less stress on the need to secure convictions, 'since the Security Service is primarily concerned with safeguarding the State and keeping itself informed about dangers to its security'.[95] For besides securing convictions, wrote Birkett, 'the Security Service has the duty to keep up to date its information covering espionage and subversion and to inform Ministers and Departments of State about security matters that concern them'.[96] Indeed, the Committee attached great importance to interception by the Security Service as a means of discharging its responsibilities. Without providing any evidence, the Committee was convinced that interception by the Security Service was highly effective, having contributed to the identification of major spies, the discovery of highly secret material, and the detection of Communists operating secretly in the civil service.[97]

The result is that the Committee gave the government a second free pass, by appearing simply to endorse the existing grounds for granting warrants. There was no question of challenging the boundaries within which MI5 worked, or in examining whether MI5 always operated within the scope of its still secret Directive when using the powers of interception. In an age of deference to and misplaced trust in government, there did not appear to be any inclination to engage in such critical scrutiny, which in any event MI5 had taken precautions to avoid. Thus the Committee was told that the 'Security Service also destroyed detailed records before 1952',[98] and that the only Home Office records now existing were 'the covering minutes' relating to warrants issued since 1954, these containing only 'very brief summaries of the reasons for the issue of each warrant'.[99] That said, as we have seen,

94 See Chapter 3 above.
95 Cmnd 283, 1957 (n 82), para. 68.
96 ibid.
97 ibid., para. 113.
98 ibid., para. 81.
99 ibid., para. 80.

there was abundant information in the MI5 files had anyone been interested in conducting a systematic exercise rather than a whitewash.

3. Procedure

Birkett thus delivered on two grounds for the government: legality and substance. That left two other grounds: procedure and accountability. So far as the procedures for granting warrants are concerned, it seems implausible that Birkett could have been satisfied with a procedure of the kind we described in relation to Burgess and Maclean, which revealed a practice of interception by MI5 authorization which would trigger interception, and ministerial approval which would effectively endorse it, retrospectively.[100] This was certainly not consistent with details of the procedure conveyed to Lord Birkett, who revealed a careful process in which applications for warrants for the detection of crime were considered initially by senior officials in the criminal department of the Home Office, who would refer any approved application to the PUS. If the latter thought a good case had been made out, he in turn would submit the application to the Home Secretary for his personal decision.[101]

So far as Security Service applications for warrants were concerned, Birkett appears again to have had the wool pulled over his eyes, just as Stewart had been misled some 11 years or so earlier. MI5 applications were said by Birkett to go 'direct' to the PUS and then to the Home Secretary for his personal decision if the PUS thought a case had been made out.[102] The PUS was thus simply a filtering not an authorizing stage, the decision being exclusively the personal decision of the Home Secretary. There is no suggestion that it would be appropriate for telephone tapping to begin before the warrant was issued, and no discussion of a warrant being issued retrospectively. As might be expected, all the Secretaries of State who appeared before the Birkett Committee 'said that they gave close personal consideration to every request for a warrant *submitted to them*'.[103]

Although potentially ambiguous, there is no suggestion in the Birkett Report that these words in italics were intended to convey the impression that not all applications were submitted to the Home Secretary or that the PUS had authority to make the decision and personally approve those that were straightforward. The impression conveyed is clear: all applications were sent to the Home Secretary, unless weeded out because they failed to meet the criteria; all applications were

100 See pp. 105–9 above.
101 Cmnd 283, 1957 (n 82), para. 70.
102 ibid.
103 ibid. Emphasis added.

personally considered by the Home Secretary, and no interceptions took place until this procedure had been exhausted. The evidence of successive Home Secretaries seemed enough for Birkett, who wrote disarmingly that the power to issue warrants is 'used with the greatest care and circumspection, under the strictest rules and safeguards, and never without the personal considered approval of the Secretary of State'.[104]

The official account reveals how the procedure ought to have operated, and given Birkett's belief that best practice was in fact adopted, it was necessary to make only modest changes. The government was thus handed a third free pass, subject to a number of mildly irritating tweaks that would make the Birkett report almost respectable. Although broadly satisfied, Birkett nevertheless thus recommended that warrants should be reviewed more frequently than once a quarter, as was then claimed to be the practice,[105] suggesting 'not less than once a month both by the Home Office and by every authority that is granted a warrant to intercept'.[106] Birkett also addressed the practice that once granted, a warrant was valid until cancelled, there being no time limit on the life of a warrant. It was now proposed that warrants normally should be issued only for a fixed-term period of no longer than one month, with any extension to be approved by the Home Office (though not necessarily by the Home Secretary).[107]

[104] ibid, para. 8.

[105] ibid, para. 71. In the course of the latter review (conducted by the PUS), it was reported that the relevant departments would be summoned, and asked to make a case for the continuation of all warrants that had not been cancelled. Note, however, a minute by D. Mumford dated 15 December 1950 in TNA, KV 2/2565 (Palme Dutt) in response to an instruction from the Home Secretary that the retention of HOWs then in operation *for more than a year* had to be justified. Mumford provided fairly perfunctory justification in relation to Dutt, who was said to be 'Vice-Chairman of the Communist Party and Chairman of the International Department of the Communist Party. It will no doubt be agreed that the telephone check should remain in existence on account of REDACTED which have lately produced information of interest to B1G and to other B1 sections.'

[106] This review would be not only of the number of warrants issued, but also of each particular warrant, which in some cases we might expect to be rather perfunctory (Cmnd 283, 1957 (n.82), 109 328–33; 337–41, para 74).

[107] ibid., paras 74–76. The Lawson file subsequently revealed that this was unlikely to make much difference in practice; in that case, a warrant that had been issued on flimsy grounds, had been in force for over a year, had failed to yield any relevant security information, and had already been extended on four occasions. The documentation reveals that little was required to justify the extension of a warrant, the grounds for extension being given as follows:

> This warrant enabled us to acquire useful information regarding LAWSON'S Communist friends and contacts. There is a continuing interest in them as he is expected to visit Malaya again (28 November 1957); This warrant enabled us to acquire useful information regarding LAWSON'S Communist friends and contacts. There is a continuing interest in them as he is expected to visit Malaya again (30 December 1957); We have learned from this warrant that LAWSON is to visit Ghana in February. No details are available of the purpose, duration, etc, of this journey but it is hoped that the warrant will in due course provide this information (30 January 1958); As well as to Ghana we learn that LAWSON may go to Ceylon. On return we hope that the warrant will indicate whether or not there were ulterior purposes (28 February 1958) (TNA, KV 2/3594 ('Review of Home Office Warrant')).

4. Accountability

These were easy though perhaps inconvenient recommendations for the government to accept, which it duly did. They were a small price to pay for the fourth pass Birkett gave the government. This was on the question of accountability and the right of the Home Office to continue not only to make the substantive and procedural rules for the granting of warrants to intercept communications, but the power also to grant warrants in individual cases without any external accountability beyond the Home Office itself. The idea that the government should have the power to grant warrants for example to arrest someone, or to search someone, or to enter and search someone's property without (i) legislative or common law authority; and (ii) without the authority of a judicial warrant would be regarded as utterly unconstitutional. That was certainly the view taken in *Entick v Carrington* and cases since,[108] and it was a view with which Birkett would have been very familiar.

Dissatisfaction in some quarters generally with the lack of judicial oversight of the security procedures is to be seen in the emergence of a small ad hoc committee of individuals under the banner of the Campaign for the Limitation of Secret Police Powers. Established in 1956 by playwright and sometime Labour MP Benn Levy, the Group enjoyed support from within the ranks of the three parliamentary parties at the time, and briefly enjoyed a high profile.[109] Despite its broad title, the group reflected its origins in the public anxiety said to have been created by the well-known case of John Lang, in which a solicitor had been dismissed by ICI on political grounds following government pressure.[110] But although the group concerned itself specifically with investigations of civil servants and employees of firms engaged in business with the government, it also made an intervention on phone tapping when the Birkett Committee was set up in 1957.

The main significance of the campaign for present purposes lay in its 'five demands' (to which we return in Chapter 11), one of which was for a greater role for judges in the administration of some of the emerging security measures. This thinking inevitably made the agenda of the Birkett Committee, which reported that it had been urged in some quarters that the issuing of warrants should not be left 'exclusively in the hands of the Secretary of State'.[111] One idea was that 'warrants should be issued only on a sworn information before magistrates or a High Court judge'.[112] For reasons already explained, this seemed obvious: indeed, it has to be asked what kind of constitutional arrangement allows for a warrant for the invasion of privacy (telephones) and the interference with private property (letters) to be issued to the Secret Service by the government department to which the Service

108 (1765) 19 St Tr 1030.
109 See pp. 328–33; 337–41 below for a fuller discussion.
110 See HL Debs 21 June 1956, col. 1226 (see Chapter 11 below).
111 Cmnd 283, 1957 (n 82), para. 85.
112 ibid.

is operationally responsible. Birkett, it seems, was happy to answer—'the British Constitution', taking the view that:

> If a number of magistrates or judges had the power to issue such warrants, the control of the use to which methods of interception can be put would be weaker than under the present system. It might very well prove easier in practice to obtain warrants. Moreover, it would be harder to keep and collate records.[113]

This was a big prize for the Home Office and MI5, which (i) was grounded in ignorance of the real procedures for intercepting communications; and (ii) would have been unthinkable in countries with a more sophisticated constitutional understanding.[114] Birkett was not in a position to make a judgement about whether it would be easier to obtain warrants from judges than from civil servants, without knowing the success rate of applications under the regime he was investigating, the records of which he was told had been largely destroyed. While no one could be sanguine about robust judicial scrutiny, it is hard to believe that better respect for constitutional principle would have been less effective than a cosy arrangement all the more lamentable for the claim that, 'Secretaries of State and all the officials and authorities concerned have taken, and continue to take, scrupulous care to ensure the strict observance of the purposes to which it is intended by the Home Office that the interception of communications should be directed and confined.'[115]

V. Making Use of Information

So far, we have highlighted a number of surveillance methods by which information was obtained by MI5. We have also seen the claims of the Birkett Committee that much of the information relating to one of these means was destroyed, with the Home Office destroying its card index of warrants in 1947, and the Security Service destroying 'detailed records' in 1952.[116] Yet at least some of the pre-1952 HOWs (or minutes relating thereto) are to be found in personal files released to the National Archives, along with a great volume of material (in the form of transcribed conversations) they produced. This is intermingled in the files of surveillance targets with the information yielded by the other surveillance methods identified, and in this part, we give an account of how all this information was stored, used, and shared (both within and beyond government). The storage and filing arrangements in

113 ibid., para. 86.
114 See *Katz v US*, 389 US 347 (1967)—only ten years later.
115 Cmnd 283, 1957 (n 82), para. 90.
116 ibid., para. 81.

particular were an impressive administrative achievement, even if much of it was of questionable utility.

1. Routine Processing of Information

As already suggested in Part II, the question that does arise from these sometimes massive files is the purpose of collecting so much information about individuals. It is clear that information of this kind would not be required for all the activities of the Security Service, to the extent that the purpose of the Service was to supply Departments with information and advice on the nature and scale of the various threats to the security of the State, and to give advice on how to deal with them. This might include:

- Responding to Departmental requests to conduct detailed inspections of their various premises, giving advice on a wide range of subjects directly related to security, while also acting as a security inspector of the premises of government contractors; and
- Participating in the inter-departmental security committee structure within government (such as the Committee on Security), often taking the initiative to submit to these committees proposals relating to security policy.[117]

But as the Radcliffe Committee subsequently pointed out, it also included 'dealing with personal vetting inquiries from Departments, which involved checking individual names against intelligence records'.[118] As we shall see in Chapter 10, the information gathered by the Security Service was to form what was in effect a large national blacklist, used to exclude people from certain forms of employment in both the civil service and amongst government contractors in the private sector. This, however, would not justify the retention of information about an individual beyond the fact that he or she was a member of the Communist Party, or indeed information about the Communist Party itself. So apart from collecting information about people and organizations for the sake of it, information had to be collected for other purposes as well, though it is a striking feature of most of the files we examined that there are only glimpses of these other purposes, as in the case of individuals like Neil Lawson, who were being targeted because they were wrongly suspected of subversive activity.

What would these other purposes be? One purpose of watching the Party and Party members would be to generate information about other organizations and

[117] Report on Security Procedures in the Public Service (Chairman, Lord Radcliffe), Cmnd 1681, 1962, para. 16.
[118] ibid.

individuals. If the purpose was to compile a blacklist of Communist Party members and supporters, it would be necessary to identify the new recruits and the additional supporters. As suggested in Part II, a prominent feature of Special Branch reports of political meetings was thus the identification of unknown people who played a prominent part in the meeting in question, with a full personal description, no doubt for follow-up and checking. But as the Attlee statement to the House of Commons in March 1948 made clear, the policy was to exclude not only Party members from work 'vital to the security of the State', but also those 'associated with [the Party] in such a way as to raise legitimate doubts about his or her reliability'.[119] This would have created a need not only to discover who these associates might be, but also (and paradoxically more intrusively) to enquire into their reliability.

But apart from obtaining the names of Party members for the purposes of the Attlee statement, it is not clear what justification there was for the routine, constant surveillance of the Party itself. Why, for example, were listening devices permanently in place and why were its phones constantly tapped? There must come a point at which MI5's own surveillance serves a purpose, meaning that if the intelligence shows that the Party was not an espionage risk, then this should be reflected in the security response. Evidence of any change of position by the Party would soon emerge, without the need to be eavesdropping on personal conversations between Betty and George Matthews,[120] or retaining transcripts about the fitting of Harry Pollitt's car radio.[121] By the same token, if there was evidence of espionage activity, then, as in the Burgess and Maclean cases, steps could be taken quickly to introduce surveillance to the extent necessary; better still if it were to follow the procedures. It is as if the surveillance had become a ritual; the Communist Party was under surveillance because it was the Communist Party, and no one knew how or why to stop it.[122]

2. Exchanging Information (1): Lawson

As already seen above, the information obtained by the Security Service was shared between departments and with foreign governments. Information about D. N. Pritt was supplied to the South African police (with a request they refer back to London if they proposed 'to make this information the grounds for any action'),[123] and to the United States Foreign Service (provided with a brief

[119] HC Debs, 15 March 1948, col. 1703.

[120] TNA, KV 2/1045 (filed in Harry Pollitt's file).

[121] TNA, KV 2/1046.

[122] Much of the surveillance was simply picking up travel arrangements, the state of Harry Pollitt's health, and divisions within the Party. The last is interesting; but is it really any business of the State?

[123] TNA, KV 2/1065 (Sir Percy Sillitoe to R. J. Palmer, Commissioner of South Africa Police). Pritt was referred to by Sillitoe as a 'person of eminence'; hence the reasons for the caution. The South Africans had written to say that they had heard that Pritt was travelling to represent a defendant in a

summary of Pritt's 'activities and connections').[124] But although information appears to have been exchanged freely, caution was required in some cases for both political and legal reasons. Such concerns were centre-stage in the Neil Lawson affair,[125] when questions arose about whether the Malay Rulers, on behalf of whom he was acting as a barrister, should be told about the security concerns (it apparently being assumed in government that they did not already know). The information having been conveyed to the British High Commissioner, he was initially strongly of the view that the Rulers should be told as soon as possible. Sir Donald MacGillivray expressed concern that Lawson's Communist associations must have been known in the legal profession and among MPs, and that it would 'greatly discredit' the Rulers if it got out in circumstances which surprised them.[126]

After consulting the Security Service, however, the Colonial Office took the view that 'no immediate overt action' should be taken against Lawson. Here, it seems the Director General of the Security Service was exercised 'not so much about the security of our sources, as about the risk of LAWSON bringing an action for defamation'.[127] It was therefore agreed that information could be passed orally by the High Commissioner, 'provided that the Colonial Office realised that if LAWSON brought an action we should claim Crown Privilege, and provided that the telegram authorising the High Commissioner to pass this information on was sent by the Colonial Office and not by us',[128] the 'us' being the Security Service, who would nevertheless provide the information to be passed on by the High Commissioner. This was conveyed by the Colonial Office to Malaya, the telegram highlighting the risk of legal action against the High Commissioner for defamation in the event of the termination of Lawson's agreement, while also pointing out that, 'Lawson is acting professionally in this matter and without political bias.'[129]

fraud case and had learned that he was a Communist. They sought 'anything of interest' from 'a security point of view'.

124 TNA, KV 2/1065 (G. R. Mitchell to J. A. Cimperman, 20 November 1950).

125 TNA, KV 2/3592–4. According to the National Archives:

> Neil LAWSON: British. A barrister and a Communist Party member from about 1931, LAWSON (who became a QC in 1955) first came to notice in 1932 when he acted for the *Daily Worker* in a contempt of court case and in 1933 he was briefed, with D N Pritt, to defend the communists accused in the Reichstag Fire trial. By 1938 he was Treasurer of the secret Legal Group of the Communist Party and Secretary of the Communist fraction of the National Council of Civil Liberties [sic.]. He later allowed his overt connection with the Party to fade but continued to make undercover financial contributions until 1957. In the same year he was appointed legal adviser to the Rulers of the Malay States on constitutional matters, a job which he carried out in a notably objective manner.

126 TNA, KV 2/3593 ('Telegram Received', 1 February 1957).

127 TNA, KV 2/2593 (Telegram for the Secretary of State for the Colonies, 4 February 1957).

128 TNA, KV 2/2593 (Minute from Head Office, 12 February 1957).

129 TNA, KV 2/2593 (Minute, 6 February 1957).

The interest in this dialogue lies in the acknowledgement of the potential legal risks involved in the exchange and use of information, as well as the willingness to use Crown privilege as a weapon to defeat any such action against the State.[130] Unsurprisingly, Sir Donald changed his mind, despite concerns that it would be 'intensely embarrassing' were he required to disclose the information later on and it was revealed then that he 'had deliberately kept them in ignorance'.[131] Not only did he see the force of the arguments presented by the Colonial Office, but MacGillivray contributed a few of his own, including the suggestion that disclosure at this stage in the proceedings would look like a wrecking device, the Rulers being likely to find it hard to believe that the government was unaware of Lawson's associations when they (the Rulers) first engaged him.[132] So although he was in favour of disclosure, the High Commissioner agreed that the timing could not be worse and that expediency argued in favour of silence. If, however, the Rulers wished to retain Lawson after the negotiations were completed, an opportunity would then arise to inform them.

It seems that the Security Service had been barking loudly up the wrong tree. A note on the investigation of Lawson dated 14 June 1957 reported that, 'having begun as an extreme radical', Lawson 'has now swung to the right of PRITT and . . . does not at present take any part in the working of the National Council for Civil Liberties or in [the Communist Party] or legal circles'.[133] Reports from non-security sources indicated great satisfaction with his work as an adviser by both the Colonial Office and the Malay Rulers, whose interests he effectively protected from the Chinese.[134] The question of Lawson nevertheless came up again in the following year, with his business trips to Ghana and Ceylon (one of which coincided with a visit by Pritt, though MI5 were unable to read anything into the coincidence).[135] Although there was no reason to suppose that 'he has some sinister or ulterior motive' in making these trips on legal business, it was nevertheless thought appropriate by the Security Service to inform the 'local authorities' in both countries so that they may inform Special Branch in each jurisdiction about Lawson's visits. In passing on this information, assurances would be sought that no action would be taken 'from which Lawson could infer that HMG had informed against him'.[136]

[130] On Crown privilege, see *Duncan v Cammell Laird & Co.* [1942] AC 624, not overruled until *Conway v Rimmer* [1968] AC 910. Such a claim would allow the Crown to refuse to disclose any documents that might assist a plaintiff in his or her action.

[131] TNA, KV 2/3593 (MacGillvary to Colonial Office, 8 February 1957).

[132] ibid.

[133] TNA, KV 2/3593 (Report on Neil Lawson, 29 May 1957) (from 'a regular source in touch with progressive lawyers').

[134] TNA, KV 2/3593 (Note for File, 1 February 1957).

[135] TNA, KV 2/3594 (Cover Minute).

[136] TNA, KV 2/3594 ('A. J. Keller, Letter to SLO Ghana (Copy to SLO Ceylon), 17 February 1958').

3. Exchanging Information (2): Bing

A more vivid example of MI5 'processing' information to undermine a prominent individual relates to the case of Geoffrey Bing, a Labour MP and barrister, who in 1949 started to take cases in the Gold Coast. According to MI5, Bing quickly gained a reputation as 'the Pritt of West Africa', and to the considerable dismay of the British government, he was instructed by the CPP led by Kwame Nkrumah, under the leadership of whom the state headed towards independence. Bing's status as an MP appeared to generate caution rather than respect in the Security Service, and this was reflected in the approach of the security and intelligence services to his activities in the Gold Coast. In response to an enquiry from SIS about Bing early in 1949, Graham Mitchell:

> explained that, since the subject of the enquiry was evidently the MP, it was difficult for us to put a summary down for transmission to SIS. I reminded [name of SIS officer redacted] that BING was popularly believed to be a fellow traveller and that our information tended to confirm that view. It was agreed that the SIS copy should be returned direct to [SIS officer] with the words 'As spoken' on it.[137]

Following Bing's defeat at the general election in 1955, serious steps were taken by MI5 to use the information they had to sabotage his close relationship with the CPP. After alerting London that Bing was being considered for the official role of Constitutional Adviser to the Prime Minister, on 30 August 1956 MI5's West African SLO was given permission to show Nkrumah a brief biographical 'personality note' placing emphasis on Bing's Communist associations. Bing nevertheless got the government job, and with it the accolade as 'the greatest security problem we were now facing in the Gold Coast'.[138] Regarded as a likely conduit for Soviet—or at least Communist—influence on Ghana, the SLO was advised by London that 'efforts are being made in this country to obtain the termination of BING's appointment', by applying pressure to the Ghanaian government. MI5 told the SLO of government plans to lure Bing away with 'appetising briefs elsewhere', 'special activities', financial inducements, and persuading the Ghanaians of US reluctance to invest in a State relying on Bing as a constitutional adviser: 'everything possible will be done to remove Mr Bing'.[139]

137 TNA, KV 2/3813 (Minute sheet note, 10 January 1949 by G. R. Mitchell B1).

138 TNA, KV 2/3816 (Roger Hollis, citing the opinion of the Deputy High Commissioner designate, Ghana. Minute sheet note, 30 January 1957).

139 TNA, KV 2/3816 (To: SLO From: Head Office, 21 February 1957). We can only speculate about 'special activities'. The signal also revealed to the SLO that on Bing's arrival in London they decided not to 'operate' a procedure the name of which has been redacted (possibly 'Legal Eagle', the A4 observation operation they had prepared), and 'although GARDEN PATH was put into readiness, he was not in fact used', probably because they had learned on Bing's arrival that he would only be in the country for three days. Quite who 'Garden Path' was and what he did is unknown, but the expression 'to lead someone

Bing was placed under close surveillance. His mail was intercepted and when he was in London his phone was tapped. During April and May of 1957, he was followed around town by the A4 watchers as he went about official Ghanaian government business, the watchers exercising special caution because it was thought that if he realized he was under surveillance he would be likely to publicize the fact. MI5 considered installing telephonic electronic eavesdropping SF in his Great Portland Street flat but, initially at least, decided not to do so,[140] very likely for fear that he might realize he was being bugged. Director General Roger Hollis noted that the new Home Secretary R. A. Butler, when discussing 'the danger of the position BING held and the risk of compromise of the Accra postal warrant',[141] had 'said that he took the poorest view of Bing and was willing to do anything he could to assist'.[142] On his return to London, Bing was observed by 'Jim' Skardon's watchers associating with, among others, a woman 'E':

> Aged 40 to 43 years. 5'3–4" in height, slightly built. Short, straightish copper coloured hair. Fair complexion. Dressed in a yellow cardigan, white blouse and medium grey straight shirt.

This was Barbara Castle MP, her description 'extracted' to her Security Service file PF 52,052.[143]

Inspired by what they considered to be Bing's unsatisfied domestic political ambitions, MI5 contemplated attempting to persuade the Labour Party NEC to lure Bing away from West Africa by telling him that there was no prospect of him being selected as an official Labour candidate at the next election unless he returned to the United Kingdom.[144] At the end of April 1957, a meeting of the

up the garden path' derives from luring a domestic pig to slaughter—not that we are suggesting MI5 wanted to do the same to Bing.

[140] Bing's February visit was shorter than MI5 envisaged, 13–16 February, and it appears that very little surveillance took place. The February telecheck was cancelled by a phone call to Mr Harlow at the GPO 'as from mid-day on 16th unless he heard from me'. The MI5 officer 'also warned him of the danger of compromising this check', indicating the extent to which Bing was considered to be alert to the possibility of surveillance (TNA, KV 2/3816 (Note by E2 [E Division had responsibility for 'the colonies'], 15 February 1957)). SF seems to have been ruled out in advance of his arrival. However, Bing's April visit was much longer, the surveillance effort intense, and despite MI5's concerns about alerting their target, it seems likely that SF was employed during this period. Certainly, there are redactions in file entries relating to the April surveillance, 'telechecks', and HOWs that could be seen to suggest that such references had been removed. The A2A briefing sheet has been removed from the file, but an extract from the 'E Branch Weekly Note for E and DG' states at para. 9 that, 'Our coverage of Bing during this visit has been an example of how information from REDACTED can aid and simplify.'

[141] After Hollis had discussed the matter with PUS Frank Newsam.

[142] TNA, KV 2/3816 (6 February 1957). Butler signed the warrant for the interception of Bing's post addressed to the Gold Coast after consulting with the Secretary of State for Commonwealth Relations (Douglas Home).

[143] TNA, KV 2/3816 (A4 surveillance report, 15 April 1957).

[144] TNA, KV 2/3817 (Redacted remains of a letter from MI5 to the Commonwealth Relations Office, 18 April).

Cabinet Committee on Communism attended by Hollis discussed suitable individuals for an appointment to an academic post in Ghana 'to supplant Mr Bing'.[145] On 30 April 1957, Skardon's people followed Bing and Professor Bernal to the Houses of Parliament.[146] They did not, however, follow the pair inside. The watchers also waited outside the Palace of Westminster on 1 May while Bing met with Lord Farringdon (a Labour hereditary peer), and subsequently followed him to Transport House, where he met Morgan Phillips. We can only speculate whether the latter passed on details of what was said to Special Branch.[147]

4. Processing of Information

One final question is the extent to which the surveillance harvest could be shared with private individuals or organizations for purposes other than those for which the information was collected. NCCL files provide examples of employers who were informed by the police that certain employees were members of the Communist Party, the employees in question being dismissed as a result. They include Chris Koupparis, who was Joint Secretary of the National Cypriot Committee in Britain, who claimed that his accounting firm had fired him after a visit from the police to inform his employer that he was 'a Communist who speaks in Hyde Park'.[148] They also include Patricia Wiggins, who claimed to have been dismissed by the *Liverpool Daily Post and Echo* after only five days of employment on the ground that she had been a press officer at the World Peace Congress in Sheffield in 1950 and had failed to disclose this in her application. In a letter to the NCCL, she added that 'I am also given to understand that the clipping shown to me [indicating her role at Sheffield] came from a police file (although I have no criminal record whatsoever).'[149]

While there are other allegations of information being passed on in this way, there are correspondingly few examples of its misuse being challenged successfully, if only because for official purposes it did not exist and was not disclosed. It may be, of course, that the allegations are just that—allegations without substance. We do know nevertheless that police officers disclose other information held on police records to third parties and that they have been prosecuted for doing

[145] TNA, KV 2/3818 (Letter from CRO to MI5, 1 May 1957).

[146] Bernal was a famous physicist with progressive political views, also active in the peace movement (on which see pp. 63–72 above). His Security Service files have been released to the National Archives as TNA, KV 2/1812–14.

[147] TNA, KV 2/3818 (A4 surveillance report, 2 May 1957). See TNA KV 4/475 (Liddell Diary, 27 January 1953) for Morgan Phillips' liaison with the Director of Special Branch, Leonard Burt. Liddell made it clear that he had no intention of giving Phillips any information, but that Burt would let MI5 have any information if it came his way. In the same entry he was similarly emphatic about MI5's 'unofficial' contact with the TUC.

[148] *Daily Worker*, 16 October 1953.

[149] J. Mahoney, *British Civil Liberties and the Cold War: 1945–1956* (Ph.D. Dissertation, University of Cambridge, 1977, Cambridge University Library), p. 196.

so. Security Service files—like police records—would have been protected by the Official Secrets Act 1911, but it would only be an offence to communicate official information to a third party without official authorization.[150] What little security this offered would be even less effective to deal with threats, such as those recorded by Fred Dallas of the Esher League of Co-operators, visited at home by a uniformed police officer ('number 426') who wanted to ask questions about his 'political activities', which Dallas refused to answer. In describing what reads like conspicuous harassment, the letter continues:

> He asked me if I was working against the state; I said no. He asked for the name and address of my employers. I refused to tell him, but he said the information could be obtained. He implied that my employers would be questioned if I did not cooperate in answering his questions, also that enquiries would be made of my neighbours.[151]

It was only in relation to phone tapping that this matter was specifically considered at an official level, the disclosure of telephone intercepts to the Bar Council in relation to the Marrinan proceedings being the activating reason for the establishment of the Birkett Committee. Birkett reported that it was the settled policy of the Home Office that, save in the most exceptional cases, information obtained by interception of communications 'should be used only for the purposes of detection, and not as evidence in a Court or any other Inquiry'.[152] An example of an exception to this practice occurred in 1953 in a disciplinary inquiry before the Metropolitan Police Board into charges of corruption against two officers.[153] The Home Secretary granted permission for evidence from the intercepted telephone calls to be used in the proceedings, a decision questioned by Birkett, as was the decision to allow the Chairman of the Bar Council and others to have sight of the intercepted telephone calls of gangster Billy Hill for the purpose of the inquiry against Marrinan. The latter decision was 'mistaken',[154] though in light of the highly exceptional circumstances relating to the administration of justice, not 'unreasonable'.[155]

Birkett concluded that 'the power given to the Secretary of State to issue a warrant to intercept communications, whether by letter or by telegram or by telephone, is a power of such importance and consequence that it should be most rigorously confined to the purposes which convinced the Home Secretary that it was right to issue the warrant in the first place'.[156] Consequently, it was

[150] *Lewis v Cattle* [1938] 2 KB 454.
[151] University of Hull, NCCL/DCL/18/4 (Dallas to Allen, 31 May 1954).
[152] Cmnd 283, 1957 (n 82), para. 92.
[153] ibid., para. 99.
[154] ibid.
[155] ibid., para. 100.
[156] ibid.

recommended that there should be no disclosure of the information obtained on 'public grounds' to 'private individuals or private bodies or domestic tribunals of any kind whatsoever'.[157] Although a welcome recommendation for several reasons, there is an important caveat, in the sense that there was no procedure recommended to ensure that data misuse did not take place, and no remedy to deal with situations where it did. It is also the case that confining the use of the information in the manner proposed would make it even less likely that the existence and extent of the practice would become known. Heightened secrecy was thus likely to have been a doubtful benefit of the Marrinan and Birkett processes, as it would also ensure that wire-tap evidence would not be available in legal proceedings, even though the fruits of that evidence would almost certainly be consumed in these proceedings.

VI. Conclusion

Although the Security Service had extensive powers of surveillance, it is a striking feature of the collection, storage, and use of information that MI5 appeared to be subject to so little accountability. It is also striking that the Birkett Committee left no statutory legacy and no statutory regulation. Birkett had proposed legislation only if there was continuing uncertainty about the legal basis of telephone tapping.[158] But this was strongly resisted by politicians on all sides, with the strongest public opposition being voiced by Herbert Morrison, Communist-hating Home Secretary in the wartime coalition government. Writing in the press post-Birkett, Morrison wrote to oppose legislation to 'curb possible abuses', for although the idea appeared sound:

> I am frightened members [of Parliament] might be tempted to put in so many restrictions and provisos that the Home Secretary's powers would be seriously hampered. My suggestion is leave the power as it is.[159]

The lack of accountability surrounding surveillance is not the same as saying that there were no restraints. There were limits on what the Security Service could do under its mandate, in the sense that any means of investigation adopted for the defence of the realm were 'strictly limited to what is necessary for the purposes of their task'. And while MI5's budget increased steadily in the post-war years, there would still be fiscal restraints, not to mention technological ones. It has been plausibly suggested by Bunyan that until the late 1960s cumbersome technology

[157] ibid., para. 101.
[158] ibid., para. 52.
[159] Morrison (n 84).

and human limitations rather than legal restrictions and ethical scruples would have curbed an even greater excess of zeal on the part of MI5.[160] But whatever the restraints in the mandate there was no independent voice to determine whether these restraints were being observed.

Although rightly dubbed a 'whitewash',[161] this is not to deny that Birkett's procedural reforms were welcome, particularly his suggestion that warrants should be issued for only a month at a time, subject to review and renewal.[162] But in terms of countervailing civil liberties concerns, Birkett was otherwise mute, able confidently to conclude in relation to phone tapping that:

> The interference with the privacy of the ordinary law-abiding citizen or with his individual liberty is infinitesimal, and only arises as an inevitable incident of intercepting the communications of some wrong doer. It has produced no harmful consequences.[163]

This was a breath-taking conclusion—patronizing, meaningless, and disingenuous: we are unaware that members of the Communist Party or the peace movement were anything but law-abiding, or that they were 'wrongdoers'. It was also misleading—surveillance generally (and phone tapping in particular) was not used only in relation to those who broke the law or who were otherwise engaged in 'wrongdoing'.

Surveillance was also used to identify Communist Party members, as Birkett acknowledged elsewhere in the report.[164] Unlike the United States, membership of the Communist Party was not—and never has been—a criminal offence. In a nutshell, what we have is an extensive system of multiple forms of surveillance by an agency that was largely self-regulating, with only limited administrative and political oversight. It is a system from which the judiciary were largely excluded, though quite whether greater judicial involvement would have made much difference is moot. Such uncertainty is a pitiful indictment of the judiciary, whose reputation Birkett—a judge of great experience, who was to sit as a Law Lord by virtue of his hereditary peerage—did nothing to enhance.

Such uncertainty also raises alarming questions about the robustness of judicial supervision in granting warrants for other purposes, on the importance of which another judge—Lord Camden—in another era was so eloquent.[165]

[160] T. Bunyan, *The History and Practice of the Political Police in Britain* (London, 1977), p. 196.

[161] P. O'Higgins, *Censorship in Britain* (London, 1972), p. 53.

[162] Cmnd 283, 1957 (n 82), para. 123. Birkett recommended that full records should be kept, including the grounds on which an application is made, a copy of the warrant or a note that the application had been rejected, and a record of the date of its cancellation.

[163] ibid., para. 8.

[164] ibid., para. 105.

[165] See p. 113 above.

6
Democracy under Surveillance

I. Introduction

In chapter four we considered the use of surveillance powers against a wide range of organizations and individuals. The other group to stand out are MPs, about whom concerns are rightly raised when questions turn to who is a legitimate surveillance target. MPs enjoy a special place in a parliamentary democracy, received constitutional wisdom suggesting that they have responsibilities to their electors, to their party, and to the country as a whole.[1] In discharging these responsibilities, MPs provide advice to constituents who have disputes with government departments; they provide political opposition to government, which they have a responsibility to hold to account; and, of course, they form the government, with constitutional practice requiring ministers to be recruited from Parliament. It would be hardly consistent with the performance of these duties if for uncertain purposes a State agency should snoop and pry on MPs to find out the advice they are giving, the steps they are taking to oppose the government, and the policies they are developing while in government.

As we saw in Chapter 3, the Attlee Directive introduced a number of key principles, including the direct responsibility of MI5 to the Prime Minister, the obligation to confine its activities to those necessary for the defence of the realm, and to avoid intervention in matters of a party-political character. But neither the Attlee Directive nor the Maxwell Fyfe Directive thereafter said anything about the legitimate targets of MI5's surveillance, and notably made no direct reference to MPs. This raises questions about whether MI5 should concern itself with the actions of MPs. Should MPs be protected from surveillance by the Security Service, or should they be treated in the same way as any other citizen, regardless of the constitutional role they perform? While it might be hard to argue that MPs should always be protected from surveillance (such as where there is suspicion of having committed a serious offence), the circumstances in which such action might be authorized ought nevertheless to be quite exceptional.

The difficulties raised by the foregoing questions are compounded by the fact that the Security Service acted under political direction, and it was the Prime Minister, and subsequently the Home Secretary, on whom lay the unenviable duty

[1] See the classic discussion in *Amalgamated Society of Railway Servants v Osborne* [1910] AC 87, esp. per Lord Shaw of Dunfermline.

MI5, the Cold War, and the Rule of Law. K. D. Ewing, Joan Mahoney, and Andrew Moretta, Oxford University Press (2020). © K. D. Ewing, Joan Mahoney, and Andrew Moretta. DOI: 10.1093/oso/9780198818625.001.0001

to attempt to ensure that the Service must not concern itself with party-political matters. But apart from the Attlee and the Maxwell Fyfe Directives, parliamentary privilege provided the only other possible restraint, though it appears to have been accepted since 1735 that 'it is a high infringement of the privileges' of MPs for their letters to be 'open[ed] or looked into', without the authority of a warrant signed by a Secretary of State.[2] These terms of a House of Commons resolution were subsequently interpreted to be 'a clear recognition by the House of the right of the Secretary of State to intercept Members' postal packets by the use of an express warrant'.[3] In the absence of any question having arisen about phone tapping, it was thought 'probable that the rulings concerning letters would extend by analogy to telephones'.[4]

So far as MPs are concerned, MI5 and its political masters otherwise had pretty much a free hand. In this chapter, we consider some of the evidence from the KV files as to how that hand was played. In the course of doing so, we examine the reasons why an MP might have been under surveillance (usually 'subversion'—essentially a suspected connection of some kind with the Communist Party); the different forms that surveillance might take; and the role of the Prime Minister in encouraging or forbidding surveillance of particular MPs. Although there is some evidence of letter opening and phone tapping, much of the material collected about targeted MPs came principally from collateral sources. The close surveillance of the Communist Party in particular helped to keep watch on the two Communist Party MPs elected after the war, and also helped to nourish many other KV files, including those of prominent Labour MPs, by no means all of which have been released.[5]

II. Phil Piratin MP

At the general election in 1935, William Gallacher was the first MP to be elected on an exclusively Communist Party platform, winning West Fife from Labour, a seat

[2] The text of the resolution is reproduced in the Report of the Committee of Privy Councillors appointed to inquire into the Interception of Communications (Chair: Lord Birkett), Cmnd 283, 1957, para. 124.

[3] ibid., para. 125.

[4] ibid., para. 127.

[5] According to MI5, between 1909 and the early 1970s in excess of 175,000 files considered to no longer be of any relevance to the defence of the realm were destroyed, and since the end of the Cold War an estimated 200,000, mostly ones 'opened for counter-subversion reasons' have been destroyed (www.mi5.gov.uk/managing-information). Nevertheless, after the 1940 fire at Wormwood Scrubs (a temporary wartime home for MI5), when numerous files were lost and damaged, 'Duplicate copies of all files and indexes were routinely made on microfilm, and stored in a specially protected MI5 warehouse in Cheltenham to prevent the catastrophe of Wormwood Scrubs occurring again': P. Wright, *Spycatcher: The Candid Autobiography of a Senior Intelligence Officer* (Toronto, 1987), p. 37). It is possible, perhaps even likely, that the post-war incineration of paper files was not followed by the destruction of the microfilmed copies.

he held until 1950.[6] Following the general election in 1945, Gallacher was joined by Phil Piratin, with Harry Pollitt just missing out in South Wales. As the experience of Phil Piratin in this Part shows, Communist Party MPs were subject to intense levels of surveillance, their parliamentary candidature being an excuse for more rather than less surveillance: there was little respect by MI5 for the office the MPs held, or the choices made by their constituents. Although there is no evidence of HOWs being issued to intercept their communications, the HOWs in place in relation to the Party allowed MI5 to pick up a lot of information about the Party's MPs, as did the hidden microphones in King Street. It is also the case that surveillance was used for wholly destructive political purposes, and could not conceivably be said to be limited to the defence of the realm.

1. Special Branch and Elections

It started with the election campaign, with Communist candidates subject to very close surveillance by Special Branch, with detailed Special Branch reports being written in the aftermath of each constituency campaign.[7] These were all deposited in the candidates' MI5 files, as well as in their Special Branch files. In the case of Phil Piratin, a notable entry is a Special Branch report of an election meeting he addressed on 1 June 1945 as prospective parliamentary candidate. The officer present was clearly unimpressed, commenting that Piratin's speech contained 'nothing new or novel in the annals of communist addresses', and 'the same time worn phrases were given from the rostrum'.[8] In a file entry a few weeks later, an intercepted phone conversation between two Party activists (Roland Berger and Alf Maizels) records one (Berger) asking the other (Maizels) if he had 'any stuff on Frankel', Frankel being the incumbent Labour member for Mile End, the constituency being contested by Piratin.[9]

After the election, a tightly typed seven-page account of Piratin's campaign was produced by Special Branch. The report highlighted various strengths of Piratin's candidature and a number of weaknesses of the Labour incumbent. These strengths related to Piratin's prodigious work in Stepney, where he was well known, and the efficient campaign waged by the local Party which ensured that Piratin's message was widely promoted. Full details were also reported of his proposer and

[6] The first Communists (Shipurji Saklatvala and Walter Newbold) were elected as Labour Party candidates in 1922, but following the proscription of the Communist Party by Labour, this ceased to be a possible route to Parliament.

[7] It is to be noted that it was not only parliamentary elections that were subject to Special Branch surveillance. The same was true of local authority elections.

[8] TNA, KV 2/2033 (Metropolitan Police, Special Branch Report, 1 June 1945).

[9] TNA, KV 2/2033 (Minute of Outgoing Phone Call from Roland Berger to Alf Maizels, 17 June 1946). As it happens, in one year the indolent Frankel had made no speeches, asked four questions (of which two were stooge questions), one supplementary question, and five words of interjection.

seconder, as well as his assentors, and the identity of prominent supporters (such as Professors Levy and Haldane) who spoke at his rallies. It was also thought necessary to include in the report the details of the printer of Piratin's election address, said to be Porteous Ltd (TU), whose chief printer was 'a close friend and keen supporter' of Piratin. Finally, the report noted that Piratin had established a close association with the local press, the *East London News*, which had been 'more than generous' in giving space to Piratin's letters and Communist Party propaganda generally.[10]

Piratin lost his seat in 1950. So far as the election on 23 February 1950 is concerned, a detailed Special Branch report in Piratin's MI5 file records that his campaign started as early as 27 October 1949 with a meeting of the Stepney YCL Youth Brigade.[11] From that date onwards, the Youth Brigade was involved 'almost daily' in an active canvass of the district in favour of Piratin, concentrating mainly in the vicinities of the Limehouse and Watney Street markets and in Petticoat Lane, with Piratin being represented as the candidate for peace. Three individuals were named in the report as being the main organizers of the campaign. In addition, a series of election meetings addressed by Piratin was kicked off by a meeting at Stepney Public Library on 18 January 1950, with three other venues identified (St George's Town Hall and two schools), along with the organizer of the meetings, who was said to be the newly appointed organizer of the Stepney Communist Party. According to Special Branch, there were no developments of special interest at these election meetings.

In addition, the report gave an account of Piratin's election literature, with a summary of its content and an account of a pamphlet outlining Communist Party policy. As with the meetings, the literature was said to contain 'nothing of particular note'. What was significant, however, was the concluding paragraph of the report, in which it was said that:

> During the course of the Stepney Communist Party election campaign about thirty motor cars were officially registered as being in use on behalf of the communist candidate. Enquiries are in hand regarding the registered owners of these vehicles and a further report will be submitted in due course.

As it is, the report had already identified the name and address of Piratin's election agent, as well as his eight 'assenters' (along with what appear to be their Special Branch file reference numbers), and eighteen representatives to act as scrutineers, in this case along with their addresses and what appear to be their Special Branch

[10] TNA, KV 2/2033 (Metropolitan Police, Special Branch Report, 3 August 1945).

[11] TNA, KV 2/2033 (Metropolitan Police, Special Branch Report, Stepney Branch Communist Party Parliamentary Election February 1950, 27 February 1950).

file reference numbers. Only in three cases was it not possible to identify the individual from Special Branch records. Quite a haul.

2. Parliamentary Privilege

Once into the House of Commons, the Communist Party MPs were not to be treated with the same respect as the others, or accorded the same courtesies as other members, several of whom revealed themselves as keen combatants in the class war. The latter included the fifth Earl of Winterton, who had served in the House of Commons since 1904 as the Conservative member for Horsham. He had briefly served ignominiously in the Chamberlain government, and in that latter capacity had led the British delegation to the Evian Conference, established to consider the plight of the Jewish refugees in 1938. If his exchange with Phil Piratin in the House of Commons on 12 December 1946 is any guide, he may not have been the best man for that particular job (depending, of course, on the true intentions of participating governments). Although it is quite likely that Piratin was very irritating to non-Communists, on this occasion he interrupted a speech by Brigadier Rayner in a debate on the Indian Constitution, with the following consequences:

Mr Piratin Surely, the question is not whether the majority—

Earl Winterton We do not want the views of foreign Communists.

Mr Sorensen Mr. Deputy-Speaker, is it in Order for the noble Lord to insinuate that anybody is a foreign Communist?

Hon. Members Withdraw!

Earl Winterton I shall withdraw nothing of the sort. I said the hon. Gentleman was a Communist, and, if he likes, I will substitute 'of foreign descent'.

Mr Piratin On a point of Order. May I ask whether it is not in accordance with the custom of this House that the noble Lord, who made a slight upon me and on my descent, should withdraw that remark, and may I ask if you propose to order him to do so?

Mr Deputy-Speaker (Major Milner) I do not think that sort of remark ought to be made and certainly not unless the noble Lord has proof of his statement.

Earl Winterton I have proof of my statement. I say that the hon. Gentleman is a Communist and that he is of foreign descent.

Mr Sorensen Is that not also a reference to our own monarchy?

Mr Piratin May I ask if you, Mr Deputy-Speaker, propose to take any steps in this matter? Otherwise, I shall have to consult Mr Speaker to see what redress I can get in the matter. I will make my position quite clear. I am British born. My father came here 50 years ago, running away from the pogroms in

> Russia which were supported by people like the noble Lord. My father was a Russian. I am British born. I am a Member of this Parliament, duly elected, and I have as much right to be here as the noble Lord. He has no right to make such a remark about me.
>
> **Earl Winterton** That was exactly what I said. I withdraw it, if the hon. Gentleman does not like it. I used the term 'foreign Communist'. I repeat, he is a Communist of foreign descent, and he has now admitted it. What is there to withdraw?[12]

A week later, Phil Piratin made a personal statement in the House of Commons about his 'nationality', which he thought had recently been called into question.[13] Referring to the debate on India, Piratin pointed out that he had been described as a 'foreign Communist', and subsequently 'a Communist of foreign descent'. In order that there may be no misunderstanding either to his nationality or allegiance, Piratin rose to make it clear that:

> I am a British subject by birth. My father was a Russian. He found refuge in this country, as many before him had done with gratitude, after fleeing from Tsarist persecution in his own country. While it is true, therefore, that I am of foreign descent, that description would apply to many British-born subjects in some degree. For my part, I would merely emphasise that I am a British subject and that I have never considered myself as having any other allegiance.

This was followed by an unseemly row between Winterton and the Speaker, in which the Leader of the Opposition shamelessly intervened on behalf of the oafish Lord. Piratin was by now a spectator, but within an hour of this farce he found himself involved in an altercation in the tea-room with the journalist Thomas Lucy, in which blows were struck, and in the course of which the member for Mile End claimed that anti-semitic views had been expressed by his allegedly racist adversary:

> When people want to be offensive, as I have found, to Jewish people . . . the expression is often used 'You people'. The words 'You people' in themselves really have no meaning at all, but when those words are used in an offensive tone, and so on, that is what is implied there . . . I would like a happy conclusion to this investigation, and therefore I am prepared to say this: that if any Member of the Committee asks me, did he at any time say to me 'You Jew', I would have to answer 'No, I cannot

12 HC Debs, 12 December 1946, cols 1415–16.
13 ibid., cols 2191–16.

> recall that'. But he kept on making sneering remarks about 'You people' and 'I am better', and so on and so on.[14]

Piratin made these latter claims in the course of oral evidence to a Committee of Privileges that had been established to examine the incident in the tea-room after a complaint had been that there had been a breach of privilege.[15] The Committee upheld the complaint, finding that the blow struck by Piratin—an amateur boxer in his youth—was a gross contempt of the House, bound to lower the House in the estimation of the public.[16] While Lucy escaped censure for this incident, he was called to heel for another matter later that day that was sufficiently insulting as also to constitute a contempt of the House.[17] But apart from the fact that the Committee's report makes no reference to the context within which the altercations took place (the unrepentant abuse by Winterton),[18] the Committee (whose members included the Leader of the Opposition) failed completely to address the anti-semitic remarks allegedly made by Lucy. Despite being alluded to consistently by Piratin in the course of his evidence,[19] not only were these remarks ignored by the Committee, but the verbatim report of its proceedings show that Piratin was prevented from pursuing the issue, having asked the Committee why they had failed to raise it with Lucy when he appeared before them.[20]

The report of the Committee of Privileges was debated in the house on 10 February 1947, the debate being opened by Arthur Greenwood, the Lord Privy Seal. Referring to the war, Greenwood continued by saying that:

> The country saved its democratic institutions, and especially the Mother of Parliaments, but democracy can live healthily only if people show tolerance to one another. The success of a democratic State depends as much on the conduct of its citizens as on the soundness of its principles. It is sad that, after the House of Commons had vindicated itself and when it had been nourished and re-invigorated by a large number of new hon. Members, whose duty it is to cherish

[14] HC Committee of Privileges, HC 353 (1946–7), 15 January 1947, Q 93–4. Earlier in the course of his evidence, Piratin claimed that Lucy had said that, 'You people are too sensitive', and that, 'You people must learn to behave like Englishmen', and that, 'I am a Welshman and I can fight, not like you people': ibid., Q 72.

[15] HC Debs, 19 December 1946, col. 2323. On this occasion, in view of the apologies from the two men involved, Morrison, as Leader of the House, had proposed to let the matter lie without a reference to the Committee of Privileges; Churchill insisted otherwise.

[16] HC Committee of Privileges, 3 February 1947.

[17] ibid. The police reports on the incident can be read in TNA, MEPO 3/2625.

[18] Winterton appeared to acknowledge his part in the drama, asking the Speaker on 19 December 1946 whether 'in view of certain circumstances' he could be 'excused from adjudicating on this particular matter' (HC Debs, 19 December 1946, col. 2329).

[19] See initially, HC Debs, 19 December 1946: 'He not only insulted me, but he also insulted my race' (col. 2324).

[20] HC Committee of Privileges, 15 January 1947.

> the honour and dignity of the House, that a Member of this Assembly, and a member of the Press Gallery should have been guilty of high breach of Privilege.[21]

Stirring words, even if they do seem a bit over the top for what Churchill referred to as a 'scuffle in the cafeteria'.[22] But it was not unruly behaviour in the tea-room that was the problem revealed by this incident so much as the casual racism of the time, which is encountered also in the Special Branch reports of Piratin's political meetings, where on one occasion it was apparently necessary for the police officer to report that a meeting of the Stepney Communist Party he attended had 'an average attendance of 500, mostly Jewish'.[23] Nevertheless the House accepted the report of the Committee of Privileges, and—to the evident anger of William Gallacher—placed on record 'its high displeasure with [Lucy's and Piratin's] conduct and its determination to proceed with the utmost severity against future offenders in like cases'.[24]

3. Surveillance as an MP

Apart from the surveillance of Communist Party electoral candidates, Communist Party members were also subject to surveillance while serving as MPs. This took several forms, including a police presence at a wide range of meetings they addressed outside the House of Commons. One example from Piratin's file is a meeting at Mile End Baths, organized by the Stepney branch of the Communist Party on 27 January 1946. Addressed by Piratin, the meeting was on the subject of *Poland—The Truth*, Piratin having recently visited Poland as a part of a parliamentary delegation with seven other MPs. These were the days before television, and the audience of around 500 was on a scale that modern-day backbenchers could only dream, whatever party to which they happened to belong, all the more impressive for the fact that admission was by ticket only at a cost of 1/- or 2/- each. After reporting a few introductory remarks by Jack Gaster and Sam Aaronovitch (both with their Special Branch file numbers), the Special Branch officer reported that Piratin 'rose to much applause', before delivering an 'extremely disjointed' speech.

Other meetings attended by Special Branch and recorded in MI5 files included a Communist Party meeting at Ilford Town Hall later in 1946 on international relations. This 'quiet and orderly' meeting was addressed by Phil Piratin on the subject of 'Communist Policy on Foreign Affairs', the essential principles of which are

21 HC Debs, 10 February 1947, cols 42–43.
22 ibid., col. 43.
23 TNA, KV 2/2033 (Metropolitan Police, Special Branch Report, 1 August 1945).
24 HC Debs, 10 February 1947, col. 62.

helpfully and admirably set out in the report. The 'five points' to distinguish the foreign policy of a 'socialist government' were said by Piratin to be as follows:

> (1) co-operation with the Soviet Union; (2) removal of reaction and fascism everywhere; (3) co-operation with all countries governed by socialist and working class movements; (4) freedom and justice for the colonial peoples; (5) the raising of the standard of living everywhere.[25]

Thus tailed in his own constituency, Piratin was also followed when he travelled to other parts of the country to address public meetings. His MI5 Personal File includes the report of Detective Sergeant G. F. Roper of the Devon Constabulary, who attended a Communist meeting at the Village Hall, Dartington along with his wife and two other friends, who no doubt enjoyed a good night out in the company of forty or so other people in the middle of February 1949. The report contains an account of a speech made by Piratin in support of Mrs Leila Seyd, wife of the Secretary of the Totnes Communist Party, who was seeking election in forthcoming local government elections.

But it was not only his Party work outside Parliament that was monitored by the State. Surveillance of the Communist Party also enabled the Security Service to find out about Piratin's parliamentary work, including his relations with his parliamentary colleagues and their parliamentary strategy; the relationship between the two Communist MPs and Party HQ; and also the matters Piratin raised with ministers. MI5's interception of correspondence from King Street picked up a letter about Piratin's views on the Health Bill,[26] significant because he was able subsequently to get onto the Standing Committee considering the Bill in the Commons. No doubt there was little that was unpredictable. The interception of phone calls in and out of King Street (where he appears to have spent some of his time while an MP) picked up messages to and from the Private Secretary to the President of the Board of Trade,[27] and to the personal secretary of the Foreign Secretary, the latter being about a matter Piratin proposed to raise in the House about the execution of Communist Party members in Iraq, described controversially as 'even sharper than anything Hitler had done'.[28] There is no evidence on his file of Piratin's personal constituency case-work being monitored, but the surveillance of the CPGB did pick up telephone messages from MPs other than Gallacher,[29] and the identity

[25] TNA, KV 2/2033 (Metropolitan Police, Special Branch Report, 30 July 1946).

[26] TNA, KV 2/2033 (Cross-Reference to Intercepted Letter from National Health Advisory Committee of Communist Party, 10 April 1946).

[27] TNA, KV 2/2033 (Minute of Incoming Phone Call to Phil Piratin from Private Secretary to the President of the Board of Trade, 19 April 1949).

[28] TNA, KV 2/2033 (Transcript of Outgoing Phone Call by Phil Piratin to Bevin's Secretary, 30 June 1947).

[29] TNA, KV 2/2033 (Transcript of Incoming Phone Call from Leslie Solley MP to Phil Piratin, 18 September 1947). Piratin was in Committee and Solley spoke to Hymie Fagan instead.

of advisers to Piratin on parliamentary matters (such as Michael Shapiro, who was asked to give weekly briefings on the Cotton Buying Bill).[30]

Otherwise, we find that the surveillance of the Communist Party picked up a telephone call between Piratin and Hymie Fagan, a Party official, dealing with the report of the Committee of Privileges discussed in section 2 above. For whatever purpose it served, the Security Service knew what Piratin privately thought of the report, what the Party thought of it, and how they all planned to deal with it. For what it was worth, it also gave some insight into the legal advice that the Party had received on the matter from Jack Gaster. The transcript of the call reads as follows:

Temple Bar 2151 (Communist Party HQ)

Phil (PIRATIN) rings Hymie FAGAN

Phil says the Privileges Committee report is out. It is very bad. It is distorted in the summary of evidence. They make no reference to Phil's allegations about anti-semitic remarks.

Hymie says it could not be worse.

Phil says there is going to be a debate on the matter of Monday. He thinks 'we' should meet to discuss what we should do . . . He will come back as early as possible in the afternoon.

Hymie has seen Harry (POLLITT) and Jack GASTER. Harry's opinion is that we did not expect anything more and that we were wrong to hope for anything better about this type of thing. He does not think it will harm Phil particularly, and he should repeat what he said in his first statement, just what happened, make his apology, and sit down. Jack thinks Phil should apologise and Bill (GALLACHER) and others should come in on his side.[31]

4. Bankruptcy and Disqualification

Phil Piratin's parliamentary career came to an ignoble end, partly as a result of the surveillance to which he had been subject as the Communist member for Mile End. Chief Superintendent Satterthwaite of the Hackney Police brought legal proceedings for slander following remarks made in October 1949 at

[30] TNA, KV 2/2033 (Transcript of Outgoing Phone Call by 'Murphy' to Michael Shapiro, 6 March 1947).

[31] TNA, KV 2/2033 (Transcript of Incoming Phone Call by Phil Piratin to Hymie Fagan, 6 February 1947). In the same file, there is also a transcript of an incoming phone call by Jack Gaster to Harry Pollitt, 20 January 1947, which appears to be on the same subject, discussing possible witnesses.

Communist meetings in the East End, the case being heard in June 1950, after Piratin had lost his seat in the 23 February 1950 election.[32] Speaking from a loudspeaker van at open-air street meetings, Piratin was claimed to have said at one meeting that:

> Police protection in the East End is given to Fascists, and when the police take any action against Fascist thugs it is because they are forced to do so by public opinion. I don't blame the ordinary policeman; he carries out the instructions of his superiors. One in particular is chief of police for Hackney, Satterthwaite. He is detested by his men and is one of the worst enemies of the working class. He should have been kicked out of the police years ago.[33]

Similar remarks were expressed at a subsequent meeting, where Piratin was claimed to have said that:

> There is one man who is not fit to be in charge of policemen. That man is Superintendent Satterthwaite, of Hackney. He is a friend of the Fascists and is hated and despised on all sides, even by his own men. I have asked the Home Secretary several times to have him removed from his job. I am still trying and will mention his name at every street corner until I do.[34]

Superintendent Satterthwaite had clearly upset Piratin, perhaps because of his well-known role in policing Communist protests against Fascist marches in the East End and elsewhere after the war. There is mention of Satterthwaite in Dave Renton's *Fascism, Anti-Fascism and Britain in the 1940s*, where he is referred to in one study as a 'first class anti-Semite who would have done a good job at Belsen'.[35] According to press reports of the subsequent legal action, however, Superintendent Satterthwaite said in evidence that 'police were at the meeting' and 'noted it all down'. That is almost certainly the case, and it is almost certainly the case that they would have noted it down very fully, though we cannot be confident that Piratin's remarks were noted as accurately as they were extensively. Piratin's defence was that while he had spoken some of the words complained of, 'the ones he admits having spoken were ones that were more or less harmless or not so damaging'. According to Mr Justice Sellars on the second day of the trial, the allegations about Satterthwaite being hated and despised by his men were the words with the 'greatest sting'. Piratin again denied 'saying anything like it that could be misunderstood',

[32] This account is based on a press reports in the *Evening Standard*, 6 and 7 June 1950, a copy of which is to be found in Piratin's MI5 file.
[33] *Evening Standard*, 6 June 1950.
[34] ibid.
[35] D. Renton, *Fascism, Anti-Fascism and Britain in the 1940s* (London, 2000), p. 104.

and that he was saying that people were beginning to hate the police, but that they should not misdirect their hatred, which was as a result of the policy of the government. Denying also that he used the term 'Fascist thug' (an expression he 'hardly ever' used), Piratin admitted to saying something like, 'I do not blame the ordinary policeman. He carries out the instructions of his superiors, one of whom is the chief of police of Hackney.'

The court believed the policeman, Satterthwaite being awarded £1,500 in damages plus costs, following the conclusion of the trial on 8 June 1950. It would have been possible, of course, for the damages and costs to be paid by the Party. However, a Special Branch report dated 6 September 1950 suggests that the Party had decided not to do so. Referring to Piratin, the Special Branch report continues:

> after he lost his court action some weeks ago, many prominent communists felt that his libellous remarks concerning police officers were, to say the least, most imprudent, and in view of the electric state of international affairs, very damaging to the British Communist Party. Furthermore, many communists commented adversely on the expectation that the damages of £1500 awarded against him would be met from Party funds. It was considered that as he was a comparatively new member and not one of the 'old brigade', he should have been more discreet, especially as he held a position of importance as an MP.[36]

The report concludes by saying that now that it was generally known that the Party was not paying Piratin's damages, 'his prestige in communist circles has fallen even lower'.

Although the *Daily Worker* had on several occasions been on the wrong end of libel writs,[37] this is thought to have been the first time the police had used slander against Communist Party activists and the first time defamation had been used against Communist Party activists in this way for things said or done at a political meeting. It was certainly the first time in living memory that slander had been used by a police officer against someone who had been a Member of Parliament at the time of the alleged defamation. Without financial means of his own, Piratin thus faced bankruptcy, the bankruptcy proceedings being initiated by the Chief Superintendent he was found to have slandered.[38] This meant that Piratin was compelled to stand down as a candidate at the forthcoming general election,[39] a

36 TNA, KV 2/2033 (Metropolitan Police, Special Branch Report, 6 September 1950).

37 See e.g. p. 172 below.

38 *The Times*, 5 December 1950, *Daily Worker*, 13 January 1951.

39 *Daily Telegraph*, 2 November 1950. This information about Piratin not being the Stepney Branch Party candidate was known to the Metropolitan Police Special Branch (TNA, KV 2/2033, Metropolitan Police, Special Branch Report, 6 September 1950), before it was reported in the press. It was also known to the Special Branch on 23 October 1950 that Piratin had been replaced by Ted Bramley as Party candidate, Bramley being a reluctant replacement, (i) because he did not have a

bankrupt being disqualified from membership of the House of Commons.[40] But this was not the only disability he suffered, as revealed by the *Daily Telegraph*, the latter not only reporting on a visit by Piratin to Sheffield on Party business, but also inaccurately stating that his room on the fourth floor of the Grand Hotel 'will cost him £1 14s 8d a day with all meals. Extras and tips are not included.'[41] Although making clear that the bill was the Party's responsibility, Piratin was nevertheless embarrassed by the revelation, but also powerless to do anything about it despite the inaccurate content, as the following exchange from an intercepted phone call to solicitor Jack Gaster makes clear:

Temple Bar 2151 (Communist Party HQ)

PIRATIN rings Jack GASTER

Phil Piratin refers to something in today's 'Telegraph'. Has he seen it?

Jack says yes and advises him to do nothing.

Phil has a postcard, one of the usual scarlet postcards which referred to that £1 14s 8d. he has a bill which will show it was really 14/-.

Jack says that as a bankrupt, he is not entitled to incur legal costs, so cannot take proceedings.

Phil asks if he could write a private letter.

Jack says he can do that. He could say that his attention has been drawn to this report which is quite inaccurate. If they cared to check the amount of the hotel bill they would find it was 14/8. That this was causing him some inconvenience, and he must ask them to correct it. As a receiving order had been made against him, he would not be able to take proceedings, and looked to them to make good the error without further difficulty.[42]

car; and (ii) because he did not have any money. He was promised a car for the election and that Stepney would foot the bill for his campaign: TNA, KV 2/2033 (Minute of a Source Report re Ted Bramley, 23 October 1950).

[40] E. C. S. Wade and G. G. Phillips, *Constitutional Law* (6th edn, London, by E. C. S. Wade, 1960), p. 103.

[41] *Daily Telegraph*, 2 November 1950.

[42] TNA, KV 2/2033 (Transcript of Outgoing Phone Call by Phil Piratin to Jack Gaster, 8 November 1950). Piratin did, however, secure a minor victory. A public examination of his affairs took place as part of the bankruptcy proceedings on 12 January 1951. The Official Receiver was aware that his wife had a successful clothing business and suggested that 'she should pay part of this', to which Piratin replied that 'she had absolutely refused to do so', claiming that 'She holds very, very strong views on the matter': *Daily Worker*, 13 January 1951. Piratin had earlier claimed that he had no assets other than the suit of clothes he stood up in. He was now employed as a Party worker, for which he received a wage of £5 15s weekly (plus a travel allowance and expenses). Although he received £1,000 annually while an MP, he had to use this to pay office and secretarial expenses, leaving him with a weekly income of £6 10s: *The Times*, 5 December 1950.

III. D. N. Pritt MP

Denis Nowell Pritt, was elected as a Labour MP for Hammersmith North in 1935 and became a member of the Party's NEC. He was expelled from the Party in 1940 because of his pro-Soviet views and stood successfully as an Independent Labour candidate in 1945, continuing to serve Hammersmith North until his defeat at the general election in 1950. Despite Attlee's suspicions, the best guess is that Pritt was not and never had been a member of the Communist Party, though he had visited the Soviet Union, and took a leadership role in many of the friendship organizations. His devotion was unequivocal and his closeness to the Communist Party beyond question. It is thus unsurprising that Pritt was subject to the most intense surveillance by MI5, probably more intensive than the Communist Party MPs, with whom he was suspected to have been in ideological collaboration, though there was very little else that they would have had in common.

1. Wartime Surveillance

Pritt was the subject of close surveillance on a periodic basis, including the opening of his mail, the evidence suggesting that this started during the war. When his wife visited Egypt in 1940, his letters to her were intercepted in Egypt and the copies sent back to Roger Hollis at MI5's wartime headquarters at Blenheim Palace. There is no evidence that we have seen of a HOW having been either applied for or granted. It appears that information on Pritt provided by GRU officer Walter Krivitsky, who had defected at the end of 1937 eventually to be given asylum in the USA, had provoked Security Service interest in Pritt beyond the routine monitoring of his extra-parliamentary political activities and speeches. Krivitsky had been interviewed in England by MI5 during January–February 1940.[43] A list of Soviet agents was produced, and Pritt was on the list, though despite these dramatic allegations, it appears that domestic telephone and letter interception were not seriously contemplated until later in 1940.

A note on Pritt's file from Miss Ogilvie to Roger Hollis, dated 20 December 1940, included Pritt's addresses and telephone numbers.[44] Hollis had added a handwritten comment, dated 12 January 1941: 'Spoke DSS, who decided that it would *not be advisable* to apply for either a telephone check or a letter check on Pritt.'[45] It is not clear why it was thought not to be advisable, though Pritt's position as

[43] Pritt was expelled from the Labour Party in March 1940, ostensibly for his support of the Soviet invasion of Finland.

[44] TNA, KV 2/1063. Hollis was then head of B4 (to become F2 under the Petrie re-organization). See Appendix.

[45] TNA, KV 2/1063. DSS: Director Security Service, Jasper Harker. Harker became DDG when Petrie was appointed DG in April 1941.

an MP would no doubt make such surveillance risky; that said, at least one other MP (Captain Ramsay, discussed below) was subject to much worse treatment.[46] However in July 1941, after Pritt had been 'bombed out', Hollis wrote to Colonel Allan at the GPO asking about changed postal and telephone arrangements for Pritt's chambers.[47] This suggests that an interception arrangement was ultimately put in place, although there is no HOW on the file, or any evidence of an application for one. And despite the obvious unease, an intercept nevertheless appears to have been placed on Pritt's House of Commons mail on 20 March 1942, though again there is no mention of a HOW.

Instead, there is mention of 'the special watch instituted for MI5 on the 20 March'. Rather than the usual exchanges with the GPO, there is a note to a Mr Pilkington (an MI5 officer attached to Shillito's F2(c), who evidently directed the 'Special Examiners'), stating that Pritt:

> has just been added to the Security List, but I have considered it desirable to confine this name to the sorters list only. I have asked that any letters intercepted are transferred to Special Examiners, and I should be glad if you would submit to MI5 either full comments or copies of the correspondence.[48]

On 4 April 1942, a Miss Moore advised Pilkington that:

> other than two letters delivered on the 21st and 22nd Pritt had received no other mail. Since that day we have not seen one single letter to or from him, can it be that, as has happened before, he has been put on a special direct sorting list for another department?'

At the bottom of the note Pilkington has scrawled 'Of course it may only be an Easter recess!'[49] It seems that these special measures may have related not only to mail addressed to Pritt at the House of Commons, but also to mail sent by him from the House of Commons.

[46] It is to be noted, however, that Mrs Pritt is recorded in a Security Service report dated 16 May 1951 as having stated that in 1941 Pritt was in immediate danger of being prosecuted under the Defence Regulations. Pritt had been warned to moderate his utterances by an Intelligence Service friend, a warning that was said to have had some effect (TNA, KV 2/1065). The author of that report was evidently unaware that in June 1941 MI5, principally Hollis, had contemplated instigating a prosecution for spreading alarm and despondency and making 'him a laughing stock among his fellows' (TNA, KV 2/1064). It is almost certainly this episode that Mrs Pritt was referring to. Pritt had allegedly told a barrister (Sir Patrick Hastings) that the Churchill government was negotiating peace terms with the Germans, word got to 'Buster' Milmo, who then reported back to MI5. On Milmo, see pp. 102–3 above.

[47] TNA, KV 2/1064 (Hollis to Col. Allan, 5 July 1941). Allan replied in longhand at the bottom of Hollis' letter (8 July 1941).

[48] TNA, KV 2/1064 (Alan Grogan to Pilkington, 19 March 1942).

[49] TNA, KV 2/1064 (Miss Moore to Pilkington 4 April 1942).

It is not clear under what legal authority this interception took place. It was clearly not done under the normal procedures, though there may have been wartime powers that ensured that it had a measure of legal authority.[50] Nor is it clear that any such interception could be justified. In a note to Miss Ogilvie, Pilkington had reported on 4 October 1941:

> As requested I have considered this case but am unable to find any suggestion that Pritt is, or has been engaged in espionage. It is true that Krivitsky said that he believed Pritt to be 'one of the chief recruiting agents for Soviet underground organisations in the United Kingdom', but this, I think, should be treated with some reserve in view of Krivitsky's admittedly limited knowledge of Communist Party affairs here. I do not think, therefore, that there is sufficient evidence to justify enquiries by my section into Pritt's activities.[51]

This reflected the Service attitude towards Krivitisky. Dick White, who had interviewed the Russian, had been unimpressed and 'discounted' the NKVD officer: 'I didn't wholly trust Krivitsky. He wasn't using his real name and he wasn't a general.' Which begs the question: why the surveillance in the first place?

Mr Pritt and Special Branch

At some point in the early years of the first Attlee administration Pritt had his car stolen. A few hours later, it turned up about a mile away from where he had left it with about one mile registered on the odometer, and he records that the police were very friendly, 'but oddly firm in their request that I should look over the car carefully to see if anything had been stolen'. Nothing had, but every bit of paper in the car had been gathered together and placed in a briefcase he had left in the vehicle. The circumstances indicated to Pritt that, 'some bright boys in the Special Branch of the Metropolitan Police were trying to be clever'. He spoke to the Home Secretary who promised he would check with Special

[50] This did not mean that MI5 had been give *carte blanche*: HOWs still had to be applied for. However, the procedure allowed for the interception of all mail entering the country from abroad or sent abroad, and permitted the suspension of the usual six-monthly review by the Home Office of existing HOWs. Crucially, it permitted Petrie to issue the following 'Director General's Circular' on HOWs:

> In urgent cases it is sometimes necessary to put on a letter or telephone check immediately, and in such cases the General Post Office are prepared to act on a telephone request in advance of the receipt of a Home Office Warrant. Such requests should only be made on the authority of the head of a Division or, in his absence, the head of the section concerned; the authority should be noted on the file and the HOW must be submitted for signature without delay (TNA, KV 4/222, 13 August 1941).

It appears that this flexible approach was maintained after the war.

[51] TNA, KV 2/1064 (Minute sheet note, Pilkington to Ogilvie, 4 October 1941).

Branch—but heard no more. A year or so later, the Deputy Commissioner of the Met had a meeting with Pritt about some other matter, and at the conclusion the policeman remarked, 'That was a curious thing about your car being apparently stolen in your constituency wasn't it?' Pritt took both responses as tacit admissions that the culprits were indeed the Special Branch.[52] At the time, it was believed that MI5 restricted themselves to collecting and analysing intelligence, leaving the physical side of investigation to their 'executive arm', the Special Branch.

2. Post-War Surveillance

There is no evidence that we have seen of Pritt's letters being opened or his phone tapped while he served as an MP in the immediate post-war era. He was nevertheless closely watched at this time provided by Special Branch reports from the airports he used on his many travels. Access to legal advice he gave to the Communist Party was obtained—on one occasion whether the Connolly Association in Ireland should sue for libel over a publication in Dublin (by means of an undisclosed Special Branch source). And his election or appointment to various positions in various organizations already referred to was closely monitored (again, usually by means of Special Branch reports). Security Service surveillance of the Communist Party (by means of listening devices at King Street, on one occasion picking up a meeting of the Political Committee) was also able to monitor Pollitt's irritation that Pritt would neither rejoin the Labour Party (though it seems that an application had been rejected by the Labour Party NEC), or declare himself for the Communist Party. In Pollitt's view, 'Pritt must do one of two things—either come out openly for the CP or go back into the LP.' He did neither.[53]

An interesting feature of the post-war period, however, was the willingness of MI5 to share information about Pritt with other intelligence agencies, uninhibited in doing so, it seems, by the lack of any legal power or by the existence of any legal restraint (notably the Official Secrets Act 1911). But although uninhibited by law, MI5 was clearly aware of the risks involved in sharing such sensitive information, which was typically given in response to a request from an overseas intelligence agency, because Pritt had been asked to provide legal representation in the country in question. Thus, following Pritt's agreement to assist in the defence of the

[52] D. N. Pritt, *Autobiography of DN Pritt, Part Two, Brasshats and Bureaucrats* (London, 1966), pp. 50–1.

[53] Pollitt was also heard to say that he thought that Pritt 'didn't really want to join the CP and his wife didn't want him to', and that he was pretending that he wanted to join (TNA, KV 2/1064, 16 August 1944).

Canadian MP Fred Rose,[54] the Royal Canadian Mounted Police requested information 'concerning [Pritt's] antecedents and present activities' from MI5. This was provided, though Pritt's Security Service file contains a guarded covering letter by Roger Hollis:

> you will, I am sure, treat the information sent to you herewith as for your personal use only as it would be a considerable embarrassment to us if it were known that we were transmitting information about a man holding a position such as that of Mr Pritt.

An indication of the kind of information provided is revealed following a similar request from the South African police, which was passed on with a similar health warning.[55] A brief biography was sent telling the South Africans that Pritt—an MP, it is to be recalled—was under surveillance as a 'prominent Communist sympathiser and champion of the Soviet Union'.[56] He was also connected with several organizations which, 'whilst nominally independent', were said to be 'controlled or exploited' by the Communist Party. These included the NCCL, the Society for Cultural Relations with the USSR, the Haldane Society of Socialist Lawyers, the British Soviet Society, the League for Democracy in Greece, and the Student Labour Federation. Attention was drawn to several books and pamphlets authored by Pritt praising the Soviet Union, which he visited in 1946, also visiting Czechoslovakia and Romania in 1948. Reference was made to his wife, who was said to share his views and activities, being prominently connected with International Women's Day.[57]

Apart from thus continuing to watch, accumulate information, and share information about him during his period in Parliament, Pritt was also subject to surveillance while a candidate at the 1950 election (at which he was defeated). Pritt's file contains his election literature (in which he revealed himself a supporter of Queens Park Rangers Football Club), and a Special Branch report dated 3 March 1950, in which it is noted that he unsuccessfully defended his seat in Hammersmith (North). The report gives details of the address of Pritt's

[54] Fred Rose was a Communist MP revealed to be a Soviet spy by Gouzenko. See Chapter 10 below.

[55] 'You will appreciate that Pritt is a person of some eminence both as a lawyer and a politician in this country. We should therefore be grateful if you would refer to us if you propose to make this information the grounds for any action': TNA, KV 2/1065 (Letter from Sillitoe to Commissioner of South African Police, 2 June 1949). See also, p. 121 below.

[56] ibid. Both the documents sent to South Africa are recorded in the minute sheet of KV2/1064, rather than KV2/1065.

[57] Similar details were provided for the FBI in 1950, following the approach to Pritt by the members of the Communist Party of America, who asked him to represent them in their appeal to the Supreme Court. Additional organizations Pritt was reported to be associated with included the BPC and the British–Romanian Friendship Society, while it was also reported that he had visited the Soviet Union again in 1950, and that in recent months he had been in touch with the Soviet Ambassador, as well as other Soviet diplomats and officials in London.

committee rooms, as well as the identity (and address and age) of his agent. The latter was Malcom Purdie (PF402/44/154), said to be 'well known to Special Branch as a member of the executive committee of the National Council for Civil Liberties', who had also 'come to notice as a member of the London District Committee of the Communist Party'. There was also a list of those who had proposed and by this time seconded Pritt's nomination, as well as eight 'attestors', two of whom had PF numbers.

3. Re-Examination

Krivitsky's allegations against Pritt were re-examined on 29 April 1949 for a purpose not recorded.[58] The details were again extracted from the registry on the 10 and 12 October 1951.[59] By this time, Pritt was no longer an MP (having lost his seat in the February 1950 general election), and the disappearance of Burgess and Maclean had sent MI5 into a frantic search for the Soviet spies.[60] Also by this time, Krivitsky's allegations had been given renewed credence when it was realized that in 1940 he had provided sufficient information about a Soviet spy in the Foreign Office for it to have become clear with the benefit of hindsight that he had been referring to Donald Maclean.[61] This most recent investigation developed into something more than merely routine, with Pritt's file indicating very considerable renewed interest during 1951–2. Notably, numerous documents have been removed from that section of the file, and the minute sheets have been weeded with particular care.

Nevertheless, some remaining documents indicate that MI5's 'penetration agents' had been reporting on Pritt and his wife, and phrases used in relation to the sources, together with the nature of some of the information, suggest that MI5 may have installed 'SF' in their telephone, allowing the Service to eavesdrop on domestic conversations when the phone was on the hook.[62] A 'B1A source report' of information that 'has been obtained under very delicate circumstances' indicated an intimate knowledge of the goings on at Decoy Cottage, the aptly named home of Mr and Mrs Pritt located provocatively on the Aldermaston perimeter:

58 TNA, KV 2/1064.

59 TNA, KV 2/1065.

60 Wright (n 5), pp. 122, 222.

61 Even Dick White took a fresh interest, and Krivisky's information was crucial in convincing White of Harold 'Kim' Philby's guilt in 1951.

62 For instance, there are references on 14 and 15 May 1946 to 'a most secret and delicate source', indicating that Mrs Pritt had been in contact with the Russian Embassy to discuss travel arrangements: (TNA, KV 2/1064). Although this may not relate to an electronic source or an informant close to Mrs Pritt, it does illustrate the type of language generally used to refer to these types of very intrusive surveillance.

> Mrs Pritt is at the moment very worried and in a state of high nervous tension in connection with Pritt's health, and also his political activities. It appears that Pritt is a diabetic, but he obstinately refuses to follow his doctor's advice. He eats all the wrong things and is, curiously enough, 'a secret eater.' It is perhaps not uninteresting to note that, at times, Mrs Pritt is not above going the pace in the drink line. Mrs Pritt is also obsessed with the fear that Pritt will get himself in serious trouble and get himself arrested; and it is thought that her fears are not entirely based on a wife's anxiety for her husband's welfare, but are the outcome of her inordinate conceit, which is so marked as almost to constitute an abnormality.[63]

MI5 were very interested in the Pritts' domestic help—Mr and Mrs West:

> It is believed that the man West has applied for a post as a fireman at the new atomic station. It is known that in conversation Pritt has remarked that he, West, would be unlikely to get such a job if it came out that he was employed by the Pritts. Mrs Pritt's comment was, "Oh, but *he* is not employed by us"—laughter.[64]

The use of SF in relation to the Pritts might help to explain Percy Sillitoe's response to the Chief Constable of Berkshire in an exchange of correspondence in 1949. The Chief Constable wrote a somewhat censorious—and revealing—letter to Sillitoe, referring to 'circulars' sent by MI5 the previous year:

> in which you outlined your arrangements for the recording of information concerning the Communist Party and your ultimate aim of keeping accurate records of all members of that Party. I now enclose a list of those persons who have been the subject of an enquiry in connection with Communism and for whom no Photostat copy records have been received. In the past officers from this Force have made enquiries about a number of people at the request of your Department, and often it was an isolated enquiry which revealed little of a concrete nature, but I have maintained these records as being persons connected with the Party. I feel, that in a number of cases, these records could very well be allowed to lapse but, before doing so, I should like to know if you are in possession of any information concerning any of them which would justify their inclusion in such a list.[65]

It was some five months later before Sillitoe managed a reply, though if SF had been installed, the last thing MI5 would have needed or wanted would have been a local copper bumbling onto the scene at Decoy Cottage. Sillitoe replied, somewhat

63 TNA, KV 2/1065 (D. N. Pritt KC,16 May 1951).

64 Security Service emphasis. A later report which is clearly from the same source and refers back to West's ambition to work at the Atomic Weapons Research Establishment is marked as originating from B1K/MK—Maxwell Knight.

65 TNA, KV 2/1064 (30 January 1949).

disingenuously, to suggest that Pritt, who had been on the list referred to by the Chief Constable, was of no interest to MI5:

> In the list of persons which you sent to us in your letter . . . dated 30th January you included D N Pritt, Decoy Cottage, Aldermaston. D N Pritt is the present Member of Parliament for Hammersmith North. He makes no secret of his sympathy with certain Communist aspirations but he is not and has not been known to be a member of the Communist Party. It is not necessary for you to maintain any special record of him or to embark on any investigation.[66]

It cannot be said with certainty when SF were installed or for how long, and in particular whether this was done before the re-examination in either 1949 or 1951. In the end, however, there was nothing against Pritt, to whom we return in Chapter 7.

IV. Geoffrey Bing MP

In terms of MI5's mandate (defence of the realm, as threatened by subversion and espionage), what we have here is a situation in which progressive MPs were the subject of fairly intrusive MI5 and Special Branch surveillance on two grounds. In Piratin's case, he was the subject of routine surveillance of his electoral and political activities (which included his parliamentary work, though there is no evidence that this was specifically targeted). The file of Piratin's comrade, Willie Gallacher, reveals much the same, without the added spice of the privileges complaint, Gallacher a shrewder, wiser, and more experienced character. In Pritt's case we see the same, but with the added spice of surveillance for the purposes of an espionage investigation as well. Indeed, such an investigation was undertaken at least twice, at least once when Pritt was an MP. But what about Labour Party MPs, with the PLP intake of 1945 including a number of progressive figures on the Left? Beginning with the case of Geoffrey Bing, if anything here we find the levels of surveillance even more intense, as not only MI5 but also the Prime Minister were keen to find out which members of the PLP if any had Communist Party connections, and what they were doing to develop these connections.

1. Generating Information by Surveillance

We have already encountered Geoffrey Bing in Chapter 5 above, and the steps taken in an attempt to derail him after he ceased being an MP. But what about

[66] ibid.

the time between 1945 and 1955 when he served as Labour MP for Hornchurch? Bing—who was a barrister—had been of interest to MI5 since his association with the NCCL came to their attention in 1935. He had thereafter been involved with a number of other noble causes, not least his support for the Spanish Republic. His file—released in February 2014—reveals that throughout the Second World War, various attempts to 'do his bit' had been stalled by the intervention of the Security Service. As a consequence, Bing spent a great deal of the war testing parachutes—fortunately, they all worked reasonably well. Soon after eventually being allowed to see active service he was badly wounded while fighting in Germany.

A document in Bing's file, dated 1 February 1945, and much annotated with the pencilled exclamation marks of MI5 officers, records a meeting of the CPGB Political Committee held at King Street, overheard by MI5's hidden microphones, recorded and transcribed by section B4B.[67] Present at the meeting was a stellar cast of twentieth-century British Communists: Raj Palme-Dutt, Johnny Campbell, Peter Kerrigan, Emile Burns, William Gallacher, Ted Bramley, Bill Rust, and Jimmy Shields. They discussed parliamentary candidates for the forthcoming general election, primarily the candidatures of Bing and John Platts-Mills, the barrister and friend of Bing, who was soon to be returned as MP for Tottenham in the 1945 election. The report reveals Platts-Mills to be a Party member, and records that Kerrigan read out extracts from a letter Bing had sent to King Street along with his Party subscription. The report continues:

> Kerrigan . . . reminded the comrades that Harry Pollitt was very against Party members getting themselves adopted as undercover members of the Labour Party . . . Bill Rust thought it would be very difficult to stop him and he did not see what it had to do with the Party. Bing should be allowed to stand for the Labour Party if he wanted to. Kerrigan replied that it was to do with them, as he is a Party member and paid his subscription to the Party.

A meeting of the Political Committee convened shortly after the July 1945 general election was also eavesdropped and transcribed by B4B, and remains in Bing's file. During the meeting, Kerrigan was asked by Emile Burns how many MPs would be 'working for the Communist Party'. It seems that Burns was not thinking about Gallacher and Piratin. MI5's file records that:

> Dutt gave a polite little laugh, as though he had made a good joke, but Peter replied in a firm and rather cross voice, that there would only be two. There was a pause, and then Peter repeated aggressively, 'Nobody more than these two.'

[67] More often known by the post-1953 designation 'A2A' used in Wright (n 5), and favoured in C. Andrew, *The Defence of the Realm—The Authorised History of MI5* (London, 2009).

It is assumed here that Kerrigan was referring to Gallacher and Piratin. Questions were raised in further discussion about four Labour MPs—Platts-Mills, Bing, Lever, and Solley. Notably, it was claimed by Kerrigan that Platts-Mills, Bing, and Solley were no longer Party members and that he did not know Lever.[68]

Bing was subsequently appointed by Attlee to be an assistant whip in the Commons, though he did not last long, resigning on 15 November 1946, ostensibly having chosen to spend more time dealing with the housing and transport problems in his constituency. It is not known for certain whether at this stage Attlee knew of Bing's links with the Communist Party, though, as is discussed below, it is known that Sillitoe told Attlee at some time before 22 November 1946 that Bing was a Communist Party member, at the same time as he named four other members of the PLP.[69] It is not clear, however, whether this was accurate information in Bing's case, with a note from Graham Mitchell tending to corroborate Peter Kerrigan's comment above. According to Mitchell, 'Bing is known to have been a subscribing member as late as the beginning of 1945',[70] that is to say before the general election. The question, of course, is this: why did it matter (particularly at that time)?

2. Foreign Office Inquiries

Having acquired this and other information about Bing, the question for MI5 was with whom it should be shared, and on what grounds. The Attlee Directive refers to MI5 being authorized to carry out inquiries on behalf of government departments (para. 5), but refers also rather more opaquely to the 'well-established convention whereby Ministers do not concern themselves with the detailed information which may be obtained by the Security Service in particular cases, but are furnished with such information only as may be necessary for the determination of any issue on which their guidance is sought' (para. 6). In what circumstances, if any, were ministers other than the Prime Minister entitled to be supplied with information obtained by MI5 about ministerial and parliamentary colleagues? These were provisions that were to be tested by Hector McNeil MP, then a Minister of State at the Foreign Office, later to become Secretary of State for Scotland in Attlee's brief second administration.

Guy Liddell's Diary reports a conversation that took place on 4 November 1946 between Liddell and the chief of SIS, apparently prompted by the concern that an assistant whip was a security risk (presumably Bing). The Diary entry in question,

68 TNA, KV 2/3412. On 28 July 1945, B4B [the transcript was extracted in 1954 so A2A is the division and section credited on the document] overheard Peter Kerrigan stating that 'Bing and Platts-Mills had once been Party members' (Meeting of the Political Committee discussing the general election).

69 See below, p. 156.

70 TNA, KV 2/3412 (22 November 1946).

no doubt released by MI5 as a contribution to a better understanding of the Labour movement, records that Liddell:

> told 'C' that . . . MacNeal [sic.] had asked for information about Bing the Labour Whip. We were not prepared to give this information and were suggesting that MacNeal should apply to the Prime Minister. If he presses us to hand over the information, I shall be forced to see the PM.[71]

Unfortunately, that particular entry has been heavily redacted, this being the only paragraph of the entry in question to have been released to the National Archives. It appears, however, that the Foreign Office was looking for evidence that while working for a 'section of the War Office which handled the dropping of British agents over France', Bing had 'passed on certain top secret plans to the Communist Party Executive'.

Roger Hollis made a note on the minute sheet of Bing's file on 7 November:

> DDG [Liddell] instructed me to see Mr Halford (Foreign Office) and tell him we did not feel we could supply the information about Bing direct to Mr McNeil. I did this, saying that there were three possible ways of handling the matter:
> 1) That we should arrange to forget it.
> 2) That we should explain to Mr McNeil that this information we could not give to him, but would have to give it to the Prime Minister only; and
> 3) That we should consult the Prime Minister without first telling Mr McNeil what we were about to do.

The Foreign Office civil servants told Hollis that McNeil was not likely to forget about the matter, and they would 'try to persuade him that the right course was for him to report such matters direct to the Prime Minister and not ask for information from the Security Service'.[72]

However, Bing's file indicates that although the Foreign Office's specific concerns about Bing were groundless, MI5 nevertheless told McNeil that they possessed a 'large file' relating to Bing's activities—all grist to the Westminster rumour mill. McNeil would, however, have been better advised to look elsewhere for evidence of espionage or subversion. Not only was he a close friend of Guy Burgess, but McNeil had also employed him as his personal assistant.[73] Such was Burgess' closeness to McNeil (a Foreign Office Minister, it is to be recalled), that he evidently:

[71] TNA, KV 4/468 (Liddell Diary, 4 November 1946).

[72] TNA, KV 2/3412 (Minute Sheet Note).

[73] Burgess worked for McNeil from the time of McNeil's appointment as a Minister of State at the Foreign Office in the wake of the July 1945 election. McNeil offloaded Burgess onto Christopher Mayhew at the IRD in December 1947: C. Mayhew, *A War of Words: A Cold War Witness* (London, 1998), p. 24.

> had the complete run of the inner sanctum. If he needed the minister's keys he asked for them. If *he* wanted access to classified files, he secured the necessary authorization without question by saying that *his minister* wanted such and such at once. Since, to the growing chagrin of such ministerial colleagues as Aneurin Bevan, the Foreign Secretary [Ernest Bevin] and his junior minister [McNeil] seemed obsessed with the growing Soviet threat to the Western world, much of the material on the files was of considerable interest to the Soviet masters of Burgess in London.[74]

Burgess had been working in the War Office in the late 1930s, and had worked for the SOE until he had returned to the BBC in 1941. Any stories Burgess might have chosen to tell McNeil about air drops to France being betrayed would at least have had the virtue of being believable.

3. War Office Inquiries

Hollis was clearly unhappy with passing on information about one 'minister' (Bing) to another (McNeil), insisting that his responsibility was to the Prime Minister alone. But it seems nevertheless that MI5 were prepared to convey more detail to ministers than was necessary, with the Foreign Office not the only beneficiaries of MI5 information. In a Diary entry for the 18 November 1946, three days after Bing's resignation as Assistant Whip, Liddell recorded that he went over to see Frederick Bellenger, the newly appointed Secretary of State for War. Bellenger told him that he:

> had a note from the PM containing a suggestion that Bing had abused his position during the war in giving away military information to Communists, and whether, in fact, Bing was a member of the Party?

That the rumour should have resurfaced in this manner might be seen to lend weight to the argument that Bing had been obliged to resign over his links to the Communist Party. However, Bing was one of the twenty-one 'rebel MPs' who in April 1948 were threatened with expulsion from the Labour Party for opposing Party policy, his independent spirit alone likely to render his position as assistant whip untenable by all concerned.[75] Liddell went on:

[74] A. Boyle, *The Climate of Treason: Five Who Spied for Russia* (London, 1979), p. 282.

[75] See *The Daily Telegraph* 30 April 1948: '21 MPs Expected to Give Pledge.' The Hornchurch Labour Party voted ninety-two to four in support of a resolution of 'full confidence' in Bing. Platts-Mills was expelled from the Party.

> I said that I was a little surprised that the PM had not, in fact referred this matter to us direct, in view of a somewhat similar case that we had on a previous occasion, where he more or less directed that he wanted to deal with matters of this kind personally . . . however Bellenger had a letter from the PM . . . I felt I was authorised to go ahead . . . I told him I would consult our files and come and see him again. I thought it wise to tell him personally, because it seemed to me that the case involved certain principles on which we should like to be quite clear. Did, for example, the PM expect us to volunteer information of this kind. If so, was it to be done to the Minister responsible or to the Prime Minister himself? I explained that our aim and object was to remain entirely non-party in all these matters and to avoid any suggestion that the department was a *Gestapo*.[76]

In Bing's file, Liddell noted that:

> It had always been the policy of our office to keep entirely clear of politics, and this particular case seemed to be a border line one. We might be open to the criticism that we were using our records for the purpose of conducting a heresy hunt within the Labour Party, although it seemed to me in this instance that we were covered by the fact that Bing, until a few days ago, had been one of the Whips, and in that sense a person who was given certain access to Government information.[77]

Shortly thereafter, Liddell was able to tell Bellenger that there was no 'indication' there was any truth in the allegations about Bing, while adding that 'it was proved beyond reasonable doubt that he was actually a member of the CP . . . perhaps a slight shock to Bellenger'. That evening Liddell met Attlee, told him of his dealings with Bellenger, and sought advice on the action to be taken about MPs 'belonging to subversive movements, and in the case of MPs who had close contacts with subversive movements'. Attlee replied that 'he alone should be informed in every case where we had positive information . . . whether that member was a member of the Labour Party, the Conservative Party, or any other Party'. According to Liddell, this reflected Attlee's view that 'he had a responsibility to the House and country to see that such members did not get into positions where they might constitute a danger to the State'. It also reflected the terms of the Attlee Directive of April 1946, which placed considerable emphasis on keeping 'the Prime Minister constantly informed of subversive activities likely to endanger the security of the State'. In cases of doubt, 'the Director General was instructed to refer to the Prime Minister'. As we have

[76] TNA, KV 4/468 (Liddell Diary, 18 November 1946).

[77] TNA, KV 2/3412 (Minute sheet note, 19 November 1946). The paragraph ends here with an emphatic handwritten full stop. However, a final five words, although scribbled out, are legible. They say 'outside the purely Party sphere'.

seen, Attlee later described the constitutional position succinctly: 'MI5 . . . is under the direct control of the Prime Minister.'[78]

The relationship between Attlee and Liddell was to produce an unwelcome surprise for the Prime Minister. At a meeting sometime in November (but before the 20th), Liddell gave Attlee the names of five MPs who were members of 'subversive organisations':

> I thereupon gave him the names of Platts-Mills, Hutchinson, Leah Manning and Mrs Braddock. He was not surprised to hear about Hutchinson, and had already taken it for granted that Platts-Mills was a CP member. He was, however, considerably shaken to hear of Leah Manning and Mrs Braddock. He then volunteered the information to me that he thought Dodds was a CP member; that Swingler probably was, and that D N Pritt almost certainly was. I said that only in the cases of Bing, Platts-Mills, Hutchinson, Leah Manning and Mrs Braddock had we positive proof.[79]

That said, it is not clear how accurate was this information. The same file entry (22 November 1946) has a note added by Graham Mitchell (dated 21 May 1947) responding to a request from Liddell for the names of those Labour MPs for whom 'we could say with assurance that they are members of the Communist Party'. Those of whom there is no reasonable doubt were said to be Platts-Mills, Bing, and Swingler, even though the evidence against (i) Platts-Mills was simply that an unnamed Party member had said in November that he was still in the Party; (ii) Bing was that he was a member as late as the beginning of 1945; and (iii) Swingler that he was a member as late as June 1943 and had done nothing since to suggest that he had ceased being a member![80]

4. Surveillance and Parliamentary Business

Aside from Communist Party surveillance and the assertion of Prime Ministerial authority under the Attlee Directive, the Bing case is important also

[78] Attlee made this statement in his Foreword to the autobiography of Percy Sillitoe, *Cloak without Dagger* (London, 1955). Attlee, although then still Leader of the Opposition, was apparently unaware that ministerial responsibility had been shifted to the Home Secretary in September 1952, with the minister's supervisory powers much reduced. See Chapter 3 above.

[79] TNA, KV 2/3412 (22 November 1946). This is the date the note of the meeting is written up for the files. Liddell's Diary has an entry for the meeting on 19 November 1946. The latter has not been released intact, and a couple of lines are missing before we are able to read that Attlee had 'kept on repeating their names and saying: "Really, I should never have thought it"'. Liddell considered this response 'quite interesting', since 'REDACTED has, in fact, been a member of the Party since 1920': TNA, KV 4/468 (Liddell Diary, 19 November 1946).

[80] TNA, KV 2/3412 (22 November 1946). In other cases, such as Hutchinson (the only one named), the individual was said to be close to the Party but there was room to doubt their current membership.

for revealing MI5 surveillance of Bing's parliamentary activities. This is perhaps even more significant. Returning to Bellenger, as Secretary of State for War he had been asked parliamentary questions by Bing about the political vetting of army education personnel. Bing had been unhappy with the answers, and planned to make an attack on both Bellenger and MI5 during the Commons debate on the army estimates. It was thought that Bing would be alleging that the Service was incompetent and as a consequence was prone to wasting money. In 'Austerity Britain', these were dangerous accusations for a Service which, the Cold War as yet undeclared, was considered by some to be unaffordable. For Bing, this was an opportunity for revenge, having fallen foul of the vetting system during the war, initially obstructed at every turn in his attempts to join a fighting unit.[81]

Bing's file contains a document provocatively entitled 'Attack on MI5'. Dated 6 March 1947, the memo was addressed to Dick White, then Director of 'B' Division and warned of the imminent parliamentary attack on the Security Service by Bing. It was to be an 'open and concerted attack on MI5, with detailed evidence from MI5's ex-victims, some of them now MPs'. The author of the warning was Maxwell Knight, who had infiltrated various progressive organizations as Director of Intelligence for the British Fascisti during the 1920s,[82] and continued with this 'penetration' work following his recruitment by MI5 in 1930. As such, Maxwell Knight features in MI5 files on Dudley Collard, D. N. Pritt, Neil Lawson, and of course Bing. He also ran a number of informers for MI5, one of whom—agent M/7—was identified in 2017 as barrister Vivian Hancock-Nunn.[83] Revealing a failure to protect MI5's sources, the identity of agent M/7 has been left on the back of a circular sent to him by the Haldane Society, which he had evidently then passed to MI5. The circular related to Bar Council elections—Pritt was one of the candidates, so MI5 added it to Pritt's file (though it is also in other files). Postmarked 28 June 1946, the document was addressed to V. W. Hancock-Nunn, South Lodge, Headingly, Sussex.[84]

Returning to the 'Attack on MI5', Knight implicated MPs Charles Smith, Donald Bruce, and—remarkably—Christopher Mayhew, as being among the plotters, while offering 'a reasonable prospect of our being able to get further

[81] Others on the Left suspected that they too had fallen victim to similar politically motivated interventions by MI5, including Pritt, who had been refused permission to give law lectures to audiences of servicemen. See the correspondence following Pritt's offer to lecture troops on subjects like the English legal system on 29 May 1941. Also, the note by E. M. Furnival Jones to the Joint Military Chiefs of Staff, 13 April 1946, and the accompanying internal memo on the advisability of continuing to ensure that Pritt was not permitted to lecture the military: TNA, KV 2/1064.

[82] J. G. Hope, 'Surveillance or Collusion? Maxwell Knight, MI5 and the British Fascisti' (1994) 9 *Intelligence and National Security* 651, at pp. 652–3. According to Hope, Knight was at various times, Deputy Chief of Staff and the British Fascisti Publicity Officer, and was a British Fascisti member between 1923 and 1930. Knight was associated with MI5 from 1925 and became an MI5 officer in 1930.

[83] See H. Hemming, *Maxwell Knight, MI5's Greatest Spymaster* (London, 2017).

[84] TNA, KV 2/1064.

and more detailed inside information on this',[85] which begs the question where the information was coming from. In the meantime, no attack materialized during the army estimates debate and Knight predicted instead an attack on the Service during the forthcoming conscription debate,[86] and reported that agent M/8 had heard that Bing's proposed intervention was to be linked to the NCCL's campaign against the vetting of civil servants. Needless to say, no attack was mounted in either debate. Coming close to revealing that M/8 was an MP, Knight claimed that his agent:

> gives it as his personal opinion that, what with the pressure of really important Parliamentary business, and the increasing seriousness of the economic position which tends to draw out nearly every debate in the House, the Bing group is in danger of missing the boat completely. He will let us know the moment he gets anything more definite.'[87]

All of Knight's ludicrous predictions went to Dick White, and then on to Liddell and Sillitoe.

So here we have MI5 monitoring parliamentary business, and having a ringside seat about matters relating to its accountability. They were fed the names of witnesses on whose testimony the MPs would rely and the nature of the complaints likely to be made, as well as the identity, character, and tactics of those who had planned to raise them. Notable also in this file is the transcript of an intercepted telephone call from Peter Klugmann (whose phone (Museum 0191) was obviously tapped) to Bing's extension in the House of Parliament. Although this is the only example we have found, it is presumably not the only time that calls to MPs were intercepted in this way.[88] Quite how this can be defended under MI5's Charter is hard to understand, unless criticism of MI5 is itself evidence of subversion or espionage. Also important, of course, is the identity of Maxwell Knight's source M/8, who figures prominently in file entries at this point. It has been known for some time that Tom Driberg MP was M/8, journalist Chapman Pincher exposing him as Maxwell Knight's agent in *Their Trade is Treachery*,[89] this confirmed by Knight's wartime assistant in B5B, Joan Miller,[90] in a controversial book that MI5 had tried to ban. Clear evidence, if evidence was still needed, that it was not only the Communist Party that was subject to MI5 surveillance; so too was the PLP.

[85] TNA, KV 2/3412 (Maxwell Knight to Dick White, 26 February 1947).
[86] TNA, KV 2/3412 (Memo to White and Hollis, 27 March 1947).
[87] TNA, KV 2/3412 (Knight to White, 30 April 1947).
[88] TNA, KV 2/3412 (Klugmann to Knight, 5 May 1947). The subject matter was trivial.
[89] C. Pincher, *Their Trade is Treachery* (London, 1981), p. 116. Pincher got most of his information for the book from Peter Wright.
[90] J. Miller, *One Girl's War, Personal Exploits in MI5's Most Secret Station* (Kerry, 1987 edn), p. 65.

V. Wilfrid Vernon MP

The Bing file is significant for a number of reasons, not least for revealing that MI5 had infiltrated the governing party. Also important, however, was Attlee's tight grip on surveillance and the desire to ensure that information was not shared with anyone but him, though there is no evidence to suggest that Attlee discouraged this information-gathering activity of MI5. But like Piratin (and Gallacher), Bing was the subject of surveillance, ostensibly for reasons of subversion. There was, however, also an example of a Labour MP suspected of espionage, which was handled very differently from the wartime handling of Pritt. This was the case of Major Wilfred Vernon, elected as Labour MP for Dulwich in 1945. He had also been convicted before the war under the Official Secrets Acts 1911–20, a fact that had re-emerged during the January 1948 interrogation of Ernest David Weiss, a German-born British citizen who confessed to having recruited Vernon, and Vernon's colleague, Frederick Meredith. Both had been employed at the RAE Farnborough, and both had provided the Soviets with information on aircraft design.

1. Revelation of Espionage

Following Weiss' revelations, MI5 thought it necessary to consult Attlee, mindful no doubt of the adjuration that the Prime Minister should be 'constantly informed of subversive activities likely to endanger the security of the state', though here the concern was more with espionage than subversion. According to a note on Vernon's file:

> Recommendations for Future Action . . . That having regard to the fact that Wilfred Foulston Vernon is now (although he was not at the material time) a member of Parliament, a statement of Weiss' testimony against him should be laid before the PM and that the latter should be invited to decide what, if any, action should be taken with regard to him. That the Prime Minister should be further invited to decide whether, if he considers that Vernon should be directly approached, it would not be desirable for this approach to be made by a member of the Government.[91]

It was decided that Meredith, a brilliant Dublin-born scientist, long known to have been a Communist, would be approached at the same time it was judged appropriate to interview Vernon.[92]

[91] TNA, KV 2/996 (Wilfred Vernon, 25 May 1948).

[92] ibid. Meredith first came to the attention of MI5 via the reports of an informant at Farnborough, who identified him as a Communist 'known to hold extreme Sinn Fein views'.

Vernon evidently no longer posed any threat to the State. The account Sillitoe presented to Attlee acknowledged that there was no evidence that Vernon's espionage had continued after 1937, describing the material and information he had supplied to the Soviets as 'low grade'.[93] Vernon's dismissal from Farnborough, following his conviction for a relatively minor offence under the Official Secrets Acts 1911–20, had been something of a *cause célèbre* in the 1930s, and the subject of a NCCL pamphlet.[94] After a burglary by a group of Fascists at Vernon's home, a number of official documents were retrieved by the police, following the arrest of the burglars. When he subsequently attended Kingston Police Station to get his papers back, Vernon was charged with 'retaining information' and 'not taking proper care of information' under the Official Secrets Acts 1911–20.[95] He was convicted and fined £50.[96]

After Weiss' confession to MI5 in 1948, B2's J. H. Marriott recorded that on being shown a note on Vernon's involvement in espionage (some ten months after Weiss had made his statement), Attlee 'was shocked at its contents which came as a complete surprise. He appeared to have no idea of Vernon's previous record.'[97] Two weeks later, in another note for the record, Marriott stated that:

> The DG told me yesterday that he did not think that the PM would wish to take any action with regard to Vernon. In these circumstances the DG has decided it will not be possible to interrogate Meredith.[98]

Shortly thereafter, however, further information on Meredith came to light, it being revealed that 'the DG saw the PM this morning and showed him the note on Meredith's case . . . The PM agreed that in the circumstances we should proceed to interrogate Meredith, and he asked to be informed of the result'.[99]

By 1948, Meredith was an important scientist at Smiths' Instruments, and it had been proposed to use him on a project 'of exceptional importance and secrecy in connection with Guided Weapons'. If he were to be permitted to work on the weapons it would be necessary to speak to Meredith in order 'to explore his

[93] Weiss claimed that one of his own handlers had complained that Vernon and Meredith had provided 'poor quality material': Extract from Weiss' interrogation, 20 January 1948. Extracts from the interrogation relating to Vernon and Meredith feature in both KV2/996 (Vernon) and KV2/2200 (Meredith).

[94] NCCL, *The Strange Case of Major Vernon* (London, 1938).

[95] ibid., p. 17.

[96] The ubiquitous D. N. Pritt KC managed to convince the magistrates that Vernon had committed only 'technical' breaches of the Act. W. H. Thompson was Vernon's solicitor. Pritt discussed the case—without using Vernon's name—in D. N. Pritt, *Autobiography of DN Pritt, Part One, From Right to Left* (London, 1965), pp. 154–55. According to Weiss, Meredith had told him that Vernon had confessed to Pritt that he was a spy (TNA, KV 2/2200, 'Extract from Interrogation Report on WEISS Mentioning MEREDITH', 20 January 1948). Vernon's defence is also discussed in NCCL (n 94), p. 20.

[97] TNA, KV 2/996 (Note by J. H. Marriott, B2, 5 October 1948). The document is dated 25 May 1948.

[98] TNA, KV 2/2200 (Note by J. H. Marriott, B2, 19 October 1948).

[99] TNA, KV 2/2200 (Note by J. H. Marriott, B2, 20 December 1948).

political attitude and reliability and to discover the nature of his relations, if any, with the Communist Party. Such an interrogation would include confrontation of Meredith with our knowledge of his pre-war espionage activities.' Essentially it was thought that if MI5 let Meredith know they were aware he had spied for the Soviets in the past, he would not be foolish enough to do it again. The difficulty was that 'there would be a possibility of Meredith imparting this information to Vernon',[100] and there were concerns about what Vernon's reaction would be. The Ministry of Supply, meanwhile, took the view that 'Meredith is of such outstanding ability in the field of aircraft stabilisation and control that from the technical point of view there is no one in this country whom the Department would be more anxious to employ.'[101]

2. Protection from Investigation

MI5's 'Jim' Skardon was despatched to Cheltenham to speak to Meredith. There, the latter confirmed Weiss' story and remarkably in his initial interview with Skardon, described Vernon as 'the most Christ-like person he had ever known', 'begging' Skardon to 'be gentle with him' should he be subject to interrogation.[102] However, Vernon was not interrogated by MI5 while he remained an MP, even though Attlee was unlikely to have felt in any way indebted to him—in April 1948, Vernon, with twenty other MPs, had been threatened by the NEC with expulsion from the Labour Party, for 'organised opposition to party policy'. Apart from an understandable caution about interrogating a Member of Parliament, there is no obvious legal reason why Vernon should have been protected in this way for, as we have pointed out, there is no privilege attaching to an MP which would have insulated him from full MI5 investigation and eventual prosecution should this have been merited. Contrary to the claims of historian Andrew Roberts, Vernon did not enjoy any 'immunity from prosecution'.[103]

It is true that parliamentary privilege gives MPs freedom from arrest.[104] But the scope of this privilege was quite limited, as had been revealed in the case of the Fascist Captain 'Jock' Ramsey, the Tory MP for Peebles, who was the subject of indefinite detention under the notorious wartime Regulation 18B as a result of his outspoken views, which appeared sympathetic to the Nazis.[105] Having

[100] TNA, KV 2/2200 (From the Note Shown to P. M. on 20 December 1948).

[101] TNA, KV 2/2200 (Joe Jaggers, Ministry of Supply to Martin Furnival Jones, MI5, 6 December 1948). Meredith was eventually moved away from secret work.

[102] TNA, KV 2/2200 (Frederick William Meredith, by W. J. Skardon, 30 December 1948).

[103] A. Roberts, *A History of the English-Speaking Peoples since 1900* (London, 2010), pp. 401–2.

[104] For the position at the time of writing, see A. W. Bradley, K. D. Ewing, and C. J. S. Knight, *Constitutional and Administrative Law* (17th edn, Harlow, 2018), pp. 221–2.

[105] There is some discussion of Ramsey in A. W. B. Simpson, *In the Highest Degree Odious* (Oxford, 1992), the leading study on Regulation 18B.

unsuccessfully appealed against his detention, Ramsay claimed that the detention was a breach of parliamentary privilege, a claim rejected by the House of Commons Committee of Privileges, which concluded that while 'it is plain that arrest in civil proceedings is a breach of privilege', 'arrest on an indictable offence is not'.[106] Nor was executive detention under wartime powers. Vernon's alleged activities not only fell within the orbit of the Attlee Directive, as relating to espionage, but more importantly within the scope of the Official Secrets Acts 1911–20. There was no reason why claims of espionage against him could not have been fully investigated.

The reasons for 'protecting' Vernon were thus almost certainly political and diplomatic rather than legal, though we should not overlook the likelihood that Vernon was no longer thought to have been involved in espionage activity, given Sillitoe's report that there was no evidence of Vernon's espionage activity having continued after his conviction in 1937. Roberts' view is that another reason why nothing was done is that the Labour government was concerned not to prejudice Anglo-American relations,[107] a view which seems more plausible. Any prosecution would have been at best pointless, and at worst damaging to the national interest.[108] Nevertheless, the political protection from prosecution extended to Vernon appeared to apply also to surveillance, the file suggesting that there was no surveillance while he was an MP. It was not until after he lost his seat in 1951 that warrants were obtained to intercept Vernon's mail and tap his phone, as the investigations into his activities were revived.[109]

Vernon was interviewed by MI5's 'Jim' Skardon in February 1952 (after Labour had left government), Skardon pointing out that 'WEISS and MEREDITH were both at liberty in spite of our knowledge', and that 'the authorities were not anxious to embark on a prosecution. We desired to fill in the gaps in our knowledge . . . so that we might arm ourselves against present enemies of the Service.'[110] Vernon confessed to '*active and paid espionage*'. Skardon visited him again in March, after which Skardon concluded that 'It is quite certain that Vernon is extremely embarrassed at being found out as a spy . . . I doubt whether any great profit will ensue from further interrogation.' However, this relaxed attitude was questioned

[106] HC 164, 1939–40, para. 15.

[107] Roberts (n 103). MI5 removed all mention of Vernon's status as an MP from the report on George Weiss—the ex-Soviet agent who had revealed Vernon's pre war role—that was sent to the FBI in Washington. They were 'fully conscious of the necessity of not making embarrassing remarks to the Americans about Labour MPs': TNA, KV 2/996 (R. T. Reed to T. A. Robertson, 31 July 1948).

[108] Skardon had reassured Meredith as best he could back in December 1948. When 'interrogating' him, Skardon claimed to have told Meredith that 'so far as I knew, no prosecutions were intended in respect of offences upwards of ten years old and I said he need not worry on that score': TNA, KV 2/996 (Extract from Report of Interrogation of F. W. Meredith on 6 January 1949 by B2A Mr Skardon).

[109] Note also that despite MI5's interest in Geoffrey Bing, there is no evidence in Bing's file to indicate that MI5 put him under technical surveillance, intercepted his mail, or set Skardon's watchers on to him until after he had lost his seat in the 1955 election. It may be that it was not until Bing was no longer an MP that he was considered to merit such attention.

[110] TNA, KV 2/996 (Interview with Wilfred Foulston Vernon on 4 February 1952, by W. J. Skardon).

by counter-espionage officer C. A. G. Simkins (B2A), after it was discovered that Vernon was standing for the London County Council, and was said to be interested in returning to the Commons. Describing Vernon as having been 'virtually uncooperative', Simkins argued forcefully that:

> There can be no excuse for the Security Service to allow VERNON to pursue a public and political career unhindered by some attempt to have his position assessed by the authorities of his political party. Mr Attlee was made aware of the facts when he was Prime Minister and we now have VERNON's confession to active and paid espionage. I submit that it would be proper at least for the present Prime Minister to decide whether or not as an act of duty if not ordinary courtesy this fact should be made known to Mr Attlee.

3. Resumption of Investigation

In April 1952, Vernon was elected to the London County Council. Yet Simkins had changed his mind, very likely having been influenced by his colleague Evelyn McBarnet, who as the voice of sanity in counter-espionage had argued that now Vernon had admitted his guilt, 'unless or until we obtain any new information bearing on his past espionage activities, I think it is unlikely that we shall get any further admissions by interrogation'.[111] Simkins now advised Dick White that:

> As Mr Attlee is no longer in office, it is probably unnecessary to mention the latest chapter in this case to anyone outside the Security Service, but before the file is put away, you may want to raise this point with the DG.[112]

Sillitoe did speak to Attlee (now Leader of the Opposition) about Vernon, it would appear with the intention of preventing Vernon standing as a Labour MP. In the last minute sheet entry on the file (followed by a redaction blanking out the remainder of the page),[113] Sillitoe recorded in an extraordinary hand-written scrawl that he had met with Attlee to discuss Vernon, and did not intend to trouble Maxwell Fyfe with the matter: 'I saw Mr Attlee this morning. He was very appreciative. I do not propose telling the H S.'[114]

[111] TNA, KV 2/996 (Minute sheet note by E. McBarnet, B2B, 13 May 1952).

[112] TNA, KV 2/996 (Minute sheet note by C. A. G. Simkins, B2A, 20 May 1952).

[113] The last minute sheet entry released to the National Archives. The date stamps on the cover indicate that MI5 was periodically consulting or adding to Vernon's file up until his death in 1975.

[114] TNA, KV 2/996 (Minute sheet entry 781) (the date has been removed but the entry follows a note on the DG's brief for use at his meeting with Attlee dated 24 June 1952, and it appears that Sillitoe probably met with his old boss on 25 June 1952).

So, what are we to make of the Vernon case? That *he was protected because he was an MP*? Perhaps, though as we have seen, it is *because* they were MPs that others *were* subject to surveillance. Certainly, Sillitoe believed that he required Prime Ministerial permission to interview Vernon when he was an MP. That *he was protected from surveillance to avoid diplomatic embarrassment*? Perhaps, though fear of diplomatic embarrassment would at best have been a reason to conceal the fruits of the surveillance, rather than a reason for not doing the surveillance in the first place. That *he was not suspected of any wrongdoing*? Perhaps, but why then the intense interest after he lost his seat? Whatever the reason for restraint in the Vernon case while he was an MP, there was no such restraint after he left Parliament. At this point, however, the evidence reveals much about the autonomy of MI5 and the lax oversight under the new Conservative government which empowered Sillitoe to feel free to share information with Attlee without even informing Maxwell Fyfe.

Following Skardon's visit to Vernon in February 1952, the MI5 man had recorded that Vernon 'is prepared to make a full statement but expressed his intention of consulting Frederick William Meredith (PF 42,780) his associate in espionage'.[115] A fresh telecheck by MI5 was supplemented by one for mail interception, and it was revealed that Meredith had invited Vernon to Cheltenham. MI5 was keen to identify any others who may have been involved with the pair, and particularly in identifying a man known to the Service as Harry II, the man who gave orders to Weiss, who in turn had recruited Vernon. The next step was to get a telephone HOW for Meredith:

> As a direct aid to discovering the content of Vernon and Meredith's discussions we are anxious to know when Vernon intends to stay with Meredith. I therefore apply for a Home Office Warrant telecheck on Cleeve Hill 178.[116]

The need to establish the date of the visit was listed on the application to Mr Saffery at the GPO, along with a telling reference to the need to find where Meredith kept his telephone: 'We know that Vernon intends to spend a week-end with Meredith and we are anxious to discover the location of Meredith's telephone in his house, and this may well be disclosed by this operation.'[117] It is obvious that they intended to set up an eavesdropping arrangement in Meredith's house, using the 'SF' system discussed in Chapter 8 below.[118]

[115] TNA, KV 2/996 (5 February 1952). There is a copy of Skardon's report of his visit on file.

[116] TNA, KV 2/996 (Minute sheet entry 341 B2A, 18 February 1952).

[117] TNA, KV 2/996 (Doc. 343a, 19 February to G. F. Saffery at the GPO).

[118] Briefly, 'SF' was a system whereby a microphone in the telephone handset continued to transmit after the handset had been replaced in the cradle. In all other respects the telephone would operate normally, but when 'SF' had been installed, the MI5 B2B team in London would be able to listen to conversations—and much else besides—in the room where the telephone was situated. If, however, a telephone was installed at the end of a long hall, for example, away from the living area, it was rarely of much use to the MI5 eavesdroppers. A telephone in the living room, on the other hand, could pick up a considerable amount of domestic conversation. Knowledge of the date of the proposed meeting was

In Meredith's file it is notable that most letters from the Ministry of Supply, and all of those from the Gloucestershire Police reporting on Meredith's activities have been removed.[119] It is apparent too that a number of documents from around the time of the proposed meeting between the two ex-spies have also been removed from the file, and that most of those which remain have been heavily redacted: MI5 do not want us to know about the bugging of private houses, and, very likely, the role of the police in monitoring the activities of Meredith and his wife. The original B4B 'briefing sheet', recording the details of the Meredith telephone-tapping arrangements, has been replaced with a photocopy, and the place on the form where the SF arrangements are likely to have been recorded have been blanked out, suggesting that SF was installed. The 'weeder' has also removed the second purpose of the telecheck—to find what room the telephone was in. The sheet reads:

> We are anxious to discover two things by this telecheck: 1. The date upon which Vernon intends to spend the weekend with Meredith.

It appears that the SF, if it was installed, produced no information of any value. Despite MI5's efforts, Simkins later conceded that 'we . . . do not know what passed between them . . . I think it is unlikely that we can extract anymore information from VERNON about his espionage.'[120] The HOWs on Vernon were suspended.

VI. Conclusion

The surveillance of MPs gives rise to difficult constitutional questions. On the one hand, democratic propriety requires MPs and other elected officials to be in a protected category in relation to State surveillance, though as is widely acknowledged, MPs should enjoy no immunity from investigation when there are grounds to believe that they may have committed an offence. As we have seen, this latter principle is recognized by parliamentary privilege, which was reinforced in 1956, when the surveillance of MPs was raised in the House by Francis Noel-Baker (then a Labour MP). Noel-Baker complained to the Speaker that letters he had sent to

also crucial: these were not voice-activated devices connected to tape recorders. If MI5 wanted to 'listen in' back in 1952, the GPO employees at Leconfield House (the MI5 offices in Mayfair) working for B4B had to connect to the line and record the meeting on an acetate disc.

[119] That these letters referred to Meredith and his wife's activities is confirmed by comments by MI5 officers elsewhere in the file. MI5's arrangements with local police forces are touched upon at pp. 23, 71, 79–80, 94–6, and 126 above.

[120] TNA, KV 2/996 (Minute sheet note 771 dating from May 1952) (the sheet has been photocopied in order to make redactions and the days of the month have been semi-obscured). A note in the file in which Simkins refers to recording the results of the telephone and mail checks, which would very likely have referred to what information the SF turned up, has been entirely redacted.

British subjects in the Seychelles had been 'interfered with'.[121] According to the Speaker in a ruling subsequently relied on to inform the conclusions of the Birkett Committee, established in the following year to conduct a general examination into the interception of communications (for reasons wholly unrelated to the surveillance of MPs):

> The law on that subject, as I understand, is that letters can be detained and opened by a warrant of a Secretary of State. There is a long series of Acts on this subject, the principal one being that passed in 1912. The fact that Act was passed by this House, and that there is no exception for letters addressed either to or from Members of Parliament shows that there can be no question of privilege involved in that.[122]

But also important, of course, is MI5's mandate, the Attlee Directive making clear that while part of its task is counter-subversion insofar as it affects the defence of the realm, MI5 is to have 'no connection whatsoever with any matters of *a Party political character* and that they must be scrupulous to avoid any action which could be so misconstrued' (para. 4). On that basis, it is difficult to justify the surveillance of the electoral activity of candidates or the political and parliamentary work of parliamentarians, unless standing for election and working as an MP can by some perverted logic be deemed to be subversive. It is clear from the files that one purpose of such surveillance was to secure information about Communist candidates' supporters in order to nourish the Registry; to monitor the parliamentary activities of progressive MPs of different parties in order to be informed of their position on live questions (with an opportunity then to take pre-emptive action as required); and in Piratin's case to monitor the extra-parliamentary activities of an MP with a view to destroying his career. With that in mind, there is no evidence of police officers attending the meetings of Tory MPs to record what they said and feed MI5 files.

Yet perhaps the most striking feature of the four cases discussed in this chapter is what they tell us about the role of the Prime Minister, to whom much of the information was fed back. What is particularly interesting is the extent to which information about Labour MPs in particular made its way to Attlee, in a manner that tested the principle that MI5 should not engage in matters of a party-political character. In the case of both Bing and Vernon, information was supplied to keep them out of office, in Bing's case despite the fact that there was no evidence against him, and in Vernon's case despite the fact that there was no evidence that he was any longer a security threat. The Vernon case is especially shocking for the fact that in

[121] It seems Noel-Baker was in contact with some of the leaders of the Cypriot independence movement who were detained in the Seychelles.

[122] HC Debs, 2 August 1956, col. 1597.

clear breach of protocol Sillitoe saw the Leader of the Opposition behind the back of the Home Secretary, with a view to preventing his selection as a parliamentary candidate. There is a sense too that while information was being supplied to Attlee in his capacity as Prime Minister, it was being received by Attlee as Leader of the Labour Party, and used for the purposes of a party hostile to Communists, rather than a government with wider responsibilities. MI5 was in effect a political police force, deciding who could hold political positions.

This is not to deny that where there is credible evidence that an MP has been involved in espionage it is right that the matter should be investigated. If Krivitsky was credible and gave credible information about Pritt, then it is right that Pritt should have been investigated. As we have seen, however, there were doubts about Krivitsky's credibility, and nothing was ever found. In the case of Vernon (who did not appear to have any direct Communist Party connections), there was evidence and ultimately a confession, though no subsequent prosecution. Yet Attlee prohibited any examination of Vernon for the lifetime of the Parliament, exposing himself to the charge that he did so in the interests of his party in government, which would be seriously embarrassed were there to be any publicity about Vernon's activities. He did so without knowing what information any questioning of Vernon might yield and without knowing whether he was still engaged in espionage. If nothing else, this was a case that exposed serious shortcomings with the Attlee Directive. It is all very well for the buck to stop with the Prime Minister. But what happens if the Prime Minister is paralysed by the information received?

7
The Rule of Law under Surveillance

I. Introduction

Lawyers had no immunity from MI5 surveillance during the Cold War, and progressive lawyers had even less. Solicitors and barristers who were members of the Communist Party or who were associated with the Communist Party were watched. So too were organizations of radical lawyers, as well as individuals who were connected with these groups. As we have seen, being a Member of Parliament provided no immunity from surveillance either, with one of the thickest files being that of D. N. Pritt KC MP, who was close to the Communist Party and carefully monitored, even during his parliamentary career. But there is no need to be too alarmed; membership was not always a barrier to elevation to the Bench, as the example of Mr Justice Lawson (PF 41,933) makes clear.

MI5 files reveal that the Service was troubled by radical lawyers and uncertain about how to deal with them. Files were opened on law firms such as Thompsons, famous for their involvement in a number of prominent cases since the First World War, including *Roberts v Hopwood*.[1] But although Harry Thompson's Personal File has been opened, those of his sons, associates, and employees generally remain closed. An important exception is that of Francis Loeffler, who came to the attention of MI5 not as a lawyer but as a member of the family of Ursula Buerton (née Kuczynski), a Soviet spy. A file entry nevertheless notes that:

> Francis Herbert Loeffler, a solicitor employed by W H Thompson & Sons, the Communist solicitors, is registered as a member of the Communist Party for 1953 under the alias of Francis Herbert Keeling. His wife . . . is also registered under the name of Keeling. Loeffler's professional status might be regarded by the Party as a reason for his adopting an alias but this appears to be inadequate justification when one considers that he is employed by a firm of solicitors which is well known as communist. Sabine Loeffler is a member of a family (Kuczynski) who have come to frequent notice in connection with Soviet espionage.[2]

[1] [1925] AC 578.

[2] TNA, KV 2/2930 (Kenneth Morton Evans B1A, 3 June 1953). 'Keeling' was a middle name of Loeffler which he used as a surname briefly during the1950s for Party membership purposes, presumably in a bid to separate his professional and political identities. It certainly had nothing to do with espionage, as MI5 would be well aware.

MI5, the Cold War, and the Rule of Law. K. D. Ewing, Joan Mahoney, and Andrew Moretta, Oxford University Press (2020). DOI: 10.1093/oso/9780198818625.001.0001

It is not clear how successful or significant Loeffler was as a lawyer. It is also unclear just how many other files were opened on solicitors and barristers,[3] the number of surveillance targets acknowledged to exist being limited and almost certain to misrepresent the full extent to which lawyers were the subject of surveillance. So although there may be a dozen or so opened files of lawyers who were targeted, there are perhaps several more dozen referred to in the various files we have examined. The numbers subject to some kind of surveillance would run into hundreds when account is taken of the interest shown in organizations such the Haldane Society of Socialist Lawyers, which MI5 had infiltrated and for which it had membership lists and other information.

The targeting of lawyers reveals a sense in which lawyers were thought to be important, and reveals also a sense of incomprehension about a group of people seen clearly by MI5 as traitors to their class, never mind their country. But just as the surveillance of MPs was an affront to the principles of parliamentary democracy that MI5 was under a mandate to defend, so the surveillance of lawyers was just as great an affront to the Rule of Law, another core liberal value that the Service was bound to respect and sustain, albeit that it did neither convincingly. There is no legitimate reason why lawyers should be targeted, unless there was reason to believe that they were involved in espionage or subversion, of which there is evidence of neither. In the absence of any such suspicion, radical movements are entitled to confidential legal advice, as are radical individuals involved in litigation, while lawyers who provide support for unpopular causes are entitled to expect freedom from harassment by the State—for obvious reasons.[4]

II. The Surveillance of Lawyers

The files suggest a number of reasons for the surveillance of lawyers. The first is the general interest in left-wing organizations, which in the case of lawyers would include the Haldane Society and the Communist Party Lawyers' Group (CPLG). Second, lawyers would be targeted in relation to individual cases or events where there was a suspicion of subversive activity. Were they serving the interests of the Party rather than their client? Third, lawyers with a public profile and a reputation for criticizing government would be targeted to monitor and record their anti-government conduct, leading in some cases to attempted retribution.[5] And finally,

[3] Apart from those considered below, lawyers under surveillance about whom there is no open file who are mentioned in MI5 dispatches include Stanley Moore (PF 61,512), L. E. P. Tyler (PF 295,722) (of Coward Chance, 'a well known and reputable firm'), and Bill Sedley.

[4] The treatment of Gaster—whatever his irritating faults—was a monstrous violation of the Rule of Law. See pp. 174–6 and 188–9 below.

[5] For detail, see K. D. Ewing, J. Mahoney, and A. Moretta, 'Civil Liberties and the Korean War' (2018) 81 *MLR* 395.

lawyers with close links to the Soviet Union would be the subject of close surveillance, presumably for all of the foregoing reasons, but also perhaps because of exaggerated concerns about espionage.

1. The Lawyer as Access

Francis Loeffler's National Archives pen picture records by way of justification of his surveillance:

> Francis Herbert LOEFFLER and Sabine LOEFFLER nee KUCZYNSKI: British and German naturalized British. This split file deals with the sister and brother-in-law of the Russian spies Ursula BEURTON and Juergen KUCZYNSKI. Both LOEFFLERS were secret members of the Communist Party of Great Britain (CPGB) using the alias KEELING, and Francis, a lawyer who read law at Downing College Cambridge 1937–1940, belonged to the CPGB Lawyers' Group and was associated with the Haldane Society.[6]

Some context is provided by the following four paragraphs from a tribute by Loeffler's son, following his father's death in 2007:

> When my father was born, his father was 63. He had no brothers, sisters, aunts, or uncles. Dad was brought up in the Channel Islands and attended Victoria College, a boarding school in Jersey. At 16 he was sent to Germany to a college in Marburg an Lahn for one year and to France for six months . . . At Cambridge [he studied] law and qualified as a barrister . . . At this time his parents were living in Jersey under Nazi occupation. His father probably died of malnutrition there . . .
>
> Frank joined the Communist Party at Cambridge, as did many other students. He was in the anti-fascist movement there and chairman of the Socialist Club. He supported the Spanish Republic against Franco. During the war he worked in an engineering company in Aylmer Road near East Finchley that made Lancaster bombers. He worked alongside Czech engineers from Skoda factory who were advising on the assembly line. He worked in an air raid shelter. He also ran a hostel for German refugees fleeing Hitler and it was there he met my mother Sabine, who had left Germany with her family in 1933. They married in June 1941. Frank took over as secretary of the Labour Committee in Warwick Avenue, Paddington.
>
> . . . In 1944 my sister Harriet was born and in 1946 Caroline. The family moved to Guernsey, where my father worked as a barrister in the Attorney General's office in St Helier. They returned to London and I was born in 1950 . . . He began

[6] TNA, KV 2/2927–33.

> working for a firm called Thompsons,[7] and took his final exams to become a solicitor, after which he joined a firm called Garber and Vowles, which finally amalgamated with others to become Gaster, Vowles, Turner and Loeffler. They were all socialist lawyers. He stayed with them until he retired at the age of 72 in 1992. My father specialised in conveyancing . . . He also worked helping socialists and communists who had been imprisoned. He went to Spain to advise the defence team of Senor Grimau, the freedom fighter who was eventually murdered by the Franco regime. He also met Senor Negrin, the exiled President of the Spanish Republic, in London . . .
>
> He was a trustee of the Marx Memorial Library, also giving them legal advice and drawing up the deeds for Marx's grave in Highgate Cemetery . . . and was a director of Marx House Ltd. My father was also at one time legal adviser to the *Morning Star* newspaper
>
> . . . When my uncle Jock Nicholson stood as a communist candidate for Camden, Frank was his election agent . . . I can remember a dinner in our flat with John Platts-Mills, who was the defence counsel for the Kray twins. Frank was also a member of the Haldane Society, a group of socialist lawyers. He was secretary of the Lawyers' Party Group, who advised the Communist Party on legal matters.[8]

It was as a result of his family connections that Loeffler first came to attention and it was because of his family connection that he was subject to what was at times intense surveillance. By 1952, MI5 had discovered that Loeffler was now a solicitor with Thompsons.[9] Around this time, the Loefflers appeared, to become briefly covert CPGB members, using the name 'Keeling', one of Loeffler's middle names. Loeffler was simply dropping his surname for CPGB purposes. This pointless and wholly ineffective measure indicates that Loeffler must have been conscious of the possibility of unwelcome attention, but unaware of the extent of Security Service knowledge of his activities. As pointed out in the National Archives pen picture of Loeffler referred to above, his sister-in-law was Ursula Beurton, the infamous Soviet spy Sonya, who had played a major part in Klaus Fuchs' affair. Loeffler was caught up in the surveillance of the wider family as a result of her espionage.

We return to the surveillance of the Loefflers in Chapter 8. In the meantime, the surveillance of Francis Loeffler in relation to the activities of Sonya was to yield an

[7] Loeffler's Security Service file reveals that he was a pupil at Platts-Mills' chambers in 1947–8, and between 1948 and 1952, prior to joining Thompsons, he attended a number of trials of Communist activists in Greece and Spain on behalf of the Haldane Society of Socialist Lawyers, as well as the International Association of Democratic Lawyers, and later served on the Executive Committee of the League of Democracy in Greece. Between 1948 and 1950, Loeffler was employed in the Attorney General's Office in Guernsey, although MI5 lost track of him while he was in the Channel Islands.

[8] Frank Loeffler, by his son: Lissenden Gardens.com (undated). See also D. Carrier, 'The Lawyer who Fought Franco and some Over-Charging Builders', *Camden New Journal*, 20 July 2007.

[9] Special Branch were slower off the mark. A Special Branch report dated 13 June 1952 describes Loeffler as working in the 'gramophone record department of Collet's': TNA, KV 2/2930.

unexpected dividend, as he continued to be monitored by MI5 long after it had become obvious that the Loefflers were not engaged in espionage. A minute sheet entry from January 1955 to Roger Hollis, the DDG, and signed for in his absence by Sir Dick White, the DG, indicates at least a rational if not wholly legitimate reason for MI5's continued interest:

> Investigations were made by B2A in 1951 and 1952 to discover if the Loefflers themselves were, like other members of the Kuczynski family, involved in espionage activities. Although no evidence for this was forthcoming, the letter check on the Loefflers produced a considerable amount of material about the Lawyers' Group of the British Communist Party, including minutes of its meetings. Loeffler has been a member of the Lawyers' Group for many years and in April 1954 became a member of its Management Committee. He is also currently a member of the Executive Committee of the Haldane Society.
>
> *At present we have no continuing source about the activities of the Lawyers' Group and I am anxious to keep abreast of its work.* It is hoped that the re-imposition of a letter check on Francis Loeffler will produce routine information about the group. I attach for your signature, if approved, forms for the imposition of a Home Office Warrant (letter check) on Francis Herbert Loeffler @ Keeling, 57 Aberdare Gardens, NW6 and 1 Milton Park, Highgate, N.6.[10]

2. The Lawyer as Subversive

After 1952, Loeffler was under surveillance, largely for collateral reasons—because of what he could tell them about his family and the activities of other German Communists in the United Kingdom, and because he could provide access to the CPLG and the Haldane Society. In the case of Neil Lawson PF 41,933, in contrast, there was a great deal of interest in his work and activities in a very extensive and detailed file.[11] Lawson was reported to have been one of three lawyers who joined the Communist Party in 1932, and in that year he handled a number of important cases, including a libel case and a contempt of court case for the *Daily Worker*. His performance in the latter was such as to move 'M/7' (the Security Service informer/agent present in court, barrister V. W. Hancock-Nunn) to write that:

> I was very favourably impressed with Neil LAWSON. I regard him as definitely a gentleman, and he has a distinct idea of advocacy. I had expected to see a rather

[10] TNA, KV 2/2931 (Minute sheet entry by Miss J. H. Money (F1A), 25 January 1955) (emphasis added).

[11] TNA, KV 2/3592–5. Lawson was also the subject of a separate Special Branch file (RF 405/42/2356), as doubtless were the others mentioned in this chapter.

> bumptious young man, but I was wrong. In my view he is far too clever and intelligent for the CP to have at their elbow, and when he feels his feet he will undoubtedly have considerable influence within his own sphere. The Attorney General regarded LAWSON with expressions of amused contempt, but none the less LAWSON is far above the average member of the Left Wing Group, and should be carefully watched.[12]

A full account of various pre-war activities is contained in volume 1 of Lawson's file, including meetings he addressed and cases in which he was involved, and much was made of his membership of both the secret CPLG of which he was treasurer, and the executive committee of the NCCL. It is reported that by the outbreak of war, Lawson had developed 'a large practice at the Bar and some reputation as an international lawyer', 'highly thought of by the leaders of the Communist Party'.[13] In a letter to the Chief Constable of Oxford in 1945, the then Head of the Security Service (Sir David Petrie) wrote that Lawson had not come to his attention during his wartime service, but that he had 'no reason whatever to think that he is likely to have changed his views'.[14] For that reason, the Security Service wanted to know where Lawson was, and asked the advice of the Oxford constabulary to track him down, apparently without success.

Lawson was nevertheless picked up again, with his file recording that in 1947 he was part of a deputation to the Home Secretary to plead for a reduction in the sentence of Alan Nunn May and was reported in 1948 to have been elected to the NCCL Executive Committee. Notes in Lawson's file also make clear that 'from top secret and delicate sources' he renewed his contact with the Communist Party, and that he continued to contribute liberally to Party funds after the war.[15] It was thought significant that these contributions were not affected by the 'anti-Stalin' allegations in 1957 or the events in Hungary in 1956, for which Lawson 'entirely accepts the Communist Party line'.[16] But it was in the mid-1950s that the Security Service became delirious and his file expanded exponentially, as Lawson became the target of active and acute surveillance, rather than someone about whom the Security Service appeared simply to accumulate information.

For the moment, it is sufficient to say that the activating cause of this remarkable interest in Lawson was his instruction by the new Malay Rulers to advise on constitutional matters, an instruction which after much intrusion was eventually revealed by the Colonial Office to have no sinister overtones but to have arisen

12 TNA, KV 2/3592.

13 ibid.

14 ibid.

15 The files also reveal that a mistake was made in describing Lawson as a secret member of the Party: TNA, KV 2/3593 (W. H. Oughton to SLO 'Security Liaison Officer' Malaya, 30 January 1957). Officially Lawson became a Party sympathizer.

16 TNA, KV 2/3593 (Neil Lawson QC).

because Lawson had been a personal friend of one of the Malay Rulers since university. Indeed, the Colonial Office 'formed a very high opinion of [Lawson's] ability and good sense', and found him 'most helpful in furthering HMG's [Her Majesty's Government's] policy'.[17] Indeed, so highly regarded was Lawson by the Colonial Office that they thought that in the interests of fairness to him, the security assessment should be reconsidered.[18] In the words of one Colonial Office official, if Lawson was a 'true Communist he is certainly the most consummate dissembler we have ever encountered'.[19] He became a High Court judge in 1971, having previously made an unsuccessful application to be Recorder of Hastings, a matter that led one especially stupid MI5 officer to question whether it was appropriate for a Communist to hold such a position.[20]

3. The Lawyer as Propagandist

Jack Gaster was born in 1907 in Maida Vale, his father having been expelled from Romania in 1885. Initially a member of the ILP, Gaster joined the Communist Party along with many others in 1935.[21] According to his Security Service file, Gaster became a London District Officer of the Party, and was prominent as an anti-Fascist speaker and author.[22] He served in the army between 1942 and 1945, and was discharged to work on the Communist Party's election campaign in 1945. Following the general election in 1945, Gaster was employed in the Parliamentary Department at King Street, and worked closely with William Gallacher and Phil Piratin, his intercepted phone calls with the latter revealing a sometimes difficult relationship between the two MPs. In 1946, Gaster was elected to the London County Council, served on the National Appeals Committee of the Communist Party, and acted as Secretary of the CPLG.

Gaster was the subject of routine surveillance in the sense that references to him in other surveillance activities would be added to his file. Thus, telephone conversations to him at King Street—and from him to King Street—are picked up by the telephone check on the Communist Party; meetings in which he participated at King Street are picked up by the listening devices and transcribed; and public meetings he attended and demonstrations he organized are written up in Special Branch Reports. Political advice given to Phil Piratin MP is recorded, legal advice

[17] TNA, KV 2/3593 (Minute from N. D. Watson to W. H. Oughton, 19 June 1957).

[18] The surveillance nevertheless continued, and the file continued to grow, notwithstanding this embarrassing discovery.

[19] TNA, KV 2/3593 (Minute from N. D. Watson to W. H. Oughton, 19 June 1957).

[20] TNA, KV 2/3594 (Loose minute by H. P. Goodwyn, 6 February 1958). Lawson also acted for Conservative Central Office in the Bank Rate Leak Inquiry in 1957: TNA, KV 2/3594 (Telecheck, 8 December 1957). See Cmnd 350, 1958.

[21] For a fuller account, see *The Guardian*, 13 March 2007 (Victoria Brittain).

[22] TNA, KV 2/1558 et seq.

given to various people who consulted him about various matters is retained, as also is information about his private life, such as details of the lease of a flat to Joe Kopelmanas, an employee of *Soviet Weekly*, who was also the subject of surveillance, and who indeed appears to have been 'interviewed' by the Security Service. To all of this is added any relevant information already in the public domain, such as Gaster's nomination of parliamentary candidates, his defeat in LCC elections (1952), and newspaper reports about him or referring to him.

Interest in Gaster was stepped up in 1952, when under the auspices of the International Association of Democratic Lawyers (IADL) (denounced by the British government as 'another international Communist "front" organisation'), he took part in an investigation into the use by the Americans of germ warfare during the Korean war. A Foreign Office minute of 24 March 1952 (addressed, we presume, to the Security Service) requested a 'little background information' about Gaster (who was joined in this mission by representatives from a number of other countries), to be given to the Charge d'Affaires at Peking 'for his own guidance'.[23] The author of the minute then asked whether there was anything that the Charge d'Affaires at Peking could say publicly there to discredit Gaster. A short note was duly provided as requested, making clear that it was general knowledge that Gaster was an 'active Communist', on many occasions making public speeches on behalf of the Party.[24] A little extra colour from the files was nevertheless provided, though there is no mention of what could be said to discredit Gaster, the note struggling to find anything notable that was not already in the public domain.

Gaster went to Korea as a member of the IADL inquiry to investigate allegations of war crimes. Allegations about the conduct of UN forces in Korea had already been made by a number of others.[25] But the account reported by Gaster in the press and elsewhere was devastating,[26] alleging altogether barbaric behaviour, and the use of 'germ warfare, shootings without trial, burning alive, torture and organised destruction'.[27] As a result, Gaster met strong parliamentary criticism on his return, with one backbencher no doubt reflecting the misplaced patriotism of one section of British society when he called on the Attorney General to initiate a prosecution in relation to the 'publication of a seditious pamphlet, circulating in this country through a Mr Jack Gaster', sent by IADL 'to consort with the enemy in North Korea

[23] TNA, KV 2/1559 (Copy of FO Minute from L. M. Minford to B1, 24 March 1952).

[24] TNA, KV 2/1559 (K. Morton Evans to Minford, 27 March 1952).

[25] See K. D. Ewing, J. Mahoney, and A. Moretta, 'Civil Liberties and the Korean War' (2018) 81 *MLR* 395.

[26] See J. Gaster, *Korea—I Saw the Truth* (London, 1952) (based on material published previously in the *Daily Worker*). Also IADL, *Report on US War Crimes in Korea* (London, 1952) (details in the *Daily Worker*, 23 April 1952). It is to be noted that the CPGB phone tap picked up an incoming call—a woman rang 'Gollie' to say that copies of the pamphlet had been sent to Pollitt, but that none were to be sent out as a libel had been found on the front page. If it went out, Gaster would be in 'serious trouble', with a handwritten codicil attributing to Gaster the view that it would constitute 'professional misconduct of a grave character'. The pamphlet was to be reprinted: TNA, KV 2/1559 (Telecheck, 2 May 1952).

[27] *Daily Worker*, 23 April 1952.

and North-East China'.[28] The Attorney wisely thought that no criminal proceedings were called for, the blimpish Colonel Gomme-Duncan, the masonic Tory MP for Perth, who asked the question, succeeding only in raising the temperature for making accusations in breach of parliamentary protocol.[29]

4. The Lawyer as Enemy Agent

As previously noted in Chapter 5, Denis Nowell Pritt joined the House of Commons as the Labour Member for North Hammersmith in 1935.[30] His politics were characterized by his admiration for the Soviet Union, his hatred of fascism, and contempt for the British ruling classes. He was a barrister, a highly successful King's Counsel, who saw himself as a political lawyer: 'I was not merely willing—and most willing—to conduct cases for the Left, but was unwilling to conduct any case against working-class people at all.'[31] MI5 had long taken an interest in Pritt, Vernon Kell observing in a note dated 14 June 1933:

> I understand from current gossip that he is a very disgruntled man who has gone 'Bolo' [Bolshevik] for some reason which nobody seems quite able to explain . . . I have heard it suggested that Pritt has adopted an extreme left wing attitude in the hope of getting a high legal appointment in a Socialist Government which he is convinced will be in power within the next few years, but on the other hand, his bitter attacks on our judges and judicial system generally would hardly be in keeping with this suggestion. Pritt . . . had a very lucrative practice at the bar which I understand is suffering rather as a result of his present attitude. Personally, from the tactless way in which he conducted the Incitement to Mutiny trial and from his attitude on the other occasion on which I saw him, I should say he was getting slightly wrong in the head![32]

There was thus a cloud following Pritt for most of his life, fuelled by claims by Walter Krivitsky, a GRU officer, who had defected at the end of 1937, and had eventually been given asylum in the USA.[33] This is a matter that we considered in Chapter 6 above in the context of Pritt's parliamentary career. Here we add some detail held back from that earlier discussion. As pointed out in Chapter 6, Krivitsky was interviewed

28 HC Debs, 21 July 1952, col. 4.

29 Sydney Silverman rose to point out that the accusation that Gaster had committed an offence ('seditious pamphlet', 'consorting with the enemy', etc.) was an abuse of privilege, which assumed that an offence had been committed, the Speaker agreeing that it was an 'old rule' of the House that 'words condemnatory of other people should be avoided until the matter is disposed of' (ibid.).

30 See p. 143–50 above.

31 D. N. Pritt, *Autobiography of DN Pritt, Part One, From Right to Left* (London, 1965), p. 126.

32 TNA, KV 2/1062.

33 Krivitsky was found dead in a Washington DC hotel room in 1941—a result of a bullet to the head.

by MI5 in 1940, producing a list of Soviet agents, naming two spies in the Foreign Office—King and Oldham. Oldham, an alcoholic with behavioural problems, had committed suicide by the time of the revelations, but King however had still been in place at the Foreign Office. He was quickly interrogated, prosecuted, and convicted *in camera* following the initial allegations Krivitsky had made following his defection. Maclean was described but not identified,[34] Philby was described (he would have recognized himself immediately),[35] and Pritt was named and condemned.[36]

Following the Krivitsky allegations, there is evidence of MI5 interest in Pritt beyond the usual monitoring of speeches.[37] However, as we saw in Chapter 6, those allegations were discounted in 1941,[38] but then again apparently taken seriously after Maclean was revealed to be a spy and Philby's association with Burgess had indicated that he too had likely been working for the Soviets. [39] Krivitsky had said that Pritt was:

> a man who supplied agents for Soviet Organisation in the UK. This man's personal staff, his contacts and activities should be very carefully examined as people like Pritt are increasingly valuable to the Soviet who have means of bringing great pressure to bear on them. In case of War with the Soviet they will not hesitate to use such pressure. Pritt will work in the interests of the Soviet without pressure, but should he hesitate he will be made to do what he is told. His book [on Soviet show trials] was written to order of the Soviet. Pritt occupies a special position and his activities must be examined from a different point of view to that adopted when looking into Soviet espionage organisations.[40]

As we also saw in Chapter 6, Pritt was the subject of intense investigation following the re-examination of Krivitsky's claims.[41] But the claims were once again discounted. Evelyn McBarnet of MI5's B2A had been given the task of examining the letters and paperwork Burgess had left behind. As a result of her work, the following note was placed in Pritt's MI5 file:

> As a result of a re-examination of the Krivitsky material I have looked at all files of this PF. In my view Krivitsky's remarks (serial 180d, vol. 2) should

[34] TNA, KV 2/805 (Information Obtained from General Krivitsky during his Visit to this Country), p. 20.

[35] ibid., p. 82. See also K. Philby, *My Silent War: The Autobiography of a Spy* (London, 1968), p. 130.

[36] TNA, KV 2/805 (Information Obtained from General Krivitsky during his Visit to this Country), p. 84.

[37] See pp. 143–5 above.

[38] TNA, KV 2/1064 (Minute sheet note Pilkington (F2C) to Ogilvie (F2A), 4 October 1941).

[39] See TNA, KV 6/142 (Leakage of Top-Secret Foreign Office Telegrams in the USA–Evidence and Investigation). See also pp. 148–9 above.

[40] TNA, KV 2/1062. This passage is from an interview with Krivitsky on 3 February 1940. The first and last sentences of the passage do not appear in the corresponding note on deposit in Krivitsky's file in the National Archives: TNA, KV 2/805.

[41] Excerpts from Krivitsky's file were extracted on 10 and 12 October 1951 and placed in Pritt's file.

> not be taken to mean that Pritt is or was a spy or a recruiter of spies, but rather that he was a dangerous propagandist and agent of the Communist Party, possibly of the Russian Communist Party and examination of files seems to bear this view out. I would not suggest any action from B2 in the case of D. N. Pritt.[42]

III. The CPGB Lawyers' Group

It is hardly surprising that there should be a group of lawyers who were either members of or sympathetic to the Communist Party. Indeed, some lawyers were so valuable that it appears they were relieved of the obligation to join the Party. There were thus sympathizers, members, and active supporters, who operated as the CPLG. According to a Special Branch report in 1938 (which included the names of the known members of the Group, now conveniently redacted), the Legal Group was 'one of the "secret" groups the members of which are not bound to disclose their adhesion to the Party unless they wish and which are controlled directly by party headquarters, via the Middle Class Bureau there'.[43] MI5 were very keen to find out the identity of all the members of this group. But it is not clear why, and it is not clear how surveillance of lawyers could be said to be consistent with either the Rule of Law or the the Directives under which the Service operated.

1. Sources of Information

Information about the Lawyers' Group was obtained in a number of ways, one by agents and informers. At some point it seems that Hancock-Nunn (M/7) infiltrated the Group, and while he appears to have dropped out of the picture by the 1950s, there is clear evidence that the Group was infiltrated again by 1956. Dudley Collard's file reveals that barrister and Haldane Society member Muir Hunter had in 1940 supplied a list of names to a barrister C. Harkforth Jones, 3 Elm Court, Temple, who duly passed on the information to MI5.[44] Harkforth Jones assured MI5 that Muir Hunter 'tells me that he will tell me anything further that comes to his notice'. But infiltration was not the only source of information about the

42 TNA, KV 2/1065 (10 January 1952).

43 TNA, KV 2/2159 (Dudley Collard).

44 ibid. (Harkforth Jones to Baxter, 28 May 1940). Muir Hunter's name has been redacted from the copy of the letter but has been left in the minute sheet entry. Neil Lawson's file reveals subsequently that one Special Branch agent had been 'blown' in 1943 (perhaps Harkforth Jones or Muir Hunter), significant not least because the Party would have known from that date, if not before, that MI5 now had this information: TNA, KV 2/3593 (Lawson Overt Information, 4 February 1957).

Lawyers' Group, with other techniques having to be found when informers were not available for whatever reason, as in the early 1950s.

The latter techniques included old-fashioned mail interception, following Dick White's minute of January 1955 referred to in Part II above in relation to Francis Loeffler. As a result of the latter minute, Miss Money, F1A wrote to Mr Harlow of the GPO asking for a re-imposition of a HOW on Loeffler.[45] It seems that she was asking him to re-activate a HOW that had been suspended, rather than apply to the Home Secretary for a fresh warrant.[46] The Loeffler file indicates that by the end of November 1955 Money was warning Harlow that the next meeting of the CPGB Lawyers' Group was on 8 December, urging him to 'try to arrange 100% interception . . . from the 9 December until you close down for Christmas in the hope of intercepting the Minutes of this meeting'.[47] Remarkably, Miss Money had started to compile a list of where and when John Hostettler, as Secretary of the Lawyers' Group, posted notice of the monthly Group meetings to Loeffler, with similar letters presumably sent to other members of the group at the same time.[48] For example:

DATE	TIME	PLACE	DATE OF MEETING	INTERVAL
7.4.56 (Wed)	1.45pm	Croydon, Surrey	14.6.46. (Thurs)	6 days

The interval refers to the time between posting the letter and the date of the meeting. There were six such entries covering the six months from November 1955 to May 1956, and a reminder appended to the entry above, recording the fact that there was 'presumably an earlier notice, which was not intercepted'. The intention was to intercept all of the notices Hostettler sent out, and thus obtain the names and addresses of all the members of the group.[49]

MI5 also had the King Street 'bug' as an aid to monitoring the CPGB Lawyers' Group. However, even when conversations were within the reach of the microphones, they could be difficult to follow, not helped by the fact that the transcribers obviously had little knowledge of the people involved in the group, as the following cryptic extract indicates:

> Well anyway the point is that Eltons asked me my opinion, and he said that if he's got to choose between the Peace movement and the 'Soviet' (ph) he'd choose the

[45] For a fuller account of the role of Harlow and his colleagues generally, see Chapter 6 above, and Chapter 8 below.

[46] TNA, KV 2/2931 (29 January 1955).

[47] TNA, KV 2/2932 (30 November 1955).

[48] TNA, KV 2/2932 (13 June 1955).

[49] See pp. 90 and 103 above for the extension of HOWs to cover the interception of letters *sent by* the individual subject to the warrant. That the code name RATCATCHER was used for such operations is confirmed by the F1A/GMB (the latter are the initials of the MI5 officer concerned) note dated 23 July 1957 in TNA, KV 2/2933.

> Peace movement any day. Bill then became inaudible. He eventually said that in spite of what the Lawyers Group said and thought about John (Elton) he had the confidence of people like 'Les Harkin'(??ph).[50]

Nevertheless, with a little perseverance such transcripts could provide a revealing picture of the activities of the Group—even if the intelligence value was arguably slight.

2. The Surveillance 'Harvest'

Apart from questions about compatibility with MI5's Charter, the obvious question is why this group was being watched. Miss Money's minute on deposit in Loeffler's file suggests a desire to obtain 'routine information' about the group, though for what purpose? It also begs the question what is meant by 'routine information', whether information other than routine information was obtained, and if so the purposes—if any—for which it was used. Routine information would be intrusive enough, if only because it would provide data about members of the group, though by the 1950s many of these would be well known. It is easy to understand that many in MI5 would be very curious about which legal practitioners were Communists, but curiosity does not provide justification for surveillance. This desire for information could perhaps have been explained retrospectively if that routine information had provided data of vital interest to national security.

But the determination to find out about the Lawyers' Group did nothing of the kind, revealing only trivial information about a small group of lawyers, most of whom may have had influence within their own families but would almost certainly have been largely unknown elsewhere. An example of the fruits of this surveillance which was deemed worthy of retention and now released is the report of a meeting on 1 April 1954, at which David Phillips, Maurice Tarlo, Sigmund Seifert, Ralph Milner, David Turner-Samuels, and Jack Gaster were 'believed present' to elect a new management committee.[51] The latter consisted of David Turner-Samuels, Frank Loeffler, Bill Sedley, David Phillips, and John Hostettler, with Turner-Samuels and Ralph Milner appointed as delegates of the Group to the British Communist Party Congress. According to the transcript, David Phillips would replace Jack Gaster on the Management Committee, with 'a special contribution to make ih his work on the industrial side', those present accepting that

[50] TNA, KV 2/2931 (LASCAR, 16 May 1955). 'Ph' stands for phonetic. Around this time the code name for an SF source changed from 'North' to 'Lascar'.

[51] TNA, KV 2/2931 (NORTH, 1 April 1954), and TNA, KV 2/2931 (Note by Miss Russell F1A, 21 April 1954).

Phillips, as a younger man, would provide a contrast to the 'old die hards' who had dominated the group for so long.

Apart from routine meetings of this kind, the surveillance served only to expose internal squabbles and bickering, particularly in relation to the Haldane Society of Socialist Lawyers, of which members of the CPLG were all formally members. At best, the surveillance confirmed (if this were necessary, even assuming it was relevant) that Haldane was Communist penetrated, surveillance allowing MI5 to determine the extent of the influence (though, again, for what purpose?). That said, the surveillance did enable MI5 to learn about splits within the Lawyers' Group in relation to Hungary in 1956, revealing also that while the Haldane Society might have been Communist penetrated, it was by no means Communist dominated. The surveillance revealed further that CPGB members did not act in a co-ordinated way on major issues, and indeed had consciously refrained from making the Haldane Society 'Party minded'.[52]

This was clear in relation to Hungary, where any idea that there could be a common position was a forlorn hope, with unity within the Group absent at a special meeting of the Haldane Society to consider the Soviet action. Listening devices installed at Communist Party HQ picked up a meeting 'on a small matter concerning the Haldane Society' between Ralph Milner (one of the Lawyers' Group) and George Matthews (Assistant General Secretary of the Party).[53] Matthews appears to have been surprisingly ill-informed about the Group, with Milner explaining that he was part of a Party faction on the Haldane executive committee.[54] According to Milner, this faction had 'disintegrated', and he was now the only committee member toeing the Party line. Milner claimed that he could not really talk to anyone else about it, but any hope that Matthews might be able to help (which seems to have been the point of the meeting) was ill-founded.[55]

3. Learning too Much

It is one thing to engage in routine monitoring of this kind, even if it is of questionable legitimacy. But it is clear that was not the only purpose of the surveillance, as is made apparent by correspondence in the file of Kenelm Digby, sometime legal

52 TNA, KV 2/2933 (LASCAR, 16 January 1957).

53 ibid.

54 Along with Loeffler and Turner-Samuels.

55 Milner reported to Matthews that the Hungarians had agreed to see a Haldane deputation (including Shields, Pain, and himself representing the minority position). Milner suggested to Matthews that he approach the Hungarians to let them know the views of the Haldane in advance of any visit (for reasons unknown)—although Milner acknowledged that if such an approach became known to the Haldane, he would 'be in trouble'. Matthews was unenthusiastic about making an intervention: he said he would 'make some enquiries and consider the matter further . . . normally his advice would be, as it would be to a trade union member, that Milner would have to abide by the majority': TNA, KV 2/2933 (LASCAR, 16 January 1957).

adviser to the NCCL, who we encountered in Chapter 4. There, it will be recalled, we find Roger Hollis addressing the CPLG in correspondence with a Colonial Office official in Borneo, where Digby had accepted an appointment. According to Hollis, the Group was one MI5 viewed with 'considerable suspicion', because of its secrecy and because it included 'men of education and intellectual power'. The correspondence may have satisfied more than curiosity, however, Hollis also indicating an interest in the legal and tactical advice the Group provided to the Party.[56] This is altogether different from the routine surveillance referred to above, suggesting that the surveillance also had a much more instrumental purpose, in terms of finding out legal advice and legal tactics. This immediately reinforces Rule of Law concerns, not just because the surveillance appeared to be conducted without mandate authority, but also because it violated a sacred private space, namely the relationship between the lawyer and his or her client.

We find file entries on more than one occasion reporting on legal strategies and tactics while cases were live and prosecutions were being conducted. It is true that it is difficult to find evidence of phone taps of law firms or of barristers' chambers, and also difficult to find evidence of letters addressed to either being tampered with. But as we shall see, there is a clear evidence of mail checks and telechecks on lawyers' home addresses, while it is impossible to say whether such interference with work addresses is concealed by redaction and weeding, or whether it was genuinely exceptional. But quite apart from such brazen activity, there is evidence of equally brazen activity by those who had infiltrated the Group, and were supplied with information about cases involving Communist Party members which was innocently provided in the course of conversation. Again, it is difficult to find evidence of this, but an entry on Dudley Collard's file suggests that sensitive strategic information was actively sought and inadvertently provided, though it is known how the information was then used.

Dudley Collard first came to the attention of MI5 in 1932. A brief minute on his file records that he was 'strongly sympathetic' to the Party, but notes that 'for some reason as yet unknown he cannot do anything openly'.[57] He visited Leningrad in 1933, and that same year he was recorded as being a member of the Legal Defence Committee of the ILP. By 1934, MI5 was aware of his association with the NCCL and the Haldane Society. Together with Pritt, Collard appeared for Percy Glading and fellow defendants in the 1938 official secrets trial, which is discussed in Chapter 4 above, and which exposed a spy ring at Woolwich Arsenal, led by a leading Communist Party member. It also unwittingly revealed the extent to which the Communist Party had been infiltrated at the highest level by MI5 agent Olga Gray (referred to as Miss X in the Glading trial). During the trial in 1938, Collard met Hancock-Nunn (MI5's M/7), the purpose of which was to pump Collard for

[56] TNA, KV 2/3809 (4 July 1940).
[57] TNA, KV 2/2159 (10 November 1932).

information.[58] Collard explained that both he and Pritt had been trying to drive a bargain with the prosecution and that all but one of the accused would plead guilty.[59]

In the following week, the pair met again, this time for lunch, Collard reported as being 'very affable' and 'quite prepared' to discuss the Glading case.[60] The following were said to be the principal points to have arisen in the discussion:

1 Collard informed M/7 of Miss X's name and reminded him that she had frequently taken down the Minutes of *Daily Worker* staff meetings and that therefore his (M/7's) name was probably in the hands of the Intelligence Department.
2 The defence had made the closest enquiries possible regarding Miss X's morals, but all the results were in her favour.
3 He and Pritt are very surprised that the Intelligence Service would throw over Miss X for the sake of prosecuting an individual who is not such a big cog in the machine as apparently the authorities think.
4 Collard was greatly impressed with the fact that Miss X had been able to remain for six years amongst people with political opinions different from her own.
5 [Collard] says that the Party are exceedingly thankful that the Moscow aspect was kept fairly dark.
6 [Collard] made no secret of the fact that Glading was literally acting on behalf of Russia, and he indicated that he quite approved of such activities.
7 While picking holes in the efficiency of the Intelligence Service, Collard said that when the two Brandes [the Russian NKVD husband and wife combo] were leaving Victoria station for the continent they actually had on them the complete plans of the 14" gun, a portion of which was mentioned in the case (sic). He said: 'It appears they actually did this under the nose of two intelligence agents'.[61]

A few weeks after his 1938 conversations with agent M/7, a Special Branch report revealed that Collard was a member of the Party's 'secret' legal group. Post war, conversations picked up by the 'King Street bugs', and his contacts with Gladys Draper (who collected subscriptions from covert members of the Party) indicated that, despite his overt support for the Soviet Union, the Eastern bloc, and for domestic Communism, Collard continued to prefer to keep his links with the Party covert.[62]

58 TNA, KV 2/2159 (11 and 16 March 1938). The report on the earlier meeting was dated 14 March, and the report of the later meeting undated, but very likely written on same day.
59 ibid., 11 March 1938.
60 ibid., 16 March 1938.
61 ibid.
62 There is an odd letter on Collard's file in which he wrote to MI5 saying that he was 'anxious to be doing something of rather more service to the country than merely practising at the Bar'. He said he was

4. Back to Sources

Prior to November 1956, MI5 appears to have had more information on the Lawyers' Group than it had on the Haldane Society. It appears that the Service had been able to infiltrate the CPLG more effectively than the Haldane Society, despite the fact that the former was secret, while the latter operated in plain sight. Nevertheless, it is clear that MI5 had sources operating within Haldane, an entry in Francis Loeffler's Security Service file referring to a recent meeting of the Haldane Society AGM in 1956. In the form of an extract from a Special Branch report, the information is 'from a source believed to be fairly reliable'.[63] Details of the 1956 AGM of the CPGB Lawyers' Group, on the other hand, were obtained from an MI5 source considered 'reliable and well placed'.[64] The latter report of the Lawyers' Group indicated that Jack Gaster was back, this time as Chairman, Hostettler remained as Secretary, and David Phillips remained Treasurer. There was also a new man on the committee, whose name was duly recorded in the MI5 source report.[65]

Like other figures in the CP Lawyers' Group, the new man was also a member of the Haldane Society, and as such the files suggest he unwittingly provided information about the latter. A source report dated 21 November 1956 refers to what is now described as 'a regular source in touch with the Haldane Society', the file entry subtitled: 'The Haldane Society meeting on Friday 23 November 1956', reporting the comments of the new man on the CPLG committee about a split on the Haldane Executive.[66] The new man in question is said to have 'spok[en] to a friend who is a member of the Haldane Society about the Society's special meeting to be held on Friday 23rd November'. This entry is notable for a number of reasons, not least for the fact that the identity of the person who spoke to the MI5 undercover agent was not redacted (though, unsurprisingly, the MI5 agent is not named), despite the fact that the individual was still alive at the time of the release. The individual providing the information about the Haldane Society, it seems, had been betrayed by a friend, and had *not* betrayed his colleagues.

As we will see, the betrayal of friendships was not the only unscrupulous behaviour employed by MI5 in relation to the Lawyers' Group. The absence of scruples was clearly on display in relation to the use of HOW's for the interception

due to register for military service and wondered whether he should express a preference for military work: TNA, KV 2/2159 (Collard to Hinchley Cooke, 3 July 1940). MI5 was unable to help: TNA, KV 2/2159 (Hinchley Cooke to Collard, 16 July 1940), and Collard joined the navy as an Ordinary Seaman.

[63] TNA, KV 2/2932 (Extract from Special Branch Report, 29 October 1956). As they were already reading Loeffler's post, the date of the Haldane AGM seems unlikely to have been much of a discovery.

[64] TNA, KV 2/2932. What remains of this heavily redacted F4/KAPH Source Report is dated 15 November 1956.

[65] ibid.

[66] TNA, KV 2/2932 (F4/AGS Source Report, Received 21 November 1956).

of mail. It appears that in 1949, there was a HOW in force in relation to Betty Wallace, Dudley Collard's wife (or partner—their marital status being unclear), who was an active member of the friendship societies.[67] In any event, it was of course a criminal offence to open mail, unless in accordance with the duty of the official in question or unless with the authority of a HOW.[68] It appears that this was a part of the criminal law that was observed in the breach, with a nicely worded note from Harlow of the GPO's Special Investigation Unit to H. M. Gee of MI5 to tell him that he was sending a letter addressed to Collard that 'may be of interest'. Harlow continues:

> Your HOW (No 10665) is on Mrs Elizabeth Wallace only, so if you wish to see any further letters of Dudley Collard's it will be necessary to obtain a new HOW either on him personally, or an Any Name.[69]

This, of course, was highly irregular. But it also raises lots of unanswered questions. How did Harlow happen to stumble across a letter to Dudley Collard that contained information that might be of interest to MI5? Was this letter to Collard rather than Wallace opened by mistake? If so, how many other mistakes were made, and by what legal authority did Harlow pass the letter to Gee? If it was not a mistake, how many other letters to Collard or anyone else were improperly opened, photographed, and retained in this way? That is to say, how often did the Investigations Unit open letters addressed to third parties residing at a location where a HOW was in place for a named resident?[70] As it happens, in this case the intercepted mail contained a sealed letter to Gerhart Eisler (a prominent German Communist) from an indecipherable correspondent who did not know the latter's address, and asked Collard to pass it on. But that was no justification for MI5 to open Collard's mail at the time the packet was opened.[71]

[67] TNA, KV 2/2160. A note dated 19 June 1950 records that Wallace was the editor of the *Russia Today Newsletter* and that 'It is not known whether [Collard] and Betty Wallace are in fact married, but they are living together at 9 Landsdowne Crescent, W11 and have a baby.'

[68] See p. 103.

[69] TNA, KV 2/2160 (Harlow to Gee, 30 May 1949).

[70] Recall the provisions of the Post Office Act 1908, by which it was a criminal offence for a Post Office employee 'contrary to his duty' to open, or wilfully detain or delay a postal packet, unless one of a number of defences applied, as where the employee in question acted 'in obedience to an express warrant in writing under the hand of a Secretary of State' (s. 56(1)).

[71] *Ghani v Jones* [1970] 1 QB 693. The Special Investigation Unit's relaxed and informal approach is reflected in the Loeffler files. Although the 1955 HOW only covered mail sent to Francis Loeffler, Sabine Loeffler's mail on one occasion (a letter sent by Sabine to Germany) was opened by the GPO. Miss Money was told that 'Strictly it should not have been intercepted. In view of the fact that it appears to have emanated from Loeffler, on whom there is a warrant, I am sending the copy to you personally.' The Loeffler HOW did not cover mail emanating from either Frank or Sabine (TNA, KV 2/2933 (E. R. Fisher of the Special Section, Investigation Branch, GPO to Money, 8 June 1957)).

IV. The Haldane Society of Socialist Lawyers

The other lawyers' organization singled out for surveillance was the Haldane Society of Socialist Lawyers, one of a number of bodies on the Left that had been attacked by a government front organization.[72] Formed in 1929, the Society was named after Lord Haldane, who had been Lord Chancellor in the first Labour government.[73] As a Labour Party affiliate, the Haldane Society was caught up in the post-war Labour government's proscription of Communists,[74] its membership including socialists of different stripes. An attempt in 1949 by the Labour faction to purge anyone 'who is a member of a political party other than the Labour Party or of any body membership of which renders him [sic.] ineligible for membership of the Labour Party' was defeated, leading to a breakaway and the creation of what has been the largely invisible and ineffective Society of Labour Lawyers. The Haldane Society's multi-volume organizational file (OF) has never been released (and nor has the similarly substantial special file (SF) relating to the Lawyers' Group).[75]

1. The Society Splits

It is clear that Haldane—with its blue-ribboned Labour Party members—was subject to surveillance long before the Society split in the late 1940s, MI5 agent M/7 having been put up for membership by Dudley Collard, who was unaware that his candidate was an MI5 informer. Collard was close to the Communist Party, and as we have seen represented Party members in high-profile cases. The Society was also the subject of Special Branch attention, Special Branch working closely with the Home Office. Indeed, a Home Office file compiled by F3 Division, a relatively small division of the Whitehall Police Department which worked closely with Special Branch, makes clear that Special Branch submitted regular monthly reports about the Haldane Society to the Home Office—as well as an interim report on ballots and meetings.[76] Unfortunately, the latter have been removed from the file, and all that remains in the file are a report from 'The Foreign Office', a handful of circulars, minutes of meetings, and ephemera.

Nevertheless, the sometimes scarcely legible long-hand minute sheet entries remain in the Home Office file, and they tell us much about the contents of the

[72] IRIS, *The Communist Solar System* (London, 1957), pp. 61–2.

[73] For a very good account of the origins and activities of the Society, see N. Blake and H. Rajak, *Wigs and Workers: A History of the Haldane Society of Socialist Lawyers* (London, 1980).

[74] See J. Mahoney, 'Civil Liberties in Britain during the Cold War' (1989) 33 *American Journal of Legal History* 53.

[75] We rely here on extracts on deposit in a few personal files that have been released.

[76] TNA, HO 45/25523.

missing Special Branch reports. During 1949 the interest of the political police lay primarily in the battle fought between the Communist Party and the Labour Party factions of the Society. The 'Foreign Office Report' is the first item in the file, which appears to date from 22 December 1948. It gives a brief account of the Society's aims and membership, and lists the principal officers of the Society—an interesting mix:

President: the Rt Hon Sir Stafford Cripps, KC, MP
Vice-President: the Rt Hon Sir Frank Soskice, KC, MP
Vice-President: Mr D. N. Pritt, KC, MP
Chairman: Mr Stephen Murray
Hon. Secretary: Mr John Elton
Hon. Treasurer: Mr Edgar Duchin

F3 acknowledged in the minute sheet that 'We have long known that communists and fellow travellers have secured a foothold in the executive, and as is normally the case, have been more vigorous than fellow members', concluding that the Foreign Office Report confirmed 'that concern about the influence of the CP in the Society is widespread'. However, it was not known whether any of the Foreign Office suggestions to rein in the Communists had been implemented, with nothing having come to public notice. Extraordinarily, the F3 commentary indicates that F3 was uncertain of the provenance of the Foreign Office document, which appears to have fallen into the lap of Special Branch in the course of their work, the latter handing it over to the Home Office. It seems likely to have been the work of the IRD, the Foreign Office's shadowy counter-propaganda outfit in which Christopher Mayhew was prominent, F3 believing it to have been written by either the Foreign Office or the PLP, 'probably the former'.[77]

The first of the Special Branch reports in the file was received on 11 March 1949. The minute sheet note considered the manoeuvrings of the Labour Party loyalists, and concluded that it 'remains to be seen whether the "purgers" return to the charge: so far the whole episode seems very schoolboy-ish'.[78] A Haldane document, dated 'February 1949' and headed 'IMPORTANT AND PRIVATE', recording the motions tabled by both sides, remains in the file. It appears that Pritt led the Communist elements of the Society against the attempts of Labour Party members to change the constitution to permit the exclusion of the left-wingers. At the end of March 1949, the rule change was put to a postal ballot of all the members, the members voting to defeat the motion. Following the subsequent departure of the Labour Party members led by Gerald Gardiner (later to be Lord Chancellor in the Wilson government), the Haldane Society disaffiliated from the Labour Party.

[77] TNA, HO 45/25523. The document is undated, but the minute sheet suggests that the report was issued on 22 December 1948.
[78] ibid.

2. Korea—an Informer Unmasked

As might be expected from an organization whose office-holders included the Chancellor of the Exchequer (Cripps) and the Solicitor General (Soskice), the split attracted some press attention,[79] and was said by the Home Office to have caused 'uproar'.[80] One effect of the split was that the Society lost the Labour Party members on its executive to the Society of Labour Lawyers, so that the remaining members of the Committee were either Communists or suspected Communists. It seems clear, however, that at least initially the great bulk of the 520 members did not defect to the Labour Party-affiliated Society of Labour Lawyers, and that not all the members who remained were associated with the Communist Party.[81] It is certainly not the case, as claimed by IRIS, effectively that the surviving Haldane Society was 'little more than a Communist rump'.[82]

The Society nevertheless continued to court controversy, partly as a result of its affiliation to the IADL and the activities of prominent members such as Jack Gaster, to which we have referred in Part II above.[83] IRIS drew attention in particular to the IADL commission's allegations (in which Gaster participated), as well as Gaster's visit to prisoners of war in North Korea,[84] pointing out that Haldane had 'never publicly accounted for the extraordinary part it played', in the 'now discredited' germ warfare campaign.[85] It is not clear for what Haldane was to 'publicly account', though it did provide Gaster with a platform for his views on Korea. Reinforcing the view that the Society was not the exclusive preserve of the Communist Party, these latter activities were to cause some offence, and led to complaints to the police by a disgruntled member of the Society, whose identity unusually has not been redacted.

File LO 02/227 contains correspondence between the Tory backbencher Cyril Black and the Attorney General (Major Sir Reginald Manningham-Buller) in 1955.[86] Here we find the Member of Parliament for Wimbledon writing to the Attorney about a constituent who would prefer 'if possible not to have his identity revealed'.[87] The constituent in question, said to be 'a strong anti-Communist', had attended a meeting of the Haldane Society at which Jack Gaster is alleged to have made a speech of 'treasonable character' about the Korean conflict. The matter was taken sufficiently seriously to involve the DPP (Sir Theobald Mathew), who

[79] *Evening Standard*, 8, 9 December 1948.
[80] TNA, HO 45/25523 (Minute sheet entry by Miss H. E. Harting of F3, dated 18 May 1949).
[81] ibid.
[82] IRIS (n 72), p. 61.
[83] See pp. 175–7 above.
[84] On which see pp. 176–7 above.
[85] IRIS (n 72), p. 62.
[86] TNA, LO 02/227. This file has the title 'Subversion Treason—Sedition. Jack Gaster—Remarks at Meeting of Haldane Society 1955'.
[87] ibid. (Black to AG, 11 March 1955). On the significance of the 'outing' of Lindner by MI5, see K. D. Ewing, J. Mahoney, and A. Moretta, 'Tinker, Tailor, Lawyer, Spy?' (2015) 69 *Socialist Lawyer* 18.

advised that it would be very difficult to establish that anything said at a Haldane Society meeting was treasonable, but suggesting also that it would do no harm to interview the informant 'since he is apparently prepared to supply information on request'.[88] It is unclear whether this suggestion was followed.

Unusually, however, the brief exchange of correspondence between Black, Manningham-Buller, Mathew, and officials revealed the identity of the informant, the MI5 censor apparently not consulted when this file was opened in December 2007. On 22 March 1955, Black wrote to Manningham-Buller in the following terms:

> I have been in communication with my constituent who has authorized me to disclose his name. He is Mr A. F. H. Lindner, Solicitor, practising at 17, Soho Square, W1, whose private address is 2, Ridgeway Gardens, Wimbledon, SW 19.
>
> Mr Lindner tells me that he has not retained his notes that he took of various statements made at meetings of the Haldane Society which he attended, but, following each meeting, he sent a full report to the Special Branch as to the statements made which he regarded as being of a treasonable character. You can presumably obtain access to these reports sent by Mr Lindner to the Special Branch. Mr Lindner would be available for interview if desired.[89]

We know nothing about Mr Lindner, but note that an A. F. H. Lindner had been an unsuccessful Labour candidate at the 1945 general election. We do not know at this stage whether they are the same person. We have no idea whether Mr Lindner provided other information, or who were the other 'sources'.

3. Hungary—Internal Controversy

By the mid-1950s, the Haldane Society was deeply penetrated, with sources on the inside supplying information to MI5 officers. A glimpse of the nature of the relationship between officer and informer is afforded by an extract from an F4/AS source report in the Lawson file.[90] A 'flyer' for Haldane meetings in October and November had been part of the latter report. The officer had added 'Please indicate whether you have a particular interest in any of these meetings, so that I may brief source to go.' The subsequent report on the talk Lawson gave at the meeting was a Special Branch report written by one 'CT'.[91] An extract in the same file from a report by F4/ARTS (A. R. T. Stewart) provides an example of the kind of

[88] TNA, LO 02/227 (Alastair Macdonald, Law Officer's Department to DDP, 15 March 1955).
[89] TNA, LO 02/227 (Black to Attorney General, 22 March 1955).
[90] TNA, KV 2/3593 (3 October 1956).
[91] TNA, KV 2/3593 (Special Branch Report, 25 October 1955).

second-hand trivia that the Service considered worthy of a file entry, though also the extent of the infiltration: it was reported that Lawson had entertained house guests on 1 December 1955 by playing a recording of the Reichstag fire trial in 1933. Reassuringly, the 'Source is reliable and sub-source is well placed'.

MI5 was thus well placed in 1956 to discover how developments in Hungary affected the Society, a matter of extraordinary concern to the Service. The work of MI5's snitches is retained for posterity in the file of Francis Loeffler, and elsewhere. A special meeting convened on 23 November 1956 was particularly significant, having been called to condemn the use of Soviet armed forces in Hungary, and to demand their early withdrawal. MI5 was fully informed about this meeting *before* and *after* the event, though quite why this should be anyone's business but the Society's is far from clear. Nevertheless, as we have seen earlier, it is clear that an MI5 informant had befriended a well-placed member of the Haldane Society, who was also on the CPLG committee. The informant duly reported that 'there were three factions in the Executive Committee of the Haldane Society, as shown at its meeting at the end of the previous week'. It was at that meeting that '"Paine" [we assume Peter Pain] had put up the resolution which was to be the subject of the special meeting, "hammering it out as he went along"'.[92]

The same source was in fact able to provide very detailed information about the three factions:

1 The resolution as it stands is supported by Shields, Elton, Witty and Paine. Shields in particular is said to be severely shaken by events in Hungary, and is particularly distressed by their implications for the future of the International Association of Democratic Lawyers.

2. The second group favours the resolution as it is, with the omission of Israel as an aggressor. This group consists of Smith, Loeffler, and Marder. The third group, which includes Milner and Gaster, considers that there is no parallel between the British action in Suez and the entry of the Russians into Hungary at the request of the lawful Hungarian Government.

3 .... Turner-Samuels favours the resolution and thought that Collard probably did. He considers that the resolution will be carried and the society split as a result.

4. Pritt's line, which he gave to a young acquaintance who is a member of the Haldane Society on Monday 19th November, is that the Society is acting rashly and they should wait until they have facts on Hungary.

5. On the morning of 21st November, Elton was asked by a friend who is a member of the Haldane Society, what he thought about it and why the resolution had been pushed forward when it would almost certainly split the

[92] TNA, KV 2/2932 (F4/AGS Source Report by N. A. H., Received 21 November 1956). As we have seen, the Haldane Society had an MI5 file: OF 14/23. This report was filed in Volume 10!

Society. He said that he agreed with this view; he thought the resolution was a mistake, but he expressed concern that the Soviet Union should have acted in the way it did in Hungary. He said 'In six months time everybody will have forgotten the British action in Suez, because this is the sort of thing the world expects from the British, but that the Soviet Union should behave in this way is a terrible thing and will not be forgotten quickly'.

6. . . . Gaster and Milner might not turn up, or if they did, they would suggest caution in the interests of the proverbial cool heads and unity.[93]

The controversial motion was carried.[94] It was followed by a meeting of the CPLG on 13 December 1956, the report of which tells us that the latter Group had convened before the Haldane meeting held on 23 November in order to decide tactics. They elected to vote as conscience dictated, concerned that to have voted *en bloc* against the motion would have split and possibly led to the end of the Haldane Society. In the end, the CPLG group apparently divided fifty/fifty on the Haldane motion. But despite the 'free vote', there was nevertheless grave disquiet at the CPLG's 13 December meeting. Apparently incandescent, Ralph Milner complained that the 'rebels' (including Loeffler) had breached Party rules. Not only that: the disunity had 'greatly weakened the Party's position in the Haldane Society'.[95] This information was supplied by a source described as 'reliable and well placed',[96] the informer likely to have been one of the twenty-four members of the Group present at the meeting.[97] The informant noted that Gaster was absent and that Turner-Samuels took the chair. Their informant told MI5 that he did not know why the Chairman was absent, suggesting that the informant had been specifically briefed to report on Gaster.

4. The Surveillance Continues

If the Haldane Society was at one time Communist dominated, post 23 November 1956 that could no longer be said to be the case. The surveillance nevertheless

93 TNA, KV 2/2932 (F4/AGS Source Report by NAH, Received 21 November 1956).

94 The motion 'firstly condemned British action in Egypt as being contrary to the principles of justice and specifically contrary to the United Nations Charter, and secondly condemned Soviet action in Hungary on the same grounds'. The motion was amended to drop the reference to the UN Charter, but the criticism of the USSR stood, and the motion was passed: TNA, KV 2/2933 (F4/KAPH Source Report on LG meeting, 13 December 1956).

95 As we have seen, Milner took his concerns to King Street, where he met a dusty response (p. 181).

96 TNA, KV 2/2933 (F4/KAPH Source Report on LG meeting, 13 December 1956).

97 The reference indicates that this source was run by an F4 officer with the initials KAPH. The report appears to have been edited for Loeffler's file. It moves on from section 1, recording Gaster as Chairman and an attendance of roughly twenty-four to section 4(d) on Milner's letter. It records only Loeffler's vote on the 23rd. Presumably other versions of the report in the files of other members record the way they voted at that meeting.

continued, and it seems that there was a regular and continuous check on Haldane Society correspondence, with copies of intercepted letters turning up in the files of prominent members. One notable extract in the file of Neil Lawson (copied there only because Lawson was Vice-President) indicates that it was from an intercepted letter from the Chairman of the Haldane Society, 2 Crown Office Row, Temple, London EC4 to the Chairman of the Preparatory Commission of a World Youth event in Moscow.[98] The purpose of the letter was to introduce John Lebor, 'a valued member of the Haldane Society', well able 'to convey to you the feelings of British lawyers of progressive views about recent events, particularly the tragic events in Hungary'.[99]

It also appears that informers had been working on the inside on a range of other matters, with a 'reliable source' informing Special Branch that Stanley Moore was responsible for a telegram expressing concern about the persecution of defence lawyers in Greece on behalf of some members of the Society.[100] Returning to Neil Lawson, one entry in his personal file from 1956 is his name on the membership list of the Haldane Society, confirming that by virtue of a mail intercept on Francis Loeffler, MI5 had obtained the list of all the members of the Society as at 30 June 1954.[101] An intelligence report from about the same time (November 1957) revealed that an MI5 officer had recently enjoyed lunch with a Haldane source. This 'regular source' appears to have been a young lawyer 'in touch with the Haldane Society, and its members'.[102] The identity of this source is unknown, MI5 succeeding on this occasion to protect his or her anonymity. But whoever he or she was, the source had met Lawson for coffee and a chat.

It appears that much of the chatting related to Malaya and colonial problems, a matter of great interest to the Security Service which, at the time, was concerned that Lawson had been instructed by the Malay rulers to advise on independence. Because of his background, MI5 suspected that Lawson was a Chinese plant to subvert the negotiations. The truth was much more benign: after *intense* surveillance, it was realized that Lawson—one-time Communist Party member and donor—had been at university with one of the rulers, by whom he was known personally. It also appears, however, that Lawson did 'not rise at all' to the source's impertinent interrogation about the Malay question, even when the source 'threw in the odd reference' to John Elton and John Platts-Mills and the Haldane Society. The only

[98] We are unaware of any connection between this address today and the Haldane Society, or indeed with Security Service surveillance!

[99] TNA, KV 2/3593 (Letter dated 5 July 1957).

[100] TNA, KV 2/1559 (Extract from Special Branch Report, Extracted 6 December 1954). This is extracted from Volume 6 of the Haldane Society's unreleased file.

[101] TNA, KV 2/3593 (Extract from Intercept List sent to Francis Loeffler, Extracted 21 March 1956).

[102] TNA, KV 2/3594 (Report, 13 November 1957). It is not clear if it is this source or another 'reliable source' who provided information about the proceedings of the AGM held on 6 November 1957: see TNA, KV 2/3594 (Extract from Special Branch Report 're Annual General Meeting of the Haldane Society (Communist dominated Lawyers' Society) held 6 November 1957').

concession the source was able to extract was an agreement that Lawson would assist him with colonial cases that sometimes came his way, whereupon they parted 'on good terms'.[103] The report concludes:

> Source has been instructed to follow up this lead as best he can to get closer to Lawson, with the aim of finding out the latter's opinions on the Haldane Society activities and policy, and on Malayan problems.[104]

It is difficult for any rational person to anticipate the national security value of much of the foregoing information relating to Haldane and its members. Indeed, a little insight into the futility of the surveillance was provided when John Bowden visited Greece in the 1960s on behalf of the Society, to investigate alleged human rights violations. The Foreign Office advice to the Embassy in Athens was that Haldane was to be 'refuse[d] any assistance beyond routine courtesies'.[105] The other advice from the Foreign Office was that while Haldane remained 'under strong Communist influence',[106] John Bowden (who had been 'on the Society's executive since about 1958') was not 'known as a Communist'.[107] On the contrary, John Bowden, PF 719,284, was likely to have taken this as an insult, having previously been monitored on the occasion of a visit to Warsaw as a guest of the Polish Lawyers' Association in 1958.[108] Indeed, he was known to be a member of CPLG, as confirmed by the *Morning Star* after his death.[109]

V. D. N. Pritt KC and the Rule of Law

As we have seen, Pritt's surveillance started before the Second World War and continued for sometime thereafter. On the evidence available to us, Pritt was never a member of the Communist Party, though he was very close to the Party and its leadership, and under some pressure from Pollitt to become a member, pressure he appears to have resisted. Yet, he was closely associated with the CPLG, and he regularly visited King Street to meet senior Party officials. In addition to his other work, Pritt was a great activist, associated with many organizations and causes. These included the NCCL, the Haldane Society of Socialist Lawyers, the British Soviet Society, the League for Democracy in Greece, the Student Labour Federation, and

[103] TNA, KV 2/3594 (Report, 13 November 1957).
[104] ibid.
[105] TNA, FCO 95/410 (J. S. Champion to Athens, 6 June 1967). Champion worked in the IRD.
[106] ibid.
[107] ibid.
[108] See TNA, KV 2/3594 (Neil Lawson) (Extract from Summary of World Broadcasts, 29 March 1958). The file also contains a Special Branch Report of Lawson and Bowden's visit to Poland in September 1958.
[109] *Morning Star*, 29 November 2013.

the BPC. But he was also in great demand as a lawyer, appearing in many of the seminal British civil liberties cases, as well as important cases overseas. He was, however, thwarted from appearing before the US Supreme Court in the first big case of the Cold War.[110]

1. The *Dennis* Case

Pritt's proposed appearance before the US Supreme Court caused almost as much anxiety in London and Washington as did Krivitsky's claims that Pritt was a Soviet agent.[111] It certainly cemented the latter's reputation as a bold and fearless defender of the Communist cause, while exposing the extent of the illiberal clampdown on the Communist Party in the USA. Formal legal proceedings started in July 1948 when—at the beginning of a presidential campaign Truman was expected to lose—the government sought from a grand jury indictments against eleven members of the national board of the Communist Party of America, including Eugene Dennis, the General Secretary.[112] The proceedings were brought under the Smith Act of 1943, which had been introduced with a view to combating the threat perceived to be posed by that substantial section of the US population of German origin.

Charges brought against the Communists were not for attempting to overthrow the government, but for conspiring to advocate and teach the duty to overthrow the government. The indictment charged the petitioners with:

> willfully and knowingly conspiring (1) to organize as the Communist Party of the United States of America a society, group and assembly of persons who teach and advocate the overthrow and destruction of the Government of the United States by force and violence, and (2) knowingly and willfully to advocate and teach the duty and necessity of overthrowing and destroying the Government of the United States by force and violence.

The indictment also alleged that the Smith Act, section 2 proscribed these acts, and that any conspiracy to take such action was a violation of the same Act, section 3. The trial began after the election in 1948 and lasted for just over nine months, generating in the process some 16,000 pages of evidence.[113]

Perhaps predictably, the defendants were found guilty and jailed for the maximum five years' imprisonment and fined $5,000 each (with the exception of Robert Thompson, who was given a reduced sentence in recognition of his war

[110] *Dennis v US*, 341 US 494 (1951).
[111] On which, see pp. 143, 148, and 176 above.
[112] The case against a twelfth member was discontinued for reasons of ill health.
[113] See M. R. Belknap, *Cold War Political Justice: The Smith Act, The Communist Party and American Civil Liberties* (Westport, CT, 1977).

service). Along the way, five lawyers who represented the defendants were convicted of contempt of court and were also imprisoned.[114] The guilty verdict was upheld by the Court of Appeals, which took the view that:

> the leaders of the Communist Party in this country, were unwilling to work within our framework of democracy, but intended to initiate a violent revolution whenever the propitious occasion appeared. Petitioners dispute the meaning to be drawn from the evidence, contending that the Marxist-Leninist doctrine they advocated taught that force and violence to achieve a Communist form of government in an existing democratic state would be necessary only because the ruling classes of that state would never permit the transformation to be accomplished peacefully, but would use force and violence to defeat any peaceful political and economic gain the Communists could achieve.[115]

Despite the charges against them, there was no allegation that the defendants had actually tried to overthrow the government, or even that they had made incendiary speeches that might have resulted in the overthrow of the government. The defendants each appealed to the Supreme Court, but such was the temper of the time that before the appeal was heard on 4 December 1950, Congress passed the Internal Security Act of 1950, the most important provisions of which were (i) the requirement that Communist and Communist front organizations register with the government; (ii) the establishment of the Subversive Activities Control Board to determine whether an organization was 'Communist'; and (iii) the denial of passports to members of any organization required to register under the Act. The Act also rendered members of registered organizations ineligible for government employment, though Communists, former Communists, and Communist sympathizers had already been purged from these positions.[116]

2. The Role of Donald Maclean

The US proceedings are not without British interest, following the refusal of US attorneys to argue the case before the Supreme Court on behalf of the appellants.

[114] The judge found that the defence had conspired to undermine the administration of justice by challenging the selection of the jury, adducing as evidence details of one of the defendant's work for the US civil rights movement, and calling witnesses to explain the principles of Marxism–Leninism. See D. N. Pritt, *Autobiography of DN Pritt, Part Three, The Defence Accuses* (London, 1966), p. 15.

[115] That the constitution of the American Communist Party expressly prohibited the use of violence and that many of the defendants were on record as stating that they sought change only by persuasion and the ballot box, counted for nothing.

[116] The Internal Security Act of 1950 was followed by the Communist Control Act of 1954, which denied to the Communist Party or any of its successors all the rights, privileges, or immunities of legal entities created by the laws by the United States, and made any member of the Party subject to the provisions of the Internal Security Act of 1950.

Seventy US attorneys had rebuffed the appellants, with no American lawyer with sufficient experience being willing to risk freedom and livelihood by representing them. The *New York Times* reported that this was 'in spite of the asserted fact that some of the American counsel considered the conviction illegal'.[117] In the face of this shocking collective cowardice of the US legal profession, an approach was made to Pritt to appear in the appeal. Whether Pritt's involvement would make any difference is of course another matter, Pritt having observed with some prescience in 1947 that:

> . . . the interpretation of the Constitution by the Supreme Court of the United States illustrated perfectly the natural and inevitable process whereby the Courts of any country protect the interests of its real rulers. Cornelius Vanderbilt had plenty of common sense when he snorted, 'Law! What do I care about law? Hain't I got the power?'[118]

Nevertheless, the prospect of Pritt appearing in the Supreme Court and revealing the realities of freedom in the 'Land of the Free' was of concern to both the US and British governments. The problem for the appellants, however, was that Pritt was scheduled to appear before the Supreme Court of India in the *Telengana* case to plead for another group of Communist defendants, though this group was under sentence of death. On 17 November 1950, Pritt had sent a telegram from London to Elizabeth Gurley Flynn of the Communist Defence Committee in New York. Intercepted by MI5, the telegram advised that:

> . . . Indian Supreme Court definitely offered set hearing either first December or January. Thinking over possibility of delays in obtaining visa and reservation for travel to America am strongly inclined think it better not to try to go to America December but request your Supreme Court postpone case to February. Please cable fully your views and present position on this. Anxious to do both cases if possibility exists.[119]

That same day, the eleven American Communists applied to the Supreme Court for permission for Pritt to lead their appeal.

On the following day (18 November 1950), the matter was first brought the attention of the Foreign Office in a discreet enquiry made by Mr C. E. Steel of the British Embassy in Washington:

> We have heard this very confidentially from the State Department, who asked us whether foreign lawyers were allowed to practise in England, no doubt in

[117] *New York Times*, 18 November 1950.
[118] D. N. Pritt, *Star Spangled Shadow* (London, 1947), p. 12.
[119] TNA, KV 2/1065.

> order to help them make up their minds whether they could refuse to allow a foreigner to defend these Communists here . . . I need not point out to you that it would not do us much good in the public relations field in the present state of public opinion here if these Communists were to be defended by a British lawyer. On the other hand, it is possible that the Americans may find themselves in some difficulty if they refused to allow a foreigner to take part in the proceedings in view of the efforts which I think they and we have made in the past to arrange for foreign lawyers to take part in trials of anti-Communists in satellite countries.[120]

By a remarkable coincidence, the matter was handled in London by Donald Maclean, ex-First Secretary in Washington, now head of the American department at the Foreign Office, having taken over the American desk on 1 November 1950. Shortly to leave London for a life elsewhere,[121] Maclean was presented with the wonderfully ironic opportunity to defend the Rule of Law in the United States by ensuring legal representation for the senior officials of the Communist Party of America.[122] Responding to Steel, Maclean observed sweetly that:

> As Mr. Steel says, it might do us harm in the public relations field if a British lawyer undertook this job. On the other hand, I do not see any ground on which we could hinder a British lawyer from doing so, and I do not think that we should try: I doubt if we can do much more than answer the State Department's question whether foreign lawyers are allowed to practise in England. I shall be grateful for Mr Best's help over this.[123]

A Foreign Office legal adviser, Mr R. S. B. Best, suggested that if Pritt was allowed by the Americans to appear in the *Dennis* case, then:

> The most that might be done would be to explain the position confidentially to the General Council of the Bar and ask that body to consider whether it would be prepared to express an opinion on the professional propriety of a member of the English Bar's accepting the brief in question.[124]

120 TNA, FO 371/81757 (Letter from C. E. Steel of the British Embassy Washington to the FO, 18 November 1950).

121 On which, see Chapter 5 above and Chapter 8 below.

122 After taking up the post, Maclean is alleged to have had a conversation at a dinner party with an old FO friend, Mark Culme-Seymour. Maclean was drunk, and he asked Culme-Seymour, 'What would you do if I told you I was working for Uncle Joe?'. He is said also to have told Culme-Seymour that 'everything he did in the Department was designed to assist Communism': P Knightley, *Philby, The Spy Who Betrayed a Generation* (1968), pp. 219–20.

123 TNA, FO 371/81757 (Note by Maclean, 21 November 1950).

124 TNA, FO 371/81757 (Note by R. S. B. Best, 22 November 1950).

In a handwritten *addendum* to Mr Best's opinion, Sir Eric Beckett (Chief Legal Adviser to the Foreign Office) added the comment that the Attorney General would have to be consulted before anything was done. Beneath this, Maclean scribbled: 'I do not think the political consequences of Mr Pritt's appearing would be so serious as to justify extraordinary measures of this kind.'[125]

3. The Problem is Solved

MI5 subsequently cooperated fully with an enquiry from J. A. Cimperman, the FBI's man at the American Embassy in London, for a brief summary of Pritt's background and activities, 'which would be of interest to the Bureau'. A note had been duly sent by MI5's Graham Mitchell on 20 November 1950—'for the information only of the FBI'—advising the Americans of Pritt's various activities, claiming that he was a 'prominent Communist sympathiser and champion of the Soviet Union'.[126] He was also said to be 'connected with several organisations which whilst nominally independent are controlled or exploited by the British Communist Party': the BPC, the Society for Cultural Studies with the USSR, the British–Soviet Society, the League for Democracy in Greece, the Student Labour Federation, and the British–Romanian Friendship Association.[127]

On the day after the note was sent to the FBI, the *Washington Post* carried an interview with Pritt ('former left-wing member of the House of Commons') who said that he was ready to act if permitted to do so. First he said, the Supreme Court would have to give him permission to appear, and he would have to obtain a visa to enter the United States, and he was unsure whether this would be granted in view of his 'known left wing views'.[128] On 25 November 1950, however, Reuters revealed that the Indian case was to be heard on 4 December—the same day as the Dennis appeal.[129] The US Supreme Court acknowledged Pritt's right of audience on 27 November, but having already set the date for the Dennis appeal, as might be expected, refused to reschedule it. On the following day, Maclean responded formally

[125] TNA, FO 371/81757 (Maclean Addendum to Note by R. S. B. Best, 22 November 1950, 24 November 1950).

[126] The letter was sent on the twentieth, the request sent from Cimperman on the twenty-first. The pair had evidently met or spoken on the phone on the twentieth. See TNA, KV 2/1065 (D. N. Pritt KC). On Mitchell see pp. 67–8 above, and pp. 238, 253–4, and 454 below.

[127] TNA, KV 2/1065 (D. N. Pritt KC). It was noted further that Pritt had made a number of visits in recent years to Eastern Europe, and that most recently he had been in touch with the Soviet Ambassador and other Soviet diplomats and officials in London. As pointed out, the same service had been undertaken for the South African Security Services in response to an inquiry from them relating to Pritt's support for defendants in that jurisdiction in June 1949 (pp. 122 and 148).

[128] *Washington Post*, 21 November 1950. This piece, and the *New York Times* piece were sent to MI5 by the British Embassy in Washington, and are in Pritt's Security Service file TNA, KV 2/1065.

[129] *Reynold's News*, 26 November 1950 (cutting in Pritt's Security Service file TNA, KV 2/1065).

to Steel at the Embassy in Washington (more than a week after the enquiry had been received), to the effect that:

> . . . our view is that her Majesty's Government should not attempt to intervene. We share your concern about the harm that might be done to us in the public relations field if Mr Pritt were to defend these men. But, on the credit side, it strikes us that some Americans, even if only a few, might draw the moral not that 'the British' (Mr. Pritt) are blacklegging but that the apparent inability of eleven convicted men to persuade any leading member of the American Bar to argue their appeal in a case of admitted constitutional importance reflects on the American Bar. There is the further consideration that even if we were willing to try, we have no ready made means of preventing Mr. Pritt from taking this brief and that any attempt to do so would expose us to severe attack from many non-communist quarters in this country.[130]

Marginal notes on the draft of this letter written by Maclean reveal that Eric Beckett was by now only to *consider* passing a copy to the Attorney General, and that 'today's *Times* [28 November] says that the Supreme Court will allow Pritt to plead, but that the case would be heard on Dec[ember] 4, which is thought to be too early for him'.[131] A paragraph was duly tacked on to the end of the letter advising Steel that 'the question may by now be academic'. The matter was at this stage referred to Sir Hartley Shawcross (on 1 December 1950), the unpleasant Labour Attorney General, who welcoming the turn of events, commented in a predictably and typically disrespectful way to the effect that, 'Pritt has found the attractions of the case in India greater than those in Washington, in the result we are saved some embarrassment'.[132] There was, of course, no question of Shawcross or his ilk taking on cases such as that which preoccupied Pritt in India. There was equally no question that Pritt had been presented with a horrible dilemma, or that in the circumstances he responded appropriately in terms of priority and need.

The twelve convicted 'Telengana' Communists were some of the surviving leaders of a 'peasants' revolt' in Hyderabad, where they had helped establish a briefly flourishing rebel state. Under sentence of death, and with no funds, they were fighting merely to have their appeals *heard* by the newly established Indian Supreme Court. The men had been tried and convicted as India gained independence, and their petitions were rejected, despite the very many doubts raised by Pritt about the fairness of the trials in Hyderabad, rejected.[133] Pritt, however, remained

130 TNA FO 37/81757 (Donald Maclean to CE Steel, 28 November 1950).

131 *The Times*, 28 November 1950: 'If Mr Pritt can reach Washington in time—and a postponement was requested because it was understood he could not—he will be the first foreign lawyer ever to appear before the United States Supreme Court.'

132 TNA, FO 371/81757 (Note to Sir Eric Beckett, 4 December 1950).

133 See T. C. Sherman, *State Violence and Punishment in India* (London and New York, 2010), p. 163 et seq.

in India campaigning and lobbying, and the death sentences were eventually commuted to imprisonment. In his understated style, Pritt recalled that: 'When the news reached me, I was on the platform of a meeting at Calcutta, and for a moment I was not able to continue with my work.'[134] In the USA in the meantime, the legal team that had appeared for the Communists in the early stages of the litigation in *Dennis* handled the appeals before the Supreme Court, which divided six:two to dismiss claims that the convictions violated the First Amendment.[135]

4. The Appeal is Dismissed

The majority in *Dennis* held that the Smith Act was perfectly consistent with the First Amendment's guarantee of free speech. According to the Chief Justice, the 'obvious purpose' of the Act was to 'protect existing Government not from change by peaceable, lawful and constitutional means, but from change by violence, revolution and terrorism'.[136] There was no question that it was 'within the power of the Congress to protect the Government of the United States from armed rebellion'. 'Whatever theoretical merit there may be to the argument that there is a "right" to rebellion against dictatorial governments', the Court continued, was 'without force where the existing structure of the government provides for peaceful and orderly change'.[137] The Act being valid, the appellants were properly convicted, on the ground that they:

> intended to overthrow the Government of the United States as speedily as the circumstances would permit. Their conspiracy to organize the Communist Party and to teach and advocate the overthrow of the Government of the United States by force and violence created a 'clear and present danger' of an attempt to overthrow the Government by force and violence. They were properly and constitutionally convicted for violation of the Smith Act.[138]

[134] The story of the Telengana Rebels case is an extraordinary one. See Pritt, *The Defence Accuses* (n 114).

[135] *Dennis v US*, 341 US 494 (1951).

[136] ibid., p. 501.

[137] ibid.

[138] ibid., pp. 516–17. It has been estimated that the Communist Party of America had a membership of 100,000 in 1945, a membership that had likely declined by the time of the indictments in 1948, making it difficult to understand how the Party could have been seen as a clear and present danger to anyone. Nevertheless, the way was now clear for further use of the Smith Act, and the government proceeded accordingly. Prosecutions were brought against so-called second-rank Communist leaders, with additional prosecutions being brought against both leaders and members under the provisions of the Smith Act. By 1957, ninety-six convictions had been secured, in addition to the eleven in the *Dennis* case, of whom twenty-nine served prison terms. Prosecutions under the Smith Act were effectively brought to an end by *Yates v United States*, 341 US 494 (1957), which imposed higher evidentiary standards.

It was perhaps implausible to expect a different outcome, though it now seems bizarre to read from Mr Justice Frankfurter that 'civil liberties draw, at best, only limited strength from legal guarantees' as a justification for deferring to the legislature.[139] As recognized by the dissenting opinions, the whole point of legal guarantees is that they should be used where possible to protect civil liberties, rather than be mute in the face of their attack. But this of course was grist to the mill for Pritt, who wrote subsequently of the majority decision reinforcing the point he had made in earlier writings referred to above, and providing striking illustrations:

> (1) of the way in which the ruling class in any country will break all its most cherished rules and traditions of civil liberty whenever it is—rightly or wrongly—frightened by critics or opponents who seek to exercise the civil liberty to criticise or oppose it;
> (2) of the particular tendency of a ruling class, in such circumstances, to practise the double hypocrisy of boasting of its observance of civil liberties whilst violating them;
> (3) of the powerful influence to which judges even of the greatest eminence are unconsciously subjected by the opinions and fears of the class from which they are drawn.[140]

As is often the case, however, it was the dissenting opinions—by the great liberal justices Black and Douglas—that shed most light on the decision. As pointed out by the former:

> These petitioners were not charged with an attempt to overthrow the Government. They were not charged with overt acts of any kind designed to overthrow the Government. They were not even charged with saying anything or writing anything designed to overthrow the Government. The charge was that they agreed to assemble and to talk and publish certain ideas at a later date: the indictment is that they conspired to organize the Communist Party and to use speech or newspapers and other publications in the future to teach and advocate the forcible overthrow of the Government.[141]

[139] 341 US 494 (1951), p. 555. Mr Justice Douglas in dissent, in contrast, turned this argument on its head (p. 595):

> The First Amendment makes confidence in the common sense of our people and in their maturity of judgment the great postulate of our democracy. Its philosophy is that violence is rarely, if ever, stopped by denying civil liberties to those advocating resort to force. The First Amendment reflects the philosophy of Jefferson.

[140] Pritt, *The Defence Accuses* (n 114), p. 18.

[141] 341 US 495 (1951), p. 579.

In condemning 'a virulent form of prior censorship of speech and press', which the 'First Amendment forbids', Justice Black held that there was no 'clear and present danger' such as would justify the Smith Act, or the prosecutions thereunder.[142] Alluding to the politics of the prosecution, Black concluded with the forlorn observation that:

> Public opinion being what it now is, few will protest the conviction of these Communist petitioners. There is hope, however, that, in calmer times, when present pressures, passions and fears subside, this or some later Court will restore the First Amendment liberties to the high preferred place where they belong in a free society.[143]

If the politics of the prosecution were not lost on Black, they were certainly not lost on Pritt, who with years of experience at the Bar in England and Wales could reflect with authority on 'judges, who are the product of their environment—generally a rather narrow "establishment" one', and who 'always tend, often unconsciously, to find ways of so deciding cases as to support government policy and decisions, and to save governments embarrassment'.[144] So wrote the defeated combatant of *Elias v Passmore* and *Liversidge v Anderson*,[145] observing also that 'most laymen take this as a matter of course'.[146] It will probably never be known why Pritt was denied his opportunity to appear before the US Supreme Court. One explanation is that bureaucratic indifference got in the way of the interests of justice, both in determining the date of the trial and the refusal to change it. That would be marginally better than the alternative explanation, that the Court—informed by the FBI or not—was disinclined to give an international platform to a British Communist sympathizer.[147]

[142] ibid.

[143] ibid, p. 581.

[144] Pritt, *The Defence Accuses* (n 114), p. 20, citing an article of his in *Labour Monthly*, September 1962, p. 425.

[145] [1934] 2 KB 164, and [1942] AC 206, respectively.

[146] Pritt's views were in contrast to 'many lawyers [who] feel a duty to deny it; and most lawyers know in their hearts that it is true': Pritt, *The Defence Accuses* (n 114), p. 20, citing his *Labour Monthly* article (n 144).

[147] Nevertheless this was not Pritt's only engagement with the anti-Communist laws of the United States, in 1955 penning an amicus brief for the IADL in a case brought under the Internal Security Act, in which he argued that the Act was invalidated by the Constitution and by the more freshly minted Universal Declaration of Human Rights:

> The Act seeks to penalise Communists simply because they believe in the principles of Communism . . . it destroys free speech, and freezes public opinion at the point at which it had arrived at the disturbed period when the Act was passed. If it were to be held to be valid, it would almost certainly lead to further inroads on the liberties of citizens in general, to further straining of the constitution, and to further departures from the concrete modern expression of those traditions in the Declaration of Human Rights (Pritt, *The Defence Accuses* (n 114), pp. 22–5).

VI. Conclusion

It is not suggested that lawyers should have immunity from investigation. If a lawyer has committed a crime he or she should be proceeded against like anyone else, and prosecuted accordingly. But that is not what we are concerned with here, with the surveillance of lawyers giving rise to two concerns. The first is the extent to which it was consistent with the legal authority of MI5 under the Attlee and Maxwell Fyfe Directives, which it will be recalled gave the Security Service the task of defence of the realm and provided explicitly that it was to take 'special care' to do no more than was 'strictly necessary'.[148] Yet although the defence of the realm was defined to include espionage, sabotage, and subversion, it is hard to see how the surveillance of the internal machinations of the CPLG or the Haldane Society could be justified by these terms of reference, having regard in particular to the requirement of 'strict necessity'.

What public interest was served by knowing the office holders, the schedule of meetings, or the minutes of the meetings of these groups? What public interest was served by knowing the splits and turmoil in these groups around Hungary in 1956 or anything else? And what public interest was served by recruiting lawyers to snitch on their colleagues? The question becomes more urgent after 1956, when the surveillance appeared to confirm that there was absolutely no justification for it ever having been undertaken in the first place. Both the CPLG and the Haldane Society were revealed to be split, and the latter was revealed to have at best a Communist presence, but could not by any stretch of the imagination be said to be Communist dominated or controlled. So why did the surveillance continue, and on what basis was it 'strictly necessary' for the defence of the realm? And given the ignorance revealed in Bowden's case, what purpose did it serve?[149]

But there is, of course, another concern about the surveillance of lawyers, which is not whether it was strictly necessary, but whether it was strictly lawful. Neither the Attlee nor the Maxwell Fyfe Directives authorized the Security Service to act unlawfully. Yet it is clear that the reason why MI5 wanted to penetrate the CPLG is because its 'main vocation' was 'to advise the Party on their legal position'. Similarly, it is clear from Dudley Collard's file that MI5 was obtaining information about litigation that would almost certainly have been confidential, and from Neil Lawson's file that they were seeking information relating to professional advice to the Malay clients. This runs counter to a fundamental common law principle conferring legal privileges on professional advice between lawyer and client, which 'should be secure against the possibility of any scrutiny from

[148] See Chapter 2 above.
[149] On the Bowden case, see p. 193.

others, whether the police, the executive, business competitors, inquisitive busybodies or anyone else'.[150]

As has been pointed out judicially, this is a privilege which is not available on such absolute terms to any other relationship, whether doctor and patient, husband and wife, or priest and penitent.[151] It may be that the lawyers' claims in defence of this privilege are exaggerated in view of its undoubted potential to 'impede the proper administration of justice in the individual case'.[152] Yet it is nevertheless real and strongly defended on 'Rule of Law' grounds,[153] recognized not only by the common law for hundreds of years,[154] but also more recently by statute.[155] That being the case, it could only be in the most exceptional circumstances, if ever, that the principle could be compromised, and only by Parliament. But there was no statute authorizing MI5 to poke its nose into the legal advice given by lawyers to clients, whether members of the Communist Party or not. Indeed, there is no evidence that powers of this kind were ever contemplated by governments, raising questions about the quality of the legal advice supplied to MI5 by its own lawyers.

[150] *Three Rivers District Council v Bank of England* [2004] UKHL 48, para. 34 (Lord Scott). Lord Scott draws freely on Australian, Canadian, New Zealand, and US authority, as well as earlier English cases in affirming the importance of this privilege.

[151] ibid., para. 28.

[152] ibid., para. 61 (Baroness Hale).

[153] ibid., para. 34, citing A. A. S. Zuckerman, *Civil Procedure* (London, 2003), paras 15.8–15.10.

[154] *Three Rivers District Council v Bank of England* [2004] UKHL 48, para. 54 (Lord Rodger), citing Sir George Mackenzie's *Observations upon the 18th Act of the 23rd Parliament of King James the Sixth against Dispositions made in Defraud of Creditors etc* (Edinburgh, 1675).

[155] Police and Criminal Evidence Act 1984, s. 9—no access by police by search warrant or otherwise to communications between lawyer and client. See also Terrorism Act 2000, Sch. 5.

8
The Guilty Secret

I. Introduction

There have been several references in the previous chapters to 'Special Facilities' or 'SF' as a surveillance method. This was a controversial surveillance technique, the use of which historically MI5 to this day seems keen to conceal. In this chapter as a result, we consider the use of SF more systematically so far as is possible given the limited amount of information currently available. As we have seen,'SF' was the code name for telephonic electronic eavesdropping, and sometimes for the use of microphones by MI5 for covert purposes in any circumstances. SF in the former sense was often—but not always—used in conjunction with a telephone interception, which was almost invariably set up at the telephone exchange, or at least outside the target's home or office.

The deployment of SF usually saw the GPO/MI5 Special Investigations Unit entering the target's premises posing as ordinary Post Office engineers, usually following the arrangement of a 'faulty line' with the Post Office. Where the surveillance target was likely to be particularly vigilant, and an overt entry likely to alert them to outside interest, then it appears that the premises were entered covertly. The telephone would be converted into an electronic 'bug' by a remarkably simple procedure, which was effective enough in permitting the eavesdroppers to listen to conversations and activity within the vicinity of the telephone even when the phone was not in use. The targets had to be fairly close to the telephone for conversations to be picked up by the microphone, but in the early 1950s the sound quality was improved by new technical arrangements introduced by Peter Wright.[1]

During the Second World War, MI5 had used hidden microphones fairly extensively, even employing the technique to assist the Ministry of Food and the Inland Revenue in their investigations into the black market.[2] MI5 installed microphones into the chairs of a London Restaurant in order to listen to the conversations of foreign diplomats,[3] as well as employing the technique in more conventional Security

[1] See P. Wright, *Spycatcher—The Candid Autobiography of a Senior Intelligence Officer* (Toronto, 1987), p. 48.

[2] TNA, CAB 301/31 (Findlater Stewart, Report on the Security Services), 'Stewart Report' Stewart records that all the special powers of investigation (which would include SF/hidden microphones) were employed in those cases (para. 40). The use of phone taps and mail interceptions in the Inland Revenue and the Ministry of Food investigations between 1940 and 1944 is noted in Appendix I of the Birkett Report, Cmnd 283, 1957.

[3] C. Pincher, *Dangerous to Know: A Life* (London, 2014), pp. 285–7. This occurred 'early in the war' and was fairly primitive, with stenographers upstairs making a written record of the conversations.

MI5, the Cold War, and the Rule of Law. K. D. Ewing, Joan Mahoney, and Andrew Moretta, Oxford University Press (2020). © K. D. Ewing, Joan Mahoney, and Andrew Moretta. DOI: 10.1093/oso/9780198818625.001.0001

Service enquiries. If not quite common practice, the use of SF had become a familiar enough form of intelligence gathering by 1945. The wartime diaries of Guy Liddell, then the Director of 'B' Division and later the post-war DDG, betrayed a marked familiarity with the use of hidden microphones as an aid to investigation, and in a 1951 entry he recorded that MI5 possessed a wireless microphone that could be hidden in a jacket pocket.[4]

The technology soon developed to enable the microphone in the telephone to be used for eavesdropping purposes, without entering the premises either to tamper with the phone, or to install a bug. Peter Wright's first work for the MI5 involved research into radio microphones,[5] and when he joined MI5 officially in 1955 as a scientific officer, Wright recorded that the Special Investigations Unit's laboratory at Dollis Hill was working on a technique for using a radio beam to engage the microphone in a telephone without having to enter the target's premises. Wright described the first use of 'wireless' SF to listen to conversations in Khrushchev's hotel room at Claridge's during his 1956 visit to Britain:

> Normally Claridge's has permanent Special Facilities installed on the hotel telephone system, because so many visitors stay there who are of interest to MI5. But we knew the Russians were sending a team of sweepers in to check Khrushchev's suite before he arrived, so we decided it was the right time to use for the first time the specially modified SF.[6]

Wright continued by saying that 'the new SF did not require a washer to be fitted, so it was virtually undetectable. The telephone could be activated over short distances using shortwave high frequency megacycles. We set the SF activation up in an office of the Grosvenor Estates near Claridge's. It worked perfectly.'[7] It is significant that Wright was referring to this new technique as 'SF', despite the fact that Post Office telephone lines were not employed.[8] 'SF' thus referred to different forms of

According to Pincher, the restaurant continued to be bugged long after the war, and when MI5 finally removed the microphones, they came across another set of microphones that had been installed by the Russians.

4 TNA, KV 4/282 (Liddell Diary, 29 March 1951):

> Cumming (Head of B4) has produced a gadget from America. It is a small wireless set which can go easily into the inside breast pocket with an aerial up the arm. We have tried it out and can hear speech quite distinctly from someone walking in the park or in the streets, or anywhere in the building.

5 Wright (n 1), p. 18. Wright started working with MI5 in 1949.

6 ibid., p. 72 (emphasis added)—one more of Wright's astonishing revelations, which appears to have been overlooked. Successful as the new approach was, it did not replace the less labour-intensive standard form of SF.

7 ibid., pp. 72–3.

8 We do not know whether a warrant was obtained for this operation, or whether a warrant permitted the permanent installation of SF in Claridge's. It would be a brave or foolish Home Secretary or Foreign Secretary, who would want to know anything at all about such activities. We would expect

electronic eavesdropping, and was often used by the Security Service to refer to methods other than those that employed the handset of a telephone. If the legal implications of either form were considered at the time, it can only have been in the most perfunctory manner, for there is no record of any serious consideration of the question by either the Home Office or MI5.

II. Legal and Political Authority

In fact, the legal questions raised by the use of SF were never properly addressed until 1989. At the heart of it, however, is the question whether the placing and use of covert listening devices was lawful. It would be lawful if the placing of the bugs was done with the consent of the property owner. But if SF were used without consent, the legal position would be much more complex. The latter situation takes us back to *Entick v Carrington*,[9] where the Home Secretary (the Earl of Halifax) had granted a warrant to the King's Messenger (Carrington) to enter and search the home of John Entick for seditious material. In an action for trespass brought by Entick, it was held that the conduct of the government officials was utterly illegal, and was not saved by a warrant the issuing of which was not authorized by law. Nor could the action be saved on the ground of state necessity, the compelling principle established in 1765—which survives to this day—being expressed as follows:

> By the laws of England, every invasion of private property, be it ever so minute, is a trespass. No man can set his foot upon my ground without my licence, but he is liable to an action, though the damage be nothing; which is proved by every declaration in trespass, where the defendant is called upon to answer for bruising the grass and even treading upon the soil.[10]

But although of doubtful legal effects, a HOW was nevertheless initially required as a matter of administrative practice to authorize the use of SF. This is suggested by the first recorded use of the practice we have been able to find, Guy Liddell writing in his wartime diaries that:

> Brooman White later telephoned to say that a man answering to POGO's description but wearing glasses has been followed to an address in Glasgow. A HOW

operations mounted against the visitors to be undertaken by SIS and any warrants to be issued by the Foreign Office.

[9] (1765) 19 St Tr 1029.
[10] ibid.

> is going to put on the address. Doust was consulted as to the possibilities of installing microphones in POGO's flat and in the meanwhile a HOW has been imposed.[11]

The Home Secretary's role in authorizing the use of SF was also revealed by Anthony Blunt in a report to his Soviet spymasters during the war. According to West and Tsarov:

> the Soviets were fascinated by MI5's procedure for inserting listening devices. Blunt explained that upon an officer's recommendation Guy Liddell endorsed an application which was then passed to Brigadier Jasper Harker, MI5's Deputy Director, for approval. Having gained his initials it went to the Home Secretary for a warrant which, if signed, was sent to Sir Raymond Birchall at the Post Office.[12]

The significance of this is that the use of SF at that stage was politically sanctioned. This was true in relation to the use of technology generally (such as it was), as well as its use in individual operations. Formal confirmation of sorts is provided by Sir Findlater Stewart, whose report we encountered in Chapter 2.[13] Unfortunately, however, paragraph 20, along with part of paragraph 19, has been excised from the copy released to the National Archives—the only redaction in the entire report. Nevertheless, paragraphs 18, 19, and 21 provide that:

> 18 Formal application to the Home Secretary for a warrant is made in each case by MI5 accompanied by a statement of the reasons for it and it is the practice for the Home Secretary to satisfy himself personally for the need for a warrant.
>
> 19 The interception of telephone messages is subject to the same legal restrictions as apply to letters, and a Home Office Warrant is equally required for its employment **REDACTED**.
>
> 21 Adequate safeguards are imposed on the use and custody of information obtained by these special means [telephone taps and hidden microphones][14] and it is recorded by specially selected operators. It must necessarily be put on record in the files in cases where it appears likely to have a material bearing on the future conduct of the case in question; but it is never used in any way which might expose its origin, eg in the interrogation of a suspect or as evidence in a prosecution.

[11] TNA, KV 4/187 (Liddell Diary, 10 October 1940).

[12] N. West and O. Tsarev, *The Crown Jewels: The Secrets at the Heart of the KGB Archives* (London, 1998), p. 169. The Liddell Diary indicates that Birchall was a very senior man at the GPO to whom the head of the Special Investigations Unit reported (see TNA, KV 4/471, Liddell Diary, 11 October 1949). Postal and telephonic HOWs went to the Unit, but it seems that SF HOWs went to the top tier of management.

[13] Stewart Report (n 2).

[14] Stewart refers back to the redacted para. 20. The summary and conclusions of the Report indicate that para. 20 refers to the use of hidden microphones.

> Although the existence of material from these sources may have to be made known to the Public Prosecutor in the course of discussions in the case it is never revealed to the police or any outside party.

MI5 no doubt still does not want publicly to acknowledge that it covertly entered people's homes or improperly used hidden microphones, even though both are by now well known. Yet the likelihood that the censored material in the passage above dealt with by SF is suggested by the 'Summary and Conclusions' at the end of the Stewart Report, which by point (v) recommended that: '*Specific authority should be obtained from the Home Secretary or in certain cases from the Foreign Secretary,*[15] *whenever it is proposed to install a microphone (paragraph 20).*'[16] Apart from confirming that the use of SF was acknowledged and discussed, this is important also for Stewart's suggestion that the use of SF should continue to be subject to the same formal control and accountability as mail checks and phone taps. That suggestion appears to have been accepted by Attlee, with MI5's original Directive stipulating in paragraph 7 that any use of 'SF' required the supervision of the Home Secretary, the DG being instructed that:

> You will be subject to the directions of the Secretary of State for the Home Department in all questions concerning the use of 'special facilities' in the discharge of your responsibilities, and you will report to him in cases where your investigations show that action should be taken.[17]

It is true that paragraph 7 did not require a HOW to be granted before SF were used as Stewart appeared to suggest, though it is equally true that the Attlee Directive did not require a HOW to be granted before mail or telephone interception were authorized. It is clear from various sources subsequently, however, that in practice a HOW was required in all three circumstances, despite the fact that paragraph 7 is also opaque in failing to define what 'special facilities' refers to. To this end, a particularly notable internal document is to be found in File KV4/162 on B Division. Dated 19 December 1946, the document in question refers to the 'Central index of HOWs (letter checks, telephone checks *and SFs*)', a rare slip on the part of the MI5 'weeders', clearly indicating that HOWs were issued when SF were installed for a period after the Attlee Directive had been issued. This of course does not tell us who granted the warrants, but further evidence that 'the buck stopped' with the Home Secretary is confirmed by Liddell's record of a conversation with Newsam, who had advised that 'in his view it would be undesirable to spread knowledge

[15] This presumably would be for domestic SIS (MI6) operations.

[16] Stewart Report (n 2), p. 27.

[17] This is para. 7 of the Attlee Directive, which was issued to all officers 'for information and guidance' by the DG on 16 May 1946. It had been issued to Sillitoe by Attlee on 20 April 1946 (see Chapter 3 above).

[about SF] to Foreign Office personnel',[18] and that MI5 should tell the Foreign Office 'that the Home Secretary had a grave responsibility on these matters and was opposed to spreading the knowledge unless it was absolutely necessary'.[19]

As we have seen, however, the more permissive Maxwell Fyfe Directive replaced the Attlee Directive in 1952, the former more permissive in the sense that it conveniently dropped paragraph 7. That said, Sillitoe commented in a contemporaneous note that, 'it has always been the established practice to obtain the Home Secretary's authority' when SF were employed,[20] thereby suggesting that the removal of paragraph 7 was inconsequential. In or out, it would make no difference: a warrant would be required. That, however, was disingenuous, with the removal of paragraph 7 either reflecting or precipitating a change of practice. This is confirmed by Christopher Andrew, who claims without acknowledging the antecedents, that:

> there was no HOW system for the installation of eavesdropping devices, which usually required burglary (although the Service did not use the word), mostly against Communist and Soviet Bloc targets. Approval was given instead by the Home Office PUS. The belief at the time that 'bugging and burgling' in defence of the realm was covered by the royal prerogative was probably mistaken.[21]

Such a belief at the time about what was covered by the prerogative is hard to credit in light of well-established legal principle: *Entick v Carrington* is quite clear that entry to a private home without legal authority is a trespass and that the trespass cannot be justified by State necessity.[22] By disposing of the Attlee Directive's paragraph 7, Sir David Maxwell Fyfe, the Home Office, and MI5 senior personnel (who were actively involved in drafting the revision) thereby abandoned not only any semblance of legality, but also any semblance of political control or accountability in relation to SF. This is a matter to which we return later in this chapter.

III. Special Facilities and Counter-Subversion

Documents relating to eavesdropping—other than from the voluminous collection of transcripts of conversations from the Communist Party's King Street HQ—are a comparative rarity in the Security Service files (though, as we shall see, careful reading of the files does reveal some). It appears that, where possible, MI5 preferred to avoid referring to the practice on paper, and it is clear that an attempt—not entirely successful—has been made to withhold from the National Archives

18 TNA, KV 4/470 (Liddell Diary, 18 November 1948).
19 TNA, KV 4/471 (Liddell Diary, 28 January 1949).
20 TNA, CAB 301/128 (Letter from Sillitoe to Mr R. J. Whittick of the Home Office, 18 July 1952).
21 C. Andrew, *The Defence of the Realm—The Authorised History of MI5* (London, 2009), p. 338.
22 *Entick v Carrington* (n 9).

those documents which do refer to SF, and to bugging in general. The wartime installation of SF at King Street was revealed in Harold 'Kim' Philby's 1968 memoir, *My Silent War*.[23] Although Philby did not give a date, his account indicated that MI5 was listening to King Street after the Soviet Union had entered the war as an ally in 1941. In 1986, Peter Wright elaborated:

> One of the first things Anthony Blunt had betrayed to the Russians was the existence of SF, immediately after it was installed in King Street, and they had alerted the Party and instructed them to remove all telephones from sensitive areas. But the Party did not really believe it. They took precautions only for very sensitive matters.[24]

The transcripts of conversations recorded by the SF installed at the CPGB might at first sight be mistaken for transcripts of telephone conversations. Indeed, to judge by other accounts we have seen of the Security Service files released to the National Archives, these transcripts are almost invariably confused with transcriptions of telephone conversations. However, close inspection reveals comments inserted into the text referring to people 'entering the room'; or transcripts of conversations involving several people which make the nature of the surveillance obvious. Closer study of a CPGB transcript will reveal the letters 'KS' (King Street) typed in the administrative references, and the then current code name for electronic eavesdropping/SF printed at the top of the paper. Intelligence obtained was typed up in the Security Service files as if communicated by an informant or agent—a 'source'. In the 1940s and early 1950s, the code name for SF was 'Table'; during the 1950s it became source 'North' and by the late 1950s it was source 'Lascar'. In addition, MI5 had specially printed headed paper for the transcripts of bugged conversations.

The activity recorded is of a wide and varied kind, including general office activity such as dictation of letters and outgoing phone calls, making both letter checks and phone taps redundant.[25] Otherwise, multiple examples in Chapters 4, 6, and 7 above, included notably the meetings about the internal affairs of the ETU. But they also included on the one hand meetings of the Communist Party's Political Committee; and on the other hand informal meetings between senior officials and King Street visitors (such as Pritt), as well as everything else in between. It may be, however, that sensitive meetings were held elsewhere as a result of suspicions (or knowledge) of the bug(s). An interesting note in the Pollitt file reveals that

[23] We cannot discount the likelihood that this would have been done using war-time powers, perhaps even prerogative powers. But the use of war-time powers would not justify continuing the surveillance after the war. That said, some war-time powers survived the war: E. C. S. Wade and G. G. Phillips, *Constitutional Law* (5th edn, London, 1955), pp. 387–9.

[24] Wright (n 1), p. 56.

[25] TNA, KV 2/1754 (TABLE, 27 February 1951).

'the old man' sometimes used a flat in Muswell Hill for meetings of 'a secret nature', the flat belonging to Joyce Smith (PF 203,926), who then worked for the Kentish Town-based WFTU.[26] According to the note, Smith gave Pollitt her key whenever he asked, it being reported that Pollitt 'goes up there for top secret meetings which are even too secret for King Street, especially for meeting foreigners who do not like to be seen going in and out of King Street, though few people in King Street know about this' (suggesting that King Street was watched, as well as bugged).[27]

MI5 in fact installed multiple bugging devices in King Street during the Cold War, and appeared able to monitor what was going on in different parts of the building. Thus, Peter Wright recalls receiving information from an F4 source that CPGB Executive Committee meetings had been moved to a windowless room, presumably a cellar.[28] As a result, Wright and a colleague installed a microphone into the door of an old coal chute, which led directly into the room.[29] MI5 was able to remove this device after it had become apparent that the Party had realized the room had been bugged. Similarly, in 1975 a news item from *The Times* recorded the discovery of a long defunct listening device:

> Builders at work in a room in the London headquarters of the Communist Party in King Street, Covent Garden, yesterday found a transistorized bugging device in a section of wood. The men, who were redecorating the room and demolishing an old raised dais in one corner, took the device, measuring 6in by 2in, to the office staff... The transmitter had been hidden in a hollowed- out section of wood, about 2ft long, attached to a panel on the dais. It would have been about ankle level to anyone sitting on the dais. One of the components was marked '397.5Hz', presumably the wavelength, with the number 'STE 7112.' The Party called in an electronics expert, a university researcher, who said that the device could pick up conversations in the large ground floor room and transmit them up to 50 yards. Conversations could be transmitted further with additional equipment. The section of wood in which the device had been hidden was stained to appear as old as the panel to which it was attached. A battery had also been pushed into the hollow, and the device was covered with a black metal casing.

The report continues by reporting Mr George Matthews (the Party's publicity officer) as saying that the electronics' experts referred to above had estimated the device to be ten to twelve years old: 'It was too new to have been installed when we took over this part of the building in 1949, and too obsolete to have been installed

[26] See Chapter 4 for MI5 interest in her involvement in the BPC and the Sheffield Peace Conference.

[27] TNA, KV 2/1046 (Minute, 9 July 1951).

[28] An F4 source would be either an informant who visited or worked in King Street or one who had gleaned the information from a 'sub-source' who worked there.

[29] Wright (n 1): 'in the late 1950s Hugh Winterborn and I installed yet another microphone into its King Street headquarters' (p. 56).

very recently', noting also that, 'there are far more sophisticated devices now available'. According to Matthews, the Party used the room in which the device was found 'for meetings, press conferences, and by the Young Communist League (YCL), when about 50 people attend'. It was not used for illegal purposes, and while the Party had 'nothing to be afraid of', this was 'a serious infringement of our civil liberties', Matthews insisting that the CPGB 'have as much right to privacy as any other political party', expressing the hope that 'some MP, when he knows that this has gone on, will take the matter up in the House of Commons, as we do not like being spied on any more than anyone else'.[30] And while the Party may actively have repudiated the idea that 'the great end, for which men entered into society, was to secure their property',[31] this 'sacred' right applied as equally to the Communist Party as it did to others.

This in turn raises questions about how the SF were put there and with what authority. The Pollitt files contain a note on ownership of Communist Party Headquarters. This claims that the building occupied at 16 King Street was 'a freehold property [which] is privately owned by Harry Pollitt'. Other property at 17–18 King Street and 27–28 Bedford Street bought by 'Pollitt and Gray' were transferred to a company called Rodell Properties Ltd, a company formed for this purpose in 1943, and still trading. Proposals to transfer 16 King Street to Rodell Properties Ltd had not yet been carried out.[32] We can of course never be sure, but at this stage it seems implausible to contemplate the possibility that either Pollitt or Rodell Properties—if the owners of the premises—would have consented to bugs being placed in a way that would allow Pollitt's conversations and those of others to be monitored. That being the case, it is difficult to see how in using SF, MI5 acted lawfully in accordance with its mandate, a failure all the more serious for the fact there is no evidence of any intelligence harvest that would in any event have justified the surveillance on grounds of counter-subversion. This is presumably why it was undertaken in the first place.

IV. Special Facilities and Operation Party Piece

SF was thus used as a means of routine surveillance of the CPGB, along with various other methods. However, MI5 did not want to know only what the Party was doing; it also wanted to know who its members were. Professor Andrew has

30 *The Times*, 5 February 1975.

31 *Entick v Carrington* (n 9).

32 TNA, KV 2/1047 (Minute by G. R. W. Spencer, 10 November 1952). The identity of Gray is not known, though it will be recalled that Olga Gray, who worked with Pollitt, was an MI5 agent. If she is the Gray referred to in the text, this gives rise to the astonishing possibility that an MI5 agent was part-owner of MI5 premises under MI5 surveillance. Conversely, a Mr Grey was thought to be bringing in money to finance the Sheffield Peace Conference (see Chapter 4 above).

claimed that the Service enjoyed 'extraordinary success' in accessing Party records 'through both agents and a series of operations collectively codenamed STILL LIFE which gained covert entry into all British and Northern Irish local Party offices'.[33] SF was one of the surveillance devices used for this purpose, the others being mail checks and telechecks, as well as the embedding of an MI5 officer in a family home. Operation Party Piece was the most famous and by all accounts the most successful of the STILL LIFE operations,[34] enabling MI5 to leap from a perhaps over optimistic estimate of between eighty and ninety per cent coverage of Party members in the Registry,[35] to near complete coverage. After the summer of 1955, MI5 had a list of Party members past and present, as well as access to CPGB files, along with the 'personal statement' or 'biography' which very many of those files contained.

Communist Party records were kept at the elegant north-west London Georgian town house of Roland and Nancy Berger, who had been monitored by MI5 for years. Mr Berger was a businessman believed by MI5 to be involved in channelling Soviet money into the UK to subsidize the CPGB; Mrs Berger was a statistician who, by 1951, was working from home for the Communist Party, while looking after their two young daughters.[36] Surveillance had led MI5 to believe it 'very likely' that Mrs Berger collected Party registration forms for civil servants, and that they were sent to her through the post.[37] In the note sent by MI5 to Colonel Allan at the GPO requesting a mail check, it was also explained that she compiled 'biographies of Party members who are either suspects or being vetted for special work'.[38] At the same time, MI5 re-imposed a suspended telecheck 'on Nancy BERGER because of her connexion with the Betty REID group'.[39] Reid was then the Party's Assistant National Organizer, based at King Street, and as such a 'formidable figure', whose home was penetrated by MI5 in the shape of her domestic help.[40]

It appears that in April 1951, MI5 was ready to make a covert entry into the Berger home. A note from the minute sheet of another unnamed file has been attached to a heavily redacted document in Mrs Berger's file,[41] stating that 'The operation referred to in minute 81 [from the unnamed file] was abandoned on 13.4.51 when it was learnt from Sources SEAT and TABLE [covert microphones] that

33 Andrew (n 21), p. 400. The first of these operations, RED KNIGHT, took place in 1949.

34 ibid.

35 TNA, KV 4/473 (Liddell Diary, 20 October 1952).

36 Nancy Berger had been awarded an OBE for her work at the Ministry of Fuel and Power, with ambitions to become a writer.

37 TNA, KV 2/2525 (Minute sheet note by 'B1A/Investigation', 6 April 1951).

38 TNA, KV 2/2525 (7 April 1951). The reason given on the face of the HOW was that:

> The person who lives at this address is a member of the Communist Party and connected with a clandestine Communist group. It has recently been learned that she is responsible for collecting the Communist Party registration forms for Civil Servants. It is hoped by this check to learn more of these activities.

39 Reid was then Assistant National Organizer, based at King Street.

40 *The Guardian*, 11 February 2004 (Obituary by Kevin Maguire).

41 Very likely the minute sheet note was from an OF file on the Party itself.

although BERGER was away there were definitely other people staying at the house.' (Presumably, these were the Bergers' lodgers whose presence had been picked up by SF thus installed at least four years before Party Piece.[42]) The monitoring of Mrs Berger continued thereafter, but interest seemed to fade and the watchers were eventually called off. It appears, nevertheless, that SF continued to be active in the Berger home, a note dated 20 August 1951 stating that 'Nancy BERGER holds in her home at 7, St. Katherine's Precincts, Regents Park many, if not all, of the biographies with which Betty REID is dealing . . . source TABLE on Nancy BERGER is particularly productive since the group meet at her home fortnightly.'[43]

Yet while SF enabled MI5 to find out what was on the Berger premises and the nature of Party work undertaken by Mrs Berger in particular, it was traditional mail checks and telechecks that eventually enabled them to secure access to the Party membership lists some four years later. By this time, Mrs Berger had inherited money from her mother, and in 1953 the family had moved to a Georgian town house at 5 Grove Terrace, London NW5, which was to become the target for an operation revealed for the first time by Peter Wright. However, the account in *Spycatcher* appears to have been conflated with the covert entry operation mounted shortly after Operation Party Piece against Reuben Falber in an attempt to gather intelligence on Party funding.[44] As Wright has it, an MI5 agent 'learned from a source inside the Communist Party of Great Britain, that the entire Party secret membership files were stored in the flat of a wealthy Party member.'[45] The flat was placed under observation, and 'MI5 had a piece of unexpected luck', in the sense that:

> The woman of the House rang her husband at work to say that she was going out for an hour. She told him she would leave the key under the mat. Within twenty minutes of the call's being monitored in Leconfield House [MI5 HQ] we were around the flat taking a plasticine imprint of the key.[46]

Sure enough, a 'Note for File' dated 14 March 1955 states that 'A copy of the key to Nancy BERGER's flat at 5 Grove Terrace, Highgate Road, NW5 is in an envelope in the safe in F4 Officers room—402.'[47] There is, however, another account

42 TNA, KV 2/2525 (The then head of the B5 Watchers noted on 13 April 1951 that there were two women and three men listed for that address on the electoral roll.)

43 Although this again makes it abundantly clear that the NW1 house was bugged, only one inconsequential SF transcript of a conversation that appears to have been held there can be found in Mrs Berger's file. A note in TNA, KV 2/2525 indicates that SF had been operating in her and Falber's house in London, NW1 since at least January 1949 (Note by G. S. Weldsmith, B1A, 14 January 1949).

44 This is understandable—Wright was relying on his memory. Falber was also a businessman, believed by MI5 to be involved in fund raising for the Party. See Wright (n 1), pp. 54–6 (OPERATION PARTY PIECE), and p. 175 (Falber operation).

45 ibid., p. 54.

46 ibid., pp. 54–5.

47 TNA, KV 2/2525.

of this operation no less shocking for the intrusive nature of the surveillance used. According to Christopher Andrew, 'An MI5 officer, who became a tenant of a flat in the Berger household, organised the first phase of Operation Party Piece in June 1955 during which about 6,000 documents were copied inside the house.'[48] Thereafter, on 1 July a note to Harlow of the GPO from MI5 stated that they:

> wished to re-impose a letter check on Nancy BERGER . . . The reason for doing so is a proposed operation involving access to the Berger household and we are particularly anxious to have advance information about their holiday plans and movements in the next few weeks. For this reason I am asking for a check on both the BERGERs.

The family went on holiday to the continent during August—September 1955, and Professor Andrew confirms that PARTY PIECE was completed in August, when '48,000 documents were secretly removed at night' from the Berger household and photographed at MI5 HQ, Leconfield House.[49] The Bergers returned from their holiday on 9 September. The operation complete, the letter check was suspended on 30 September.[50]

Whether Wright's or Andrew's account is correct, it was mail and telephone interception that were decisive in Party Piece. Nevertheless, SF continued to be deployed at Grove Terrace, a Lascar file entry from May 1956 picking up a series of conversations apparently made close to the telephone during a party at the Berger household. The conversations were interrupted by a telephone call in which the monitor was apparently able to hear both sides of the conversation sufficiently to describe the unidentified 'distant' as having a 'cultured English voice'.[51] A later Lascar report contained brief notes of a telephone conversation in which Roland Berger had mentioned the address of a house he and his wife were interested in buying,[52] and a third noted that during a conversation with a number of visitors Berger made a phone call which 'was not audible owing to loud chatter'.[53] With an MI5 officer embedded in the house as a lodger as recently as 1955, it may well be that a 'free standing' microphone(s) rather than a telephone installation was used for this Lascar surveillance, which shows considerable interest in conversations about plans to alter the interior of the house.

[48] Andrew (n 21), pp. 400–1.
[49] Wright (n 1), recalled that '55,000 files were copied' (p. 55).
[50] TNA, KV 2/4242.
[51] TNA, KV 2/4242 (LASCAR, 7 May 1956). At the time the 'telecheck' had been suspended.
[52] ibid. (LASCAR, 24 September 1956).
[53] ibid. (LASCAR, 21 October 1956).

V. Special Facilities and Counter-Espionage

As we have seen, the Klaus Fuchs' case was a seminal moment in post-war counter-espionage.[54] It was important for a number of reasons, not least for what it revealed about the activities of the Soviet Union after the war. That apart, another aspect of the case was the role of Ursula Beurton as Fuchs' handler, and the use of SF to secure information about her and her siblings. Code named 'Sonya', Beurton was in fact a GRU officer with the rank of Colonel, and had been awarded the Order of the Red Banner for espionage work in China in the 1930s.[55] From a well-known German Communist family, Beurton was the sister of Jurgen Kuczynski, an economist, statistician, and some-time spy who had moved to live in the German Democratic Republic in August 1947. Other than her pedigree, Beurton was known by MI5 to have worked for Soviet intelligence, and MI5 believed that she was still in the United Kingdom when Fuchs identified her from his cell in Stafford Prison.[56] Fuchs had picked her out in photographs shown to him by 'Jim' Skardon.

'Sonya' had been running agents in the United Kingdom for some time, and had been in regular radio contact with Moscow between 1941 and 1947. Although she lost both radio and 'dead letter box' contact thereafter, this was revived before her departure to the East early in 1950, following Fuchs' arrest.[57] Even before Fuchs identified her in 1950, Beurton unsurprisingly had been under suspicion, with MI5 mounting a surveillance operation against her. But this could not be done effectively in Beurton's adopted community of Great Rollright—a small Oxfordshire village, which was reliant on one public phone. However, Beurton had siblings in London, and this provided an opportunity for MI5 to use their 'special powers of enquiry'. Indeed, MI5 took a close interest in Buerton's extended family, all of whom it seems were the subject of suspicion, the files of all six Kuczynski siblings having now been released to the National Archives.[58] Nevertheless, when Fuchs was shown photographs of the Kuczynski family, he failed notably to identify any of them, except Ursula Beurton.[59]

54 See pp. 10, 30, 34, 37, 38–9, 58, and 102.

55 For full details of her career, see her autobiography: R. Werner, *Sonya's Report: Fascinating Autobiography of One of Russia's Most Remarkable Secret Agents* (London, 1991). Ursula features heavily in Chapman Pincher's work on Roger Hollis (see particularly C. Pincher, *Treachery, Betrayals, Blunders, and Cover Ups: Six Decades of Espionage* (Edinburgh and London, 2011)). However, according to Ursula in her autobiography:

> I was never asked by Centre to contact anyone from MI5, and I had no contacts there . . . I know no Fifth Man, and I must also spoil the speculation or, as some writers state 'the fact', that I ever had anything to do with the one time Director of MI5, Roger Hollis. I resent the way journalists try to turn me into a sensation, simply in order to make money (p. 239).

56 TNA, KV 6/44 (Interrogation Report on Fuchs by Mr Skardon, 1 December 1950).

57 Werner (n 55), pp. 277–8, 291.

58 For Sonya's file, see TNA, KV 6/41–5.

59 TNA, KV 6/44 (Interrogation Report on Fuchs by Mr Skardon, 1 December 1950).

Special facilities were thus installed in the north-west London home of Sabine and Francis Loeffler, and in the nearby house belonging to Barbara and Duncan Taylor.[60] Sabine and Barbara were two of Beurton's London-based sisters. The Taylors moved shortly afterwards, and the whole process in relation to HOWs and SF (although there is no reference to SF installation in the Taylor files) had to be repeated. Oddly, MI5 went no further than sporadic mail and telephone interception of the remaining London-based sister, Brigitte, although they knew—from the same informant who had told them of Ursula's espionage past—former 'Rote Drei' operative Alexander Foote—that Brigitte had definitely been involved in espionage work.[61] It seems that MI5 had assumed Communist lawyer Francis Loeffler to have been the mastermind of any putative espionage ring, having concluded that Ursula Beurton—arguably the most successful female spy of all time—was a disillusioned Communist exiled in rural poverty: 'We are reasonably satisfied that they [Ursula and her husband] are not at present active, and there is no reason to suppose that they have been active for some years.'[62]

The Loeffler and the Taylor files make it very obvious that electronic eavesdropping was taking place. A number of transcripts of eavesdropped conversations (intelligence attributed to source TABLE) remain in the files, and many of the same transcripts feature in the files of Ursula Beurton and her husband.[63] Yet it appears that the documentation relating to the *installation* of the facilities has been removed. In all KV personal files, there is a minute sheet at the beginning of the file. This is essentially a list of the contents of the file, with an entry being made as each fresh document (serial entry) is placed on file—effectively an index of the documents in the file compiled in date order. On the minute sheet of one of the Loeffler files there is a very brief entry referring to a document in the main part of the file on the installation of SF—the minute sheet entry evidently overlooked by the MI5 censor before the file was deposited in the National Archives. The document referred to on the minute sheet has been removed from the file. It is not known what happens to documents that have been censored in this way, though if the evidence of the Donald Maclean file minute sheet entries is representative,[64] it seems likely that such was the level of secrecy surrounding the installation and warranting of SF that the documentation was stored in separate volumes.

[60] Much of the following is drawn from the MI5 Personal Files of the individuals in question. See TNA, KV 2/2927–33 (Loeffler) and TNA KV 2/2935–7 (Taylor).

[61] Foote was to find fame of a sort as the author of *The Handbook for Spies* (London, 1949), a book written for him by MI5 officer Courtney Young. Foote's identification of Ursula Beurton as a Soviet agent features in TNA, KV 6/41. His own comprehensive Security Service file is available at the National Archives: KV 2/1611–16.

[62] TNA, KV 2/2935 (Note by W. J. Skardon, 15 September 1947). Chapman Pincher rated Ursula the most 'influential female secret agent of all time': *Treachery, Betrayals, Blunders* (n 55), p. 47.

[63] TNA, KV 6/41–5 (MI5 Personal Files).

[64] See pp. 221–2 below.

While the SF transcripts make very entertaining reading, this was presumably not their purpose. What they reveal is the futility of the operation, which appeared not to yield any significant information. In 1947, MI5 officers 'Jim' Skardon and Michael Serpell had interviewed Beurton in her Oxfordshire home. Following the interrogation, the officers returned to London, and Francis Loeffler made a flying visit to Beurton, for reasons about which we can only speculate. Thereafter Loeffler visited the Taylors, when his visit to Oxfordshire was discussed, the discussion being picked up by SF. But whatever benefit may have been secured from the SF in 1947, there were no such benefits when the Loefflers and Taylors re-entered the orbit of MI5 in 1950, after Ursula had been identified as one of Fuchs' contacts. Francis was followed around London for a couple of weeks, but neither this surveillance, nor the SF and mail and telephone intercepts produced anything of interest. By 1951, the counter-espionage (B2) officers were forced to conclude that, 'No information has been obtained since the present checks were imposed to show that the Loefflers are engaged in any covert activities.'[65] Interest in the Taylors was finally lost in 1952, after abortive attempts by Skardon to persuade them to reveal what they knew about Ursula.[66] Before Skardon's final attempt to lock the stable door long after the horse had bolted, his colleague, Evelyn McBarnet, had commented:

> I wonder if we have much to gain from a B2 point of view in pursuing this matter any further. We do not need confirmation of the guilt of Ursula Beurton and Jurgen Kuczynski and even if we learned from Taylor that members of the Kuczynski family knew what Ursula and Jurgen were doing, it does not get us much further.[67]

When, nevertheless, an appointment was made and Barbara Taylor was visited by Skardon at her home, there was no need for 'Jim' to take notes—the interrogation was being picked up on the SF. Realizing he was going to get nothing out of Barbara, SF reveals that Skardon attempted to 'lean on' Duncan, implying that his job at the BBC was at risk if he failed to cooperate. Skardon had been unable to mention the Fuchs connection—this had been ruled out by the B2 counter-espionage team, and he was obliged to avoid raising any details that had been picked up using the 'special powers of enquiry', for fear of alerting the couple to the surveillance that they

[65] TNA, KV 2/2929 (Minute sheet note by Miss Small, 5 June 1951). Miss Small also noted that 'Sabine Loeffler is in fairly regular contact with her sister, Ursula Beurton. The letters passing between them, however, have been purely personal . . . Source TABLE at this address is completely unproductive, and would not be of any assistance following an interrogation'. Her boss, J. C. Robertson, agreed that the 'Loefflers are at present unlikely subjects for interrogation', but suggested that the decision might be reconsidered following interrogation of the Taylors (Minute sheet note, 5 July). Two days later, the 'telecheck' (the 'tap', not the SF) on the Loefflers' phone was suspended.

[66] For a celebration of Skardon, see *Daily Telegraph*, 22 May 2003.

[67] TNA, KV 2/2937 (Minute sheet note by Evelyn Barnet, 22 February 1952).

had been subject to—*for fear of publicity*. The man who had broken Fuchs had to admit defeat, concluding that:

> Duncan Taylor was unwilling to see me except in the presence of his wife, and equally I decided that to do so would be no more profitable than seeing his wife on her own . . . I felt unwilling to advise otherwise than that an interview with the pair of them seeking intelligence information was likely to be unprofitable, and that an interview at which I spoke my mind and detailed my views and the view of the Security Service about her family, might easily, since it would have to be advanced in the presence of both, *lead to repercussions for the Security Service*.[68]

On 1 April 1952, B2 accepted that 'further interrogation of the Taylors would be a bad thing . . . all the checks at present imposed upon the Kuczynski family would be suspended'.[69]

VI. Special Facilities and the Cambridge Spy Ring

Given the use of SF for counter-surveillance and counter-espionage, it would be remarkable if SF were not used in relation to the suspected spies in their own midst, including most notably Burgess and Maclean. Thus, MI5 had become aware that Maclean was a suspected Soviet agent only some three weeks before his disappearance, overlooking suspicions that had been harboured for many years. In a Diary entry for 11 April 1951, Liddell recorded that Dick White had told him:

> about the case of a Soviet agent that we had been looking for . . . It is now thought that this individual may be identical with the Foreign Office agent reported by KRIVITSKY as supplying information on Imperial Policy back in 1937 . . . Recent ACORN material served to narrow the field; this material has been in the possession of the Americans for a long time, but for some unknown reason has only just reached us. There are two people who might possibly fit the bill; one Donald Maclean and the other John Russell.[70]

A lot has been redacted from the diaries around this time, but in his entry for 29 May 1951, Liddell recorded that, 'The Watchers failed to pick up MACLEAN since his departure from the country on Friday, and we now learn from the Foreign

[68] ibid. ('Barbara Macrae Taylor and Duncan Burnett Taylor', by W. J. Skardon, 27 March 1952) (emphasis added).

[69] Suspended rather than cancelled. If a HOW was suspended, it could be re-imposed without re-applying to the Home Office. Until Birkett recommended otherwise, HOWs were 'open-ended'.

[70] TNA, KV 4/467 (Liddell Diary, 11 April 1951). Krivitsky was a Soviet defector who had provided MI5 with a lot of intelligence when the Service interviewed him in 1940 (see TNA, KV 2/802–5). ACORN was the then current code word for US communications intelligence shared with the UK as part of the joint US/UK interception programme best known today as the Venona project.

Office that he was given a day's leave on Saturday. He has not apparently been seen since and TCs indicate considerable anxiety in the family.'

Heavy redactions notwithstanding, Guy Liddell's Diary indicates that it was likely that both SF and a telephone tap were used to monitor Donald Maclean shortly before his disappearance. In his entry for 1 May 1951, Liddell records that:

> We are trying to get **REDACTED** on MACLEAN, but meanwhile we are entirely dependent upon Watchers, who in any case are an essential ingredient in an enquiry of this kind.

As a telecheck was already in operation it seems likely that the words 'special facilities' have been removed from the entry. In the MI5 files despite the usual censorship with regard to SF, enough has been left to confirm that SF was installed. A note from Cumming of B4 dated 5 June 1951 refers to a conversation with Saffery at the Post Office Special Investigations Unit about:

> the interruption on Tatsfield ** REDACTED** and TC for several hours during each of the last two nights . . . it appeared likely either that Mrs. CURZON [Maclean] was taking off the bedroom telephone overnight or, alternatively, the power supply to the local exchange was being cut off at these hours in connection with (eg) local repairs.[71]

The minute sheet entry has, however, been overlooked by the 'weeder' and records the document as a 'Note by B4 re interruption on Tatsfield SF and TC'.[72]

SF Redactions

A rare glimpse of evidence of the preparations for the installation of SF is provided by a sequence of minute sheet entries recorded in Maclean's file.

Such is the context that it is apparent that the letters 'SF' have been redacted from each entry in preparation for the release of the file to the National Archives.[73]

Curzon is the code name used by MI5 to identify Maclean for the purposes of this investigation.

4 May 1951: 'B4 plan for **REDACTED** at CURZON's house & note by B2 stating plan not feasible'.

'B4 note of discussion with B2 re ** REDACTED**.'

[71] TNA, KV 2/4142.

[72] ibid. Corroboration of sorts—not that it is required—is offered by Chapman Pincher, who claimed that the Security Service had managed to conceal 'several hidden microphones' in Maclean's house: C. Pincher, *Their Trade is Treachery* (London, 1981), pp. 224–5.

[73] TNA, KV 2/4140. The usual approach of the 'weeders' is to obliterate the entire entry, which is what appears to have happened in the Loeffler and Taylor files.

7 May 1951: 'B2 note of meeting re sources of investigation in CURZON case.'
'B4 note of meeting re sources of investigation in CURZON case.'
8 May: 'B4 re operation of ** REDACTED** on a green line.'
'B4 note of discussion re ** REDACTED** in CURZON's home.'
[Dates unclear, but circa 10 May]: 'B4 note of discussion re installation of ** REDACTED** at CURZON's home.'
'B4 note of message from GPO re ** REDACTED**.'
'From GPO re ** REDACTED** on Curzon.'

Each entry also has had a line scored through it and a handwritten note added, indicating that the documents they relate to have been removed and placed in a 'link volume'. This step was apparently taken many years ago and is unconnected with the release of the file to the public. Very likely the motivation was a desire to keep knowledge of electronic eavesdropping, and of MI5 covert entries, restricted to the smallest possible number, even within the Security Service.

Following the disappearance of Burgess and Maclean, attention turned to Kim Philby, whose interrogation by 'Buster' Milmo we have already encountered in Chapter 5. In order to get evidence against Philby, it seems that 'enquiries' were made of others, including Edith Tudor-Hart, who was believed to have been involved in his recruitment.[74] An Austrian national married to an English doctor, Tudor-Hart had been 'a trusted courier and go-between' for Russian Intelligence, and was an overt Communist all her adult life.[75] In a news report on her file at the time of its release, *The Guardian* states that in the 1930s Tudor-Hart had:

> acted as a courier for Burgess, Philby's Cambridge University contemporary. But it was only in 1964, with the confession of the fourth member of the spy ring, Anthony Blunt, that the full truth emerged. Tudor-Hart had, Blunt told his MI5 interrogators, been 'the grandmother of us all'.[76]

The Guardian also notes that Tudor-Hart was placed under close observation and that MI5 subjected her 'to round-the-clock surveillance, opened her mail, tapped her telephone, bugged her home and eavesdropped on the conversations of her friends and associates. The agency even set up an observation post from which they could see her retiring to bed.'[77]

[74] This was eventually confirmed in 1985 in one of many interviews granted by Philby to Genrikh Borovik: G. Borovik, *The Philby Files, The Secret Life of the Master Spy—KGB Archives Revealed* (London, 1994), p. 31. Documents in the KGB archive corroborated Philby's claim (pp. 39 and 133).

[75] TNA, KV 4/4093 (A Note on the Case of Edith Tudor-Hart). This is from 1965, the most recent of the released MI5 documents on her activities. By this time, Tudor-Hart had apparently 'settled down to a responsible bourgeois life'.

[76] *The Guardian*, 20 August 2015.

[77] ibid.

Such was the importance of the Philby investigations, HOWs relating to Tudor-Hart were applied for and obtained in one day, 2 October 1951. There is a gap in the minute sheet of Tudor-Hart's file where it appears that the arrangements for the SF installation have been redacted. Entry 142 has also been removed and a sizeable amount of text in the minute sheet has been taken out. The file refers to the visit made by 'Jim' Skardon to interrogate Mrs Tudor-Hart on 3 October 1951.[78] According to *The Guardian* again:

> Two MI5 officers, one of them Jim Skardon, considered to be the agency's most effective interrogator, burst into the flat, brandishing War Office identity cards, and questioned her for an hour.[79]

Another 'note' on file KV2/1014 appears to have had the reference to 'SF' in paragraph 3 redacted—'The telephone check and **REDACTED** on Tudor-Hart will be placed on an immediate monitoring basis.' Security Service redaction of any references to the installation or use of SF in files released to the National Archives is standard practice, but nevertheless remarkable in the case of the Tudor-Hart file, given the numbers of SF-based reports and transcriptions in the file.

If the existence of SF is a secret, the fruits are there for all to see. File KV2/4091 includes a document from source NORTH (the code name for electronic eavesdropping which replaced TABLE in January 1952). This particular document reveals that Edith had returned home at 15.30, and 'could now be heard talking to her mother and WOLF. URSULA was also there.' The marginal notes added by MI5 indicate that they were perhaps surprised and amused to see that Edith suspected that her telephone had been interfered with. The fact that it appears that no telephone repairmen, or any other tradesmen had been in the flat rather suggests that the SF had been installed following an undetected entry by MI5 and the GPO Special Investigations Unit. Arranging a faulty line, then sending the Special Investigations Unit to install SF when 'repairing' the line, would very likely have led Mrs Tudor-Hart to stop using the telephone.[80] Yet even at her most paranoid she would have been unlikely to suspect that MI5 were listening to her through the mouth-piece of her telephone while it was still in the cradle.

Interest in Tudor-Hart waned in 1952, but revived early in the following year. The Security Service sought fresh HOWs to permit postal and telephone

[78] TNA, KV 2/1014 (Minute sheet, Edith Tudor-Hart).

[79] It was arranged so that Skardon would turn up without notice. The MI5 note did not raise any concerns that he would not be able to conduct the interview. So much for MI5 officers having no legal powers. The interview was timed to take place at least twenty-four hours before the interrogation of Philby, to allow time to consider the results.

[80] There are a number of documents in that file to indicate that Mrs Tudor-Hart was regarded by her friends as suffering from a persecution complex, believing as she did that she was being followed, that her phone was tapped, and that certain of her friends were passing information to the Security Service about her—and, of course, she was right. The B5 'watchers' were on her tail. She may even have suspected that her home was bugged. As also picked up by *The Guardian* report (n 76), she suffered a nervous breakdown, and became in the 'early 1950s unbalanced to the point of insanity': TNA, KV 4/4093 (A Note on the Case of Edith Tudor-Hart).

interception, on the ground that she 'is **REDACTED** reported to have been involved in Soviet espionage in this country and it is desired to re-examine her current activities as closely as possible'. An accompanying briefing sheet suggests that Tudor-Hart had fallen out of favour with the Communist Party and that she might now be in a 'better frame of mind' as a result. This, however, seemed optimistic, and there is no evidence that this wily operator gave anything away. It is unclear whether MI5's attentions were responsible for or contributed to her subsequent mental illness. Although MI5 officers were instructed to familiarize themselves with previous NORTH reports, there is no evidence that SF were used on the occasion of this re-examination of the Tudor-Hart case. It is possible that there have been some documents redacted, but, unlike KV2/1014, there are no obvious gaps in the minute sheet of KV2/4092 in the relevant period.

VII. Political Accountability

It is at this point we return to questions of accountability. As noted in Part II above, the Attlee Directive required 'specific authority' from the Home Secretary 'whenever it is proposed to install a microphone' (para. 7). Some of the incidents discussed in this chapter—the CPGB, Beurton, Maclean, and Tudor-Hart—took place while the Attlee Directive was in force, yet there is no evidence on file of any authority from the Home Secretary, whether in the form of a HOW or otherwise. Other incidents discussed in this chapter—the CPGB and Operation Party Piece—took place after the Maxwell Fyfe Directive had replaced the Attlee Directive, and there is no evidence of a warrant there either. Although in the latter case this might be unsurprising, it should be pointed out that the removal of paragraph 7 of the Attlee Directive was not supposed to signal an end to HOWs for SF, its removal being supported by Sillitoe as principal author of the Maxwell Fyfe Directive on the ground that the formal reference to SF in the Directive was not necessary because a warrant was always sought and obtained anyway.

It should be added that although there is no evidence of a warrant on file, it remains possible, though unlikely, that political authorization was given in all of these cases. Unlikely because it does not seem plausible that MI5 would wish today to convey the impression that it routinely broke the rules. Nevertheless, if it is unclear just how faithfully the paragraph 7 obligations were met prior to the revision of the Attlee Directive, it is now very clear that there was little ministerial supervision thereafter, as many different sources confirm. An intervention by Rupert Allason in a House of Commons debate in 1989 corroborates Professor Andrew's account of Home Office procedure referred to above when he said in relation to MI5 operations:

> Until fairly recent times the attitude of the Home Secretary has been, 'I do not wish to know about these things'. When Security Service officers have had to

> conduct some clandestine entry they have obtained permission, but have done so through the Permanent Under Secretary. I know that on at least one occasion the Home Secretary was consulted, but that was on the basis that he could more or less deny that he knew what was going to happen if anything went wrong.[81]

While some MI5 officers may have preferred to have less deniable political procedures in place, there were presumably others who embraced the de facto and unconstrained powers the Service appeared now to enjoy.

Yet it was not only ministers who were uncomfortable about any sense of complicity in or responsibility for MI5's activities; Home Office officials were also not always happy either. So although senior Home Office officials had engineered themselves into a position of de facto authority, Newsam as PUS nevertheless revealed himself as nervous, following a lively discussion about ministerial responsibility with Guy Liddell. As we saw on page 38 above, Liddell reported being told by the Home Office mandarin that MI5:

> should go back to our former status, where we were more or less responsible to everybody and nobody; he thought there was much too much publicity given to MI5 . . . the affairs of the Department could not be discussed in Parliament any more than those of the Secret Service [MI6]. *The Home Secretary would deny knowledge of our activities and suggest that if we had infringed the law in any way the appropriate remedy was to bring an action against us.*[82]

Nevertheless, it is clear that under successive Home Secretaries since Maxwell Fyfe, all responsibility for supervision and accountability had drifted to officials. As a brief on ministerial responsibility prepared in 1963 for Burke Trend pointed out, the role of the Home Secretary in relation to MI5 became 'blurred' after 1952, and of the 'four officials to whom the Director General of the Security Service can turn for advice or authority' named in the brief, the first was the PUS at the Home Office.[83]

This was true generally, but also true specifically in regard to specific operations or special procedures, ministers also managing to avoid scrutiny of their retreat by the Birkett Committee on the interception of communications. It appears that witnesses before the latter were not asked about 'bugging' and apparently chose not to trouble the committee with any details of the practice. It might be argued that use of a hidden microphone does not amount to an 'interception'—though this would clearly be as unconvincing a claim as it would be unacceptable. The practice was

81 HC Debs, 16 Jan 1989, col. 62.

82 TNA, KV 4/473 (Liddell Diary, 21 March 1951) (emphasis added).

83 TNA, CAB 301/230 (Note by 'JHR' [J. H. Robertson of the Cabinet Office] to Burke Trend, 19 June 1963). The others were the Cabinet Secretary, the Joint Permanent Secretary to the Treasury, and the Prime Minister's Personal Private Secretary.

nevertheless clearly outside the committee's brief—otherwise it would have featured in their report. However, it is remarkable that such a closely related matter was not even *mentioned*. It appears that at some point between 1945 and 1957 electronic eavesdropping became defined as a surveillance technique, and came to be regarded, in government and security and intelligence circles at least, as distinct from the interception of communications. This ensured that any discussion of mail or telephone interceptions—distasteful as such matters are in a democracy—did not draw the use of covert microphones into the debate.

Whatever arrangements were or were not in place, it is apparent that opaque practices were stretching constitutional principle to breaking point: at best, actions were being taken benignly on behalf of ministers who deliberately knew nothing about them; at worst, the decisions in question were taken malignly by a State agency in circumstances where the responsible ministers were deliberately kept in the dark. It may be that one-time DG Stella Rimington's response to ex-MI5 officer Peter Wright's now famous confession is a better indication of how the Home Office and MI5 co-ordinated their activities before the Security Service Act 1989. Perhaps thinking of Norman Brook, it will be recalled that Wright claimed that, 'we bugged and burgled our way across London at the State's behest, while pompous bowler-hatted civil servants in Whitehall pretended to look the other way'.[84] Rimington, in a very measured, but nevertheless very revealing passage in her autobiography observed that:

> To eavesdrop effectively it is obviously important to plant the microphones where they will have the best chance of picking up the targeted conversations and also where they will not be discovered, and that is usually somewhere inside the premises where you expect the conversations to take place. Such operations . . . were carefully controlled and scrutinised for the appropriateness of the targets and though judgments were made about the balance of risk and reward, and though *they were known about and tacitly approved of in Whitehall*, the fact remains that those operations had no explicit statutory basis.[85]

It is unclear whether Rimington is here acknowledging impropriety by MI5. But returning to our immediate concern, 'known about' suggests either the Home Office merely knew the practice went on, or that they were informed of each operation. Peter Wright revealed that 'Every microphone installed is recorded in the A Branch Index, which logs technical specifications, a history of its operation, and, most important of all, its precise location.'[86] In other words, a list of SF installations

[84] Wright (n 1), p. 54.

[85] S. Rimington, *Open Secret: The Autobiography of the Former Director-General of MI5* (London, 2002 edn), p. 194.

[86] Wright (n 1), pp. 59–60.

was made and maintained (though we have not seen it). 'Tacit approval' suggests either that the Home Office intervened in cases where they disapproved of an unlawful entry, or the use of a microphone; or—and this appears to be the more likely interpretation—the Home Office simply let the Service get on with their activities. Certainly, Rimington appears to imply that MI5 rather than the Home Office made the judgements as to risk, reward, and propriety. While it is very likely that Wright's 'list' was available for Home Office inspection, (i) knowledge; and (ii) tacit approval at best are a long way short of the Attlee Directive's obligations of (iii) acting under the directions of; and (iv) reporting to, the Home Secretary.

VIII. Conclusion

In practice, during the early Cold War, little distinction appears to have been drawn between the use of SF and the use of hidden microphones, with 'Special Facilities' being used as a convenient catch-all term for electronic eavesdropping generally, although this may have changed in later years. Such were the political implications of any prospective Fleet Street coverage of the use of covert eavesdropping techniques by MI5, it appears that all concerned were more comfortable using either this euphemistic term or using the acronym 'SF'. Yet while the existence of SF was kept secret, inevitably some telephone engineers and telephone exchange staff became aware of these eavesdropping operations. An article in the *Sunday Pictorial* in 1952 had referred to the use of SF after a GPO employee had shown a number of local councillors around a telephone exchange in Slough, telling the surprised worthies that telephone calls were sometimes monitored by the police and MI5, and that telephones could be activated as listening devices.[87]

However, the substance of the story was about telephone tapping, and the muddled, but fundamentally accurate, description of SF was overlooked by other newspapers, Parliament, and the wider public. It was not until 1965 that we find the first academic engagement with the question, with D. G. T. Williams reflecting in his pioneering *Not in the Public Interest* on 'technical aids to espionage through microphones and transmitters', and concluding that:

> Some limitation should be imposed upon the use of these new technical devices just as some limitation is imposed on the interception of letters, telegrams and telephonic communications.[88]

[87] The *Sunday Pictorial* article was cited by T. Bunyan, *The History and Practice of the Political Police in Britain* (London, 1977), p. 203 and subsequently by P. Fitzgerald and M. Leopold, *Stranger on the Line: The Secret History of Phone Tapping* (London, 1987), pp. 114–15 and p. 202.

[88] D. G. T. Williams, *Not in the Public Interest—The Problems of Security in Democracy* (London, 1965), p. 136.

Little did he know that there had been a form of regulation under the Labour government in the shape of the Attlee Directive.

Professor Williams was not the only one operating in the dark. As late as 1967, Gordon Campbell, Conservative MP for Moray and Nairn, ended a speech on a debate on the rights and liberties of the individual in the Commons by adding:

> One further matter which has not been touched on so far in this debate is the problem of eavesdropping with technical devices. Here I do not blame the Government, because it is a new problem. A great deal has been said in the House about telephone tapping . . . But if that is thought to be reprehensible, it is even more reprehensible to use electronic or other devices to eavesdrop on ordinary conversations or business discussions, unless it is being done for the security of the State under special regulations authorised by the Home Secretary and the Secretary of State for Scotland.[89]

There were, of course, no special regulations for these special powers, though there had once been special procedures under Attlee, which in 1967 were unknown.

We can easily speculate that the Attlee Directive's requirement that the use of 'SF' should have the authorization of the Home Secretary could well have evolved into a requirement only for telephonic SF to require a HOW, and for mikes more generally to break free from the HOW system, particularly as technology advanced and free-standing microphones were no longer reliant on GPO cables. Squeamishness about publicity for bugging nevertheless continued for the next twenty years or so, and to its exclusion from the regulatory provisions of the Interception of Communications Act 1985, even after journalists Nick Davies and Ian Black had revealed that the then current code word for SF was CINNAMON, and that for hidden microphones it was AZURE.[90] Political qualms were overcome only when the Thatcher government's hand had been forced by Peter Wright's *Spycatcher* revelations and the litigation embarked upon by the government to silence him had served to turn the book into an international best seller.[91] The immediate response was the Security Service Act 1989, which provided that 'no entry on or interference with property or with wireless telegraphy shall be unlawful if it is authorised by a warrant issued by the Secretary of State'.[92]

[89] HC Debs, 17 July 1967, col. 1580.

[90] *The Guardian*, 18 April 1984. According to the same authors, CINNAMON arrangements required HOWs (which did not sanction trespass), while warrants were not issued for 'free standing' AZURE microphones.

[91] See K. D. Ewing and C. A. Gearty, *Freedom under Thatcher: Civil Liberties in Modern Britain* (Oxford, 1990), ch. 5.

[92] Security Service Act 1989, s. 3. See L. Lustgarten and I. Leigh, *In from the Cold: National Security and Parliamentary Democracy* (Oxford, 1994), pp. 55–9. The power is now contained in the Intelligence Services Act 1994, s. 5, which also includes powers to grant warrants to MI6 and GCHQ. The minister issuing the warrant must be satisfied that it is 'necessary', for the purpose of 'assisting' MI5 in carrying out its functions, and 'proportionate' to what the action seeks to achieve. The functions of MI5 are set out in the Security Service Act 1989, s. 1.

The latter provision was significant because it introduced a long-overdue legal formality to a practice that was now engaging Convention rights as well as property rights.[93] But it was significant also because it was a back-handed way of acknowledging that what MI5 had been doing in relation to electronic eavesdropping otherwise had been potentially 'unlawful' for many, many years.

[93] *Hewitt and Harman v United Kingdom* (1992) 14 EHRR 657.

9
Surveillance and the Purge

I. Introduction

Perhaps the most significant step taken in relation to the Communist Party was to exclude Communist Party members from various forms of employment, ostensibly to prevent them from coming into contact with State secrets. In this chapter we provide an account of the so-called civil service 'purge procedure' announced in 1948. This was not the only security procedure using MI5 material in the civil service, with developed forms of vetting being announced in 1952, and similar procedures operating in the private sector for employers handling government contracts formally announced in 1954. All three procedures were in operation long before they were formally made known, and indeed one of the motivations for announcing the civil service purge was the fear that the existing informal purge of Communists would be publicized, and the ensuing need for an official procedure to limit the potential embarrassment to MI5 and to the government. The different procedures were augmented in 1962 by the purge of Communists from civil service trade unions, and we deal with each of them in the chapters that follow.

For now, however, we are concerned only with the civil service purge, and its application to the 750,000 or so civil servants. MI5 had been involved in the vetting of prospective recruits to the civil service, as well as existing civil servants prior to their 'establishment' or transfer to secret work long before 1948. This running of a name past police and MI5 records was a purge—those who were found to have a questionable record could find themselves denied employment, refused establishment as a fully fledged public servant, or denied access to secret work. As we will see, these informal practices continued after 1948 alongside the official purge announced by Attlee, which is best seen as a political firewall employed exceptionally in a very few cases where vetting had indicated that a civil servant involved with secret work was closely associated with the Communist Party, and where it was too risky to resolve the problem informally. The purge thus refers to the official procedure, which required ministerial approval for dismissal, unlike the unofficial purge, which was executed by officials informed by MI5.

Britain is a country with an ambivalent and contradictory relationship with constitutional principle, whether it be parliamentary sovereignty (in the sense that Parliament is the source of legal authority), or the Rule of Law (in the sense that government must have legal authority for its actions, and that such legal authority must be grounded in clear rules fairly administered). The purge procedure was

MI5, the Cold War, and the Rule of Law. K. D. Ewing, Joan Mahoney, and Andrew Moretta, Oxford University Press (2020). DOI: 10.1093/oso/9780198818625.001.0001

introduced without statutory authority, by means of a statement to the House of Commons by the Prime Minister, which did not lead to a vote,[1] with revision of the procedures announced by way of written answer, the process no longer thought sufficient to merit an oral statement.[2] Not all security procedures—notably pre-recruitment 'negative' vetting for civil servants, were announced to Parliament even by written answer—and there is evidence of anxiety lest the existence of these and other procedures received publicity. The importance of the purge procedure, however, is that by the appointment of Three Advisers to scrutinize its operation, the Attlee government introduced what was to be MI5's only direct accountability until 1985.

The purge procedure was thus important because it both empowered and potentially contained MI5. It empowered MI5 in the sense not only that it required the collection and use of information about Communist Party members and sympathizers, but also in the sense that it enabled MI5 to make the assessments about who was to work and who was not, and to work where, and under what circumstances. But it potentially constrained MI5 in the sense that these assessments would now be the subject of scrutiny, albeit to a body of officials appointed by the government who would not pass any judicial test of independence. As we will see, MI5 had lobbied for an official purge procedure, principally to give them political cover in the event of the existing practice spilling out. But the Service strongly opposed even the mild and limited scrutiny of the The Three Advisers as an affront to its integrity and independence. The speed with which MI5 moved to contain and neutralize the accountability mechanisms is salutary, leading eventually and perhaps coincidentally to a purge of the Three Advisers and the appointment of a new chair.

II. Origins

According to received wisdom, the purge was introduced in 1948. Some scholars have suggested that the government jumped the gun and started the process before it had been formally announced. Writing in 1982, Hennessy and Brownfeld cite private information that transfers of civil servants to less sensitive posts were already taking place some two years before the purge was formally announced, while Schneer claims that six Communist civil servants lost their jobs in 1948 before Attlee's speech to Parliament.[3] But the position is more complex than the government itching to implement a new policy before its formal announcement, with MI5 having orchestrated a purge which was taking place informally at least since

1 HC Debs, 15 March 1948, col. 1703.

2 HC Debs, 29 January 1957, col. 152 WA.

3 J. Schneer, *Labour's Conscience: The Labour Left, 1945–51* (London, 1988), p. 156. Further evidence that the purge had already started covertly is provided by E. Bontecou, 'The English Policy as to Communists and Fascists in the Civil Service' (1951) 51 *Columbia Law Review* 564, at pp. 566–7.

1943, this reflecting a failure of a political vetting process already in place but evidently lacking in rigour.

1. War-time Proposals

In October 1943, the Prime Minister, Winston Churchill, and the Home Secretary, Herbert Morrison received a paper from the then chair of the Security Executive, Alfred Duff Cooper, also Chancellor of the Duchy of Lancaster (and former Secretary of State for War in the Baldwin government). The paper contained proposals by the Security Service following the conviction of Communist Party organizer Douglas Springhall for espionage.[4] Duff Cooper proposed a purge:

> It may fairly be stated that any member of the Communist Party should be regarded as a potential agent . . . Attached to this memorandum is a list of known members of the Communist Party employed on secret work in various Government departments . . . It would be a comparatively simple matter to arrange for the transfer of all known Communists now engaged on secret work to other branches of national service.

Roger Hollis, then Assistant Director of MI5's F Division, unmoved by the Party's very considerable support for the war effort, had long been warning of the danger he saw posed by domestic Communists, and there can be little doubt that he regarded the Springhall case as a vindication. Hollis had sent Duff Cooper a memo by David Clarke, F2A, with a list of 'fifty seven known members of the Communist Party who are believed to have access to secret information and in some cases information of the highest secrecy'.[5]

Clarke's memo gives us a good grasp of the vetting process as it then stood, and as it appears to have continued until 1948:

> It is not intended to suggest that the fifty seven members of the Communist Party referred to above have obtained their position through any wholesale failure of the vetting system . . . In certain cases there is a real difficulty in balancing the requirements of the work against the risk of disclosure, for example, in the employment of such a man as Prof. J. B. S. Haldane. In a few cases, but not the least secret posts, the name has not been submitted for vetting until after employment has begun.[6]

[4] See p. 19 above.

[5] TNA, KV 4/251 (Policy Re Communists Already Employed on Secret Work in Government Departments). The memo, dated 21 October 1943, 'Communists Engaged on Secret Work', has a long-hand note at the foot of it indicating that in 1955 Hollis had identified it as the work of David Clarke.

[6] ibid.

Clarke went on to admit that the Service had made some serious mistakes, and that some Party members employed as clerks had been able to see confidential documents because there were no vetting arrangements for certain categories of civil servant or military rank. Significantly, Clarke conceded that:

> In a large number of cases the individual has come to notice as a member of the Communist Party only after he has already been engaged on secret work for some time. It is the general practice of the Security Service in such cases to notify the Government Department concerned of the information which has come into their possession. There are, however, obvious difficulties in advising drastic action which might reveal the sources of our information. In many cases of this type no action is taken.[7]

Clarke, however, cited a recent case where the Service discovered an 'Air Ministry Group of the Communist Party which has resulted in the transfer of several established civil servants to less secret work without friction or publicity'. In the light of these cases, Clarke was calling for procedures to avoid the bureaucratic mistakes he had referred to, and was also pressing for a ban on Party members being employed in secret work, where that was possible without revealing that the individual in question had become of interest to the Security Service, and without threatening the Service's sources:

> No . . . uniformity is to be found in the final outcome of cases, either of the pre-vetting or of those already employed who are found to be communists, because there is no general policy towards employment of members of the Communist Party on secret work . . . it is not wholly a wartime problem . . . After the war it [the Party] will be just as anxious to guide its policy by foreknowledge of the Government's domestic programme. The political advantage of such information should be denied to the Communist Party. The need for a uniform policy will remain after the war.[8]

The Springhall case had supposedly revealed the Party's interest in secret work, although the headstrong and independent 'Springy', who had been the Party's pre-war link with the Communist International (Comintern) and consequently had personal contacts in Moscow, appeared to have been operating without the knowledge of the Party in London.[9] The latter had expelled him following his conviction

[7] ibid.

[8] ibid.

[9] Springhall was believed to have played a key role in running the 'Cambridge Five' (see A. Boyle, *The Climate of Treason: Five Who Spied for Russia* (London, 1979), pp. 102 and 112), and arguably he can be seen as a spy who worked for the Party in much the same way as Blunt and Philby were spies who worked for MI5 and SIS, although his work for the Party would not have revealed much that would have

under the Official Secrets Acts, and had changed its name to the Communist Party of Great Britain (CPGB) to emphasize that it was not in thrall to the Russians. Clarke argued that with the Party 'in no mood to refresh the public's memory by raising an outcry',[10] the departments should take the opportunity to work with the Service to weed Party members out of secret work. Apart from pressing for a ban on Communists being engaged in secret work, Clarke's memo thus also revealed that there was a well-established vetting process in place, but one of limited effectiveness that would require a purge of those who had slipped under the wire.

2. MI5 Rebuffed

Churchill approved of a purge, but did not think a public announcement was appropriate 'at this stage'. Nor did he agree with MI5 that individuals should be removed from office on the say-so of MI5 alone, proposing a more formal process.[11] Thus, in accepting MI5's case for a civil service purge, Churchill nevertheless proposed that:

> When MI5 knows or believes that any person concerned is a member or adherent of the Communist Party, the evidence should be laid before a small panel under the Chairman of the Security Executive. This panel should include Mr Isaac Foot and Mr Wall. It will decide what action is necessary in face of the evidence laid before it.[12]

The chair of the Panel was to be Sir Herbert Creedy, the head of the small committee on Communism that reported to the Security Executive. However, both Sir David Petrie (then Head of MI5) and Roger Hollis were unhappy about the 'the panel procedure *suggested* by the Prime Minister'.[13] MI5 had merely wanted a Cabinet ruling 'in order to strengthen the attitude' of the departments to the advice of the Service;[14] it had not wanted a 'Panel' to which it had to justify its claims, and most certainly did not want to be obliged to reveal any evidence. Earlier in the war, the Service had been severely embarrassed in a number of Regulation 18B detention cases when the committee scrutinizing individual cases had revealed to detainees evidence that could only have come from clearly identifiable

been of interest to Moscow. See also F. Beckett and J. Murray, *Enemy Within—The Rise and Fall of the British Communist Party* (London, 1995), pp. 85–7.

[10] 'Policy Re Communists Already Employed on Secret Work in Government Departments', n 5 above.

[11] TNA, KV 4/251 (Prime Minister's Personal Minute, 31 October 1943, Serial No. M 762/3).

[12] TNA, KV 4/251 (Prime Minister's Personal Minute, 13 December 1943, Serial No. M(S) 10/3).

[13] Emphasis added—it was an order, as they well knew.

[14] TNA, KV 4/251 (Minute sheet note by Hollis, 10 November 1943).

sources.[15] Phone taps, mail interception, and penetration agents aside, the Service had been eavesdropping on King Street by the use of SF since 1942, and as we have seen, was very wary about referring to the practice, even in its own files. Disclosing evidence culled from SF transcripts to a committee of politicians and civil servants was unthinkable.

Petrie's concerns were nevertheless dismissed, Edward Bridges (Cabinet Secretary) sending a brusque letter on 11 February 1944, telling him that:

> the Prime Minister has given instructions that a panel should be set up . . . charged with weighing that evidence and deciding whether it ought to be brought to the notice of the Department concerned. The decision as to what action should be taken in regard to the evidence will rest with the Department concerned.[16]

Churchill had ordered that the decision lay with the panel but Morrison and Bridges appear to have decided to permit the department and the minister to weigh the value of the individual against the security risk, and to permit the minister to buck the advice of the panel where appropriate, further undermining the authority of MI5. The first meeting, an introductory meeting of the panel which was addressed by Petrie, was held on 1 March 1944. However, it appears that no cases were ever brought to its attention, Hollis stating on more than one occasion in internal memos that concerns about sources meant that it was unlikely any cases would take the formal route set by Churchill.[17]

A lengthy semi-redacted minute sheet note by Hollis from November 1944 indicates that MI5 were carrying on as they did before the panel was established, investigating and advising on suspects on the Left. Duncan Sandys' private secretary, for example was found to be politically undesirable, and MI5 suggested 'that Mr Sandys, who has only just taken over, might be advised to find that he did not suit him'.[18] A Home Office case was brought to the attention of Sir Alexander Maxwell (PUS at the Home Office) by Hollis in November 1944. Rather than transfer the individual, the normally pliant Maxwell nevertheless suggested that it was a case for the 'Prime Minister's Panel'. Hollis told Petrie 'we have never used the Panel and were not anxious to do so, a point with which Sir Alexander Maxwell was in sympathy'. After a disagreement with Maxwell on what had been decided earlier in the year, Hollis later agreed that the case did appear to fall within the jurisdiction of the panel. However, after Hollis and Creedy had discussed the possibility 'that the panel be brought into operation', the paper trail stops, and it seems very likely

[15] See TNA, KV 4/470 (Liddell Diary, 19 March 1948). On the procedures, see generally A. W. B. Simpson, *In the Highest Degree Odious* (Oxford, 1992), pp. 92–3, 264–6.

[16] TNA, KV 4/251 (11 February 1944).

[17] It was for the Security Service rather than the departments to bring cases to the Panel, see TNA KV 4/251 (Minute sheet notes by Hollis, 4 March 1944).

[18] ibid., 29 November 1944.

that the case was dealt with informally.[19] The numbers affected by this unofficial purge are unknown.

3. After the War

It seems that the responsibilities (such as they were) of the Creedy Panel were taken over in 1945 by a new panel. This was 'the Bridges Panel'—'the Panel on Security Arrangements in Government Departments'. Bridges was Head of the Home Civil Service, and although not much is known about these arrangements, it appears that it was departments rather than MI5 that referred difficult cases for determination or guidance.[20] MI5's responsibilities thus continued to remain uncertain, and the Service started to lobby for a new procedure within a few weeks of Churchill leaving office. Displaying impressive optimism, Petrie told Hollis on 6 September 1945 that:

> the position ought to be reviewed. We could not do better than begin by consulting Sir Herbert Creedy in doing which we stand to gain something and lose nothing . . . if exclusion is to be decided upon, Cabinet approval is essential.

But in the first months of the Attlee administration, with the focus on civil liberties, and Churchill's election jibe about a Labour *Gestapo* a very recent memory, there was little chance that Hollis and Petrie would get their way.

That said, circumstances were to change quickly. The defection of KGB officer Igor Gouzenko in Canada in September 1945, and the gradual realization that Soviet intelligence had mounted an extensive espionage campaign, were triggering factors for a reconsideration of the need for a formal purge procedure.[21] As discussed in Chapter 4, Gouzenko's defection led directly to the arrest and conviction of Dr Alan Nunn May, who had spied for the Russians while working on a joint American–British–Canadian atomic project. The government responded immediately with a review of security procedures for the civil service, a Committee appointed to develop better arrangements. Led by Sir Edward Bridges, and Sir Percy Sillitoe, now MI5's Director General, most of the Committee's work was done primarily by John Winnifrith (a senior civil servant at the Treasury, who later became

19 TNA, KV 4/251 (Minute sheet notes from Hollis to Petrie, 30 November 1944). These were part of a series in which Petrie's handwritten responses (where they remain) counselled 'utmost caution'.

20 We do not know a great deal about the work of the Bridges' Panel. It is almost certain that it already existed and very likely indeed that it assessed important vetting cases.

21 Gouzenko defected in September 1945, but many were reluctant to 'think the worst of our former allies'—Liddell referring the reaction of a member of the Canadian Department of External Affairs (TNA, KV 4/467, Liddell Diary, 25 April 1946).

Permanent Secretary at the Ministry of Agriculture), and notably Graham Mitchell (MI5).[22]

These unexpectedly changing circumstances presented MI5 with the opportunity to continue to press for a formal purge procedure to be agreed with government and the departments.[23] In the meantime, however, vetting and advice on purging continued in the absence of a formal procedure, as revealed by the following extracts from the Liddell Diaries:

> November 1945: 'Marriott tells me that Street of the HO [Home Office] is being moved to the Ministry of Town and Country Planning. Street is a CP member and is an embarrassment to us as he sits in the same room as Hill and Bromley'.[24] [Hill and Bromley worked closely with MI5].
>
> October 1946: 'Hollis raised the question of two historians who were members of the Communist Party working in the Cabinet Office. Although they might not be engaged on confidential subjects, it was not unlikely that they mixed with other people who were. These people would not know that they were talking to members of the Communist Party. I suggested to Hollis that he should have a talk with Colonel Walker, who spoke to me about them at the club the other day—one of them was taken on against our advice and the other was taken on before the result of the vetting was received'.[25]
>
> January 1947: 'I spoke to the DG about a [**REDACTED**] who is a communist and said to be working in the private office at the Home Office. The DG went over and saw Maxwell, who was much perturbed and undertook to look into the matter immediately. The danger from our point of view was that [**REDACTED**] might be seeing all our HOWs'.[26]
>
> February 1947: 'I went to see Newsam [then Deputy PUS at the Home Office] about three checks on civil servants . . . [the three names have been redacted]. I asked him to make special arrangements to see that the warrants were not handled by the staff as [**REDACTED**] and [**REDACTED**] had both been in the Home Office'.[27]

[22] P. Hennessy and G. Brownfeld, 'Britain's Cold War Security Purge: The Origins of Positive Vetting' (1982) 25 *Historical Journal* 965.

[23] At an MI5 meeting in January 1947, Liddell also argued that Sir Edward Bridges should be asked:

> to revert to the system of vetting of civil servants temporary or permanent who were to be employed on secret work. Secondly we ought to vet temporary civil servants at the outset and thereafter rely on their being brought to notice if they were to be employed on secret work, and thirdly that the DG should bring to the notice of Brides [presumably Bridges] the question of PAs and secretaries brought in by Ministers and Parliamentary Under Secretaries. Normally these people are not vetted . . . Fourthly, that the Bridges' panel should ask Departments for an assurance that their outstations knew about vetting procedure for secret work (TNA, KV 4/468, Liddell Diary, 7 January 1947).

[24] TNA, KV 4/466 (Liddell Diary, 1 November 1945).

[25] TNA, KV 4/468 (Liddell Diary, 1 October 1946).

[26] TNA, KV 4/468 (30 January 1947).

[27] TNA, KV 4/468 (11 February 1947).

July 1947: 'It seemed to us all that there was a clear case for the dismissal both of BODDINGTON and EWING, in that they as responsible civil servants were actually assisting the Economic Committee of the Communist Party to frame its policy. It was thought that the case would have to go up to Bridges, and possibly to Morrison, and it was agreed that if necessary we would state the full facts to the latter'.[28]

October 1947: Liddell mentioned the case of a civil servant, Jack Parine at the War Office: 'the first case of its kind that would come before the new Minister . . . Shinwell was basically anti Communist and might therefore be quite amenable to action being taken . . . He [Eric Speed, PUS at the War Office] said that as soon as we had obtained confirmation he would get in touch with Bridges and ask for guidance . . . it would be most undesirable to leave PARINE where he is, and if he moved him it would be difficult to do so without stating the reasons'.[29]

These cases referred to by Liddell are in addition to the cases identified by others, suggesting that there were many more victims of this informal purge. Writing in 1949, Bontecou (who appears to have been well informed at a very early stage) claims that one of the civil service trade unions had complained that 'MI5 investigators had been inquiring at local Post Offices concerning the political opinions of some of its members', and that late in 1946 'two scientists had their assignments to the Atomic Energy Establishment and the Control Commission in Germany cancelled, while a third had been denied permanent civil service status—all without explanation'. The cases were taken up with Bridges by the civil service unions, complaining that 'if nothing more is attributed to a Civil Servant than membership of a political party, this fact of itself affords no ground for dismissal, refusal of employment, or any special departmental policy'.[30] But just as important as the reasons for the removals was the lack of any formal policy by which they were implemented.

4. MI5's Need for Formality and the Emergence of the Purge

An entry in the Liddell Diary from October 1947 recorded that a Working Party 'had considered the question of Communists in Government employment', and had 'put forward certain recommendations regarding the elimination of these people which had been accepted by the Defence Committee'.[31] We return to these recommendations in Chapter 10 in our consideration of the related and overlapping question of vetting. The entry continues rather dolefully, however,

[28] TNA, KV 4/469 (Liddell Diary, 22 July 1947).
[29] TNA, KV 4/469 (14 October 1947).
[30] Bontecou (n 3), pp. 566–7.
[31] TNA, KV 4/469 (Liddell Diary, 14 October 1947).

with Liddell recording that 'the matter was to be referred to the Cabinet, but so far we had heard no more'.[32] At this stage, there was thus still 'no positive Cabinet policy on the subject',[33] an omission that left MI5 with an ill-defined role and vulnerable to criticism should things go wrong.[34] Clearly, in such circumstances they would prefer to be able to say that the de facto piecemeal purging they were undertaking was being done at the behest of government.

Backing a formal procedure of political discrimination had, however, the potential to damage reputations and for a Labour government elected on a platform which included restoring civil liberties, it would be potentially toxic, even if hostility to the Communists within the government ran deep. At some point late in 1947, Sir Stafford Cripps as the responsible minister nevertheless ordered that Communist Party members could not be employed on 'secret or very secret work'. Liddell commented that:

> this ruling has to receive final approval from the Cabinet: once it has been obtained the way will be clear for us to discuss with relevant departments how these people can be side-tracked without giving rise to too much comment. Personally I do not see how they can escape telling a man the reasons for his removal.[35]

This matter would fall to Cripps (Chancellor of the Exchequer) because at the time HM Treasury was responsible for civil service employment, a responsibility which may help to explain Cripps' opposition to the European Convention on Human Rights. This opposition was strongly expressed at a Cabinet meeting in 1950, Cripps fearing that the Convention would impede the work of an administration committed to a socialist planned economy, as well as endanger steps being taken by the government to deal with Communists.[36]

In late December 1947, Attlee responded to a minute from the Minister of Defence (Albert Alexander) also calling for an official purge of the civil service:

> I agree. We cannot afford to take risks here, and the general public will support us. Fellow travellers may protest, but we should face up to this. Action should be taken in regard to Fascists as well as Communists, although the former are feeble.[37]

[32] ibid.

[33] ibid.

[34] TNA, KV 4/469 (Liddell Diary, 3 November 1947).

[35] TNA, KV 4/469 (Liddell Diary, 5 December 1947). Liddell reported that Sillitoe had seen the Minister of Defence, 'who produced for him a document drawn up by Cripps on the question of Communist Party membership of Government employees'.

[36] TNA, CAB 128/18 (Cabinet Conclusions, 1 August 1950). According to the Cabinet Secretary (though not recorded in the Conclusions) the concern was with Articles 4, 5, 8, and 13: TNA, CAB 195/8 (Cabinet Secretary's Notebook, 1 August 1950). It is not clear what Cripps had in mind that would engage Articles 4 (no slavery or forced labour), or 5 (right to liberty and no arbitrary detention).

[37] TNA, CAB 21/2278 (Prime Minister's Minutes, 21 December 1947).

One key advantage of the official procedure for MI5 was that the question of who they should purge—in the civil service at least—was now agreed, thereby securing the Service an officially acknowledged role, which threw off the last vestiges of post-war uncertainty about its future. MI5 also now knew who it was *obliged* to purge, making it less likely that the Service would be blamed if an individual outside of the purge criteria was found to have been engaged in espionage. One disadvantage was that the departments, arguing it was impossible in most cases to distinguish between those who had access to secret material and those who did not, wanted the Service to vet almost all staff, which would impose an extraordinary burden.[38] Even more troubling for the Service, however, was the prospect of having to produce evidence to back its allegations. As we have seen in relation to the wartime purge procedure, the Service saw this fundamental requirement as a threat to its sources.

Yet more troubling still for MI5 was the proposed appointment of Three Advisers, effectively to deal with appeals from civil servants who were to be purged on political grounds. In one sense, this was better than what had been proposed in wartime: the composition of the panel was not nearly as challenging for MI5 as had been the wartime panel, while it was not now proposed that *all* cases would have to go to the panel, which would hear cases only at the request of the accused. In fact, the Three Advisers was a radically different form of panel than the one to which MI5 had taken exception during the war. Then, the Service was to have acted as the 'prosecutor' albeit in a procedure in which the 'accused' was denied a right of audience or a right to make representations of any kind. Under the new procedures, in contrast, MI5 would be the 'respondent' required to justify the steps taken against individuals who would have an opportunity to appear in person before the panel. It was nevertheless a threat, and it was met by both capturing the procedures and by working around them.

III. Announcement and Reaction

The announcement of the civil service purge in March 1948 can arguably be seen as an acknowledgement by the government that vetting and purging were being undertaken, the announcement being made to permit the government and MI5 to manage the response to political blacklisting on their own terms, rather than

[38] See TNA, KV 4/470 (Liddell Diary, 4 February 1948, 21 June 1948). Also most notably, the meeting of the Cabinet Committee on Subversive Activities, 5 April 1950, chaired by Attlee, where the Committee heard that MI5 was inundated with departmental vetting requests: 'Only in around 1% of cases did this process produce an adverse report of any real substance; and in more than 90% of cases there was no record of the person's being a member of or associated with the Communist Party.' Vetting requests were coming in at a rate of 2,500 a week and Sillitoe wanted the Departments to reduce their demands to permit 'more searching enquiries over a narrower field'. It was agreed that a Committee of Officials would be briefed to look into the problem (TNA, CAB 130/20).

be forced to defend the practice after it had been revealed in the Courts, or in Parliament, or by the press. Exposure had been considered inevitable, by both the government and MI5, and neither wanted it to be presented to the public as the work of the government and the government's '*Gestapo*'. The purge was thus presented as an initiative—as if they wanted the whole distasteful business to be as transparent as was possible in the circumstances. In reality, a purge had been in progress for years, and the new purge procedure, although of great value to those who were told they were subject to the purge and permitted access to the Three Advisers, can be seen as something of a cosmetic exercise.

1. Prime Minister's Statement

In announcing the new security procedures to the Commons on 15 March 1948, Attlee made clear the government's view that 'there are certain duties of such secrecy that the State is not justified in employing in connection with them anyone whose reliability is in doubt'.[39] This was said to be because 'experience, both in this country and elsewhere', has shown that 'membership of, and other forms of continuing association with, the Communist Party may involve the acceptance by the individual of a loyalty, which in certain circumstances can be inimical to the State'.[40] While not suggesting that 'all those who adhere to the Communist Party would allow themselves thus to forget their primary loyalty to the State', there were those who 'would be prepared to endanger the security of the State in the interests of another Power', and there was no way of distinguishing between the two. Thus:

> The Government have, therefore, reached the conclusion that the only prudent course to adopt is to ensure that no one who is known to be a member of the Communist Party, or to be associated with it in such a way as to raise legitimate doubts about his or her reliability, is employed in connection with work, the nature of which is vital to the security of the State.[41]

Attlee added that the same rule would govern those who were known to be actively associated with Fascist organizations, though this was as feeble a gesture in the direction of even-handedness as the acknowledged feebleness of the Fascist organizations themselves. There was only one target of this action (members and sympathizers of the CPGB) and ostensibly one principal reason (the prevention of information being leaked to the Soviet Union). The extension of the procedure to Fascists and a non-existent external Fascist threat tended to diminish the Prime

[39] HC Debs, 15 March 1948, col. 1703.
[40] ibid.
[41] ibid., col. 1704.

Minister's claim that 'this action is being taken solely on security grounds'.[42] On the other hand, an undertaking was made that 'as far as possible alternative employment on the wide range of non-secret Government work will be found for those who are deemed for the reason indicated to be unsuitable for secret work'.[43] There was nevertheless a brutal coda from the Prime Minister in the sense that it may 'happen that' it is 'impossible to find suitable employment elsewhere in the Civil Service for individuals with specialist qualifications', in which case 'there may be no alternative to refusal of employment or dismissal'.[44]

Three days later (18 March 1948), a motion was tabled in the House by Harold Davies, on behalf of himself and forty-two other members, regretting the Prime Minister's statement on the ground that it constituted a departure from the principles of democracy and civil liberty, arguing that adequate safeguards had been provided in the past by the Official Secrets Acts 1911–39 and other measures.[45] The Prime Minister's announcement had clearly excited parliamentary opinion, with a debate scheduled for 25 March 1948, in anticipation of which Attlee informed the Cabinet of the procedure to be followed in purge cases. Communicated to the Cabinet shortly before the Commons debate on 25 March, the need for a full explanation on the Prime Minister's part perhaps reflected a measure of ministerial unease. Ministers were informed that:

1) Civil servants hold office at the pleasure of the Crown and are not able to claim the protection of the courts if they are dismissed because their 'conduct or ability fell below the standard required.'
2) Where there was serious doubt about a person's reliability, that person should be suspended until enquiries were complete.
3) While persons who had been members of the Communist Party during the war or earlier might have changed their views, they should not be presumed to be reliable. 'Full enquiries should be made in such cases' although 'no stigma should attach to a person merely because he had been the subject of enquiries.'
4) The final decision to dismiss or transfer would rest with the Minister in charge of the department. [The Prime Minister] proposed to appoint an advisory board, composed of three retired civil servants, to assist the Minister. The civil servant would be entitled to make written representations to the advisory body and, if he wished, to appear personally, but he would not be permitted to be represented by either counsel or a member of his union, although he could ask the advisory body to see witnesses who could testify as to his character. He

[42] ibid.
[43] ibid.
[44] ibid.: 'refusal of employment or dismissal'—an admission of pre-entry normal or negative vetting.
[45] HC Debs, 18 March 1948, col. 2305. On the reaction to the announcement outside Parliament, see J. Mahoney, 'Constitutionalism, the Rule of Law and the Cold War', in T. Campbell, K. D. Ewing, and A. Tomkins (eds), *The Legal Protection of Human Rights: Sceptical Essays* (Oxford, 2011), Ch. 7.

would be given sufficient particulars of the information against him to enable him to bring rebutting evidence, but it would be impracticable to disclose to him the sources from which the information had been obtained.

5) The Government would need to resist any suggestion that the report of the advisory body should be made public.
6) The majority of cases would be dealt with by transfer and few civil servants would be dismissed. Those that were should be given the option of resigning, although in either case, whether they resigned or were dismissed, they would lose their pension rights.

The Prime Minister added that the armed forces were taking similar measures.[46]

Later that day, Parliament debated the new security measures at some length. William Gallacher, one of the two Communists then in Parliament, suggested that the purge had been prompted by the United States and mentioned a case of political discrimination that had already occurred in private employment.[47] Most of the members who spoke, however, conceded the need to take steps to protect the security of the State, but as suggested above, many were concerned about the process and whether there would be sufficient protection for the rights of civil servants. In reply, Attlee again stated that there would be 'no general purge, no general witch hunt', and that most of those affected would be transferred to other work. He set out the procedure that would be followed, as described at the Cabinet meeting, pointing out that the final authority in every case would rest with the minister in charge.[48] And in a passage that greatly annoyed MI5, he also said that individuals should 'not be merely informed that [they are] suspected, but should be given, as far as possible, chapter and verse, saying, 'You are a member of this organisation, you did this or that, can you explain it?' He ought to have the case put before him perfectly clearly.'[49]

2. Reaction outside Parliament

The reaction of groups outside of Parliament was mixed. While most newspapers supported the government, the *New Statesman and Nation* in contrast ran a column on the purge that included the following:

> Past experience of MI5 . . . suggests it would be administered by people lacking any of the necessary 'intelligence or fair-mindedness'. MI5 found it difficult in

46 TNA, CAB 128/12 (Cabinet Conclusions, 25 March 1948).
47 HC Debs, 25 March 1948, col. 3398.
48 ibid., cols 3421–3.
49 ibid., cols 3423–4.

> the last war to pay attention to Fascists because they had always been trained to watch Communists. If given their heads now, these custodians of our liberties will readily start the kind of witch-hunt which has recently disgraced American public life . . . It won't be long before Labour Ministers will find their own pasts raked over, to the delight of newspapers which always declared that Socialism and Communism are the same thing.[50]

As we saw in Chapter 4, the NCCL strongly opposed the purge, as did a number of civil service trade unions. The General Secretary of one of these unions—L. C. White of the Civil Service Clerical Association (CSCA)—was also Chairman of the NCCL, and took to the pages of the Council's newsletter, *Civil Liberty*, to express his opposition. By modern standards, with about seventy organizations proscribed by legislation, the purge as a form of political discrimination seems rather innocuous. It is also relatively innocuous by the standards of other countries, such as the United States and Australia, which had banned the Communist Party, in the case of Australia leading to a strong rebuke from *The Times* calling for modifications that 'will check the Communists but at the same time preserve the precious tradition of liberty'.[51] But whatever the view of hindsight, the actions of the government were genuinely shocking to many, and not all of the shock was confected.

White's article made a number of predictable but nevertheless salient points. In terms of principle, the purge was challenged for cutting across 'the deepest principles of civil liberties and the maintenance of the best British traditions'. Historically, there was no precedent apart from wartime to penalize people for their political opinions or religious views since Roman Catholic emancipation. The civil service had always been non-political and there had never been political tests for those who sought admission to it. To the extent that there was a risk of disloyalty, there was no justification for concluding that because some civil servants held certain political views that they would betray their trust as public officials as a result. In any event, the Official Secrets Act was available in cases of breach of trust, and far from being inadequate, the NCCL had constantly pointed out that the powers under the latter Act were 'too comprehensive'. In short, the purge was 'wholly repugnant and alien to British traditions'.[52]

But not everyone—not even all those on the Left—shared the NCCL's concerns. The Co-operative Party Conference met on 28 March, a resolution opposing the purge being loyally defeated.[53] The Conference of the white-collar Clerical and Administrative Workers' Union held a special session on the same day, at which they passed a resolution drawing a distinction between civil servants who 'accept

[50] *New Statesman and Nation*, 20 March 1948, p. 229.

[51] *The Times*, 8 May 1950.

[52] L. C. White, 'Political Discrimination', *Civil Liberty*, May 1948.

[53] D. N. Pritt, *The Labour Government, 1945–51* (London, 1963), pp. 165–6. The Co-operative Party was affiliated to the Labour Party and was larger and more significant then that it is now.

the democratic premises', and those 'prepared to endanger the security of the State in the interest of a foreign power'. It was concluded that the latter group should be withdrawn from positions affecting security, with concern expressed only about the need to secure full protection of civil rights for those involved.[54] In September of that year, however, the TUC defeated a motion demanding that civil servants under investigation should have the right to be represented by officers of their union.[55] With a few exceptions, the Labour movement closed ranks behind the Labour government, the TUC's support being crucial but expected.

3. Effect on the Communist Party

The Communist Party was thus left largely isolated, save for the support from a number of Labour MPs. The Party had become accustomed to attacks in Parliament and to proposals that it should be rendered unlawful. In Chapter 4, we referred to the sniping by right-wing Tory back-benchers such as Sir Waldron Smithers MP, demanding in 1947 that the Communist Party should be banned, a proposition taken seriously by very many. Nevertheless, although the civil service purge the following year appeared, in contrast, to be quite modest, it was nevertheless a massive blow for the Communist Party. It may not have been banned, but it was now officially beyond the pale in what was a very British condemnation. As already suggested, the significance of this should not be underestimated. Not only was this the first time other than during armed conflict that legal powers had been used formally to discriminate against the members of a political party, but in taking this power (all the more striking for having no statutory authority), it was exercised against a political party with parliamentary and local government representation.

The impact is to be seen when four weeks after the statement in Parliament, Liddell reporting to Attlee that there was a 'general atmosphere of depression in the Communist Party in view of recent happenings', the Party having realized that the possibility of a 'united front' on the Left was 'blown'. Not only did it feel that it had lost the initiative, but the Party feared that it might be suppressed, and was now in the process of 'destroying indexes, issuing warnings about talking on the telephone and taking other precautions'.[56] Liddell revisited this last point in his Diary two days later, as he reflected on the Prime Minister's 'ruling'. There he wrote that:

> There is a considerable consternation in the CP over the PM's ruling. All fields of Party activity are to be surveyed with the object of improving security. The names of comrades in the civil service, the GPO, and Government factories are to be

[54] ibid.
[55] TUC Report, 1948, p. 279.
[56] TNA, KV 4/470 (Liddell Diary, 14 April 1948).

> removed from Party records, registration forms are to be destroyed and list [sic.] kept at Party headquarters at all levels destroyed wherever possible.[57]

It was reported also that it was now assumed within the Party that all telephone lines to Party offices were tapped. As a result, any call mentioning Party members was to be made from outside lines, and a strict review of membership lists was now underway to hunt for informers. The Party may not formally have been suppressed, but this was not how it seemed to a bruised organization, with the Tory Right—led by Sir Tufton Beamish (later Lord Chelwood)—now emboldened to renew their demands for a statutory ban, the Australian Parliament showing how it could be done. Thus, the Communist Party Dissolution Act 1950 began by declaring the Australian Communist Party an unlawful association, which was dissolved 'by force of this Act', its property confiscated without compensation and transferred to a receiver appointed by the government.[58] It was thereafter a criminal offence (punishable with five years' imprisonment) to be a member or official of the Communist Party, to display anything indicating support for it, to contribute to it financially, or to take part in any activity in which it was engaged.

But the Act did not only dissolve the Party: it also required the Governor General to compile a list of Communist Party members and Communist Party supporters who were engaged or likely to engage in activities prejudicial to the security and defence of Australia, membership being widely defined for this purpose to include those who attended Party meetings or spoke publicly in support of the Party or its objects at public events. The public denunciation of Party members and supporters in this way had additional adverse consequences, in the sense that a person so declared to be a Communist by the Governor General would be disqualified from being employed by the federal government, incapable of holding office in a federal government agency, and incapable of holding office in a trade union operating in any 'vital industry', a term widely defined.[59] He or she would also be barred from holding any contracts with the federal government. Although the Act was quickly declared unconstitutional by the High Court of Australia,[60] it was nevertheless a warning from a country distant in miles but close in spirit.

[57] TNA, KV 4/470 (16 April 1948).

[58] These provisions also applied to any organizations deemed to be Communist Party front organizations, if so declared by the Governor General (effectively the Prime Minister) after consulting a committee to include the Director General of Security. In the case of such organizations there was a right to apply for a court order to set aside the Governor General's declaration on the ground that the organization in question was not Communist dominated.

[59] A vital industry was defined to mean 'the coal-mining industry, the iron and steel industry, the engineering industry, the building industry, the transport industry, or the power industry, or any other industry which, in the opinion of the Governor-General is vital to the security and defence of Australia' (s 10(3)).

[60] *Australian Communist Party v Commonwealth* (1951) 83 CLR 1.

4. The Scope

The procedural safeguards announced by the Prime Minister on 25 March left much to be desired. They nevertheless probably helped to deflect much of the resistance to his proposals, which was limited and restrained. This is not to say, however, that the procedures were above criticism or, conversely, that the scheme proposed would be easy for MI5 to operate with. An obvious criticism is that the proposals were disingenuous in their attempt to appear non-partisan by including Fascists as well as Communists. If there had been pretence of even-handedness in 1948, then that was abandoned in 1951, when a meeting of the MI5 Working Party on Communism:

> agreed to put lower category people on the Index instead of on the files—fascists, pacifists, and certain other individuals would be regarded as NRA ['Nothing Recorded Against']; Communists, whose membership dated from January 1948 onwards would be stopped, as well as anybody engaged in espionage[!]. Doubtful cases and in particular Communist Party members prior to 1948 would be marked ' enquiries needed' and should be resubmitted by departments for a full-scale vet [effectively an investigation] if necessary.[61]

This, however, was a relatively minor concern, though it would have been a test of the integrity of the NCCL (which, as we have seen, had been strongly critical of the purge) had they been asked to represent a Fascist who had been removed for political reasons. A more serious concern was the vagueness of the terms used by the Prime Minister, highlighting one of the advantages of governing by administrative fiat rather than legislation, namely the opportunity to avoid precision and definition of core provisions. The scheme would apply to secret work 'the nature of which is vital to the security of the State'. But there was no definition of what this would cover, it being left to departments themselves to decide what posts were included. As suggested above, the problem for MI5 was that some departments classified the entire department as secret, Liddell complaining that these departments were now 'putting forward cases about which we have informed them in the past, but which have never been hotly pursued because the individual in question was not really employed on secret work'.[62]

[61] TNA, KV 4/473 (Liddell Diary, 29 June 1951). The case of a Mr Shelley—a Fascist who was dismissed from the civil service in the war—is nevertheless of interest. After the war, he was taken on by the Home Office 'with their eyes open and with the official approval of the Treasury' and known to be 'Mosleyite'. Shelley was a legal adviser and when Liddell brought the case to Newsam's attention in 1951—possibly with the intention of 'needling' him—Liddell reported that the PUS 'does not intend to take any action, but he thought it right that we should have brought the matter to his notice. Our letter will be placed on the record' (ibid., 30 July 1951).

[62] TNA, KV 4/470 (Liddell Diary, 21 June 1948).

Returning to the question of who was to be purged, the concern here was not the spurious inclusion of Fascists, but the fact that the purge would apply both to members of the Communist Party, as well as to those 'associated with it in such a way as to raise legitimate doubts about his or her reliability'. In the course of the House of Commons debate on 25 March 1948, the question was raised by W. A. Brown, Independent MP for Rugby (and previously right-wing General Secretary of the CSCA, whose relationship with Brown was the subject of a seminal parliamentary privilege complaint concerning his relationship with the union). In seeking clarification, Brown referred to 'Communist "front" organizations' generally and the NCCL specifically, adding that the 'only liberty that that body ever seems to me to defend is the liberty of Communists to take other people's liberty away'.[63] But although not responding to the question directly, Attlee made it clear that the purge would be both deep and wide:

> In addition to all these classes of professed Fascists and Communists, there are also the crypto-Communists. The question was asked whether we could have a list of the bands or organisations, but anyone who has had experience of Communist activities over a number of years will know the number of disguises in which Communists appear, with a litter of 'Friends' of various countries—that is the general title. Therefore, one cannot lay down something quite as simply as that.[64]

Both the vagueness of the grounds for the purge and the uncertainty about to whom it would apply would, of course, greatly empower MI5, subject to any unexpected intervention by the Three Advisers announced by Attlee. But so too would the legal environment in which this procedure operated, civil service employment being governed by the royal prerogative, under the terms of which civil servants were engaged at the pleasure of the Crown, with no contractual rights or remedies.[65] Although in practice most civil servants at the time enjoyed secure tenure and relatively good conditions of service,[66] they could nevertheless be hired and fired at will, with no remedy in the event of a transfer or termination on security grounds, however unfounded and unsubstantiated the case against them might be. For MI5, that too was real power: there were few legal restraints to worry about. The position had been made perfectly clear by the Prime Minister in his statement to the Cabinet on 25 March, and in his statement to the House on the same day, when he said that:

[63] HC Debs, 25 March 1948, col. 3409.
[64] ibid., col. 3421.
[65] *Dunn v R* [1896] 1 QB 166.
[66] See E. C. S. Wade and G. G. Phillips, *Constitutional Law* (6th edn, London, by E. C. S. Wade, 1960), pp. 644–5.

> The civil servant holds office at the pleasure of the Crown. He can be dismissed. There is no remedy at law if he is dismissed if his conduct and efficiency do not come up to standard. Further, he has no right to occupy a particular office and to be in a particular Department. Even promotion does not come of right. A man can be transferred from any part of the Civil Service.[67]

IV. The Three Advisers

MI5 had been relaxed about the purge procedures being made public, and having been given a draft copy of the Prime Minister's first statement to the House on 15 March, thought it to be 'extremely good'.[68] But it was also strongly opposed to the appointment of the Three Advisers, which MI5 saw as a challenge to its authority, as well as a threat to its sources, and the creation of extra work in defending cases. Its concerns being dismissed by Attlee, the task now was to contain the damage and to take control of the process, in such a way as to ensure that the suspect would not in fact be given 'chapter and verse', as Attlee had promised. There was thus an early indication that this might be straightforward, with Liddell welcoming the appointment of Sir Thomas Gardiner as Chairman of the Three Advisers,[69] and early meetings suggesting that he would be very responsive to MI5's concerns.[70] But the procedure was to prove unduly onerous for MI5, which was required to devote too much time preparing cases for the Three Advisers, who were to become much more rigorous and independent than the initial (arguably irregular) meetings between MI5 and the adjudicator might have suggested.

[67] HC Debs, 25 March 1948, cols 3418–19.

[68] TNA, KV 4/470 (Liddell Diary, 4 March 1948). Liddell later saw Attlee to discuss, among other matters, 'CP penetration of the civil service' in relation to the statement (ibid., 12 March). MI5 were involved to some extent with the preparations (ibid., 22 and 24 March) for the debate on 25 March, although it appears that on the day Attlee went his own way. While relaxed about the announcement on 15 March, Liddell heard 'the account of the speech [on 25 March] on the BBC'. He wrote that it seemed to him:

> to be singularly unsatisfactory, and as I rather anticipated, not only have we been used as whipping boys, but we are now committed to disclosure to the the suspect of the evidence on which he is being dismissed or transferred. The whole of the tone of the speech gives the impression that appalling stupiditys [sic.] have been committed by the security authorities in the past, but that the Labour government are now going to see that we are properly supervised (TNA, KV 4/468, Liddell Diary, 7 January 1947).

[69] It was thought that as a result of Gardiner's background in the Post Office, he would have a full knowledge of HOWs, though quite why that would be necessary for this job was unclear. See TNA, KV 4/470 (Liddell Diary, 4 March 1948).

[70] In preliminary discussions with Liddell, it was Gardiner who counselled against keeping a verbatim record of the proceedings of the Three Advisers, on the ground that 'it would be difficult to resist a request from a suspect to receive a copy'. And according to Liddell, it was Gardiner who initiated the request for information about the Communist Party and its penetration of the civil service unions: TNA, KV 4/470 (Liddell Diary, 12 April 1948).

1. Treasury Memorandum

The Three Advisers' procedures were subsequently published after consultations with the civil service trade unions in a Treasury Memorandum to the civil service trade unions on 20 May 1948.[71] As had been announced by the Prime Minister, the procedures were to apply to a civil servant employed or intended to be employed in connection with work 'the nature of which is vital to the security of the State', and who is believed to be either a member of the Communist Party or of a Fascist organization, or associated with either the Communist Party or a Fascist organization 'in such a way as to raise legitimate doubts about his reliability'.[72] The memorandum gave no account of what would constitute work 'vital to the security of the State'; that was a matter for the government. Nor did it indicate what type of association with the Communist Party or a Fascist organization would be deemed to raise doubts about a civil servant's reliability. Indeed, it was expressly stated that no statement of general application could be made for this purpose, though the fact that someone had been a member of the Party would not necessarily be sufficient evidence, unless the membership was fairly recent.[73]

Where the minister ruled that there was a prima facie case under these procedures, the civil servant would be so informed and would be given particulars of the alleged membership or the nature of the alleged association so that he or she could clear himself or herself. But 'there would have to be limits to the information given', for the civil servant cannot be given such particulars as might disclose the sources of the evidence'.[74] At the same time as being informed of the minister's ruling, the civil servant would be sent on 'special leave' with pay, and care would be taken 'as far as possible not to disclose the reason for his absence to his colleagues'.[75] If the civil servant accepted the allegations, he or she would be posted to or retained in non-secret work in his or her own department, or if this was not practicable, to non-secret work in another department. If, however, the official:

> belongs to a category which it is impossible to employ in any other than a secret branch or if his [or her] qualifications or experience are such that no alternative employment elsewhere in the Government Service can be found, he [or she] will have to be dismissed, unless he [or she] accepts the option, which should always be afforded in such cases, of resigning.[76]

[71] A copy of the *Statement of Procedure to be Followed When the Reliability of a Civil Servant is Thought to be in Doubt on Security Grounds*, is to be found in TNA, BA 28/6 (Three Advisers: Miscellaneous Papers (B)).

[72] *Statement of Procedure*, ibid., para. 1.

[73] *Statement of Procedure*, ibid.

[74] *Statement of Procedure*, ibid., para. 3.

[75] *Statement of Procedure*, ibid., para. 2.

[76] *Statement of Procedure*, ibid., para. 9. Dismissal or resignation would have important implications for pension entitlement, in the sense that someone who left the Service below the age of fifty would lose

Where the civil servant denied the allegations, the minister would be required to reconsider his or her initial ruling in the light of the representations made. If on receiving these representations, the minister confirmed the initial ruling, the matter would, if the civil servant requested it, then be referred to the Three Advisers. Composed initially of three retired civil servants, none of whom was required to have legal training or qualifications relevant to assessing the credibility of evidence, the jurisdiction of the Three Advisers was extremely narrow. Thus it was expressly provided in the Treasury Memorandum that their function was limited to advising the minister on questions of fact, that is to say whether the civil servant was either a member of the Communist Party or of a Fascist organization, or associated with either in such a way as to raise legitimate doubts about reliability.[77] In other words, the Three Advisers were not authorized to comment on whether the work was vital to the security of the State, though questions of judgement would be required in assessing someone's reliability where the ground for exclusion was association rather than membership, where unreliability was assumed and not open to challenge.

The civil servant in question would have the right to appear in person before the Three Advisers. However, it was expressly provided in the Treasury Memorandum that 'the proceedings must be governed by the requirement that neither sources of evidence nor evidence which might involve the disclosure of sources can be given to the person concerned'.[78] This was designed to protect the Security Service, in terms of the identity of its officers, its methods of its operation, and its sources of 'evidence'. The Advisers were, however, to consider it an important part of their functions to ensure that anyone appearing before them was able to make his or her points effectively, and were therefore to adapt their procedures 'in such a way as to give [the civil servant] the best possible opportunity of bringing out the points which [he or she] wishes to bring to their notice'.[79] And as anticipated by Attlee, while the individual whose reliability had been called into question could ask third parties to appear as a witness to vouch for their 'record, reliability and character', it was expressly provided that the civil servant 'may not be accompanied and/or be represented by a third party before them'.[80] There was thus no right to either legal representation or to representation by a trade union official.

all pension benefits, while someone over the age of fifty who left would have his or her benefits frozen until the age of sixty.

[77] *Statement of Procedure*, ibid., para. 6 (referring to the *Terms of Reference of the Three Advisers*—a separate document).

[78] *Statement of Procedure*, ibid., para. 7.

[79] *Statement of Procedure*, ibid.

[80] *Statement of Procedure*, ibid.

2. MI5 and the Three Advisers

Questions of scope and application to one side, the primary objection to the arrangements introduced in 1948 was the transparent lack of fairness in procedures which MI5 played a part in developing, thereby creating a system that looked well and truly rigged in its favour. Liddell lost little time in educating the Advisers, none of whom had a security background.[81] Having already had a meeting with the Advisers, on 20 April 1948 Liddell sent to A. J. Bligh (the Secretary to the Three Advisers), 'certain basic documents' which might assist Bligh and the Advisers in their deliberations.[82] The documents in question were:

- *The Communist Party, its Aims and Organisation*, 1945;
- An article by Douglas Hyde ('late of the *Daily Worker*') in the *Catholic Herald* of 25 March 1948, said to show how Party members employed by the government were 'made use of';
- *The Communist Party, its Strength and Activities, its Penetration of Government Organisation and of Trade Unions*;
- a Note on the Civil Service Clerical Association; and a separate Note on the Association of Scientific Workers; and
- details of the Springhall case and the Canadian espionage case (presumably the investigations and prosecutions that followed the Gouzenko defection).

Preliminary meetings took place thereafter to thrash out a number of issues relating to the proceedings of the Three Advisers. Senior officials from a number of government departments attended, as did all the Three Advisers, along with Liddell from MI5. A revealing minute dated 11 May 1948 indicates that a meeting had taken place a week earlier between Sir Thomas Gardiner (one of the Advisers) on the one hand, and Liddell and Hollis on the other, in which it was recorded not only that the three of them discussed the procedures to be followed in cases brought before the Advisers, but also that MI5 had undertaken to 'consider a list of questions which [the Advisers] intended to ask the "accused" '.[83] In effect, the Advisers were seeking approval from MI5 about the questions they could put to the people appearing before them, Hollis replying to Gardiner's proposed list of questions as follows:

> So far as I can see the questions are likely to cover the points on which we shall have information, and I am doubtful only about the last question: 'Are you a

[81] TNA, BA 28/4 (Three Advisers: Miscellaneous Papers (A) (Letter from Liddell to Bligh, 20 April 1948)).
[82] ibid.
[83] TNA, BA 28/5 (Three Advisers: Formal Minutes 1–150) (The Three Advisers, 11 May 1948).

member or in any way associated with any of the of the organisations mentioned on this list'? I feel it might be advisable to put this question in the form: 'Are you a member of or in any way associated with any organisation which is under Communist influence or control? leaving it to the untrustworthy civil servant to name the organisation.[84]

The Three Advisers heard their first cases in early June 1948, the minutes revealing a rather curious procedure, in which MI5 official Graham Mitchell was present for all or most of the proceedings, except the part where the suspect appeared.[85] Individual cases were dealt with initially in batches of four or five, and considered at a preliminary meeting attended by a representative of the government department concerned, where the individuals in question were 'talked about'.[86] It was at this preliminary meeting that the government's representative submitted evidence in the presence of the Advisers and MI5's Mitchell, who would also chip in with 'evidence' or undertake to provide some more.[87] The case would be discussed in the presence of both the government representative and Mitchell (in the absence of the 'suspect'), before being adjourned to hear the individual 'suspect', with the audience of the latter in the early cases varying according to the redacted minutes from no more than 20, 30, or 35 minutes to about two hours in an exceptional case.[88]

Although the minutes of these proceedings do not suggest that Mitchell was present when the suspect appeared (or when decisions were taken), they do indicate that he had a longer presence at the preliminary meetings than the government representative who presented the case against the 'suspect'. A further indication of MI5 oversight of the procedures was to be found in a complaint from civil service unions that suspects were given insufficient notice of the cases against them,[89] an assessment with which Mitchell agreed in correspondence with Winnifrith of the Treasury.[90] Mitchell was concerned that by releasing less information to suspects than MI5 authorized, the departments risked opening the procedure to public criticism, of which MI5 was 'likely to be the favourite target'.[91] In order to deflect any such criticism, paradoxically MI5 was seeking the agreement of departments not to dilute the 'Statement for Suspect' issued by the Service without prior consultation, making clear that MI5 officers were the sole 'arbiters of what safely can be disclosed'.[92]

84 TNA, BA 28/4 (Three Advisers: Miscellaneous Papers (A)) (Hollis to Bligh, 13 May 1948).
85 TNA, BA 28/5 (Three Advisers: Formal Minutes 1–150).
86 TNA, BA 28/5 (Minute 57).
87 TNA, BA 28/5 (Minutes 30, 57, 96).
88 TNA, BA 28/5 (Minutes 19, 29, 139).
89 TNA, BA 28/3 (Purge Procedure: Correspondence with Civil Service Clerical Association (CSCA)) (L. C. White to Sir Thomas Gardiner, 1 October 1948).
90 TNA, BA 28/3 (Mitchell to Winnifrith, 6 October 1948).
91 ibid.
92 ibid.

3. The Procedures

The first requirement of a fair procedure is the right of the individual to know the case against him or her, a requirement recognized by the Prime Minister in the course of parliamentary debates in March 1948, when he agreed that 'when anyone's reliability is in doubt', the person in question 'will be told the charge against him, and given an opportunity to answer it'.[93] Indeed, as we have seen in Part III above, Attlee was later to say that the civil servant should not merely be informed that he is under suspicion, but 'should be given, as far as possible, chapter and verse', and 'ought to have the case put before him perfectly clearly'.[94] The correspondence between Mitchell and Winnifrith referred to above suggests that the reality may have been rather different, and that no effort was made to inform the civil servant of the evidence in the record, but that on the contrary efforts were made to conceal evidence for fear that knowledge of it might lead to the disclosure of sources of information.

It is not clear whether Mitchell's directions to Winnifrith would seriously address the unions' concerns. The unions had complained that the statement issued to 'suspects' frequently contained no more than a bare allegation of 'association with the Communist Party in such a way as to raise legitimate doubts of reliability'.[95] In his complaint about the conduct of departments, Mitchell claimed that in 'association' as distinct from 'membership' cases MI5 had always included something beyond the bare allegation of association, before then admitting that their Statement for Suspect sometimes 'contains little beyond that, for the reason that little beyond that is known'.[96] But as if to confirm that MI5 was the source of the problem, Mitchell then proceeded to reveal by way of explanation that the very least MI5 had ever submitted was this: 'Your are believed to be associated with the Communist Party in such a way as to raise legitimate doubts about your reliability (or and) you have recently been a member of the Party'.[97] If this is what MI5 were supplying for suspects, it is difficult to see how departments could be blamed.

Apart from failing to ensure that people knew the case against them, the procedural aspect about which there was greatest objection was the denial of the right of individuals to be represented by a trade union official at the hearing before the Three Advisers. Although the civil service unions now 'agreed that the decision of the Government to exclude Communists and Fascists and persons closely associated with those bodies from work vital to national security was right and proper', they had been wrongly led to presume that such representation

[93] HC Debs, 25 March 1948, col. 3422–3.

[94] ibid., col. 3422.

[95] TNA, BA 28/3 (Purge Procedure: Correspondence with Civil Service Clerical Association (CSCA)) (L. C. White to Sir Thomas Gardiner, 1 October 1948).

[96] TNA, BA 28/3 (Mitchell to Winnifrith, 6 October 1948).

[97] ibid.

would be permitted by the Prime Minister's comment in the House that the 'accused' civil servant' would be 'able to ask other people to speak for him'.[98] The trade unions expressed astonishment that no more was in mind than that third parties, including a trade union representative if desired, could testify to the civil servant's character and reliability, and were even more surprised to discover at a later stage that the representative would not be permitted to appear before the Three Advisers at the same time as the civil servant under threat of dismissal. In the end, the matter was referred to the TUC, asked by the civil service unions to use its influence with the government to ensure that the unions' claim was granted. But TUC representatives were to have only limited success in two meetings with the Prime Minister.[99]

At the first of these meetings in July 1948, it was argued forcefully that the denial of trade union representation before the Three Advisers 'appeared on the face of it to strike at the very basis of trade unionism'.[100] The claim was 'strongly resisted' by Attlee, the government side fearing 'the risks of disclosure of sources of information if one person were able continuously to watch the Advisory Committee at work'.[101] At the second meeting in December 1948 (attended also by the Chancellor of the Exchequer and the Minister of Labour), the TUC made two requests: representation at the hearing and the appointment of a person from the trade union movement to the panel of Three Advisers. The Prime Minister again turned down the first request, but agreed to the latter. In a brief prepared for the Prime Minister before the meeting, it was pointed out that the TUC had narrowly defeated the call for trade union representation of civil servants at their Congress in September, and though the security issues raised earlier were still a consideration, there was no objection to the appointment of an appropriate trade union person as a member of the Three Advisers. Accordingly, J. W. Bowen, former General Secretary of the Union of Post Office Workers, was appointed to replace Sir Maurice Holmes, who conveniently had been given a position in the West Indies.[102]

4. Asserting Independence

We should be careful not to fall into the lawyer's trap and presume that only courts are capable of providing the kind of scrutiny necessary to protect the individual

[98] See p. 243 above.

[99] TUC Report 1949, p. 279.

[100] ibid.

[101] ibid. Attlee also said that given the need to safeguard sources of information, the government could not agree to have cases investigated by a judicial tribunal under forensic procedures: ibid.

[102] Bowen joined Sir Thomas Gardiner (formerly Director General of the General Post Office) and Sir Frederick Leggatt (formerly Deputy Secretary at the Ministry of Labour): HC Debs, 24 January 1949, cols 556–7.

from the abuse of executive power. Administrative tribunals have been established as an alternative to courts, and have many advantages in terms of access, cost, and expertise.[103] The arrangements described in section 3 above were nevertheless a travesty, being controlled by the very people they were designed to scrutinize, and failing to comply with the most basic requirements of procedural fairness—in terms of the right to be given notice of the charges to be met; the right to be represented; and the right to see and comment on the evidence supplied by the department and by MI5. Yet for all that, the Three Advisers were remarkably to win the respect of trade unions for integrity, MI5 control and supervision of their activities perhaps being suspected but almost certainly unknown outside a small government circle. Initially concerned that the procedure should deflect public criticism, MI5's Mitchell came to take the view that the Advisers had become too keen to question whether the Security Service and the civil service were adhering to those procedures, and that 'the tail was now wagging the dog'.

An early indication of this independent spirit within the MI5 straitjacket was revealed in a testy exchange between Sir Thomas Gardiner and the Ministry of Supply, with Sir Edward Bridges (Permanent Secretary to the Treasury and Head of the Civil Service) being drawn into what was a dispute about a case in which the Ministry had overruled the Advisers.[104] This was perfectly permissible under the procedures (and accepted as such), but what clearly irritated Gardiner was the reason for being overruled, namely a rule allegedly adopted by the minister that any previous Communist Party membership would forever be a disqualification for atomic work. This was said to violate the Prime Minister's instructions and the principles by which the Three Advisers were operating, which seemed to imply that renounced Communist Party membership ought not to be a barrier if there was no evidence of continuing unreliability. Not mincing his words, Gardiner wrote that:

> Apart from this aspect of the matter, the submission to us of cases in which the Minister has already made up his mind is not only a waste of our time but seems to us an abuse of the procedure under which we are working. If therefore the procedure laid down by the Prime Minister is to be varied in the sense in which, according to our information, it has been varied in the case of NAME REDACTED we suggest that the variation should be only stated, and that cases coming within its ambit, in which past membership of the Communist Party or of a Fascist Organisation is admitted, should not be referred to us.[105]

[103] For a contemporary defence of administrative tribunals, see W. A. Robson, *Justice in Administrative Law* (London, 1947).

[104] TNA, BA 28/2 (Complaint about Refusal by the Three Advisers to Hear all Witnesses) (Gardiner to Bridges, 11 August 1948; Turner to Gardiner, 13 August 1948; Bridges to Gardiner, 16 August 1948; Rowlands to Gardiner, 8 September 1948; Gardiner to Bridges, 7 October 1948; Gardiner to Rowlands, 7 October 1948).

[105] TNA, BA 28/2 (Gardiner to Bridges, 11 August 1948).

Following emphatic denials from the Ministry of Supply that past membership of the Communist Party was taken as conclusive proof of unreliability or that cases were sent to the Advisers even though the minister had already made up his mind,[106] the correspondence was brought to an end when Gardiner wrote again to Bridges to say that the Three Advisers had hoped that his earlier letter 'might act as an astringent' so far as the Ministry of Supply was concerned, and now 'surmise that it has had that effect'.[107] This combative approach was hardly likely to win friends, and appears to have set the train on a track that led to the derailment of Gardiner in 1956. In the meantime, however, this was not the last run in with the Ministry of Supply, which happened to be the source of most references to Gardiner and his colleagues. The files reveal another concern (which was to be revisited by the Radcliffe Committee in 1961),[108] namely the by-passing of the procedures by quietly moving suspects from secret to non-secret work—the informal purge which we address below—said by Gardiner to be 'indefensible'.[109]

But although revealing a streak of independence at an early stage in the life of the procedure, perhaps the most interesting aspect of this spat with the Ministry of Supply is that the findings of the Advisers were sometimes overruled, despite the very narrow nature of their jurisdiction, as outlined in the Treasury Memorandum. The procedures were, of course, quite clear that the role of the Advisers was to give 'advice', but that the final decision was that of the minister, taking into account factors that may be excluded from the purview of the Advisers as well as the recommendations of the latter. In other words, Gardiner was not chairing an appeal committee but an advisory committee. The fact that the power was used sparingly does not, however, detract from the fact that MI5 got the last word, despite their assessments of risk appearing often to have been grossly inflated. Thus, in the first four years of the purge being in operation, fifty-five cases were received by the Three Advisers, of which only twenty-five decisions were 'substantiated', the Advisers being overruled in three of the cases not substantiated.[110]

106 TNA, BA 28/2 (Rowlands to Gardiner, 8 September 1948).

107 TNA, BA 28/2 (Gardiner to Bridges, 7 October 1948).

108 Report on Security Procedures in the Public Service (Chair: Lord Radcliffe), Cmnd 1681, 1962, para. 56.

109 TNA, BA 28/4 (Three Advisers: Miscellaneous Papers (A)) (Note of a Meeting held in Room 57 Cabinet Office, 10 August 1951).

110 TNA, BA 28/4 (Three Advisers: Miscellaneous Papers (A)) (Note prepared for Sir Thomas Gardiner by Secretariat). The overruling of the Advisers could give rise to difficulties, as in one case where on hearing the 'suspect' the Advisers felt it unnecessary to hear his witnesses before finding the case against him unsubstantiated. The overruling of the Advisers by the Ministry of Supply gave rise to criticism of the Advisers who were presumed by the suspect to have upheld the original decision of the minister in breach of procedures and without giving the suspect a full hearing: TNA, BA 28/2 (Complaint about Refusal of Three Advisers to Hear all Witnesses) (Cherry to Winnifrith, 26 July 1948).

V. Containment

It is nevertheless the case that MI5's demand for a formal procedure was by no means an unqualified success, even if it was not backfiring altogether. Other figures recorded by Liddell reveal that by 18 May 1950:

> 89 cases have been dealt with under the purge. In 44 cases there was no counter-challenge by the accused. Among the 40 challenged who were seen by the Advisers, 14 had the charge upheld, and in 3 the accused declined to appear. There are some 185 cases being investigated, where there is only suspicion. In some 67 cases Ministers to whom a prima facie case has been submitted have decided to take no action, owing to the innocuous employment of the accused.[111]

These figures are quite striking, the Advisers upholding more than half of the appeals received. There were two ways of responding, one being to continue to deal with an unknown number of cases informally to keep them away from Gardiner, and the other was to get rid of Gardiner. Both strategies were adopted.

1. The Impact of the Purge

Before dealing with these strategies, we should first revisit the numbers involved, the figures at best being opaque. It is hard to know just how many civil servants were purged formally or informally and what form the purge took, whether dismissal, transfer, resignation, or retirement.

- At the time of Attlee's announcement, there were thought to be about almost *750,000* civil servants.
- Of these 750,000, MI5 estimated (in 1950) 'about' *14,047* were Communists, 'of which roughly a third are in the GPO'.[112]
- In October 1952, Liddell told the Official Committee on Communism that Party membership was about 35,000 plus 3,000 YCL.[113]

By October 1952, however, Liddell told the Official Committee on Communism (Home) (the 'Brook Committee' as it was referred to by Liddell) that: 'In the Civil Service there were now some *2,600* Communists, none of whom had access to secret work. Under the purge we had dealt with *95* cases.'

[111] TNA, KV 4/470.

[112] TNA, KV 4/472 (Liddell Diary, 5 August 1950). Compare TNA, KV 4/472 (Liddell Diary, 27 July 1950): Liddell recorded that MI5 had notified the GPO of 569 Communists since 1949.

[113] TNA, KV4/474 (Liddell Diary, 20 October 1950).

The figure of *2,600* is considerably less than the *14,047* estimated to be present in 1950, and Liddell himself remarked that the figure seemed low. However, the 1950 figure was an *estimate* (albeit a remarkably specific figure), and the 1952 figure referred to those who had, by that date, been identified as Communists and *remained employed as civil servants*. Yet only *95* had been put through the purge procedure. This means that there was a difference of *11,447* people to account for, in terms of the difference between the estimate in 1950 and the information provided in 1952. There are three possible explanations for this.

- The first is that the 14,047 was a guess at a time when Liddell's reporting of figures was very fluid,[114] though even before Operation Party Piece gave MI5 access to all Communist Party members, Liddell had nevertheless expressed confidence that they had reasonably accurate information about all Communist Party members.[115]
- The second is that the 14,047 included people who had previously been members of the Communist Party, rather than just current members. This may help to account for Liddell's explanation in September 1952 that the large number of HOWs then current was 'partly accountable to the fact that we had so many cases whether [sic.] it was desirable to clear up one way or another an individual serving in a secret department was a current member'.[116]
- The third is that between 1950 and 1952 there had been a major cull of 11,447 Communists from all grades within the civil service, Attlee's statement giving a green light to discriminatory conduct regardless of whether or not the person in question was engaged in work 'vital to the security of the State'.

It is also the case, of course, that all three of these explanations can be true: the figures in 1950 were inflated but not by as much, that they included lapsed as well as current members, and that there had been a cull. The other point to bear in mind, however, is that the purge applied not only to Party members but also to civil servants who had an association with the Communist Party that would lead to questions about their reliability. Liddell's original figure almost certainly included this

[114] Compare, e.g., TNA, KV4/472 (Liddell Diary, 1 October 1948):

> Research shows that there are roughly 200 Communists in the Civil Service. A number of these are in positions where they can do no harm, and we should not, therefore, recommend the Ministry to take any action. In other cases the evidence is not sufficiently strong. There are some fifty cases under investigation and a limited number are ready for action.

[115] TNA, KV4/472 (Liddell Diary, 25 July 1950): 'we had a considerable coverage although we do not presume to know the identity of every single Communist' (TNA, KV 4/472, Liddell Diary, 20 October 1952): 'we thought that with our present coverage we had between 80% and 90% of these people on our records'; (TNA, KV4/474, Liddell Diary, 27 November 1952): 'we had a reasonable coverage of the Communist Party and on several occasions we had been able to test this out'.

[116] TNA, KV4/474 (Liddell Diary, 17 September 1952).

category as well, for it seems that a significant number of those purged formally and informally were people who fell into this latter group. This is made clear in a parliamentary written answer to Major Tufton Beamish, who had asked in 1950 in relation to the formal purge (we must go along with the façade and assume he was unaware of the informal purge):

> how many civil servants have been moved from their employment since 15th March, 1948, for security reasons for alleged Communist connections; how many of these were members of the Communist Party when moved; how many were not members of the Communist Party but had been in the past; and how many had never been members of the Communist Party;[117]

The answer at that stage was forty-eight, 'of whom 22 have been removed on grounds of membership of the Communist Party, one on grounds of membership of the Fascist Party, and 25 on grounds of association with the Communist Party in such a way as to raise legitimate doubts as to their reliability'.[118] The point is that although it may be possible to say how many people were removed formally under the purge, it was impossible to say how many people were removed informally, other than that we have an implausible ceiling in Liddell's figures. The other point, however, is surely this. What the information tells us is that MI5 were seeking to find out the identity of Communist Party members in the civil service as a whole, rather than the identity of Communist Party members engaged in secret work vital to the security of the State. What this tells us in turn is that MI5 was vetting individuals, rather than posts. This is not what Attlee announced. The purge was to apply to secret work only and gave no licence to assess individuals engaged in other activity, or to conduct a census of the civil service estate for signs of Communist Party membership. For the record, the official line was that by the end of 1953, twenty-three civil servants had been dismissed, and another nineteen had resigned as a result of the purge.[119]

2. By-Passing the Procedures

It is apparent that there was a flourishing informal process in operation for dealing with security cases, operating in the shadow of the formal procedure, which avoided accountability to the Three Advisers. Liddell had explained to the Brook

117 HC Debs, 14 March 1950, col. 42 WA. He also asked the same question in relation to Fascists.

118 ibid., col. 43 WA.

119 *Daily Herald*, 16 January 1954. For some unknown reason, this information about the number of dismissals was provided by Sir Hartley Shawcross in a speech in New York on 15 January 1954, unusual given that he had ceased being Attorney General in the post-war Labour government some three years earlier.

Committee that 'Communists and their sympathizers in the Civil Service were identified and reported to the Departments concerned, when the purge procedure *could, if thought desirable, be put into operation*.'[120] Only a tiny proportion of them were put through the purge procedure. Some, it is true, will simply have been left alone, but many will have been dealt with informally in one way or another. Some evidence of two approaches in operation is found in Liddell's Diary where he refers to the:

> rather puzzling case of a man who has recently been posted to the Cabinet Office from the Ministry of Education and now comes into the secret field for the first time. His wife is a Communist, but his own sympathies are not known. The Cabinet Office are, therefore, considering whether or not they can deal with this case on the lines of discipline, since the man did not disclose the fact that his wife was a Communist before being taken on. We have warned them, however, that our information is not the kind we can put before the Tribunal, since there is nothing on the man himself. They have agreed to refer the matter to us before taking any action.[121]

In an entry ten days later, Liddell reveals that the Cabinet Office man was being 'groomed' to become Norman Brook's personal assistant, that he had been sent back to Education, and that he was to be reprimanded, Liddell recording his personal view that 'it is difficult to believe that [REDACTED] himself is not pretty far to the left if he is married to a Communist woman'.[122]

But this was not the half of it, for the informal purge was covertly sanctioned at the very highest levels. Concerns for 'the danger to . . . sources, particularly in London', were raised early in 1951, and Bridges and his Permanent Under-Secretaries had 'decided to go slow on purging London Civil Servants, and to do so only when it is not possible to remove them by other means i.e. transfer to non secret posts—and only to take a risk of overt action when security demanded it. The Prime Minister agreed to this.'[123] Attlee, Bridges, and Sillitoe also agreed a policy for dealing with cases of civil servants 'about whom there were doubts', but whose work could not be said to be vital to the security of the State. At an MI5 DG's meeting in January 1951, Sillitoe told his colleagues that he and Bridges had asked Attlee 'if he would encourage Ministers to uphold prima facie cases of this kind, in spite of any ruling to the contrary by the purge tribunal. The Prime Minister agreed.'[124] Procedural flexibility was evidently second nature to MI5 (to

[120] TNA, CAB134/737 (Cabinet Committee on Communism (Home) 20 October 1952).
[121] TNA, KV4/472 (Liddell Diary, 21 February 1950).
[122] ibid., 2 March 1950.
[123] TNA, KV4/473 (Liddell Diary, Minutes of the Director General's Meeting held on 23 January 1951, para. 1).
[124] ibid.

say nothing of Attlee and senior civil servants). At another DG's meeting on 27 February 1951, the minutes record that:

> In connection with the purge, the DG asked what the outcome had been regarding an objection raised by Sir Frederick Leggett, one of the three advisers, that we had been going behind their backs to the Prime Minister.

Evidently Sillitoe had given his 'personal assurance that there was no intention of going behind their backs and that any intervention by the Prime Minister would be *post hoc* and not *ante hoc*'. Dick White concluded that the answer 'must have been accepted since nothing more had been heard of the matter'.[125] At that meeting on 27 February 1951, the MI5 officers returned briefly to a matter at a DG's meeting held three weeks earlier, the minutes of which reveal that the Service connived with the Ministry of Supply to circumvent the purge procedure in cases where they had taken workers on without a negative vet.[126] It had been proposed that this be done by the introduction of a 'probationary period', 'so that a man could be fired without the purge being invoked', should a post-recruitment vet indicate that there were 'doubts'. The Security Service favoured a one-month probationary period—very likely because a longer period would be too obviously an attempt to get round the necessity of invoking the purge procedure. Talk of probationary periods had nothing to do with the illegality or legality of any putative dismissal. It was merely that a dismissal made during that period could be passed off more easily as one made for reasons of competence or suitability.

An entry in Guy Liddell's Diary later still in 1951 noted that Mitchell had reported that the Three Advisers had suggested 'that the purge procedure was being circumvented by the departments with our connivance'. They were, of course, absolutely right. Indeed, even those who had been cleared by the Three Advisers were not immune from the informal purge. Liddell again: 'I had a talk with Hollis about the case of one REDACTED, a compositor in the Stationery Office, who has in my view been somewhat doubtfully cleared by the Three Advisers.' The redacted compositor was a one-time member of the Communist Party who had recently rejoined, but had claimed that his membership had been renewed without his consent. 'Assuming the best', wrote Liddell, 'do we know whether if he became disgruntled REDACTED would not be prepared to betray secrets to the CP?'. Liddell questioned the man's access to secret papers, whether arrangements could be made to keep him on alternative duties, whether 'his case could be written off or whether it could be periodically reviewed', and, most notably, whether B1A rather than C

[125] TNA, KV4/473 (Liddell Diary, Minutes of the Director General's Meeting held on 27 February 1951, para. 10).

[126] TNA, KV4/473 (Liddell Diary, Minutes of the Director General's Meeting held on 6 February 1951, para. 10). The subject was revisited on 27 February (para. 9).

Division should be involved. That is to say whether an active investigation be set in train, rather than a mere periodic trawl through the records relied upon.[127] If the former, it would mean the use of the various surveillance techniques described in Chapter 5.

3. Purging the Three Advisers

The purge procedure was thus, to the few with a grasp of what was going on, a rickety façade of respectability hiding the true nature of the purge, and yet the Three Advisers were evidently thought by MI5 to be taking their responsibilities much too seriously. The appointment of the Conference on Privy Councillors by Anthony Eden in 1955 provided MI5 with an unexpected opportunity to do something about it. Almost certainly dancing to MI5's tune, the Conference accepted without demur the MI5 case that the purge procedures went too far in protecting the individual (in those cases where they applied) and not far enough in protecting national security. The Conference reported unequivocally that the terms of reference of the Three Advisers encouraged it to place too narrow an interpretation on the suspect's association with the Communist Party, and did not provide for action where a person was neither a member nor an associate of the Party but clearly had Communist sympathies, or associated himself or herself with members of the Party but not the Party itself.[128] The purge was to be deeper and wider, though it is hardly a failing on the part of the Advisers that they felt constrained by their terms of reference.

The Conference was also concerned that the terms of reference of the Three Advisers requiring them to advise whether the minister's prima facie ruling about a civil servant was substantiated 'seemed to put the onus of proof on the State in a way which [was] not altogether consistent [with the intention of the government]'.[129] This led the Tribunal simply to report 'Yes' or 'No' to the minister without giving the detailed background and evidence on which its decision was reached. The interpretation placed by the Advisers on their terms of reference had also made them unwilling to pronounce against an individual 'unless current or very recent membership, or association with, the Communist Party can be proved'.[130] This narrow approach of the Three Advisers was said to have had two consequences, one of which was that departments were side-stepping the procedures (as indicated above) by moving suspects to non-secret work. The other, however, was that 'the recommendations of the Tribunal have been of much less value to Ministers than they might have been'.[131]

127 TNA, KV4/472 (Liddell Diary, 20 February 1950).
128 TNA, PREM11/1587 (Report of the Security Conference of Privy Councillors, 24 January 1956).
129 ibid., para. 55.
130 ibid., para. 56.
131 ibid., para. 57.

The Privy Councillors thus indicated that the role of the Advisers should change, and that their role should be what their title suggested: they were there to advise ministers not to sit in judgement as a de facto appellate body. Thus, the Advisers were to perform what would be revised terms of reference 'in such a way as to give the Minister the utmost help in deciding himself what course to take', the report continuing:

> It should provide him with all relevant facts, while taking precautions to safeguard any very secret methods by which they have been obtained. The decision on what employment is to be regarded as 'work vital to the security of the State' should remain, as at present, one for the Minister in charge of the Department. But especially in cases where the Minister's decision will be a difficult one, the Tribunal has an important duty in assessing the evidence, and in indicating to the Minister the weight which it has attached to particular factors and the reasons for its recommendation.[132]

It is unlikely that the Three Advisers then in post would have seen these recommendations. If they had done so, they would have been right to have taken them as a personal slight, the Privy Councillors also recommending that they should be replaced.

But although Gardiner was duly replaced, in truth the Three Advisers had very little to do after the initial spate of cases. Indeed, the figures suggest that numbers had fallen dramatically by the time the new procedures were announced in 1957, which makes these later debates about the Three Advisers slightly surreal. Nevertheless, the new team were to be assisted by further guidance, with the Privy Councillors proposing to widen the meaning of Communist association to include association by marriage:

> 65 One question on which we think that guidance is needed is the case where it is discovered that an individual has a close relative who is a Communist, or a Communist sympathiser, but where there is nothing to show that the individual is a Communist. He may, indeed, have an unimpeachable record. The most obvious case is a man with a Communist wife. Another instance is an unmarried man who is living with his parents, one or both of whom are Communists.
>
> 66 We consider that such a situation entails a security risk and that it must be deemed to be a Communist association, though the individual is not himself responsible. We recommend, therefore, that an individual who is living with a sympathiser, should be moved from secret work; and that the same should apply to an

[132] ibid., para. 60.

individual who is living with someone as a husband or wife, or with a parent, who is a communist or communist sympathiser.[133]

4. Revision of the Procedures

The Privy Councillors' Report was not published, the government producing, in a white paper, a much-truncated summary, the censors predictably careful not to reveal the criticism of the Three Advisers.[134] On 29 January 1957, Mr Enoch Powell announced the government's response and the revisions to the purge procedure,[135] though, as might be expected, these appeared to reflect almost exactly the recommendations of the Privy Councillors and wholly to reject the demands of the 'pop-up' Campaign for the Limitation of Secret Police Powers that had been established to lobby for security procedures reform.[136] Under paragraph 1 of the new procedures (which were announced to Parliament, but were not the subject of legislation), a civil servant was to be regarded as suspect if:

(a) he is, or is to be, employed in connection with work the nature of which is vital to the security of the State; and simultaneously;
(b) he is or has recently been a member of the British Communist Party, or in such a way as to raise reasonable doubts about his reliability, is or has recently been sympathetic to Communism, associated with Communists or Communist sympathisers, or is susceptible to Communist pressure.

It was expressly provided again that 'No statement of general application can be made as to what constitutes sympathy or association under (b) above. Each case will be assessed in the light of the particular facts.' Once the minister decided that there was a prima facie case, the civil servant would be suspended, and would be given details of the alleged membership or the nature of the alleged sympathies or associations, to enable him or her to respond. However, there continued to be 'limits to the information given for [the civil servant] cannot be given such particulars as might involve the disclosure of the sources of the evidence'. If, on receiving this information, the civil servant contested the matter, he or she would be given an opportunity to respond in writing to the minister, who would reconsider the initial finding. Where the latter was confirmed, the

133 This was very convenient in light of the Lang case, which we encounter in Chapter 11 below. That case suggests that association by marriage was already enough, as does the case of the official in the Ministry of Education denied a transfer to the Cabinet Office referred to above at p. 261.

134 Statement on the Findings of the Conference of Privy Councillors on Security, Cmd 9715, 1956.

135 HC Debs, 29 January 1957, col. 152 WA.

136 See pp. 334–7 below for more detail on the Campaign for the Limitation of Secret Police Powers.

civil servant would have a right to complain to the Three Advisers, where he or she would continue to have a right to be heard in person, and to have third parties testify on his or her behalf as to his or her 'record, reliability and character'. But it remained the case that the individual 'may not be accompanied and/or represented by a third party'.

In line with the Privy Councillors' recommendations, the Three Advisers were now instructed that when determining whether a prima facie case in relation to an individual was substantiated, they should answer the following questions:

> (i) Are there or are there not reasonable grounds for supposing that the individual has or has recently had Communist sympathies or associations of the type described in paragraph 1 above?
> (ii) If you are in doubt about the answer to (i) above, how do you assess the evidence whether presented to you or elicited at the hearing before you?

In answering these questions, the Advisers were also directed that their aim 'should be to give the Minister the utmost help in deciding himself what course to take'. In addition, they were required to give reasons when they agreed with a prima facie ruling, and in other cases to 'assess the evidence for the Minister reporting the weight which [they] attached to particular factors'.

Where the minister was inclined to uphold the initial decision following consideration by the Three Advisers, the civil servant would continue to be entitled to make representations to the minister or his representative (a third opportunity to make representations). If the prima facie ruling was finally upheld, 'the civil servant would continue to be posted to or retained in a non-secret branch within his [or her] own Department, or, if this is not practicable, will be posted to a non-secret branch in another Department'. If for a number of reasons, no other work could be found, the civil servant in question would either be dismissed or given the opportunity to resign. At no point was there to be any input from a High Court judge as demanded by the recently established but Campaign for the Limitation of Secret Police Powers. Indeed, there was little improvement for the individual in the procedural changes, which were conspicuously designed to tilt the balance more clearly in favour of the State. As with the original procedures, it remained fundamental to this process that:

> In the special circumstances of these cases the proceedings must be governed by the requirement that neither sources of evidence nor evidence which might involve the disclosure of sources can be given to the person concerned.[137]

[137] HC Debs, 29 January 1957, col. 152 WA.

VI. Conclusion

Whatever else may have been achieved by the Privy Councillors and the revised procedures announced by Powell, it is unlikely that they had much effect on the purge procedure. Although the changes were designed to enable more people to be removed more easily, evidence provided to the Radcliffe Committee in 1961 suggests that in the four years after the changes were introduced, the number of cases to the Three Advisers declined to a total of only four (compared to twelve in the previous four years). Indeed, in only two of these cases between 1957 and 1960 was the complaint/original decision substantiated, compared to nine (out of twelve) in the previous four years.[138] Paradoxically, MI5 was no more likely to succeed under the new arrangements than they were under Gardiner. In truth, however, the system was petering out for two reasons, one being that when the procedure was introduced in 1948, it had to be applied to the existing body of the civil service in vital posts, whereas now it had to be applied only to those moving into these posts each year.[139]

A second explanation is that there were now much more extensive security measures operating in the civil service and elsewhere to prevent people of questionable political views being hired in the first place, in relation to which MI5 insisted there should be no scrutiny or accountability.[140] More effective screening at the point of recruitment meant that there ought to be only a limited need to purge individuals who slipped in beneath the procedures or who in an epiphany joined the Party after their recruitment. As anticipated by MI5 in 1948,

> Party members fall, almost without exception, into one of two categories; either they have come to light as Party members (or themselves have become Party members) since obtaining the employment, or the nature of their work is not such as to afford them access to secret information. The Ministries have been acquainted with the particulars of those falling within the first category and take every opportunity to divert them into the second; equally, they have been acquainted with the particulars of those in the second category lest they should be transferred or promoted to secret work.[141]

But these considerations apart, it appears from the Radcliffe Committee that there were other factors to explain the decline in the use of the formal purge procedures,

[138] TNA, BA28/11 (Closed Extract: Schedule of Cases) (Note of a Breakdown by Departments of the Appeals Considered by the Three Advisers).

[139] Report on Security Procedures in the Public Service (n 108), para 54.

[140] See also Bontecou (n 3) who claims that the 'process of elimination of communists and fascists from sensitive positions was practically completed by May 25, 1949, so far as present incumbents were concerned' (p. 572). The claim is unsourced.

[141] TNA, BA 28/9 (Closed Extracts: Letter dated 7/6/1948, two undated briefs) (Penetration of Government Technical Assistance).

the most important of which was the reluctance to adopt a more 'regular resort to the purge procedure whenever there is any security misgiving on a matter of Communist association'.[142] Thus, Radcliffe suggests not that the purge had fizzled out but that there were other ways of dealing with the problem, which should by now be no surprise. According to the Radcliffe report, 'a pattern of departmental treatment' of security cases 'emerged fairly early' from their enquiries.[143] True, establishment officers were 'careful in their recognition' of the principles in the purge procedure. 'On the other hand', however, they were said to 'remain watchful about any man who, through vetting or otherwise, is marked with some suspicion of current or recent Communist association and they accordingly welcome an opportunity of posting such a man to a post in which there is little or no chance of his coming into contact with secret information'.[144]

The Committee continued:

> If the opportunity for such a transfer occurs, they take it, provided that it is not to the man's prejudice. If it does not, they remain so far as possible on the watch, choosing, if a sensitive post cannot be altogether avoided, a post as little sensitive as possible. No one can say that this is an altogether satisfactory situation and we have had to consider whether there is any feasible improvement that we can recommend. But it is fair to say that, worked as the system is, *it does not, in our view, deprive the individual of any safeguard to which he is entitled, nor does it suggest a major security risk*.[145]

So, while procedural justice may have been a casualty of the Cold War, it was for reasons even more profound than merely the failure of the purge procedure to provide a sufficiently independent forum in which individuals had a right to know the case against them—the procedures were simply ignored. Even the more heavily rigged system introduced in 1957 was insufficient to persuade MI5 and departments to adopt a more 'regular resort to the purge procedure whenever there is any security misgiving on a matter of Communist association'.[146] It is true that Radcliffe resisted more demands to tilt the balance even more in favour of the State. But given the context, it was not necessary to do so.

[142] Report on Security Procedures in the Public Service (n 108), para. 57.
[143] ibid., para. 56.
[144] ibid.
[145] ibid. (emphasis added).
[146] ibid., para. 57.

10
Vetting and the Secret Blacklist

I. Introduction

VVetting took two forms—normal (or negative) and positive (or PV)—and both were used to screen recruits and to 'purge' those already employed. References to 'normal vetting' rather than simply 'vetting' became usual in the early 1950s to distinguish the standard security assessments from the new enhanced PV procedures introduced in 1952. The latter procedures were announced a few years after their introduction,[1] so that like the civil service and industrial purge announcements of 1948 and 1957 respectively, the announcement was a belated and limited acknowledgement of existing practices, none of which had statutory approval. Pre-entry normal vetting was not acknowledged until 1990, it being impossible for the government to try and conceal the more intrusive PV, involving as it does the formal questioning of the individual concerned, and enquiries made of associates—sometimes of relatives.

While the arrangements for vetting no doubt had lawful authority under the prerogative, this is not to say that these procedures satisfied the demands of lawyers concerned about civil liberties and the Rule of Law in the context of national security. The concerns were twofold. So far as civil liberties are concerned vetting is done for a purpose: the exclusion of certain people from certain positions because they share certain prohibited characteristics. It is a way of sanctioning discrimination, raising questions about the grounds on which discrimination is taking place, as well as the justification for such discrimination. While in this case it may be hard to argue with the justification of keeping certain individuals away from work involving national security if there is evidence to believe that they may betray State secrets, it is nevertheless also the case that the grounds for any such exclusion need to be public and transparent, as well as proportionate to the ends being pursued, with appropriate forms of accountability of those doing the vetting.

The need for caution is informed in part by the potential impact of vetting on the lives of vetting subjects, in some cases locking out individuals from certain forms of employment for which they may have been highly trained. The need may be all the greater for the fact that the State or its agencies may be a monopoly employer, with the result that exclusion by vetting may have life-defining consequences.[2]

[1] Announced in general terms as an initiative in January 1952, details of the procedure were not slipped out until 1954. See pp. 274–5 below.

[2] It also denies the State the benefit of the best talent in what are often highly specialist areas, which is why in some cases exceptions were made.

MI5, the Cold War, and the Rule of Law. K. D. Ewing, Joan Mahoney, and Andrew Moretta, Oxford University Press (2020). © K. D. Ewing, Joan Mahoney, and Andrew Moretta. DOI: 10.1093/oso/9780198818625.001.0001

But apart from these substantive concerns about the reasons for vetting, there are also concerns about the procedures associated with vetting. Vetting involves the creation of a database and the checking of the individual against the database, but also intrusive inquiries and investigations by the State. This will involve others giving assessments about the vetting subject, and may encourage these others to collect information about colleagues or clients to pass onto agents of the State. Some of this information may be inaccurate; some of it may be malicious.

This in turn raises other concerns. If people are to be subject to intrusive investigation by the State, the Rule of Law demands not only that this should be for a clear purpose proportionately applied, but in accordance with a purpose contained in clear rules legitimately created. These rules should indicate the circumstances in which this power will be used, the means adopted for the vetting of individuals (without giving such detail as to compromise the purpose of the exercise), and the safeguards against abuse. The latter should include the right to challenge any negative assessment before an independent tribunal. As we have seen, although there was much wrong with the purge procedure, some of these core requirements were nevertheless met, even if not to the extent desirable. As we will now see, there was, in contrast, no attempt to meet these requirements in the case of vetting, which just grew and grew without external validation and without adequate safeguards.

Unravelling Security Procedures

As we pointed out in Chapter 9, there is a great deal of overlap and confusion about the different security procedures (normal vetting, the purge, and PV), in terms of where one starts and another ends. The most lucid summary we have encountered was provided by Sir Laurence Helsby, Joint Permanent Secretary to the Treasury and Chairman of the Official Committee on Security. In a memorandum in his latter capacity (TNA, CAB 134/2498 (Ministerial Committee on Security: Meetings 1–3, Papers 1–6 (1962); Meetings 1–2, Papers 1–8 (1963); Meeting 1, Paper 1 (1963); Meetings 1–2, Papers 1–6 (1964)) (Normal Vetting—Memorandum by the Chairman of the Official Committee, 30 April 1963, para. 2), Helsby wrote that:

> Normal or (negative) vetting in the field of employment is applied to all persons inside or outside the Government service who are required to have access to information graded CONFIDENTIAL or higher. It is a covert process. Only those who fail to pass normal vetting and have access to information 'vital to the security of the State'—which is usually held to mean SECRET information or higher—are dealt with openly under the Purge Procedure and given the right to appeal. Positive vetting is applied to persons with regular and constant access to TOP SECRET defence information or material.

II. From Normal to Positive Vetting

It is clearly the case that some system of vetting potential employees has existed in some departments of government from time immemorial,[3] long before the formal check it is said had been introduced in 1945 for all new recruits to and all temporary employees of the Foreign Office.[4] The latter was introduced to ensure that 'no adverse security record is held against candidates for employment'.[5] We now know, however, that normal vetting was introduced for most of those employed in government departments shortly thereafter, following the Gouzenko spy scandal in Canada.[6] The information he passed to the West revealed that a spy ring was operating in Canada and that American, British, and Canadian nuclear weapon technology had been compromised, in a plot that implicated not only British scientist Alan Nunn May, but also Canadian MP Fred Rose.

In May 1947 a Working Party established by the Cabinet Committee on Subversive Activities had claimed that all but two of those who had been charged following the Gouzenko defection had been civil servants, with the Communist Party 'the principal organ of recruitment' of the Canadian spies, citing Glading and Springhall as evidence that the Party was likely to be associated with espionage in the United Kingdom.[7] The report revealed security arrangements in the British civil service to be chaotic and arbitrary,[8] the officials 'forced to the conclusion that the only safe course is to decide that a member of the Communist Party is not to be employed in work where he may have access to secret information', and that 'adult entrants to the Departments or branches should be vetted before appointment'.[9] It was also recommended, however, that those appointed to posts

[3] The file of Wilfred Vernon (TNA, KV 2/994) contains an entry revealing that vetting at RAF Farnborough had been taking place since 1936, recording complaints that the employment of a man called Mearns had shown that the 'vetting of applicants' for employment there were 'not working satisfactorily'. The department which had hired this man was not told that he was not to be employed and that 'they must get out of it as best they can', the procedures being reviewed to make sure that they applied to 'local men' as they did for those recruited through more formal channels for scientific work.

[4] HC Debs, 7 November 1955, col. 1499 (Foreign Secretary). According to the Report of the Conference of Privy Councillors appointed in 1955, normal vetting had been operating since the First World War (TNA, CAB 21/4035, Report of the Security Conference of Privy Councillors, 24 January 1956, para. 18).

[5] HC Debs, 7 November 1955, col. 1499 (Foreign Secretary).

[6] See pp. 16–17 and 236 above, and p. 458 below.

[7] TNA, CAB 130/20 (The Employment of Civil Servants etc. Exposed to Communist Influence, 29 May 1947, paras 2, 3, 4, and 5). They consisted of twelve scientists, academics, and military men, some of them associated with the Canadian NRC, plus Canadian MP Fred Rose, British physicist Alan Nunn May (who had worked for the NRC), and Kay Willsher, who had worked for the British High Commission. Most could loosely be described as *public servants*.

[8] Although the report did not use such frank terms, what it reported did indicate that vetting was patchy and arbitrary.

[9] 'The Employment of Civil Servants etc. Exposed to Communist Influence' (n 7), para. 16.

in atomic energy or research and development for the armed forces should be dealt with on an 'individual basis', questionable political views sometimes being seen as a risk that could be taken when the worker concerned was possessed of scientific expertise.[10]

The Working Party's recommendations were largely adopted by the Cabinet Committee on Subversive Activities on 16 June 1947. But although normal vetting was thus extended to new and existing staff, and although vetting was rapidly extended beyond secret work,[11] the procedures were nevertheless thought to be insufficient, in the sense that it was only 'a negative check' that would catch people who had already come to the unfavourable notice of the Security Service.[12] These failings were thought to have been highlighted by the unmasking of Klaus Fuchs in 1950, the precipitating event leading to the introduction of additional and more intrusive PV of individuals. A German émigré who had worked as a scientist in the United States and the United Kingdom on the development of the hydrogen bomb, Fuchs had been a Communist since his youth in Germany. It seems that for reasons of ideological conviction, he provided secret information to the Soviets, enabling them to develop their own bomb, and thereby alter the balance of power between East and West.

It is almost incredible that MI5 had cleared Fuchs for establishment at Harwell after two senior officers had independently suggested that he could be a spy.[13]

[10] ibid., para. 17. The draft report listed the 'unsafe' departments which handled material 'of great interest to the Communists': Cabinet Office; Service Departments; Ministry of Defence; Foreign Office; Home Office; Department of Scientific and Industrial Research; Control Office, 'and possibly, some branches of the Scottish Office, the Board of Trade and the Ministry of Supply'. In the final report, the officials had woken up to the importance of the Ministry of Supply—'much of their secret work [is] concerned with the development of atomic energy or research and development for the Services'. The 'safe' departments were the likes of the Inland Revenue, Housing or Agriculture, although by 1953 MI5 were vetting civil servants who handled material classed merely as 'confidential'.

[11] By 1953, Liddell was boasting that MI5 'now vets any government official who in the course of his normal duties is handling confidential information and upwards': TNA, KV 4/475 (Liddell Diary, 4 February 1953). In a minute from the Colonial Secretary to the Prime Minister in February 1953, it is said that 'My office has an arrangement with MI5 for the checking of the political reliability of applicants for appointment to the Colonial Service. I have just seen an analysis of the 86 applications rejected last year. Most of the rejects either were members of the Communist Party or associated with it.' The Colonial Secretary's letter also suggests that the process screened out large numbers of people, while in itself being a valuable source of intelligence. Thus it was pointed out that sixty-one of the eighty-six applications were for educational appointments, suggesting a plan to 'penetrate educational institutions, presumably because they are most likely to produce the political leaders of the future': TNA, PREM 11/537 (Arrangements between Colonial Office and MI5 for Checking Political Reliability of Applicants for Appointment to Colonial Service) (Colonial Office to Prime Minister, 27 February 1953).

[12] HC Debs, 7 November 1955, col. 1499 (Foreign Secretary).

[13] Of Fuchs' Harwell 'establishment' vet, the Liddell Diary records on 8 December 1947 that 'it was agreed that although our information was entirely negative, we should tell Atomic Research that in our view the information does not really amount to anything. The alternative was to say nothing which seemed undesirable': TNA KV 4/469. Yet after Fuchs' conviction for espionage, Sillitoe addressed senior MI5 officers, and according to Liddell, the DG 'drew attention in particular to a minute by T. A. R. Robertson in which he had expressed the view that Fuchs might be a spy, and also to one by Michael Serpell expressing the view that both Fuchs and another scientist Rudolph Peierls might be spies' (TNA, KV 4/472, Liddell Diary, 17 March 1950).

Nevertheless, the case appears to have been the trigger for the introduction of the PV procedure, and preparations were made for additional steps 'to check the reliability of persons holding important positions in the public service',[14] the sense of urgency reinforced by the defection of Burgess and Maclean in 1951, with existing procedures having revealed 'nothing about the subversive political associations of their early days'.[15] Immediately after this latest security disaster, another committee, this time chaired by Sir Alexander Cadogan, approved the plans for PV already prepared, recommending that PV should apply to all members of the senior branches and the senior grades of the junior branches of the Foreign Service.[16] But Cadogan also proposed that vetting should cover not only 'political unreliability' but extend more widely to 'character defects, which might lay an officer open to blackmail, or otherwise undermine his loyalty and sense of responsibility'.[17]

Also triggered by the Burgess and Maclean case was the introduction of the policy of questioning those seeking to work on secret atomic energy projects on their political beliefs—whether he or she was, or ever had been, a member of the Communist Party—an initiative that the minutes of the Cabinet Committee on Subversive Activities indicates was specifically proposed in order to 'lessen American doubts about the efficacy of our security arrangements and remove obstacles to greater co-operation in atomic energy matters'.[18] It was conceded that the 'new procedure could not be kept concealed . . . a public statement should be made by the Government'.[19] Director General Percy Sillitoe had attended the meeting and told Guy Liddell that Home Secretary Chuter Ede had 'hotly opposed' the proposals, 'on the grounds that we were on the slippery slope of the Gestapo and pandering to American procedure'.[20] Ten days later, the Cabinet Committee on Atomic Energy Security (Chuter Ede was on it) agreed that a 'right of appeal' to the Three Advisers would be restricted to applicants who were already in government service,[21] and gave its approval to the new policy.

[14] A phrase used five years later by Foreign Secretary, Harold Macmillan: HC Debs, 7 November 1955, col. 1499.

[15] ibid.

[16] See Report Concerning the Disappearance of Two Former Foreign Office Officials, Cmd 9577, 1955, para. 27.

[17] HC Debs, 7 November 1955, col. 1500 (Foreign Secretary). According to the Report Concerning the Disappearance of Two Former Foreign Office Officials:

> since 1952 searching enquiries have been made into the antecedents and associates of all those occupying or applying for positions in the Foreign Office involving highly secret information. The purpose of these inquiries is to ensure that no one is appointed to or continues to occupy any such post unless he or she is fit to be entrusted with the secrets to which the post gives access (ibid., para. 28).

[18] TNA, CAB 130/20 (Cabinet Committee on Subversive Activities, Minutes of Meeting, 17 August 1951).

[19] ibid.

[20] TNA, KV 4/473 (Liddell Diary, 17 August 1951).

[21] TNA, CAB 130/20 (Cabinet Committee on Atomic Energy Security, Minutes of Meeting, 27 August 1951).

Subsequently held up by the October 1951 election, PV thus received its first publicity at the beginning of 1952, when the enhanced security measures for atomic energy were announced, although forms of PV had obviously been in use in relation to atomic work for some time before. It was not until 1954 that Parliament was given any real detail about PV being applied more widely, and then only in response to an oral question from the Liberals (about which the government would have had notice). In the words of Henry Brooke (who as Financial Secretary was the responsible minister):

> In 1952, the Government introduced a special security procedure for investigating the reliability of civil servants employed on exceptionally secret work. It was then estimated that, outside the atomic energy field, not more than 3,000 posts would be involved. Experience has shown that further posts need to be included in order to work to a consistent and reasonable definition of exceptionally secret work, and the revised estimate is that about 10,000 posts will be subject to this procedure.[22]

As suggested by Brooke's statement, 'PV' was thus not confined to the Foreign Office, as appears initially to have been anticipated, but operated in all government departments 'having access to classified material involving the security of the State'.[23] It also applied to a wider range of staff than proposed by the Cadogan Committee, with 'many more junior grades, which must inevitably be employed on highly classified work', being positively vetted.[24] As a result, the 10,000 posts subject to PV revealed by the Financial Secretary was well beyond the Cabinet Secretary's initial estimate of 1,000, though it seems that 1,000 would have been about right if the procedure had been confined to the Foreign Office.[25] While this exponential increase in the scale of PV would not, of course, have been known to Parliament at the time the procedures were formally disclosed (the initial estimate not having been revealed), the new procedure nevertheless generated only limited concern from MPs.

These concerns—such as they were—appeared to dissipate following assurances that the PV arrangements had been discussed with the civil service unions, and that PV would not require an expansion in the numbers employed by the Security Service.[26] MPs were equally restrained a year later when the Foreign Secretary Harold Macmillan gave an unusually vivid account of the process, his guard down

22 HC Debs, 21 October 1954, col. 1367. According to Brooke, the increase in numbers had been the subject of discussion, with trade unions representing civil service staff.

23 HC Debs, 7 November 1955, col. 1500 (Foreign Secretary).

24 ibid.

25 ibid.

26 MI5 appeared to be very sceptical about the value of PV. Liddell, after Hollis had returned from a visit to the USA, reported that he had been told:

> of the enormous number of field enquiries conducted by the FBI only four-tenth of one percent had led to the rejection of a candidate. Our objections, through vetting on the basis of our records, amounted to 1.2 percent . . . either the Americans as a whole were whiter than

in a moment of shared anxiety. During a Commons debate on the 'disappearance' of Burgess and Maclean, in which he reported that about 900 Foreign Office staff (in senior, junior, and clerical branches) had been subject to PV, Macmillan said that:

> This procedure entails detailed research into the whole background of the officer concerned, including his school and university career and any previous employment before joining the Foreign Service. In a large number of cases, personal inquiries are made of university tutors, past employers and others who have personal knowledge of the candidate.[27]

In contrast to the heated debates in 1948 about the purge, the mood was now very different: there were no concerns expressed about PV in a debate dominated by lengthy ministerial speeches peppered with backbench concern about the failures of MI5 and the need to tighten up the procedures to avoid the risk of repetition.

III. The Conference of Privy Councillors

As a result of pressure to have some kind of independent review of security procedures in the light of the Burgess and Maclean affair (concern about which had been revived in 1955), the Prime Minister did what was perhaps the least possible to allay parliamentary and public concerns. Thus, with the prior agreement of Attlee as Leader of the Opposition, Eden (who succeeded Churchill in April 1955, before increasing the Tory majority at the general election in the following month) announced at the end of an Adjournment Debate on 7 November 1955 that he was proposing 'to convene a small, informal conference of Privy Councillors from both sides of the House', in order to 'consider whether any further precautions can properly be taken to reduce the risk of treachery'.[28] The possibility that this task might be given to a judge was not seriously considered, the Prime Minister explaining that:

> Behind all that the House has been discussing this afternoon, behind the anxieties, the fears—to some extent the confusion—there is a larger question, and it is this. How far are we to go in pursuit of greater security at the cost of the essential liberties of the British people? That is why I have suggested Privy Councillors—who are not judges. This is not, I think, a matter for judges, but for Parliament. The

we had reason to think, or that the field enquires were ineffective . . . on the average [in the US], each one takes 44 days, and in one case . . . no less than 32 people had been interviewed, all with completely negative results (TNA, KV 4/474, Liddell Diary, 5 May 1952).

27 HC Debs, 7 November 1955, col. 1499.
28 ibid., col. 1609.

> only reason that I said Privy Councillors is that they are Members of Parliament. It is essentially Parliament's decision.[29]

Apart from the slight to the judicial profession, who today might (wrongly) be seen by some lawyers as the guardians of civil liberties, Eden's disarming remarks reflect a view that it was Parliament that had the primary responsibility for the protection of political freedom. This is a view that has much to commend it, and it is one that was to be rehearsed by ministers in governments of both parties throughout the period of this study. It did not follow, however, that Privy Councillors were the only parliamentarians able to perform this role, a restriction which meant that the work was being done not by Parliament but by the government. Those picked for this task were senior representatives from both sides of the House, with the Lord President of the Council (Salisbury), the Lord Chancellor (Kilmuir), and the Home Secretary (the little-known Lloyd George) representing the government, and three Cabinet ministers in the Attlee government (Jowitt, Morrison, and Strauss) representing the Labour Party.[30] There were no backbenchers and no representatives of the awkward squad, the team being completed by Sir Edward Bridges, Permanent Secretary to the Treasury, and Head of the Home Civil Service.[31]

As might be expected, the Privy Councillors adopted a crude assessment of the security threat, which seemed ironically to confound MI5's more subtle assessment in a Conference briefing.[32] According to the Privy Councillors, the security problem was not the informant motivated by greed or moved by blackmail; but rather that posed by the ideological zealot moved by a commitment to a political cause.[33] The result was the need to identify and exclude from access to secret work the members of the Communist Party, all the more curious given that the wrath of the Conference was directed at the failings of PV, which was designed as much for character defects (creating vulnerabilities of the first kind) as for Communist sympathies (creating vulnerabilities of the second kind). For the most part, however, the report of the Conference avoided making any radical proposals for change, more concerned to tighten the existing procedures to ensure they worked more effectively. In this endeavour the Conference may well have been constrained by the Prime Minister, who had revealed his hand when he indicated that he was looking for options within the law rather than seeking new powers, and looking to improve

29 ibid., col. 1610.

30 See TNA, CAB 21/4037 (Public Service Security: Conference of Privy Councillors; The Lord Chancellor's Papers) (Letter from Bridges to Viscount Kilmuir, 30 December 1955). The Conference had been established following a Commons debate on 7 November 1955. The proposal for the Conference was announced to the Commons on 23 November 1955: HC Debs, 23 November 1955, col. 1462.

31 Bridges appears to have drafted the report. See TNA, CAB 21/4037 (Public Service Security: Conference of Privy Councillors; The Lord Chancellor's Papers) (Letter from Bridges to Viscount Kilmuir, 30 December 1955).

32 TNA, CAB 134/1325 (Security Conference of Privy Counsellors [sic.]: Meetings 1–8 (1955); Papers 1–20 (1955); Meetings 1–5 (1956); Papers 1–6 (1955) (Memorandum on 'Communism as a Security Problem').

33 Report of the Security Conference of Privy Councillors (n 4), para. 6.

security procedures consistently with the 'essential liberties of the British people',[34] which 'this House so far has always been determined to defend'.[35]

This defence of liberty by the Prime Minister at a time of crisis was superficially impressive, but overlooks the fact that Parliament had been kept in the dark about the full extent of the PV procedures for two or three years, and was still being kept in the dark about the proposals hatched in February 1955 to extend them to government contractors.[36] In their (confidential) report (to the Prime Minister), the Privy Councillors found that PV applied to the 'more secret categories of work' (whereas normal vetting applied to 'a wide category of secret work'),[37] and confirmed that PV had developed significantly since it was introduced in 1952, notably by:

(a) widening the categories of post subject to this procedure and;
(b) pursuing enquiries openly and 'in the field', which was not considered acceptable when positive vetting was first instituted.[38]

However, the plans to extend PV to government contractors in line with what was now a US treaty obligation had yet to be implemented because of problems developing an appropriate appeal procedure that would not also apply to the victims of negative vetting, a prospect that greatly alarmed MI5, though the Conference seemed less concerned.[39]

As we saw in Chapter 9, the Privy Councillors made a number of recommendations about the purge procedure that would tilt the balance more in favour of the State and away from the suspect. They did the same in relation to PV, excoriating in their criticism of the inefficiency of its operation, arguing for tougher procedures. In a remarkable passage, the Privy Councillors wrote:

> We enquired about the progress made in positive vetting. It is true that this procedure was only started four years ago and has had to expand from small

[34] HC Debs, 7 November 1955, col. 1610.

[35] ibid., cols 1610 and 1631, respectively.

[36] TNA, PREM 11/1587 (Review of Security Procedures: Setting Up of Committee of Privy Councillors) (Minute from Home Secretary to Prime Minister, 24 January 1955), informing the latter that the Ministerial Committee on Security (which the Home Secretary chaired) had recently decided that PV should be extended from members of the civil service, Atomic Energy Authority and the armed forces), to a 'limited number of persons outside the public service—namely, consultants and senior staff of firms handling top secret Government contracts'. It is clear that this step was taken partially to satisfy the USA, which would not have been willing to exchange atomic energy information 'if we have to tell them that we are not prepared to extend PV to any person outside the public service' (ibid.).

[37] Report of the Security Conference of Privy Councillors (n 4), para. 18. This is contained in TNA, CAB 21/4035, which was not released until 2008. What appears to be the original signed copy of the report is in a file in another series, TNA, PREM 11/1587, which was opened in 1996. The name of this file ('Review of Security Procedures: Setting Up of Committee of Privy Councillors') does not indicate that it contains the report. Bridges' draft of the report is in a Lord Chancellor's file relating to the Conference: TNA, CAB 21/4037 (Public Service Security: Conference of Privy Councillors; The Lord Chancellor's Papers).

[38] Report of the Security Conference of Privy Councillors (n 4), para. 22.

[39] ibid., paras 74–84.

> beginnings; and that the field to be covered has since been greatly widened. Nevertheless we were dismayed to find what a small proportion of the positive vetting which needs to be done has so far been carried out. We were shocked to hear from one Permanent Secretary who gave evidence to us that he had estimated that, at the present rate, it would take another ten years to clear up the cases waiting for positive vetting in his Department.[40]

With the exception of the Atomic Energy Authority (where an agreement with the United States in the sharing of atomic secrets required the vigorous application of PV), progress in PV was said to lag far behind what was necessary to cover all the posts with access to highly secret information.[41]

The main cause of these 'deplorable delays' (no wonder the Privy Councillors did not want their report to be published) was the size of the Ministry of Supply team of field investigators, who conducted all the inquiries except those on behalf of the Foreign Office and the Atomic Energy Authority. About to be increased from eighteen to twenty-seven, this was 'not nearly enough' and should be 'expanded rapidly' to compare with the Atomic Energy Authority's team of 121 members. One reason for the disparity was said to be the difficulty in recruiting suitable people from the retired ranks of the Special Branch, thought to be the best qualified for this kind of work, but increasingly hard to find. The Privy Councillors noted, however, that the Atomic Energy Authority had found that retired officers from other police departments (such as the Criminal Investigation Department) were just as good, and recommended that the Ministry of Supply should follow this example, giving consideration as well to 'suitable men from other walks of life'.[42] The vetting rules also applied to the Atomic Energy Authority, notably with statutory authority, Authority employees not being engaged like civil servants at the pleasure of the Crown.[43]

As suggested above, the full report of the Privy Councillors was not published, the Privy Councillors explicitly advising against publication because of the subject

40 ibid., para. 44.

41 ibid. Indeed, an appendix to the report revealed that a total of 35,480 posts required PV, with vetting to have been completed in 14,190 cases. While the bulk of the Atomic Energy Authority staff had been vetted, this was true of less than half of the civil servants identified for vetting and only about half of the members of the armed forces who were covered by the procedure. Since the Russians already had the knowledge to enable them to make nuclear weapons, it was thought by the Privy Councillors that secrets 'in other spheres, including particulars of certain other weapons, deserve at least as much protection'.

42 ibid., para. 47.

43 Atomic Energy Authority Act 1954, Sch. 1(4). This allowed for staff of the Atomic Energy Authority to be dismissed on security grounds in circumstances where a civil servant might also be dismissed. This presumably would include a failure to secure PV clearance where relocation was not an option. See pp. 326–6 below.

matter.[44] They were, however, content that a general statement should be issued about the nature of the security threat, with an indication of some of their recommendations, which in their view would have to be acknowledged in any event at the time the latter were implemented.[45] The government agreed, and the sixteen-page (ninety-seven paras) report was reduced to a three-page white paper (twenty-one paras),[46] which stood in sharp contrast to the relative candour that had been on display during the debate that had prompted the appointment of the Privy Councillors in the first place. The summary contains an assessment of the security risk (members of the Communist Party), which reveals just as starkly as the unpublished full report the crude security assessment of the Privy Councillors in terms of risk. It also contains an assessment of the areas of vulnerability, from the type of establishments to the individuals vulnerable because of 'serious defects or failings'. But the summary is very shy about revealing the methods deployed to eliminate these risks.

In particular, there is no reference to vetting, negative or positive, the latter according to the full report now applying to 10,890 civil service posts.[47] The British citizen reading this summary would be left with no idea about the operation of these practices, and even less idea about their scope and extent. In this sense, the attempt at transparency was a step back into the shadows. The only information about PV thus continued to be the rather cryptic remarks of Henry Brooke in 1954 about 'special security procedure for investigating the reliability of civil servants employed on exceptionally secret work', and Harold Macmillan's description of the 'positive vetting procedure', which 'now operated in all Government Departments having access to classified material involving the security of the State', both referred to in Part II above. Nor was there any discussion in the white paper about the proposed extension of these procedures to the private sector in the shape of government contractors, although it was acknowledged that there did exist 'procedures for the security of secret Government contracts involving persons outside Government employment'.[48] But what were these procedures and how did they operate lawfully in practice?

[44] Indeed, so embarrassing was the report that the government was unwilling to share it with foreign administrations. The government was embarrassed by the failure to honour undertakings to introduce PV to 'certain categories of contractors' employees' (on which see Chapter 11), and by the role of trade unions at GCHQ (on which see Chapter 12). The latter was said to 'expose a gap in our defences at one of our most vulnerable points'. It was also thought that the Americans would be 'very much disturbed' by the lack of progress on 'field inquiries', and deficiencies in relation to the purge (TNA, CAB 21/4036 (Official Committee on Security, Transmission of the Security Conference of Privy Councillors to Commonwealth and Foreign Governments, 17 April 1956)).

[45] Report of the Security Conference of Privy Councillors (n 4), paras 90–95.

[46] Statement on the Findings of the Conference of Privy Councillors on Security, Cmd 9715, 1956. The white paper was published in March. For the insipid parliamentary debate on the white paper, see HC Debs, 21 March 1956, col. 1255.

[47] Report of the Security Conference of Privy Councillors (n 4), Appendix B. This was out of a total of 35,480 posts altogether when the Atomic Energy Authority and the armed forces were included.

[48] Statement on the Findings of the Conference of Privy Councillors on Security (n 46), para. 21.

IV. Operational Concerns

So here we have a review recommending the intensification of PV and the recruitment of a bigger army of snoopers to make sure that it was carried out effectively. The Privy Councillors were well aware of the significance of these procedures, which were 'different from anything we have previously had to carry out in this country'.[49] They were also well aware that their procedures 'go deeper into the lives and habits of a very large body of people who handle state secrets',[50] while arguing that they needed to go further. At no point did it appear to occur to anyone that such powers ought to have been fully transparent, or that they ought to have statutory authority, or that those who exercised the powers ought to have been fully accountable for the way they were used.[51] But if these powers needed an army of snoopers, they would also need an equivalent army of snitches, as the source of information and misinformation about candidates for various positions. It did not take long for this furtive process to be exposed still further.

According to the Privy Councillors, the full PV procedure included the 'completion by the individual of a questionnaire, letters to referees named by him, and a field investigation carried out by a professional team entirely employed on this work'.[52] This, of course, was not revealed by the white paper, though as both the Foreign Secretary and the Prime Minister had earlier revealed during the 7 November 1955 debate, the army of snitches would be recruited largely from the academic community,[53] leading to real concern about what some saw as the infiltration of the universities by MI5. The army of snoopers descending on campus soon made their presence felt,[54] Lord Chorley complaining during a Lords' education debate in 1957 about the intrusion of the Security Services,[55] as well as university teachers being called upon to disclose secrets not only about their students but more and more frequently also about their colleagues,[56] at a time when there was clear evidence of academics being refused employment or dismissed on political grounds.[57]

[49] Report of the Security Conference of Privy Councillors (n 4), para. 8.

[50] ibid., para. 9.

[51] At this point, we should not exaggerate the significance of the Atomic Energy Act 1954, Sch. 1(4), which effectively offered a blank cheque by writing into statute the opaque and unspecified civil service procedures. See p. 278, n 43.

[52] Report of the Security Conference of Privy Councillors (n 4), para. 20.

[53] HC Debs, 7 November 1955, col. 1499 (Macmillan), 1604 (Eden).

[54] See pp. 283–7 below.

[55] HL Debs, 22 May 1957, col. 1122.

[56] ibid.

[57] See J. Mahoney, *British Civil Liberties and the Cold War: 1945–1956* (Ph.D. Dissertation, University of Cambridge, 1989, Cambridge University Library), pp. 186–91, discussing the dismissal of Andrew Rothstein by the University of London, and other cases. Early in 1952 Liddell had recorded that Home Office PUS Newsam had given him the particulars of four individuals who were being considered for a Russian professorship at Nottingham University: 'He was anxious that we should let him know if any of them were undesirable. He did not wish for anything to be put in writing': TNA, KV 4/474 (Liddell Diary, 14 February 1952).

A Labour peer (ennobled in 1945), Lord Chorley was a distinguished scholar in the law department of the LSE, as well as an office-holder in the AUT, then the trade union for university staff. Clearly angry, Chorley complained about what 'many teachers regard as spying for the State on the activities of their students', which was 'one of the cruellest dilemmas of the modern world'.[58] He also complained about the 'subterfuges and tricks used by security officers' for the purpose of obtaining information, and 'the evils which result from material which they do get'.[59] In terms of the procedure used by the Security Service (at least in relation to students; staff inquiries seem to have been less formal), it appears that university teachers were asked 'to answer quite elaborate questionnaires as to the political associations of [their] students, very often as to the political associations which ex-students who have left [them] years before formed while they were under [their] supervision at University'.[60]

The problem that concerned Chorley was not one that occurred 'only now and then': it was 'going on all the time'.[61] Nor does it appear only to have been a problem of PV of students past and present, with colleagues in the University of London complaining about being asked to report on their own colleagues. Here Chorley said that some of the information he had received was 'almost unbelievable', claiming that if teachers were being asked to report on the general loyalty of colleagues, they were being 'encouraged to act as spies; to find their way into their colleagues' studies, even to pry into the drawers of their desks',[62] the latter a claim Chorley was to regret, the claim being reported as a fact which he was unable to substantiate. In a statement to the House a week later, Chorley ate humble pie, explaining in a statement on University Teachers and Security:

> As some of your Lordships will remember, I spoke last week in the debate on the universities, and in my speech I drew attention to what I regarded as objectionable aspects of the methods used by the security services in collecting information as to happenings in the universities. I have been widely reported in the Press as having stated that a teacher had been asked to find out what documents a colleague had in his room. I wish to correct this. I did not intend to convey that this had actually happened—that a teacher had in fact been asked to do that. I have no evidence that that is so. I was simply arguing that that was the sort of thing that would be likely to happen if this type of method were used. I do not want to make any accusation of misreporting. I have no doubt that I was not speaking as accurately as I should have liked to do. But as this is a matter of importance, I should

58 HL Debs, 22 May 1957, col. 1123.
59 ibid.
60 ibid.
61 ibid., col. 1123.
62 ibid., col. 1124.

> like to make it quite clear that I did not intend to make any imputation of this kind.[63]

Chorley appeared to have been right: some of the information may have been unbelievable, a matter to which we return.[64] But despite this unwelcome embarrassment, Chorley's intervention was timely, with the matter to be considered by the AUT Council at its meeting later in the same month.[65] The *Manchester Guardian* reported resentment among AUT members about having to make private reports about students, and that this had prompted a standard form of refusal being issued by the Executive Committee of the Association. The form had been drawn up in response to an AUT Council decision in 1956, which stated that teachers ought not to be asked questions about a student's politics or religious opinions and activities. It was also stated that no report should be made without the prior knowledge of the student in question. There appears, however, to have been some uncertainty about (and some opposition to) the policy,[66] and it is unclear to what extent some academics were willing to assume the new role that PV demanded.

Chorley's intervention nevertheless generated a response from the government, with the *Manchester Guardian* reporting that the AUT Council in 1957 had before it a circular issued by the Ministry of Supply outlining government policy. The circular denied that any suspicion attached to those individuals who were the subject of government inquiries, claiming that the inquiries were made in all cases where the individual was a candidate for a post giving access to 'exceptionally secret information'. Apparently, only a 'comparatively small' proportion of those employed on defence work 'and other secret and confidential matters' were engaged on work of such secrecy that such inquiries were necessary. But the reason why there were so many inquiries in the universities is simply because the universities were such an important ground for recruitment of staff, the Ministry making it quite clear that the object of the inquiries was to prevent information vital to the security of the country getting into the hands of unreliable people.

Unreliability for this purpose meant those with Communist or Fascist sympathies, or 'character defects' which 'might render them susceptible to pressure'. However, it was claimed by the Ministry that it should not be supposed that an early association with Communists as a student would automatically bar an individual from access to secret information. The response from the Ministry of Supply was thus utterly unapologetic, it being further explained that the reason why tutors were approached was because it was felt that 'they had a unique opportunity of seeing many sides of a man', while 'scrupulous care' was taken to cross-check

[63] HL Debs, 29 May 1957, cols 59–60.

[64] It should also be added in his defence that there were a number of allegations of discrimination against academics on political grounds to make such claims easily plausible. See Mahoney (n 57).

[65] See *Manchester Guardian*, 27 May 1957.

[66] ibid.

the information obtained from tutors. There was, moreover, 'nothing surreptitious' about the inquiries, which were 'considered essential to the security of the State'. But as the *Manchester Guardian* pointed out in a persuasive leader, the objection was not with the principle of the employer checking out potential recruits before recruitment, but with the manner in which it was done in this case.

The objections here were that inquiries were made from people the candidate did not name as referees, and were made 'secretly and without his knowledge'. This was thought to put teachers in 'a very invidious position', and it is small wonder some of them revolted against it. Although the nature of the objections appeared rather feeble, they nevertheless concealed a more fundamental point about the transparency of the process and transparency about the purposes for which the information might be used. Agreeing with Lord Chorley that the matter could be dealt with in a 'more humane way', the *Manchester Guardian* asked:

> Why should not the Ministry say to an applicant, 'In addition to the references you give, we should like to ask Professor X and Dr Y about your suitability for this post. Have you any objection?' Apart from the manner of these inquiries, there is the use to which they are put. Many teachers would be more ready to answer if they knew more of the methods of evaluation. They may suspect that great weight is given to points which they regard as unimportant, and the questions actually put may have encouraged this belief. The AUT is well advised to seek from its members now a clear picture, not of their feelings about these inquiries but of what they are being asked and how. And the government may soon find it prudent to lift a corner of the security curtain in order to reassure them.[67]

V. Spies on Campus—More than Vetting

Spying on students may have been the major concern at the heart of this spat between the AUT and the government. But as the intervention by Lord Chorley makes clear, it was not the only one, with concerns also being expressed about a more sinister intervention on the campus. This related to allegations of MI5 snooping on academics, and fellow academics snitching on their colleagues. Although Chorley was right that some Cold War claims are unbelievable, his claim in the House of Lords on 22 May 1957 may not have been one of them after all. The role of the Security Service on campus inevitably made its way to the floor of the House of Commons, with the most significant intervention taking place on 6 June 1957, when former Labour minister George Strauss asked the Home Secretary (R. A. Butler) 'what changes or extensions have been made during the last twelve

[67] *Manchester Guardian*, 27 May 1957.

months in the arrangements for checking teachers and students in universities for security purposes'.[68] Back came the answer:

> special inquiries are made, at the universities where appropriate, about the reliability of Government staff to be employed on exceptionally secret work. *Apart from these special inquiries, investigations have also to be undertaken in the universities as elsewhere from time to time to protect the security of the State.* It would not be in the public interest to disclose the nature of the arrangements made to carry out these investigations, but I can say that no significant changes or extensions have been made in the last twelve months.[69]

This suggested that there was more than PV taking place on campus. Not satisfied, Strauss returned with more. He claimed that 'the need for checking formally, through tutors, students applying for secret jobs is generally accepted', but expressed disquiet about 'the belief that there may be on the staff unidentified persons who are passing on information to MI5 about their colleagues, or about students', and asked Butler to look at the evidence 'to see whether he cannot allay the real anxieties which now exist in many university circles'.[70] In a lamentable performance, the Home Secretary sought to reassure the House that 'there is no need to exaggerate the position', the government simply 'following the practice which was approved by the Conference of Privy Councillors, which, the House will remember, concluded that there was nothing organically wrong or unsound about the Government's security arrangements'.[71]

This was almost as stupid as a related claim was patronizing, the latter being the claim that as someone closely associated with the universities, he [Butler] could assure the House that there was no abuse in the matter.[72] It was stupid because his tormentor had been a member of the Privy Councillors' Conference (representing the Labour side), Strauss venturing to suggest that Butler was likely to have been aware that the Conference 'did not go into this aspect of the problem at all and did not consider the detailed arrangements for security in universities'.[73] Perhaps unable to avoid the patronizing tone of those born to rule, Butler acknowledged the 'useful service' given by Strauss 'in this connection', adding that:

> the Conference approved the general outline of our arrangements, and, as I said in my answer, the arrangements have to be applied wherever they are necessary, whether it be in the universities or elsewhere. The undertaking which I can now

68 HC Debs, 6 June 1957, col. 1457.
69 ibid.(emphasis added).
70 ibid., col. 1458.
71 ibid.
72 ibid.
73 ibid.

> give is that this matter will be very closely watched by myself as the guardian of private liberty.[74]

The last sentence genuinely appears in Hansard, as does the claim in an exchange with Kenneth Younger (previously a junior minister in the Attlee government) that while 'universities have a certain licence of liberty and speech', at the same time, 'there are general considerations affecting the security of the State', which 'must apply all round in the State wherever it may be'.[75]

These questions were revisited on the following day in a debate initiated by Hilary Marquand, the Labour member for Middlesbrough East.[76] On this occasion, Butler sent his junior minister into bat. However, Jocelyn Simon—then the member for Middlesbrough West and a future Law Lord as Lord Simon of Glaisdale—fared little better with a hopeless brief. After another Home Office peroration about liberty and security, Simon did, however, confirm that in relation to the universities, 'the activities of the security services fall under two heads':

> First, there are general inquiries to guard against subversion of our freedom and, secondly, there are specific inquiries to ensure that anyone taken into certain work of great secrecy is reliable.[77]

So far as the 'specific inquiries' are concerned, Simon thought there was 'no objection on the part of university dons to answering references from Government Departments any more than to their answering references by, say, commercial undertakings'.[78] In an unusual moment of reconciliation, however, he did say that this was subject to the proviso that 'those inquiries are reasonably circumscribed'.[79] But there was no attempted reconciliation in relation to the 'general inquiries': to say what the arrangements were for dealing with espionage and subversive activities would 'obviously be contrary to the public interest', and would destroy 'the whole purpose of the security investigations'.[80]

This was thus an important debate in which the government conceded that MI5 had a presence on campus that was not only for the purpose of PV. But

[74] ibid.
[75] ibid., col. 1459.
[76] HC Debs, 7 June 1957, col. 1572.
[77] ibid., col. 1582. In his ode to liberty, Simon had referred to the 'age-long relationship between security and freedom', adding that:

> without security there can be no freedom. The problem on the one hand, as the right hon Gentleman suggested, is to prevent freedom from being used to destroy freedom; but equally, on the other hand, we must take care that the measures we take for the preservation of freedom do not themselves result in its impairment (col. 1580).

[78] ibid., col. 1584.
[79] ibid.
[80] ibid., col. 1585.

despite Strauss' concession about PV being generally accepted, not everyone was as complacent. For although concerns about PV had thus developed into wider concerns about MI5 involvement on campus, there were still serious concerns about inquiries relating to a person's suitability for appointment to a government job. Thus, in what sense would inquiries be 'reasonably circumscribed'? Would views expressed in the course of tutorials be used against a student in the context of PV? This led to more fundamental questions about whether Security Service questioning is consistent with the professional integrity of academics. According to Marquand—himself an academic before his election to the House:

> the profession has its professional honour to safeguard, and the relationship between the university teacher and his pupil, though it may be somewhat different, is not very greatly different in character from the relation between the doctor and his patient or the priest and the penitent.[81]

The real meat in this story, however, related to the 'general inquiries' referred to by Simon, and the suggestion that academics were being used to snitch on their colleagues to the Security Service, Marquand raising one such case in the course of the debate:

> I have taken steps to check the accuracy of the story that at least one university teacher has been asked to report on the activities of his fellow teachers in his university institution. I have prima facie evidence that the story is true. I will say no more. I have no intention of mentioning names. The name, I shall, of course, give freely to the right hon. Gentleman and to the hon. and learned Gentleman; indeed, the person who gave me the information has asked me to do so.[82]

In responding to this very grave allegation, Simon chose his words very carefully, as the following exchange suggests:

> Mr Simon: I entirely agree with the right hon. Gentleman that it would also be a severe loss if the confidential relationship between tutor and student were destroyed, and that academic life as we know it could hardly continue to exist if it were thought that a spy was planted in every common room. I can assure the right hon. Gentleman that there is no justification for any such apprehension, no justification for the belief that university teachers are encouraged to spy upon their colleagues or their students.

[81] ibid., col. 1576.
[82] ibid., cols 1577–8.

As I have said, I will investigate any case which is—[Interruption.] I used the word 'encouraged'.

Mrs. Castle: That is the whole allegation.[83]

But having successfully exposed the matter, the parliamentary process revealed its limitations by being unable to resolve it. Although clearly not confined to PV, the nature and scale of Security Service involvement on campus was never revealed. Indeed, although Simon undertook to ensure that the whole matter would be examined by the Home Secretary, who would also investigate the specific instance referred to by Marquand, he refused to give an undertaking that the Home Secretary would report on his findings to the House. One of the benefits of a ventriloquist's dummy is that he cannot speak without being told what to say. In any event, it would all depend on the nature of the inquiries, or more probably what they were likely to yield. Simon was unprepared to accede to a request that the Home Secretary's inquiry should take place in consultation with the AUT, or the university vice chancellors and principals. So far as he was concerned, this was simply a question relating to the 'method of approach to university teachers', and as such no doubt could easily be resolved.

The legacy of this reluctance to explain the role of the Security Service on campus is still with us. It seems likely that facts relating to some of the speculation ventilated on 6 and 7 June 1957 are submerged in a Home Office file (HO 325/158), 'Parliamentary Question—Government Security Services; Vetting Potential Recruits to Government Departments'. It seems likely that this was prepared as part of the background to the exchange between Butler and Strauss (and others) referred to above, with the Home Secretary's response giving a flavour of some of its content in terms of the prepared line to take. There appears, however, to be more in the file than has been revealed publicly, whether to the House of Commons or elsewhere. There is otherwise no reason why it would remain closed. As we know, under the Public Records Act 1958, government files must be transferred to the National Archives 'not later than twenty years after their creation'.[84] This is subject to the proviso that records may be retained 'if, in the opinion of the person who is responsible for them, they are required for administrative purposes or ought to be retained for any other special reason', subject to the approval of the Lord Chancellor.[85]

[83] ibid., col. 1586.
[84] Public Records Act 1958, s. 3(4).
[85] ibid. For whatever reason, the Home Office retained file HO325/158. A request was duly made under the Freedom of Information Act 2000 to secure access to the file, without success, on the ground that it has been 'misfiled' and that it would exceed the cost limit to seek to retrieve it, the cost limit providing an exemption from the duty to comply with a request for information under the Freedom of Information Act 2000, s. 12. See also pp. 458 and 481–2, below.

VI. Radcliffe's Re-Assessment

To recap: officially introduced in 1952, PV was the subject of intense criticism, with initial concerns of the security establishment about its lack of rigour giving way to parliamentary, press and academic concern about the engagement of snitches, the presence of MI5 on campus, and inadequate regard for the interests of vetting subjects. Despite being barely transparent and acknowledged by government to only a limited extent, it was thus attacked from three sides. The critics were to be joined by others, as further security crises were to lead to three judicial inquiries in the early 1960s, two of which were chaired by Lord Radcliffe, reinforcing concerns about the inadequate protection for and accountability to vetting subjects, as well as expressing doubts about the practical value of PV, though nevertheless leading paradoxically to the procedures being tightened still further.

Radcliffe had been appointed for the first time in 1961 to look again at security only five years after the Privy Councillors had reported. The reason for his appointment was yet another security scandal (this time the George Blake espionage case), in what seemed like a continuous security and intelligence crisis in the 1950s and early 1960s. As with the Privy Councillors' Report in 1956, the full Radcliffe Report was not published, with a summary again being produced as a white paper, albeit longer and more detailed than the summary of the Privy Councillors' Report.[86] It is clear from the white paper that while Radcliffe was not concerned exclusively with PV,[87] he had serious reservations about its 'inherent weakness'.[88] In a nutshell, the 'inherent weakness' was the failure of PV to 'throw up material' which is 'hard' enough for any conclusive action to be founded' on the material in question.[89]

This was hardly a ringing endorsement of the value of PV, with Lord Radcliffe reinforcing these doubts by acknowledging that 'traces of Communist association' would normally be picked up 'from intelligence records', in other words normal vetting.[90] No explanation was given for these 'intelligence records' and no one asked; it seems that everyone knew all about them. Nor as we shall see, was there any reference to normal vetting in the white paper, even if allusion to it seemed unavoidable. It was, moreover, only rarely that PV would uncover evidence of character defects, such as 'insobriety, financial instability, untruthfulness, irregular sexual or marital relations, family connexions behind the Iron Curtain, etc'.[91] But according to Radcliffe, even where such information was uncovered, it would not necessarily be troublesome, its significance depending on the context.

86 Report on Security Procedures in the Public Service (Chair: Lord Radcliffe), Cmnd 1681, 1962.
87 For a fuller account of the Radcliffe Report, see Chapter 13 below.
88 Report on Security Procedures in the Public Service (n 86), para. 62.
89 ibid.
90 ibid.
91 ibid.

While 'in theory' such 'defects of character' (as they were referred to in the moralistic timbre of the day) would 'constitute vulnerability to temptation and pressure', Radcliffe was of the view that such traits were not necessarily the most dangerous from a security point of view and did not 'in practice' make a 'very firm base for action against a person as a security risk, *unless he is to be envisaged as placed in some special situation, such as service behind the Iron Curtain*'.[92] The latter qualification (in added italics) was prescient, as we will see when Radcliffe turned his attention in his second report to Christopher Vassall almost immediately after completing his wide-ranging security review. For the moment, however, the concern was not to go overboard and treat all character traits in the same way for fear of 'imposing an excessively high standard upon the morals and conduct of a particular section of the public service'.[93]

Radcliffe's scepticism about the value of PV did not, of course, suggest a lack of concern with the defence of the realm on his part. On the contrary, though the main focus of his concern was with lax document classification and security. But on PV in particular, scepticism about its value was reinforced by an awareness of a lack of protection for those who had failed to obtain clearance. Radcliffe was concerned in particular that the consequences of PV for 'character defect' had not been worked out, noting the absence in such cases of any procedure equivalent to the purge procedure applicable to those with Communist sympathies or associations. According to Radcliffe, where PV clearance was refused on character grounds alone, departments appeared 'to follow no consistent practice as regards intimating to [the individual concerned] any formal finding or decision adverse to him or providing him with a right of appeal to the Head of Department under normal departmental procedures'.[94]

Unlike someone refused PV clearance on the grounds of Communist associations alone (here PV merged with the purge), there was thus no right of appeal to the Three Advisers for someone refused clearance on grounds of character defect. It was important that this should be addressed, though in recommending the introduction of an appeal in character defect cases, Radcliffe did not propose that there should be parity of treatment with people denied clearance for political reasons. Nevertheless, it was recommended that minimum standards of procedural fairness should be introduced so that an officer was told that PV clearance had been refused and the reasons for it, and that there should be a right of appeal by the individual to his or her Head of Department. However, Radcliffe expressly rejected the suggestion that there might be a right of appeal to the Three Advisers on the

92 ibid. (emphasis added).
93 ibid., para. 63.
94 ibid., para. 52.

bizarre ground that it would cause 'the tribunal appealed to' in effect 'to take over the whole responsibility of a man's department for his posting and promotion'.[95]

The latter argument was very unconvincing, for it is hard to see how a review of evidence by a body such as the Three Advisers could remotely be said to represent a transfer of responsibility for the departmental management of staff. It already took place in the case of those refused clearance on political grounds (without any suggestion that responsibility had been transferred to the panel). As we discussed in Chapter 8, the procedure was very clear about where final responsibility lay, particularly after the Privy Councillors had reinforced the advisory role of the panel. It was up to the minister to decide how to respond to advice from the Three Advisers. All of which suggests that there may have been undisclosed reasons for the refusal to allow external scrutiny. Yet although a little sceptical about the value of PV, and although concerned about the absence of procedural safeguards, Radcliffe nevertheless accepted that the government would not be able:

> easily to defend a situation in which it failed to take reasonable steps to satisfy itself as to the general background and character of the people to whom it was entrusting its most important secrets.[96]

giGiven Radcliffe's scepticism about PV, it is nevertheless remarkable that the Committee was unable to resist the temptation of making the process even more demanding by imposing additional vetting requirements. So, because 'men are capable of changing their behaviour and way of life and to some extent their character', he recommended that PV should be reviewed periodically rather than be a once-and-for-all exercise. Here it was proposed to follow the practice of the Foreign Service to require PV clearance in appropriate cases every five years, and more often should the circumstances require.[97] And reflecting first Radcliffe's views about the vulnerability of youth,[98] those under twenty-one would have to be vetted annually. It is true that the PV reviews would be conducted with a lighter touch than the original assessment, but it is also true that this marked a significant step up in the application of scrutiny of those employed by the State.

VII. The Limits of Transparency

One of the virtues of the Radcliffe Report was that it shed more light on the practice of PV than had been seen in the past, though it would take another Radcliffe

[95] ibid., para. 60. See pp. 312–20 below on resistance to extending the remit of the Three Advisers to private-sector cases.
[96] Report on Security Procedures in the Public Service (n 86), para. 69.
[97] ibid., para. 75.
[98] ibid., para. 73.

inquiry for more complete transparency. But in this spirit of greater openness and critical examination, there was one extraordinary omission, this relating essentially to the practice of normal vetting, which we referred to above. We thus have the paradox of the more benign security checks remaining a closely guarded secret, with the more intrusive now being openly discussed. This is despite the fact that checking the name against information already held was part and parcel of PV and, the focus on political views and activities aside, a procedure that would scarcely surprise anyone who gave the matter any serious thought. It was extraordinary. So although there is no mention of normal vetting in the published summaries of the reports of either the Conference of Privy Councillors or the Radcliffe Committee, it was nevertheless considered by both, with the former reporting that the procedure applied systematically in the government service to all civil servants engaged in a 'wide range of secret work', with a 'considerable proportion of the posts in the civil service' now subject to the process, which entailed a search of the Security Service records 'to see if anything adverse is recorded against an individual'.[99]

We knew that the practice of normal or negative vetting of existing employees engaged merely on confidential work was also the subject of discussion by the Radcliffe Committee (which also appears to confirm that it was operating on an industrial scale), even before a fuller version of the report was released in 2018. We knew this because shortly after it was submitted on 21 November 1961, the report was the subject of discussion by both the Official and Ministerial Committees on Security, the minutes of both of which have been available at the National Archives for some time. In a memorandum to the Ministerial Committee, the Chairman of the Official Committee (Sir Norman Brook) makes it clear that Radcliffe deals with both normal and positive vetting in chapter 5, expressing concern that publication of this chapter would 'probably involve the Government in some embarrassment'.[100] This was thought to arise from the fact that 'while the latter [PV] is an overt process which the Government have publicly announced and justified, the former [normal vetting] is covert and, apart from occasional references in Parliament which have attracted no attention, its existence has not been officially avowed'.[101]

[99] This suggests that the process was undertaken on a large scale, albeit that 'a considerable proportion' is not quantified. The report is all the more tantalizing for the fact that in another section, it is made clear that normal vetting applied also in the private sector to the employees of government contractors, where it appears to have operated quietly and unobtrusively, an issue to which we return in Chapter 11.

[100] TNA, CAB 134/2498 (Ministerial Committee on Security: Meetings 1–3, Papers 1–6 (1962); Meetings 1–2, Papers 1–8 (1963); Meeting 1, Paper 1 (1963); Meetings 1–2, Papers 1–6 (1964)) (Report of the Committee on Security Procedures in the Public Service: Memorandum by the Chairman of the Official Committee, 24 January 1962, para. 5).

[101] By the early 1960s, existing staff would largely have been assessed, and normal vetting would principally have affected those applying for civil service work. Government service aside, prospective and existing BBC employees were also subject to normal vetting; the ground-breaking M. Hollingsworth and R. Norton-Taylor, *Blacklist, The Inside Story of Political Vetting* (London, 1988) is particularly good on the BBC, and has some interesting examples of applicants to public-sector employment falling foul of security vetting.

Sir Norman thought it 'doubtful whether we can hope to maintain this secrecy indefinitely', and accepted that 'the publication of Radcliffe's findings provided an opportunity to acknowledge the existence of the practice. But on the other hand:

> the area over which normal vetting is applied is very wide, as is illustrated by paragraph 60 of the Report. An admission that normal vetting is applied on this scale would provoke a demand, from Parliament and from Departmental staffs, for an appeals procedure similar to that of the Three Advisers who constitute the court of appeal in the more limited field of positive vetting. It would be wholly impracticable; but it would be embarrassing to have to refuse to do so.[102]

In the light of the foregoing concerns about the consequences of making a disclosure about normal vetting, the Official Committee thought that the balance of advantage lay in omitting from the published report the entire section dealing with normal vetting, as well as all other references to the practice. If this advice was accepted, Sir Norman pointed out that there would be a need to amend the section of the report on PV as well prior to publication. This was because the 'initial check against intelligence records, which constitutes the whole of normal vetting' is itself also the 'initial stage of positive vetting'.[103]

The Official Committee was led to conclude that in preparing the abridged version it would be 'wise to admit that this check is made as one element in the process of PV but to delete all references which could lead the reader to identify it as constituting the separate and distinct process of normal vetting'.[104] These recommendations—set out in a memorandum by Sir Norman Brook—were duly accepted after some discussion but little resistance by the Ministerial Committee, which met to consider the Radcliffe Report in late January 1962.[105] At this point, it appears to have been accepted that because Radcliffe had made 'no adverse comment' on the system, 'it seemed better not to advertise its existence'.[106] The general view was that it would be inexpedient to disclose the extent to which normal vetting operated, for 'even if it were practicable to meet the demands which would

[102] Report of the Committee on Security Procedures in the Public Service: Memorandum by the Chairman of the Official Committee (n 100). In fact, the Radcliffe Report eport stated that 162,805 posts were now subject to NV, and an additional 26,937 to PV, out of a total complement of 530,340 (just under 40 per cent of all non-industrial civil servants): TNA, CAB 301/258 (Report of the Committee on Security Procedures in the Civil Service), para. 60.

[103] TNA, CAB 301/258 (Report of the Committee on Security Procedures in the Civil Service, para. 6).

[104] ibid.

[105] TNA, CAB 134/2498 (Ministerial Committee on Security: Meetings 1–3, Papers 1–6 (1962); Meetings 1–2, Papers 1–8 (1963); Meeting 1, Paper 1 (1963); Meetings 1–2, Papers 1–6 (1964) (Ministerial Committee on Security, Minutes of a Meeting, 29 January 1962).

[106] ibid., p. 2. This meeting was dominated by a consideration of another Radcliffe recommendation, namely the purge of Communists from the civil service unions.

be made for an appeals machinery', it would be 'dangerous' to do so because 'each appeal might reveal some part of the sources relied upon by the Security Service'.[107]

In a note to the Cabinet circulated by the Prime Minister on the eve of publication of the summary of the Radcliffe Report, it is revealed that 'the Opposition leaders agree that public reference to [normal vetting] is best avoided'.[108] Pointing out that 'all references to normal vetting have been left out' of the Radcliffe report, the afore-mentioned note by the Prime Minister also repeated the line that normal vetting was a 'covert process which is carried out without the knowledge of the individual concerned and it has never been publicly avowed by any government'. Which is not quite true, for as the note also pointed out somewhat apologetically, it had been 'incidentally mentioned in Parliament on a few occasions'.[109] No doubt to his great embarrassment in view of the policy stated in the note, the culprit on both occasions was the Prime Minister himself, once as Foreign Secretary during the Burgess and Maclean debate in 1955,[110] and again in a statement in 1961, when he said that

> One of the questions involved is whether positive or negative vetting should be applied, and to what groups of people. There is a very big difference between them. We may have to go to positive vetting over a wider field.[111]

It should be noted, however, that on neither occasion did the Prime Minister use the term 'normal vetting', and there was no explicit reference to it in the white paper, which contained what was the heavily censored version of Radcliffe. So while paragraph 60 of the report submitted by Radcliffe dealt with normal vetting, paragraph 60 of the white paper dealt with positive vetting, the crucial section on the former omitted. All references to normal vetting were forensically removed, with the result that generations of scholars were misled, writing incomplete accounts about security procedures in the public services, which were widely thought to consist only of the purge and PV. As indicated above, however, it is possible to detect passages in the white paper which strongly imply that there is a procedure of some sort in operation, though there is not enough information to say what that procedure might be. A section in general terms on the Security Service refers to MI5's role in dealing with personnel vetting inquiries from departments, explained to mean the checking of individual names against intelligence records.[112] But as pointed out above, no explanation is given for these intelligence records, and there

[107] ibid.
[108] TNA, CAB 21/6015 (Security Procedures in the Public Service, 'Radcliffe Report') (Publication of Part III, D Notices).
[109] ibid., para. 4(i).
[110] HC Debs, 7 November 1955, col. 1499.
[111] HC Debs, 23 March 1961, col. 587.
[112] Report on Security Procedures in the Public Service (n 86), para. 16.

is no discussion of why or how often such checks would take place, or in relation to whom.

Another section of the white paper contains Radcliffe's account of the purge procedure, which is initiated 'in the light of information obtained from the Security Service or from other sources';[113] there is no explicit acknowledgement that formal security checks or vetting will take place as a precursor to this information being provided. Nevertheless, there is an express acknowledgement in the white paper that PV begins with 'a check with the Security Service, to ascertain whether intelligence records contain any adverse information about the individual in question.'[114] There is thus a lengthy section in the white paper about the 'Role of the Security Service', and two passages in which it is expressly acknowledged that the Security Service keeps intelligence records about individuals. This all seems obvious now, but it is to be recalled that only a month earlier the Cabinet was being reminded that the government denied the existence of MI6, and that this was offered as a reason for not publishing Part I of the white paper (though there were probably more compelling reasons for not doing so).

What is remarkable is that none of this generated any concern. So far as we are able to tell, parliamentarians did not ask awkward questions about the authority or mandate of the Security Service (though in fairness that was about to be fully exposed by the Profumo affair, which was by now smouldering).[115] Nor did they ask awkward questions about intelligence records (such as who collected them, what was recorded about individuals and why, and how this information was used, or with whom it was shared). These were obvious questions, to which the white paper invited a follow-up. Perhaps the problem was that the Radcliffe Committee was followed so quickly by the Radcliffe Tribunal of Inquiry into the Vassall affair,[116] revealing security lapses that opportunistic politicians on the Opposition benches could exploit more easily and more willingly than concerns about civil liberties, in the violation of which they appear all to have been complicit. Paradoxically, the late 1950s and early 1960s created demands for better security rather than better civil liberties, even from the most unlikely sources, as revealed by the following exchange in a debate about the Radcliffe Tribunal of Inquiry rather than the Radcliffe Committee on Security:

> LORD CHORLEY The next point is in respect of this homosexuality vetting by the Security Service. In paragraph 24, at the top of page 8, the Report says that information of this kind is not in general 'collected and recorded by the Security Service.' That is an extraordinary statement. I hope that that is still not the case,

[113] ibid., para. 52.
[114] ibid.
[115] See Chapter 11 below.
[116] See pp. 295–9 below.

and I wish that the Tribunal had indicated that they thought this was not a satisfactory situation.

VISCOUNT HAILSHAM The noble Lord should look at the bottom of page 48. There are two types of vetting. If the noble Lord looks at the bottom of page 48, I think he will see that homosexual tendencies certainly do raise a presumption that anyone like that is unfit to occupy a 'positive vetting' post.

LORD CHORLEY That is true, but the point is that you have to take steps to discover whether they have these tendencies. During the war this certainly was done, because I was working in the Home Office, under my noble friend Lord Morrison of Lambeth, and for a time in a section where we had the security reports, and I know that it was one of the matters to which they paid very great attention. The fact that in the interval they seem to have given it up indicates to me once more the general feeling of slackness which seems to have come over this very important branch of the work of the community.[117]

VIII. Scepticism Vindicated

TThese concerns about keeping the lid on normal vetting would continue to haunt the government. In the meantime, however, Radcliffe was right to be sceptical about the value of PV, though perhaps for different reasons than those expressed in the first Radcliffe Report. Unknown to Radcliffe at the time he was writing his report, the security-cleared Christopher Vassall was about to compound the various problems identified so far. One problem was not just that PV would rarely throw up fresh evidence as Radcliffe had suggested, it was also that the process would not always be carried out effectively, even where there was evidence to find. Like any other intelligence-gathering system, PV could only be as effective as those responsible for its administration were diligent. If nothing else, the Vassall case would have caused Radcliffe to have had second thoughts were he ever to have re-read the passage from his 1962 report, in which he had said that:

> We also considered whether the Positive Vetting procedure could in some way be made more effective. At present the Investigating Officers are for the most part retired Police Officers (many with experience in the Special Branch) or retired officers from the Armed Forces, Colonial Services, etc. In general we found that Departments are quite well satisfied with the tact and perspicacity with which these officers go about their tasks and with the quality of the reports which they

[117] HL Debs, 8 May 1963, col. 779. The two forms of vetting referred to by Hailsham were not normal and positive vetting, but lifestyle and political vetting.

> submit on each case. We ourselves saw a number of such reports and thought that they were entirely adequate in quality.[118]

If nothing else, the Vassall case raised question about the rather complacent tone about vetting that had been struck by Lord Radcliffe. This was markedly different from the urgency of the Privy Councillors some six years earlier,[119] an urgency that *Vassall* appeared to vindicate. Vassall had been caught in a 'honey-trap'—photographed taking part in a homosexual orgy while posted to Moscow, at a time when homosexual activity could still attract a criminal conviction (both in London and Moscow). He had been blackmailed by the Russians since 1955, and had passed documents to his handler in Moscow, until he was posted back to London to work in Naval Intelligence, the private office of Mr Thomas Galbraith MP (the Civil Lord of the Admiralty), and the Military Branch (the secretariat serving Naval Staff in the Admiralty), where the arrangements continued until he was arrested in 1962. His method of operating was to remove documents overnight and to photograph them with a camera supplied by the Russians before their return the next day.

It seems that Vassall had no ideological commitment to the Soviet Union, and was motivated in part by greed, living an ostentatious lifestyle unsustainable on a civil servant's salary, a factor also in the downfall of Henry Houghton of Portland spy ring infamy. Like Houghton and the rest of the Portland team, Vassall was exposed by a defector, and on 2 October 1962 he too was convicted under the Official Secrets Act 1911, after pleading guilty in an hour-long trial before the Lord Chief Justice,[120] much of which was held in camera. Despite his subsequent claims to have been a 'pygmy of a spy',[121] Vassall's passing to the Russians of classified information dealing with British torpedoes and anti-submarine devices led to an eighteen-year prison sentence, though he was released after serving only ten. And despite the fact that the press had been excluded from the trial, the matter attracted a great deal of damaging coverage for the government, journalists uncovering 'a hapless saga of incompetence, extravagance combined with foolish penny-pinching, and sexual corruption'.[122]

But just as the Blake case led to the appointment of the Radcliffe Committee discussed above, so the Vassall case led to the appointment of a Tribunal of Inquiry to investigate various aspects of the affair, including 'any breaches of security arrangements that took place'. Appropriately, the tribunal was chaired by Lord Radcliffe, appointed by the Home Secretary on 15 November 1962, under the authority of the Tribunal of Inquiry (Evidence) Act 1921. Unlike the first Radcliffe Report,

[118] Report on Security Procedures in the Public Service (n 86), para. 70.
[119] Report of the Security Conference of Privy Councillors (n 4), para. 36.
[120] *Camden New Journal*, 29 May 2003.
[121] *Independent*, 9 December 1996 (Obituary of John Vassall).
[122] *Independent*, 30 June 2006: article on the opening of the papers relating to the trial of John Vassall.

the second was published in full, revealing clearly a number of security lapses, including the selection of staff for posting to Moscow, the supervision of staff when they were in Moscow, and the physical security of documents.[123] But the second Radcliffe Report also raised questions about PV, while in the process informing us for the first time that the procedures were set out formally in a Treasury circular of 31 March 1954, by which the following posts were subject to PV:

- Those which required regular and constant access to the most highly classified defence information or material; and
- Those which gave access to classified atomic energy information.[124]

According to Radcliffe, no one was to blame for failing to detect Vassall's 'acts of abstraction',[125] the report taking the view that 'no precaution short of a 'strict personal search either of all persons leaving the building or of persons selected for snap checks from time to time' would have offered any protection against the methods used by Vassall. Although better document security had been a big issue in the earlier Radcliffe Committee on Security Procedures, such steps were not recommended by either Radcliffe report.[126] But if document security could not be guaranteed, what about PV, which was designed to stop people like Vassall slipping through, and which in the case of the Admiralty was being applied on a five-yearly basis? By 1956, Vassall had been successfully put through all stages of the PV process, despite being exposed to the risk of blackmail by his lifestyle, PV clearance coinciding with Vassall's recruitment by the Soviet intelligence machine.

An account of the procedures under the Treasury circular of 31 March 1954 are also set out in the second Radcliffe Report. After checking MI5 records, the vetting subject would be asked to complete a questionnaire and to nominate two referees. Field enquiries would then be conducted by members of the investigating team based at the Ministry of Supply, where by 'means of personal interviews with the subject and such other persons as might be able to assist the investigation, a sufficiently firm and coherent view of the subject's background, character and interests could be established to enable the employing Department to determine his fitness to occupy a Positive Vetting post'.[127] The Treasury circular gave only limited

[123] Report of the Tribunal of Inquiry Appointed to Inquire into the Vassall Case and Related Matters (Chairman Viscount Radcliffe), Cmnd 2009, 1963. For an assessment, see R. West, *The Vassall Affair* (London, 1963).

[124] Report of the Tribunal of Inquiry Appointed to Inquire into the Vassall Case (n 123), para. 153. It was also pointed out that Under-Secretaries were all subject to PV, a belated recognition that the government had accepted the Privy Councillors' recommendation that Communist Party members should be excluded from these positions.

[125] ibid., para. 40.

[126] ibid., para. 43. See Report on Security Procedures in the Public Service (n 86), Ch. 8.

[127] Report of the Tribunal of Inquiry Appointed to Inquire into the Vassall Case (n 123), para. 158.

guidance for the conduct of field enquiries (interviews, background checks), and left to the discretion of the investigating officer what further enquiries were to be made. That said, it was the 'invariable practice to interview the two nominated referees and to seek to interview the people who had been the subject's supervisory officers or previous employers'.[128]

In this case, the investigations by Mr E. S. Sherwood 'followed closely the standard pattern'.[129] But rather than accept the inevitable limitations of an imperfect system, it was necessary to find a scapegoat and to engage in a process of public humiliation of the 'not inexperienced' investigating officer.[130] Mr Sherwood was found to have made a mistake for failing to interview anyone to cover Vassall's two-year period in Moscow,[131] which had ended shortly before the commencement of the PV inquiries. This is despite the fact that he had tried to speak to Captain Bennett, the person who was best able to speak about Vassall, but gave up on being informed by the Admiralty that Bennett—who had returned from his posting in Moscow—was now on his way to the Far East. According to Radcliffe, this was 'clearly an error, as Captain Bennett was then stationed at Portsmouth'.[132] No explanation is given for this error about Bennett's whereabouts and no one is named for having committed it, the finger of blame pointing only at Sherwood for having relied on information about Vassall's time in Moscow solely from someone in London to whom Bennett had reported.

Radcliffe's criticisms could only be justified if it was plausible to expect PV to operate 100 per cent effectively in all cases. But such an expectation would be to set impossible standards for a procedure that could not possibly bear the burden that was now demanded. Rather than point the finger at Sherwood for an 'initial error of judgment', Radcliffe would have been better engaged revisiting some of the scepticism about PV rehearsed in his earlier report, scepticism that now seemed to have been amply vindicated. Not only did he fail to do so, but he proceeded to compound the injustice to Sherwood (and to a lesser extent his line managers, who were 'supposed to direct and check his investigation with the aid of their greater skill and experience'), by concluding that Bennett was neither 'remiss or careless' in failing to report his suspicions about Vassall's homosexuality.[133] More importantly in terms of the scapegoating of Sherwood, Bennett had reported to the Admiralty from Moscow in November 1955 that Vassall was:

[128] ibid., para. 159.

[129] ibid., para. 161.

[130] Sherwood was not alone as a junior official who was scapegoated, as we discuss when we return to the Vassall Report in Chapter 13.

[131] Report of the Tribunal of Inquiry Appointed to Inquire into the Vassall Case (n 123), paras 170–171. See further, pp. 378–9 and 394–405 below, where this matter is revisited.

[132] ibid., para. 170.

[133] ibid., para. 129.

> A pleasant young man of first-class appearance and manners. Never ruffled. Always helpful. His moral standards are of the highest. A distinct social asset to the Embassy staff.[134]

IX. A Startling Discussion

Anxiety on the part of officials that publication of the first Radcliffe report would expose the existence of normal vetting were reinforced shortly thereafter when Radcliffe's second report was published in April 1963, only a year separating the two documents. The problem here was that the latter of the two Radcliffe reports stated that at various stages Vassall had been 'subject to checks against security records',[135] leading to renewed concerns that there might be pressure for a statement about 'the extent of checking against security records'.[136] So the matter was revisited quickly by the Official Committee on Security on 26 April 1963,[137] in anticipation of a debate in the House of Commons—which duly took place on 7 May 1963—about the Vassall Report in the belief that ministers would want to look again at the decision not openly to disclose the existence of normal vetting (or Criminal Record Office checks).[138]

Chaired by Sir Laurence Helsby, those present at the meeting of the Official Committee on Security held in the Cabinet Office on 26 April 1963 included Philip Allen from the Treasury (Second Secretary), Sir Harold Caccia from the Foreign Office (PUS), Sir Charles Cunningham from the Home Office (PUS), Sir Maurice Dean from the Air Ministry (PUS), Sir Roger Hollis from the Security Service (DG), and Sir Clifford Jarrett from the Admiralty. There were two subjects on the agenda of this most illustrious of Establishment company (several of the members of which in time were to add peerages to their knighthoods), the first subject being the Vassall case and the second being normal vetting, in relation to which the

[134] ibid., para. 124. Nevertheless, Radcliffe insisted in a manner invoking memories of a famous proverb ('For the want of a nail . . .') that (para. 169):

> It is, we believe, quite possible that if Captain Bennett had been interviewed and his full assessment of Vassall sought, he would at any rate have mentioned the suspicion that he had held that Vassall had homosexual tendencies. Mr Sherwood would, we believe, have heeded such an opinion and he might well have returned to a closer questioning of Vassall or have sought to make a wider circle of enquiries about him. Where this would have led can only be conjecture.

Exactly.

[135] ibid., paras 78, 82 (for example).

[136] TNA, CAB 134/2498 (Ministerial Committee on Security: Meetings 1–3, Papers 1–6 (1962); Meetings 1–2, Papers 1–8 (1963); Meeting 1, Paper 1 (1963); Meetings 1–2, Papers 1–6 (1964)) (Normal Vetting—Memorandum by the Chairman of the Official Committee, 30 April 1963, para. 2).

[137] TNA, TS 58/632 (Report of Cabinet Office Official Committee on Security) (Official Committee on Security, Minutes of a Meeting, 26 April 1963). The Committee considered a number of issues raised by Lord Radcliffe's report.

[138] HC Debs, 7 May 1963, col. 240.

Home Office had presented yet another paper to ventilate the question whether the existence of the practice should be made publicly known.

In the course of the discussion, it is clear that there was concern about the public reaction not so much to the fact that vetting took place, but to the size of its application. The minutes of that meeting make clear that:

(a) The real embarrassment arising from disclosure of the existence of normal vetting lay not in the check itself but in the scope of its application. If it became known that large numbers of persons were being subjected covertly to the check and that their future employment was at stake, there would be a powerful demand for an appeal procedure.
(b) The existing appeal procedure—the Purge Procedure—did not cover the whole field of Normal Vetting. It applied only to persons, in the Civil Service or in Industry, who were or who were about to be employed on work 'vital to the security of the State', which was interpreted as work giving access to SECRET information. But Normal Vetting was to apply to anyone who was to have access to CONFIDENTIAL information. Moreover, applicants for employment were not regarded as falling within the scope of the Purge Procedure.
(c) Such a volume of appeals would lead in a very short time to the compromising of the Security Service's sources of information. This was a decisive argument against the institution of an appeal procedure.[139]

But these were not the only arguments against disclosure, with the most remarkable being the claim that the secrecy of the process allowed departments to deal with cases where there was doubt but not proof, 'by confining the persons concerned to work of little security importance'.[140] According to the minutes of this particular meeting, if normal vetting became an 'overt procedure, with right of appeal, this freedom of maneouvre would be lost'.[141] 'In most cases', the minutes continue, 'such individuals would have to be allowed normal vetting clearances, despite the doubt about them'.[142] Nevertheless, the Chairman concluded that the balance of argument for and against disclosure was 'narrow' and that ministers 'should be given the opportunity to decide where that balance lay',[143] a rather interesting insight into sources of power in British government. If, however, ministers decided in favour of disclosure, they should be advised that it was essential to the security system that the government should resist any demands for an appeals mechanism for those denied clearance.

139 TNA, TS 58/632 (Report of Cabinet Office Official Committee on Security) (Official Committee on Security, Minutes of a Meeting, 26 April 1963).
140 ibid.
141 ibid.
142 ibid.
143 ibid.

Four days after the meeting of the Official Committee, Sir Laurence prepared a briefing for a forthcoming meeting of the Ministerial Committee, in which he conveyed a view not reflected in the minutes (though perhaps otherwise expressed at the meeting) that the officials felt on balance that 'it would be better not to disclose the normal vetting procedure'.[144] There was no question now of the matter being left to a minister to decide. The issue was in turn the subject of an undated minute by the Cabinet Secretary to the Prime Minister, in what looks like a briefing for the forthcoming meeting of the Ministerial Committee.[145] The Prime Minister was being alerted to the fact that the meeting would be attended by Helsby, with the practice of normal vetting being one of the matters for consideration, and in particular whether 'the existence and scope of the undisclosed processes of Normal Vetting and the Criminal Record Office (CRO) check (which forms part both of Normal and Positive Vetting) should now be openly admitted'.[146]

The Cabinet Secretary expressed concern that the details would leak in due course because 'so many people now know of them',[147] and it would be all the more embarrassing for the fact that normal vetting had been in force for such a long time, with the result that many people, could claim 'with some justification' that their careers had been adversely affected by the checks.[148] The question now was whether to open up in the forthcoming security debate, which would minimize the embarrassment by demonstrating the thoroughness of the security procedures in force. The Cabinet Secretary's concern, however, was that disclosure would lead to a 'strong demand' for an appeal procedure for those who failed to pass normal vetting, which was said to number as many as 1,200 annually (the equivalent of five for *every* working day), compared to a total of less than ninety appeals in the fifteen years since 1948 under the existing purge procedure.[149] The latter

[144] TNA, CAB 134/2498 (Ministerial Committee on Security: Meetings 1–3, Papers 1–6 (1962); Meetings 1–2, Papers 1–8 (1963); Meeting 1, Paper 1 (1963); Meetings 1–2, Papers 1–6 (1964)) (Normal Vetting—Memorandum by the Chairman of the Official Committee, 30 April 1963, para. 9).

[145] TNA, PREM 11/4459 (Changes in Security Arrangements: Follow-Up to Recommendations in Radcliffe Report) (Normal Vetting).

[146] ibid., para. 1(a).

[147] ibid.

[148] ibid.

[149] Similar claims were made by Sir Charles Cunningham, then Home Office Permanent Under-Secretary, who feared that there could be as many as 1,200 normal vetting appeals annually, half of them from contractors' employees: TNA, TS 58/632 (Report of Cabinet Office Official Committee on Security) (Official Committee on Security, Minutes of a Meeting, 26 April 1963). Information supplied to the Radcliffe Committee in 1961 suggested that there were 55,000 posts subject to negative vetting in the Admiralty alone. All non-industrial staff were vetted, as were industrial staff with 'direct access to classified work'. Some of the 55,000 would no doubt also be subject to PV. See TNA, T 216/914 (Radcliffe Committee of Enquiry into Civil Service Security Procedure) (R. J. Jones to A. J. Platt, 20 July 1961). A handwritten ledger style list in the same file suggests that over 100,000 non-industrial posts were subject to NV at the time. We now know that it was a staggering 189,742. See p. 292, n. 102 above.

consideration was seen to outweigh any political advantage that might otherwise accrue.

The concern was twofold. First, such a volume of appeals would 'raise formidable political and administrative problems', all the more so since pressure for an appeal procedure would come not only from the civil service staff associations but also from the 'big trade unions', with more than 600 workers in industrial employment failing normal vetting annually. The second problem was that an appeal mechanism on this scale would damage the Security Service's sources of information about subversives, the old chestnut being uncovered for another roasting, again a 'decisive argument against the institution of an appeal procedure'.[150] For these reasons wrote Sir Burke, the Official Committee took the view that normal vetting should not be disclosed and that the risk of future political embarrassment should be accepted. This meant that the CRO check forming part of normal vetting should not be disclosed, and that the CRO check as a feature of PV should also not be disclosed, 'in case we are pressed for further information about the use of this check'.

It is now very clear that the security establishment no longer expected to be second-guessed. Running with the grain of official advice would nevertheless not be without risk, with Sir Burke concluding that it would be necessary to address several questions in anticipation of the forthcoming parliamentary debate on security. These included the following:

> (i) what answer should be given if in the course of parliamentary debate there is pressure for a statement on the extent of 'checking against security records—the periphrasis which we have adopted, in the published versions of both Radcliffe reports, in substitution for the explicit reference to normal vetting. Could this be refused on security grounds?
> (ii) what we should say if by any chance we are reminded of your earlier public reference to Normal Vetting . . . which seems to have passed unnoticed at the time.[151]

Yet, as we have seen, they managed to get away with it until 1990, when the practice was eventually acknowledged. Even then, however, the Security Vetting Appeals Panel (chaired by a High Court judge) established to hear complaints under a much more elaborate security clearance procedure was denied jurisdiction to deal with recruitment cases.[152]

[150] TNA, TS 58/632 (Report of Cabinet Office Official Committee on Security) (Official Committee on Security, Minutes of a Meeting, 26 April 1963).

[151] TNA, PREM 11/4459 (Changes in Security Arrangements: Follow-Up to Recommendations in Radcliffe Report) (Normal Vetting, para. 1(f)).

[152] A. W. Bradley, K. D. Ewing, and C. J. S. Knight, *Constitutional and Administrative Law* (17th edn, Harlow, 2018), pp. 553–5.

X. Conclusion

There can be no objection to the principle that governments have a duty to ensure that sensitive security information does not get into the hands of the enemy, whether in war or peace. To that extent it would be hard to argue against the practice of vetting to protect information from being compromised. That said, it must also be recognized that the consequence of vetting was to discriminate against individuals, either on grounds of their political affiliations or beliefs, or on the ground of their lifestyle. It must also be recognized that while some of the individuals in question would be found work of a non-security nature, the effect of vetting would be to blight careers and opportunities.[153] This would be done without the individuals knowing the case against them (at least in lifestyle cases), and in many cases without having a right of appeal against a vetting decision. There was often no opportunity to challenge the malicious or mistaken source of information, and no way of challenging decisions which may have been based on information revealed by PV.

For a constitutional regime ostensibly grounded in the Rule of Law, however, the main concern with this arrangement was its total failure to meet the basic requirements of legality, in the name of which it would no doubt be defended as one of our safeguards against totalitarianism. In the case of normal vetting, the procedure was secret, with decisions being made about people on the basis of procedures that were largely unknown. Although there are suggestions that normal vetting was referred to again in the House of Commons in the 1970s,[154] it remained unclear just precisely how the procedure operated. Indeed, it was not until 1990 that the then Prime Minister formally acknowledged that it had been 'the long-standing practice of successive Governments to carry out a more limited range of background checks, including criminal record checks, for access to less sensitive information and, increasingly, for the purposes of countering terrorism: this system has been known within the Government as normal vetting (NV)'.[155]

In the case of PV, which at least had the virtue of having been made known, the concern here is that it too was introduced in secret and then gradually extended in secret, with details of the procedure and its extensions only being announced at some time after the event. Despite the impact on civil liberties, the procedure was not introduced with the approval of Parliament, which had to make do simply with an announcement. There was thus no opportunity for the merits of the process to be tested, or for the procedures to be considered, or for the safeguards to be examined. As it was, the safeguards were patchy, applying differently to different

[153] See Report on Security Procedures in the Public Service (n 86), para. 64.

[154] S. Fredman and G. S. Morris, *The State as Employer—Labour Law in the Public Services* (London, 1989), p. 236.

[155] HC Debs, 24 July 1990, col 159 WA. See also Fredman and Morris (n 154), p. 236.

types of vetting, with inadequate information being made available about the procedure, and a lack of a right of independent external review of PV refusals on lifestyle grounds. It is perhaps a measure of these shortcomings that they should have been highlighted by Lord Radcliffe, a security-conscious judge, whose record suggests that he would not have compromised security on the anvil of liberty under any circumstances.

But perhaps the real point about vetting (whether negative or positive) is what it tells us about the State and the nature and extent of State surveillance. Although the figures were never published, it appears that both negative and positive vetting were conducted on a vast scale, both requiring a check of Security Service records, as Radcliffe made very clear. The most remarkable feature of this process, however, was that no one saw fit to take a step back and ask questions about the Security Service and its database. What was the legal authority for the database? By what means was information collected and recorded? And by what means could individuals challenge any mistakes or malicious entries? By failing to ask these questions, Radcliffe (a senior judge) not only gave the vetting process a stamp of approval (subject to few, but important procedural criticisms), he also gave the same stamp of approval to the infrastructure without which that system could not operate. By their silence, parliamentarians were just as guilty of a neglect of duty.

11
Surveillance and the Industrial Purge

I. Introduction

We have been concerned so far with the security procedures in the civil service. But even before the programme of mass privatization initiated by the Thatcher administrations in the 1980s, the government relied to some extent on private companies for various purposes. It was the private sector that built the roads and schools, and it was the private sector that built the military hardware needed for war. Workers in at least some parts of the private sector were likely to come into contact with government secrets, and these workers would be members and supporters of a range of political parties, including the Communist Party. It was thus inevitable that security measures would be implemented for private-sector workers, at least to the extent of preventing Communist Party members or supporters from coming into contact with secret government information.

This chapter is concerned with the vetting and purging of workers in the private sector. These are questions governments were reluctant to address in public, for fear of revealing the full extent and ever-widening scope of surveillance and the Security State. It was the 'longstanding practice' even before the Cold War that the purge and other security procedures extended well beyond the civil service into private industry. This 'longstanding practice' could operate only because of the surveillance work undertaken by MI5, in both compiling and maintaining the blacklist of Communist Party members. And contrary to the claims by Lord Denning made later about MI5 having no executive authority,[1] in the case of the private-sector exclusion of Communists, it was left to MI5 to secure the removal of workers to whom the Service objected: MI5 may have had no authority, but it had power.

One question for this chapter is thus the legal issues surrounding such intervention and the potential legal liabilities to which it could give rise, while another is the scope of the authority and the manner and circumstances in which intervention might take place. But the underlying theme is the question of accountability. As we saw in Chapters 8 and 9 in relation to the civil service, accountability has two dimensions in this context, publicity being the first and most obvious, so that people affected and the public generally are aware of the procedures and the

[1] Cmnd 2152, 1963, para. 273.

MI5, the Cold War, and the Rule of Law. K. D. Ewing, Joan Mahoney, and Andrew Moretta, Oxford University Press (2020). © K. D. Ewing, Joan Mahoney, and Andrew Moretta. DOI: 10.1093/oso/9780198818625.001.0001

circumstances in which they might be used. But publicity is only the start, a second dimension of accountability being the responsibility to defend decisions taken or advice given. It is this latter dimension that MI5 railed against in relation to both the purge and PV, for a number of spurious reasons.

As we saw in Chapter 10, it was also this latter dimension in the case of normal vetting that led MI5 to oppose publicity for fear that it would lead to heightened demands for responsibility. In this chapter, we see the same game being played: resistance to accountability of even the most elementary kind for fear that publicity about the existence of the procedures might lead to demands for accountability in the manner of their exercise. If in this case MI5's influence was not quite as effective, it was able nevertheless seriously to constrain the scope of the accountability procedures eventually introduced by the government. For the most part, security procedures in industry thus operated in a *sub rosa* manner, on the basis of informal practices only latterly acknowledged, in a manner for which there was no accountability, and on scale unknown.

II. 'Communists in Industry'

MI5 had for years been approaching firms engaged on secret government contracts and 'advising' them unofficially about Communist employees. The majority of such firms had contracts with the Ministry of Supply, although a few worked for other departments, notably the Admiralty, the Ministry of Works, the Ministry of Defence, and HMSO.[2] A standard term of these contracts provided that:

> Clause 59. This Clause is made a Condition of TOP SECRET and SECRET Contracts ONLY.
>
> 59(3) when called for by the Authority the Contractor shall furnish full particulars of persons of British or other nationality who are to be concerned with any work in connection with the contract. The Contractor shall take all reasonable steps to ensure that . . . No alien or persons of dual nationality or naturalized British subject, unless the prior permission in writing of the Authority has been obtained, or any person whatsoever whom the Authority decides is undesirable (which decision shall be final and conclusive) shall be concerned with any work in connection with the contract.[3]

[2] The HMSO contracts merely required that the contractors have in place 'satisfactory' security arrangements, although in practice this made no difference (see below p. 322).

[3] TNA, AVIA 46/541 ('Communism in Industry Secret Contracts—Advisory Tribunal'). Details of a revised version of Clause 59 appears in the file (Note to Sir Harold Parker, 25 November 1952). The amended contract expressly prohibited the contractor from disclosing information about a secret matter to a person in relation to whom the department had notified the contractor in writing that such information was not to be provided to the person in question.

In practice, however, MI5 rarely raised Clause 59(3) with private contractors, a government working party on subversive activities noting in May 1947 that 'only in projects connected with Atomic Energy has the right been used freely of demanding the names of the actual employees'.[4] Rather than running 'white lists' of names through the Registry, the Service preferred a more informal approach, based largely on the links forged with such contractors during the war. It was not until later that more systematic normal vetting took place, as suggested by a Liddell Diary entry on 31 May 1949, where he referred to the proposed 'vetting of the 150,000 industrials' employed by government contractors. Liddell noted that it had been suggested to the DG that MI5 should 'cease to receive names and particulars but should check the place of employment of any Communist who comes to our notice against the list of establishments provided to us by the Admiralty and Ministry of Supply'.[5] It had evidently not been taking place beforehand.

Workers had thus been singled out if they were brought to MI5's attention, which might be as a result of inquiries made by an employer of those who were deemed disruptive. A good example—if nevertheless, a rare find—is the case of Bert Edwards, sometime aircraft fitter and 'ardent communist'[6], whose file we encountered in Chapter 4. Edwards' file reveals the attitude taken prior to the entry of the Soviet Union into the war in June 1941, and perhaps also gives us a flavour of the 'informal approach' preferred by MI5 in the immediate post-war period. In 1940, following a visit to Edwards' place of work, a coach-building firm given over to aircraft manufacture, the Security Service's representative (Flying Officer G. C. Laws)—there, let it be remembered, to assess and give advice on security rather than on industrial relations—had looked up Edwards in the Registry and told the Managing Director, a Mr Black, that:

> what you already suspect is true and that he has, in fact, been for some time a fairly militant communist... legally this is nothing against the man. The obstructive activities which you mentioned to us were not, if I remember right, directly aimed at slowing down production; and it seems that this is one of those cases which the employer should deal with as an internal matter. If this man should cause you further trouble and you are unable to dismiss him for named 'trade' reasons, I have

[4] TNA, CAB 130/17 ('Vetting of Industrial Employees Engaged on Secret Work', presented to the Defence Committee by the Joint Secretaries (J. A. Drew and S. H. E. Burley)).

[5] TNA, KV 4/471. On 26 July, Liddell recorded that those departments had agreed to 'rely on our bringing to their notice the names of any of these individuals who might come up in the course of enquiries. As regards any new intake, they would be subject to the normal vetting procedure'.

[6] TNA, KV 2/3062. The description 'ardent communist' is from a Special Branch report, which goes on to reveal that Edwards 'loses no opportunity to voice these views in the Kenton area [where he lived, near Wembley] and amongst his workmates'. The report gives some indication of his activities in the period 1948–52, recording that at the TUC annual conference in 1948 he was seen to be a 'Communist sympathiser' and he was a member of the deputation of the BPC to the American Embassy in 1949. The file also records his contributions to various trade union meetings in 1950, 1951, and 1952, as an official of the NUVB. See further on Edwards, pp. 81–2 above.

> little doubt that that the local Trade Union Area Organiser will prove helpful and I suggest that you enlist his help.[7]

In a carefully worded response, Black thanked Laws 'for the information concerning one of our employees. We appreciate the position and will act with discretion.'[8] In an appendix to his June 1941 report on the firm, Laws stated that at Park Royal, Edwards,

> After getting himself elected chairman of shop stewards and causing a certain amount of friction—vide my report of 10.8.40—this man was discharged on an excuse. He went to Ernest Turner at High Wycombe [manufacturer of aeronautical instruments] and thence [in spite of a warning from Black] to Handley Page Ltd, where he remained for 8 days. He is believed now unemployed.[9]

Unfortunately, evidence of the presumably more permissive 1941–5 attitude taken towards Edwards, and of the post-war handling of this vocal trade unionist, has been denied to us. The Security Service has redacted every minute sheet entry, and every document placed in his file between 1941 and 1952,[10] although a Special Branch post-war chronology indicates that by 1948 Edwards was working as a coachbuilder in car manufacturing.

The exclusion of Communists from some private-sector jobs was thus well established, but generally not well known. Remarkably, MI5 had managed to maintain and operate the blacklist without attracting attention or publicity, though no doubt its victims would have their well-informed suspicions. But that was to change, with allegations about the purging of Communists in industry being raised in Parliament for the first time in 1948. D. N. Pritt MP had initially tabled a motion condemning the civil service purge, stating that it 'has been imitated by various private firms', though the charge initially made little impression. Having been asked to raise the case of S. J. Manley,[11] Pritt subsequently tabled two questions, this time triggering alarm in security circles. Indeed, according to a Liddell Diary entry, 'the

[7] TNA, KV 2/3062 (Flying Officer G. C. Laws, MI5, to the Managing Director Park Royal Coach Works, London NW10, 19 August 1940). Handley Page Ltd was an aircraft manufacturer, best known for the 'Halifax' bomber.

[8] TNA, KV 2/3062 (Reply, 21 August 1940).

[9] TNA, KV 2/3062 (Appendix to report of visit to Park Royal Coach Works, Abbey Road, NW10 by Flying Officer Laws on 11.6.41).

[10] The last discernible wartime date is August 1941, and entries resume, with some significant further redactions, in September 1952. It is unusual to see the redaction of both the minute sheet entries and the serial entries for a full eleven years. It seems likely that MI5—the file was released in 2009—was anxious to conceal very intrusive Security Service interest and interference in political and trade union affairs.

[11] See D. N. Pritt, *Autobiography of D N Pritt, Part Two, Brasshats and Bureaucrats* (London, 1966), pp. 178–80. Pritt appears to have been asked either by Manley's union, or—more likely—by the NCCL to raise the matter in Parliament. Pritt does not mention Manley by name in the book.

government would now be obliged to reveal that ministers had the contractual right to ask for the removal of "undesirable" persons from secret contracts'.[12]

A few days later, Liddell went to Whitehall accompanied by MI5 legal officer Bernard Hill to discuss the matter with Norman Brook, armed with an MI5 memo on the *Danger of Leakage of Information Through the Employment of Communists in Industry on Secret Government Work* ('*Communists in Industry*').[13] According to Liddell, the Prime Minister 'was urged to stall'—advice he appeared to accept. Asked by Pritt 'what steps he proposed to take to procure alternative employment for people dismissed by private employers on political grounds at the suggestion of MI5 or other Government organizations, in order that the hardship they suffer may be no worse than that of civil servants similarly dismissed', Attlee refused to rise to the bait. Avoiding the question, he merely stated that 'The position of a civil servant dismissed from his post is no different from that of any other person who has become unemployed. In both cases the machinery of the Ministry of Labour and National Service is available to help him find other employment.'[14]

Pritt's second question specifically raised the Manley case. He asked 'why and how often officials of MI5 called upon the engineering firm who were employing Mr Manley . . . prior to his dismissal from that firm on account of his political opinions . . . [and] what representations these officers made to the firm'. On this occasion, Liddell had recommended that the question be answered by the Home Secretary as the Manley case concerned Special Branch, not MI5. So it was Chuter Ede rather than the Prime Minister, who confirmed that a police officer had visited the employer 'for the purpose of making certain enquiries',[15] but denied that the police officer had made 'representations' concerning Manley.[16] Liddell's Diary reveals that the Special Branch officer had visited the firm following a request from MI5 for information about Manley's work for the CPGB. Manley had thereafter written to Herbert Morrison (Lord President of the Council) to complain about his dismissal,[17] and the case had received some publicity, though Manley must have known that he would get little sympathy from such a notorious anti-Communist.

But with the civil service purge procedures now in the open, it was hard to argue that the similar procedures relating to government contractors should not also be published. Nevertheless, MI5 was opposed to a procedure for industry similar to that introduced for the civil service: it wanted to avoid publicity, threats to its sources, and—where possible—to avoid responsibility. To that end, it also wanted to withdraw from direct contact with employers and instead advise the departments as to who should be excluded from secret work without being required to

[12] TNA, KV 4/470 (Liddell Diary, 13 July 1948).
[13] TNA, KV 4/470 (Liddell Diary, 16 July 1948).
[14] HC Debs, 19 July 1948, col. 4WA. Also Pritt (n 11), p 179.
[15] TNA, KV 4/470 (Liddell Diary, 19 July 1948).
[16] HC Debs, 20 July 1948, cols 35–36 WA. Also Pritt (n 11), p. 180.
[17] TNA, KV 4/470 (Liddell Diary, 15 July 1948).

produce any evidence to support its pronouncements. This was effectively the primary recommendation made by the Security Service in its *Communists in Industry* paper—that 'MI5 should place the facts before the authority'. That authority, usually the Admiralty or the Ministry of Supply, should then, in consultation with MI5, and 'in appropriate cases' the contractor, weigh the threat to security posed against the threat of industrial action, possible loss of 'technical efficiency', and 'political repercussions'. Dismissals would be justified, if justification became necessary, by reference to clause 59.[18]

III. MI5 Overruled

Communists in Industry was presented to Sir Harold Parker, PUS at the Ministry of Defence by Liddell and Hill on 19 July 1948, and on that seemingly informal occasion they discussed 'all the implications of the document' on an unofficial basis with both Parker, and the PUS at the Home Office, Sir Alexander Maxwell. The paper was considered subsequently at a formal meeting called by Parker for 28 July 1948 at the Ministry of Defence.[19] That meeting was attended by representatives from the Admiralty and Ministry of Supply, as well as Winnifrith and Hankey from the Treasury Solicitor's Department, together with unidentified 'representatives of the Security Service'—Liddell and Hill. Parker's note of the proceedings reveals that the Ministry of Supply and the Admiralty were at that point not engaged with concerns about the political views of their contractors' rank-and-file workers. Thus, the Assistant Secretary at the Ministry of Supply reported that the Ministry was only 'beginning to review the position as regards their own industrial employees', and had not yet looked at contractors' workers, but agreed 'that there was a risk of possible leakage if particular senior staff . . . were Communists or fellow travellers'. The Admiralty position was apparently 'much the same'.

What the Ministry of Supply and Admiralty officials meant was that there were no formal policies or procedures in place, Parker obliged to note that 'the present practice was for the Security Service to have direct, though informal contact with the contractors'. If MI5 objected to an individual and the firm did nothing, 'they did not get a contract. Alternatively, they might move the objectionable individual or dismiss him.' It was 'generally agreed' by those present that it was inevitable that this *sub rosa* approach would ultimately receive widespread publicity and 'the risk which the Security Service feared was that legal action might be taken against the Government for conspiracy with the company to get rid of the men'.[20] Parker

[18] For Clause 59, see p. 306 above.

[19] TNA, AVIA 46/541 (Ministry of Defence, Meeting, 28 July 1948, untitled note of the meeting by Parker, 29 July).

[20] ibid.

recorded that the 'general view' was that the 'legal position could be safeguarded', particularly if action was taken after the contract had been placed, it having been thought also that it would be best for any communication to be made to the firm by the minister 'under his contract powers than direct by the Security Service', although with 'careful watching it should not be impossible, even in advance of a contract, for intimation to be conveyed to a firm that in the event of their getting a secret contract there might be difficulties about certain of their employees'.

So far, so good for MI5. But the prospect of a 'political row', even if the government was seen to be acting lawfully, gave rise to a discussion of the advantages of 'some sort of tribunal procedure', and the possibility was considered that the jurisdiction of the Three Advisers be extended from the public to private sphere in industrial cases where there was direct ministerial involvement. Thus, it was suggested that 'before a Minister took a decision he might be advised by the Civil Service Tribunal on the paper facts'. Liddell and Hill were strongly opposed, with Parker recording that:

> Objection to such a course was seen on two grounds. First, the man would not have the opportunity to appear in person and, secondly, *such a procedure might seem to impugn the integrity of the Security Service*.[21]

Liddell had focused on this latter argument in his account of the meeting in his Diary, where he had stated that 'an important principle is involved here', insisting that 'a Minister must be prepared to accept the assessment of the evidence given to him by the Director-General of the Security Service without calling in the opinion of an outside body'.[22] Another way of expressing the principle is that MI5 should never be required to explain or account.

Surprisingly, Liddell's position was supported by a Ministry of Defence paper,[23] the unnamed author reasoning that the invocation of Clause 59, permitting the minister to exclude from any work in connection with a secret contract any person he considered 'undesirable', meant that the question was purely a contractual matter, and any dispute a matter to be settled by the civil courts. The establishment of a tribunal was 'not only unreasonable but unnecessary'.[24] Thus, it was claimed that a worker targeted in a particular case had no standing in relation to the contract agreed between contractor and the government, while the employer could lawfully dismiss the worker as long as the contract of employment was complied with. In these circumstances, a tribunal would be 'a direct interference with the powers of the Courts and with the ordinary commercial rights of the parties to

[21] ibid (emphasis added). Not that they *wanted* the individual to appear in person before any tribunal.
[22] TNA, KV 4/470 (Liddell Diary, 28 July 1948).
[23] TNA, AVIA 46/541 (Ministry of Defence, 'Communism in Industry Secret Contracts— Advisory Tribunal', 20 July 1948).
[24] ibid., para. 4.

the contract', while 'any such contemplated machinery would be hotly contested by all commercial interests'.[25] The role of the Three Advisers in civil service purge cases was said to be an entirely different matter: 'In the case of the Civil Servant, the Crown is the employer and by the setting up of a tribunal, the Crown has agreed to some extent to fetter its right to transfer and dismiss a Civil Servant.'

The problem with feeble and unconvincing claims is that they can be easily overcome, and the foregoing arguments by the anonymous official were never seriously relied on. By 9 March 1949, the position had swung the other way, with the Ministry of Defence now claiming in a paper to the Cabinet Committee on Subversive Activities that in view of 'the international situation, the spread of Communism among scientists and the publicity given to the measures for "purging" the civil service', it was 'no longer possible to rely on the long-standing direct contacts between the Security Service and firms'.[26] In what would be a significant overhaul of the procedures, it was proposed that Clause 59 should be invoked overtly,[27] with names submitted by employers to the departments and workers subject to negative vetting. According to the minutes:

> The general feeling of the Committee was that given the changed circumstances which rendered inadequate the existing practice (though that practice was still maintained) the course proposed was right in principle and should subject to Cabinet approval be adopted. The likelihood and the intensity of protests and industrial or political outcry would depend upon the status of the workers affected, unskilled men and men not engaged on secret work would under the proposals not be affected in any case . . . There must be no question of a witch-hunt which could be represented as a move to a 'purge' of all Communists from work on Government contracts.[28]

At its meeting on 9 March, the Committee on Subversive Activities asked Parker at the Ministry of Defence to prepare a report on the vexed question of an 'appeals' procedure, and the legal implications of the proposed new overt approach. MI5 was obviously consulted and continued to press the case against, concerned about 'disclosing sources of information to a tribunal which is almost certain to be composed of trade unionists'.[29] But despite being overruled, it looks like MI5 achieved some success in restricting the right of appeal only to 'skilled men' engaged on

25 ibid., paras 4 and 6.

26 TNA, CAB 130/20 (Minutes of Meeting of Cabinet Committee on Subversive Activities, 9 March 1949, p. 3). The Committee was chaired by A. V. Alexander (who, as Minister of Defence, was responsible for the memo under consideration), and included on this occasion Bevin, Ede, Isaacs, Strauss (Minister of Supply), Parker (Ministry of Defence PUS), Bridges, Sillitoe (MI5), Baker (Home Office), the Minister of Works, and the First Lord of the Admiralty.

27 Alexander also proposed that Clause 59 be extended to merely 'confidential' work, but that suggestion appeared to be quickly forgotten.

28 TNA, CAB 130/20 (Minutes of Meeting of Cabinet Committee on Subversive Activities, 9 March 1949, p. 2).

29 TNA, KV 4/471 (Liddell Diary, 18 March 1949), reporting on a draft of the Parker Report discussed at a meeting attended by Furnival-Jones, Mitchell, Hill, and Liddell.

secret work.[30] Indeed, when the Committee on Subversive Activities met again on 30 March, it was suggested that only around thirty men in important posts would be covered by the new approach.[31] The vital question for the Committee was whether 'the present informal methods' should 'still be used in as many cases as possible, overt exercise of contractual rights being reserved only for those cases in which publicity and trouble were to be expected?'[32] That vital question was never answered, despite concerns by some of those present that the existence of an appeals procedure would alert workers purged informally that they were likely to have been the victims of a political witch-hunt, it being predicted that such a scheme would break down as a result.

Nevertheless, Albert Alexander (Minister of Defence) was 'forced to the conclusion that there was a need for an overt procedure for excluding untrustworthy employees of contractors from secret Government work and that that procedure must embody the opportunity of cases being referred to independent advisers', the right course being 'to extend the functions of the existing civil service advisers'.[33] This was despite renewed MI5 objections expressed (again) at the meeting on 30 March, the minutes revealing that Sillitoe had told the committee that 'the Security Service know which employees were a real danger to national security and he would undertake to be personally responsible for putting before the minister concerned only cases on which ministers could safely act'.[34] This in itself was a compelling indictment of the status quo, in the sense that MI5 knew very well who were the serious potential security risks employed by government contractors in various positions, but constrained by the fear that these individuals might go to the press, to law, or to a sympathetic MPs, had felt powerless to do anything about them. MI5 energies had thus been concentrated instead on the misplaced and unnecessary attempt to purge industry of Communists operating in junior positions, as a form of displacement therapy. It was pointless and ineffective, but no doubt wholly rewarding.

So, on 19 May 1949—barely a year after Attlee's announcement of the civil service purge to Parliament and with it a few weeks later the procedural safeguards for those to be purged—the Cabinet approved proposals for similar procedures for industry. The minutes are disingenuous to the extent that they refer to the proposed announcement of a 'policy which was to be adopted', given that the policy had been operating for many years. What was new were the procedures that were now agreed, the extensive minutes—on a matter that seemed unlikely to have been the greatest concern facing the government at the time—reading as follows:

[30] TNA, CAB 130/20: ('An Advisory Body for Industry', Report by a Group of Officials, 26 March 1949) (signed by Parker), was considered by the Committee, along with 'Legal Position Arising from Proposed Measures for Safeguarding Government Contracts', a Note by the Treasury Solicitor's Department, 26 March 1949.

[31] TNA, CAB 130/20 (Minutes of Meeting of Cabinet Committee on Subversive Activities, 30 March 1949).

[32] ibid., p. 3.

[33] ibid., p. 4.

[34] ibid., p. 3.

The Cabinet had before them a memorandum by the Minister of Defence (CP (49) 107) reporting the conclusions of the Committee on Subversive Activities on the measures to be taken to improve the arrangements for excluding untrustworthy persons from employment in connection with Government contracts for secret work placed with outside contractors.

The Minister of Defence explained that under the existing form of contract for secret Government work the Department could require the contractor to furnish particulars of all persons who would be employed on the secret aspects of the work, and could require him not to employ on such work any person whom it decided to be undesirable. There would, however, be serious political trouble if Communists and Fascists were summarily excluded from work at the request of a Department, without any public announcement of a general policy or any provision for hearing appeals. It was therefore proposed that a general statement should be made explaining the policy which was to be adopted, and that the advisory body which considered similar cases in the Civil Service should operate also in this field. The functions of this body would be purely advisory and final responsibility would rest with the Minister concerned.

In discussion the following points were made:

(a) The Service and Supply Departments had evidence that unreliable persons were being employed on highly secret work by firms with which the Government must place contracts because of their specialised knowledge and equipment.

(b) Both the TUC and the British Employers' Confederation should be consulted on these proposals, through the National Joint Advisory Council. The Trades Unions might take exception to the use for this purpose of the advisory body which dealt with Civil Service cases, though from this point of view it was advantageous that that body included a prominent trade unionist and a former official of the Ministry of Labour.

(c) The procedure in industrial cases would be broadly similar to that applicable to Civil Servants. A Civil Servant had the right to make representations to his Minister, or to an official designated by his Minister, after the Minister had received the findings of the advisory body. Although in industrial cases the Minister would not be the employer, it was right that the final appeal should be to the Minister since it would be an appeal against his direction that the man concerned should not be employed on secret Government work.

(d) The field within which the new arrangements operated should be kept as narrow as possible. Care would have to be taken not to encourage employers who might be over-zealous in this matter.

The Cabinet

(1) Approved the arrangements proposed in CP (49) 107 for excluding untrustworthy persons from participation in secret Government work undertaken by contractors, subject to consultation with the National Joint Advisory Council.
(2) Invited the Prime Minister, after the concurrence of the National Joint Advisory Council had been obtained, to make a public announcement about the arrangements proposed.

IV. MI5's Unexpected Reprieve

By July 1949, the government was thus on the verge of announcing an industrial purge procedure incorporating the Three Advisers,[35] albeit for mixed reasons not all related to an unequivocal commitment to procedural fairness as an end in itself. Indeed, so close was the government to going ahead with the scheme that Attlee's announcement to the Commons had been drafted.[36] The government held back, however, when the TUC sided with the employers' representatives on the NJAC to oppose the plans.[37] According to a handwritten note on the matter by Joe Jaggers, the security officer at the Ministry of Supply who played a prominent part in developing the procedures, the TUC was unhappy about the Three Advisers and had not been placated by the appointment to the panel of a former trade unionist (J. W. Bowen).[38] The TUC believed that industrial transfers and dismissals on security grounds would be better handled unofficially, with the employer and the Security Service consulting the relevant union. That said, whatever the real reason for their objections, the TUC was no appeaser of Communists.

The NJAC veto was a blow to Ministry of Supply officials like Jaggers who had argued strongly in favour of a tribunal, believing—wrongly as it turned out—that the TUC and the employers could be placated. A subsequent Memorandum for the Cabinet by the Minister of Labour and the Minister of Defence (written, of course, by their senior civil servants),[39] had nevertheless bolstered the arguments of the

35 An announcement had been approved by the Cabinet on 19 May 1949. The Prime Minister was authorized to make an announcement that the agreement of the NJAC had been obtained, the agreement having been taken for granted, but not forthcoming: TNA, CAB 125/15 (Cabinet Conclusions, 19 May 1949).

36 TNA, AVIA 46/541. The file contains a number of drafts of announcements of an industrial purge procedure dating from 1949.

37 The NJAC was a standing body of trade union and employer representatives established to advise the government on labour matters generally. On the NJAC, see Ministry of Labour, *Industrial Relations Handbook* (London, 1961), pp. 16–17.

38 See p. 255 above.

39 TNA, CAB 129/34/37 ('Communists and Fascists: Secret Contracts', 24 November 1949).

NJAC. Adding that 'the appeal procedure proposed would cut across the established conciliation machinery in industry', this became the standard justification for the TUC's strange approach in official accounts thereafter.[40] But although the NJAC position would have been welcomed by MI5, some consideration was given in government to the possibility of overruling the opposition to forestall any accusations of 'underhand means', by going ahead with the proposal for an overt procedure. But it was in no one's short-term interests to do so, and although obviously aware that extending the Three Advisers' jurisdiction was at some point inevitable, by the end of 1949 the senior civil servants at the various Ministries affected reluctantly advised the Cabinet to abandon plans for a tribunal.[41]

The advice was accepted and the decision to abandon the proposal for what the Cabinet called a 'special appeal tribunal', and to permit ministers to continue to require dismissal under the terms of Clause 59, was taken by the Cabinet after a full discussion on 8 December 1949.[42] As on 19 May, there was a full discussion here too, the minutes recording that:

> On 19th May the Cabinet had approved, subject to the views of the National Joint Advisory Council, the scheme outlined in CP (49) 107 for excluding untrustworthy persons from participation in secret Government Work undertaken by contractors. This had included provision for a general statement of policy, to be made before action was taken against any particular individual, and for a right of appeal to a special tribunal . . . The Cabinet now had before them a memorandum by the Minister of Defence and the Minister of Labour (CP (49) 233) reporting that the Council had expressed the considered view that the proposed statement of policy would provoke controversy out of all proportion to the issues involved, and that the creation of a special appeal tribunal would cut across the established machinery for conciliation in industry. The Council therefore recommended that the Departments concerned should proceed, without any general announcement of policy and without establishing any special rights of appeal, to remove untrustworthy individuals from participation in secret Government work by administrative action under the terms of their contracts, which empowered them to require contractors to remove from secret Government work any persons whom they regarded as unreliable.
>
> In discussion it was pointed out that, where an untrustworthy person denied membership of a political party and ascertained that he was being

[40] See, e.g., TNA, AVIA 46/541 (Ministry of Supply, 'The Provision of Appeal Procedure for Government Contractors' Employees on Secret Work', 24 May 1956, Memo to Cabinet Security Committee).

[41] TNA, AVIA 46/541 (Note on a meeting of Permanent Under-secretaries by Joe Jaggers, 22 November 1949).

[42] TNA, CAB 128 (Cabinet Conclusions, 8 December 1949).

excluded from secret work at the request of the responsible minister, the procedure preferred by employers and workers would provide no forum where the facts could be tested. It was, however, clear that both sides in industry were opposed to the appointment of any appeal tribunal which might seem to cut across the established conciliation machinery. Both sides agreed that the security of the State must be paramount, but considered that the responsibility for safeguarding it must rest with the Government. If a suspected person were a member of a trade union, he could make representations through his union; but a technician might not be a member of any union and in such cases it might be represented in Parliament that there were no safeguards for the individual. The view of the Cabinet was that, if a minister were pressed to indicate in what respects an individual was untrustworthy, he would be well advised to refuse to go beyond the general statement that he was satisfied that the individual could not safely be employed on secret Government work.

It was stated in CP (49) 233 that the Admiralty and the Ministry of Supply were the only Departments concerned with this problem. In discussion, however, it was pointed out that the Ministry of Works were also concerned in respect of contracts under the atomic energy programme.

The Cabinet

(1) Agreed that, in view of the advice given by the National Joint Advisory Council, there should be no general policy statement about the Government's intention to exclude untrustworthy persons from employment on secret Government work undertaken by contractors, and that the proposal for a special appeal tribunal should be abandoned.
(2) Agreed that, where the responsible minister was satisfied that the removal of an untrustworthy individual from secret work was essential, the minister should request the firm, under the terms of their contract, to remove the man from secret work.

Apart from displaying a power of the TUC that would be unthinkable today, the abandoning of plans to bring the longstanding industrial purge into line with the civil service purge also reveals an unholy community of interest between the TUC and MI5, though each had its own reasons for eschewing procedural fairness. It was nevertheless another clear victory for MI5, cemented in the memorandum by the joint Minister of Defence and Minister of Labour and National Service referred to above,[43] which was approved by the Cabinet also on 8 December 1949. The

[43] See n 39 above.

procedures to be operated in the future were outlined as follows in the Ministry of Supply brief on the joint ministerial memorandum:

> As in the past, information that an employee is an untrustworthy will continue to reach the contractor direct from the Security Service. *In the lower grades of employees, preventative action will continue to be taken without the intervention of the Ministry of Supply*. The department will be concerned only in the following cases:–
>
> (a) Where the employer is recalcitrant and chooses not to take steps to minimise a security risk which has been explained to him;
>
> (b) Where the employer is reluctant to take any action because of the risk of industrial disputes etc;
>
> (c) Where the employee concerned is in such a 'key' position that his withdrawal from secret work cannot fail to excite comment.
>
> We should require the Security Service to report to us in all cases under (a), (b) and (c) above.[44]

The first of the procedures identified by the Ministry of Supply brief was the one that would apply to the great bulk of workers: the skilled trades, secretarial and administrative staff, and unskilled labourers. They would be removed or transferred at the insistence of MI5 alone, the foregoing procedures confirming that in these cases there would be no Ministry of Supply authorization, knowledge, or supervision of what MI5 was up to *in individual cases*, the Service constrained—if at all—by no more than its own reading of the Attlee Directive. It would be only when an employer refused to move on a security risk that MI5 could then approach the minister for authority for a more formal intervention under paragraph (a) of the Ministry of Supply brief. But patriotic employers were generally willing to co-operate with MI5 in the removal from security work of workers who were alleged to have Communist sympathies, particularly where the workers were unskilled. In retrospect, this was a remarkable power to invest in a secret police force, with the capacity to disrupt lives on what may well have been the flimsiest evidence, which no one was permitted to assess or challenge.

The second procedure was one in which there was clearly departmental involvement, reserved principally for the higher-grade staff: the chief designers, engineers, and draughtsmen, who were to be afforded a greater courtesy than their blue-collar counterparts. In these cases, by virtue of paragraph (c) of the ministerial brief referred to above, MI5 would present the information to the department, which would then authorize the action to be taken, whereupon it would fall to MI5 to make the first contact with the employer. It is only if that contact failed to deliver the required

[44] TNA, AVIA 46/541 (Arrangements for Excluding Untrustworthy Persons from Employment on Government Contracts for Secret Work, Brief for Minister, October 1949).

outcome that the minister would be involved and that formal steps would be taken by the department under Clause 59 of the contract. So, within the formal procedure for senior personnel, it is important to note the significance of the informal element and that formal steps to invoke Clause 59 would be taken only as a last resort. Much of the work under the formal procedure would thus also be undertaken by MI5—both in bringing the case to the department and in carrying out the department's wishes. Very few cases would require the formal invocation of contractual powers.

The words in added italics in the ministerial brief thus not only (i) *reveal* clearly that there were, in effect, two procedures in operation; but also (ii) *conceal* the amount of autonomy that was vested in MI5 in running these procedures. MI5 (i) identified the Communist suspects on the basis of its covertly collected data; (ii) made its own unchallenged security assessment about the individuals in question; and (iii) albeit reluctantly in some cases, approached the employers to dispose of the suspects. What is not clear from the foregoing, however, was how to decide whether someone was a 'lower grade of employee', or conversely an employee engaged 'in such a "key" position that his withdrawal from secret work cannot fail to excite comment'. In the absence of guidance, we can only presume that this would be a decision for MI5 to make, which would be constrained not by any sense of rule-based obligation, but principally as a result of its anxiety about the secrecy of the procedure being compromised, and its ability to persuade employers to do as they were told. Such flexibility would certainly be consistent with the informality of the procedures as they were continuing to evolve.

Returning to *Communists in Industry*, however, it will be recalled that MI5 had sought both to remove itself from direct contact with employers, and also to avoid any responsibility for advice given to departments. The effect of abandoning the proposed formal procedure of 19 May 1949 was that MI5 retained the former role as a condition of not having to accept a limited form of tribunal oversight. There was, however, now an important difference which had parallels with the civil service purge. There it will be recalled, MI5 had welcomed the publicity about the scheme because it gave them legitimacy for what was a de facto executive role, even though they railed against the tribunal.[45] In the same way, the arrangements emerging after 8 December 1949 gave express authority to MI5's informal methods in the industrial purge, which would be well known in government, if not beyond. There was thus a sharing of liability, so that any problems in the future could not be passed off as MI5's fault alone. MI5's other achievement to emerge from this episode is that even if the extension of the tribunal's supervision was inevitable, it had been accepted that it should have a very limited jurisdiction, the impact of which could be reduced even further by delaying for as long as possible the introduction of such a scheme.

[45] See Chapter 9 above.

V. The New Government

As revealed by the experience of the Attlee government, the industrial purge was thus potentially more complex than its civil service counterpart. It was also a source of friction between MI5 and the Ministry of Supply about how the procedure should operate in practice, the files suggesting that the Ministry's Joe Jaggers thought that MI5 was continuing to take liberties even after the supposed clarification of policy in 1949 referred to in Part IV above.[46] The two-tier arrangement nevertheless continued, but now its operation appeared to depend more on the likely response of the employer than on the status of the employee. This is confirmed by the review undertaken by a 'group of officials' who met MI5 DG Roger Hollis under the chairmanship of Sir Harold Parker (Permanent Secretary, Ministry of Defence), following the change of government and the dilution of the Attlee Directive. The meeting was held on 13 November 1952 'to take stock' of the past three years, 'to find out whether difficulty had resulted from the need to avoid the risk of publicity; and to consider whether a report on the present policy should be made to the present Government'.[47] Those attending included Under-Secretaries and executive officers, as well as Hollis.

A memorandum prepared by Sir Harold Parker after the 13 November 1952 meeting acknowledged—uncritically—that there were two ways by which the industrial purge now operated—informal and semi-formal.[48] The former continued to be the preferred method and the one adopted in by far the overwhelming number of cases, applying mainly to 'untrustworthy' employees 'in the lower ranges'.[49] By virtue of the informal procedure, an estimated 150 workers had been 'removed from secret work by unobtrusive means' in the preceding three years, the figure of 150 being based on information provided by Hollis to the meeting on 13 November. However, it is likely that many more were purged in the sense that their employment prospects had been blighted, with Liddell having told the Brook Committee (Official Committee on Communism (Home)) three weeks earlier that 'There were about 3,100 Communists employed in firms which had secret contracts, but they were all excluded from Government work under a special clause in the contract.'[50] These 3,100 individuals had been 'purged' without dismissal—transferred, or sidelined.

The semi-formal approach in contrast had been applied in only seven cases where it was doubtful whether the employer would be responsive to an informal approach, some of the individuals concerned being in receipt of 'substantial

46 See pp. 316–17.

47 TNA, AVIA 46/541 (Security–Secret Government Contracts, Record of a Meeting held in Sir Harold Parker's Room, Ministry of Defence, 13 November 1952).

48 ibid.

49 ibid.

50 TNA, KV 4/474 (Liddell Diary, 20 October 1952).

salaries'.[51] The semi-formal purge now in operation was said in contrast to be a 'five-step' procedure, as follows:

- MI5 was required to present the case to the department, and the case would have to meet civil service purge standards in the sense that the suspect would have to be a member of the Communist Party or associate with the Party in such a way as to raise doubts about 'his' reliability. The suspect would also have to be 'employed in connection with important and secret work';
- When the Security Service provided the case to the department it would be submitted to the minister through the Permanent Under-Secretary;
- The minister would then decide whether a request should be addressed to the firm to remove the employee concerned from secret work;
- If the minister decided that the individual should be removed from secret work, a meeting was then arranged between the firm, the MI5 officer handling the firm and a departmental representative at which the firm's representative is given information about the individual. The meeting would also discuss the consequences of retaining or removing the suspect;
- Thereafter the minister had to decide whether to invoke formal contractual powers to direct the firm to remove the employee either immediately or at an agreed date.[52]

The Parker memo provided an account of some of the seven cases in which the 'formal exercise of contractual rights' had been deployed, though it is not clear in all the cases how far into the procedure it was necessary to go in order to secure the removal of the worker concerned. That said, one Admiralty case was dealt with by dismissal, with the victim apparently well aware of why he had been dismissed. There had been no adverse publicity. A case at the Ministry of Works had also resulted in a dismissal, though on this occasion 'certain difficulties had arisen'. However, as was evidently customary in the trade, an industry-based tribunal ('a local industrial tribunal') dealt with the dispute, and there was no subsequent publicity. The Parker memo also highlighted a number of cases other than the seven disposed of under formal contractual procedures, these arising in HMSO, where the contractual arrangements between government and supplier were different. Thus, there was no Clause 59 in HMSO contracts, only a requirement that security arrangements be 'satisfactory'.[53] HMSO had used contractors to print classified material and MI5 had been consulted, with twenty employees in these firms

[51] ibid.

[52] ibid. This was slightly different from the procedure described in the Record of the Meeting, where the fifth step involved the firm breaking the news to the worker that he or she was being removed on security grounds at the request of the government, though the worker was not on any account to be told that the reasons related to Communist Party membership or association.

[53] See p. 306 above.

identified as security risks, and in seven cases the individuals were moved to non-secret work.[54]

Having thus fully reviewed the operation of the procedures (such as they were) since 1949, it was the informal approach that was to prevail. The assembled officials (and Hollis) at the meeting on 13 November agreed that:

> it would be best to carry on with present arrangements, placing reliance in most cases on direct informal contacts between the Security Contract and employees [sic.] and resorting, in a limited number of cases, to the semi formal procedure of exercising contractual rights. There should be no public statement about this.[55]

This means a result that the approach in the Bert Edwards case discussed in Part II above was to continue to be the template for the immediate future, despite the fact that conditions had changed greatly since the beginning of the war:

> Before the war it was easy for a firm to sack a man without having to give a reason and without having to placate shop stewards, joint consultative committees, etc. Until 1949 the number of classified contracts placed with firms was small and it was comparatively easy for firms to switch unreliable employees from classified work. Nowadays managements have to account to various works committees for any dismissals and many employers dare not act to remove a man from employment for security reasons without being able to point to the Ministry of Supply as being responsible.[56]

Nevertheless, one of the benefits of the informal method highlighted by Parker in an accompanying memo to his 13 November minute was that:

> the informal contacts between the Security Service and contractors which dispose of the great majority of the cases do not involve the Government at all. The action taken is to all appearances entirely the responsibility of the contractor, and in many cases the employee probably has no suspicion why he has been transferred to non secret work or discharged.[57]

This endorsement of the status quo would be music to Liddell's ears, given MI5's then anxiety about the Three Advisers, along with the generally co-operative

[54] TNA, AVIA 46/541 (Security—Secret Government Contracts. Memorandum by a Group of Officials, First Draft, 13 November 1952).

[55] TNA, AVIA 46/541 (Security—Secret Government Contracts, Record of a Meeting held in Sir Harold Parker's Room, Ministry of Defence, 13 November 1952).

[56] TNA, AVIA 46/541 (Minute Sheet).

[57] TNA, AVIA 46/541 (Gen. 399 First Draft, 'Security—Secret Government Contracts. Memorandum by a Group of Officials', 13 November 1952).

response of employers. But there was nevertheless a danger on the horizon, Parker acknowledging that 'at least one Minister' in the new government was inclined to the view that some more formal procedure, with safeguards, was necessary.[58] That minister was Duncan Sandys, the new Minister of Supply. Sandys was an experienced politician, not unsympathetic to security concerns,[59] though he was evidently conscious that if bad practice were to be exposed he would be the one to suffer politically. Sandys' support for an overt rather than covert industrial purge procedure and access to the Three Advisers was raised by Hollis at a directors' meeting.[60] Guy Liddell recorded the reaction:

> We considered this matter to be fraught with considerable danger . . . If we bring these people under the purge procedure, it means that someone, presumably the employer, has to tell him that he is accused of being a Communist or associated in such a way with Communists as to cause reasonable doubts about his reliability, and if he so desires he can go before the Three Advisers. This would seem to lay the Government open to libel action and if such a case were brought we should be called upon to produce the evidence. This would land us in an impossible position since the evidence would be of such a nature as to preclude the possibility of it being used in court.[61]

On taking on board these concerns, it is likely that too much reliance was being placed on the sometimes questionable advice of legal officer Bernard Hill. In a separate Diary entry on the same date, Liddell noted that Hill 'has very strong views on extending the purge to industry, and is surprised that the Treasury Solicitor has not been brought into the discussion'.[62] The Treasury Solicitor had at one point been sounding similar dire warnings about defamation, claiming that allegations presented at a tribunal were more likely to provoke legal action than allegations made during covert informal meetings between MI5/ministry representatives and employers. However, by the time Hill was expressing his 'strong views', the Treasury Solicitor had, if not recanted, then acknowledged that the risk of a successful legal action was very remote. Thereafter, concerns tended to be focused on the publicity associated with threats of legal action, or attempts to bring claims, rather than on their likelihood of success. Indeed, it is notable that the Treasury

[58] ibid.

[59] Duncan Sandys had famously raised concerns about the country's military preparedness for war in 1938, leading to claims that he had been threatened with prosecution under the Official Secrets Acts, leading in turn to the appointment of a Select Committee to consider the application of the latter to the parliamentary duties of MPs: HC 101 (1938–9).

[60] A draft procedure produced by the Ministry is to be found in TNA, AVIA 46/541 (Ministry of Supply, 'Appeal Machinery for Communists in Defence Industry'). The document is undated and unattributed.

[61] TNA, KV 4/475 (Liddell Diary, 2 March 1953).

[62] ibid.

Solicitor's advice incorporated into the record of the meeting at the Ministry of Defence on 13 November 1952 was altered to make that point, by pasting new text over the old, after the Ministry of Defence issued a 'corrigenda' to the minutes on 24 November 1952.

The legal concerns were thus a smokescreen, to hide MI5's reluctance to risk its sources, a recurring preoccupation since the end of the war. Two days after the MI5 director's meeting had exposed the dangers in Sandys' proposals, Liddell spoke to Maxwell Fyfe (the Home Secretary with notional responsibility for MI5 under the terms of its mandate). In doing so, Liddell took the opportunity to advise Maxwell Fyfe that the NJAC, the Ministry of Defence, and the Treasury were all against the Ministry of Supply's proposals. Without apparently referring to any fears about defamation, Liddell focused on the danger of publicity in such cases with the disingenuous argument that 'it would be virtually impossible for us to disclose our sources to such a tribunal',[63] without explaining that it may not have been necessary to reveal sources, and certainly not necessary to do so in the presence of anyone other than the Three Advisers. On 9 March 1953, Liddell was able nevertheless to report that the Cabinet has decided in 'our favour': 'It was quite clear to all that Duncan Sandys' proposal would get everyone into trouble.'[64]

VI. Government Acknowledgement

MI5's pleasure was to be short-lived, its fears vindicated when the procedure broke into the open, encouraging Duncan Sandys finally to acknowledge in 1954 the existence of contractual procedures empowering ministers to remove workers from security projects.[65] The acknowledgement was made in relation to the case of Mr A. Chambers, whose removal from employment by Rolls Royce at their Hucknall works had been raised by the progressive Labour backbencher, William Warbey in 1954. In response to a rather pointed question from Warbey, the Minister of Supply (Duncan Sandys) claimed that he did not order the dismissal of Mr Chambers,

[63] TNA, KV 4/475 (Liddell Diary, 5 March 1953).

[64] TNA, KV 4/475 (Liddell Diary, 9 March 1953).

[65] HC Debs, 8 March, col. 1735; 15 March 1954, col. 23. Another case was that of G. F. Clarke, who was dismissed from his position as a technical assistant at the Armstrong Whitworth aircraft factory in Coventry where he worked on guided missiles. Mr Clarke was told that he was sacked for being a Communist Party Branch Secretary, although in fact he was an active member of the Labour Party in Coventry and had been for a number of years. It turned out that there was *another* Mr Clarke in Coventry who was involved in the Communist Party, but he was not the Mr Clarke who worked at the aircraft factory. The matter would have been comical were the consequences not so serious. It was all the more serious for the fact that having acknowledged that Mr Clarke was not a member of the Communist Party, the minister nevertheless refused to change his decision that Mr Clarke was a security risk. The matter was pursued by Richard Crossman (Labour MP for Coventry East). Mr Crossman produced a lengthy statement about the case that was released to the press, where the matter enjoyed some good coverage: *Daily Worker*, 16 November 1955; *The Times*, 16 November 1955; also, *Daily Herald*, 12 November 1955.

but rather instructed the company not to give Mr Chambers access to information about secret defence projects. This led to a supplementary from Warbey, who asked whether the minister was 'aware that as a result of the instruction which he gave to Rolls Royce this man lost his employment with that firm, because it was unable to find suitable alternative employment for him'. The minister was also asked 'whether there was any inquiry, and whether this man had an opportunity of being represented at that inquiry, either directly or through his trade union representative', and in addition whether 'any specific breach of security or specific criminal act was alleged against this man'.[66]

According to the minister, Chambers found suitable alternative employment within a week or two of leaving Rolls Royce, but neither of the other questions was addressed. The government appeared, however, largely to have washed its hands of the matter, for when asked by Warbey at a later date whether Chambers would be compensated for his loss of earnings, the minister responded that any claim for compensation lay against the company, not against the government.[67] The importance of this case and the exchanges between Warbey and Duncan Sandys, however, is that it led to an admission that the government had the contractual power to instruct an employer to deny an individual employee access to secret information, and that this had been a part of standard-form government contracts used since before the war. According to Duncan Sandys, the power had been used to deny certain individuals *access to secret information* seven times since the war, three times by Duncan Sandys and four times by his predecessor as Minister of Supply in the Labour Government (George Strauss), though none of these seven individuals would have had any procedural redress.

Duncan Sandys' accurate but misleading claim that the power had been used to deny certain individuals access to secret information only seven times since the war was both feeble and disingenuous. It may have seemed persuasive enough when parroted behind closed doors, but it was less persuasive when tested in Parliament. More importantly, this acknowledgment of the contractual power and its exercise made it all the more difficult for the government to continue to refuse access to the Three Advisers, though it also laid the government open to accusations of dishonesty should the full extent of the industrial purge be exposed. The absence of any procedural redress was also hard to justify given that the Atomic Energy Authority Act 1954 introduced safeguards for workers removed from employment on security grounds by the newly created Atomic Energy Authority (to which Liddell was coincidentally appointed as head of security on his retirement from MI5).[68] The 1954 Act was concerned principally to establish the Atomic Energy Authority as a public corporation, though unusually statutory provision was also made to

66 HC Debs, 8 March 1954, col. 1735.
67 HC Debs, 15 March 1954, col. 23.
68 Atomic Energy Authority Act 1954, Sch. 1, para. 4.

authorize the dismissal of staff on security grounds, the staff in question not being civil servants and so not subject to the civil service procedures announced in 1948 and 1952.

Under the Bill as originally drafted, the Authority required the consent of the Lord President of the Council before dismissing any employee on the ground that 'his political associations render his continued employment undesirable in the interests of national security'. The latter proposal was considered too wide in the House of Lords, where it was argued that there was a need to apply the same test to employees of the Authority as to civil servants.[69] As a result, an amendment was tabled by Lord Silkin and accepted by the government, this providing that the Authority would not dismiss anyone on security grounds, except with the permission of the Lord President. The amendment also provided, however, that the expression 'security grounds' meant 'grounds which are grounds for dismissal from the civil service . . . in accordance with arrangements for the time being in force relating to dismissals from that service for reasons of national security'. In this way, explained Silkin, whatever arrangements were in force for the civil service from time to time would be applied to employees of the Authority.[70]

Now the cat was out the bag, there was little option but also to provide some kind of appeal for some of the employees of government contractors prejudiced by the industrial purge procedure. The Conference of Privy Councillors established by Eden in 1955 had considered this, along with a number of other related issues, and reported that the procedures for excluding Communists from secret work with contractors had worked 'fairly well'.[71] But they also reported that a number of cases had arisen—presumably including those referred to in Parliament—in which the individual concerned had suspected the reason for the action taken against him and made it known.[72] Some contractors had handled these cases 'clumsily', letting out that the action against an individual had been taken in response to a request from a government department.[73] This was somewhat unfair when the final step of the five-step procedure explained above was in theory supposed to culminate with the employer telling the unfortunate worker exactly that (while avoiding directly accusing the individual concerned of suspected Communist associations), which must have been known to the Privy Councillors, whose numbers included Strauss and Kilmuir.

The Privy Councillors were aware, however, that ministers had contemplated introducing a right of appeal in 1949, but that both employers and trade unions

69 HL Debs, 11 May 1954, col. 512 (Lord Silkin).

70 HL Debs, 19 May 1954, col. 799. See pp. 326–7.

71 See TNA, PREM 11/1587 (Report of the Security Conference of Privy Councillors, 24 January 1956).

72 For other cases, see J. Mahoney, 'Constitutionalism, the Rule of Law, and Cold War', in T. Campbell, K. D. Ewing, and A. Tomkins (eds), *The Legal Protection of Human Rights – Sceptical Essays* (Oxford, 2011), p. 135.

73 Report of the Security Conference of Privy Councillors (n 71), para. 76.

were 'emphatic' in regarding an appeal machinery as being 'undesirable',[74] with the result that the practice of dealing with suspects 'unobtrusively' continued. They also noted, however, that it had been decided to extend the practice of PV to government contractors as well as to civil servants,[75] but the decision had not yet been implemented because of uncertainty about the nature of the appeal procedures to be put in place. The Privy Councillors acknowledged that as the individuals concerned would by the very nature of 'PV' be aware that they were being vetted, it was politically desirable to give them the right of appeal. But if safeguards were to be introduced in the case of PV, it was thought that 'there would inevitably be demands that it should be available also to the much larger class of employees who, under the present normal vetting, are unobtrusively removed from their posts because their reliability has become suspect'.[76] Although by this stage it seems that many contractors' employees were being normally vetted with extraordinary consequences,[77] MI5 nevertheless was still opposed to the creation of 'a further special tribunal' to 'hear a much larger number of cases'.

The Privy Councillors appear thus to have swallowed the standard line about 'the risk to Security Service sources' being 'greatly increased'.[78] It was a 'difficult' matter, and although they did ultimately come down in favour of extending the right of employees to have their case considered by the Three Advisers, this would be only 'if suitable arrangements can be made', in 'certain types of case',[79] an apparently guarded acknowledgement of the Security Service's perennial concerns about its sources. The Privy Councillors had either failed to grasp the true scale of the industrial purge, or more likely were indifferent to it. Following consultations with TUC General Secretary (Sir Vincent Tewson) and his counterpart in the British Employers' Confederation, the Committee proposed in its secret report that the only solution would be to limit access to the appeals tribunal to those cases where, as a result of a ministerial directive that an individual should not be employed on secret work, the individual in question is either dismissed, or 'in the Minister's opinion', is liable to suffer a pay cut.[80] Since the numbers involved were considered likely to be 'very few' it would be possible to give these contractors' employees access to the same tribunal as civil servants (that is to say, the Three Advisers).[81]

In this way, it seems that the Conference overcame the remarkable resistance of the TUC, which, as we have seen, was quite content that 'untrustworthy persons

74 ibid., para. 77. This, of course, is a reference to the NJAC (see above, p. 315, n 37).

75 ibid., para. 78.

76 ibid., para. 79.

77 TNA, AVIA 46/541 (Appeal Machinery for Contractors' Employees, undated and unattributed, but it appears to be from January 1955).

78 Report of the Security Conference of Privy Councillors (n 71), para. 79.

79 This phrase was not in the formal report, but appears only in the summary published as a white paper: Statement on the Findings of the Conference of Privy Councillors on Security, Cmd 9715, 1956, para. 21.

80 ibid., para. 88.

81 ibid., paras 80–81.

could not be allowed to remain on this work', and content also that if there was no non-secret work available, 'the man would simply have to be dismissed'.[82] But what was being proposed was wholly inadequate in relation to the problem. Now that normal vetting had been (secretly) introduced in relation to contractors' employees, the government was enforcing the contractual term that departments be furnished with details of contractors' personnel. Ministry of Supply files coinciding with the Conference of Privy Councillors inquiry reveal that contractors' employees were being submitted for vetting at the rate of 5,000 a month, with 100 a month being referred to the Ministry as 'doubtful' cases, and about fifty a month (600 every year) being rejected for classified work. Not all of these rejections culminated in dismissals, but a proportion undoubtedly did. As was pointed out, 'in a larger proportion of cases there can be little doubt that individuals' career prospects are seriously impaired by our action', the figures revealing the wholly inadequate proposals of the Privy Councillors and the extent of continuing impunity for MI5.

VII. The Lang Case

But for the case of John Lang, however, it is not clear if even these very limited proposals would have been accepted, and unclear whether MI5 would have been permitted to retain total impunity.[83] John Lang was a solicitor with ICI who had married a former member of the Communist Party in 1951.[84] He was on MI5's radar almost immediately thereafter, Liddell recording on 19 October 1951 that:

> Hollis spoke to me about a rather awkward case of a man called [REDACTED] who is legal adviser at ICI and has complained that he is not in the confidence of the board. He suspects that this is due to adverse reports from MI5 and threatens legal action. The fact is that we did give a warning to ICI and that they are reluctant to take him on the board, where highly secret matters may be discussed.[85]

[82] TNA, AVIA 46/541 (Arrangements for Excluding Untrustworthy Persons from Employment on Government Contracts for Secret Work, Ministry of Supply Note, October 1949), para. 3. The employers were opposed to giving the Three Advisers jurisdiction to apply civil service methods to the private sector.

[83] On the Lang case, see HL Debs, 21 June 1956, col. 1269.

[84] One of the ironies to which Mr Lang drew attention was that during the war he had joined the army, and 'throughout the war was concerned with various aspects of the security of important military secrets', serving in a number of different capacities (including MI9 at the War Office). In one of his capacities, not only was he generally brought into contact with 'top secret information', but he also specifically 'dealt with the investigation of security cases, ie communists, fascists, etc'. Not only that, but he was 'in direct correspondence with the Security Service and had all their current information on security matters, eg Communist under-cover organizations, etc': University of Sussex, Benn Levy Papers, Campaign for the Limitation of Secret Police Powers, 4/8 (Statement of Representations by Mr J. H. A. Lang, 14 February 1956). He was thus fully conversant with security procedures, claiming that it was most unlikely that he would inadvertently disclose security information.

[85] TNA, KV 4/473 (Liddell Diary, 19 October 1951).

Subsequently, an ICI deputy chairman told Lang that as a result of the attitude of the Security Service, the company had been placed in an impossible position and had been required to request his resignation. So far as Mr Lang was aware, there was no complaint about his work or his conduct of the company's affairs, but that the request for his resignation had come about solely because of pressure from the Security Service—not it would seem the Ministry, suggesting that this was a *sub rosa* approach.

Mr Lang expressed frustration that he had never been officially informed of any grounds on which he was considered to be a security risk. He had received information from a previous solicitor to the company that the reason was 'almost entirely' that his wife had for a long time been a member of the Communist Party. But this had been before they were married in 1951, and although certain other matters were raised, Lang understood that these had been withdrawn. In forceful terms, Mr Lang made it clear that he had 'never been a communist nor held any communist views or been in sympathy in any way with communist views or been in sympathy in any way with communist ideas'. On the contrary, he had been 'persistently and strongly anti-communist',[86] though he does appear in the files as an active member of the Haldane Society.[87] So far as his wife was concerned, by the time of their marriage she had renounced her Communist views, had ceased all contact with the Communist Party, and had no intimate Communist friends.[88] Nevertheless, this suggests that family associations would be a disqualifying security risk long before it had been recommended by the Conference of Privy Councillors in 1956,[89] which seems to have endorsed what had been the practice for some time, as the following entry from Liddell's Diary revealed was taking place:

> Hollis said that he had had a discussion about vetting. Cases arose fairly frequently of a man's relative being a Communist. We felt bound to tell the employing department and to express a view as to whether such facts had any real significance in the case of each candidate. The DG was rather reluctant to accept this responsibility, but finally agreed. We were the only people who could express a view and that provided it was done with due caution and the final responsibility remained

[86] University of Sussex, Benn Levy Papers, Campaign for the Limitation of Secret Police Powers, 4/8 (Statement of Representations by Mr J. H. A. Lang, 14 February 1956).

[87] Mr Lang had told Sir Cyril Musgrave (see below) (who would almost certainly have known!) that 'he had in years past been a member of two societies—the British–Soviet Friendship Society and the Haldane Society, to which objection might be taken by the Security Services'. However, 'he had not been a member of them for a long time past; and, in fact, he left both of them because they became, in his view, Communist-infiltrated': HL Debs, 21 June 1956, col. 1229.

[88] HL Debs, 21 June col. 1227 (Lord Chorley).

[89] The recommendation is reproduced in the white paper, which contained a brief summary of the report: Statement on the Findings of the Conference of Privy Councillors on Security, Cmd 9715, 1956. It was recommended that 'an individual who is living with a wife or husband who is a Communist or a Communist sympathiser may, for that reason alone, have to be moved from secret work' (para. 15).

> with the employing department, we should endeavor to assess the value of this information in accordance with the circumstance in each case.[90]

It appears that Lang and ICI had come to some arrangement in 1951, and the matter lay dormant for four years until for some undisclosed reason it was revived in 1955, at which point the company indicated that it was difficult to exclude Mr Lang from secret information altogether. This time the firm was dealing with the departments rather than the Security Service, and the Treasury Solicitor wrote to ICI on 4 January 1956 to criticize the firm's handling of the situation, 'indicating that since there was no chance of Mr Lang's acquiring any further secret information in connection with current contracts, which were nearing completion, no practical purpose would be served by issuing a formal notice in respect of these contracts requiring that secret matters should not be disclosed to Mr. Lang'. The letter went to say, however:

> On the other hand, to wait until further secret contracts have been negotiated and signed when, as you point out in your letter, the process of negotiation may well result in secret information coming into the hand of the individual concerned, would be to take an unjustifiable risk. In these circumstances, I have been instructed to inform you that the responsible Ministers regard it as an essential condition to the placing of further secret contracts with your company that you should be able to undertake that this individual will not have access to secret information disclosed in connection with such contracts.[91]

In the light of this threat, ICI felt that it had no option but to dismiss Mr Lang, who claimed to harbour no grudge against the company, by which he believed he had been treated fairly. Mr Lang did, however, have concerns about the way the government had treated him, these concerns being raised in the House of Commons on 11 June 1956, when Will Griffiths asked the Minister of Supply why ICI had been informed by his department that Mr John Lang was a security risk, and not to be given confidential information.[92] In the course of the short exchanges that followed, it was confirmed that Sir Cyril Musgrave (the Second Permanent Secretary at the Ministry of Supply) had told Mr Lang subsequently in the proceedings discussed below that 'it was because of his wife's former membership of the Communist Party that this action was being taken against him'. Predictably, the minister was unable 'to make public' the information available to the government, though he did say that 'Mrs Lang's political associations were one of a number of matters taken into consideration',[93] adding subsequently with some

[90] TNA, KV 4/473 (Liddell Diary, 17 December 1951).
[91] HL Debs, 21 June, cols 1271–2 (Lord Chancellor).
[92] HC Debs, 11 June 1956, col. 18.
[93] ibid. (Mr Reginald Maudling).

circumlocution that 'Mr Lang was not informed that Mrs Lang's previous political connections were the only matter taken into account by the Government',[94] which, of course, is not the same as saying that other considerations were taken into account. When pressed by Emmanuel Shinwell about possible other considerations, Mr Maudling replied that:

> Ministers have a solemn responsibility to safeguard State secrets and, in the course of that responsibility, not only have the right but the duty to exclude from access to those secrets people whom they do not think suitable. In such circumstances, it has been recognised that it is not possible in those cases to publish the information upon which a decision has been reached by Ministers.[95]

It is one thing for action to be taken against a solicitor because of the alleged political associations of his wife. But it is another matter to take action against someone whose wife no longer has these associations. And it is another matter altogether to take action against someone because of the political associations of his wife at a time when official government policy did not formally authorize such action. A source of burning indignation was the repeated claim that 'Her Majesty's Government have followed the recommendations of the Conference of Privy Councillors on Security' (a brief summary of which was published as a white paper),[96] and that 'Mrs Lang's political associations were one of a number of matters taken into consideration.'[97] But this does not answer the charge levelled by Lord Chorley—in a 'masterly and moving speech' in what at times was an unusually bad-tempered House of Lords debate[98]—that Mrs Lang had:

> formerly been a member of the Communist Party, from which, according to her own statement (which I think has not been challenged at any stage in the history of this case), she had resigned some time before the marriage. She had then severed all connections with it, and has had no business whatever with that Party since.[99]

As with the employees of other government contractors, Mr Lang had no right of access to the Three Advisers. However, when he was informed by ICI of the government decisions, Mr Lang made written representations and asked for an interview, being seen by Sir Cyril Musgrave, as explained above. He also asked that his

94 ibid., col. 20.
95 ibid., col. 22.
96 Statement on the Findings of the Conference of Privy Councillors on Security, Cmd 9715, 1956.
97 HL Debs, 21 June 1956, col. 1275.
98 ibid., col. 1239 (Viscount Stansgate).
99 ibid., col. 1227 (Lord Chorley). Lord Chorley was also heard to doubt whether the Lang case was covered by the white paper, and more seriously to accuse the minister of 'not honestly or reasonably' applying it (ibid., col. 1234).

wife should be interviewed, together with three friends, a request that was granted. Before the interview took place, Sir Cyril Musgrave wrote to Mr Lang, drawing his attention to the white paper and 'asking him whether he would prefer to wait until it was known whether machinery for cases like his to be put to the Three Advisers would be put into effect'.[100] But because this might take 'some time' (and indeed might never happen), Mr Lang accepted the offer of an interview with Sir Cyril Musgrave as a representative of the ministers instead. The inquiries subsequently made by Sir Cyril Musgrave were said by the Lord Chancellor to have followed the same course as those of the Three Advisers, which he conducted on the same lines as the Three Advisers, before tendering his advice to ministers, who took their decisions.

Apart from the nature of his employment and the reasons for his removal, concern was also expressed about the foregoing procedure on a number of scores, the first of which related to the independence of Sir Cyril. According to Lord Chorley, who, referring to Sir Cyril, said in a manner that clearly stung the Lord Chancellor Kilmuir, better known as David Maxwell Fyfe :

> But since he was judging a case which had already been decided against Mr Lang by his own officials, in his own Department, I cannot regard his decision as being an impartial one. The Department is, in fact, the prosecutor in cases of this kind, and the head of the Department, in giving judgment, is giving judgment in a case in which he himself is concerned. That is an infraction of one of the most elementary principles of natural justice, and one to which I am sure the noble and learned Viscount the Lord Chancellor has frequently drawn attention, and in which he must believe to the bottom of his soul.[101]

Apart from these allegations of bias in the process established by the government to review Lang's case, a second and altogether more serious concern, however, related to the fairness of the proceedings themselves. Lord Chorley again:

> One of the most evil features of the present security inquisition, I think, is that its victims are not allowed to know the case which is being made against them, what the charges are. They are not told; they are given no opportunity to answer. Can anyone imagine a more terrible fate for a sensitive, honourable and patriotic man than to have his honour and patriotism traduced in this way? Here is a man who knows that he is being unjustly charged, unjustly impugned, and yet he is not allowed the elementary right of defending himself.[102]

[100] ibid., col. 1272.

[101] It was this speech that drew from Kilmuir the defensive response alluding to his role in drafting the European Convention on Human Rights.

[102] See also HC Debs, 11 June 1956, col. 20

The government nevertheless resisted calls for the case to be reconsidered by the Three Advisers. Mr Lang had been offered this route and had rejected it, the Lord Chancellor also letting it be known that after his interview with Sir Cyril, Mr Lang had written to say that:

> This note is just to thank you very much for the most kind and patient hearing you gave me this morning. Whatever the outcome I feel that at least I have had a fair opportunity of stating my case.[103]

It is not clear whether the noble Viscount had the permission of Mr Lang to communicate private correspondence with Sir Cyril in this way, or why it should be appropriate to make public Mr Lang's response but not the government's reasons for having moved against him in the first place. If nothing else, it hardly provides reassurance to those who thought Sir Cyril to have been biased (at least in the administrative law sense).[104] In any event, Mr Lang was duly dismissed, the government absolving itself of any responsibility for what it had done, the Minister of Supply (Reginald Maudling) subsequently telling the House of Commons that any action taken in relation to Mr Lang's employment thereafter 'is the responsibility of the Company'.[105]

VIII. New Procedures: Accountability Contained

The Lang case caused uproar: not only was it the subject of an angry debate in the Lords (with Maxwell Fyfe, alias Kilmuir—since incongruously beatified by the centre-left[106]—the butt of that anger), but it also led to a government announcement accepting the recommendations of the Privy Councillors, as they had been published in the white paper less than a year earlier.[107] According to the Lord Chancellor, fresh discussions with the NJAC recommended by the Privy Councillors had taken place (the TUC's objections to worker protection presumably overruled),[108] the government deciding as a result to give effect to the recommendation of the Conference of Privy Councillors that 'contractors' employees who, '*as a result of a directive by a Minister, are dismissed, or in his opinion are liable to suffer financial loss*, should have the same rights' as civil servants.[109] This

[103] HL Debs, 21 June 1956, col. 1273; also HC Debs, 11 June 1956, col. 21 (Mr Maudling).

[104] On which see E. C. S. Wade and G. G. Phillips, *Constitutional Law* (6th edn by E. C. S. Wade, London, 1960), esp. pp. 615–17.

[105] HC Debs, 11 June 1956, col. 19.

[106] Sadiq Khan, 'The Left's Favourite Tories: David Maxwell Fyfe', *New Statesman*, 6 October 2011.

[107] Statement on the Findings of the Conference of Privy Councillors on Security, Cmd 9715, 1956. For the amended procedures, see HC Debs, 29 January 1957, col. 152 WA. For a stinging criticism of the revised procedures, see D. C. Jackson, 'Individual Rights and National Security' (1957) 20 MLR 364.

[108] HL Debs, 21 June 1956, col. 1268.

[109] ibid., cols 1268–9 (emphasis added).

meant that the 'Three Wise Men' procedure would be applied to contractors' employees, but in practice only those at the small tip of the iceberg, the words in added italics meaning that the vast bulk of political discrimination cases would continue without redress.

Apart from leading to a government announcement to reform the procedures governing government contractors, the publicity around Lang's case also helped to fuel the demands of the Campaign for the Limitation of Secret Police Powers, established initially because of concerns about the Privy Councillors' report giving too much power to MI5. Despite its broad title, the Campaign reflected its origins in the public anxiety said to have been created by the industrial purge. It thus concerned itself mainly with representing civil servants and employees of firms engaged in business with the government, though it is true as we have seen that an intervention was made on phone tapping when the Birkett Committee was set up in 1957. As discussed in Chapter 5, playwright and former Labour MP Benn Levy was the driving force behind the Campaign, which was also supported by Will Griffiths (Labour MP for Manchester Exchange) and Stanley Mayne (General Secretary of the Institution of Civil and Public Servants, a civil service trade union). Together the three held the offices of Chairman, Vice Chairman, and Secretary respectively, and they were joined by a glittering sponsoring council of parliamentarians from all parties and both Houses (including Tony Benn, Aneurin Bevan, Barbara Castle, Michael Foot, and Gerald Gardiner), as well as non-politicians such as J. B. Priestley and Peter Ustinov.[110]

The arrival of the Campaign was announced by a huge rally at Caxton Hall, Westminster on 18 July 1956—addressed by Jo Grimond (Liberal), Aneurin Bevan (Labour), Will Griffiths (Labour), and J. B. Priestley.[111] The group did not, however, suggest that security screening by the government should be abandoned, but they did advance a five-point plan intended to protect those caught up in it, and to enhance the accountability of MI5 as follows:

1) Rules governing employment on security work should be approved by Parliament and made known to every person engaged upon it.
2) No person should be removed from their employment on a pretextual charge, ie, if they are considered a security risk, they should not be discharged for inefficiency.

[110] There were, however, a number of prominent people who declined to become involved, including John Gilguid, Graham Greene, Frank Cousins (General Secretary of the TGWU), and A. L. Goodhart (Master of University College, Oxford, and author of some sharp criticisms of the police in the 1930s, as well as a seminal article on the legality of the General Strike in the 1920s). Graham Greene wrote to say that he was 'very much in sympathy' with the objects of the Campaign but had a 'rooted objection to appearing as a sponsor', which 'always seems a way of easing one's conscience rather than *doing* something, like hitting a policeman!'.

[111] Full details of the rally are to be found in the University of Sussex, Benn Levy Papers, Campaign for the Limitation of Secret Police Powers, 4/11.

3) Any person considered a security risk should be informed of the charges, the right to appeal, and the right to be supported by either legal or trade union representation.
4) There should be an appeal to three High Court judges, sitting *in camera*, whose proceedings would be protected by the Official Secrets Act.
5) If the Court should find evidence of misconduct, it should be reported through the Lord Chancellor to the Privy Council.[112]

Apart from the Caxton Hall rally and several pamphlets, the Campaign's other major achievement was to have the matter addressed at the 55th Annual Conference of the Labour Party at Blackpool in October, 1956.[113] Mr Lang attended the Labour Party Conference as an observer, and as such he would have seen the NEC introduce a document entitled *Personal Freedom*. In the debate that followed, a representative of the Association of Engineering and Shipbuilding Draughtsmen conceded that there may have been good reasons for the security measures introduced in 1948, but claimed nevertheless that since then 'the ramifications of the Act [sic.] have gone much wider', and that now employees of private industry were more exposed to 'what is happening' than highly placed civil servants. He mentioned that a number of union members had been dismissed because of pressure put on the employers by government departments, even though some of those dismissed were neither Communists nor Fascists, but were thought to have sympathies 'in one direction or another'.

In the course of the same debate, Dick Leonard, the Labour MP for Harrow, expressed concern about the recommendation in the Privy Councillors' white paper that the balance between security and liberty should be tilted more clearly in the direction of the former. 'What appalls me about this', he said, 'is that this sentence might very well have been written by Senator McCarthy.' Also participating in the debate, Benn Levy then moved an amendment to the NEC document, which consisted essentially of the above-mentioned five-point plan proposed by the Campaign, adding, 'I would lay odds that there are dossiers in MI6 files [sic.] about a great many more of you here than you suppose.' But although supported by Will Griffiths, the amendment was opposed by George Strauss MP. Not only had the latter been Minister of Supply in the Labour Government, he was also a signatory to the Privy Councillors' report. Strauss defended the existing system, stating that an average of only seven civil servants a year had been removed from their posts and that an average of only one person a year in private industry had been affected.

[112] These demands were set out in handbills distributed at meetings, and in publications such as M. Jones, *The Secret Police and You* (London, 1956). Copies are on deposit in University of Sussex, Benn Levy Papers, Campaign for the Limitation of Secret Police Powers, 4/19. The same file also includes an interesting anonymously written pamphlet published by the Campaign entitled *A Year with the Secret Police* (1956).

[113] Labour Party, *Annual Report 1956*, pp. 83–91.

The Levy amendment was defeated by a vote of 3,478,000 to 2,625,000, following an NEC decision not to support it.

Despite its high profile it is doubtful whether the Campaign had any impact, the government announcing the revision to the civil service procedures on 29 January 1957, and to contractors on 12 February 1957. The latter was in response to a written question from Labour's Kenneth Younger, inquiring about the procedures 'followed when the reliability of a person not in Government employment, whose work is vital to the security of the State, is thought to be in doubt on security grounds; whether such cases are now referred to the Three Advisers; and what terms of reference have been given to these advisers'. Responding for the government, Enoch Powell replied that:

> employees of Government contractors engaged on secret Government contracts who, as a result of a directive by a Minister are dismissed or, in his opinion, become liable to suffer financial loss, are given the same right as persons in the public service of having their case considered by the Three Advisers. The terms of reference of the Three Advisers in any such cases are the same as those where civil servants are concerned.[114]

Following this exchange in the House of Commons, Stephen Mayne wrote to Younger, fastening on the phrase 'as a result of a directive by a Minister', used by Powell in his announcement. According to Mayne, it was in the nature of the case practically impossible to get details of what really happens in practice, but that a formal directive was rarely the way in which these cases were dealt with:

> What happens is that one of the security people sees a relatively high official in the firm and just mentions to him privately for his information that x is regarded as a doubtful customer and that it might become necessary for him to take steps with the department. Then, in some cases, at any rate, the firm takes action on some completely invented reason.[115]

Mayne then gave the example of a case he had encountered in his role as Secretary of the Campaign, the case being that of an unnamed manager of a factory engaged on work for the Ministry of Supply. It was suggested to the individual in question that he might like to attend a technical conference, to which he agreed. He was then told that it would be necessary to obtain security clearance, at which point the individual in question declined, only to be told that this would have 'awkward consequences'. Shortly before this incident, the unnamed man had received a Christmas bonus from the employer with 'congratulatory comments', but shortly after the

[114] HC Debs, 12 February 1957, col. 564.

[115] University of Sussex, Benn Levy Papers (Mayne to Younger, 17 February 1957).

incident he was dismissed with three months wages in lieu and told to go 'literally at once'. According to Mayne, the individual had asked to know the reasons for his dismissal, only to be given 'the usual story of re-organisation', which in the circumstances of the case was 'obviously nonsense'.[116]

The implementation of the Privy Councillors' recommendations was a far cry from the demands of the Campaign for the Limitation of Secret Police Powers. Thus, there was no legislation governing employment on security work (1).[117] Indeed, there was not even a parliamentary statement, the revised procedures being published in a parliamentary written answer by the Financial Secretary to the Treasury within a few weeks of his appointment. Still less was there any guarantee that 'no person should be removed from their employment on a pre-textual charge' (2), as the case referred to by Mayne in his exchange with Younger revealed was taking place. So far as the Campaign's other demands were concerned—such as an appeal to three High Court judges, sitting *in camera*, whose proceedings would be protected by the Official Secrets Act (4)—these were for the birds. Sir Cyril Musgrave's review in the Lang case had shown that MI5 thus had little to fear from the extension of the Three Advisers' jurisdiction, which was by now little more then a gesture to political criticism rather than a meaningful form of accountability. On the contrary indeed, such a procedure might help to diminish the risk of unwelcome publicity.

IX. The Empty Threat of Legal Liability

If the Lang case was responsible for the implementation of an ineffective form of scrutiny by the Three Advisers, it also laid to rest any latent concerns about legal liability in the implementation of the industrial purge, whether informally or formally. These concerns have already been referred to, having been raised by MI5's Bernard Hill and then by Sir Harold Parker after the meeting on 13 November 1952. Such concerns are not to be diminished, though the degree of risk would depend on the nature of the employment and the status of the worker. As we have seen, there were not only two procedures but also two categories of workers, for

[116] Mayne concluded rather ruefully: 'Has this man been treated in this way on the directive of a Minister? Indeed, do we know that this is a security case? Personally I have no doubts on the subject but equally I have no evidence that would stand up for a moment in a court of law.' Younger replied in a similar tone, tending to agree that the most worrying feature of the situation was not so much the procedure that had been published as the doubt he had about its application. He too had no doubt that an employer looking for an opportunity to get rid of someone who was troublesome would find ways and means of doing so 'by methods outside the established procedure'. He was also concerned about so-called security cases existing outside the scope of the procedure, as in the case of people dismissed as a result of information supplied by bodies like the Economic League, a militantly anti-Communist organization that kept a blacklist of Communist Party activists (University of Sussex, Benn Levy Papers, Younger to Mayne, 18 February 1957).

[117] Except in the case of those employed by the Atomic Energy Authority; see pp. 326–7 above.

present purposes wage earners on the one hand and salary earners like Lang on the other. The starting point for any legal claim in both categories would be wrongful dismissal for breach of contract, though for the overwhelming majority of cases liability could be avoided by the employer giving reasonable notice to terminate, generally measurable in hours, days, and weeks rather than months.

In the days before statutory unfair dismissal laws, the dismissal with notice would be lawful whatever the cause—none need be specified—and there would be no cost to the employer. This was clearly revealed when shop stewards raised concerns about the operation of the security procedures representing electricians employed at the Aldermaston Atomic Site. The shop stewards in question wrote to the General Secretary of their union (the ETU) on 18 December 1951, complaining that workers were being removed from the security zone without a reason being given, and asking to know by what statutory authority these actions were being taken. The matter was referred by the union to the NCCL, which sought advice from Stuart Shields at 10 KBW, the NCCL expressing concern that security was being used as a cover for dismissing workers for other reasons, such as trade union activities, which in turn would have a chilling effect on trade union organization at the site.

Mr Shields required additional information from the ETU, which was sought by the NCCL on 21 March 1951. In the course of the latter correspondence, NCCL General Secretary Elizabeth Allen wrote to say that:

> On the general question of the position of an unestablished Government employee, or the employee of a contractor on Government work, challenged on security grounds, we are extremely perturbed at the information now coming to us. We understand from a local trades council, who has referred the issue to us, that in the case of the building industry, employment on sites where security issues arise is subject to the employee obtaining a pass from the Security Officers. If a pass is refused or withdrawn, the employers then claim to be in a position where employment terminates for reasons beyond their control.
>
> We would point out that the situation here is far more serious than it is in respect of the established civil servant, who is dealt with under the 'Purge' procedure, since, in the case of the unestablished worker, or the worker on contract, there is no special machinery of any kind, no investigation which can be checked and no guarantee that the powers are not being used for purposes other than security. Moreover, there is no obligation on the employer to arrange a transfer of employment if it is practicable.

It appeared, however, that the workers were in a precarious position, the employers effectively free to dismiss at will. There was no statutory authority for the removals because none was needed. In a remarkable insight into the condition of contemporary employment standards, the General Secretary of the ETU wrote to the

NCCL to say that under the terms of the collective agreements between the union and the employers' association then in force, the employer was free to terminate employment on giving one hour's notice, 'on any grounds he may deem permissible'. This lack of protection is important because it meant that when MI5 was operating the informal system against non-'key' personal, they were doing so with legal impunity in an environment where there were effectively no legal constraints on the power of the employer (which is not to say that there would be no industrial constraints).[118] It was also important because employers could hide behind the claim of security without having to substantiate it, and use security as a pretext for getting rid of people on other grounds.

That said, the Lang case revealed that there were exceptions, with the Benn Levy archive yielding correspondence in which Lang indicates that he had been employed on a five-year contract (with an expectation of renewal to the retirement age) with an annual income of just over £5,000. This is a contract that could not lawfully be terminated by notice, though it could have been terminated summarily for cause. It is an open question whether it would have been lawful under such a contract to dismiss Lang because of government pressure following security concerns related to his political views or connections. It was, however, unnecessary to address such matters, ICI diplomatically offering a settlement of £20,000, somewhere in the region of £500,000 at 2019 values. The offer was accepted, the Treasury Solicitor subsequently making clear that this was a matter for the company and not the government, which had been faced with the choice of dismissing Mr Lang or retaining him and losing government contracts.[119]

In these circumstances, the only possible threat to MI5 would be an action in tort rather than contract, not against the employer but against the Crown as tortfeasor. The question of liability had been considered briefly by Sir Harold Parker and officials in 1952, and indeed it is notable that the legal concerns expressed between 1948 and 1952 did not relate to the employers' liability in contract, or fear that MI5 could be dragged into potential litigation between worker and employer. But although actively considered, government liability in tort at the suit of a dismissed worker appears also to have been quickly discounted at the time.[120] Nevertheless, the Benn Levy archive suggests litigation on this ground was seriously contemplated by Lang, who instructed Gerald Gardiner QC, a supporter of the Campaign for the Limitation of Secret Police Powers, and later Lord Chancellor in the Wilson government. There is no record of why the claim was abandoned,

[118] This is not to deny that there would be industrial relations rather than legal constraints that would have to be navigated. These are alluded to in the minute sheet to file TNA, AVIA 46/541, considered at p. 322 (n 56).

[119] University of Sussex, Benn Levy Papers, Campaign for the Limitation of Secret Police Powers, 4/8.

[120] Liability on these grounds was acknowledged by the government but the threat was swiftly and rightly dismissed: TNA, AVIA 46/541 (Gen. 399 First Draft, Security—Secret Government Contracts. Memorandum by a Group of Officials, 13 November 1952, Annex 2).

though the settlement by ICI in Lang's favour may have rendered any such litigation pointless.

The possible cause of action would be conspiracy to injure or inducing breach of contract of employment. Substantively, however, it was a defence to a claim for conspiracy to injure that the defendant was acting to promote his or her own self-interest,[121] and it would have been hard to argue at the time that the protection of State secrets as a reason for causing harm to the plaintiff did not constitute a sufficient interest for this purpose.[122] But although the risk had been raised by Parker in 1952, there is no serious mention of conspiracy to injure in any of the Lang files that we examined.[123] Inducing breach of contract is rather different. Although in the great majority of cases this would stumble on the ground that the contract had been lawfully terminated rather than breached, that is a defence that may not have been available to ICI in the Lang case. One of the issues in any litigation, however, would have been whether there was a defence of justification to any such inducement to breach, a matter on which there was only limited authority,[124] the scope of which Mr Lang would nevertheless have been ill-advised to test. As Lang himself acknowledged in correspondence, 'the constitutional issue whether the Government is "justified" in inducing breach of contract on the ground of protecting State secrets is . . . an interesting and fundamental one'.[125]

It is also one a court at the time was unlikely to decide in Lang's favour. So while an action for inducing breach of contract was contemplated in the Lang case, it was not followed through. But even if it had been, the procedural obstacles to bringing a claim would have been formidable. In any proceedings in which it was involved, the Crown would have claimed Crown privilege (now public interest immunity) to prevent the disclosure of any sensitive material that the plaintiff might need to substantiate the claim.[126] This might include the terms of the contract, and in particular the provisions of 'Clause 59' or its equivalent, as well as any correspondence between the firm and the government, or any correspondence or records of meetings with MI5 of the kind we encountered in Bert Edwards' file in Part II of this chapter. Even today, with the Crown having no absolute right to prevent the disclosure of evidence under public interest immunity, any claim of the kind discussed would be challenging; in the 1950s, however, procedural law joined forces with substantive law effectively to empower the State and its agencies. And while

[121] *Crofter Hand Woven Harris Tweed v Veitch* 1942 SC (HL) 1.

[122] See *Scala Ballroom (Wolverhampton) Ltd v Radcliffe* [1958] 1 WLR 1057 for the scope of the defence (authorizing action in resistance to racial discrimination).

[123] Except to be dismissed in the short account in TNA, AVIA 46/541 (Gen. 399 First Draft, Security—Secret Government Contracts. Memorandum by a Group of Officials, 13 November 1952, Annex 2).

[124] *Brimelow v Casson* [1924] 1 Ch 302.

[125] University of Sussex, Benn Levy Papers, Campaign for the Limitation of Secret Police Powers, 4/8 (Lang to Kimber, 19 February 1957).

[126] *Duncan v Cammell, Laird & Co Ltd* [1942] AC 624.

there was sometimes concern on the part of MI5 of defamation, this was notably not a serious issue raised in the Lang correspondence.

X. Conclusion

The government was right to have been concerned that the secrecy of the industrial purge would be blown and that there would be demands for its operation to be supervised. That said, no one could have anticipated the Lang case, with none of the earlier victims of the purge able to call on the services of an LSE law professor elevated to the hereditary peerage, or the same intense support of a campaign group endorsed by a wide range of politicians and celebrities. Nevertheless, the system of supervision implemented in response was already well in hand following the Privy Councillors' report, which went no further than the minimum necessary to deal with the problem from a political perspective. By the passage of time MI5 had been able greatly to diminish the role of the Three Advisers in the industrial purge in particular, having already succeeded in persuading the Privy Councillors to limit the Three Advisers' input in civil service cases.

If experience since the war was any guide, the new jurisdiction would increase the Three Advisers' workload by an average of less than one case a year, with the need for their services soon exhausted. For as in the case of the civil service, the problem to which the extended jurisdiction was addressed will have been largely dealt with by vetting procedures, which would stop people being appointed in the first place. The Three Advisers would thus be dealing mainly with people who got in before vetting was stepped up and who could not otherwise be removed by informal means. In fact, the recently released report of the Radcliffe Committee on Security Procedures reinforces the view that MI5 had got off the hook by the delay in extending the Three Advisers' jurisdiction:[127] by 1961 there had been only one reference to the Three Advisers by an employee of an independent contractor since 1957.[128]

The real problem of the industrial purge was thus left unresolved, that being the problem of the informal, two-tier system, MI5's lack of accountability for the manner of its operation, and the large number of workers who were likely to have been prejudiced in various ways as a result. As we saw in Chapter 8, this was also

[127] TNA, CAB 301/258 (Report of the Committee on Security Procedures in the Public Service). A censored public version was published as a white paper: Report on Security Procedures in the Public Service (Chair: Lord Radcliffe), Cmnd 1681, 1962.

[128] TNA, CAB 301/258 (Report of the Committee on Security Procedures in the Public Service), para. 132. The information is not included in the white paper. The reference had been made only a few weeks before the report was published. Writing in 1990, Fredman and Morris point out that the Three Advisers had not met since 1969, which is not to say that people would not still be purged from firms engaged on government contracts: S. Fredman and G. Morris, *The State as Employer—Labour Law in the Public Services* (London, 1989), p. 236.

a feature of the civil service purge procedure, highlighted by Radcliffe. In the case of the industrial purge, however, that two-tier system appears to have been institutionalized, in a manner that did not attract any adverse comment from Radcliffe (unlike in the case of the civil service purge). Perhaps he was unaware of what was happening. But of particular interest in a part of the report that was published was the revelation that 'in addition to the formal procedures, contracting firms are helped in various ways to carry out their security obligations'.

Here Radcliffe referred expressly to the fact that the 'Security Service employs a team of officers who act as Security Advisers to Government contractors', the report continuing to say that 'these officers, who act as agents for the contracting Departments, visit contracting firms to inspect their security arrangements and to offer help or advice on any security problems that may arise'.[129] We can readily imagine the type of problems likely to arise and the nature of the advice given, this reading very much like an explanation of the MI5 role in the Bert Edwards case some twenty years earlier. But although the procedure was now out in the open, there was no suggestion that there should be any accountability for the way in which MI5 officers carried out these duties, notwithstanding the impact that any advice might have on the individuals affected. MI5 officers remained free to act with impunity.

[129] TNA, CAB 301/258 (Report of the Committee on Security Procedures in the Public Service), para. 132; Cmnd 1681, 1962, para. 100.

12
Purging the Trade Unions

I. Introduction

One of the notable developments of modern public law was the decision of the House of Lords in the *GCHQ* case.[1] There, it will be recalled, the government moved unilaterally to ban trade unions from the security and intelligence establishment, and introduce a 'house union'. This gave rise to litigation in which it was held that the exercise of the royal prerogative was in principle subject to judicial review.[2] It was also held, however, that in some circumstances those exercising prerogative power could claim in their defence that they were acting in the interests of national security, a claim that succeeded in the *GCHQ* case. The case was nevertheless of huge constitutional importance, not only for breaking new legal ground, but also for helping to expose what had been hitherto one of the most secret arms of the British security machinery.

What is now clear from material available at the National Archives is that in taking steps to ban trade unions at GCHQ, the Thatcher government had succeeded where previous Conservative administrations had failed. In this chapter, we provide an account of these earlier attempts to ban trade unions and provide an explanation for their failure. We also consider the steps that were taken in lieu of an outright ban on trade union membership, steps taken because the more drastic option was unavailable, despite being the recommended course of action. Our account also provides some insight into the role of the senior judiciary in the 1950s and 1960s, a role which is very different from that at least superficially on display in the *GCHQ* reasoning of the House of Lords in 1984.

Consistently with other measures taken at the time under the cover of security, government intervention to deal with the alleged menace of Communist infiltration of the civil service trade unions did not take the form of legislation, which would at least have had the virtue of transparency in the course of which evidence of a mischief would have had to be produced, and proposals for legislation justified and tested in an open forum. It was simply not necessary, just as it was unnecessary

[1] *Council of Civil Service Unions v Minister of Civil Service* [1985] AC 374.

[2] On the constitutional significance of the decision, see H. W. R. Wade, 'Procedure and Prerogative in Public Law' (1985) 101 *LQR* 180.

MI5, the Cold War, and the Rule of Law. K. D. Ewing, Joan Mahoney, and Andrew Moretta, Oxford University Press (2020). © K. D. Ewing, Joan Mahoney, and Andrew Moretta. DOI: 10.1093/oso/9780198818625.001.0001

to legislate for the purge or vetting procedures in the civil service, or the security procedures in industry. Despite the severe consequences of the government's action for trade unions, their officials, and their members, no one appeared to contemplate legal action as a response. There was no legal remedy.

The legal position reflected both the lack of statutory regulation of industrial relations generally at the time (though this is not to be mistaken for an absence of government intervention in industrial relations), and the lack of statutory regulation of public-sector employment in particular. There was a heavy reliance in industrial relations on administrative rather than legislative power, and in the case of the civil service on the royal prerogative rather than legislation, as the legal foundation of that power. In practice, however, governments rarely needed to reveal or justify the legal foundations for their actions. The benefit for government is that although security policies might well be announced and made public, there would be little accountability thereafter if operated unobtrusively.

II. The Communist Presence in the Trade Unions

Government concerns about Communist Party influence in the trade unions were not confined to the civil service. As we saw in Chapter 4 above, trade unions and trade unionists were the subject of MI5 surveillance on a scale still unknown. In terms of MI5's Charter, this surveillance was related more to concerns about 'subversion' than 'espionage', which could not plausibly be a concern in relation to unions representing members with no access to secret establishments. To this end, the Cabinet Secretary records an exchange in which Attlee asked Bevin whether Communism was growing in the trade unions, to which the latter replied by saying that Communists were 'getting control through office'.[3] This in turn led immediately to a proposal that the TUC—the Fifth Estate—should be asked to re-issue its 'black circular' which had been produced in the 1930s, to deal with disruptive elements, that is to say the Communists, organizing within the Movement.[4]

Circular 16 prohibited trade councils from admitting delegates who were associated with Communist or Fascist organizations, while Circular 17 requested affiliated unions to amend their rules to enable them to exclude members of disruptive bodies from membership. The circulars were removed in 1943.[5] But in

[3] TNA, CAB 195/5/68 (Cabinet Secretary's Notebook, 25 November 1947).

[4] TUC Annual Report 1935, pp. 110–12. See *McCormick v Transport and General Workers Union, The Times*, 30 July 1935. For background, see TUC Annual Report 1929, p. 169.

[5] The circulars were withdrawn in 1943 at a time when apparently the country was in awe of the Red Army: TUC Annual Report 1943, pp. 337–9.

light of the government's request, the TUC General Council apparently found it necessary in 1949 to 'direct the serious attention of all trade unionists to the malignant character of Communist agitation and organisation'.[6] Communist penetration was a concern in several unions and gave rise to a number of bitter internal conflicts. In the case of the mighty TGWU these conflicts led to a rule change in 1949, prohibiting members of the Communist Party from holding office in the union.[7] Other unions followed suit, including the painters' union, which—in its desire quickly to amend its rules to ban Communist sympathizers from office—found itself on the wrong end of a High Court judgment.[8] But by no means all unions took this course of action.

It is thus difficult to tell just how serious was the alleged Communist penetration of trade unions, it being reported at a Cabinet meeting in 1949 that there was no Communist Party member on the TUC General Council, which typically included the most senior figures in the Movement.[9] But the government had other issues, expressed by the Minister of Labour at the same meeting, in the course of which it was reported that the Communist Party appeared to be actively engaged in disrupting the transport system and had formed a rail and road transport section for the purpose.[10] The main concern—which, as we saw in Chapter 4, was not shared by Liddell—was with unofficial action in the docks, it being claimed in Cabinet discussions that the Communists had embarked on a programme of political warfare:

> Hitherto they had tried to obtain representation in Parliament and to secure control of the trade unions: they had now abandoned parliamentary action and were concentrating on fomenting industrial troubles. They would doubtless continue their efforts to capture control of the key unions.[11]

Six years later an MI5 security assessment of the Communist Party reported that at least one in eight full-time trade union officials was a Party member or sympathizer, and that of the thirty-six major unions, 'at least eight have General Secretaries of whom there is recent evidence of their being Communists or Communist sympathisers'. This was said to reflect the industrial strategy of the Party, much of which was devoted to the 'penetration of the Trade Union movement', a process

[6] TUC Annual Report 1949, p. 275.

[7] See J. Goldstein, *The Government of British Trade Unions* (London, 1953). It was reported at the Cabinet on 14 September 1950 that the General Secretary of the TGWU was pressing for action to be taken against the Communist Party. See TNA, CAB 128/18/18 (Cabinet Conclusions, 14 September 1950).

[8] *Bisset v National Amalgamated Society of Operative House and Ship Painters and Decorators*, *The Times*, 20, 21 April 1951. The union was pulled up, not for acting in a discriminatory manner, but for having implemented the ban without following the rule-change procedures in its constitution.

[9] TNA, CAB 128/18/18 (Cabinet Conclusions, 14 September 1950).

[10] ibid.

[11] ibid.

that was said to have being going on 'steadily for nearly thirty years'.[12] MI5's risk assessment was nevertheless counter-intuitive. For although the Communist Party had a 'vested interest in industrial unrest' and was 'sufficiently strongly represented in some of the most important Trade Unions to bring it about', it was only 'exceptionally' that the Party dared 'use its influence to start a strike or to prolong and spread a strike started by someone else'.[13]

So far as the civil service specifically was concerned, both MI5 and the government feared that the CSCA was Communist dominated in the years after the Second World War, which would be a particular concern given that the Association was the largest of the civil service unions.[14] But as was the case with several other unions at that time, Communist Party domination of the union was short-lived, the right-wing faction taking control of the union in 1949 showing little tolerance for the regime it replaced. But while there was no civil service union that could be said after 1949 to have been Communist dominated, in government terms all but three of the civil service unions were thought to be Communist penetrated. According to MI5, the latter unions had at least one national officer who was either a Party member or a Party sympathizer—that appears to be all it took to stimulate heightened anxiety.

But so what? It is clear that there was no issue with subversion, there being 'no evidence of any deliberate attempt by the Communist Party to penetrate the Civil Service or to use communist civil servants to influence policy'. The Party's aim was thus thought to be 'long-term—namely to build up communist cadres within the Civil Service for use should the Party ever come to power'.[15] The Party was thus 'constantly emphasizing that a communist civil servant's main duty is to maintain and improve his position in the Service'.[16] Nor was there any evidence that Communist Party members in the civil service unions were using their position to foment industrial action. Indeed if this was their purpose, they were singularly ineffective, it being noted in a memorandum by the Home Secretary in 1949 that 'in recent times there have been very few strikes by civil servants and those that have occurred have been trivial in nature and short in duration'.[17]

This was by no means surprising. While the levels of industrial action exercised the Labour government immediately after the war (giving rise to the

[12] TNA, CAB 134/1325 (Security Conference of Privy Counsellors [sic.]: Meetings 1–8 (1955); Papers 1–20 (1955); Meetings 1–5 (1956); Papers 1–6 (1956); Memorandum on 'Communism as a Security Problem').

[13] The threat the Communist Party presented through its role in the trade unions was thus said to be a 'potential one' only, albeit potential for reasons of 'political expediency'. According to MI5, that potential could be 'turned into a reality' only when the Party considered it to be 'politically safe' to do so.

[14] See E. L. Wigham, *From Humble Petition to Militant Action: History of the Civil and Public Services Association* (London, 1980), ch. 12.

[15] 'Communism as a Security Problem' (n 12).

[16] ibid.

[17] TNA, CAB 129/35/33 ('Civil Servants and Industrial Disputes', Memorandum by Chuter Ede).

famous Cabinet discussion of 14 September 1950), it is a problem that is even easier to exaggerate in the period after 1951. Thus, in a memo circulated in 1957, we find the Prime Minister remarking complacently that the post-war years had been:

> 'free from widespread and protracted stoppages', with 'much less working time [having] been lost even than in the 1930s' (and 'trivial compared with the 1920s').[18]

But if there was no evidence of subversion, nor was there any evidence that the Party was engaged in illegal espionage activities or used well-placed civil servants or union officials for this purpose, tending to undermine the need for the measures discussed later in this chapter.

The point was made clearly enough in MI5's security briefing 'Communism as a Security Problem', where it is said that:

> The importance which the Party attached to its political role imposes severe limitations on its illegal activities. This does not mean that individual Party members will not be allowed to take risks when the Party considers them absolutely necessary, but the general party line is now so cautious that members are only allowed to transgress the law in the most exceptional circumstances.
>
> There is an additional reason for caution when it comes to espionage as the Party is ever mindful of the shock it received when its then National Organiser, SPRINGHALL, was successfully prosecuted for espionage in 1943. The Party is once again faced with its fundamental dilemma. Its basic loyalty to the Soviet Union which must make it a duty to carry out espionage for the Russians has to be balanced against its constitutional ambition to be seen as a respectable British political party. This ambition is in direct conflict with treasonable activity and the Party as a party therefore shies away from it.[19]

It was pointed out that the Russians themselves no longer used Communist Party members or sympathizers for espionage purposes, though it may be that this practice was not invariably followed.[20]

18 TNA, CAB 129/88/32 ('The Economic Cost of Industrial Disputes', Memorandum by Harold Macmillan).

19 The Springhall case is discussed in F. Beckett and J. Murray, *The Rise and Fall of the British Communist Party* (London, 1995)— 'an appalling embarrassment' for the Party (p. 86).

20 Note also that 'Sonya' confirmed in her memoirs that, when she was active as an agent, 'In accordance with the rules, I kept strictly away from the British Party' (R. Werner, *Sonya's Report: Fascinating Autobiography of One of Russia's Most Remarkable Secret Agents* (London, 1991), p. 242). She also states that she had been told by Moscow to have 'no contact with the British party' (p. 188), though she admits that after she had lost contact with Moscow, she and her husband joined the Banbury branch of the CPGB (p. 277).

III. The Proposal to Ban Trade Unions at GCHQ

It appears that the MI5 briefing referred to in Part II above was prepared for the Conference of Privy Councillors that had been established in 1955 to review security procedures in the public service and to consider whether additional measures were necessary.[21] An appendix to the full report of the Privy Councillors reveals that Communist Party penetration of the civil service unions in particular had been raised at a ministerial meeting on 31 March 1955,[22] there being no record available to us of any earlier consideration of the question. This meeting led to a rather drastic proposal, which was simply to ban trade unions and trade union membership from some locations, the Foreign Office being 'invited to take the first suitable opportunity for putting forward proposals for the introduction of a house union in certain secret Foreign Office establishments'.[23]

A scheme was duly prepared by the Foreign Office in consultation with other interested departments, though it was thought that in order to ensure proper security for the matters dealt with by GCHQ,

> the house union or unions would have to include not only the non-industrial employees of GCHQ and Diplomatic Service Wireless Establishments for which the Foreign Secretary [was] responsible, but also the civilian members of the radio, traffic handling and radio maintenance classes employed at the Service Intercept Stations, for which the Service ministers answer.[24]

The question of how this was to be done—whether by legislation or by administrative action—was referred back to ministers, though it appears to have been thought that the security debate initiated by the Burgess and Maclean defections 'provided as good an opportunity for tightening security measures as was likely to be offered'.

The Foreign Office scheme was, however, the subject of powerful criticism by the senior civil servants responsible for security policy and its implementation. It is true that the Official Committee on Security thought that the Foreign Office scheme was 'well devised to meet the security risk' at the security establishments where staff were said to belong to unions that had been 'penetrated by Communism'.[25] But thereafter the officials saw only 'difficulties and objections', and

[21] See Report of the Security Conference of Privy Councillors, 24 January 1956. As explained in Chapter 10 above (n 37) this report is contained in TNA, CAB 21/4035. Notably this copy is absent from the National Archives, being used by the Cabinet Office, we have been informed. It is not clear why the Cabinet Office should have special access to these documents and why they ought not to use them on the same terms as anyone else. The idea that documents should be removed from the Archives seems extraordinary. We have relied instead on what appears to have been Bridges' original signed copy of the report.

[22] Report of the Security Conference of Privy Councillors (ibid.), Appendix D.

[23] ibid., para. 1.

[24] ibid., para. 3.

[25] ibid., para. 6.

proceeded to take the proposals apart, layer by layer. Thus, although it might be possible to make membership of a house union (and non-membership of an independent union) a condition of employment of 'new entrants', how could such conditions be imposed on existing staff, who were said to number some thousands? If it was to be done by administrative means and without legislation, what would happen to those members of staff who refused to accept the new terms?[26]

The prospect of dismissal was viewed with some alarm: not only would strong objections be expressed in some quarters about the dismissal of established civil servants for refusing to accept an important change in their conditions of service, but more importantly it was thought that 'the last thing the State wishes to do with individuals whom possess such knowledge of secret operations is to discharge them'.[27] While the possibility of legal action under the Official Secrets Acts 1911–39 might be contemplated if the individual 'continued to discuss details of his employment with the officials of his original union', there were thought to be 'considerable administrative and legal difficulties in doing this effectively'.[28] Although proceeding by way of legislation would overcome the problem of worker resistance (in the sense that the new terms could simply be imposed), such an initiative was also thought to 'hold awkward consequences' if the imposition of the new terms 'was resented by the staff concerned'.[29]

There was, however, another reason for caution about legislation, which related to the effect on security of the publicity that would necessarily be associated with the introduction of legislation. In a beautifully ironic passage, it was argued that 'since the Russians almost certainly know of the existence of these establishments, publicity about them would not very much matter'.[30] But on the other hand, the introduction of a house union would 'certainly advertise the existence and the size of the organisation', about which in this country 'remarkably little' was known.[31] In what must almost certainly have been a crucial argument against taking action by way of legislation, it was argued further that:

> It would seem certain that the surprise which would be shown at the large numbers employed in this activity would certainly provoke discussion as to the importance which must be attached to it. And there might also be awkward enquiries as to how the expenditure of this organisation, which is largely met by hitherto undisclosed contributions from the Service Departments' Votes, was provided for in the Estimates.[32]

[26] ibid., para. 7. This itself is an interesting insight into de facto job security in a service where staff had no legal protection by virtue of their engagement under the prerogative.
[27] ibid., para. 7.
[28] ibid., para. 8.
[29] ibid., para. 9.
[30] ibid., para. 10.
[31] ibid.
[32] ibid.

But secrecy was not the only reason for secrecy. So was one of the reasons for intervening in the first place, namely the need to maintain good terms with the United States. In another extraordinary passage, officials thought it necessary to raise the effect of publicity on Anglo-American collaboration, with any public discussion likely to concentrate public attention on the fact that (what was now) all but two of the civil service unions were to some degree infiltrated by Communists. Sooner or later, it was argued, 'people would ask why the risk to security of such infiltration cannot be allowed in certain Foreign Office establishments, but is permitted elsewhere'.[33] As a result, it was said, Anglo-American collaboration could be compromised if the Americans—who would have been very critical of a Communist presence—discovered that employees in—for example—guided weapons establishments had contact with Communist trade union officials.[34]

In light of these concerns, the Official Committee charged with the task of examining a trade union ban at GCHQ and elsewhere thought that the appointment of the Conference of Privy Councillors provided a good opportunity to give further (and presumably more authoritative) consideration to the question. Appointed by Anthony Eden at a time of deep parliamentary and public anxiety about Russian espionage in the wake of publicity about the Cambridge spies,[35] this was not a conference as that term would be understood today, but a high-level committee with senior representation from both sides of the House. As we have see, the Lord President of the Council (Salisbury), the Lord Chancellor (Kilmuir) and the Home Secretary (Lloyd George) represented the government, while three Cabinet ministers in the Attlee government (Jowitt, Morrison, and Strauss) represented the Labour Party.[36]

In the end, the Conference dealt only very briefly with the proposed trade union ban in a wide-ranging twenty-five-page report—boiled down at the time to a three-page white paper for public consumption.[37] Apart from the absence of any discussion of the legal implications of a ban on trade union membership, it is also striking that there was no consideration of principle, or the question whether the proposal to ban trade unions would be consistent with the international treaties and freedom of association conventions to which the country

[33] ibid., para. 11. The example was given of the low-grade officials in the Ministry of Supply who, if questioned by trade union officials about the nature of their work, might be able to give general information on the development of particular weapons and the deployment of resources.

[34] ibid.

[35] The Conference had been established following the Commons debate relating to the 'disappearance of two members of the Foreign Service' (HC Debs, 7 November 1955, col. 1483): TNA, CAB 128/30/243 (Cabinet Conclusions, 6 March 1956). The 'appointment' of the Conference was announced to the Commons on 23 November 1955: HC Debs, 23 November 1955, col. 1462.

[36] Sir Edward Bridges, the senior civil servant at the Treasury, completed the team. As suggested above, it seems that it was Bridges who drafted the report. See TNA, CAB 21/4037 (Letter from Bridges to Viscount Kilmuir, 30 December 1955).

[37] On the abbreviated white paper, see Statement on the Findings of the Conference of Privy Councillors on Security, Cmd 9715, 1956.

had only recently subscribed.[38] Consideration of such matters was perhaps as unnecessary as it was opaque,[39] for we were now deep into the territory of the royal prerogative, addressing questions of the defence of the realm. These were matters that would be resolved not by considerations of obligation, but by considerations of expediency.

IV. The Triumph of Pragmatism

This is not to say that the Conference was unsympathetic to the Foreign Office proposal, which appears to have been rejected on purely pragmatic grounds. Thus, it was acknowledged that there was a major political obstacle to the implementation of this proposal, in the sense that '[t]he feasibility of introducing house unions mainly turns on the attitude of the trades union movement as a whole to this idea'.[40] But indicating that they were neither unsympathetic to the proposal to ban trade unions from certain government establishments, nor unaware of the general hostility of trade unions to house unions, the Conference thought that 'in the special circumstances of this case', the trade unions 'might be prepared to accept the scheme proposed'.[41]

So they decided to consult Sir Vincent Tewson, the General Secretary of the TUC. Not by a long stretch a supporter of the Communist Party, Tewson confirmed that even non-Communist trade unionists would find the idea of house unions to be repugnant, a judgement powerfully reinforced some thirty or so years later. Speaking in a personal capacity and making it known that he had already been 'sounded out' on this matter, Tewson made clear in evidence to the Conference 'his firm opinion' that 'a proposal to introduce a house union would encounter strong opposition from all the [trade unions] concerned and that the trades union movement would unquestionably support them'.[42] In his view, to proceed with these proposals over the objections of the trade unions would prejudice other security measures that the Conference might be recommending to government.

That was enough for the Privy Councillors, no doubt consoled by Sir Vincent's judgement that the existing arrangements—whereby Communist officials were so far as possible kept away from direct negotiations relating to staff at the establishments in question—were working reasonably well, and should be persevered

[38] Notably ILO Convention 87 (Freedom of Association and Protection of the Right to Organise Convention, 1948) and the European Convention on Human Rights, art. 11, which Kilmuir (as Sir David Maxwell Fyfe) had a hand in drafting, a role to which he was willing defensively to refer when in a tight spot: HL Debs, 21 June 1956, col. 1261.

[39] On the contemporary legal position relating to the employment of civil servants, see E. C. S. Wade and G. G. Phillips, *Constitutional Law* (5th edn, London, 1955), ch. 16.

[40] Report of the Security Conference of Privy Councillors (n 21), para. 87.

[41] ibid.

[42] ibid. With some prescience, Tewson said that the unions would 'certainly raise a storm of protest'.

with. According to the Conference, a decision to set up a house union against the opposition of the trade unions would make matters worse, the establishments in question being brought to public notice and given wide publicity, leading to 'much speculation by the press as the exact nature of the secret work in which they are engaged, some of which might well be near the mark'.[43] Although conceding that the 'present position is certainly a most unsatisfactory and dangerous one', the Privy Councillors had no solution.

It appears that the Prime Minister accepted the recommendation to leave matters as they were, despite the fact that this was a problem that had 'confronted Ministers and successive governments for several years past',[44] and despite the fact that political proposals had been made in the Foreign Office to address the problem. It does not follow, of course, that the matter could not be revisited, the Privy Councillors assuming that 'the position will be constantly watched in order that any favourable opportunity may be taken to introduce changes which will lessen if not remove the dangers inherent in the present arrangement'.[45] This was consistent with Tewson's view that 'if circumstances changed and there seemed a better prospect of acceptance of a house union by the [trade unions], then the proposal could be considered again'.[46]

It seems that the government had no room for manoeuvre in light of the compelling reasons provided by both the Official Committee on Security and the Conference of Privy Councillors. If problems of implementation and adverse publicity were not enough, the resistance of the TUC was decisive. But what is also clear is that while the Foreign Office might have been the source of damaging leaks to the Russians, there is nothing in the Privy Councillors' Report—or in any of the documents referred to the Conference—to suggest that there had been any breach of security caused by a trade union official at a secret establishment or elsewhere. Putting to one side the contestable calumny that trade unionists were traitors, the lack of evidence tended to confirm Tewson's view that existing safeguards were adequate.

So although the Cambridge spy ring was being used as an opportunity for proposals to ban trade unions, there was no connection between trade unionism and espionage that anyone had mentioned. However, it was on neither principle nor evidence that policy was based, but ultimately on the fear that organized resistance would compromise secrecy (which is not the same as security). The full extent of the secrecy surrounding GCHQ and other establishments is, with retrospect, difficult to fathom, especially as it was recognized that their operations would have been well known to the Russians. Nevertheless, a remarkable insight into the

43 ibid., para. 88.
44 ibid., para. 89.
45 ibid.
46 ibid., para. 87.

extent of that secrecy was revealed in exchanges involving the Home Secretary, the Cabinet Secretary (Norman Brook), and the Prime Minister shortly after the Privy Councillors had submitted their report.

Having taken delivery of the report, Eden now had to decide what to do with it, a matter on which the Privy Councillors had themselves given some advice. They assumed that their report would not be published, but suggested that some of the changes proposed (on matters not dealt with in this chapter) could be made in a public announcement, which might include some of the general background material in the report.[47] The Privy Councillors were of the view that a document of this kind 'might be felt likely to have a useful effect on public and parliamentary opinion'.[48] It was suggested by the Ministerial Committee on Security that a white paper could be produced outlining some key points, a proposal which met the approval of the Home Secretary.[49] In a minute to the Prime Minister, however, the latter cautioned against circulating the report to ministers:

> I think your attention has already been drawn to the fact that Appendix D to the Report deals with certain very secret activities of the Foreign Office, the details of which are not known to all Cabinet ministers. My own view is the Report is not a document that ought to be circulated to the Cabinet.[50]

The latter minute from the Home Secretary to the Prime Minister thus revealed the full extent to which the government was handcuffed by its own secrecy from taking steps that it might otherwise have contemplated. Advising Eden on how best to proceed, the Cabinet Secretary (Sir Norman Brook) wrote on the same day to say that:

> The Cabinet ought, I think to be made aware of this announcement before it is made. If they are to consider it, the report of the Conference ought to be before them at the same time. I think they ought in any event to see the report: it deals with a subject that is of great importance and of close interest to all Ministers in charge of Departments. There is, however, one section of the report, on GCHQ establishments, which contains information not generally known to Ministers; and this part of the report ought to be omitted from those copies of the report which receive general Cabinet circulation.[51]

47 ibid., para. 92. It was written on the assumption that it would not be published.

48 ibid., para. 94.

49 For the white paper, see Statement on the Findings of Privy Councillors on Security (n 37). On the parliamentary statement, see HC Debs, 8 March 1956, col. 2313. There is no reference to the proposed ban of trade unions at GCHQ in the white paper.

50 TNA, PREM 11/1587 (Minute from Home Secretary to Anthony Eden, 1 March 1956).

51 TNA, PREM 11/1587 (Minute from Norman Brook to Anthony Eden, 1 March 1956).

To which Eden replied by scrawling 'Good' in red pen in the left-hand margin. Even by the standards of the time it is extraordinary that information should be deliberately withheld from ministers in this way, not least because they were collectively responsible for the decisions which were to be taken.[52]

V. The Pressure Continues . . .

Notwithstanding the government's concerns about banning trade unions at GCHQ, political pressure to deal with Communist penetration of trade unions continued. The matter was back on the agenda within a period of five years, following an initiative by James Prior, then a Tory backbencher. In a question to the Prime Minister, Prior asked whether the latter was satisfied about the adequacy of precautions where full-time officials of civil service trade unions had 'access to information in departments where security is necessary'.[53] It was perhaps not a coincidence that this matter had been raised shortly after the appointment of yet another security review, this time following spy scares at Portland Down and the conviction of George Blake under the Official Secrets Act 1911.[54] On this occasion, the matter was not referred to a Conference of Privy Councillors, but to an independent Committee of five defence and intelligence experts under the chairmanship of Lord Radcliffe, a Lord of Appeal in Ordinary.[55]

This Committee was charged with the responsibility of reviewing again a wide range of security matters, including the classification and security of official documents, as well as the operation of the purge and PV procedures. But following Prior's prompting, the Prime Minister asked the Committee to look yet again at the question of trade union membership by civil servants employed at a number of secret establishments, including GCHQ. Quite whether Prior alone was responsible for this reference is unclear, though there is no evidence to suggest that his was a planted question to enable Macmillan to make a pre-arranged statement. There is also evidence, however, that a number of Labour MPs—notably Douglas Houghton and Christopher Mayhew—had subsequently written privately to Macmillan expressing concern about 'security risks flowing from the infiltration of Communists and fellow travellers into full time posts in civil service staff associations'.[56]

52 For Cabinet consideration of the report, see TNA, CAB 128/30/243 (Cabinet Conclusions, 6 March 1956).

53 HC Debs, 13 July 1961, col. 59 (WA).

54 See *R v Blake* [1962] 2 QB 377.

55 See Chapter 13 below.

56 TNA, T 216/914 (Radcliffe Committee of Enquiry into Civil Service Security Procedure). The file contains a draft letter from Macmillan to Houghton and Mayhew in relation to their letter of 27 July 1961 about the 'security risks flowing from the infiltration of Communists and fellow travellers into full time posts in civil service staff associations'. They appear to have proposed that trade union officials should be vetted by MI5 and refused access to secret establishments if they were 'believed to be unreliable'. Houghton had been General Secretary of the Inland Revenue Staff Association from 1922 to 1960. He was also Chairman of the Staff Side of the Civil Service National Whitley Council from 1956 to

So the process started again of getting information from officials about the nature of the problem. To this end a Treasury official prepared a lengthy briefing on the issue for the Committee,[57] in which it was acknowledged that the Security Service now estimated that one-third of full-time officials in civil service unions were Communists or Communist sympathizers.[58] These officials were said 'inevitably to obtain some information of security value', which 'could represent a security risk'.[59] In practice, however, it seems that these concerns were greatly exaggerated, a Communist being defined not only to mean a Communist sympathizer but also someone who associates with Communists, which could include the great bulk of the trade union movement. Nevertheless, the official identified a number of areas of potential vulnerability in the work of trade union officials (physical access to establishments, collective bargaining negotiations, and pay and grading claims), and the steps taken to deal with them to ensure that security was not compromised.

It was thus already the case that a number of safeguards were in place to prevent the leaking of information via trade union officials. Some of these were identified in the Treasury briefing, in the course of which a number of precautions were explained. These included the exclusion of full-time officials from Whitley Council discussions that would involve revealing secret information, while staff in establishments dealing with secret work were warned not to disclose information to anyone who did not need to know it, though the warning did not specifically refer to trade union officials. So far as special precautions taken when dealing with pay and grading claims of staff employed on secret work are concerned, the elaborate nature of these precautions was described as follows:

> If the investigation [of the claim] is [undertaken] by the Civil Service Pay Research Unit the research staff employed on the investigation (who are themselves civil servants) are positively vetted and steps are taken to exclude from the Unit's report any specific references to the nature of the secret work done. In some instances the nature of the work is so secret that it has not been thought desirable to have it investigated even by positively vetted research officers of the Pay

1958. On Houghton, see *The Independent*, 3 May 1996 (obituary). Before becoming an MP, Mayhew had worked for the IRD during the post-war Labour government. This was a shadowy black propaganda unit. On Mayhew, see *The Independent*, 9 January 1997 (obituary).

57 TNA, T 216/914 (Radcliffe Committee of Enquiry into Civil Service Security Procedure). The file contains a memo 'Committee on Security Procedures in the Public Service—Communist Officials in Civil Service Trade Unions', CSP (61) 37, 8 August 1961. The memo had been cleared with the Foreign Office, the Ministry of Aviation, GCHQ, the Atomic Energy Authority, and the Security Service (letter from A. J. Platt, 21 July 1961, filed in TNA, T 216/914, Radcliffe Committee of Enquiry into Civil Service Security Procedure).

58 Notable examples were said to be the Civil Service Union (which represented radio-operators), the CSCA. and the Institution of Professional Civil Servants.

59 'Committee on Security Procedures in the Public Service—Communist Officials in Civil Service Trade Unions' (n 57), para. 5.

> Research Unit. This is because they could not produce a sensible report without referring to the nature of the work and the report would have to be put in the hands of Civil Service Trade Union officials. In such cases the investigation has been made by Civil Servants nominated solely by the management in conjunction with Civil Servants nominated for this purpose by the Civil Service Trade Unions and acceptable on security grounds to the management.[60]

But this was by no means the end of it. There also existed at that time a Civil Service Arbitration Tribunal for the resolution of disputes.[61] Precautions were taken here to ensure that there was no public reference to secret work, whether in documents prepared for the Tribunal or otherwise. The opening statements of the case would be made in public but would not contain any reference to secret work, the Tribunal members were all vetted, and proceedings would be heard *in camera* to deal with any secret matter, with only civil servants present. Little wonder the civil service unions (whose official would be excluded from the *in camera* hearings) were heard to complain that they were 'hamstrung' by the precautions in conducting pay negotiations on behalf of their members engaged on secret work, simply because these members were unable to tell them about the work they do, a complaint ventilated in the pages of the *Sunday Times* by the CSCA.[62]

Otherwise, steps were taken to limit access to secret establishments by trade union full-time officials, who had to be 'escorted as necessary to and from meetings in the establishment', while secret work was concealed when 'joint inspections' took place. In the case of especially secret establishments such as GCHQ and the Atomic Energy Authority, the Security Service was said to supply 'security assessments of Trade Union officials who may have opportunities of acquiring secret information'.[63] In these cases, it seems that unspecified precautions were taken, subject to a proviso that 'precautionary action must not prejudice Security Service sources'.[64] Nevertheless, it appears that for access to these secret locations to be given to a trade union official, the 'Security Service require a special case to be made and to be fully informed of the circumstances'.[65] There was no suggestion that these arrangements were ineffective for the purposes for which they were devised, though they raise intriguing questions.

[60] ibid., para. 8.

[61] See S. Fredman and G. S. Morris, *The State as Employer; Labour Law in the Public Services* (London, 1989) and B. A. Hepple and P. O'Higgins, *Public Employee Trade Unionism in the United Kingdom: The Legal Framework* (Detroit, MI, 1971).

[62] *Sunday Times*, 9 July 1961: 'National security is preventing a trade union from pressing a wage demand for some of its members, because neither the workers concerned nor their employers can tell the union what the men's duties are.'

[63] 'Committee on Security Procedures in the Public Service—Communist Officials in Civil Service Trade Unions' (n 57), para. 11.

[64] ibid.

[65] ibid.

The only real weak spot identified in the procedures related to 'personal grievances and informal discussions', claimed to be 'the major hazard'.[66] This was said to be 'regarded seriously in specially secret establishments, eg, by GCHQ, the Diplomatic Wireless Service and the Composite Signals Organisation'. It was also said to cause concern in 'secret, usually research, establishments of the Defence Departments and Ministry of Aviation, and in local negotiations held by the Atomic Energy Authority covering both secret and non-secret areas of work'.[67] (In relation to the AEA, it was said 'incidentally' to be the policy of the Authority not to employ Communists.) The other concern of the Foreign Office in particular was the risk of 'talent spotting for possible hostile intelligence agents', the advice now on thin ice conveying a 'belief' that Communists are 'on the look out for persons who are thought likely and suitable to act as hostile intelligence agents'. Trade union officials 'could be' favourably placed to do this.[68]

But what was to be done about it? The Treasury official canvassed a number of possible options to deal with this matter, as follows:

(i) the establishment of a house union or house unions in establishments dealing with secret work;
(ii) barring any trade union with any Communist officials from negotiations affecting staff in any establishments dealing with secret work;
(iii) barring Communist officials of trade unions from negotiations affecting staff in any establishment dealing with secret work;
(iv) warning staff in such establishments against disclosing information to trade union officials.

As the official pointed out, the last was not necessarily an alternative to (i), (ii), or (iii), but could be combined with any one of them. It is clear, however, that he thought that (iv) was the only realistic option.

VI. . . . And Almost Prevails

It is easy to understand why officials might conclude that the last was the only practical solution. The first option had been considered by the Privy Councillors in 1956, who had consulted the General Secretary of the TUC to be told that 'house unions were anathema to trade unionists', and would 'meet with the strongest trade union opposition'. The second would be 'a very drastic step' that would effectively bar most of the major civil service trade unions from negotiations and could be

[66] ibid., para. 13.
[67] ibid., para. 16.
[68] ibid., para. 17.

'represented as penalizing those unions and their members because of the presence of even one security risk among their officials'. And the third would not deal with the problem of the concealed Communist or Communist sympathizer, nor prevent a security-cleared trade union official from passing on information—unwittingly or otherwise—to someone not security cleared. This left the last option as the 'only solution', if the others were thought to be 'impracticable or not worthwhile'.[69]

But it appears that Radcliffe did not accept this advice, though until recently the full details were unknown. This is because only a brief part of Radcliffe's recommendations on trade unions was included in the white paper published subsequently to summarize the main provisions of his report, for reasons to which we return in Chapter 13. In the meantime, however, it is now clear that Radcliffe proposed in strong terms the banning of trade unions at the 'most highly secret organisations', including GCHQ. According to Radcliffe:

> We ourselves recognize the delicacy of this question. But we do not think that the known and natural antipathy of trade unionists to the concept of 'house unions' can safely or properly be regarded as decisive in a special situation of this sort. Our view is that the present situation, in these highly sensitive organisations, is so unsatisfactory and so dangerous that no government would be justified in allowing it to continue. We think that the only effective remedy in the establishments we have mentioned lies in the formation of 'house unions' and we accordingly recommend that the Government should take this step, basing it openly on security considerations. The spy trials earlier this year and the light recently thrown on the administration of the Electrical Trades' Union suggest that public opinion might be more receptive of this proposal than might have been the case five or six years ago.[70]

Radcliffe reported to the Prime Minister on 21 November 1961,[71] the report then fully considered by both the Official and Ministerial Committees on Security, before being considered by the Cabinet on 20 March 1962.[72] While the Ministerial Committee appeared generally to support the Radcliffe recommendations, the foregoing could not be accepted, Norman Brook making it clear that the TUC would not accept house unions in 1961 anymore than they would in 1956.[73] The matter was left open at the first meeting of the Committee to see whether the TUC would turn a blind eye to a ban, failing which consideration would be given to simply turning these establishments into 'non union shops'.[74] Within three days,

69 ibid., paras 18–28.
70 TNA, CAB 301/258 (Security Procedures in the Public Service, para. 102).
71 TNA, CAB 129/109/1 (Memorandum by the Prime Minister, 16 March 1962).
72 TNA, CAB 128/36/22 (Cabinet Conclusions, 20 March 1962).
73 TNA, CAB 134/2498 (Memorandum by the Official Committee on Security, 24 January 1962).
74 TNA, CAB 134/2498 (Ministerial Committee on Security, Minutes of Meeting on 26 January 1962).

however, there had been a change of heart, the Foreign Secretary now accepting that 'whilst the recommendation [to introduce house unions] could properly be accepted, the chances of putting it into effect in the near future were poor'.[75]

The best course of action was to implement another Radcliffe recommendation whereby the government refused to deal with certain trade union officials in certain establishments. To this end, the Chief Secretary to the Treasury (at the time Henry Brooke) was sent off to prepare such a scheme for implementation.[76] But before his scheme was circulated to the Ministerial Committee on 27 March,[77] the Radcliffe Report was finally taken to and approved by the Cabinet.[78] In line with another decision taken by the Ministerial Committee on Security, it was at this latter meeting that Macmillan proposed that a white paper should be published, containing much—though not all—of the contents of the full report. As explained above, it was decided at this time that the chapter of the report dealing with trade unions would not be among those that would be published, the subject matter thought to be too controversial.

This, however, was to change following a leak to the press about the withholding of the latter information, leading to a rethink in which some of Radcliffe's trade union proposals were published; covering only four paragraphs of the white paper, this represented only a small part of the chapter in the full report. These four paragraphs were appended to a section of the white paper dealing with 'Organisation for Security',[79] Radcliffe announcing that having enquired into the penetration by Communists of the civil service unions, he was disturbed by the number of Communists and Communist sympathizers holding positions in these unions.[80] Reflecting (though not exactly) the Treasury briefing referred to above, Radcliffe reported that:

> We enquired into the penetration by Communists of the Civil Service Staff Associations and Trade Unions and were disturbed to learn that of the permanent full-time paid officials of these bodies about 25 per cent are communists and a further 10 per cent follow the party line on union affairs so consistently that they must be regarded as working in association with their communist colleagues. Among the unpaid national officers and members of the national executive committees (who are all Civil Servants) just over 10 per cent are Communists and a slightly larger proportion Communist followers in the sense described, making a total of almost one-quarter in the Communist camp.[81]

[75] TNA, CAB 134/2498 (Ministerial Committee on Security, Minutes of Meeting on 29 January 1962).
[76] ibid.
[77] TNA, CAB 134/2498 (Memorandum by the Chief Secretary to the Treasury and Paymaster General, 27 March 1962).
[78] TNA, CAB 128/36/22 (Cabinet Conclusions, 20 March 1962).
[79] Security Procedures in the Public Service, Cmnd 1681, 1962, paras 33–36.
[80] ibid., para. 33.
[81] TNA, CAB 301/258 (Security Procedures in the Public Service, para. 99).

No evidence was provided about the number of Communist officials, who was counted as a Communist for these purposes, or what access they had to secret information.

Nor was any account given of the safeguards in place to avoid the risk of secret information being disclosed, and no assessment was made that these safeguards were inadequate. As had been revealed in draft correspondence between Macmillan's office and the Labour MPs—Douglas Houghton and Christopher Mayhew—the Official Secrets Acts 1911–39 would protect such secret information, yet no consideration was given as to the adequacy or otherwise of these notorious provisions, or how they could be improved.[82] The government thus accepted two proposals for the exclusion of Communist trade unionists, the first and most important of these being the right of any Department where staff were employed on secret work 'to deny access to or to refuse to negotiate (either by correspondence or face to face) with a named trade union official whom it had reason to believe to be a Communist under the definition used by the purge procedure'.[83]

In common with the purge procedure, Radcliffe proposed that any trade unionist suspected of being a Communist or a Communist sympathizer would be challenged formally by the department concerned in the first instance, and would have a right of appeal to the Three Advisers against any adverse decision. For obvious reasons, there is no pretence that this procedure would apply also to suspected Fascists, as the purge procedure purported to do, largely for presentational reasons.[84] In addition, however, Radcliffe's second proposal addressed the question of trade union officials outside secret departments who were Communist Party members. The plan ostensibly was not to remove all Communists, but only those with access to secret departments. In the case of other departments, however, it was proposed that:

> without jeopardizing secret sources of information, Heads of Departments and Principal Establishment Officers should be told more frankly than we believe to be the present practice the scale of Communist penetration of the Civil Service unions and *should be warned of the identity of individual Communists with whom they are likely to have dealings*. More generally we think that Civil Servants who take part in staff negotiations should be warned in general terms that the Communist representation among Civil Service union officials is disproportionately high and that they should be as careful to avoid disclosing secret information to union officials as to anyone else outside the Government service.[85]

[82] See draft letter from Macmillan to Houghton and Mayhew, referred to in n 56.

[83] Security Procedures in the Public Service (n 79), para. 34.

[84] On which see J. Mahoney, 'Constitutionalism, the Rule of Law and the Cold War', in T. Campbell, K. D. Ewing, and A. Tomkins (eds), *The Legal Protection of Human Rights: Sceptical Essays* (Oxford, 2014), p. 129.

[85] Security Procedures in the Public Service (n 79), para. 36 (emphasis added).

Although the Cabinet rejected proposals to ban trade union membership in secret establishments, it nevertheless accepted these quite extraordinary proposals. The first would require the removal of Communist Party members and sympathizers from important positions, while the second would involve spreading information about the political beliefs, associations, or connections of individuals with a wide group of people. In neither case would there be any explanation of where the information had come from. This was nothing short of a purge of Communists from the trade unions, rather than a purge of trade unions from the establishments, the mischief compounded by trade union claims that the Radcliffe Committee 'sought and had no discussion with any officer of the staff side of the Civil Service National Whitley Council, nor with any officer of the Civil Service trade unions involved in the security fields'.[86]

VII. A Purge of Trade Unions

An announcement accepting these recommendations was made in June 1962. In what seems like another cavalier disregard for procedural propriety, Radcliffe did not suggest that the change should be implemented by legislation, despite the significance of what was being proposed for civil service staff, and the officials of their trade unions who risked losing their jobs if they were blacklisted under the proposed new arrangements. It is true, of course, that the purge procedure to which the trade union blacklist was to be attached had been introduced without legislation and continued to operate in a statute-free zone. But there was to be a big difference between civil servants who lost their jobs under the purge and civil service trade union officials who lost their jobs, in the sense that the former unlike the latter were generally to be regarded as a charge on the public service and to be found non-secret work.

There was no such commitment to trade union officials. On the contrary, one of the government's objectives was:

> To make this area of exclusion as wide as possible in order to limit the usefulness of these officials to their members and to encourage their Associations and Unions to get rid of them.[87]

Following the government's acceptance of the Radcliffe recommendations, procedures were quickly worked out for their implementation, leading to a number of

[86] This is confirmed by Appendix 1 of the full report, which contains a list of those who gave written and oral evidence.

[87] TNA, CAB 134/2498 ('Memorandum by the Chief Secretary to the Treasury and Paymaster General—Draft Plan of Action', 27 March 1962).

trade union officials being challenged in June 1962.[88] One of the first was Richard Nunn, the General Secretary of the Institution of Professional Civil Servants, which represented civil service scientists, but who had been in office for just over a year.[89] Nunn replaced Stanley Mayne, who was also believed to have close Communist Party links. Some context about Richard Nunn was provided by the journalist Chapman Pincher, who claims to have 'volunteered the suggestion' in evidence to the Radcliffe Committee that 'it seemed rather pointless keeping Communists out of the secret departments when Communists or near-Communists in Civil Service unions were allowed access'.[90]

Pincher continued in what was nothing short of a smear:

> When asked to give an example I cited the case of [Stanley] Mayne, stressing that I had no evidence that he had betrayed any secrets and stating that I did not think it likely that he would ever do so. My main concern was his successor. Mayne had made it plain to me that his successor would be a man of his choice. If Mayne was of the extreme Left the odds were that he would see to it that his choice was too.[91]

On the instruction from the new Chief Secretary to the Treasury (John Boyd-Carpenter), Mr Nunn was challenged in a letter from Sir Norman Brook (writing presumably as Head of the Home Civil Service), in which it was stated that:

> It has been reported to the Chief Secretary to the Treasury that you have been a member of the Communist Party and are still sympathetic to Communism in such a way as to raise legitimate doubts about your reliability.[92]

Nunn was given the opportunity to appeal to the Three Advisers, which upheld his exclusion. Correspondence between the Chief Secretary to the Treasury and the Prime Minister about this case on 21 August 1962 also revealed, however, that following a decision of the Three Advisers, the trade union official had a right of further appeal to the Cabinet Secretary (in his capacity as Head of the Civil Service), before whom oral representations could be made. Mr Nunn had not yet done this, though in view of the fact that the Three Advisers had spent 'two whole days on his case', it was thought by the Chief Secretary that 'nothing he can now say

88 Much of what follows is drawn from correspondence in a slim file TNA, PREM 11/5087 ('Radcliffe Committee: Recommendation that Departments Should Have Right to Exclude Officials Whom They Believe to be Communists from Negotiations between Management and Trade Unions; Discussions on Cases; Part 3').

89 S. Dorril, 'Gone but not Forgotten—Stanley Mayne' (1990) 19 *Lobster Magazine*.

90 C. Pincher, *Inside Story: A Documentary of the Pursuit of Power* (London, 1978), p. 335.

91 ibid. Also, C. Pincher, *Dangerous to Know—A Life* (London, 2014), pp. 41–2.

92 TNA, PREM 11/5087 (J. A. Boyd-Carpenter (Chief Secretary to the Treasury), 'Officers of Civil Service Staff Associations with Communist Sympathies', 21 August 1962), on which the following account draws.

is likely to prevent a final decision against him'. In providing these details to the Prime Minister, Boyd-Carpenter pointed out that as a result Mr Nunn would be forbidden access to the Cabinet Office, the Ministry of Defence, the three service departments, parts of the Ministry of Aviation, the Foreign Office, and the Atomic Energy Authority.

It was not only physical access that was banned; Nunn was also 'barred from negotiations, both in person and by correspondence, with those Departments on matters concerning their staff'. He was also 'barred from central negotiations with the Treasury on the pay, etc of several classes of staff not exclusively employed by the above departments but a substantial proportion of whose members are employed in them'. These classes were thought to number some 50,000 people and to include all the major classes represented by the union. If that was not enough, Nunn was also to be warned that the Treasury reserved the right to exclude him from other central negotiations 'as they may from time to time designate', and that other departments 'may refuse him access to some of their premises and may exclude him from some negotiations'. According to the Chief Secretary, this was not only 'the first case to be settled', but also 'the salient one', it being candidly admitted that Nunn's usefulness as General Secretary would be 'so impaired that he may well lose his job', which seems to have been the intended outcome.

Not only was Nunn a very prominent figure in the civil service trade unions and the General Secretary of one of the most important unions, but he was a leading member of the Staff Side of the Civil Service National Whitley Council, and well known in trade union circles outside the civil service. It was also pointed out that:

> Quite a large number of civil servants will have to be told that Mr Nunn is to be refused access; the instruction will be marked 'Confidential' and will not contain the reason; but those receiving it will not be slow to put two and two together.

There were also concerns that other members of the Institution's Executive Committee would have to know, leading to more pressure for Nunn's dismissal. In the end, Mr Nunn in fact asked to be relieved of his post, while denying that he was a Communist.[93]

Richard Nunn was the first but not the last trade unionist to be purged, with a number of union officers being challenged, details of individual cases being sent to the Prime Minister by ministers as if they were schoolboys seeking approval.[94]

[93] Dorril (n 89).

[94] In addition to the cases below, another that stands out is the case of J. E. Morrish of the Civil Service Union, the subject of a letter from John Profumo (Secretary of State for War) to Macmillan, 13 November 1962: TNA, PREM 11/5087.

The effect of the new procedures was that by 2 May 1963 (just under a year from its introduction) seven officials from four different trade unions—the Institution of Professional Civil Servants, the Society of Technical Civil Servants, the CSCA, and the Civil Service Union—had their credentials withdrawn on security grounds.[95] Not only that, but according to a pamphlet produced by the NCCL shortly thereafter, five of the seven were required to leave trade union work after having been 'named', and only one of the seven was a member of the Communist Party, the other six accusations being of the 'vague "association" type'. The seven presumably included Nunn.

The fact that only seven people were identified in this way seems a rather thin return for the rather exaggerated claims of Radcliffe, and falls short of the numbers predicted by Henry Brooke in his memorandum to the Official Committee on Security when he said that:

> There are some fifteen to twenty full-time Union officials (representing most of the major unions) against whom the Security Service could— and would be willing—to produce evidence which they believe would satisfy the Three Advisers that a charge of communist sympathies or association was valid.[96]

But it is to be recalled that it was not proposed to ban all Communist officials, but only to ban Communist officials from secret establishments. The problem that the Nunn case revealed, however, is that this could have the effect of decapitating the trade union, as the many duties of the most senior officials might well require them to have some responsibility for staff employed in these establishments. It would cause some officials to lose their jobs as a result.[97] Finally, just as the Nunn case was notable for revealing the presence of the Prime Minister in the correspondence, other cases were also to reveal that the Prime Minister was not simply kept informed about how this policy was applied in practice. He was also responsible for determining—and expanding—its scope of application.

95 HC Debs, 2 May 1963, col. 138 WA (Reginald Maudling).

96 TNA, CAB 134/2498 ('Memorandum by the Chief Secretary to the Treasury and Paymaster General', 27 March 1962).

97 In correspondence with one of the authors in 1978, the General Secretary of the Civil Service Union intimated that by that stage all applicants for full-time officers' posts with the union were reminded of the Radcliffe recommendations, and asked to say whether they knew of anything likely to impair their effectiveness as a full-time official as a result. It was explained that if a full-time official were to be excluded from security-sensitive departments in accordance with the Radcliffe recommendations, 'this would represent a very serious disability to a union with only eleven full-time officers'. It was further explained that 'It is repugnant to us to have to enquire into the political affiliations of candidates for full-time officer posts but we cannot allow ourselves to be placed in the position where, having recruited a full-time officer, we find that he is less than fully effective': K. D. Ewing, *The Legal Regulation of Trade Union Political Activities* (Ph.D. thesis, University of Cambridge, 1980, Cambridge University Library), p. 268.

VIII. The Role of the Prime Minister

The Prime Minister thus not only initiated the witch-hunt: he also determined (with some vigour) how borderline cases were to be dealt with, sitting as final Court of Appeal in cases where there was a dispute between ministers and officials. One such case was that of G. H. Jamieson, a CSCA official. In a four-page letter on 4 May 1963, the Chief Secretary (still Boyd-Carpenter) wrote to Macmillan to say that Jamieson was one of the seven officials who had been successfully challenged under the Radcliffe recommendations as a security risk, all seven having been excluded from negotiation with the Defence Department, the Foreign Office, and the Cabinet Office.[98] The question now was whether Jamieson—who, along with his wife, was a 'known Communist'—should be barred from central negotiations about the terms and conditions of 'clerks and typists' in view of the fact that twenty-five per cent of his constituents were in the defence departments.

Although two other officials (Nunn and Cooper) had been barred from central negotiations, as Boyd-Carpenter pointed out, a much greater proportion of their 'constituents' were in the defence departments, while it was necessary for them to mix with the staff and to speak to them about their work. In the case of Jamieson, in contrast, the work of the clerks he represented was much the same, whether they filed secret or non-secret papers, and he did not need to talk directly to people in the defence departments 'because this was the responsibility of another one of the Association's officials'. As we have seen, however, ministers had decided that the Radcliffe exclusion rule should apply as widely as possible 'to limit the usefulness of these officials and to encourage their Associations to get rid of them'. The issue raised by this case was whether the exclusion of Jamieson would go beyond what was anticipated by ministers.

One of the Chief Secretary's concerns was that the exclusion of Jamieson would cause trouble with the trade unions, which so far had generally gone along with the Radcliffe recommendations. Some of the unions had also accepted the recommendations, including Jamieson's own union, which was now taking steps to remove him, Boyd-Carpenter expressing concern that any peremptory action by the government might backfire by leading the union to protect rather than remove the hapless Jamieson, risking the swinging of sympathy in his direction 'in the belief that he was being made the victim of a witch hunt'. But although it was thus tempting to do nothing and wait for the matter to be resolved by Jamieson's dismissal by the union, the Chief Secretary thought this to be 'unwise', and that a decision should be taken immediately on Jamieson's future, just in case the union decided—albeit unexpectedly—to keep him on.

[98] TNA, PREM 11/5087 (J. A. Boyd-Carpenter (Chief Secretary to the Treasury), 'G. H. Jamieson—Civil Service Clerical Association', 21 May 1962), on which the following account draws.

There was, however, a difference of opinion, with Treasury officials advising that it would be best not to exclude Jamieson from the national negotiations because of the effect such a decision would have on relations with the national staff side. The minister's view was that 'on balance the risk of allowing a known Communist to represent substantial numbers of staff in the Defence departments is too great and outweighs the strong likelihood of trouble with the Staff side'. But in view of the fact that this was a difficult and closely balanced case, Boyd-Carpenter asked the Prime Minister to consider it personally. In making this decision, the Prime Minister was supported by a short note on the file from an unidentified source, who offered the advice that 'in the present climate', it would be right to be 'tough' in security cases and not to give the individual the benefit of the doubt, and right to agree with the Chief Secretary and not the Treasury officials, advice apparently well received.

The same weakness masquerading as 'toughness' was to be seen in the casual extension to the official of a non-civil service union. On 5 February 1964, the Lord President of the Council (Quintin Hogg) wrote to the Prime Minister (by now Sir Alec Douglas-Home) about a security case he was dealing with.[99] The case concerned the Reading District Officer of the AEU, who had been 'for some years' responsible for negotiations with management at the Atomic Weapons Research Establishment at Aldermaston.[100] Referred to in the correspondence simply as Farrelly, the latter was said to have been a 'declared Communist'. According to Hogg, there was an anomaly in the Radcliffe recommendations which applied only to the civil service trade unions and did not extend also to the 'field of industrial trade unions'. As a result, he agreed with colleagues:

> A policy whereby any Communist officer of an industrial union who had dealings with a secret establishment and whose functions gave rise to a real risk that he might acquire secret information should be told that he would not be accepted in negotiations or allowed entry into the establishment.

Farrelly was duly informed, provoking the union at both branch and executive levels to protest, leading to a deputation from the Executive being received by Hogg to convey strong objections, in the light of which the latter undertook a full reassessment of the decision. But having done so, the Lord President refused to change his mind, but thought it wise to consult the Prime Minister before writing formally to the union. Sir Alec, however, was not so sure—footed as his predecessor,

[99] TNA, PREM 11/5087 (Quintin Hogg (Lord President of the Council) to Douglas-Home, 5 February 1964), on which the following account draws.

[100] The officer in question had been a target from the start, and for this reason was the subject of consideration by the Official Committee on Security of how the purge could be extended to non-civil service unions: TNA, CAB 134/2498 ('Communist Officers of Industrial Unions', Memorandum by the Chairman of the Official Committee on Security, 19 July 1963).

with his private secretary (Sir Timothy Bligh) writing to the Permanent Secretary to the Treasury (Sir Laurence Helsby) to convey the content of some marginal notes made by the Prime Minister on Quintin Hogg's letter, asking questions about what Farrelly would do in negotiations or how he could be a security risk in being present at them. The message was not sent or copied to Hogg, as the matter was thought to deal with 'a point of Civil Service policy', on which the Prime Minister 'should be advised' by Sir Laurence.[101]

The reply to Sir Timothy from Sir Laurence was most revealing, disclosing that the 'policy' in this type of case had been considered by both the Official Committee on Security (which Sir Laurence chaired) and the Ministerial Committee on Security.[102] Moreover, the problem now under consideration had been the subject of 'informal' consultation with George Woodcock, the General Secretary of the TUC, which had shown that while the formal extension of the Radcliffe policy to industrial unions would have been strongly opposed and would now be strongly resisted, 'it would not be thought unreasonable to deal with individual cases on their merits', adding that 'we might hope to do so without raising general controversy'. Sir Laurence added:

> It was, therefore, agreed that there should be no announcement of a new policy towards communist officials of industrial unions, but that action should be taken on a strictly practical basis to exclude communist officials whose negotiating position did in fact give a right of access to sensitive areas. Each case was to be considered on its merits.[103]

In the case of Farrelly, the negotiations were said by Helsby to be of such a nature that it was necessary either to make a site visit or for discussion to take place that would reveal details about the layout and method of operation of the site. In these circumstances, it was said that Farrelly could not play his part as a negotiator 'without risk to security', with the result that it would be right for the minister to confirm his decision to exclude Farrelly, while making it clear that this was an 'individual decision and not an example of the operation of a general policy'. Bligh duly wrote to the office of the Lord President of the Council (and to Helsby) to notify him that the Prime Minister agreed with the decision to exclude Farrelly,[104] though the personal and confidential letter from Hogg to John Boyd of the AEU

[101] TNA, PREM 11/5087 (T. J. Bligh to Sir Laurence Helsby, 7 February 1964).
[102] For a full consideration of the matter by the Ministerial Committee on Security leading to similar conclusions, see TNA, CAB 134/2498 ('Communist Officers of Industrial Unions', Memorandum by the Chairman of the Official Committee on Security, 19 July 1963).
[103] TNA, PREM 11/5087 (Sir Laurence Helsby to Sir Timothy Bligh, 10 February 1964, 'Communist Officers on Industrial Unions' [sic.]).
[104] TNA, PREM 11/5087 (T. J. Bligh to C. Herzig, Office of the Lord President of the Council, 18 February 1964, and T. J. Bligh to Sir Laurence Helsby, 18 February 1964).

perhaps exaggerates the extent to which the matter had been re-assessed in the light of the AEU's concerns:

> As I told you, I had considered this case very fully before reluctantly coming to the, to me at least, distasteful decision contained in the letter of 15th November to Mr Farrelly. Nonetheless, as I promised, I asked for a full reassessment of this case, and I have gone into it with great care in the light of your representations. I am sorry to say that I can find no reason to go back on my original decision that Mr Farrelly should be barred from all negotiations with the managements of Aldermaston and Burghfield.
>
> I have considered particularly your point that the negotiations for which Mr Farrelly had been responsible were of such limited scope that they could not involve any security considerations. I have enquired closely into the nature of matters that are settled by local negotiations and it is not possible to guarantee that, over an extended period, information of security importance will not become known to the negotiators concerned.[105]

IX. Radcliffe Assessed

So only seven officials were identified in the first round of the trade union purge, which tends to confirm the exaggerated nature of the problem identified by Radcliffe. The hastily composed four paragraphs of his report dealing with this matter were a mess, the Committee's anxiety about Communist penetration being directly contradicted by a judgement earlier in the report that 'the central threat' to security 'lies further back than the British Communist Party',[106] not to mention the comment in the paragraph where the anxiety was expressed that 'there is no evidence that the Communists have made any exceptional effort to gain control of these unions'.[107] Nor was there any evidence that 'Communist union officers, whether serving on a paid or unpaid basis, have been detected in any form of espionage'.[108] Even more bizarre, given that 'there is no evidence that the Communists have made any exceptional effort to gain control of these unions', was the Committee's counterclaim (in the same paragraph) that it regarded 'this presumably deliberate massing of Communist effort in these unions', to be 'most dangerous to security, however one defines it'.[109]

105 TNA, PREM 11/5087 (Quintin Hogg to John Boyd, 19 February 1964).

106 Security Procedures in the Public Service (n 79), para. 5. As the Committee acknowledged in repeating evidence previously given to the Privy Councillors, it was 'not the policy of the party . . . to give its members, open or secret, any encouragement to undertake espionage' (para. 3).

107 ibid., para. 33.

108 ibid.

109 ibid.

But why would this lack of evidence be surprising? As we have seen, the TUC had for many years taken active steps to block Communist participation in the trade unions, while several unions—which may have been Communist dominated in the past—had undergone bitter internal political struggles as a result of which Communist Party influence was in decline—at least at official level. In some cases, indeed, Communists were now ineligible to hold office in the trade union in question.[110] It is disappointing, nevertheless, that the official trade union structures co-operative in both the development of the Radcliffe exclusion policy and its extension and implementation. As pointed out by Boyd-Carpenter in Part VII above, the staff side trade unions generally accepted Radcliffe, while the official historian of the largest union—the once Communist-dominated CSCA—suggests that it could not implement the policy of Communist exclusion quickly enough.

Having been identified under the Radcliffe policy, two CSCA officials were thus dismissed, the CSCA refusing to transfer them to work that carried no security risk, the view being taken that 'since they could not perform the full range of duties, their continued employment was not in the interests of the Association'.[111] So far as the extension of the policy to the so-called industrial unions is concerned, here we find that the TUC General Secretary was prepared to turn a blind eye to the extension of the policy on a case-by-case basis,[112] while the *initial* decision by Quintin Hogg to exclude Farrelly in implementation of that policy was taken *after* George Woodcock (TUC General Secretary) and Sir Leslie Carron (President of the AEU) had both been informed. According to Hogg in his letter to Macmillan referred to in Part VIII above, 'neither raised objections to the matter being allowed to take its course'.

But whatever the failings of trade union leaders, this was above all perhaps not Lord Radcliffe's finest hour. Apart from the unconvincing evidence on which his recommendations for a purge of the trade unions was based, there was also a notable lack of evidence provided to justify the comparative judgement made by Radcliffe, namely that 'Communist representation among Civil Service union officials is disproportionately high'.[113] How would he have known, given that his terms of reference did not extend to trade unions generally? To make this judgement, Radcliffe would presumably have been supplied with data about the non-civil-service trade unions, which itself presumes a worrying level of surveillance of trade unions, of which almost all traces have been forensically wiped from the National Archives.

[110] The classic struggle was in the TGWU, on which see Goldstein (n 7). But see also Wigham (n 14), for the CPSA; and F. Bealey, *The Post Office Engineering Union—The History of the Post Office Engineers 1870–1970* (London, 1976). See also *Cohen v National Union of Tailors and Garment Workers, The Times*, 13 January 1962—one of several cases in which the plaintiff challenged his ineligibility for office because of Communist activities.

[111] Wigham (n 14), p. 113. See also D. G. T. Williams, *Not in the Public Interest—The Problem of Security in Democracy* (London, 1965), p. 178.

[112] See also TNA, CAB 134/2498 ('Communist Officers of Industrial Unions', Memorandum by the Chairman of the Official Committee on Security, 19 July 1963, para. 4).

[113] Security Procedures in the Public Service (n 79), para. 36.

If it was not based on evidence, it was pure speculation, which served simply to fuel smears about civil service trade unions and their leaders.

The other point to emerge from the foregoing is the total inadequacy of the procedures before the Three Advisers, notwithstanding its implications not only for the livelihoods of the individuals involved, but also for the autonomy of the organizations to which they belonged. (So far as the latter point was concerned, there was absolutely no discussion anywhere—even amongst the complicit trade unionists—about the nation's obligations under ILO Convention 87, even though this had recently been the subject of Cabinet engagement in another context.)[114] As Quintin Hogg rightly pointed out in his letter to Douglas-Home in the Farrelly case, the right to appeal to the Three Advisers applied only to the officials of civil service unions, but did not apply to the officials of the so-called industrial unions.[115] And as the case of Cyril Cooper revealed, the procedure was in any event a pointless formality, permitting the minister to do what he or she wanted anyway, even if this meant rejecting the Three Advisers' advice.

Cooper was General Secretary of the Society of Technical Civil Servants, accused of having 'extensive personal contacts with members of Iron Curtain diplomatic missions'. It has otherwise been claimed that he was purged because he had been a member of the Communist Party 'many years ago'.[116] Peter C[arrington]—then First Lord of the Admiralty—wrote to say that Cyril Cooper had been excluded from further negotiations in the Admiralty, the Ministry of Aviation, and the Atomic Energy Authority. In his case, however, the Three Advisers had reached a decision in his favour, only to be overruled by the minister in consultation with two other ministers. The Three Advisers were in turn consulted by the Admiralty, and agreed that the case was difficult and were said not to be surprised that ministers had decided the balance fell the other way.

Carrington was taking the precaution of informing the Prime Minister in case there should be any difficulties from being more severe than the Three Advisers, had been pointing out that there were precedents for overruling them, while 'the nature of their advice in any case remains strictly secret'. There was thus no reason to suppose that difficulty was likely to arise. Any nervousness on the part of Carrington was no doubt assuaged by the assurance from Macmillan scribbled in red ink on

114 A memorandum to the Cabinet in July 1961 by the then Minister of Labour expressed a desire to strengthen the rights of members 'to ensure that union affairs are run in accordance with the rules'. According to the minister, 'It would accord with our acceptance of the right of trade unions to run their own affairs if we could rely on them to put their own house in order.' This acceptance was to be found in ILO Convention 87, the details of arts 2 and 3 he thought fit to rehearse for the benefit of his colleagues: TNA, CAB 129/105/45 (Minister of Labour, 'Trade Union Elections', 11 July 1961).

115 A deliberate decision was made not to extend the procedure to people like Farrelly: for a full consideration of the matter by the Ministerial Committee on Security leading to similar conclusions, see TNA, CAB 134/2498 ('Communist Officers of Industrial Unions', Memorandum by the Chairman of the Official Committee on Security, 19 July 1963).

116 TNA, PREM 11/5087 (Letter from Lord Carrington (First Lord of the Admiralty) to Macmillan, 1 February 1963).

the bottom of the letter to the effect that 'you have done right'. After having thus been named and barred from certain departments, Mr Cooper was nevertheless retained in his position as General Secretary of the Society of Technical Civil Servants, at which point the Treasury was added to the list of departments barred to him, followed two months later by the Ministry of Public Buildings and Works. For some, this would look very much like the government deciding who was permitted to be a trade union officer.[117]

Yet for all that, we can hardly be surprised that the temper of the time would dictate some form of intervention by both Radcliffe and the government, irrational though it may have been. It was not helpful that shortly after the Radcliffe Committee had been appointed, the High Court exposed what has been represented as Communist Party ballot rigging in the ETU as a way of ensuring Communist domination of the union.[118] Although not referred to in the four-paragraph summary of the trade union chapter of the unpublished report, it is clear from the full report that the events surrounding this case had been in the minds of the Radcliffe Committee. The events had clearly been in the minds of the government, which had been wrestling for some time with how best to intervene to address the question of Communist dominance in the ETU, as well as how to deal with the wider question of trade union elections.[119] While no ETU officials were subsequently purged by the government,[120] it will not have escaped Radcliffe's attention that the union had a presence in secret establishments.[121]

X. Conclusion

There is no question that in purging the civil service of Communist trade union officials, the government was seeking also to purge the civil service trade unions of officials who were members of the Communist Party. It could be presented as a more proportionate way of dealing with the mischief which had led initially to the proposals to ban trade unions in the secret establishments and to introduce house

[117] If so, it would breach ILO Convention 87, which provides that 'Workers' and employers' organisations shall have the right to draw up their constitutions and rules, to elect their representatives in full freedom, to organise their administration and activities and to formulate their programmes' (art. 3).

[118] *Byrne v Foulkes*, *The Times*, 29 June 1961. For a brief account, see C. Grunfeld, *Modern Trade Union Law* (London, 1966), pp. 154–7. According to Grunfeld, the case was never fully reported, 'perhaps because it was thought, not entirely correctly, to involve questions of fact only' (p. 154, n 22).

[119] See TNA, CAB 129/90 (Electrical Trades' Union, Memorandum by the Minister of Labour, 17 December 1957). In the immediate aftermath of the decision, the Minister of Labour (John Hare) informed the Cabinet that it had 'shown that the courts could deal effectively with abuses in the conduct of union elections', but that because of the length and cost of legal proceedings, 'failing some means of reform, malpractices would continue': TNA, CAB 128/25/40 (Cabinet Conclusions, 13 July 1961).

[120] There was probably no need to, in light of the ETU rule change following *Byrne v Foulkes* (n 118), which banned Communists from holding office in the union. See *Courtney v ETU*, 30 March 1965.

[121] Committee on Security Procedures in the Public Service—Communist Officials in Civil Service Trade Unions (n 57).

unions (namely the fear that trade union members would pass on information to trade union officials). Indeed, it was the perfect answer to the objections of officials, the only other option being to ban all civil servants from any trade union that had officials who were members of the Communist Party. It was also a more proportionate response than that adopted in the USA, where there was both a total ban on Communist Party members being employed in the civil service *and* a total ban on Communist Party members being employed as officials of *all* labour unions.[122] Even in the civil service unions, officials were not banned from membership of the Communist Party if other work could be found for them by their respective unions.

The idea of a trade union ban at secret establishments did not disappear completely and was revived and executed in 1984 when a house union was imposed on GCHQ. The reason for doing so was not, however, related to Communist Party 'subversion', there being no evidence since 1955 that trade unionists at GCHQ had breached security by providing information to a trade union official, and no evidence that a trade union official had ever compromised national security. The reason for the ban was rather the prevalence of trade union action by trade union members, with the opportunity to do something about it provided when the existence of GCHQ was finally acknowledged publicly following the trial of Geoffrey Prime for breach of the Official Secrets Act 1911.[123] The implementation of the ban gave rise to the furious row that had been predicted some thirty or so years earlier,[124] though it also brought centre-stage issues that had been absent from the advice given by officials in 1955 and again in 1961, namely obligations arising under ILO Convention 87, which would have been known to officials in 1955 and 1961.[125]

The ban on trade union officials who were also members or associates of the Communist Party was perhaps a meagre return for a government that appeared to have strongly committed anti-Communists at its highest level, with Macmillan willing to provide government funds for clandestine Communist-monitoring organizations. It was all the more meagre for the fact that the government had been handed a gift by the outcome of the ETU trial, in which—rightly or wrongly—the High Court was said to have exposed what it claimed to be ballot rigging in union elections. But meagre or not, the purge of trade union officials—to say nothing of

[122] See *American Communications Association v Douds*, 339 US 382 (1950).

[123] *R v Prime* (1983) 5 Cr App R(S) 127. See TNA, CAB 128/78/3 (Cabinet Conclusions, 26 January 1984). It is not known if the Cabinet was provided with a full account of the reasons for the ban, though it would not be the first time that controversial information had been withheld. The Cabinet was told formally on the day after a parliamentary statement: HC Debs, 25 January 1984, col. 917.

[124] As Sir Vincent Tewson said, the unions would 'certainly raise a storm of protest', Report of the Security Conference of Privy Councillors (n 21). See p. 351 above.

[125] For a full account of which, see K. D. Ewing, *Britain and the ILO* (2nd edn, London, 1994). See also W. B. Creighton, 'The ILO and Freedom of Association in the UK', in K. D. Ewing, C. A. Gearty, and B. A. Hepple (eds), *Human Rights and Labour Law—Essays for Paul O'Higgins* (London, 1994), ch. 1.

the high-handed manner in which it was done—was a serious violation of an important principle (freedom of association), which seemed to be lost not only on Lord Radcliffe (who as a judge should have known better) and the government (from whom it was to be expected), but also on some senior trade unionists (about whom nothing more needs to be said). As such, the affair raises wider questions about the role of judges during the Cold War, matters explored more fully in the chapters that follow.

For the moment it is enough to say that here we have a situation of abject judicial failure: a significant violation of civil liberties keenly felt by some, by a judge who was—as we will see in Chapter 13—prepared to turn the security screw much tighter than was acceptable even to a Conservative government.[126] His proposals were made (i) on the basis of flimsy evidence; (ii) without any convincing explanation of why the purge was required (all the more necessary in view of the Radcliffe Committee's revised security assessment); and (iii) without ensuring adequate safeguards against abuse by those who would be included in the proposed purge. Radcliffe thus stands condemned not only for a 'pusillanimous report',[127] but also for failing to uphold the very qualities that a rigorous judge-led inquiry would be expected to display. The number of trade unionists purged speaks volumes about the ridiculous and exaggerated nature of Radcliffe's claims.

[126] TNA, CAB/128/36 (Cabinet Conclusions, 20 March 1962).
[127] E. P. Thompson, *Writing by Candlelight* (London, 1980), p. 157.

13
The Ubiquitous Lord Radcliffe

I. Introduction

As we saw in Chapter 1, contemporary constitutional law was based on ideas about the Rule of Law, and was understood to mean that the judges played a pivotal role *in restraining the executive* and the protection of political freedom.[1] Yet the judges are notable absentees from the story so far. They have had a part, but only a very minor one. Given the far-reaching and wide-ranging nature of MI5's mandate and powers so far encountered in the preceding pages, this limited role for the judges may strike some as a remarkable omission on our part. Apart from Lord Radcliffe, the most notable up to now is the work of Sir Norman Birkett (as he then was) reviewing the practice of telephone tapping and mail interception.[2] The largely uncritical work of Sir Norman is all the more remarkable for the fact that much of the activity he was reviewing was done without any clear legal authority, and by an agency of the State with an opaque legal base, with little coverage in the constitutional law texts of the time.[3] This fleeting appearance of Sir Norman nevertheless provides a clue to the judicial role during the Cold War.

Those looking for the judge as defender of liberty will look in vain, for reasons that may become clearer as this and Chapter 14 unfold. Here we deal with the judge as government servant, called upon to perform various acts *on behalf of the executive*, notably in the conduct of inquiries or reviews on matters of great political controversy and public concern. By using judges in this way, the government could doubtless say that it was calling on highly skilled individuals to cast an independent, dispassionate, and clinical eye over the matter at hand. But by using judges in this way, there is also a risk that the judicial currency is devalued, reinforcing the view that judges are at best 'pillars of the establishment', and at worst 'instruments of the State'. What this chapter tends to reveal is that there was a unity

[1] See E. C. S. Wade and G. G. Phillips, *Constitutional Law* (6th edn, London, 1960), Part III.
[2] Cmnd 283, 1957. See pp. 112–19 above.
[3] Wade and Phillips (n 1), ch. 40. The latter was unusual in dealing with 'Special Security Measures' (the purge and PV), but not unusual in failing to mention MI5. It also repeats the old trope as justification for these measures that 'a Communist Party member is commonly believed to be under an obligation to the Party to achieve the establishment of a Communist regime, if necessary by force' (p. 351). The first scholarly account by a legal academic appears to be D. G. T. Williams, *Not in the Public Interest—The Problem of Security in Democracy* (London, 1965).

MI5, the Cold War, and the Rule of Law. K. D. Ewing, Joan Mahoney, and Andrew Moretta, Oxford University Press (2020). © K. D. Ewing, Joan Mahoney, and Andrew Moretta. DOI: 10.1093/oso/9780198818625.001.0001

of interest and unity of purpose between executive and judiciary, at least during the 1950s and 1960s, the latter contributing to the work of government, and sharing essential assumptions that informed that work. If not 'more executive-minded than the executive', some judges at least were to show themselves as being 'as executive-minded as the executive'.[4]

So if this book is a study of the mandate, powers, and accountability, this chapter is an account of how the judges were incorporated into the process of government. In other words, of how senior judges were used as instruments of the government, rather than as defenders of political freedom. There was no independent judicial voice speaking for legality or liberty. This is despite the fact that being brought into the process of government and being called upon to exercise a unique governmental role, senior judges had a unique opportunity to ensure that the Rule of Law was promoted and liberty protected. In this and the next chapter, we also give an account of the role of the judges when performing their traditional role in the prosecution of offenders, in which—as in *Chandler v DPP*[5]—they are called upon to defend the individual against the State. We would not be giving away too much at this stage if we were to say that litigation (in the form of prosecution) was (like legislation) simply a means by which the administration governed to secure certain political ends, in which (like legislation) the government encountered few serious institutional restraints.

In addressing these questions, the main focus of this chapter, however, is the work of Lord Radcliffe, a member of the Appellate Committee of the House of Lords and evidently a man greatly trusted by government. Here we examine in more detail two important reports already encountered, the first being the Committee on Security Procedures in the Public Service, a censored version of which was published in April 1962, and the second being the detailed report of a Tribunal of Inquiry Appointed to Inquire into the Vassall Case, which was published in April 1963.[6] In Chapter 14, we consider Lord Denning's Report into the Profumo affair,[7] which is to be seen as the much better known companion to the Radcliffe Reports, though one suffering from many of the same defects as the latter. Nevertheless, Lord Denning's Report completed what had been an unprecedented and intense judicial scrutiny of State security activity, these three reports setting in train a process of safe, secure, and trusted supervision that continues to this day. It was safe, secure, and trusted because it accepted MI5's premisses and showed little concern for the values that would normally be associated with the Rule of Law.

[4] *Liversidge v Anderson* [1942] AC 206.

[5] [1964] AC 763.

[6] See Report on Security Procedures in the Public Service (Chair: Lord Radcliffe), Cmnd, 1681, 1962; and Report of the Tribunal of Inquiry Appointed to Inquire into the Vassall Case and Related Matters (Chairman: Viscount Radcliffe), Cmnd 2009, 1963 respectively.

[7] Lord Denning's Report, Cmnd 2152, 1963.

II. Context: Spy Scandals

In the early 1960s, the British State was again enveloped by a crisis of security, with one spy scandal following another: George Blake, the Portland Spy Ring, and John Vassall, all found guilty of spying for the Soviet Union and all convicted of various espionage-related offences. A sordid period in British history was topped off by the Profumo affair in 1963, which led to the resignation of the Secretary of State for War, and eventually the Prime Minister. But although devastating in their impact for several reasons, these were simply the latest in a long line of Cold War espionage scandals, with spies already exposed in this country having included Alan Nunn May and Klaus Fuchs, as well as Guy Burgess, Donald Maclean, and Kim Philby, most of these latter cases having been discussed in previous chapters. All point to inadequacy on the part of the Security Service, still preoccupied with the Communist Party, which does not appear to have had a role to play in any of these episodes.

George Blake was the most prominent of the second wave of spies unmasked in the period under review. An MI6 officer who had been recruited by the Soviet Union in the early 1950s, it was reported that for 'the next nine years, wherever he was posted for MI6—Vienna, Berlin, Milan, Beirut—[Blake] met his KGB case officer every three weeks to pass over information'.[8] His cover was blown by the defection in 1960 of a Polish intelligence officer, and he was prosecuted under the Official Secrets Act 1911, despite a request from a deeply embarrassed Prime Minister 'that Blake's treachery should be kept quiet and he be offered immunity from prosecution in return for a full confession'.[9] But despite fears that the affair could bring down the government, the prosecution took place at the insistence of the Head of MI6, partly on the ground that Blake's treachery had been more serious than that of 'Kim' Philby. Indeed, even as late as 2006 newspapers were writing about the damage done by Blake as being 'still classified'.[10]

Blake's trial under the 1911 Act on five counts relating to offences committed between 1951 and 1959 was held *in camera*. He pleaded guilty, and was sentenced to fourteen years on each count, the first three to run concurrently, and the last two to run consecutively, the total sentence being an extraordinary forty-two years.[11] In passing sentence, Lord Chief Justice Parker expressed the view that Blake's case was one of 'the worst that can be envisaged other than in

[8] *Independent*, 30 September 2006.

[9] ibid.

[10] ibid.

[11] ibid. Blake escaped in 1966, with the help of ex-prisoners. See M. Randle and P. Pottle, *The Blake Escape: How We Freed George Blake and Why We Did It* (London, 1989). By a remarkable coincidence, Randle and Pottle were two of the defendants in the *Chandler* case discussed below. See K. D. Ewing, 'The Cold War, Civil Liberties and the House of Lords', in T. Campbell, K. D. Ewing, and A. Tomkins (eds), *The Legal Protection of Human Rights—Sceptical Essays* (Oxford, 2011), ch. 8.

time of war', which in many countries would have 'carried the death penalty'.[12] The sentence was upheld on appeal, as having a threefold purpose: 'It was intended to be punitive, it was designed and calculated to deter others, and it was meant to be a safeguard to this country.'[13] Blake had challenged the sentence as being excessive and that to pass consecutive sentences was to evade the limit of fourteen years laid down in the Act. But according to Mr Justice Hilbery in the Court of Criminal Appeal:

> there is no settled principle that a judge may not pass consecutive sentences in respect of a number of offences for any one of which the maximum sentence is 14 years where each offence charged in each count is separate and distinct.[14]

Also revealed by a defector was the so-called Portland Spy Ring, a team of two British civil servants—Henry Houghton and Ethel Gee—employed at the Underwater Weapons Establishment at Portland in Dorset; a Russian agent (Konon Molody) living illegally on a Canadian passport in the United Kingdom (that is without diplomatic immunity) under the pseudonym Gordon Lonsdale; and a couple known initially as Peter and Helen Kroger, but who were revealed subsequently to be Morris and Lona Cohen, wanted by the FBI in the United States on espionage charges.[15] All five were involved in a plot to sell secrets about HMS Dreadnought—Britain's first nuclear submarine—to the Soviet Union, as well as 'the newly-developed Asdic sonar system designed to detect and track Soviet submarines'.[16] They all pleaded not guilty to the charges that between 14 April 1960 and 7 January 1961 they conspired to breach the Official Secrets Act 1911.

Leading the case against them was the Attorney General, Sir Reginald Manningham-Buller, who claimed that the two civil servants were passing on secrets to Lonsdale, who in turn took the information to the Krogers' house in Ruislip, Middlesex, where a radio transmitter was found with a capability of transmitting messages to the Soviet Union. A search of the Krogers' house also gathered a large haul of other material associated with espionage, as well as large sums of money, leading Manningham-Buller to claim that this was the 'the hub of a spy ring and, in view of the money found there, the bank of a spy ring'.[17] The jury found all five guilty, and on 22 March 1961 Lord Parker (the Lord Chief Justice) jailed Lonsdale for twenty-five years, the Krogers for twenty years, and Houghton and

[12] *The Times*, 4 May 1961. For the government's immediate response, see HC Debs, 4 May 1961, col. 1609.

[13] *R v Blake* [1962] 2 QB 377.

[14] On Mr Justice Hilbery, see *Tribune*, 3 December 1937.

[15] For a good account, see V. Dowd, 'The Spies in a Suburban Bungalow', *BBC News*, 14 November 2014.

[16] *Daily Telegraph*, 22 January 2008 (Obituary of Charles Elwell, MI5 officer said to have been responsible for breaking the Portland Spy Ring).

[17] *The Times*, 14 March 1961.

Gee for fifteen years each.[18] Neither Lonsdale nor the Krogers served their full sentences, being exchanged for British citizens held in the Soviet Union.

The Portland case was followed almost immediately by the arrest of John Vassall, a civil servant blackmailed to provide information to the Soviet Union. The background to the Vassall case is considered at pages 295–299 above and need not be repeated here. On 22 October 1962, he too was convicted under the Official Secrets Act 1911 and jailed for eighteen years by the Lord Chief Justice (Parker). What is notable about this case, however, is the way in which government ministers were drawn into the affair, albeit subsequently to be fully exonerated by the Radcliffe Tribunal of Inquiry,[19] also considered in Chapter 10, and more fully in the following pages of this chapter.[20] Indeed one minister—Thomas Galbraith—felt compelled to resign as Under-Secretary of State in the Scottish Office on 8 November 1962 as a result of 'comments in various quarters as to the nature of his relationship with Vassall', with questions having been raised 'as to the propriety of that relationship in general and, more particularly, as to his own responsibility for making possible some of Vassall's traitorous activities or failing to detect in him an object of suspicion'.[21] Galbraith had been Civil Lord of the Admiralty from 1957 to 1959, and Vassall had been working in the minister's private office while some of the espionage activities were taking place.

Lord Carrington was the other minister to be caught in the firing line as rumour surrounding Vassall was rife. Carrington had been First Lord of the Admiralty since 1959 and the allegations against him were different from those against Galbraith. It had been alleged after the Portland case that the presence of another spy had been known by the First Lord and the Service Chiefs for some eighteen months before Vassall was exposed.[22] These claims made by the *Daily Express* were, however, subsequently withdrawn unreservedly, as was the accompanying allegation that Carrington had been 'reprimanded by the Prime Minister for failing to disclose the existence of that spy'.[23] Indeed, it was one of the terms of reference of the subsequent Radcliffe Tribunal of Inquiry that it should investigate the particular allegation that the existence of a spy in the Admiralty had been known by the First Lord and the Service Chiefs for eighteen months. This was revealed to have been completely without foundation. In fact, Vassall's detection had nothing to do with the Portland case, the Admiralty first being told of a spy in its midst by MI5 on 4 April 1962, Vassall arrested, tried, found guilty, and imprisoned shortly thereafter.

[18] *The Times*, 23 March 1961. A full account of the trial is to be found in *The Times*, 14–23 March 1961.

[19] Report of the Committee of Inquiry Appointed to Inquire into the Vassall Case and Related Matters (n 6).

[20] See pp. 295–299; 401–5.

[21] Report of the Committee of Inquiry Appointed to Inquire into the Vassall Case and Related Matters (n 6), para. 213. Mr Galbraith subsequently returned to government, his integrity intact.

[22] ibid., para. 255.

[23] ibid., para. 271.

Anxiety about espionage was to become overpowering early in the following year with the breaking of the Profumo scandal, which we consider more fully in Chapter 14 below. It was not only that John Profumo—Secretary of State for War—had a short relationship with a nineteen-year-old woman (Christine Keeler), who also was friendly with Yevgeny Ivanov, Soviet naval officer and Russian GRU officer. Even more importantly, when this sorry saga began to break in the press in 1963, the forty-eight-year-old Mr Profumo denied in a statement to the House of Commons any improper relationship with Ms Keeler. This was soon revealed to be a lie, leading Mr Profumo later that year to resign from the government and his seat in the House. Although there was no evidence of any betrayal of secrets, the role of Ivanov in this affair raised questions about the competence of the Security Service still engaged in a futile and distracting preoccupation with the CPGB and its associates.

III. Radcliffe as Reviewer

Sleaze: espionage, sexual promiscuity, and corruption: so, step forward Her Majesty's judges. In response to each of the foregoing four scandals a judge was appointed to conduct a review, beginning with the investigation ordered on 29 March 1961 into the circumstances of the Portland case. This reported in June 1961 that the problems were due mainly to lax security procedures at the naval base.[24] Sir Charles Romer conducted the inquiry, having recently retired as a Lord Justice of Appeal, distinguished also as the son of a Law Lord. Before the Romer Inquiry had concluded, however, a second inquiry was appointed under the chairmanship of Lord Radcliffe. The Committee was required by its terms of reference 'to review the security procedures and practices currently followed in the public service and to consider what, if any, changes are required'.[25] This was to be done 'in the light of the recent convictions for offences under the Official Secrets Act', a reference to both the Portland case and the Blake case.

The five members of the Radcliffe Committee included a retired Field Marshal—Sir Gerald Templar—who had worked in military intelligence and with the SOE during the Second World War; a decorated former 'special operations officer'—William

[24] HC Debs, 13 June 1961, col. 211. The report was not published. According to Macmillan in a parliamentary statement, however, the findings:

> fall broadly into three groups. First, the Committee criticises, in general terms, certain defects in the Admiralty organisation for implementing security policy and procedures. Secondly, it criticises certain individuals at Portland for specific shortcomings in maintaining adequate security. Thirdly, it finds that no blame attaches to the .... authorities and that the counter-espionage operations of the Security Service in this case were carried out with efficiency (ibid., col. 211).

[25] Cmnd, 1681, 1962, above.

Deakin—who later became the head of an Oxford college; and Sir David Milne, a retired PUS in the Scottish Office. The key player, however, was almost certainly Lord Radcliffe, who was unlikely to receive any subversive advice from his colleagues. Although the fifth member of the team was Kenneth Younger, the former Labour MP—he too had a background in military intelligence.[26] A fellow of All Souls College, Oxford, Lord Radcliffe had served in the Ministry of Information during the war, becoming its DG in 1941. He was appointed as a Law Lord in 1949, after having played a part in the partition of India in 1947. Like Lord Reid, he was appointed as a Lord of Appeal in Ordinary without having held judicial office, after a career at the Bar that had been punctuated by periods of public service.[27]

The Radcliffe Committee reported to the Prime Minister on 21 November 1961. As pointed out in Chapter 13, the full report was not published, though following the precedent of the Privy Councillors' Conference six years earlier, a shortened version was released in the form of a white paper. So far as the report itself is concerned, this was not declassified (with omissions) until 2018, and here we refer principally to the censored version with references to the report itself as and when required. Beginning with a re-assessment of security concerns, the Committee identified two main threats to national security, the first being the intelligence services of foreign powers, and the second being subversive organizations, the most 'formidable' of which was thought to be the CPGB, 'with its fringe of associated bodies and sympathisers'.[28] Radcliffe was here revisiting and remapping territory previously visited by the Conference of Privy Councillors in 1956,[29] which, with poor judgement, as we have seen, had focused on the latter threat (the Party) rather than the former (foreign powers), in spite of evidence to the contrary staring them in the face.

No doubt informed by an MI5 security assessment, the Privy Counsellors' controversial assessment was thus to change with Radcliffe, which, stating the obvious, announced that the security threat now lay from the intelligence services of the Soviet bloc, which were 'steadily at work' in this country.[30] The activities of the CPGB, in contrast, were not 'of the same order as a threat to security', the Radcliffe

[26] Younger can take some credit for Labour's acceptance of the ECHR. Standing in for the ill-disposed Foreign Secretary, Younger sought Cabinet approval 'to accept at the Committee of Ministers of the Council of Europe the draft Convention on Human Rights': TNA, CAB 128/18 (Cabinet Conclusions, 1 August 1950). Some Cabinet members were very unhappy with the proposal. See p. 239 above. He also chaired a Committee on Privacy, which was sceptical of a legally protected right to privacy. See Cmnd 5012, 1972.

[27] For context and a more sympathetic account of Radcliffe than the one presented here, see N Duxbury, 'Lord Radcliffe Out of Time' [2010] 69 *CLJ* 41.

[28] Report on Security Procedures in the Public Service (n 6), para. 1.

[29] Statement on the Findings of the Conference of Privy Councillors on Security, Cmd 9715, 1956: 'the chief risks are presented by Communists and by other persons who for one reason or another are subject to Communist influence' (para. 4).

[30] Report on Security Procedures in the Public Service (n 6), para 2.

Committee noting that it was not the policy of the Party to encourage its members 'open or secret' to engage in espionage.[31] In any event, the Soviet intelligence services did not necessarily recruit people on ideological grounds: 'fear, pressure, and mercenary motives are as strong as any other'.[32] But although expressly repudiating the assumption that 'the central problem of security is to exclude Communists from State secrets',[33] the Committee nevertheless did nothing to remove the restraints under which members of the CPGB appeared needlessly to labour. Nor did it offer any clues about how to deal with the new threat or whether the existing response was adequate.

Radcliffe was thus irrationally unable to break free from the concerns about Communism, reinforcing these concerns with what he saw as the ambiguity in public policy, treating Communists as subversives, while not banning them from the public service ('provided they are not engaged in secret work') altogether.[34] Although this was an implicit recognition that Communists were not an espionage threat, Radcliffe seemed quite content that in relation to the CPGB 'a considerable effort is made by the Government to keep informed of its activities'.[35] And although the ambiguity might suggest a level of liberal tolerance on the part of the State, we now know that it concealed a menacing discussion within the Committee, with unknown members of the team supporting a total ban on Communist employment in the civil service.[36] As discussed below, this section of the report was deliberately withheld from the public in the published summary. As already discussed in Chapter 10, if Radcliffe thus revealed that the CPGB was still the subject of State surveillance, he also revealed a little more about MI5's methods, without, of course, any reference to its mandate, powers, or accountability.

As already discussed in Chapter 10, in a section on the 'Role of the Security Service', Radcliffe reported that one of MI5's tasks is to deal with 'personnel vetting enquiries from Departments', that is to say, it 'checks individual names against intelligence records'.[37] This is an important acknowledgement that there were 'intelligence records', even if there was no explanation of how they were compiled, where they were stored, how they were used, what safeguards there were for errors, and on what legal base the compilation and sharing of such information was thought to stand, if any. This was followed by a detailed discussion of a wide range of security and intelligence matters, including the classification of documents, personnel security in the public service, issues relating to the foreign service and the armed

[31] ibid., para. 3.
[32] ibid.
[33] ibid., para. 5.
[34] ibid., para. 10.
[35] ibid., para. 10.
[36] See below, p. 385.
[37] Report on Security Procedures in the Public Service (n 6), para. 16.

forces, security in industry (relating to government contractors working on sensitive projects), the protection of documents, and the D Notice procedure.[38] We have already examined the purge and vetting provisions of the report in some detail in Chapters 9 and 10, respectively, and it is unnecessary to repeat here what has already been said.

It is striking nevertheless that at the point in the report where individual liberty rubbed against State security most abrasively, little was done to advance the former at the expense of the latter. Radcliffe admittedly resisted a proposal to alter the terms of reference of the Three Advisers in a way that would 'still more positively tilt the balance in favour of the suspicion'.[39] But given the willingness of departments to evade the Three Advisers by informally purging officials, Radcliffe's recommendation that there should be 'more frequent resort to the purge procedure in marginal cases' would be at best a matter of departmental indulgence incapable of enforcement.[40] If, however, it was largely to be business as usual for the purge, it is true that important changes were to be made to PV, Radcliffe proposing in particular that there should be a right of appeal to someone denied security clearance. But as we saw in Chapter 10, the appeal would be only as far as the department head and not to the Three Advisers, where the reasons were unrelated to Communist Party membership or association, it being proposed also that vetting should increase in frequency.

The main criticism of Radcliffe (already identified above in relation to security procedures in industry, as well as the civil service) was not that he was simply tinkering with formal procedures, so much as that he was largely ineffective in responding to the informal practices that were by then flourishing. That said, Radcliffe tells us more than previous reports, the significance of his revelations overshadowed by the publicity storm created by his own inquiry into the Vassall affair in 1962, and Lord Denning's Report on the Profumo affair in 1963. Nevertheless, in the first Radcliffe Report we find the Security Service being openly discussed, intelligence files openly acknowledged, and some of MI5's methods openly disclosed. All of this in a comprehensive review of security procedures, in which the more controversial information and analysis was censored for publication. The most striking feature of the report, however, is the sense that it was tilting even more aggressively at the same windmills, apparently failing to tailor procedures to the real threat of espionage, which was unfolding even as the white paper was being prepared.

[38] This was an afterthought that had been added to the tasks Radcliffe was asked to examine: ibid., p. iii. For a brief account of the D Notice system, see A. W. Bradley, K. D. Ewing, and C. J. S. Knight, *Constitutional and Administrative Law* (17th edn, Harlow, 2018), ch. 18.

[39] Report on Security Procedures in the Public Service (n 6), para. 58.

[40] ibid., para. 59.

IV. Radcliffe Reviewed

Although dated 21 November 1961, the Radcliffe Report was not considered by the Cabinet until 20 March 1962, though in the meantime it had, of course, been ground through the Ministerial Committee on Security. All senior ministers would thus have been aware of its contents, and it was only after the Committee had finished its work that the Prime Minister brought a memorandum about the report to the Cabinet for the meeting on 20 March 1962. The latter reminded ministers of the reasons why Radcliffe had been appointed in the first place (the Portland and Blake spy cases), while advising them that in conducting his review of security procedures Lord Radcliffe had been given the fullest access to all relevant material, including the unpublished report by Sir Charles Romer.[41] The Cabinet discussion also reveals that the Report was in three parts—the first dealing with security procedures in the public service generally, the second examining the special problems of the Blake case, and the third commenting on the operation of the 'D' Notice system.

It is also recorded that the Ministerial Committee on Security (at which the Prime Minister presided) had already agreed that all the Radcliffe recommendations could be accepted, and that there would be 'advantage in making public a substantial proportion' of the parts of the Report dealing with 'security procedures in the public service generally'.[42] The parts of the report referred to here by the Ministerial Committee had highlighted the need for continual vigilance against espionage, including specifically the need for better physical safeguards, as well as better personnel security. According to the Prime Minister:

> It was desirable that as much as possible of the philosophy and reasoning of this part of the Report should be made public. For, while it illustrated the danger of the espionage threat, it also demonstrated the difficulty of countering it effectively in a free society. Publication would therefore help to secure a better public understanding both of the importance of the security problem and of its difficulties.[43]

But although the Prime Minister was keen that a large part of the report was published, even that part which was published was to be heavily censored, so that it was unknown at the time just how full an account was thus provided.

[41] TNA, CAB 128/36 (Cabinet Conclusions, 20 March 1962). The memorandum itself is to be found at TNA CAB 21/6016 (Report of the Committee on Security in the Public Service (the Radcliffe Committee), Memorandum by the Prime Minister, 10 March 1962). The substance of the latter is reproduced in the Cabinet Conclusions, which are quite full. So far as the Romer Report is concerned, a summary is to be found in 'Naval Security: Romer Committee's Report', HL Debs 13 June 1961, cols 125–129. The Romer Report was ultimately released to the National Archive in 2017 (CAB 301/248).

[42] TNA, CAB 128/36 (Cabinet Conclusions, 20 March 1962). But they quickly rowed back on their acceptance of proposals to ban trade unions at security establishments. See pp. 358–9 above.

[43] ibid.

There was, of course, no question of Part II (dealing with the Blake case) being published, the forty-one-page white paper failing even to acknowledge that there was a Part II, which is referred to by the Prime Minister in the memorandum to his Cabinet ministers, to whom it is unclear whether the full report was circulated:

> There can be no question of publishing any part of Part II. For the Government have never formally admitted that MI6 exists: they cannot therefore publicly discuss whether its security is good or bad . . . The Opposition leaders accept this, though they too realize that it may give rise to Parliamentary difficulties.[44]

Copies of the report had been shown to the Leader of the Opposition and three unnamed senior Privy Councillors from the Labour side, who had welcomed the proposal to publish a substantial part of it, notably that part relating to security procedures in the public service. They also supported the publication of the aspects of the report dealing with 'D' notices (as did the press members of the 'D' notice committee).[45] However, the Labour leader and his colleagues agreed that it would be contrary to long-standing convention to publish that part dealing with the Blake case, 'in view of the nature of the duties on which Blake had been employed'.[46]

The draft white paper now before the Cabinet thus included a version of Radcliffe's Report, edited to delete all the sensitive stuff: 'references to specially secret establishments, details of foreign intelligence services and descriptions of counter-measures'.[47] Crucially, however, there were also 'three larger omissions', which were made on 'grounds of public policy'.[48] It is not clear if these latter omissions had been agreed by the Opposition, but they were nevertheless *hugely* controversial, the government concealing (i) the true extent to which vetting was taking place; (ii) consideration by a judge-led inquiry of blanket political discrimination on the basis of guilt by association; and (iii) proposals by the same inquiry for the denial of trade union rights to some civil servants. The Prime Minister's report to the Cabinet thus proposed the following:

> (i) No reference should be made in the white paper to the procedure of normal vetting. While it had been incidentally mentioned in Parliament on a few occasions, the nature and extent of the procedure had never been fully disclosed.[49]

[44] TNA, CAB 21/6015 (Security Procedures in the Public Service Radcliffe Report: publication of Part III, D Notices) (The Radcliffe Report, March 1962).
[45] ibid.
[46] ibid.
[47] ibid.
[48] ibid.
[49] See Chapter 9 above.

(ii) No reference should be made in the white paper to a chapter of the Report which discussed whether Communists should be completely excluded from the public service. The Radcliffe Committee itself was divided on this issue and made no recommendation on it.[50]

(iii) The white paper should omit a chapter of the Report that considered the problem of Communist penetration of civil service staff associations. The situation disclosed by the chapter was said to be 'disquieting and certainly called for urgent action'.

We have already fully considered the first of these proposed exclusions in Chapter 10 above. So far as the second is concerned, it is not clear which members supported this proposal, or indeed what position Lord Radcliffe himself took in relation to it. We now know from the declassification of the report, however, that the arguments both for and against were set out in some detail, with the case in favour including the following gem:

> It is generally accepted that the Communist philosophy is basically subversive in its intention, and that no confidence can therefore be placed in the trustworthiness of adherents of that philosophy in public affairs. If so, it is arguable that there is something inherently offensive as well as illogical and dangerous in employing Communists in any capacity in the service of the State, whose social order it is their policy to undermine and ultimately to destroy.[51]

This and other 'arguments' were countered by a range of competing considerations, though the case against a total ban appears to have been clinched by the acceptance that it could not be justified on security grounds,[52] a conclusion that reflects more generally on the anti-Communist tone of the report.

So far as the third of the proposed exclusions referred to above is concerned, this has been considered in Chapter 12 above. Here it is clear from the Ministerial Committee in particular that Radcliffe had overshot the mark. According to the minutes of the meeting on 29 January 1962, it was thought that the chapter in question (chapter seven) gave an 'alarming account of the Communist penetration in the early paragraphs of the chapter (which might have been overstated)'.[53] The Ministerial Committee on Security was also reported as being concerned that 'disclosure of the extent of Communist penetration of these associations would shock public opinion in this country and, even more, in the United States'.[54] As we saw

[50] Radcliffe's own position is unknown. The sanitized white paper version deals briefly with the issue at para. 10.

[51] Report on Security Procedures in the Public Service (n 6), para. 96.

[52] ibid., para. 98.

[53] TNA, CAB 134/2498 (Ministerial Committee on Security, Minutes of Meeting on 29 January 1962).

[54] TNA, CAB 128/36 (Cabinet Conclusions, 20 March 1962).

in Chapter 12, the fuller version of the report revealed that Radcliffe had been disturbed to 'learn' that twenty-five per cent of civil service union officials were members of the Communist Party, and that another ten per cent followed the Party line so consistently that they had to be regarded as working in association with their Communist colleagues.[55]

But although it had been decided not to publish details about alleged Communist penetration of the trade unions, as this would also be likely to prejudice the evolving plans to deal with the Communist trade union officials discussed in chapter 12 above, the government was nevertheless thwarted in part by press speculation about the substance of the Radcliffe recommendations. Thus, senior ministers were concerned by a newspaper article about the contents of the report relating to alleged Communist penetration of the civil service trade unions, the newspaper article claiming that the 'Radcliffe Committee had made recommendations . . . which were so embarrassing to the Government that they were to be excluded from the white paper'.[56] This forced a re-think, the Cabinet told a week later that 'the Ministerial Committee on Security had come to the conclusion that the balance of advantage now lay on the side of including in the white paper a shortened version of this chapter of the Radcliffe Report'.[57]

Before being approved by Cabinet, this slightly amended plan had been agreed earlier on the same day by the Ministerial Committee on Security, which had been advised by Macmillan that the version of the report abbreviated for publication included the additional material, but:

> omitted the percentages quoted in the Report, the references to certain highly secret [government] organisations, and the proposal that 'house unions' should be established. It used the wording of the Report, except in the introductory paragraph which was designed to make clear that the Communists had penetrated the union organization, not the general membership. *The draft had been accepted by Lord Radcliffe*.[58]

As a result, four paragraphs on trade unions were slipped into the white paper, the only provisions of the full report published being the proposal to give departments the right not to deal with Communist officials. There is no mention of Radcliffe's reheated recommendation to ban trade unions at GCHQ, or his belief that the ETU trial would make it more publicly palatable to do so than in 1955, when the matter had last been considered by a Conference of Privy Councillors.

55 Report on Security Procedures in the Public Service (n 6), para. 99.
56 TNA, CAB 128/36/24 (Cabinet Conclusions, 29 March 1962) (emphasis added).
57 ibid.
58 TNA, CAB 134/2498 (Ministerial Committee on Security, Minutes of Meeting on 29 March 1962).

V. Radcliffe as Adjudicator

As indicated in Part IV above, Lord Radcliffe presided over two security inquiries for the government between 1961 and 1963. The first (in Part IV) was completed in November 1961, and the second (below) was started in November 1962. By an extraordinary act of dedication to national security, Lord Radcliffe also sat in his judicial capacity in the leading case on the Official Secrets Act 1911 to be decided since the Act was passed, and the first under the Act to reach the House of Lords. Although not concerned with espionage, the *Chandler* case was concerned with the range and scope of the 1911 Act, s. 1, the marginal note to which made it clear that its main purpose was espionage. But what some may see as an act of personal dedication, others might condemn as a remarkable lack of judgement that a man could think it constitutionally appropriate to slide from investigator to adjudicator to inquisitor on the question of national security within a period of twelve months. If nothing else, Lord Radcliffe's participation in the *Chandler* case reveals a lot about the promiscuous nature of the constitution and the actors who operated within it.

The background to the *Chandler* case has been told elsewhere.[59] The case was concerned with a demonstration at RAF Wethersfield organized by a group called the Committee of 100. The latter was an uncompromising anti-nuclear war group founded by Bertrand Russell, which sought to immobilize US air force airbases at which airplanes were loaded with nuclear weapons. The government went to great lengths to frustrate a demonstration held on 9 December 1961, at which the organizers had proposed to break into the airfield. But in what has been described as the biggest display of force by a government in peacetime since the General Strike, the projected thousands of demonstrators were outnumbered by about ten to one, with a 'bedraggled' 300 or so squatting 'damply in the fog outside the two gates for about four hours'.[60] Nevertheless, on 6 December 1961 the Attorney General (Sir Reginald Manningham-Buller) intervened by informing the Prime Minister that after discussion with the DPP, 'the time has come for the institution of serious criminal proceedings against the organisers of the demonstrations planned for next Saturday if necessary evidence can be secured and the organisers identified'.[61]

Although the security of the base was not breached, six members of the Committee of 100 were thus arrested and charged under the Official Secrets Act 1911 in connection with the events at Wethersfield. Consistently with the Attorney General's note to the Prime Minister on 6 December 1961, they did not include figureheads such as Lord Russell, but six leading activists in the form of Helen Allegranza (who was to die in Holloway prison), Terence Chandler, Ian Dixon, Trevor Hatton, Patrick Pottle, and Michael Randle. The charges related to

59 Ewing (n 11).
60 BLPS, CND/2008/3/5 (Independent Labour Party, *The 100 versus The State* [n.d.], p. 5).
61 TNA, PREM 11/4284 (Prime Minister's Office: Correspondence and Papers, 1951–1964).

organizing the events at Wethersfield, and they were each charged with conspiracy to commit and conspiracy to incite others to commit a breach of the Official Secrets Act 1911, section 1.[62] This provides that it is an offence for 'any person for any purpose prejudicial to the safety of the state' to approach or be in the neighbourhood of, or enter any prohibited place within the meaning of the Act. According to Lord Devlin, these provisions of the statute are 'far wider and vaguer than those usually employed in the definition of criminal offences', with 'terms such as "purpose", "interests", and "State"' being 'unfamiliar in the criminal law and [having] no settled meaning in connection with it'.[63]

The Wethersfield base was clearly a prohibited place within the meaning of the Act, but it is far from clear that Parliament contemplated that the Act might be used in this way. A clue as to the purpose of section 1 is provided by the side-note which refers to penalties for spying, while the parliamentary record provides little evidence that this was a mistake, though it is true that the only real evidence of parliamentary intention was out of bounds to the Courts by their self-denying ordinance that they would not look at Hansard. If they had, they would have discovered from the House of Lords debates that the notoriously rushed 1911 Act was designed to apply to British citizens as well as to those of other countries, but that the furthest it was designed to go was to deal with those furtive individuals who found themselves on military establishments, not necessarily to spy on behalf of foreign powers, but to obtain information that they could then sell on to such powers.[64] But the real target was German spies in the run-up to the First World War, though obviously the Act had a new purpose in a new political climate.

The trial was conducted before the seventy-two-year-old Sir Cecil Havers (father of Sir Michael Havers, who became Lord Chancellor in a Conservative government; and Baroness Butler-Sloss, who became President of the Family Division). The main strategy of the accused was to challenge the whole basis of the government's policy of nuclear deterrence. Thus, they planned to show that their purpose was not prejudicial to the interests of the State, that the aircraft carried nuclear bombs, and that it was not in the interests of the State to have aircraft armed in this way. It was also proposed to argue secondly, that the accused reasonably believed that it was not prejudicial but beneficial to the interests of the State to immobilise the aircraft, and that the jury was entitled to hold that no offence had been

[62] Crucial evidence appears to have been obtained by the police raids authorized by Manningham-Buller (and criticized in Parliament by Shinwell). A document dated 7 November 1961 stated as follows:

> The working group at this end has finally decided in favour of a demonstration that will involve an attempt to occupy the base at Wethersfield. However, the plan is for only a number of trained people to do this. The bulk of the demonstrators will squat by the entrances on the roadway. Our leaflet about the demonstration will simply state that we intend to immobilise the base and this is the information that will be released to the Press (*Chandler v DPP* [1964] AC 763, at pp. 787–8).

[63] [1964] AC 763, at p. 804.

[64] HL Debs, 25 July 1911, cols 642–4.

committed. This was the nightmare that had been anticipated by Manningham-Buller in his note to the Prime Minister on 6 December 1961 that the matter might end up before a jury at the Old Bailey, with 'the risk that the jury will contain one or more sympathisers'.[65]

Although the latter risk could be managed to some extent by the process of jury vetting (which according to the Committee of 100 would take place in the potential juror's home),[66] there was also the apparently unanticipated risk that a jury that did not contain sympathizers still might nevertheless be influenced by the case presented by the defence, with significant political consequences if the accused were to be acquitted as a result. This second risk now had to be addressed, which meant that the argument about 'the futility of nuclear warfare' had to be kept away from the jury,[67] which, despite being vetted, might not be obliging in the light of unpredictable expert evidence and evidence of fact that the defence intended to call, which would deal with the effect of exploding a nuclear bomb, no doubt to the discomfort of the squeamish. Hence the vigour of the government's argument (presented by the Attorney General who appeared for the Crown) that 'an objective test must determine whether the purpose of grounding aircraft was a prejudicial purpose, that the accused's beliefs were irrelevant and so was the reasonableness of their beliefs'.

Apart from anything else, this would mean that the defence could not ask government witnesses in cross-examination whether the aircraft were carrying nuclear weapons. Accepting the arguments of the Attorney General, the trial judge ruled that the defence were not entitled to call evidence to establish that it would be beneficial for this country to give up nuclear weapons or that the accused honestly believed that it would be.[68] As Lord Devlin pointed out, the judge's ruling did not stop with the exclusion of the evidence, Mr Justice Havers also directing the jury that 'it was no defence for the appellants to say that they intended to do something which would be beneficial to the State in the long run, namely, to induce or compel the government to abandon nuclear weapons'.[69] It is true that the jury was directed that 'it was for them to say whether they were satisfied that what the accused had conspired to do was prejudicial to the safety or interests of the State', but it was also true that 'the general effect of his summing up was that if they accepted the evidence of Air Commodore Magill they could not do otherwise than find prejudice to the safety or interests of the State'.[70]

65 TNA, PREM 11/4284 (Prime Minister's Office: Correspondence and Papers, 1951–1964).
66 BLPS, CND/2008/3/1 (Committee of 100, Policy and Planning—Report of National Conference held over weekend 11/12 April at Unity House London (1964)).
67 [1964] AC 763, at p. 802.
68 ibid., at p. 788 (Lord Reid).
69 ibid., at pp. 802–3 (Lord Devlin).
70 ibid., at p. 789 (Lord Reid).

Magill had said that the base was occupied by squadrons of the US Air Force assigned to the Supreme Commander Allied Forces, Europe, that these squadrons were combat ready and on constant alert, and that in the event of an emergency any interference with the ability of the aircraft to take off would gravely prejudice their operational effectiveness.[71] The jury duly did its duty, with Lord Devlin noting in the House of Lords appeal that Mr Justice Havers had 'indicated a fairly strong opinion in the present case, particularly at the end of his summing-up, when he hinted to the jury that there was only one verdict that they could in conscience return'.[72] Having thus secured a guilty verdict (albeit with a request for leniency from the jury), Mr Justice Havers is reported as having said that he had 'to pass a sentence which is adequate to the offences that [the accused had] committed and which will deter others from committing similar offences'.[73] They were each sentenced to eighteen months.[74]

VI. *Chandler* in the House of Lords

An appeal to the Court of Appeal was unsuccessful, and was notable only for enabling the Lord Chief Justice (Lord Parker, who we encounter again below) to quote his father (Lord Parker of Waddington) as authority.[75] The House of Lords appeal was heard as usual by a Bench of five. Sir Reginald Manningham-Buller was not yet Lord Chancellor Dilhorne and appeared again for the Crown in an appeal that took four days between 30 May and 5 June 1962, with judgment delivered on 12 July. The five men assigned to hear the case included Viscount Radcliffe. They also included Lord Reid, who had been a Tory MP and the Scottish law officer for ten years (1936–45) (first as Solicitor General for Scotland and then as Lord Advocate). He had also seen active service in the machine gun corps during the First World War and had risen to the rank of Major. As we have seen, he was appointed as a Law Lord in 1948 without having previously occupied judicial office.

Lord Hodson was appointed to the House of Lords in 1960, where he served until 1971, having previously served for ten years in the Court of Appeal. Hodson had a distinguished military career, having been wounded twice during the First World War, and been awarded the Military Cross for gallantry. Added to the foregoing was a rich educational background likely to encourage loyalty and conformity: Edinburgh Academy and Jesus College, Cambridge (Lord Reid); Cheltenham College and Corpus Christ, Oxford (Lord Pearce); and Stoneyhurst

[71] ibid., at p. 788.
[72] ibid., at p. 804.
[73] BLPS, CND/2008/3/1 (Independent Labour Party, *The 100 versus The State* [n.d.], p. 12).
[74] BLPS, CND/2008/3/5.
[75] *The Zamora* [1916] 2 AC 77, at p. 107: 'Those who are responsible for national security must be the sole judges of what national security requires.'

College and Christ's College, Cambridge (Lord Devlin), to which we can add Cheltenham College (Lord Hodson) and All Souls College, Oxford (Viscount Radcliffe). The youngest of the bunch was fifty-eight (Lord Devlin) and the oldest seventy-three (Lord Reid), at least four were Privy Counsellors, and one (Lord Reid) was to become a Companion of Honour.

Into this bewildering world of judges with distinguished government, military, and legal service with impeccable social credentials stumbled six peace campaigners. The great political importance of the case was rehearsed by counsel on their behalf, who argued that the 1911 Act 'envisages very grave incursions on the liberty of the subject',[76] and that the decision of the Court of Criminal Appeal to uphold Mr Justice Havers was 'of very great constitutional importance for it decides that where national security is involved, no evidence and no cross examination can be adduced in a criminal case on that matter'.[77] They also argued that the interpretation placed on the Act by the Court of Criminal Appeal was so wide that 'a workman on strike who approached a government establishment, for example, Woolwich Arsenal, in order to induce workers there to come out on strike would be guilty . . . of being in the neighbourhood of a prohibited place for a purpose prejudicial to the safety and interests of the State'.[78]

The appellants further contended that it is not a principle of a criminal case that the executive are the sole judges of what is prejudicial to the State, with Lord Parker having been wrong to have relied on the authority of his father in a civil case, which offered 'no authority for the proposition that in a criminal case evidence cannot be called to challenge the policy of the security of the State'.[79] In arguing that the statute should be limited because of its impact on civil liberties, counsel for the appellants provided many opportunities for this to be done, referring to the parliamentary history, as well as contending that the accused should have been allowed to have been permitted at the trial to give evidence of their beliefs in order to show what was their purpose; and that the evidence should have been at large to enable the jury to decide as a fact whether the appellants' purpose was or was not prejudicial.[80]

Yet despite the weight of the appellants' arguments, it would have been impossible to place a cigarette paper between the Law Lords and the Attorney General, who was about to join their ranks as Viscount Dilhorne. First, the House of Lords agreed that the Act was to be read widely and could not be confined to spying: the side note referring to penalties against spying was dismissed by Lord Reid as being no use as an aid to construction, while in any event it was impossible to suppose that the section did not apply to sabotage as well as spying, though there is nothing

76 [1964] AC 763, at p. 777.
77 ibid., at p. 778.
78 ibid.
79 ibid., at p. 779.
80 ibid., at p. 778–9.

on the parliamentary record to support this construction. According to Viscount Radcliffe who was to take a prominent and influential role in the decision, 'the saboteur just as much as the spy in the ordinary sense is contemplated as an offender under the Act'.[81] Second, the House of Lords adopted a narrow approach to the question of purpose, preventing the appellants from having a jury consider whether their purpose was beneficial rather than prejudicial to the interests of the State.

According to Viscount Radcliffe again:

> if a person's direct purpose in approaching or entering is to cause obstruction or interference, and such obstruction or interference is found to be of prejudice to the defence dispositions of the State, an offence is thereby committed, and his indirect purposes or his motives in bringing about the obstruction or interference do not alter the nature or content of his offence.[82]

But this was an argument that seemed to be undermined (as Lord Devlin was to point out), if not fatally weakened by a later passage in Viscount Radcliffe's speech:

> Is a man guilty of an offence, it was asked, if he rushes onto an airfield intending to stop an airplane taking off because he knows that a time bomb has been concealed on board? I should say that he is not, and for the reason that his direct purpose is not to bring about an obstruction but to prevent a disaster, the obstruction that he causes being merely a means to securing that end.[83]

Third, the House of Lords adopted an equally narrow approach to who determines what is or is not prejudicial to the interests of the State. Here there was little difficulty, with Lord Reid drawing on the royal prerogative line of cases to say that 'the disposition and armament of the armed forces are and for centuries have been within the exclusive discretion of the Crown, and 'no one is entitled to challenge it in court'.[84]

The Attorney General thus succeeded in both construing section 1 widely and in keeping the crucial question away from the jury. A sympathetic court would determine the issue. The only note of criticism was to be heard from Lord Devlin, who was at times excoriating and at others in agreement. On the question of purpose, he was unable to agree with the Crown's argument that had been accepted by Viscount Radcliffe. Exposing the contradiction in the Crown's position, Lord Devlin argued that if it is permissible for a man who has interfered with the running of an

[81] ibid., at p. 794.
[82] ibid., at p. 795.
[83] ibid., at p. 796.
[84] ibid., at p. 791.

airfield to say that all he was doing was trying to capture a criminal, 'it must also be permissible for him to say that all he was doing was trying to save the State from impending harm'.[85] For Lord Devlin, the salient question was whether 'immobilisation of this airfield [could] be regarded as the first step in a general immobilisation of all the country's nuclear weapons and, if so, would that be a good thing for the country'.[86] At this point, Lord Devlin fell into line, rejecting the idea that the trial judge should allow 'hours or days to be spent at the trial in giving an accused the opportunity of expounding his political views', in the process evoking parallel concerns with those expressed by some in relation to more recent cases about the Courts being used as a platform for the continuation of political campaigns as diverse as opposition to the war in Iraq to the re-settlement of the Chagos Islanders.

According to Lord Devlin, 'the court is not the forum for such a debate and the jury is not the body to determine what the interests of the State should be'.[87] Although appearing to dispute the view that the interests of the State are to be determined by the government, Lord Devlin nevertheless held simply that there was a rebuttable presumption that it is 'contrary to the interests of the Crown to have one of its airfields immobilised just as it may be presumed that it is contrary to the interests of an industrialist to have his factory immobilised'.[88] So despite the fancy rhetoric, Lord Devlin ended up agreeing with Sir Reginald that the '[t]hing speaks for itself', before uttering the most famous passage in his speech which acquired a significance well beyond its importance for the disposal of the case, and which is not normally quoted in full:

> Men can exaggerate the extent of their interests and so can the Crown. The servants of the Crown, like other men animated by the highest motives, are capable of formulating a policy ad hoc so as to prevent the citizen from doing something that the Crown does not want him to do. It is the duty of the courts to be as alert now as they have always been to prevent abuse of the prerogative. But in the present case there is nothing at all to suggest that the Crown's interest in the proper operation of its airfields is not what it may naturally be presumed to be or that it was exaggerating the perils of interference with their effectiveness.[89]

VII. Radcliffe as Inquisitor

Only four months after contributing as an adjudicator to a major expansion of government powers relating to national security, Viscount Radcliffe was back on the

[85] ibid., at p. 806.
[86] ibid.
[87] ibid., at p. 808.
[88] ibid., at p. 811.
[89] ibid.

security trail again. As we have seen, the Radcliffe Report had made recommendations relating to document security and to the increased frequency of the PV procedures. Perhaps by way of vindication, it was a failure of both document security and vetting procedures that enabled John Vassall to act freely for the Russians. That said, if the Radcliffe recommendations had been fully in operation during the period of Vassall's espionage, it is difficult to see how they would have prevented it.[90] If the report of the Tribunal of Inquiry into the Vassall affair is to be believed, it was two key acts of human failure at relatively low levels in the chain of command that were ultimately responsible for the failure in turn to pre-empt Vassall. These are failures against which no system of document security or PV is likely ever to provide complete protection. Although the Vassall case provides some uncomfortable lessons for Lord Radcliffe, it did nevertheless confirm the analysis of the first Radcliffe Report that it was not members of the CPGB who were the threat to national security.

Lord Radcliffe was appointed to chair the inquiry into the Vassall affair in mid-November 1962, the report being published in April 1963. The tribunal had been asked to investigate a number of questions, which included the following:

- allegations that after the Portland case, the presence of another spy inside the Admiralty was known to the authorities;
- allegations reflecting on the integrity of ministers, naval officers, and civil servants concerned with the Vassall case; and
- any breaches of security arrangements that took place in the Vassall affair, and any neglect of duty on the part of anyone responsible for Vassall's work.

Appointed with the approval of both Houses of Parliament, the Home Secretary declared that the panel would be governed by the Tribunals of Inquiry (Evidence) Act 1921.

The Bill giving rise to the 1921 Act led to some bad-tempered exchanges and extensive amendments in brief Committee proceedings.[91] As enacted, it provided that where a tribunal is created by resolution of both Houses of Parliament to inquire into a matter of 'urgent public importance', the instrument by which the tribunal is appointed may provide that the tribunal is to have the same powers as the High Court or (in Scotland) the Court of Session in relation to requiring the attendance of witnesses, the examination of witnesses under oath, and compelling

[90] Compare the following assessment:

> I am convinced that the recent improvements in security following the great 1962 Report have done a great deal to improve and tighten up the security measures in all the public services. As the Tribunal itself says, there will always be a danger of a break down because of the human factor, however carefully the regulations are made and however scrupulous our efforts to enforce them (HC Debs, 7 May 1963, col 243, Prime Minister).

[91] HC Debs, 7 March 1921, col. 189 (2R); 8 March 1921, col. 397 (Committee).

the production of documents.[92] The 1921 Act also provided that 'a witness before any such tribunal shall be entitled to the same immunities and privileges as if he were a witness before the High Court or the Court of Session',[93] the Attorney General pointing out at Second Reading that this was designed to ensure that witnesses were 'entitled to absolute privilege' from liability from defamation.[94]

Whether or not this was the 'modern day Star Chamber' condemned at Second Reading,[95] the procedures under the 1921 Act nevertheless gave a Tribunal appointed thereunder extensive powers of inquisition. The Vassall Tribunal appeared to use these powers to the full, taking evidence from 142 witnesses, including the Attorney General on behalf of the 'public interest'. Evidence was also taken from a number of journalists, who were obliged by the 1921 Act to produce any document in their power or control when demanded by the Tribunal, as well as being required to 'answer any question to which the Tribunal may legally require an answer'.[96] Failure to comply with these obligations could lead to contempt proceedings against the offender in question, the matter to be referred to the High Court or the Court of Session for disposal. Most of the Radcliffe proceedings were held *in camera*, though the Tribunal later acknowledged that it had 'possibly erred too much' in the direction of hearing evidence behind closed doors.[97]

The thirty-day inquisition led to a substantial report of eighty-seven pages, with a summary of the main findings but no recommendations about how to proceed in the future to prevent incidents of this kind from being repeated. The Tribunal made clear that in reading newspaper articles about Vassall, a number of statements of fact had been made, leading the inquiry 'to endeavour by questioning the makers as to the basis and source of their information to measure for [themselves] the validity of what was said and to assess its possible implications'.[98] The Tribunal thus thought it necessary to question the journalists about their sources and to examine the latter, so that the Tribunal members could be satisfied 'of the truth or falsity of the statements made'.[99] The journalists in question, however, claimed professional privilege, which the Tribunal was unprepared to accept, requiring the witnesses 'to answer questions' wherever it appeared 'necessary for the purposes' of the inquiry.[100]

As we have seen, the 1921 Act extended to the Tribunal the same powers as the High Court to require witnesses to 'answer any question to which the tribunal may

92 1921 Act, s. 1(1).
93 ibid., s. 1(3).
94 HC Debs, 7 March 1921, col. 189.
95 ibid., col. 192.
96 1921 Act, s. 1(2)(b).
97 Report of the Tribunal of Inquiry Appointed to Inquire into the Vassall Case and Related Matters (n 6), para. 6.
98 ibid., para. 13.
99 ibid., para. 15.
100 ibid.

legally require an answer'.[101] Although the 1921 Act also provided that 'a witness before any such tribunal shall be entitled to the same immunities and privileges as if he were a witness before the High Court or the Court of Session',[102] this was not read by the Tribunal to mean that journalists could stand in the way of its inquiry, and Lord Radcliffe and his colleagues did not consider it possible to 'concede any further immunities and privileges in any case where an answer to a question appeared to . . . be necessary for the furtherance of [its] investigation'.[103] Refusal to answer questions would be a contempt of court, punishable by the High Court on a reference by the Tribunal, a step taken in this case in relation to three journalists who refused to provide the information demanded.

The journalists certified by Lord Radcliffe as having failed to answer questions necessary for the purposes of the inquiry were employed either by the *Daily Mail*, or the *Daily Sketch*. Brendan Mulholland had written articles claiming that colleagues of Vassall had called him '"Auntie" to his face', that a girl typist in the Admiralty Office where he worked had decided that no £15 a week clerk could possibly live in the way he did honestly,[104] and that it was the sponsorship of two high-ranking officials which led to Vassall avoiding the strictest part of the Admiralty's security vetting.[105] When asked by Lord Radcliffe to provide the names of two different people from whom he claimed to have obtained information, Mulholland refused to do so, as did Desmond Clough when confronted by Radcliffe in terms to which any self-respecting journalist would have had great difficulty in responding:

> Radcliffe: I gather that you are the source in your office of the statement made by the paper that: 'Vassall's spying led to Russian trawler spying fleets turning up with uncanny accuracy in the precise area of the secret NATO sea exercise' and you have told us that you yourself derived the information which linked Vassall with that particular Russian activity from what you described as a 'someone in Whitehall'. I think I am bound to direct you that in order that we should follow up the facts alleged with regard to that we should know the name of that informant so that we can send for him and question him.[106]

Reginald Foster had contributed to one of the articles, and claimed not to know or ever to have known the names of the people of whom he had made inquiries. He nevertheless refused to answer questions designed to find out 'what kind' of informant they were. Clough eventually coughed up after his source came forward

[101] 1921 Act, s. 1(2)(b).
[102] ibid., s. 1(3).
[103] Report of the Tribunal of Inquiry Appointed to Inquire into the Vassall Case and Related Matters (n 6), para. 3.
[104] *Attorney General v Foster and Mulholland* [1963] 2 QB 477.
[105] ibid., p. 479.
[106] ibid., p. 776.

voluntarily, and he was thus spared a six-month jail sentence. The source proved to be an Admiralty employee, from whom Radcliffe was unable to conclude whether he had in fact contributed in any way to Clough's story. With no answers having been received from Mulholland or Foster, Radcliffe claimed somewhat unconvincingly that his investigations remained incomplete. Unconvincing because 'the allegations involved which we desired to follow up were not supported by any other acceptable evidence which came into our possession and some of them were in fact contradicted by other evidence that we did obtain and are prepared to accept'.[107]

VIII. Judicial Inquisition and Press Freedom

The three cases were duly referred to the High Court, Lord Radcliffe certifying that the three men had refused to answer questions that were relevant to the purposes of the inquiry and necessary for the witness to answer. First up was Desmond Clough, who argued that a journalist had legal and ethical obligations not to reveal his or her sources:

> The essence of the matter is, first, that a journalist has an obligation towards his suppliers of information and it would be dishonourable for him to reveal them; secondly, he owes a duty to his employers not to imperil their receipt of information in the future, which would clearly occur if an informant knew that the reporter would break his confidence; thirdly, he has a self-interest in the matter because he would be out of business if it were known that he revealed confidential information; fourthly, the law will not force a man to divulge trade secrets and fifthly, journalists have a conscientious objection to revealing sources of information which is part of the ethics of their profession. A person should not be asked to commit a breach of commercial ethics.[108]

But however powerful the arguments, they were firmly rejected by the Lord Chief Justice, before whom the case was heard. According to Lord Parker, 'in all the [law] reports in this country there is not to be found one single case where this so-called privilege or immunity has been raised or ruled upon at the trial of the action'.[109]

Lord Parker relied heavily on *McGuinness v Attorney General of Victoria*,[110] a decision of the High Court of Australia, confessing that he would 'hesitate very long if in a matter which pertained to the common law of England, this country should

[107] Report of the Tribunal of Inquiry Appointed to Inquire into the Vassall Case and Related Matters (n 6), para. 19.
[108] *Attorney General v Clough* [1963] 1 QB 773, at p. 783.
[109] ibid., at p. 790.
[110] (1940) 63 CLR 73.

differ, unless it had to, with another Commonwealth country'.[111] But although he had no hesitation in holding that 'in regard to the press, the law has not developed and crystallised the confidential relationship in which they stand to an informant into one of the classes of privilege known to the law',[112] Parker nevertheless also held that it would 'remain open to [the] court to say in the special circumstances of any particular case that public policy did demand that the journalist should be immune'.[113] But this was not such a case. As Lord Salmon was later to recognize at a time when the right claimed by Clough was enshrined in statute,[114] there was a nationwide crisis of confidence about security matters:

> It is certainly not surprising that the court considered that the man who informed the journalists of what they had reported in the press would probably be able to give, and, if so, ought to have given the tribunal evidence about [relevant] matters.[115]

Turning from substance to sanction, the Lord Chief Justice decided that the sentence had to be more than nominal. He did, however, give Clough ten days to reflect on his actions and also indicated that some remission of sentence would be in order if the identity of the source were to be revealed by other means (which did happen in this case, with the source coming forward). The Attorney General's application for costs was strongly resisted by counsel for Clough on the ground that the case 'raised an entirely novel point of constitutional significance which the Crown was desirous of testing as much as anybody'.[116] The Lord Chief Justice held that the Crown was entitled to costs, but with an expectation that the costs order would not be enforced. Although the Attorney General agreed, Clough would, of course, remain liable for his own costs in what would be an expensive stand on principle, if not personally, then for those supporting him.[117]

Clough was followed by Brendan Mulholland and Reginald Foster, both of whom were tried and found in contempt of court by Mr Justice Gorman, who passed a six months' sentence on Mulholland. In doing so, Mr Justice Gorman took into account the fact that the tribunal had been appointed to investigate a matter of 'urgent public importance' involving offences under the Official Secrets Acts. Not for him a discussion of 'the relative question of conscience and the rights of the State', the six months was to reflect 'the importance of the Tribunal and the far-reaching nature

[111] *Attorney General v Clough* [1963] 1 QB 773, at p. 792.
[112] ibid.
[113] ibid.
[114] Contempt of Court Act 1981, s. 10.
[115] *British Steel Corporation v Granada Television Ltd* [1981] AC 1096, at p. 1150. And as the new Attorney General had argued before Lord Parker, at stake was 'the safety and security of the State, the activities of a most dangerous spy, and the conduct of Ministers of the Crown, of officers of Her Majesty's Services and of civil servants': [1963] 1 QB 773, at p. 780.
[116] *Attorney General v Clough*, Sentence, filed at TNA, TS 58/703 (Tribunals of Inquiry (Evidence) Act 1921—Vassall Inquiry—*Attorney General v Desmond Clough* (Daily Sketch Reporter)).
[117] ibid.

of [its] terms of reference'.[118] Like Clough, Mulholland was given time to reflect, but unlike Clough he was given only five days for reflection, though the other terms of the sentence were similar, including a condition that it should not be executed until the appeal process had been concluded, which would not be for another two months. Reginald Foster was sentenced to three months on the same day, Mr Justice Gorman concluding that Foster did not need to be treated as harshly as Mulholland.[119]

Both Mulholland and Foster appealed, not for them the good fortune of a source coming forward to release them from their predicament. In their appeal, it was argued for Mulholland and Foster that—contrary to Mr Justice Gorman in the High Court—there was a general principle that a journalist should not be required to disclose the source of his information unless there were special reasons. To this end, it was contended that:

> The press has not accepted, as have doctors and bankers, that their scruples may be overruled by the direction of the court. It is contrary to public policy that journalists should be forced to disclose the sources of their information. To do so strikes at the liberty of the press. The press is the watch-dog of the public. It cannot exercise its functions if it cannot secure information. Without protection from disclosure many sources of information will cease to be available. The police do not disclose the sources of their information.[120]

But again, the defence was rejected, this time by a unanimous Court of Appeal, the reasoning and judgment of which failed to do justice to the quite substantial points raised. Indeed, in terms of its cavalier indifference to the constitutional issues raised, there are few cases in the law reports to match it.

After referring to a first-instance Irish decision of 1935 and the High Court of Australia decision in *McGuinness*, Lord Denning concluded that 'the authorities are all one way', albeit that he had remarked earlier that the authorities are 'few enough'.[121] There were in fact only the two, as well as an exchange during the Parnell Inquiry Commission in 1891which served only to highlight the unsatisfactory state of the law at the time. In truth, the Court of Appeal had a free hand to do as it pleased. Yet the best it could do in response to the important arguments presented to it was in the following passage in the judgment of Lord Denning:

> There is no privilege known to the law by which a journalist can refuse to answer a question which is relevant to the inquiry and is one which, in the opinion of

[118] TNA, TS 58/704 (Tribunals of Inquiry (Evidence) Act 1921—Vassall Inquiry— *Attorney General v Reginald William Foster* (Freelance Reporter, Daily Sketch)).

[119] By the time of the prosecutions, the Tribunal had taken evidence from Vassall ('the principal actor in this case'), who had given 'certain information'. Although that information 'did not supply to the Court the deficiency in evidence caused by Foster's refusal to give evidence', this appeared nevertheless to have been accepted by the Attorney General to be a factor in mitigation.

[120] *Attorney General v Mulholland and Foster* [1963] 2 QB 477, at p. 482.

[121] ibid., p. 491.

> the judge, it is proper for him to be asked. I think it is plain that in this particular case it is in the public interest for the tribunal to inquire as to the sources of information. How is anyone to know that this story was not a pure invention, if the journalist will not tell the tribunal its source? Even if it was not invention, how is anyone to know it was not the gossip of some idler seeking to impress? It may be mere rumour unless the journalist shows he got it from a trustworthy source (as I take it on his statement he has, which I fully accept), then however much he may desire to keep it secret, he must remember that he has been directed by the tribunal to disclose it as a matter of public duty, and this is justification enough.[122]

Both Mulholland and Foster appealed to the House of Lords,[123] with counsel arguing in the *Mulholland* case that a journalist's privilege had always been recognised in defamation law.[124] The petitioners also contended that the Court of Appeal had failed to mention an important Privy Council authority to which its attention had been directed,[125] and in which it had been held by a strong court that a newspaper editor who refused to reveal his source was not guilty of contempt of court. Referring to that latter decision several years later, Lord Justice Rigby said of it that 'the whole question of contempt was discussed in a more exhaustive manner than in any other case within my experience'.[126] Apart from referring to this 'strong persuasive authority', the petitioners also asked searching questions about the authorities on which the Court of Appeal did rely. The Parnell Commission was 'no *binding* authority at all'; and *O'Brennan v Tully* (the Irish case relied on) was only a first-instance decision in which 'the question was not fully argued'.[127]

True, the High Court of Australia decision in *McGuinness v Attorney General of Victoria* was of 'strong persuasive authority' because of its provenance.[128] But it too was of limited assistance because it had incorrectly understood English law on a relevant point. This added to the weight of the petition that claimed not only that the Court of Appeal had overlooked relevant authority and over-relied on

122 ibid., pp. 491–2.

123 The petition seeking leave to appeal (In the Matter of the Tribunals of Inquiry (Evidence) Act 1921, and In the Matter of Three Certificates Issued in Respect of Brendan Joseph Mulholland) is filed at TNA, TS 58/705 (Tribunals of Inquiry (Evidence) Act 1921—Vassall Inquiry).

124 In the Matter of the Tribunals of Inquiry (Evidence) Act 1921, and In the Matter of Three Certificates Issued in Respect of Brendan Joseph Mulholland, TNA, TS 58/705 (Tribunals of Inquiry (Evidence) Act 1921—Vassall Inquiry), para. 7, where a number of defamation authorities are referred to. According to the petitioners, 'there is a general rule that a newspaper should not be ordered by way of interrogatory to disclose its source of information', the Court of Appeal acknowledging that 'it was in the public interest that the name of a newspaper's informant should not be disclosed': *Adam v Fisher* (1914) 30 TLR 288.

125 *In re The Bahama Islands* [1893] AC 138.

126 *Seaward v Pattison* [1897] 1 Ch 545, at p. 559.

127 (1935) *Irish Law Times* 115.

128 (1940) 63 CLR 73.

unpersuasive precedent, but also claimed strongly that the matters raised in the petition were of importance to the public (as well as to journalists and newspapers) on a point where there was no binding authority. But despite the point of law in this case having been certified by the Court of Appeal as being one of general public importance, Lords Reid, Morris, and Hodson refused leave to appeal on 6 March 1963. In accordance with the usual practice, no reasons were given for this decision, a similar decision being reached by the same judges in relation to an appeal by Reginald Foster on identical grounds on the same day.[129]

IX. The Vassall Report

The imprisonment of the journalists was rightly condemned. As pointed out by *Tribune* at the time, 'they were not jailed for peddling rumours as facts', but because 'they defended a time-honoured convention governing the relations between Government and the press that should not have been challenged in this way by this Tribunal'.[130] Mulholland and Foster were, however, not the only victims of the Inquiry, much to the dismay of *Tribune*, concerned that 'for six years a Soviet spy worked in the Admiralty, ostentatiously living above his income, and nobody is to blame'.[131] Yet inviting parallels with the Hutton Report on the Iraq war some forty years later,[132] the Radcliffe Tribunal wholly exonerated government ministers and senior officials, mildly rebuked junior civil servants (with the only personal blame being attached to someone who was dead), and excoriated some newspapers and journalists, several of whom, as we have seen, ended up in jail.

As pointed out on page 296 above, Vassall had been blackmailed by the Russians since being compromised in 1955, and on returning to work in the office of the Civil Lord of the Admiralty (Thomas Galbraith), he had removed documents from the office, which he photographed and returned the following day. The photographs were then passed to the Russians. As we also saw on page 297 above, Radcliffe was unwilling to blame anyone for this lapse of procedure, though it must have been galling all the same in view of the fact that this problem—along with opportunities to make copies of documents in the office—had been identified by Radcliffe in his Review of Security Procedures in the Public Service, considered in Part III. There Radcliffe specifically addressed concerns about 'the opportunity to take classified documents out of the office'.[133] But anticipating conclusions which were more or

129 The petition in the *Foster* case is filed at TNA, TS 58/704 (Tribunals of Inquiry (Evidence) Act 1921—Vassall Inquiry).
130 *Tribune*, 3 May 1963.
131 ibid.
132 Lord Hutton, Report of the Inquiry into the Circumstances Surrounding the Death of Dr David Kelly CMG (HC 247, 2003–4).
133 Report on Security Procedures in the Public Service (n 6), para. 116.

less repeated by the Tribunal of Inquiry only a year later, Radcliffe had written in his earlier report that:

> We considered all the possible methods of detecting such practices—routine or snap checks, searches, either of the person or of bags, brief cases, etc. It is quite plain that they could never be wholly effective against a determined person; and to have even a likelihood of being effective they would be intolerable to those concerned.[134]

But if document security could not be guaranteed, what about PV, which was designed to stop people like Vassall slipping through, and which in the case of the Admiralty was being applied on a five-yearly basis? By 1956, Vassall had been successfully put through all stages of the PV process, Radcliffe noting with nice understatement that it was 'a disquieting thought that a young man of no great strength of character and only recently recruited through intimidation by the Russian Secret Service should have passed successfully through this investigation without arousing suspicion'.[135] For the purposes of PV, it was Vassall's homosexuality that at the time made him a potential target for blackmail, and it was this that was missed in the inquiries and background checks. In the view of the Tribunal, however, it was missed because Vassall's homosexual activities were 'essentially private ones', and because he was 'discreet in his conduct of them'.[136]

Contrary to press reports, Vassall thus had 'no office reputation of homosexuality', and no one had heard him called 'Auntie', though he was regarded as 'something of a joke', 'effeminate' and a 'bit of a miss', referred to by some staff in Moscow as 'Vera' and by another as 'rather a pansy little man'.[137] The main criticism of the Tribunal was reserved for H. V. Pennells, who played a major role in Vassall's recruitment for Moscow in the first place, and who was blamed for not adopting a more rigorous selection procedure in light of the dangers to which it was known staff were exposed in Moscow:

> Mr Pennells is dead and we cannot know his side of the story. His reputation is that of a keen and hard-working officer who was a little lacking in imagination, an officer to whom [Naval Intelligence] owed much. But we cannot escape the conclusion that, although he was efficient and conscientious and served the Admiralty well, he failed among his other pressing duties to give this matter the attention it deserved. It would be unjust to conclude that such a man had been negligent in his public duty. We think it sufficient to say that he was undoubtedly remiss and

134 ibid. There was a concern that searches would be resented by the staff and that they would have 'a bad effect on staff relations'.
135 ibid., para. 48.
136 ibid., para. 64.
137 ibid., paras 106, 125.

> lacking in judgment in not taking any effective action to have the system of selection reviewed within the Authority.[138]

There was also criticism of the failure to ensure 'sufficiently strict control of association between members of the Embassy staff and locally-engaged employees', and while responsibility for this must be shared between senior Embassy staff, 'the evidence is not precise enough to enable responsibility to be allocated more closely'.[139] But apart from Pennells, the strongest criticism was reserved for several officials who were responsible for the conduct of the PV. As pointed out in Chapter 10, the investigating officer who conducted Vassall's PV was E. S. Sherwood, a former Deputy Commissioner in the Nigeria Police, the investigation being conducted in accordance with the Treasury instruction of 31 March 1954. This covered not only membership of 'subversive organisations', but also 'serious character weaknesses of a kind which might make a person unreliable or subject to blackmail', with any reasonable suspicion of 'homosexual tendencies' raising a presumption of unfitness for office.

As we saw in Chapter 10, the PV investigation was conducted in accordance with normal procedures, and was generally not in any way 'remiss', though there was one respect in which it was said to be 'inadequate'.[140] The particular criticism levelled at Mr Sherwood was that he did not seek the views of anyone in Moscow and relied exclusively on Vassall's manager in London—the unfortunate Pennells again—when conducting his investigations. It is possible that if Mr Sherwood had interviewed and sought a full assessment from the man who had direct oversight of Vassall in Moscow, the officer in question (Captain Bennett) would have 'mentioned the suspicions that he had held that Vassall had homosexual tendencies', which 'might well' have led to 'closer questioning of Vassall' or 'a wider circle of enquiries about him'.[141] As Radcliffe pointed out, however, where this would have led 'can only be conjecture'.[142] It was nevertheless enough publicly to condemn Sherwood for an 'error of judgment'.[143]

[138] ibid., para. 84. Many thought this unfair, not least Pennells' daughter, who wrote to Macmillan on 1 May 1963 asking him to 'correct the injustice which has been done': TNA, PREM 11/4459. Other correspondence in this file refers to the distress caused to the family. The matter was raised in Parliament, but Macmillan would not see the family, despatching the Home Secretary instead. Standing on his dignity, Macmillan informed the House of Commons that 'It is not for me to palliate or rebut the conclusions of the Tribunal on this matter after a most careful and thorough inquiry': HC Debs, 7 May 1963, col. 243.

[139] Report of the Tribunal of Inquiry Appointed to Inquire into the Vassall Case and related Matters (n 6), para. 152.

[140] Vassall's PV report by Sherwood (3 December 1956) is filed in TNA, TS 58/632 (W. J. C. Vassall, The Tribunals of Inquiry (Evidence) Act 1921, Report on Security 1956–1963).

[141] Report of the Tribunal of Inquiry Appointed to Inquire into the Vassall Case and Related Matters (n 6), para. 169.

[142] ibid.

[143] ibid., para. 171. See pp. 297–8.

So in addition to the condemnation of a dead man, here we have the condemnation of a vetting officer and his superiors for carrying out their duties in circumstances where, as we also saw in Chapter 10, the Treasury instructions 'gave no precise guidance on how far field inquiries ought to be pressed as a minimum safeguard, apart from an interview with the person being investigated'.[144] In contrast, the two responsible ministers got off scot-free. One—Thomas Galbraith—had, as we have seen, already resigned in connection with the affair, not only in the light of unsubstantiated allegations made about his personal relationship with Vassall, but also in relation to 'his own responsibility for making possible some of Vassall's traitorous activities or failing to detect in him an object of suspicion'.[145] In contrast to Pennells and Sherwood, there was no condemnation of Galbraith for visiting Vassall at his Dolphin Square flat, or in failing to question whether such accommodation was consistent with the presumed income of a civil service clerk:

> And, even though the furnishings were not complete by the autumn, the flat was obviously well furnished and equipped with pieces of appreciable value. Should the sight of this have placed Mr Galbraith on the alert and warned him that there was something suspicious, even perhaps sinister, in Vassall's way of life? We have given this question our careful consideration, because it has a certain plausibility; but we have come to the conclusion that to answer it unfavourably to Mr Galbraith would assume a measure of critical vigilance on the part of the visitor which is out of relation to the realities of human intercourse.[146]

So, it would 'not be reasonable to pass any censure upon Mr Galbraith',[147] in whose private office Vassall worked and whose home Vassall had visited. Nor—to the disappointment of the Opposition[148]—was there any blame to be apportioned to Lord Carrington, the First Lord of the Admiralty:

> A Minister cannot be expected to be in touch with all the day-to-day security problems of a busy Service department, and in our view Lord Carrington has fairly discharged his Ministerial responsibility for security in the Admiralty in the actions he has taken.[149]

[144] ibid. Officers 'were expected to use their discretion' (ibid.), though what is striking in this condemnation of the officers for their error of judgement is any consideration of the likely response from their superiors if they had asked to travel to Moscow to interview Captain Bennett in order to make the full assessment required, or if they had asked for Captain Bennett to be brought back to London for the purpose.

[145] ibid., para. 213.

[146] ibid., para. 253.

[147] ibid., para. 254.

[148] HC Debs, 7 May 1963, col. 331–3.

[149] Report of the Tribunal of Inquiry Appointed to Inquire into the Vassall Case and Related Matters (n 6), para. 276. Compare former Attorney General Sir Frank Soskice in the House of Commons debate on the report: HC Debs, 7 May 1963, cols 352–60.

This was music to the government's ears, with similar passages in the report exonerating Lord Carrington being read out in the House of Lords by the Lord Chancellor (Dilhorne) (known before his elevation as Sir Reginald Manningham Buller), who was sure that 'your Lordships will, in whatever part of the House your Lordships may sit, welcome the conclusion of the Tribunal in relation to the noble Lord and the Service chiefs', adding that he was also 'sure that none of your Lordships who knows my noble friend would ever have dreamt that he would be guilty of such neglect of his duty'.[150]

X. Conclusion

Lord Radcliffe thus presided over what was at the time the most detailed inquisition of journalism ever conducted in the United Kingdom, to which the press was legally bound to submit by virtue of the 1921 Act. Some of his judgments on press standards were excoriating: an article in the *Daily Telegraph* was said to contain 'little truth';[151] another in the *Daily Mail* was said to be 'in all essentials a piece of fiction';[152] and yet another in the *Daily Express* was largely 'embellishment'.[153] While few would be willing to justify the reporting criticized by Radcliffe, it is to be recalled that there was no evidence of any offence having been committed by any of the newspapers: this was not 'phone-hacking', and Radcliffe was not Leveson.[154] It is also to be recalled that the purpose of the inquiry was not to discover whether there was a spy still at large in the Admiralty, but in the words of the Prime Minister, principally to investigate 'terrible accusations which were eventually made against Ministers and others'.[155]

It might have been thought that the involvement of judges would be a matter for reassurance, in the sense that a senior judge in particular would be able to stand back and ask searching questions about the Rule of Law, while tempering the need for security with liberty. But although the judicial vocation is widely believed to bend in the direction of both the Rule of Law and the protection of liberty, we know from judicial practice that these concerns are typically submerged by concerns for security.[156] What was true during the First and Second World Wars was true also during the Cold War, and what was true of the judge acting in a judicial capacity

150 HL Debs, 8 May 1963, col. 710.
151 ibid., para. 116.
152 ibid., para. 223.
153 ibid., para. 234.
154 Lord Leveson, An Inquiry into the Culture, Practices and Ethics of the Press (HC 780, 2012–13).
155 HC Debs, 7 May 1963, col. 241. It is to be recalled further that the Prime Minister did 'not think that great harm has been done to the nation, or great information conveyed to the enemy': ibid., col. 248.
156 See *Liversidge v Anderson* (n 4).

was true of the judge acting in an extra-judicial capacity.[157] In this chapter, we have encountered the contribution of Lord Radcliffe, who in two major reports confounded all expectations about the judicial vocation by displaying absolutely no awareness of the constitutional context within which security judgments were made, the two reports discussed in this chapter traversing almost the entire civil liberties frontier.

In every respect, Lord Radcliffe appears as the man from the Ministry of Information, from where he was catapulted to the Appellate Committee of the House of Lords without any prior judicial experience. The man from the Ministry not only approved existing security measures, but proposed to extend them with an enthusiasm and lack of judgement that clearly appalled the government. Where he found poor practice (such as the over-classification of documents or the informal purge by-passing administrative safeguards), his response was to do nothing (reclassification of documents would be a waste of time for people with 'more important things to do', while the informal purge 'does not, in our view, deprive the individual of any safeguard to which he is entitled').[158] He was also the author of the purge of civil service trade unions, a recommendation that seemed directly to contradict his judgement that the CPGB was not a security threat. If the Communist Party was not a source of espionage what was the reason for decapitating a number of public-sector trade unions?

It is one thing for judges to allow the authority of their office to be used for government work of this kind, but it is an altogether different matter for the judge to discard judicial robes to serve the interests of the executive in the manner revealed here. While it has been known that judges have been willing servants of government, it was perhaps not known just how willing they have been in the service of government. This is perhaps also demonstrated, but in different ways, by the contribution of the Lord Chief Justice, who was as ubiquitous a figure in this period as was Lord Radcliffe. It was rank bad luck for Desmond Clough that he should be sent by Radcliffe to appear before Parker, the latter quoted in the Dictionary of National Biography as saying that the role of the judge was to be the handmaiden of the Executive.[159] He was certainly that, acting not only in the Vassall affair, but also as the key judge in all the leading political cases of the time, being called upon also to support the government in quelling protest groups as disparate as the Committee of 100, and the National Socialist Movement.[160]

[157] See *R v Halliday, ex p Zadig* [1917] AC 260, and *Liversidge v Anderson* (n 4), respectively.
[158] Report on Security Procedures in the Public Service (n 6), paras 50, 56.
[159] D. A. S. Cairns, *Hubert Lister Parker, Baron Parker of Waddington, 1900–1972* (Dictionary of National Biography).
[160] *R v Chandler* [1962] 2 All ER 314; *Jordan v Burgoyne* [1963] 2 QB 744.

Lord Parker and the Politics of the Judiciary

Relaxing in the afterglow of the second Radcliffe Report, the Prime Minister nevertheless acknowledged that many MPs were 'wondering whether the Tribunal procedure is not altogether too heavy an instrument to be employed in this kind of case'.[161] Leading the criticism of the procedure in the House of Commons debate on the second Radcliffe Report was the Leader of the Opposition, though the impact of Mr Wilson's contribution was somewhat diminished by the very powerful defence of the 1921 Act by Sir Frank Soskice, a former Labour Attorney General (and a short-lived Home Secretary in a future Labour government).[162] Mr Wilson's main concern was with the power of the Tribunal to require journalists to reveal their sources, which he conceded could not be an unqualified privilege. However,

> What I am not happy about under the present Tribunal procedure is the way in which the public interest is decided. As far as I can understand, this question has never arisen in the 700 years' history of the courts. The Attorney-General once told us that. But it does come up, and it is liable to do so again, in tribunals. In my view—and I know that some of my hon. and learned Friends, and right hon. and learned Friends, will disagree—where there is a clash between the journalistic code of ethics, which involves the public interest, on the one hand, and the public interest and security, on the other, the decision should be made by Parliament.[163]

The Leader of the Opposition concluded by proposing that a Select Committee should be established to examine the operation of the 1921 Act, looking at a range of issues that had arisen, these including costs and press secrecy, as well as the disclosure of sources.[164] The Cabinet considered these concerns later that month, but reached no conclusion on how to proceed.[165] Thereafter, the Home Secretary and the Secretary of State for Scotland examined the matter, together with a number of senior colleagues principally concerned, a memorandum along with a note prepared by officials being presented to the Cabinet on

[161] HC Debs, 7 May 1963, col. 241.
[162] ibid., cols 352–60.
[163] ibid., col. 266. He continued by saying that 'Parliament is responsible for the Tribunals of Inquiry (Evidence) Act. We have not repealed it, or amended it. We are responsible for the decision to establish a Tribunal in a certain place. We are responsible for the terms of reference—in this case, as in all the others.'
[164] ibid., col. 266.
[165] TNA, CAB 128/37 (Cabinet Conclusions, 30 May 1963).

11 November 1963.[166] The latter note spilled well beyond the concerns raised by Wilson, to include an examination of half a dozen or so different questions, by no means all of which seemed relevant to the conduct of the Vassall inquiry. In the ministers' view, however, there was no case for changing the law, no case for setting up an independent inquiry, and no case for a Select Committee.

The Home Secretary and the Secretary of State for Scotland duly advised the Cabinet accordingly at its meeting on 14 November 1963.[167] In addressing the meeting, the Home Secretary thought that it 'appeared unnecessary' for the government 'to take any initiative to amend the Act', and that there would be no practical advantage in constituting a review of its operation.[168] He accepted, however, that 'public disquiet about the procedures adopted under the Act might be thought to make it politically desirable to institute some inquiry into its working', in which case the inquiry should be entrusted to a Royal Commission.[169] In the discussion that followed, there was general agreement on the importance of allaying public anxiety about the way tribunals under the 1921 Act were conducted, but that 'careful examination had suggested that there was little scope for improvement', given that 'most of the criticisms which could still be advanced against it related to features of its working which were inseparable from the purposes for which it had been enacted'.[170]

So what was to be done? The short-term solution did not reflect well on the independence of the judiciary, it being agreed that:

> the wisest course might be to arrange a debate in the House of Lords, in which the issues involved would be open for discussion by senior members of the Judiciary and it might become clear, as a result, that there would be little advantage in an independent inquiry into the operation of the Act.[171]

The Cabinet thus invited the Leader of the House of Lords, in consultation with the Lord Chancellor, to consider the possibility of arranging a debate in the House of Lords at an early date on the operation of the Tribunals of Inquiry (Evidence) Act 1921. An early debate would precede parliamentary debates about the Denning Report on the Profumo affair, and might satisfy the House of Commons that 'no further action was required to amend the Act of 1921 or substantially to modify the procedures adopted by tribunals appointed under that Act'.[172]

[166] TNA, CAB 129/115 (Tribunals of Inquiry (Evidence) Act 1921, Memorandum by the Secretary for the Home Department and the Secretary of State for Scotland).
[167] TNA, CAB 128/38 (Cabinet Conclusion, 11 November 1963).
[168] ibid.
[169] ibid.
[170] ibid.
[171] ibid.
[172] ibid.

The low-key House of Lords debate took place on 4 December 1963, in which the Lord Chancellor Dilhorne (Manningham-Buller) spoke, as did his immediate predecessor (Viscount Simonds). So too did Lord Parker, the ever-obliging Lord Chief Justice. Lord Parker revealed that he had been involved professionally in three such tribunals (not including the part he played in the Vassall inquiry), claiming that 'anybody who was connected with these inquiries, whether as counsel or as a member of a tribunal, or certainly as a witness, cannot have failed to realise the evils inherent in the procedure'. But in common with the views expressed by ministers, these were 'evils which are inherent in the procedure which really cannot be appreciably lessened'.[173] And right on cue:

> Now, my Lords, what of the future? Is there a case for repealing the Act of 1921? I would say certainly not. It is a weapon that must be preserved and one only hopes that its use will be comparatively rare. Is there a case for amending the Act? Again I would suggest no, unless it be in regard to costs; and here, as the Vassall case inquiry has shown, it is possible to alleviate the burden of cost without any amendment of the Act.[174]

A memorandum by the Lord Chancellor, the Home Secretary, and the Secretary of State for Scotland on 9 December 1963 informed ministers that the debate had taken place, but that it 'did not attract a very large attendance and only seven Peers spoke'.[175] These, however, included both the Lord Chief Justice and Lord Simonds, 'to whose views the House naturally paid great attention'. It was also pointed out that the debate had received 'a generally sympathetic Press', and it was now 'apparent that, at least at present, there is no pressure for any radical amendment of the procedure under the Act of 1921 or for the Act itself to be repealed'.[176] Ministerial colleagues were thus invited to agree that there was 'no case, nor any serious public pressure, for an independent inquiry into the procedure under the Act', and that government spokesmen should take this line in the forthcoming parliamentary debate on the Denning Report relating to Mr John Profumo's resignation.[177]

173 ibid., col. 987.

174 ibid. On the advice of the Radcliffe Tribunal, ex gratia contributions were made towards the costs of those who appeared before it, leading the officials who had advised the Home Secretary and the Secretary of State for Scotland to conclude that although there was a case for amending the Act to provide for the payment of costs, 'in the light of recent practice this does not appear to be a matter of urgency'.

175 TNA, CAB 119/125 (Tribunals of Inquiry (Evidence) Act 1921, Memorandum by the Lord Chancellor, the Secretary of State for the Home Department and the Secretary of State for Scotland, 9 December 1963).

176 ibid.

177 ibid.

Lord Parker's involvement in a campaign hatched by the Cabinet to protect the Tribunals of Inquiry (Evidence) Act 1921 was perhaps the most notable and damaging insight into the judicial role revealed in this chapter. A small matter perhaps, but a remarkable glimpse of the close relationship between government and bench at the highest levels, albeit not as sensational as the revelation elsewhere that Lord Parker had telephoned the Prime Minister the night before he passed sentence on George Blake.[178] The incident about the 1921 Act and its defence also highlighted the presence of another ubiquitous figure in the shape of Lord Dilhorne, who as Attorney General (Sir Reginald Manningham-Buller) appeared before the Lord Chief Justice in the Portland, Blake, and *Chandler* cases in the early 1960s. This cosy relationship not only reinforces the concerns about the highly politicized nature of the British judiciary at the time, but also casts additional light on the judicial back-story to the Profumo case, which we consider in Chapter 14.

[178] *The Guardian*, 2 February 2016.

14
Lord Denning Takes Over

I. Introduction

While the life of Thomas Galbraith was crashing around him as a result of the activities of John Vassall, another minister was implicated in a controversy of a much greater dimension. This was the hapless John Profumo, the Secretary of State for War, who resigned from government on 4 June 1963. During 1961, Profumo enjoyed a sexual relationship with Christine Keeler, an associate of Eugene Ivanov, the Russian Naval attaché, a man known to the Security Service as a Soviet Intelligence officer. They had met at Lord Astor's estate at Cliveden, where Astor's osteopath, Stephen Ward, had the use of a small cottage. Ward was a popular figure, who also enjoyed a close relationship with Keeler and a number of other young women. He was a friend of both Ivanov and Profumo.

Profumo's relationship with Keeler became well known within certain circles in London. According to the official story, gossip had reached Macmillan's ears early in 1963, as Keeler's life kiltered out of control and onto the pages of the newspapers. Macmillan's team of private secretaries had supposedly taken Profumo's word that the gossip about his relationship with Keeler was baseless, and that the relationship was not 'improper'. If not actually confirming Profumo's version of events, MI5's then DG Roger Hollis refrained from giving Macmillan the full story, despite knowing that Profumo and Keeler had been in a sexual relationship. Profumo had gone on to tell a similar story in a statement to the House of Commons in March 1963,[1] subsequently resigning after he had finally admitted that the relationship had been of a sexual nature.

The Profumo affair is, of course, one of the great punctuation marks of twentieth-century political history. It is not only that a minister admitted lying to Parliament and that he resigned for having done so. The affair was symbolic also of the sense of decay that had engulfed the governing Conservative Party, which seemed to have lost its way after twelve years at the helm. But although the Macmillan government was often portrayed as patrician and out of touch with the new spirit of the times, it was paradoxically an affair that was perhaps perfectly consistent with the swinging sixties that was the government's undoing. Lurking behind the links between Profumo, Ivanov, and Keeler were allegations of gangsterism, the use of guns

[1] HC Debs, 22 March 1963, col. 809. Profumo was later found to have committed a contempt of the House: HC Debs, 20 June 1963, col. 655.

MI5, the Cold War, and the Rule of Law. K. D. Ewing, Joan Mahoney, and Andrew Moretta, Oxford University Press (2020). © K. D. Ewing, Joan Mahoney, and Andrew Moretta. DOI: 10.1093/oso/9780198818625.001.0001

and drug-taking, as well as allegations of sexual promiscuity in high society, the last at least implicating Lord Astor, as well as John Profumo.

Lord Astor had been a Tory MP, inheriting his title in 1962. His part in this drama was immortalized by Mandy Rice Davis (a friend of both Ward and Keeler), who was a witness in the trial of Stephen Ward, prosecuted for living off immoral earnings as part of the fall-out from the affair. Confronted by counsel with Astor's denial of a sexual relationship with her, Davis replied that, 'He would, wouldn't he', a rare occasion of the lower orders impertinently turning the tables on their social and economic superiors. It has been said that Lord Astor never recovered from the allegations, his son subsequently claiming that this was 'a scandal that exposed the hypocrisy of the establishment that Ward so offended, exposed the dishonesty of the police and prosecuting authorities and of the security service'.[2] In the end, claimed Lord Astor's heir, 'the characters in the Profumo scandal were all victims'.[3] So too was the integrity of the legal system.

II. The Three Judges

The significance of the Profumo affair for our purposes relates to the insights it provided into the role of the judges in relation to the powers, activities, and accountability of MI5. We have already encountered a number of judge-led enquiries in the 1950s and 1960s, notably the Conference of Privy Councillors (led by the then Lord Chancellor, Viscount Kilmuir) (1956), the Birkett Committee (1957), the Romer Committee (1961), the Radcliffe Committee (1962), and the Radcliffe Tribunal of Inquiry (1963).[4] These were all concerned with either (i) in general terms the existing security procedures, and the powers of MI5 (the Privy Councillors, Birkett, and Radcliffe (1)); or (ii) the operation of these procedures and powers in practice (Romer and Radcliffe (2)). What distinguishes the Denning inquiry in relation to the Profumo affair, however, is that it was the first of the six inquiries established specifically to address 'the operation of the Security Service'.[5] Appointed on 21 June 1963, Denning's full terms of reference were as follows:

> To examine, in the light of the circumstances leading to the resignation of the former Secretary of State for War, Mr J D Profumo, the operation of the Security Service and the adequacy of their co-operation with the police in matters of security, to investigate any information or material which may come to his attention

[2] *Daily Mail*, 9 January 2014. The current Lord Astor was described as David Cameron's father in law.

[3] ibid.

[4] See Chapters 4, 8, 9, and 10 above.

[5] Lord Denning's Report, Cmnd 2152, 1963, para. 1.

> in this connection and to consider any evidence there may be for believing that national security has been, or may be, endangered.[6]

There were, however, three judges who had a role in the Profumo affair; this was by no means a solo performance for Denning. Indeed, the judges involved were the three most senior in the country at the time: the Lord Chancellor (by now Viscount Dilhorne), the Master of the Rolls (Denning), and the Lord Chief Justice (Parker); in other words, the heads of the House of Lords, the Court of Appeal, and the High Court, respectively. It would not be possible to say that the three of them *conspired* to protect the government, and to pervert the course of justice; but only because there is no clear evidence—nor is there ever likely to be—that they met formally or informally to co-ordinate a response to the Profumo affair. We know, however, that the Lord Chancellor recommended the appointment of Lord Denning, and that the Lord Chancellor and Lord Denning were in communication before the Denning Report was published.[7] We also know that the Lord Chancellor and Lord Chief Justice Parker were as thick as thieves afterwards, as they salvaged some of the debris from the affair.[8]

An insight into the latter is provided shortly after the Denning Report was published. In December 1963, Christine Keeler had been convicted of perjury for evidence given in the trial of one 'Lucky' Gordon, evidence she also gave at Stephen Ward's trial. As we will see, Gordon's appeal against conviction was successful, his conviction being quashed by the Court of Criminal Appeal (on the same day that Ward's trial ended), though ostensibly not for reasons relating directly to Keeler's perjury. As a result of the conviction being quashed, Gordon was free to leave the court, which at the time had no power to order a retrial.[9] Within a month of the Keeler trial, however, the Lord Chancellor (with the Lord Chief Justice also present) introduced a Criminal Appeal Bill to confer such a power on the appeal court.[10] Only three members of the House of Lords spoke in the Second Reading debate; Dilhorne being one, Parker being another, both referring freely to the Gordon case. Particularly eye-catching in a very short debate is Dilhorne's tribute to Parker:

> of all courts [the Court of Criminal Appeal] is probably subject to the heaviest pressure of business at the present time, and it is, if I may say so with the greatest

[6] HC Debs, 21 June 1963, col. 802. The inquiry and its terms of reference were reported to the Cabinet on the day before they were announced to Parliament: TNA, CAB 128/37/39 (Cabinet Conclusions, 20 June 1963).

[7] C. Pincher, *Their Trade is Treachery* (London, 1981), p. 91. This information was provided by Dilhorne to Pincher, who was a 'close friend' (ibid., p. 88). Shortly before his death, Dilhorne is said to have told Pincher that (in his capacity as Lord Chancellor) he had been the only person to have seen the Denning Report before it had been submitted (p. 91).

[8] See also pp. 407–10 above.

[9] For full details, see G. Robertson, *Stephen Ward Was Innocent, OK: The Case for Overturning His Conviction* (London, 2013).

[10] This became the Criminal Appeal Act 1964, giving the Court of Criminal Appeal the power to order a retrial: A. Samuels, 'Criminal Law Appeal Act 1964' (1964) 27 *MLR* 568.

> respect to my noble friend the Lord Chief Justice, a great credit to him and to his fellow Judges that its prestige stands so high.[11]

As already suggested, we will probably never know whether there was any collusion between Dilhorne and Parker during the Profumo affair. But whether formally or informally, the three most senior judges in the country each stand condemned for their failure to hold government and government agencies to account, and for failing to perform their first duty, which was to the Rule of Law and the procedures they were supposed to uphold. In their desire to give cover to the government, they certainly failed to hold the Security Service properly to account, and revealed themselves to be no better than the politicians it was their duty to check. The Lord Chancellor helped to create a narrative around the 'Stephen Ward affair', as the 'Profumo affair' metamorphosed in government; and although not the judge in the Stephen Ward trial, Lord Parker helped to ensure that the latter was convicted, contriving it seems to influence the jury (in a case in which he did not sit), to secure a conviction in a quite unprecedented (so far as we are aware) intervention.[12]

The Profumo affair was, of course, the stuff of theatre, film, and fiction.[13] As such, it is perhaps not easy initially to see what it had to do with the operation of MI5, or with the role of the enior judiciary in matters of national security.[14] There were, however, three barely concealed yet over-lapping questions of urgent concern, these relating to (i) the powers and accountability of the Security Service; (ii) the collusion of senior judges in a grave miscarriage of justice; and (iii) the independence of the judiciary more broadly. So far as the first of these matters is concerned, for reasons considered below the affair perhaps unexpectedly shed light on the role of the Security Service, raising profound questions about its operations and activities. Did MI5 operate in accordance with its mandate? Who was checking to ensure that MI5 was operating in accordance with its mandate? And to whom was MI5 in practice accountable for any failure to act in accordance with its mandate?

So far as the second question is concerned—that of judicial collusion—this arises in relation to the search for a sacrifice and the clinical removal of Stephen Ward, whose prosecution was every bit a political show trial as those in Moscow so vigorously condemned by Washington and London. As was understood at the

[11] HL Debs, 14 January 1964, cols 526–7.

[12] According to the Dictionary of National Biography, Parker was made a life peer on his elevation to the position of Lord Chief Justice, taking the title Lord Parker of Waddington, which was the same as his father, who had previously been a judicial member of the House of Lords (see Chapter 13 above).

[13] It also produced outstanding contemporary journalism. See L. Kennedy, *The Trial of Stephen Ward* (Harmondsworth, 1964).

[14] Apart of course from the obvious role of Lord Denning in his review of the affair.

time, Stephen Ward was a 'scapegoat' and a 'victim of British hypocrisy',[15] unusually robust language for a journal normally as upright and staid as the *Criminal Law Review*. But the language was if anything understated, a point reinforced by commentators on several occasions since.[16] The travesty of Stephen Ward's trial revealed the role of politicians in directing police investigations, and that at best the protection by the Courts of the common law rights of suspects was pure fiction. At worst, it revealed a willingness of the judges at a time of high political excitement quite explicitly and brazenly to serve the ends of the government and the State rather than the ends of justice, though we ought not now to be surprised by this.

The foregoing leads us to question the principles and practices of judicial independence more widely, doubts about which we encountered in Chapter 13 in relation to Lord Radcliffe, who seemed to be more security-minded than either Sir Norman Brook or Sir Roger Hollis. Independence means a sense of detachment from rather than engagement with the work of the subject being reviewed, and in the case of the Security Service the judge might be expected to temper the demands of national security with the need to protect civil liberties.[17] But Denning was engaged in a different exercise than that which had occupied Radcliffe, in the sense that he was charged with the duty of determining whether MI5 had operated within the scope of its lawful authority, and whether those who were politically responsible under these powers properly discharged their duty. In performing this task, it is clear that Denning was also moved by the temper of the time and the needs of the State. His task was to minimize damage rather than create it.

Sweeping up at the end, Lord Denning thus provided valuable cover, in a report he himself recognized might be seen as a 'whitewash'.[18] He was right to raise the concern: it *was* a whitewash. True, the report had two great virtues. First, it exposed the procedures under which MI5 operated and provided the first serious official discussion of the work of the Service, while second, it pointed the finger of blame fairly and squarely at the Prime Minister and his colleagues for their handling of the affair. But Denning nevertheless failed in two key respects directly related to our inquiry.[19] While not disputing that he hit the bullseye in terms of responsibility (there can be no disputing that Profumo was about the collective failure of ministers, and the collective responsibility of ministers),[20] there were two sub-themes

15 G. L. W., 'The Trial of Dr Ward' [1963] *Crim L R* 597. 'GLW' is Professor Glanville Williams.

16 Notably, Robertson (n 9), who makes a strong case for posthumously overturning Ward's conviction.

17 This brings us back, of course, to A. V. Dicey, *Introduction to the Study of the Law of the Constitution* (London, 1885).

18 Lord Denning's Report (n 5), para. 9.

19 For a contemporary assessment of Lord Denning's Report, see D. G. T. Williams, *Not in the Public Interest—The Problem of Security in Democracy* (London, 1965), pp. 156–8, 164–9.

20 Lord Denning's Report (n 5), paras 283 and 286.

central to the story that he got badly wrong, white-washing the role of the Home Secretary in the affair in particular:

- having exposed the procedures governing the Security Service, Denning fell short by (i) allowing the failure of MI5 to comply with its governing Directive (written to its demands) to pass without censure; and as a result (ii) not properly addressing the culpability of MI5 for its performance in the Profumo Affair;[21]
- having exposed political interference in the prosecution of Stephen Ward, Denning again allowed to pass without comment or censure what was a monstrous perversion of the course of justice, and contributed to the scapegoating of Stephen Ward, an innocent man the persecution of whom appears to have caused him to take his own life.

III. Denning's Principal Findings

Before addressing these issues, it will be useful to clear the air with a brief account of Lord Denning's celebrated report and its main findings, these providing the context of much of what follows. The bulk of the report was a detailed account of the relationship between Profumo and Christine Keeler: how they met (at Lord Astor's swimming-pool party at Cliveden), and her connections with Stephen Ward, who was close to a Russian diplomat called Ivanov, with whom Keeler was friendly (and with whom she claimed to be having an affair). Ward—who was well connected politically and had delusions of grandeur—is reported to have had an ambiguous relationship with the Security Service. The evidence suggests that Ward was in contact with, and under suspicion by, MI5 because of his links to Ivanov. On 31 July 1961, MI5's suspicions about Ward were passed to the Cabinet Secretary (Sir Norman Brook), who then warned Profumo privately about Ward (but not Keeler), at which point Profumo claims to have broken off his relationship with Keeler.[22]

Thereafter the narrative is largely about how the story of an old affair became public (with much speculation in the press), and of how Mr Profumo lied to everyone about it, including his Cabinet colleagues and the government's law officers. Matters began to unravel seriously when the Home Secretary finally intervened, as a result of which the focus of attention concentrated intensely on Stephen Ward, with criminal investigations leading to charges being brought against him for living off immoral earnings (of two young women, one of whom was Christine Keeler).[23] These investigations led to Ward renewing claims about the affair

21 The Directive in question is, of course, the Maxwell Fyfe Directive. It is interesting to reflect that there is no discussion of the legal status of the Directive in the Denning Report or elsewhere at the time (so far as we are aware). It probably did not matter.

22 Lord Denning's Report (n 5), paras 33–37.

23 G. Robertson, *Independent*, 19 December 2014. Neither woman had 'immoral earnings'.

between Profumo and Keeler; to rumours that Keeler had fled the country to avoid giving evidence in a previously unrelated criminal trial (of John Edgecombe) in order to protect Profumo; and to Profumo's parliamentary statement in which he not only denied the latter allegation (about Keeler's disappearance), but also claimed that he had never had an improper relationship with Keeler (with whom he had committed adultery).[24]

The foregoing account necessarily does less than justice to the full story as told by Lord Denning with its folds, wrinkles, and turns. But that is the essence of it, and buried deep in the report are two stand-out issues and two stand-out paragraphs that are crucial to the analysis that follows. The first of these issues relates to the role of MI5 and its culpability for what happened, with concerns having been expressed that MI5 had been sleeping on the job and had failed to keep ministers fully briefed as events unfolded. According to Denning, however in the first of these stand-out paragraphs,

> [The Security Service] work under a strict directive to confine themselves to danger to the Realm as a whole. Once they came to the conclusion that there was no security interest in the matter, but only moral misbehaviour in a Minister, they were under no duty to report it to anyone. They did come to that conclusion. They came to it honestly and reasonably and I do not think they should be found at fault.[25]

This is important because it applies standard administrative law principles to MI5 in the sense that it is required to use its discretionary powers 'honestly and reasonably', but important also, of course, in finding that these standards had been met.

Indeed, with a nod in the direction of his terms of reference it should be pointed out that Lord Denning absolved both the police and the Security Service of any failure of duty, and found also that cooperation between them was beyond reproach.[26] In Lord Denning's view, none of the government services was thus to 'blame' (though it is not clear for what), this being an 'unprecedented situation for which the machinery of government did not cater': 'neither the police nor the Security Service should pry into private lives',[27] Denning noting that there is no machinery for reporting the moral misbehaviour of ministers.[28] According to Lord Denning, 'it is perhaps better thus, than that we should have a "police state". That being so, when a "Minister is guilty of moral misbehaviour and it gives rise to scandalous rumour", it is for him and his colleagues to deal with it as best they can. It is their responsibility and no one else's.'[29]

[24] ibid., paras 200–8, 228.
[25] ibid., para. 283.
[26] ibid., paras 274–6.
[27] Contrast the prying into the private life of Neil Lawson, pp. 99-100 above. MI5 frequently pried into private lives.
[28] Lord Denning's Report (n 5), para. 283.
[29] ibid.

The second stand-out issue relates to the treatment of Stephen Ward and the mobilization of forces to contain and destroy him. He was the unfortunate victim of an unforeseeable random incident in which Christine Keeler was an alleged victim of another of her associates (John Edgecombe), and was scheduled to give evidence in the trial against the individual in question. This gave rise to panic on the part of Ward, Profumo, and Astor, concerned that unsavoury evidence relating to their relationship with Keeler would become public.[30] And for reasons that are not at all clear, Keeler's anxiety about giving evidence led to her informing a large number of people about her relationship with Profumo and Ivanov, so that by the end of January 1963 it was known to George Wigg MP; the *News of the World*, and the *Sunday Pictorial*; and the police and the Security Services, as well as others.[31] This in turn led to six weeks of fevered political activity culminating in Profumo's ill-fated personal statement to the House of Commons on 22 March 1963, in which he denied any impropriety in his relationship with Keeler.[32]

According to Denning, Profumo's statement left the Home Secretary (Henry Brooke) 'feeling very suspicious towards Stephen Ward',[33] though there was nothing in the short statement to arouse such suspicion. Nevertheless, Brooke asked to see both the Head of MI5 (Hollis) and the Metropolitan Police Commissioner (Sir Joe Simpson), the meeting taking place on 27 March 1963. We will return to this meeting at various points below, its significance for present purposes being Brooke's assumption of control over the prosecution of Ward, asking Simpson curtly but with clear enough meaning and intent 'whether there was a police interest'.[34] Although we are told by Denning that the Commissioner was sceptical about any prosecution succeeding, in what is the second stand-out paragraph for our purposes, we find Denning reporting that in the aftermath of the meeting on 27 March:

> the Commissioner of Police immediately gave further consideration to the question of prosecuting Ward, and on 1st April, 1963, set on foot an investigation which eventually led to his prosecution and conviction.[35]

In other words, Simpson was told to get Ward, presumably to protect Profumo. But although the need to sacrifice Ward ceased to exist when Profumo notified the Prime Minister of his resignation on 4 June 1963, there was no way back.[36] Having been targeted for the preservation of Profumo and his colleagues, the persecution

30 ibid., paras 71–74.
31 ibid., para. 68.
32 HC Debs, 22 March 1963, col. 809.
33 Lord Denning's Report (n 5), para. 68.
34 ibid., para. 197.
35 ibid., para. 199.
36 For the resignation letter, see ibid., para. 220.

of Ward now satisfied the desire for revenge by those whose house he had brought down. But while Denning also denounced Ward with unvarnished contempt, the weight of responsibility for the whole affair was found by Lord Denning to lie principally with Profumo, though the disgraced minister may nevertheless have taken some comfort from Lord Denning's judgement that despite the constant presence of Ivanov (who had disappeared back to Moscow before the closing stages), there had been no breach of security: there was no evidence that Profumo had given information to Keeler, who as a result had not given any information to Ward, who as a result had not given any information to Ivanov.

Yet the Denning Report would have made uncomfortable reading for Profumo, who lost his seat in Parliament, his position in government, and his membership of the Privy Council;[37] but not his liberty (despite having brought successful defamation claims to protect his lies).[38] It was nevertheless plausible that Denning's judgement should be directed initially at Profumo, and plausible also that some responsibility should rest with Profumo's ministerial colleagues, and ultimately with the Prime Minister, who Denning appears to suggest had been naïve and gullible in failing to press Profumo further on key questions. In the brutal assessment of Lord Denning, 'It was the responsibility of the Prime Minister and his colleagues, and of them only, to deal with this situation: and they did not succeed in doing so.'[39] But while Macmillan and his colleagues were thus clearly culpable, what seems less plausible was Lord Denning's assessment that MI5 had 'honestly and reasonably' complied with its mandate, and his judgment about the importance and value of the Home Secretary's meeting of 25 March,[40] matters to which we return.

IV. The Maxwell Fyfe Directive

Before returning to the foregoing matters, it should be acknowledged that Lord Denning won many plaudits for 'unexpectedly' uncovering the Maxwell Fyfe Directive, setting out paragraphs 1–6 of the text in his Report.[41] As we saw in Chapter 3, the Attlee Directive was the instrument by which the Security Service was governed, a secret but constitutional text drafted by Attlee and Edward Bridges to reflect the recommendations of the Findlater Stewart Report, which was subsequently diluted by MI5 to become the Maxwell Fyfe Directive in 1952. This important document had never previously been acknowledged, nor its legal authority or effects ever discussed. But apart from publicizing a document that appears to

37 Lord Denning's Report (n 5), para. 222: 'His disgrace was complete.'
38 ibid., para. 190.
39 ibid., para. 286.
40 ibid., para. 195.
41 L. Lustgarten and I. Leigh, *In from the Cold* (Oxford, 1994), p. 375. See Lord Denning's Report (n 5), para. 238, where paras 1–6 of the Directive are set out.

have been unknown even to Privy Councillors on the government benches, the Denning Report was clearly also important for bringing the constitutional position of the Security Service into full view, as well as for the sentiments expressed in the discussion of the legal powers of the Service. That said, however, Lord Denning painted a very benign picture of the Service, and avoided hard questions about its accountability.

Thus, Lord Denning made clear that Security Service operations are to be used for one purpose and one purpose only, namely the defence of the realm:

> They were not to be used to pry into someone's private conduct or business affairs, or into his or her political opinions, except in so far as they are subversive, which is to say that 'they would contemplate the overthrow of the Government by unlawful means'.[42]

This limited role for the Security Service was something with which 'most people in this country would wholeheartedly support', for 'it would be intolerable to us to have anything in the nature of a Gestapo or Secret Police to snoop into all that we do, let alone into our morals'.[43] But as Lord Denning pointed out, the Security Service is 'not established by Statute nor is it recognized by Common Law', while even the Official Secrets Acts do not acknowledge its existence.[44] He continued in an important passage to say that:

> The members of the Service are, in the eye of the law, ordinary citizens with no powers greater than anyone else. They have no special powers of arrest such as the police have. No special powers of search are given to them. They cannot enter premises without the consent of the householder, even though they may suspect a spy is there. If a spy is fleeing the country, they cannot tap him on the shoulder and say he is not to go. They have, in short, no executive powers. They have managed very well without them. We would rather have it so, than have anything in the nature of a 'secret police'.[45]

This detailed account of the Maxwell Fyfe Directive was clearly an important breakthrough in terms of the transparency of MI5 and it should not be underestimated. By the same token, however, it seems likely that it was officially sanctioned, and that the government used the Denning Report as an opportunity to put into the public domain information that ought to have been there already. The publication of the constitutional arrangements relating to MI5 had been canvassed

[42] Lord Denning's Report (n 5), para. 230.
[43] ibid.
[44] ibid., para. 273.
[45] ibid.

in an anonymous Treasury Chambers memorandum on 23 August 1963, drafted it seems for submission to Lord Denning. Although addressing the question whether a Ministry of National Security should be created (an idea roundly rejected by the authors), the memorandum inevitably addressed the existing constitutional position of the Security Service, and in doing so suggested that '[t]here is no reason why the Home Secretary's responsibility for the Security Service should not be made public', having already been alluded to in the House of Commons by the Prime Minister.[46] Indeed, after discussing the complementary duties of the police and the Security Service, the author suggested further that it would be helpful for this to be done:

> It would therefore seem to be right and appropriate for the Home Secretary's position in relation to the Security Service to be made known. This would enable him to give the Prime Minister even more support than at present, because he could then deal with Parliamentary Questions other than those of the most general importance.

But having thus made the constitutional position known (albeit with government approval), Lord Denning also exposed *the lack of awareness about the Directive within government*. The transfer of responsibility to the Home Secretary in 1952 'had never been announced: and it does not seem to have been generally known',[47] even at the highest level. Macmillan's hatchet man, Lord Chancellor and former Attorney General, Reginald Manningham-Buller, implausibly seemed uncertain, as suggested by his report to the Prime Minister on 12 June 1963. This was the point at which the 'Profumo affair' became the 'Stephen Ward affair', as the Lord Chancellor's report was headed, even though it deals in great detail with Profumo and his conduct. Here, the Lord Chancellor referred to intelligence that MI5 had obtained from the police on 7 February 1963 that Keeler had been asked by Ward to obtain information from Profumo about the delivery of atomic secrets to West Germany. The failure of MI5 to pass on the intelligence brought a rebuke from Dilhorne, who concluded that the Security Service had made an error of judgement in not making it available 'to a Minister or to one of the Prime Minister's Private Secretaries'.[48]

But although Lord Denning gently rejected this latter assessment, it was not because the Lord Chancellor had identified the wrong person to be approached.

46 TNA, PREM 11/4471 (House of Commons Debate about Denning Report: Speech by Prime Minister) ('A Minister for National Security', 23 August 1963, Memorandum drafted from Treasury Chambers). The creation of a Ministry of National Security was also rejected by Lord Denning. See Lord Denning's Report (n 5), para. 242.

47 Lord Denning's Report (n 5), para. 182.

48 TNA, CAB/129/113 ('The Stephen Ward Case', Memorandum by the Lord Chancellor, 14 June 1963).

Denning nevertheless made it plain that not even the Lord Chancellor (who had been around as a law officer continuously since November 1951) was aware of the Directive,[49] with further evidence of ignorance within government about its existence or content being revealed at a Cabinet meeting on 12 June 1963, where it was minuted that:

> It was now widely believed that the Security Service had known, from the outset, of the relationship between Mr Profumo and Miss Keeler and either that they had failed to inform the Prime Minister of this potential risk to security or that they had done so and that the Prime Minister had failed to take any action at the relevant time.[50]

Given the terms of the Maxwell Fyfe Directive, it is not clear why the Security Service should have reported to the Prime Minister, this apparently popular misconception about its responsibility having gone unchallenged at the meeting. As Denning was later to make clear, the first salient point of the Maxwell Fyfe Directive was that 'The Head of the Security Service is responsible directly to the Home Secretary for the efficient and proper working of the Service and *not* in the ordinary way to the Prime Minister.'[51]

But having exposed the formal constitutional position of MI5, and the apparent ignorance about it within government, the Denning Report also helped to expose the fact that *these procedures were manifestly not applied in practice*. So far as the channels of responsibility are concerned, Lord Denning set these out clearly enough in the following terms:

> The result of these principles is that, if the Director-General of the Security Service is in doubt as to any aspect of his duties—as, for instance, when he gets information about a minister or senior public servant indicating that he may be a security risk—he should consult the Home Secretary. The Home Secretary will then have to take the responsibility for further action, that is to say, whether to take steps to eliminate the security risk or to put up with it. If a mistake is made, it is the Home Secretary who will be responsible to Parliament.[52]

But it is just as clear that this is not what was happening, as reflected by the chain of events in the Profumo case. The Home Secretary 'had never been in the picture',[53] until he woke up and asked for a briefing on 27 March, by which time Ivanov had long been recalled. All security contact between the government and MI5 had been

49 Lord Denning's Report (n 5), para. 268.
50 TNA, CAB 128/37/37 (Cabinet Conclusions, 12 June 1963).
51 Lord Denning's Report (n 5), para. 239 (emphasis in original).
52 ibid., para. 240.
53 ibid., para. 182.

with the Cabinet Secretary, the man who had engineered the transfer of responsibility in 1952 and the man clearly in charge.

It is curious that there should be no criticism of this practice by Lord Denning. Not only was this a breach of the Directive, on which Lord Denning placed great weight to expulcate the Security Service of any wrong-doing, but it also meant that there could be no parliamentary accountability for decisions taken. To whom was the Cabinet Secretary responsible? This looked like a back-stairs operation, from which the responsible minister was cut out, and as such it was constitutionally reprehensible. Yet according to Lord Denning, it was to Sir Norman Brook that Hollis had suggested that 'it might be useful for him to have a word with Mr Profumo about Stephen Ward and Captain Ivanov'.[54] Although the circumstances were clearly difficult and Hollis had 'carefully considered what to do', it was nevertheless a breach of the Directive by both Hollis and Brook, no ministers being informed. It is true that Hollis had approached Brook rather than Profumo himself for reasons of 'awkwardness', and because as Cabinet Secretary Brook was a 'in a position to speak to a Minister' on a matter such as this.[55] Denning's silence was nevertheless all the more curious for the clarity of his understanding of the constitutional chain of command:

> It was suggested to me that, when the conduct of a Minister was in question, it would be preferable for the Director-General to approach the Prime Minister direct rather than approach the Home Secretary because the Home Secretary might find it embarrassing to have to investigate the conduct of another Minister. The majority view was, however, that in all cases there should be a clear and unambiguous channel to the Home Secretary.[56]

Yet as already pointed out, the Home Secretary had not been informed about MI5's concerns until he supposedly took the initiative to find out what was going on, by summoning Hollis and the Metropolitan Police Commissioner to a meeting on 27 March 1963. Despite the concerns referred to above, this meeting was celebrated by Denning as being 'so valuable that it affords a useful pattern as to the way in which such a problem—of mixed security and police interest—should be handled'.[57] Perhaps so. Highlighting the obvious distance of the Home Secretary from the action, Lord Denning noted not only that this was the first time any minister had been told about the request for information about the bomb, (of which MI5 had been informed by the police on 7 February), but also that the Home Secretary 'did not know he was the first to be told about it' (nor did he seem to care,

[54] ibid., para. 33.
[55] ibid., para. 247.
[56] ibid., para. 241.
[57] ibid., para. 195.

though constitutionally only he should have been informed). Indeed, he thought 'he was simply being brought up to date by the Security Service'.[58]

V. The Expulcation of MI5

Lord Denning's revelations about MI5 were thus even more revealing than was perhaps intended. While parts of the Maxwell Fyfe Directive were placed in the public domain for the first time, it was shown that the provisions of this hitherto secret text were largely unknown even in government, and that the responsible minister was kept largely in the dark,[59] the key player in government being a civil servant—Sir Norman Brook, the Cabinet Secretary and principal author of the ostensible shifting of responsibility from the Prime Minister to the Home Secretary. Denning is to be applauded for unearthing this shambles, but is open to criticism for not illuminating its consequences. He is open to criticism also for the extent to which he absolved the Security Service of any fault in the unfolding drama of the Profumo affair, MI5 being culpable on two counts, and more if Chapman Pincher (a particularly well-informed and experienced intelligence journalist) is to be believed.[60]

The first criticism is that Denning expulcates MI5 for ignorance of that which it should have known. As we have seen, MI5 had duties under the Maxwell Fyfe Directive in terms of counter-espionage, in the discharge of which it was responsible to the Home Secretary personally. Yet Denning expulcated Hollis for not knowing the true nature of the relationship between Profumo and Keeler, and accepted the DG's version of events that this information did not reach the Security Service until the end of January 1963, being provided by a 'secret source considered reliable'.[61] True, we have become accustomed to MI5—a counter-espionage agency—being over-obsessed with fears of subversion and ill-informed about espionage threats, going back to Nunn May and Klaus Fuchs, and of course to 'Sonya'. But even supposing Denning is right and the Security Service did not know about the affair (a claim which is hotly contested), on this occasion the lack of knowledge (if there was a lack of knowledge) seems wilful, rather than negligent.

As is clear from the Denning Report, Ward had had contacts with MI5 since 1961, keeping them well informed of his 'obvious admiration' of Ivanov, and his

58 ibid., para. 198. The Lord Chancellor put it slightly differently: 'The Home Secretary was under the mistaken impression that this information was already known to those dealing with the Profumo case and that was why he took no personal action on it': 'The Stephen Ward Case' (n 48), para. 39.

59 A position perhaps nicely summed up unintentionally by Denning when he wrote: 'The Home Secretary left the House immediately after the debate ended and went home. He was not called back to the meeting. The question has been asked, why was he not called back? The answer is that no one thought of it. He had never been in the picture previously' (Lord Denning's Report (n 5), para. 182).

60 See Pincher (n 7), ch. 9.

61 Lord Denning's Report (n 5), para. 259.

'friendship' with Profumo. An MI5 agent had been to Ward's house, where he met Keeler, and the same agent knew that she had been at the Cliveden party where she had met Profumo. This was described by Denning in these terms:

> There had been quite a party of celebrities there deporting themselves in the swimming pool, including Mr Profumo, the Secretary of State for War. Ivanov had been much amused by their antics. Christine was there (Ward explained that Christine was the young girl who lived in his house.) Ivanov was undoubtedly attracted by Christine. After the bathing party, Ivanov had taken her back to his (Ward's) house and they had drunk between them two bottles of whisky. Ward claimed that he and Mr Profumo were quite close friends and Mr Profumo visited him at his London house.[62]

Following a second meeting between Ward and the MI5 agent, the Security Service is said to have asked Special Branch 'to make inquiries' about 'Ward's establishment and about Christine'.[63] A week later, Special Branch reported that 'Christine could not be identified and that enquiries revealed nothing to the discredit of Ward'.[64] But although MI5's suspicions about Ward and Keeler had thus been aroused, the trail was simply allowed to go cold, Lord Denning rejecting any criticism of MI5:

> It has been said that the Security Service ought to have done differently. They ought to have set a watch on Ward's house or got permission to tap his telephone calls: for they would then have discovered that Mr Profumo was having an affair with Christine Keeler at Stephen Ward's house and that Captain Ivanov was often at the house too. But I am satisfied that this criticism is mistaken. *The Security Service knew all that they needed to know about the Ward–Ivanov relationship*: and it would not have increased their knowledge to have set a watch on Ward's house. They knew that Ivanov was a Russian Intelligence Officer. They already had from other sources information as to Ivanov's visits to and relations with Ward. They knew also that Mr Profumo was on occasions visiting Ward's house. They acted on that information by having Mr Profumo warned. I do not think the Security Service should be blamed for not doing more.[65]

But how could MI5 have known that they knew 'all they needed to know about the Ivanov–Ward relationship'? They could not have known that at the time, and with the benefit of hindsight (with which this whole affair appears to have been judged

[62] ibid., para. 246.
[63] ibid., para. 247.
[64] It is at this point that the Cabinet Secretary was told about Ward, and that Profumo was warned in turn, leading him to end his relationship with Keeler.
[65] Lord Denning's Report (n 5), para. 249 (emphasis added).

by Denning) they clearly *did not* know all they needed to know. What was known and what did give rise to suspicion were the following facts:

(i) Ward was thought to have 'peculiar political beliefs', coupled with an 'obvious admiration of Ivanov', which 'might well cause him to be indiscreet unintentionally'.[66]
(ii) Ivanov was known to be a 'Russian intelligence officer'; indeed, he had been exposed as a GRU officer (the GRU being the 'military arm of the Soviet espionage and subversion apparatus').[67]
(iii) Ivanov, a known Russian agent, visited the home of an unstable British citizen who was also visited at home by Profumo, not just a Cabinet minister but the Secretary of State for War.

It would not require a lifetime working for MI5 to wonder what Profumo was up to. Given the intensity of the surveillance of small fry like Neil Lawson, it is at best remarkable that the pathologically curious MI5 did not persist with its inquiries to discover (i) why someone like Profumo was consorting with someone like Ward; and (ii) whether by doing so he was putting the defence of the realm in jeopardy.

Yet Denning not only absolved MI5 of criticism for an intelligence failure, he also absolved it of culpability for a second failure. This was *the failure to report the information about the relationship between Keeler and Profumo and Ivanov respectively to the Home Secretary in a timely manner* once they claimed to have stumbled upon it in late January 1963. Information came MI5's way in two instalments:

- On 28/29 January 1963, information was received from a 'reliable source' that Profumo had enjoyed a 'prolonged affair with Keeler', whom Profumo had visited several times; that she had also been visited several times by Ivanov; that Profumo had written her amorous letters which were now in the hands of the *Sunday Pictorial*; and that the Russians were so certain that a scandal was brewing that they ordered Ivanov to return to Moscow.[68]
- On 7 February 1963, Special Branch reported to MI5 information they had received directly from Keeler corroborating the information obtained on 28/29 January, while adding that 'Stephen Ward had asked her to discover from Mr Profumo the date in which atomic secrets were to be handed to Western Germany'. Keeler had described Ward as 'a procurer of women for gentlemen in high places' who 'was sexually perverted', and that he had introduced her to both Profumo and Ivanov.[69]

[66] ibid., para. 246.
[67] Pincher (n 7), p. 81.
[68] ibid., para. 259.
[69] ibid., paras 266 and 280.

As Lord Denning himself made clear, MI5's mandate meant that 'it must collect information about individuals, and give it to those concerned'.[70] However, in again providing cover for Hollis, Lord Denning found that MI5 could not be blamed for failing to pass on this information to ministers. In reaching this conclusion, he accepted two arguments presented by Hollis:

- First, MI5 were 'not greatly impressed' by Keeler's statement about Ward's request for information about the atomic bombs. There was no evidence that Keeler had complied with the request or that Profumo had given her the information. The only security interest would have arisen had there been a possibility to charge Ward under the Official Secrets Act, but this was ruled out by MI5.
- Second, there was no security risk now that Ivanov had left the country, any danger having passed. In any event there was no reason to doubt the loyalty of Profumo, for although there may have been doubts about his moral behaviour, that was not a matter for MI5 to report. It was a personal matter with political implications. But it 'had no longer any security interest'.[71]

Nevertheless, it must surely have struck even Lord Denning as strange that on 1 February 1963 the government should have been told about the relationship between Keeler and Profumo and Ivanov, respectively in a telephone call from a journalist rather than from its own Security Service.[72] Indeed, the Prime Minister's Principal Private Secretary phoned MI5 on the same day to tell them about the call, only a few days after Hollis claimed that MI5 had been made aware by their 'reliable source', and on the same day that Hollis had given an instruction to colleagues not to act on the information.[73] MI5 replied by saying that this was 'recognisably the same story as they already had', and agreed that Profumo should be seen, but did not subsequently volunteer the other information that they received from the police on 7 February, about Ward asking Keeler to obtain secret information from Profumo. Indeed, this information was not provided to the Prime Minister until 29 May 1963, when Macmillan had finally asked to see Hollis as the political pressure was intensifying, shortly before Profumo's resignation.

In a serious over-indulgence of the Security Service, Lord Denning painted a benign picture of an organization remarkably self-contained and self-controlled, hugging closely to the terms of its legal mandate. Responding to the Lord

[70] ibid., para. 239. As Pincher (n 7) pointed out, those concerned would include the Home Secretary, who was placed in an embarrassing position by Hollis' inaction, especially in relation to a parliamentary debate on 21 March 1963, where he knew nothing about the details laid bare by Labour's George Wigg (p. 89). See Lord Denning's Report (n 5), para. 169.

[71] Lord Denning's Report (n 5), para. 267.

[72] ibid., para. 262.

[73] ibid., paras 259–263.

Chancellor's claims that Hollis should have shared information much earlier,[74] Denning thought that Dilhorne made a mistake. In an unusual public disagreement, Denning explained that the mistake was due to the fact that the Lord Chancellor did not have the Maxwell Fyfe Directive before him when writing his report. If he had done so, Dilhorne would have realized that MI5 are 'not to meddle with anything which is not clearly and specifically their business as a security matter'.[75] Having revealed the existence of the Maxwell Fyfe Directive, Denning thereby proceeded to make it clear that the Security Service was its own master when determining the scope of its mandate, accountable to no one and apparently under no duty to report to anyone.[76]

VI. Political Interference in Stephen Ward's Prosecution

Apart from exposing the fact that the Home Secretary had been kept in the dark and that important decisions were being taken by MI5 alone, the meeting of 27 March 1963 appears to have had a more sinister purpose, which again Denning allowed to pass without comment. This was the meeting at which a decision was taken to go after Ward, either under the Official Secrets Acts 1911–1920 or on some other ground, the Metropolitan Police Commissioner having been asked by the Home Secretary whether there was a 'police interest'.[77] There appears to have been a discussion about whether a prosecution would be possible under the Official Secrets Acts, in relation to the allegations that Ward had pressed Keeler to ask Profumo for information about the supply of nuclear weapons to West Germany. Apparently, Hollis had said that if the allegations were true 'there might well be a case against Stephen Ward under the Official Secrets Act'.[78]

It was of course an offence under the Official Secrets Act 1911, section 2 for a person (such as Profumo) in possession of confidential information to pass it on to someone (like Keeler) to whom he was not authorized to pass it on (and an offence

[74] 'The Stephen Ward Case' (n 48), para. 2(h).

[75] Lord Denning's Report (n 5), para. 268.

[76] ibid., paras 267–268, two very important paragraphs of the report where this is the clear tone. According to Pincher (n 7):

> It is clear from the Denning Report that Hollis made highly effective use of the guidelines laid down to govern the activities of MI5 when trying to explain his behaviour, as he did later when interrogated about his strange actions during the Blunt case. He stressed that under [the Maxwell Fyfe Directive], MI5's task was the defence of the realm as a whole and that no inquiry was to be carried out unless those directing MI5 were satisfied that an important public interest was at stake. In retrospect there can be no doubt that an important public interest was at stake and that it bore directly on the defence of the realm. So at best, Hollis was guilty of a series of faulty judgments (p. 90).

[77] Lord Denning's Report (n 5), para. 197.

[78] ibid., para. 196.

also for Keeler to pass it on to Ward, and for Ward to pass it on to Ivanov).[79] By virtue of section 4, the same Act also makes it an offence to attempt to procure another person to commit an offence under the Act, though this may not have been enough on its own to catch Ward if the proposed instrument of the procurement was Keeler, rather than Ward himself. It is suggested, however, that what was being contemplated here is covered by the Official Secrets Act 1920, section 7, whereby an offence is committed by any person who 'solicits or incites or endeavours to persuade another person to commit an offence, or aids or abets and does any act preparatory to the commission of an offence under the principal Act or this Act'. According to the Denning Report, Hollis thought that if the allegations about Ward pressing Keeler to ask Profumo were true, 'there might well be a case' against Ward under these latter provisions, for 'endeavouring to persuade Christine Keeler to commit an offence against the Act'.[80]

It is a striking feature of the meeting of 27 March that Hollis reported that MI5 had decided not to proceed with their invetigations on the ground that 'the witnesses in any such prosecution would prove unreliable', as a result of which MI5 was not 'inclined to pursue the matter'.[81] Perhaps there was a fear that Keeler was unreliable for what she could reveal rather than for her credibility as a witness. Although Hollis' judgement might prove to have been right, it was not known on 27 March that Keeler would subsequently commit perjury in the unrelated case of Lucky Gordon and perhaps thus be a poor witness against Ward in an official secrets case.[82] It did not, however, embarrass the police, who proceeded with a criminal investigation as directed, while in any event provision is made in the Official Secrets Act 1920, section 8 for proceedings to be held *in camera* on grounds of national security. It is true that this power is exercised at the discretion of the court and that there is no guarantee that it will ever be used when called upon. But it would nevertheless require the head of MI5 to take an unduly pessimistic view of the judicial condition to believe that a court would not be open to the exercise of the powers in a case such as this.

The real significance of this intervention did not, however, lie in the credibility or otherwise of Christine Keeler as a witness. More significant is what it tells us about the role of MI5 in the process of government, and its de facto authority to make decisions about whether or not to prosecute under the Official Secrets Acts. This was an issue that caused controversy more recently when the release of the Mitrokhin Archive triggered the revelation that in the 1990s when information supplied by a KGB officer had revealed the identities of a handful of Cold War spies, they had not

[79] It was also an offence to receive the information. The Official Secrets Act 1989 repealed the 1911 Act, s. 2, and replaced it with more tightly drawn restraints: see K. D. Ewing and C. A. Gearty, *Freedom under Thatcher: Civil Liberties in Modern Britain* (Oxford, 1990), ch. 6.

[80] Lord Denning's Report (n 5), paras 199 and 267.

[81] ibid., para. 196.

[82] Robertson (n 9), pp. 49–53, 75–7, 92–6, 113–14, 125–9, 177–8, and 184–6.

been prosecuted, with MI5 apparently preferring to 'let sleeping dogs lie'.[83] This de facto authority calls into question the famous standard account of MI5 peddled in the Denning Report, an account that bears repetition:

> The Security Service in this country is not established by Statute nor is it recognised by Common Law. Even the Official Secrets Acts do not acknowledge its existence. The members of the Service are, in the eyes of the law, ordinary citizens with no powers greater than anyone else. They have no special powers of arrest such as the police have. No special powers of search are given to them. They cannot enter premises without the consent of the householder, even though they may suspect a spy is there. If a spy is fleeing the country, they cannot tap him on the shoulder and say he is not to go. They have, in short, no executive powers. They have managed very well without them. We would rather have it so, than have anything in the nature of a 'secret police'.[84]

But although accurate as far it goes, it does not go far enough, with the Denning Report revealing that the Service did in fact have special powers, these relating to prosecution, if not arrest. The appropriate role of MI5 would have been to assemble the facts for the Home Secretary and perhaps even to have advised the Attorney General on whether to prosecute. But constitutionally these are decisions for the Attorney General acting in a quasi-constitutional capacity; not decisions for the Security Service acting off its own bat.

At the meeting on 25 March 1963, it seems that Hollis was sent packing to think again. After taking advice, however, he stuck by his original decision: *'He decided on 4th April, 1963, not to take any action on it.'*[85] That appears to have been enough, for that was the end of it. The Metropolitan Police Commissioner who, unlike the DG of MI5, did have formal or informal executive authority was nevertheless not so robust. Apparently, the Metropolitan Police Commissioner had thought there would be grounds for prosecuting Ward (for reasons not specified) if the police were able to get the full story, though he 'very much doubted whether they would succeed on this'.[86] It seems, however, that the Commissioner's resolve was strengthened, with the Home Secretary's intervention leading to the Commissioner 'immediately' giving further consideration to the question of prosecuting Ward, with a criminal investigation commencing only five days later.[87] The latter was pretty swift following an intense police investigation for such a petty matter (in this case, living off immoral earnings), leading to the eventual conviction on 31 July.

[83] Mitrokhin Inquiry Report (Intelligence and Security Committee), Cm 4764, 1999–2000, esp. paras 28–29.
[84] Lord Denning's Report (n 5), para. 273.
[85] ibid., para. 199 (our emphasis).
[86] ibid., para. 197.
[87] ibid., para. 199.

An account of the meeting of 27 March is provided in the Denning Report.[88] But as Robertson points out in his meticulous dissection of the Ward case, it does not provide a full account, which has not been released.[89] Nor does it say in terms that the Home Secretary instructed the DG and the Commissioner (Sir Joseph Simpson) to open a book against Ward. That said, however, Simpson can have been left in no doubt about what was expected of him, the Denning Report concealing very little. To repeat:

> On 27th March,1963, the Home Secretary asked the Commissioner whether there was a police interest in Ward. On 1st April, 1963, the Commissioner decided that Stephen Ward's activities should be investigated. On 4th April the police began to take statements.[90]

As Robertson has pointed out, such political interference in the criminal justice process was grossly improper.[91] Indeed, it was the Conservatives themselves who had led the attack on the first Labour government, which was brought down in 1924 because it was charged with withdrawing the *Workers' Weekly* prosecution on political grounds. According to Sir Douglas Hogg (Attorney General in Tory governments), ministers in 1924 stood condemned for using 'their political influence in party interests, in order to interfere with the even administration of justice in this country'.[92]

If it is wrong for Labour ministers to order/suggest to the law officers that a prosecution should be withdrawn, it would be equally wrong for Tory ministers to order/suggest to the police that a prosecution should be initiated. The criminal justice system does not exist for the personal benefit of the governing party, but in a democratic society must operate (so far as possible) independently and impartially. The Metropolitan Police Commissioner is not the Police Commissioner for the Conservative Party or indeed the Conservative government; he or she is the Police Commissioner for the Metropolis. Lord Denning of all people would have known this and would have known why any political interference was improper even in 1963, and even before the creation of the CPS. Indeed, it was only five years after the Denning Report that Lord Denning had the opportunity himself to set out the relevant principles, when he said that:

> No minister of the Crown can tell [the Commissioner] that he must, or must not, keep observation on this place or that; or that he must, or must not, prosecute this

88 ibid., paras 195–199.
89 Robertson (n 9), p. 41.
90 Lord Denning's Report (n 5), para. 200.
91 Robertson (n 9), p. 44.
92 HC Debs, 8 October 1924, col. 680. See K. D. Ewing and C. A. Gearty, *The Struggle for Civil Liberties: Political Freedom and the Rule of Law in Britain, 1914–1945* (Oxford, 2000), ch. 4.

> man or that one. Nor can any police authority tell him so. The responsibility for law enforcement lies on him. He is answerable to the law and to the law alone.[93]

Yet there was no response from Lord Denning about the process initiated by the Home Secretary to pursue Ward for no reason other than that he had embarrassed the government. When Ward wrote to the Home Secretary to complain about the intensive police investigations against him, he was met with the wholly disingenuous (though no doubt constitutionally accurate) response that 'the police, in making whatever inquiries they think proper, do not act under [the Home Secretary's] direction'.[94] But not only was Ward prosecuted at the behest of the Home Secretary, he was arrested and refused bail during the committal proceedings, apparently on the ground that there was a risk that he might flee the jurisdiction. Yet rather than question this scapegoating of Ward, Denning served only to contribute to it, for despite his desire not to 'do an injustice which is without remedy', he was prepared nevertheless to smear Ward. As with Pennells, the dead were easy targets and fair game.

VII. Perverting the Course of Justice?

Thus, Stephen Ward—the society osteopath, son of a clergyman—was 'utterly immoral', who procured 'pretty girls of the age of 16 or 17' to be mistresses for 'his influential friends'. He did not 'confine his attention to promiscuity', catering also for those of his friends who had 'perverted tastes'. He was 'ready to arrange for whipping and other sadistic performances', kept 'collections of pornographic photographs', and attended parties where there were 'sexual orgies of a revolting nature'.[95] But this was not the end of it, Ward being castigated for his improvidence in money matters. He did not keep a bank account but got a firm of solicitors to handle his finances, would often cash cheques received through other people or use cheques received to pay bills, and used cash transactions that left no trace.[96] No inquiry appears to have been made of the financial arrangements of Profumo or Astor. Who paid their bills? Finally, to add to the character assassination on the first page of chapter 1 of the Denning Report, we learn that Ward 'admired the Soviet regime and sympathised with the Communists', and would advocate their cause in conversation with patients.[97]

Profumo was not pilloried in this way. Yet Profumo had cheated on his wife with a woman young enough to be his daughter, had placed himself in a position

[93] *R v Metropolitan Police Commissioner, ex p Blackburn* [1968] 2 QB 118.
[94] Lord Denning's Report (n 5), para. 204.
[95] ibid., para. 10.
[96] ibid.
[97] ibid., para. 12.

that potentially compromised the defence of the realm, had lied to Parliament in a personal statement, had won damages in defamation proceedings to cover his lies (suggesting that he may have committed perjury), and had tried unsuccessfully to use the power of the State in the form of a D Notice to stop press coverage of his misconduct. None of this was judged. So far as Denning was concerned, Profumo had a 'fine war record', a 'distinguished record of service to the country', and was 'entitled to the confidence of his colleagues and of the country'. Although falling a little way short of beatification, Denning also tells that 'whatever indiscretions [Profumo] may have committed, and whatever falsehoods he may have told, no one who has given evidence before me has doubted his loyalty', in sharp contrast to Ward's dubious sympathies. There was thus no moral censure, and the choice of language (indiscretions rather than wrongdoing, falsehoods rather than lies) was such as to avoid any suggestion of criticism by Denning.

The difference, of course, was that unlike Profumo, Ward was by now a convict. He was also dead. But the fact that no one even thought it appropriate to bring charges against Profumo for perverting the course of justice is extraordinary,[98] and serves also to highlight the wilful abuse of the criminal justice process that was at the heart of this affair. In telling the story of that abuse, Robertson makes a persuasive case that Ward was the subject of the most appalling miscarriage of justice. One of the most compelling aspects of the story as told by Robertson was the role of the Lord Chief Justice in securing the conviction, the Lord Chief Justice in question being Lord Parker, who we encountered in Chapter 13. In the Stephen Ward case he intervened decisively, though as a contemporary account makes clear, the abuse of process began at the earliest stages of the trial.[99] According to Professor Glanville Williams, 'throwing the book at Ward' meant that 'senior prosecuting counsel was for some reason thought necessary to conduct the Crown's case before the magistrate as well as before the jury'.[100]

But that was only the start of it. Ward had spent twenty-six days in custody during the committal proceedings, and although he was subequently granted bail by the magistrate, what the Denning Report does not comment on was that he had

[98] See Perjury Act 1911, s. 1(1)—it is an offence for a witness wilfully to make a false statement which he or she knows to be untrue. Perjury has been said to be 'one of the most serious offences on the criminal calendar because it wholly undermines the whole basis of the administration of justice': *R v Warne* (1980) 2 Cr App R (S) 42 (Chapman J). See now Crown Prosecution Service, *Prosecution Guidance* (London, 2019).

[99] G. L. W. (n 15). The Clerk of the Court wrote subsequently to the *Criminal Law Review* to explain that the decision to put the case on the High Court judge's list was his alone, and that no pressure was brought to bear on him to put it there. The unnamed clerk explained that the reason for doing so was threefold. First, one of the charges related to conspiracy to procure an abortion, a charge normally tried by a High Court judge. Second, 150 press passes had been issued, and only one court was big enough to accommodate so many people, that court being the High Court judge's court. And third, in view of the worldwide publicity, it was important that the trial was conducted impeccably—'who better to ensure that than the High Cout judge?' [1963] *Crim L R* 798. According to Robertson (n 9), however, the Old Bailey was 'an unprecedented place' for dealing with minor sexual offences (p. 64).

[100] Robertson (n 9), esp. ch. 4.

only nineteen days to prepare for his trial. An application to have the trial postponed until September 1963 was rejected, the judge (Mr Justice Marshall) taking the view that the matter should be dealt with as quickly as possible.[101] This would clearly have suited the government, with concern that the matter was not proceeding at a fast enough pace being reflected in the Lord Chancellor's report to the Prime Minister on 13 June 1963. According to Dilhorne, there were reports circulating that proceedings were being delayed at the instance of the government. Significantly, he thought it 'inconceivable that there could be any substance to this suggestion', a thought confirmed by inquiries made of both the DPP and the Metropolitan Police Commissioner.[102] Any delay that had occurred—Dilhorne confirmed—had been due solely to the need to complete inquiries and to consider the case.[103]

In his gripping account of the Ward trial, Robertson documents a number of irregularities. But none was so extraordinary as that which took place on the last day, in order to understand which it is necessary to say something about the trial of Lucky Gordon, another associate of Christine Keeler. According to the Denning Report, Gordon was alleged to have assaulted Keeler on 18 April 1963. He was duly arrested and came up for trial on 5 June, at which point he was found guilty of causing actual bodily harm and jailed for three years. However, he had been unable to call any witnesses in his defence, including the two witnesses (of the thirty he had proposed to call) whom the police decided were the only two who could actually speak as to what had happened. On 30 July, the Court of Criminal Appeal (the Lord Chief Justice presiding) upheld the appeal on the ground that there were statements from the two witnesses Gordon had wished to call that 'might have led to the jury having reasonable doubt'.[104] There could be no mention in the Denning Report of Keeler's subsequent conviction for perjury in the Gordon trial.

The problem, however, was that on the day Gordon's appeal was upheld, the Stephen Ward trial was coming to an end, with the judge's summing up to take place also on 30 July. As explained by Robertson, Gordon's appeal was heard before the Lord Chief Justice at the unusual time of 9. 00 a.m., those assembled being 'treated to nine minutes of pre-planned judicial cover-up'.[105] The appeal was summarily upheld after Gordon's two witnesses had come forward, making statements that might have caused a jury to have reasonable doubt if the evidence had been before them. The more compelling reason that established Gordon's innocence, however, was Keeler's perjury at the original trial, which was known to the appeal court by virtue of a tape-recorded statement made by Keeler, read by the judges. If the appeal had succeeded on this latter ground, it would have had serious implications

[101] Robertson (n 9), pp. 64–5.
[102] 'The Stephen Ward Case' (n 48), para. 53.
[103] ibid.
[104] Lord Denning's Report (n 5), para. 227.
[105] Robertson (n 9), p. 94.

for the prosecution in the Ward case, in which Keeler was also a key witness for the Crown. In order to avoid any such misunderstanding, in upholding Gordon's appeal, the Lord Chief Justice wished to make it clear that Keeler's evidence was not necessarily untruthful.

Lord Parker thus stated that Keeler 'may well have been speaking the truth', and that it was the 'further evidence' (that of the other two witnesses) that might have raised a doubt in the jury's mind.[106] In order to ensure that this message was fully understood by the court in the Ward trial, due to close later that day, Parker took the extraordinary step of directing that 'a copy of his remarks in open court should be transcribed and rushed by special messenger to the Old Bailey', where 'they were used by the prosecutor and the judge to bolster Keeler's credibility',[107] 'quite incredibly' as Robertson points out 'given that [Gordon's successful appeal] had been based on sworn evidence by three witnesses, and a taped self-confession that she had lied'.[108] The prosecution in the Ward case was nevertheless able to inform the jury that although Gordon's appeal had been successful, it did not mean that Keeler had been lying, the Lord Chief Justice saying that 'it might be that Miss Keeler's evidence was completely truthful'.[109] Stephen Ward was found guilty in a trial that was little more than a farce; Miss Keeler was subsequently jailed for perjury.

There is so much to condemn about the conduct of the Gordon and Ward trials, as was noted at the time. The criticisms of the Gordon case in particular were summarized anonymously in an article in the *Criminal Law Review* in 1963,[110] where the author or authors pointed out the following:

- A court has no power to quash a conviction on the basis of evidence proposed to be given by new witnesses unless those witnesses give that evidence before the court. That was not done here, the conviction being quashed on the basis of untested witness statements only. This led the author to ask pointedly about why this case was so exceptional.
- Even if the case was exceptional, the witness statements should nevertheless have been disclosed so that the conviction was not quashed for reasons made known only to the court and the parties. As the authors pointed out, 'justice should be done publicly and reasons should be given for decisions', the public being 'unable to judge the adequacy of the reasons in this case'.

There was, however, a more damning criticism, that the court had 'brought upon itself the suspicion of yielding to external pressures', in a case 'linked with a major

[106] ibid., p. 95.
[107] ibid.
[108] ibid., pp. 95–6.
[109] ibid., p. 101.
[110] Anon, 'The Appeal of Aloysius Lincoln Gordon' [1963] *Crim L R* 600.

public and political scandal'. The fact that such suspicion had been aroused was 'manifest', with implications for 'public confidence in the judiciary'.[111]

VIII. The Denning Inquiry

The Profumo affair was a political disaster. Macmillan was made to look out of touch and out of control, while his Cabinet, and indeed much of the political establishment found themselves the focus of attention, as the press printed stories related to the case and rumour and innuendo ran rife. A Prime Minister had been ruined, a Cabinet minister's credibility had been destroyed, and Britain's reputation had been demeaned. There were, however, a number of questions that were left unresolved, not the least of these being questions relating to the defence of the realm, given the relationship between Profumo and Keeler on the one hand, and Keeler and Ivanov on the other. These questions were pressed by the Opposition and by sections of the press, and would have to be answered, particularly in view of allegations that Stephen Ward had asked Keeler to procure information that would have been useful to the Russians.[112]

For its part, the Opposition had proposed that the matter should be examined by a Select Committee, a prospect that clearly alarmed Macmillan and his colleagues.[113] Given the skilful campaign waged by the Labour Party in exposing Profumo, the last thing the government needed was for this agony to be extended, or for a fresh platform to be given to a sprightly and determined Opposition. At a meeting on 20 June 1963, the Cabinet had canvassed a number of concerns about a parliamentary inquiry, including the fear that it would be 'cumbrous and time-consuming', that it would be partisan rather than impartial and objective, and that even if sitting *in camera* it would not be appropriate for investigating the Security Service or discussing sensitive security questions.[114] As a result, the government plumped for a judicial inquiry to be conducted by Lord Denning, despite the objections of the Leader of the Opposition, who later complained that:

> This recent practice of turning to the judiciary to probe matters which are properly the sphere of the Executive and, on a failure, or alleged failure, of the Executive, the responsibility of this House, is a relatively new development which is fraught with danger both in devaluing the rôle and standing of Parliament and in blurring the edge which marks the sharp definition of the functions of the judiciary, on the

[111] ibid., 603.

[112] See HC Debs, 17 June 1963, col. 34—Adjournment debate on the Security Implications of Profumo's Resignation.

[113] The suggestion was made in the Debate on 17 June, but resisted by the government, which signalled its preference for some kind of judicial inquiry: ibid., col. 169.

[114] TNA, CAB 128/37/43 (Cabinet Conclusions, 20 June 1963).

> one hand, and the Executive and Legislature, on the other. Earlier administrations did not take this way out.[115]

It is not clear why Lord Denning was chosen for this role, having no known security background comparable to that of Lord Radcliffe. Nor is it clear why he agreed to take on the role on the terms presented. Unlike the Vassall inquiry chaired by Radcliffe, the Denning inquiry was not established under the Tribunals of Inquiry Act 1921. This was no oversight on the government's part, as revealed by the Cabinet discussion of 20 June 1963, where the Prime Minister made clear that the government had rejected a statutory inquiry for two reasons. The first was that it would have to be held in public, whereas the government preferred a more private process to avoid more damaging allegations making the press. And the second was that witnesses would not have the same protection from libel for making unsubstantiated allegations, though given the secrecy of the proceedings it is difficult to see how this would be an issue.[116] In secret proceedings, witnesses would be free to say what they liked about whomsoever they liked.

According to the Cabinet minutes, there was nevertheless anxiety that:

> If the Government established a Tribunal under the 1921 Act with terms of reference as proposed by the Prime Minister, they would appear to be acquiescing in a situation in which any person could with impunity call in question the good name of a member of the Government on the basis of rumour alone and the Government could be compelled, as a result, to adopt the most stringent methods in order to refute the allegations. It would be intolerable that public affairs should have to be conducted on this basis.[117]

This was followed by the most revealing observation suggesting further that the form of the Denning inquiry was designed to take some of the heat out of events, with those making allegations being invited to put up or shut up:

> Lord Denning's appointment should be seen as essentially an offer by the Government to provide an opportunity for individuals responsible for promoting defamatory rumours to substantiate those rumours in so far as they could. They would be protected by the normal principle of qualified privilege against the risk of subsequent action for slander or libel, provided that their action was not malicious. But, if they were prompted primarily by malice and therefore rejected the

115 HC Debs, 16 December 1963, col. 865. This is a concern reinforced on this occasion by the belief that 'the Government were saved from defeat and disintegration only by the decision to hold the inquiry' (ibid., col. 867 (Harold Wilson)).
116 ibid.
117 ibid.

> opportunity to submit their allegations to the test of enquiry, they could be dismissed as scandalmongers, from whom the government had nothing to fear.[118]

The nature of the inquiry was addressed directly by Lord Denning in the first few pages of his report, where he sought to make virtue out of necessity, conceding that the nature of the inquiry was such that it had a number of drawbacks.[119] In the first place, it was held in secret and as a result did not have 'the appearance of justice'; and the second was that in carrying out the inquiry, Lord Denning had to act as 'detective, inquisitor, advocate and judge', a combination of overlapping roles which he found 'difficult to combine'.[120] There were, however, advantages in the sense that:

> First, inasmuch as it has been held in private and in strict confidence, the witnesses were, I am sure, much more frank than they otherwise would have been. Secondly, I was able to check the evidence of one witness against another more freely. Thirdly, and most important, aspersions cast by witnesses against others (who are not able to defend themselves) do not achieve the publicity which is inevitable in a Court of Law or Tribunal of Inquiry.[121]

It is nevertheless the case that the proceedings had a number of inhibiting features, which Lord Denning openly acknowledged: no one gave evidence on oath, no one was cross examined, and no one heard any accusations against them which they were able directly to rebut.[122]

This was hardly an ideal format, and certainly not one that would lend itself to judgements about whether 'someone or other has been guilty of a criminal offence, or of professional misconduct, or moral turpitude, or even incompetence'.[123] And while no one would question the vigour of what was done, others may question the rigour of a process that saw about 168 witnesses being examined over a period of only forty-nine days. Some of these witnesses—Ward, Keeler, and Profumo—attended more than once, while Denning also managed in this time to visit MI5 headquarters, where he spoke to staff. It is not known if any of the witnesses—who included the Prime Minister, Cabinet ministers, the government law officers, the most senior civil servants, the DG of MI5, and the Metropolitan Police Commissioner—were legally represented, though all were given guarantees of confidentiality.

118 ibid.
119 Lord Denning's Report (n 5), paras 1–9.
120 ibid., para. 5.
121 ibid.
122 ibid., para. 6.
123 ibid., para. 7.

As Denning himself recognized, the nature of the process was such that it would thus inevitably lead to cautious and restrained outcomes.[124] But it is hard to argue with his 'cardinal principle', which was to operate on a generous presumption of innocence 'rather than do an injustice which is without remedy'.[125] As Denning pointed out, this was a process without an appeal, with further restraint on his part being dictated by the possibility of libel proceedings, a much underestimated restraint that as we have seen had been used maliciously as a sword by Profumo to prevent unwelcome publicity as the crisis was erupting. This was an issue to which Denning was alive, drawing the attention of the Prime Minister to the fact that while the delivery of the report would be covered by absolute privilege, this would not be true of subsequent circulation or publication to a wider audience.[126]

Given that the government fully intended to publish the report, Denning suggested that it should be published as a parliamentary paper, thereby enjoying wider protection from defamation than would otherwise be the case. It is not clear what passages in the report specifically troubled Denning, though he did appear to be concerned that the report 'contained passages reflecting on certain individuals'.[127] But again, the government dictated the terms. In order to enjoy immunity under the Parliamentary Papers Act 1840, it would be necessary to recall Parliament, which would raise the political temperature to a level the government was not prepared to contemplate.[128] Under the pretext of having to get the report out quickly in advance of the political conference season, Lord Denning was overruled, and was offered instead the promise of indemnity legislation in the event of anyone suing him.[129] It was an unsatisfactory process, from beginning to end.

IX. The Three Judges Again

Despite the shocking nature of judicial involvement in the Profumo case, this was to be the model for the future. In the debate on the Denning Report on 16 December 1963, the new Prime Minister had to pull something out of the hat to move the matter forward. Remarkably in light of the foregoing was the endorsement of an idea mooted first by Macmillan before his resignation that there should be a Standing Security Commission to conduct inquiries into security matters referred to it by the Prime Minister.[130] It was proposed that the new Commission would be chaired by a judge but would also include one or two civil servants and

124 ibid., para. 9.
125 ibid., para. 8.
126 TNA, CAB 128/37/53 (Cabinet Conclusions, 19 September 1963).
127 ibid.
128 The Parliamentary Papers Act 1840 effectively provides a wide immunity from legal proceedings arising from material published by order of either the House of Commons or the House of Lords (s. 1).
129 TNA, CAB 128/37/53 (Cabinet Conclusions, 19 September 1963).
130 HC Debs, 16 December 1963, cols 859–60.

one or two members of the armed forces with experience in security matters. The Security Commission was thus the deeply ironic ill-gotten progeny of the Profumo affair and the Denning Report. It was even more ironic in view of his criticisms of a judge-led inquiry into the Profumo affair that the Leader of the Opposition should eventually have supported this initiative, while emphasizing that such a body would not affect 'the responsibility of the executive Government for adequately controlling the security services of this country'.[131]

By their performance in the Profumo affair, the judges had shown that they could be relied upon and that they would deliver, just as Radcliffe had jumped when the government fingers had snapped a few years earlier. Any lingering doubts about judicial engagement had long gone, with the three most senior judges sharing a common endeavour to protect the integrity of the State, its institutions, and its personnel. As we have seen the Lord Chancellor's role was pivotal. Not only did he prepare the original report, steering the focus onto Stephen Ward; he also recommended the appointment of Lord Denning, presumably determined the terms of reference and the form of the inquiry, and saw an advance copy of the Denning Report, for which he was able to make suggestions for amendment, with a view to removing any possible 'implied criticisms of the Security Service and its Director-General, which, at the time, the Lord Chancellor deplored "in the national interest"'.[132] The Lord Chancellor's pivotal role in all this is perhaps best reflected in his reported remark to Chapman Pincher that his own report to Macmillan was so heavily relied on by Denning that he (Dilhorne) could have sued the latter for breach of copyright.

Denning's role was, of course, also crucial. But although it was widely applauded, and even as late as 1986 thought to have stood the test of time,[133] the Denning Report was deeply flawed. His assessment of witnesses was flawed, over-relying on status and position, and the integrity of someone whose job was to protect secrets. His judgements of events were flawed, in the sense that on crucial points they lacked credibility. And his conclusions were flawed in the sense that they were irrational in finding that the Security Service had complied with the Maxwell Fyfe Directive. The fact that the latter was apparently unknown by ministers was surprisingly not the subject of adverse comment, while it was clearly known by MI5, which just as clearly failed to comply with its obligations under the Directive. Lord Denning revisited his report in 1986, in the course of a House of Lords debate during the *Spycatcher* affair.[134] There he recalled Hollis as a man of 'integrity and

[131] ibid., col. 862.
[132] Pincher (n 7), p. 91.
[133] HL Debs, 17 December 1986, col. 176 (Lord Jenkins).
[134] The 'Spycatcher' affair is so named as the affair related to the attempts by the British government to stop the publication of Peter Wright, *Spycatcher: The Candid Autobiography of a Senior Intelligence Officer* (Toronto, 1987). For a brief account of the voluminous litigation in Great Britain and elsewhere and the political context, see Ewing and Gearty (n 79), ch. 5.

uprightness', and argued that the procedures he identified in his report were not in need of improvement. Denning's view was to 'let the position go on as it is. It is very good on the whole and has withstood the test of time.'[135]

This, of course, would not be the last time that Denning would make bad choices influenced by people's rank and position. Perhaps even more famous than his judgements about the DG of MI5 were his judgements about the police in the Birmingham Six case. Following their conviction for murder and conspiracy to cause explosives, the six brought civil proceedings against the police. Faced with the possibility that the appellants might be innocent, the Court of Appeal preferred instead to strike out the application, which as a result never made it to full trial. In the course of his decision, Lord Denning said famously that:

> Just consider the course of events if their action were to proceed to trial . . . If the six men failed it would mean that much time and money and worry would have been expended by many people to no good purpose. If they won, it would mean that the police were guilty of perjury; that they were guilty of violence and threats; that the confessions were involuntary and improperly admitted in evidence; and that the convictions were erroneous . . . That was such an appalling vista that every sensible person would say, 'It cannot be right that these actions should go any further'.[136]

This is significant, suggesting that Lord Denning appeared to be gullible in the presence of authority, and over-willing to trust those such as the Security Service, police officers, and prison officers. Of course, it proves nothing in relation to the Profumo affair except to suggest that Pincher's account of Denning being over-impressed by Hollis is not implausible.[137] But what is more alarming about this passage is Denning's cavalier attitude to the 'justice' he was keen to emphasize in the introduction to his report, and his willingness to sacrifice the liberty and reputation of individuals to the greater good of authority. He would rather innocent men were denied redress following a perversion of process than hold to account their tormentors in uniform. It was more important to uphold superficial confidence in the justice system rather than the deep integrity of justice. It was to get worse, with Denning to tell the *Spectator* magazine ten years after his Birmingham Six decision that had the (innocent) Birmingham Six been hanged, 'we shouldn't have all these campaigns to get them released'.[138] The Six were, of course, subsequently released shortly thereafter and awarded substantial compensation—fully vindicated.

135 HL Debs, 17 December 1986, col. 183.
136 *McIlkenny v West Midlands Chief Constable* [1980] QB 283.
137 On which, see Pincher (n 7), pp. 90–1.
138 A. N. Wilson, 'England, His England', *The Spectator*, 17 August 1990.

Yet Denning's commitment to 'justice' is expressed as his primary concern, claiming boldly as follows:

> While the public interest demands that the facts should be ascertained as completely as possible, there is a yet higher public interest to be considered, namely, the interest of justice to the individual which overrides all other. At any rate, speaking as a Judge, I put justice first.[139]

Like beauty, justice is in the eye of the beholder. But there is little sense that justice was done in the Profumo Report. Taking his lead from the Lord Chancellor, Denning's examination of the operation of the Security Service 'in the light of the circumstances leading to the resignation of the former Secretary of State for War, Mr J D Profumo', was said by Denning to be a 'story [that] ends, as it began, with him'.[140] But the 'him' was Stephen Ward, not John Profumo, Denning's narrative beginning with a pen picture of Ward (as the first of five 'principal persons'), ending with his death on 3 August 1963. Although Stephen Ward was the major victim of the Profumo affair, Lord Denning refrained from examining his treatment at the hands of the State, apparently content not to turn over any stones relating to the prosecution. To this end, he could no doubt say that his terms of reference related to the resignation of the Secretary of State for War, rather than the unconstitutional behaviour of the Home Secretary.

The other judge to play a part in the Profumo affair was Lord Parker, the Lord Chief Justice, whose role in securing the prosecution of Stephen Ward is discussed in Part VII above. Lord Parker's contribution came too late to be considered by the Lord Chancellor in his account of the Stephen Ward case presented to the Prime Minister in June, and of course Lord Denning does not mention it in his account of the conviction in his report. But Parker's contribution does, nevertheless, provide a very vivid insight into the Lord Chief Justice's views about the role of the judges as handmaidens of the executive. According to the *Guardian* reporting on the launch of Robertson's account of Stephen Ward's trial:

> 'In this case we have judicial misconduct from two [past] lord chief justices, Lord Parker and Lord Widgery', Robertson said at a press conference to launch the campaign to obtain a posthumous acquittal for Ward. 'They sent a misleading note to the Ward trial saying nothing they had seen cast a shadow on Christine Keeler's credibility. It's a sad moment in British judicial history that judges should have withheld evidence of great importance to the defence.'[141]

[139] Lord Denning's Report (n 5), para. 9.
[140] ibid., para. 229.
[141] *The Guardian*, 2 December 2013. Lord Widgery sat in the appeal with Parker, and was to succeed Parker as Lord Chief Justice in 1971.

We can only speculate about why judges so senior would behave like this. But there does look like a concerted effort from the time of the meeting in the Home Secretary's office on 27 March 1963 to 'get Ward', an effort in which the Lord Chancellor and the Lord Chief Justice were implicated whether wittingly or unwittingly, and in which Lord Denning helped to provide cover and justification in a report at times intemperate and ill-judged.

Yet as we have seen the pivotal role of the judges in the scrutiny of MI5 was to continue in the future, the Security Commission setting in train a model of judicial engagement that is one of the foundations of the modern law.[142] The model for the Security Commission, however, appears to have been more the Radcliffe Committee on Security Procedures that had reported in 1961, rather than the Denning inquiry, as suggested by its original terms of reference announced by Sir Alec Douglas Home:

> If so requested by the Prime Minister, to investigate and report upon the circumstances in which a breach of security is known to have occurred in the public service, and upon any related failure of departmental security arrangements or neglect of duty; and, in the light of any such investigation, to advise whether any change in security arrangements is necessary or desirable.[143]

The first chair of the Security Commission was Lord Justice Winn, who had a distinguished war-time service in naval intelligence, joined by Lord Normanbrook and Sir Caspar John. Lord Normanbrook was the title taken by Norman Brook following his elevation to the peerage, while Sir Caspar had been a distinguished naval officer. In yet another sweet irony, there is only one report of the Commission that has never been published.[144] That was the general review of security procedures ordered by Margaret Thatcher in 1981 in the wake of allegations by Chapman Pincher that Hollis was a Soviet spy.[145] It is only recently that the Security Commission was discontinued, its role—ironically yet again—having been displaced by the parliamentary Intelligence and Security Committee and the Intelligence and Security Commissioner, both appointed by statute.[146]

X. Conclusion

If the Prime Minister was the biggest political casualty of the Denning Report, the Security Service was by some way the greatest beneficiary. This is subject to

142 Lustgarten and Leigh (n 41), ch. 17 for background; A. W. Bradley, K. D. Ewing, and C. J. S. Knight, *Constitutional and Administrative Law* (17th edn, Harlow, 2018), Chs 16 and 19 for current practice.
143 HC Debs, 23 January 1964, col. 1271.
144 Lustgarten and Leigh (n 41), p. 478.
145 HC Debs, 26 March 1981, col. 1079.
146 For background, see Bradley, Ewing, and Knight (n 142), ch. 19.

the caveat that MI5's cover had been blown, with much unwanted publicity about its activities being detailed in the Report. Yet that would have happened anyway if a select committee had conducted the inquiry as the Leader of the Opposition (Harold Wilson) had demanded, while the benefit of a judicial inquiry was that it spared Hollis and his team from any direct responsibility to Parliament. The subordination of the Security Service to the House of Commons would have been quite a humiliation, and a blow for democracy that few were prepared to strike. But apart from protecting MI5 from the trauma of intense parliamentary scrutiny, Denning also protected it from the criticism many thought due. Having exposed the Maxwell Fyfe Directive, Denning used it as a shield to protect Hollis, rather than a sword with which to attack him.[147]

But having shown that the judges could be trusted politically to protect the security and intelligence services, Lord Denning nevertheless also exposed serious problems about MI5's mandate and its accountability, problems by which he seemed to be unconcerned. We began this chapter with three questions: Did MI5 operate in accordance with its mandate? Who was checking to ensure that MI5 was operating in accordance with its mandate? And to whom was MI5 in practice accountable for any failure to act in accordance with its authority? These are concerns that would normally give rise to anxiety about MI5 overreaching itself: here the concern, in contrast, was that MI5 fell short of what the mandate required. What Denning revealed was that MI5 had total control of the mandate in determining the scope of its powers and when and how to exercise them. The test was whether they acted 'honestly and reasonably' in the exercise of the wide discretion Maxwell Fyfe provided.[148]

Although in no sense justiciable in this context, this was the standard *Wednesbury* test derived from administrative law,[149] which Denning seemed to apply to the Directive, making it clear in doing so that MI5 would be given a wide berth. What Denning also revealed (albeit unwittingly and no doubt unintentionally) is that from 1951 no one was checking to ensure that MI5 operated within the boundaries of its authority and that it was not exceeding its terms in a way that was not 'honest and reasonable'. The informal supervision that had been established by Attlee had disappeared with the transfer of responsibility to the Home Secretary, who was exposed as being wholly unaware of his constitutional responsibilities. As a result, during the period of the Conservative governments from Churchill to Macmillan there appears to have been no oversight or accountability of a Service which not only had great power, but was revealed also to have presumed significant executive authority over prosecutions.

[147] As suggested also by Pincher (n 7), esp. pp. 90–1.
[148] Lord Denning's Report (n 5), para. 283. Also, paras 267–268.
[149] *Associated Provincial Picture Houses Ltd v Wednesbury Corporation* [1948] 1 KB 223. The pitch was slightly higher in principle than in *Liversidge v Anderson* [1942] AC 206, but the result was the same in practice—no intervention.

Lord Denning's Report was thus a powerful vindication of the status quo: a whitewash for MI5's past deeds, and a blank cheque for its future conduct. Going forward, MI5 would, of course, be subject in principle to greater levels of scrutiny, but Lord Denning's test would give great autonomy in the operation of a non-justiciable mandate. It had been cut free to please itself with wide powers, little supervision, and no control. This was a long way from the Attlee Directive, with its close supervision of the DG by the Prime Minister, who took a keen interest in the activities of the Service. That said, a Security Service under a tight rein directly accountable only to the Prime Minister is hardly more appealing than a Security Service with a free rein accountable to no one at all. The incoming Labour government tried vainly to restore some measure of Prime Ministerial oversight, though this was by no means a return to the days of Attlee and Sillitoe. That fox had long since bolted.

The Wigg Codicil

In Chapter 3, we saw how the then Home Secretary rewarded MI5 for the lamentable counter-espionage failures exposed by the Profumo affair by widening its counter-subversion powers to include a wider range of organizations. However, the Soskice Directive was issued without the approval of the Prime Minister, and gave raise to a row in government, as the manner of its introduction appeared to contradict attempts being made on behalf of the Prime Minister to get a grip of MI5. Determined that he would not be exposed like Macmillan (who was shown to be completely clueless and to have been kept in the dark on security matters), Harold Wilson appointed George Wigg, who was not universally liked, as Paymaster General. As such, Wigg had special responsibility for security and intelligence,[150] with powers in practice to liaise directly with the DG, without the knowledge of the Home Secretary.[151]

[150] Wigg had played a leading part in exposing the details of the Profumo affair and had been an effective campaigner. His influence on Wilson in security matters became sufficiently obvious to the House by 1966 to lead veteran Tory security and intelligence enthusiast, Sir Tufton Beamish, to ask Wilson what security responsibilities Wigg had been given. Wilson's answer was predictably uninformative: 'None . . . The functions of my right honourable friend the Paymaster General are confined to advising me on such questions of security falling within my responsibility as I may refer to him from time to time': HC Debs, 13 December 1966, col. 48. Wilson had been pressed earlier on the same issue, and without mentioning Wigg, stated that the then current arrangements for ministerial responsibility were 'as endorsed' by the previous Government (HC Debs, 6 December, col. 277 WA).

[151] Wilson was nevertheless dissuaded by MI5 from appointing George Wigg—perhaps the key Opposition politician in the Profumo affair—as the Minister responsible for the Security Service: C. Andrew, *The Defence of the Realm: The Authorised History of MI5* (London,2009), p. 523. However, the measure of his authority is to be seen in TNA, PREM 13/3471 (which includes references to meetings between Wigg and the DG on sensitive matters about which the Home Secretary was not informed).

Wigg was an obvious choice, having played a prominent role in the Profumo affair. Outlining his ideas to Sir Phillip Allen (the Second Secretary at the Treasury), on 17 November 1965 (four weeks before Soskice had issued his Supplementary Directive), Wigg said that he thought there were circumstances where if necessary the Prime Minister should issue direct instructions to the DG, and that it would be for the latter to decide whether or not the Home Secretary was to be kept in touch. Although not as extensive as Attlee's scrutiny, Sir Philip Allen nevertheless thought this latter proposal to be 'slightly heretical', and undertook to consider the matter.[152] It appears, however, that Sir Philip had not concluded his consideration when notice of the Soskice Supplementary Directive landed on Wigg's desk in the middle of December, prompting Wigg's private secretary to write to Allen to say that Wigg had received Soskice's minute on the Supplementary Directive, adding perhaps menacingly that 'Mr Wigg wonders whether he can deal with this straight away or if he should wait to receive the note you undertook to send him following your talk with him on the 17th November.'

Drafted by Allen personally, a Note was duly despatched to Wigg's private secretary on 16 December 1965, accompanied by an invitation to the minister: 'If the Paymaster General would like to discuss, I will of course be very glad to come over.'[153] The Note was in effect a Codicil to the Directive and was to be a powerful vindication of Prime Ministerial authority.[154] Wigg made two minor clarifications to paragraph 4 of the Codicil, and more importantly added to paragraph 1 of Allen's text that 'it is clearly understood at all levels and by all concerned that the ultimate responsibility for security rests with the Prime Minister'.[155] The 'Codicil'—'Ministerial Responsibility for the Handling of Security Matters'—made it clear that although the 1952 Directive provides that the DG is responsible to the Home Secretary personally (para. 2), it was implicit (without the need to have been set out in the latter Directive) that the Prime Minister could send for the DG at any time, and if necessary and desirable give him 'instructions' (para. 3). In the event of any such instructions being given, the Prime Minister's Office would inform the Home Secretary, leaving it to the DG 'to keep the Home Secretary in touch with the matter under the normal arrangements' (para. 4).[156]

[152] TNA, PREM 13/3471 ('Extract of Note of Meeting on 17 November').

[153] TNA, CAB 301/230 (Untitled Draft of 'Arrangements for Handling Security Matters').

[154] TNA, CAB 301/230 (Note from Wigg to Wilson, 21 December, 1965).

[155] TNA, CAB 301/230 (McKenna to Allen, 20 December 1965).

[156] A subsequent 'clarification' of para. 4 post-Wigg and after the General Election returning a Tory government in June 1970, was to the following effect: 'if [the Prime Minister] sent for the Director General of the Security Service and if he gave instructions to the Director General, the Private Office were required to inform the Home Secretary': TNA, PREM 13/3471 (Undated Minute, July 1970). The file also contains the various drafts of the Allen/Wigg Codicil.

The new orthodoxy was reinforced when on the same day (16 December 1965), G. J. Mitchell (Prime Minister's office) wrote to Wigg seeking his advice on the Supplementary Directive, indicating that the Prime Minister was happy with it.[157] In a reply dated 20 December 1965, George Wigg told Wilson that while he too was quite happy with the substance of the Supplementary Directive, it was wrong that Wilson had not been consulted before the Home Secretary 'took the action he did', adding that it was 'of fundamental importance that it be clearly established beyond all shadow of a doubt that ultimate responsibility for security rests with [the Prime Minister] and that in consequence no action should have been taken without [Wilson's] prior knowledge and consent'.[158] The matter was officially resolved when Mitchell wrote to Mr Ralph Shuffrey of the Home Office to say that the Prime Minister approved the Supplementary Directive, adding that the Prime Minister 'expects to be consulted before the Directive is amended'.[159] While a reminder of Prime Ministerial authority, this intervention nevertheless did not represent a restoration of Attlee-style responsibility, though it did serve strongly to reinforce the point that MI5 had broken free of any effective accountability during the long period of Conservative government.

157 TNA, PREM 13/3471 (G. J. Mitchell to Wigg, 16 December 1965). Mitchell also indicated that because it had already been signed by Soskice, the new instrument 'strictly is already in force' and should not be 'lightly undone'.

158 TNA, PREM 13/3471 (Wigg to Wilson, 20 December 1965).

159 TNA, PREM 13/3471 (G. J. Mitchell to R. F. D. Shuffrey, 18 January 1966).

15
Conclusion

I.

In the course of preparing this book we had many conversations with many people, mostly lawyers. Those to whom we spoke seemed politely interested in the project and the sources with which we were working. One response, however, remains disarming. This was the question from a senior lawyer whose relative appears in the pages above, who asked what was the point of the exercise, and what was the purpose of knowing about MI5 files during the Cold War. The question was certainly challenging, and no doubt one that political and other historians have to face on a daily basis. Why waste time unearthing the past when there is so much to be done building the future? It is a tough question, yet with simple answers, even for those for whom history has no intrinsic merit.

Although this is not the place for a detailed justification for legal history, it is nevertheless the case that the study of the past helps us better to understand the nature, influences, and values of contemporary institutions. In the case of MI5, it is important to know that Maxwell Knight,[1] the long-standing head of the 'agents and informers' 'M section' was an unsavoury character who, as Director of Intelligence for the British Fascisti (BF), had planted agents in various left-wing organizations in the 1920s.[2] Professor Andrew records Maxwell Knight having graduated from working as an agent runner for a 'private Industrial Intelligence Bureau (IIB), financed by the Federation of British Industries and the Coal Owners' and Shipowners' Associations, to acquire intelligence on industrial unrest arising from subversion by Communists, anarchists, the IRA and others'.[3] Maxwell Knight joined the BF in 1923, the SIS in 1929, and MI5 in 1931, where he worked until the 1950s.[4]

[1] Joan Miller's book, *One Girl's War, Personal Expolits in MI5's Most Secret Station* (Kerry, 1986) is of interest.

[2] Knight was also a member of the British Empire Union, and was associated with John Baker-White and the Economic League. See T. Lineman, *British Fascism 1918–39, Parties, Ideology and Culture* (Manchester, 2000) and M. Hughes, *Spies at Work* (London, 2012), ch. 3.

[3] C. Andrew, *The Defence of the Realm: The Authorised History of MI5* (London, 2009), pp. 122–3. See also J. G. Hope, 'Surveillance or Collusion? Maxwell Knight, MI5 and the British Fascisti, (1994) 9 *Intelligence and National Security* 651.

[4] By 1944, Maxwell Knight's 'M' section had successfully infiltrated the CPGB (his agent, Olga Gray, had been central to the conviction of Percy Glading for espionage in 1938), and other left-wing organizations (including the Haldane Society of Socialist Lawyers), and the trade unions, according to Tom Bower, *The Perfect English Spy: Sir Dick White and the Secret War* (London, 1996), p. 89. There is some

MI5, the Cold War, and the Rule of Law. K. D. Ewing, Joan Mahoney, and Andrew Moretta, Oxford University Press (2020). DOI: 10.1093/oso/9780198818625.001.0001

The contemporary significance of such links with big business in the DNA of MI5 is no doubt contestable. Our view is that the Left generally, and trade unionists in particular, ought to continue to be very suspicious. But apart from insight into the influences and values of contemporary institutions, the historical record is important also for informing our understanding of the origins, form, and structure of legal rules. It is important to know, for example, why the modern law on the interception of communications empowers the Home Secretary, rather than a judge, to issue warrants to authorize the opening of mail and the tapping of phones. Apart from helping us to understand the roots of this power, the historical record also more clearly casts light on the close relationship between the Security Service and the government, which by virtue of this procedure not only knows about but also authorizes MI5 targets and operations, raising doubts about the operational independence of MI5.

Following directly from the foregoing, the experience of the past helps to understand and to assess problems of the present. In particular it gives credibility and continuity to complaints about the use and abuse of surveillance powers and the corruption of the criminal justice system for political ends, whether these relate to the large-scale blacklisting of trade unionists, the role of the government in the prosecution of the Shrewsbury pickets and the Orgreave miners, or the more recent concerns about 'spycops'.[5] The last are the police officers who infiltrated political movements and protest groups, taking the identity of dead children and entering into wholly exploitative and unconscionable personal relationships with members of the infiltrated groups. The historical record suggests that there cannot now be any presumption in favour of the integrity of the police and the Security Services, with the issues now confronting the Pitchford inquiry being no more than the logical corollary of practices adopted by MI5 secret agents and Special Branch officers since before the Second World War.[6]

II.

As suggested in Part I above, the problems relating to MI5 and the Rule of Law are concerned with the secrecy of the mandate, the secrecy and arbitrariness of the powers, and the open violation of the law. It is, of course, deeply ironic that these should continue to be concerns after the Second World War, not only because the European Convention on Human Rights (ECHR) was supposed to reinforce

evidence that he also penetrated the PLP, warning MI5 in 1947 of an imminent Parliamentary attack on the Security Service by left-wing Labour MP Geoffrey Bing. See Chapter 6 above.

[5] See http://campaignopposingpolicesurveillance.com .

[6] See https://www.ucpi.org.uk. Sir John Mitting was appointed in 2017 to investigate undercover police investigations since 1968.

and enhance the principle of legality, but also because the man who was credited with its authorship was also responsible for authoring a slackening in the oversight of MI5, in an era characterized by organizational incompetence as well as institutional illegality. These concerns were nevertheless fully vindicated by the decision of the European Commission of Human Rights in *Hewitt and Harman v United Kingdom*,[7] where the surveillance regime discussed above was found to violate Article 8 (of Sir David Maxwell Fyfe's) ECHR, Article 8 guaranteeing the right to respect for private and family life.

Hewitt and Harman had been senior officers of the NCCL, and both were to become MPs and subsequently Labour ministers. The complaint was brought following the revelations by MI5 whistle-blower Cathy Massiter in a televised interview, discussed in more detail below. For present purposes, however, Massiter largely confirmed much of what has been set out in the previous chapters, including the fact that the NCCL was under surveillance on the ground that it was a subversive organization, and that its leading officials were regarded as 'communist sympathisers', therefore worthy of surveillance.[8] In the case of the complainants, files were opened on both, Massiter describing in some detail the content of Security Service files, at a time when none had been released to the National Archives, and when their content as a result would be largely unknown beyond the Service itself.[9]

Although the British government refused to confirm or deny the Massiter allegations, the European Commission of Human Rights concluded that 'the existence of practices permitting secret surveillance has been established and that there is a reasonable likelihood that the applicants were the subjects of secret surveillance and that the Security Service have compiled and retained information concerning their private lives'.[10] It was thus fairly straightforward to conclude that there had been an interference with the applicants' right to respect for their private life under the ECHR, Article 8(1), the main question being whether this interference could be justified under Article 8(2) as being 'in accordance with law' and 'necessary in a

[7] (1992) 14 EHRR 657.

[8] Massiter reported in the television programme referred to below that the NCCL had been targeted as a subversive organization by MI5 during the mid-1970s. According to Massiter, this was solely because one assistant director at MI5—Massiter did not name him—took the view that the NCCL was a subversive organization. According to the programme, one man's view became policy. Massiter stated:

> Anybody who was on the National Executive of NCCL, or who worked for NCCL or who was an active member to the degree of being a branch secretary of NCCL would be placed on permanent record and routine investigation would be instituted to identify such people . . . the police were asked to identify branch secretaries in their area and to report on the activities of the NCCL branch in their area . . . quite clearly there were agents in [NCCL] . . . people like Patricia Hewitt, who used to be its General Secretary, Harriet Harman, who used to be its Legal Officer, they would be put on record as communist sympathisers because of their involvement . . . what seems to have been the deciding factor was his [the Assistant Director's] own view that NCCL's attacks on certain institutions such as the police were deliberate attempts to undermine these institutions.

[9] *Hewitt and Harman* (n 7), para. 16.

[10] ibid., para. 32.

democratic society' for one of the prescribed reasons, including 'national security'. The crux of the matter, however, was to determine what was meant by 'in accordance with the law', a matter which the European Court of Human Rights (ECtHR) had already addressed earlier in *Malone* and other cases.[11]

Malone was also a surveillance case, brought only a few years earlier in relation to the phone-tapping procedures then operating in the United Kingdom. Although concerned with phone tapping undertaken by the police, the principles established in *Malone* applied in principle with equal force to surveillance by MI5, the Commission in *Hewitt and Harman* relying heavily on the decision in *Malone*, where it was said that '"in accordance with the law" does not merely refer back to domestic law but also relates to the quality of the law, requiring it to be compatible with the rule of law, which is expressly mentioned in the preamble to the Convention'.[12] According to the Commission:

> The 'law' in question must be adequately accessible in the sense that the citizen must be able to have an indication that is adequate in the circumstances of the legal rules applicable to a given case. In addition, 'a norm cannot be regarded as law unless it is formulated with sufficient precision to enable the citizen to regulate his conduct. He must be able—if need be with appropriate advice—to foresee, to a degree that is reasonable in the circumstances, the consequences which a given action may entail.'[13]

Applying these standards, the Commission in *Hewitt and Harman* found there to have been a failure to comply with two basic requirements of the Rule of Law, the first being an absence of clear legal authority for the activities of MI5, and the second being the lack of clarity about its powers. So far as the first is concerned, the Commission referred to the Maxwell Fyfe Directive which, although 'published', was not claimed by the government to have 'the force of law', nor to 'constitute legally enforceable rules concerning the operation of the Security Service'.[14] As to the second, the Commission noted that the Directive failed to 'provide a framework which indicates with the requisite degree of certainty the scope and manner of the exercise of discretion by the authorities in the carrying out of secret surveillance activities'.[15] Here the Commission was reflecting the views expressed by the Court in *Malone*, where it was said in relation to phone tapping that:

> the law must be sufficiently clear in its terms to give citizens an adequate indication as to the circumstances in which and the conditions on which public

[11] *Malone v United Kingdom* [1984] ECHR 10.
[12] ibid., para. 67.
[13] *Hewitt and Harman* (n 7), para. 38.
[14] ibid., para. 40.
[15] ibid.

> authorities are empowered to resort to this secret and potentially dangerous interference with the right to respect for private life and correspondence.[16]

The latter observations contrast sharply with the impoverished view of legality adopted by Sir Robert Megarry, when the *Malone* case was in the High Court.[17] In a conception of the Rule of Law much at odds with Maxwell Fyfe's ECHR, we find the High Court tucking in to protect the State by effectively holding that Home Office procedures on phone tapping were consistent with constitutional principle on the ground that England 'is not a country where everything is forbidden except what is expressly permitted: it is a country where everything is permitted except what is expressly forbidden'.[18] This applies as much to the activities of the State as to its citizens. Yet by the judgement of a Commission and a Court established under a treaty apparently authored by the man who put his name to MI5's Charter (which he did not write), the position could hardly have been clearer: Britain's Security Service operated for eighty years without legal authority, exercising powers which failed to satisfy the most basic requirements of legality.

III.

Although the Maxwell Fyfe Directive was said in *Hewitt and Harman* not to be 'law' for the purposes of the ECHR because it did not meet the requirements of the latter in terms of its quality, it is nevertheless the case that it constituted 'law' in the sense that it was a document believed to have been issued with legal authority (albeit a legal authority of questionable provenance) in order to empower but also to constrain the activities of the Service. Although secret texts that did not meet basic requirements of openness and publicity associated with 'law', both the Attlee and Maxwell Fyfe Directives were law in the sense that they were (i) issued by a 'sovereign' believed to have had authority to issue them; (ii) intended to be empowering and binding on those to whom they applied; and (iii) capable of some kind of enforcement in the event of breach, albeit by ministers and civil servants, rather than courts.

It is clear, however, that those to whom the mandates were addressed did not willingly comply with their terms, and indulged in activities which quite clearly exceeded their authority. It is true that there was some difficulty associated with the open-ended nature of the mandates, which imposed a primary duty on MI5 for the defence of the realm, specifically from threats of espionage or those 'judged' subversive of the State. These terms can nevertheless not be divorced from the

16 *Malone v United Kingdom* (n 11), para. 67.
17 *Malone v Metropolitan Police Commissioner* [1979] 1 Ch 344.
18 ibid., p. 366.

understandings of those whose work contributed to the Directives in question, notably Sir Findlater Stewart, who was—according to Liddell—clear so far as subversion was concerned that this should be 'confined strictly to people advocating the overthrow of the constitution by violence'.[19] In other words, 'the defence of the realm as a whole' no matter how widely defined in practice, did not provide a licence to operate against individuals and organizations because they held dissident views.

The monitoring of the political Left nevertheless had been MI5's core role since 1931, when the Service had assumed authority for such matters, and it is clear from various sources that this was not a role it wished to relinquish.[20] Post war, subject to a degree of accountability, and its duties delineated by the Attlee Directive, the Service thus fought to continue what was in effect its political policing work. Although justly famous for his wartime counter-espionage successes, DDG Guy Liddell had moved from Scotland Yard to join MI5 in 1931, where he was regarded as a Communist subversion specialist,[21] and it was Liddell who fought hardest to shake off the restrictions imposed by Attlee in 1946. This is despite the fact that in March 1945 Liddell had written that 'Communism seems to be the great bogey in the Western hemisphere. I cannot help feeling that a somewhat exaggerated view is taken of the whole thing.'[22]

The main focus of MI5 post-war political work thus had only a tenuous connection with the defence of the realm. The work was also undertaken in clear defiance of the Prime Minister, to whom the Service was accountable, with Liddell directly refusing to obey Attlee's express order that the Registry be systematically weeded of material not immediately relevant to the defence of the realm. Although some token destruction of 'useless' intelligence was undertaken, Liddell and Hollis connived to dispense with Petrie's 1944 ruling that only important Communists be 'carded', deciding in 1946 that to fail to keep tabs on the whole of the Party would be to fail the Chiefs of Staff and the JIC. The Registry was key to the Service's mass surveillance programme, and it had to be fed. On the evidence of the Liddell Diary,

[19] TNA, KV 4/196-2 and KV 4/196-3 (Liddell Diary, 29 May 1945). (The first file ends halfway through the entry and the second file starts with the remainder of the entry).

[20] A partially redacted document from one of the Cabinet Secretary's files relating to the post-war review of the Security Service by Findlater Stewart gives a good picture of the long-standing focus on left-wing politics. The document refers to the Central Index, rather than files (the distinction is important), noting that: 'In 1941 there were 1,250,000 cards in the index. The total in January 1946 was 1,212,000. An analysis of 1,009 cards gave the following result—Left Wing 413; Right Wing 104; Palestine 42; Espionage 107; Preventative 202; Miscellaneous 141.' This was shortly after a five-year period when interest in those on the Left had been at something of an all-time low.

[21] Andrew (n 3), pp. 129–31.

[22] TNA, KV 4/196-2 (Liddell Diary, 19 March 1945). Whatever his private thoughts, Liddell was aware that the best interests of the Security Service lay with monitoring the Communist Party, as MI5 faced being wound down after the war. Liddell and Dick White discussed the Communist Party, 'and the differences of view about keeping a close watch on all Party members. We came to the conclusion that it would probably be necessary to continue this work on as detailed a basis as manpower would allow': TNA, KV 4/466 (Liddell Diary, 13 August 1945).

it looks as if neither Liddell nor Attlee were prepared to back down on this matter, and that Sillitoe was obliged to mislead the Prime Minister about the extent of the destruction of cards and files.[23]

As we have seen, in 1952 the Maxwell Fyfe Directive had loosened the accountability of the Service in an attempt to permit it to come to grips with the espionage threat, and to minimize political 'fall out' should things go wrong. Liddell and Sillitoe retired in 1953, and Dick White was appointed DG. White reformed F Division, resurrecting the old, independent counter-subversion branch away from the close embrace of counter-espionage, effectively an official acknowledgement of the drift back to the straightforward political policing of the pre-war years. Bower's biography of White, informed by numerous interviews with White, and with colleagues in MI5 and in the Home Office, confirms that the dogs had indeed been let off the leash:

> MI5's status as a deliberately isolated, self ruling secret army prevented any investigation of its own mistakes . . . Shielded from supervision and professional management, and sealed off by perpetuation of the 'need to know' rule of confidentiality even at the highest level within Whitehall, White could assert his total dominance.[24]

White was succeeded by Roger Hollis in 1956, with Graham Mitchell (who had followed a similar career path within the Service) appointed his deputy. Both were essentially political policemen,[25] and their rise to the top coincided with the Service gaining access to the CPGB's membership records. 'Operation Party Piece' in 1955 had handed them what they had for years been obliged to glean,

[23] Although some files were destroyed, weeding on the scale envisaged by Findlater Stewart, and by the Attlee Directive, did not occur. Had it done so then the Service would have changed profoundly, arguably steering it towards active espionage investigation, and away from the intensive accumulation of political intelligence. Liddell's continuing belief in retaining old records was illustrated when the saga of CPGB funding—'Moscow Gold'—again raised its head in October 1951. Liddell noted that two men, one of them Bob Stewart, had been involved in moving money about since 1922: 'I cannot help feeling that had Miss Saunders' History Sheet on CP finance been available, this might all have been discovered long ago. This is a clear instance of the value of records which are nearly thirty years old.' However, it is likely that the History Sheet was destroyed in the Wormwood Scrubs fire of 1940, rather than in any purge of irrelevant material—few would be likely to quibble about the importance of retaining intelligence on the funding of domestic political parties by foreign powers.

[24] Bower (n 4), pp. 146–7.

[25] By some accounts Hollis had undertaken counter-espionage work very early in his career (he joined the Service in 1938), but files released to the National Archives indicate that his early work in B Division was focused on left wing subversion. In 1941 he continued this work as F2, later heading F Division. While F2(C) was tasked with countering Soviet espionage (at one time comprising of just one officer, Hugh Shillito, who Hollis considered 'idle' and 'ineffective') and was thus under Hollis' control, well over 90% of his career between 1938 and 1953 was concerned with monitoring left wing organisations. Hollis was noted for his warnings to colleagues, to Special Branch and to the Security Executive of the subversive threat he saw posed by the Party. That in 1945 Liddell chose to describe Hollis as an 'expert' on counter-espionage was arguably an accolade which reflects the dearth of knowledge about Soviet intelligence operations against the west than upon Hollis' qualities as a Security Service officer.

name by name, from observation, informants, phone taps, postal interception, and SF. Peter Wright said of the 'dour, uninspiring' Hollis that he believed MI5's role to be 'collecting files, maintaining efficient vetting and protective security, without straying too far into areas like counter espionage, where active measures were needed to get results, and where choices had to be confronted and mistakes could be made'.[26] This view of Hollis was endorsed by White, who recalled that Hollis 'was never interested in CE (counter espionage) work, having one of those crabbed minds that prefer protective security measures to the fun of sniffing things out'.[27]

Hollis retired in 1965, and by Peter Wright's account there was something of a counter-espionage resurgence under Martin Furnival Jones, who served as DG from 1965 to 1972, during the period of the Wilson administration in the wake of Portland and Profumo. Any suggestion that MI5 might be diverted away from a political policing role was, however, shattered by the Heath government, which sought to enlist the help of the Service in taming the unions. This, however, was resisted by Furnival Jones, a Cambridge law graduate who appeared to be less malleable than his predecessors,[28] clashing with Home Secretary Reginald Maudling in late 1970 and early 1971, following a 'suggestion' from Edward Heath that MI5 eavesdrop upon a meeting of trade union leaders.[29] If the monitoring of the CPGB and the peace movement on the grounds of subversion was a stretch, the monitoring of trade union officials engaged in ordinary trade union activity was clearly a stretch too far.

But rather than accept that the limits of MI5's mandate were already stretched by practice beyond their boundaries, the Heath government proceeded to redefine what was meant by subversion and in the process to expand the jurisdiction of MI5 to cover the 'far and wide Left'.[30] According to Peter Wright, 'The miners strike of 1972, and a succession of stoppages in the motorcar industry, had a profound effect on the thinking of the Heath Government. Intelligence on domestic subversion became the overriding priority.'[31] This led to the adoption by Furnival Jones' successor, the more malleable Michael Hanley, of the wide definition of subversion that had been formulated by ACPO and the Home Office in 1970 for Special Branch purposes, which was ultimately announced to Parliament by Lord Harris in 1975.[32] Like Hollis, Hanley had spent his career on political work, and between

[26] P. Wright, *Spycatcher—The Candid Autobiography of a Senior Intelligence Officer* (Toronto, 1988), p. 77.

[27] Letter to Hugh Trevor Roper, 25 April 1984, cited by Chapman Pincher, in *Treachery, Betrayals, Blunders and Cover Ups: Six Decades of Espionage* (Edinburgh and London, 2011), p. 426.

[28] *New York Times*, 16 March 1997 (Obituary of Sir Martin Furnival Jones).

[29] See Andrew (n 3), pp. 589–91.

[30] *The Guardian*, 6 January 2001 (Obituary of Sir Michael Hanley, quoting Peter Wright).

[31] Wright (n 26), p. 359.

[32] The new definition had been adopted officially by MI5 in 1972 when F Division was led by John Jones. Significantly, Jones was later appointed DG by Margaret Thatcher, and served during 1981–5.

1972 and 1978, a period when the Tory Party lurched to the Right, he oversaw the recruitment of:

> a small army of handlers, agents and informers, technical and secretarial staff . . . According to one former Security Service officer, 'literally hundreds' of trade union officials and activists were signed up in the late 1970s as informers.[33]

Subverting Student Politics

A rare glimpse of how the extended definition of subversion enabled MI5 to dig into student politics is afforded by a release relating to events in 1965–6, arguably the dawn of the serious student left-wing activism of 1966–76.

The story begins in 1952, when the NUS was said to have disaffiliated from theInternational Union of Students (IUS) 'on account of its Communist bias'. By 1966, the union was evidently retreating from full affiliation with the US-backed International Students Conference (ISC), and growing increasingly closer to the IUS, a step which provoked the IRD to send a 'confidential' circular to heads of Chancery/information officers condemning the IUS as a Soviet front organization and emphasizing the value and importance of the ISC.

Predictably, the blame for the shift was placed on 'a small communist led group of extremists', and the recipients were reminded that in a previous letter they had been told, 'it is very much to be hoped in the general interests of the West, and of students in all but communist countries, that the ISC should flourish'. While being advised to avoid arousing interest in the matter where none exists, the IRD gave a number of points that might be used in a debate on the question of support for the ISC, stating in conclusion that 'any reports of significant local reaction to those events will be most useful'.[34]

In March 1966, around the time MI5 prepared a new paper on the CPGB and the universities,[35] a paper on 'NUS Membership of ISC' evidently written by the IRD was received by the Cabinet Office. It detailed the efforts being made to ensure the NUS did not renounce full membership of the ISC, and stated that:

> It is very much in our interests that the decision taken . . . should be reversed when the NUS Council meets again . . . A decision to stay out of the ISC would represent a major victory for the Communists in the NUS, and

[33] S. Milne, *The Enemy Within: The Secret War against the Miners* (London, 1995, paperback ed), pp. 380–1.

[34] TNA, CAB 301/206 (Circular by CFR Barclay of the IRD, 17 December 1965).

[35] TNA, CAB 301/206 (Note by Heaton of the Cabinet Office, 23 March 1966). Unfortunately, the MI5 paper—'a much more detailed analysis of anything we have seen before'—is not in the file. According to Heaton, the file revealed 'that the threat is not very serious'.

> would seriously weaken the influence and the morale of the responsible non-Communists who, with discreet support from *our friends*, have dominated the NUS Executive for the last 15 years.[36]

A matter of particular importance was the election of new officers:

> The leadership of the Executive with whom our friends are in touch has now drawn up its own list of candidates. We also know from secret sources that the Communists are hoping to put up at least two candidates . . . our friends may be able to frustrate them but very little hard evidence is so far available on Communist intentions.[37]

However, it was considered imperative that 'action designed to secure a favourable outcome for the debate must not prejudice success in the elections'.[38]

Fergus Nicholson and Alan Hunt were singled out in the paper as particularly able student activists. Nicholson was said to be set to go to Prague, where the IUS had its headquarters: 'should this visit take place we are ready to exploit in order to discredit Nicholson and, if possible, Alan Hunt'.[39] The paper went on to detail the wide-ranging efforts of MI5's very well-connected 'friends' to promote the ISC and denigrate the IUS and 'rally support for full membership of the ISC' with counter-action and publicity.[40]

It also detailed the ways in which 'At our friends' suggestion, IRD are helping.'[41] Who were 'our friends'? Not MI5, because the paper concludes that 'the above measures and any further suggestions will continue to be discussed in the Interdepartmental Committee on Overseas Students, chaired by the head of the IRD, on which the CRO, our friends and the Security Service are represented'.[42] It is difficult to avoid concluding that MI5 and the IRD were colluding with the Americans. While 'our friends' could be argued to be SIS, it seems very unlikely, and, in the circumstances, even less likely that MI5 would help them.

In the event, the vote at the Exeter NUS Conference in April 1966 on membership of the ISC went in favour of the ISC. An assistant secretary at the Cabinet Office attended the Conference. Noting that under the complex election

36 TNA, CAB 301/206 (NUS Membership of ISC, no date, para. 4).
37 ibid., para. 5.
38 ibid., para. 6.
39 ibid., para. 7.
40 ibid., para. 10.
41 ibid., para. 11.
42 ibid., para. 12. Moreover, Paul Gore-Booth of the Foreign Office sent a copy of the IRD paper to Burke Trend, stating that he was also sending a copy 'to Thistlethwaite [MI5], whose service is giving all necessary help both to our friends and to IRD in the supply of relevant information'. Thistlethwaite appeared to have emerged as the Service's expert on student Communism: TNA, CAB 301/206 ('Paul' to 'Burke', 25 March 1966).

procedures for candidates for posts on the executive, Alan Hunt had failed to secure a post, despite receiving around one-third of all 'first preferences', the IRD paper prepared for the Cabinet Office referred to a number of other student activists at the time not all of whom were linked to the Communist Party. It also referred to an NUS commission on voting procedures which was to report to the November Council of the Union. The activists referred to include 'Mr Jack Straw of Leeds University', subsequently to be Home Secretary, amongst other distinctions, and as such with responsibility for MI5.[43]

IV.

The post-war focus on the Communist Party is not one that could easily be justified by the mandate with which MI5 was entrusted, even after the definition of subversion in the mandate was extended in 1972. Nor could the focus on trade unions easily be justified, whether before or after the extension of the definition of subversion in 1972. It would take a rather creative mind and a warped view of democracy to say post 1972 that the Communist Party, the peace movement, or the trade unions were involved in activities that 'threaten the safety or well-being of the State, and which are intended to undermine or overthrow Parliamentary democracy by political, industrial or violent means', as the new definition provided. None sought to overthrow parliamentary democracy, and all were engaged in legitimate activity perfectly consistent with parliamentary democracy unless that term is to be defined as narrowly as subversion was defined widely in the post-war era.

The post-war focus on the Party was not only a breach of MI5's mandate, it was also a grave political mistake, with drastic consequences. The ill-judged and misguided nature of this strategy were beginning to emerge as early as September 1945, when Russian GRU man Igor Gouzenko defected, beginning the long revelation of the Soviet espionage campaign against the West. Although there was initially reluctance 'to think the worst of our former ally',[44] MI5 realized that they were back in business, albeit the wrong business. By 1950, Guy Liddell and Dick White were able to tell Norman Brook that MI5 had:

> about 700,000 names of Communists and sympathisers on its file [Central Index CP Index] of which around a quarter of a million are more fully covered by files. *These are thought to include all potential spies.*[45]

[43] TNA, CAB 310/206 (C. Freedman, The NUS Conference, Exeter 13–17 April 1966). Someone has written 'shades of Wat Tyler' in the margin next to Mr Straw's name.

[44] TNA, KV 4/467 (Liddell Diary, 25 April 1946, Liddell's account of his visit to North America during which he interviewed the defector Igor Gouzenko). Liddell is describing the attitude of a senior member of the Canadian Department of External Affairs.

[45] TNA, CAB 301/20 (Interviews [with Norman Brook] at Leconfield House, 7 July 1950) (emphasis added).

This is despite the fact that the CPGB had long been wholly averse to espionage, and the Eastern Bloc intelligence services were similarly wary of having any contact with the Party.

Betrayal and decryption were the means by which Eastern Bloc spies were caught in the post-war era. Blake, Vassall, and the Portland ring in the early 1960s, like Nunn May in 1945, had been exposed by information from defectors.[46] Christopher Andrew, in his authorized history of MI5, refers to a number of Polish agents exposed during the 1950s—all identified by information supplied by defectors.[47] Maclean and Philby had been described, if not identified, by a Soviet defector back in 1940, and Maclean—like Klaus Fuchs—had been identified by US 'Venona' decrypts. MI5 was in a state of almost constant reorganization during 1946–53 as the Cold War escalated, and the Service struggled to catch spies. In an unguarded moment, Liddell and White in 1950, revealed to Norman Brook that after nearly five years of close scrutiny of the Party, the counter-espionage campaign had not even started; '*in order to be in a position to start a campaign against spies*, it is necessary to know all about the Communist Party, its activities and associates'.[48]

The increased commitment to vetting and the continuing failure to get to grips with the espionage offensive paradoxically sharpened the focus on the Communist Party. Liddell took to presenting vetting as if it were counter-espionage work.[49] But it was at best no more than a form of displacement therapy. The Party could be said to have provided the Service with a surrogate enemy, serving to distract from and mitigate its failure to defend the realm. Late in 1952, when addressing the 'anxiety that sufficient was not being done to deal with Communist agents' expressed by the Chiefs of Staff, Liddell explained to the Brook Committee that MI5 identified Party members and 'sympathisers' for the civil service purge,[50] passing on to the departments the names of all individuals they had associated with left-wing politics who worked for the government or on government contracts. They passed to

46 Wright (n 26), p. 129, revealed that MI5 had been given the opportunity to 'roll up' the Portland Ring back in the 1950s, when Henry Houghton's wife had reported her suspicion that he was a spy to Naval Security, who in turn had informed MI5's C Division, but nothing was done until an intelligence source revealed the identity of a man named 'Huiton' at Portland.

47 Andrew (n 3), p. 484.

48 TNA, CAB 301/20 ('Interviews [with Norman Brook] at Leconfield House, 7 July 1950).

49 TNA, KV 4/475 (Liddell Diary, 17 March 1953):

> Although it did not necessarily follow that every Communist was a spy in the accepted sense of the word, there was always a risk that if he had access to secret information he would discuss his work with his local group, and that the facts of interest to iron curtain countries might percolate through to headquarters, who would pass them on to the Russians if they thought them to be sufficiently important.

50 The ubiquitous Norman Brook presiding over a committee comprising, among others, the Metropolitan Police Commissioner; the PUS at the Ministry of Labour, Robert Gould; and Baker of the Home Office's F3 Police/Security Services Liaison Department, which appears to have had industrial policing responsibilities, having been central to the monitoring of the unofficial industrial action in 1950–1, overseen by Newsam, then Home Office PUS.

the police 'all information' on Party members and sympathizers, encouraging provincial forces to reciprocate.

Liddell went on to explain that: 'In addition, we were passing information about Communists in the Trade unions to the Ministry of Labour and also reporting strike action where Communists were concerned. We were also listing teachers, both at the Universities and at schools, in accordance with a previous decision reached by the Brook Committee.'[51] Writing in 1952, at a time when MI5 did not have access to the full Communist Party membership lists, Liddell put Party membership at around 35,000 plus 3,000 in the YCL. Remarkably, he estimated that there were 150,000 Communist sympathizers, 'although we had 250,000 on our records, who, at one time or another had come to notice with regard to Communist activity'.[52] Liddell was also able to break down the numbers of Communists in the civil service, BBC, GPO, and teaching at the universities, and in the schools, noting also that MI5 had identified some 250 Communist journalists.

All this, of course, had little to do with dealing with Communist agents, but it did indicate that MI5 was coming along in leaps and bounds as a political police force. Two months later, Liddell confessed to the Deputy Director of Military Intelligence that Soviet espionage 'presented us with an extremely difficult problem. We had made considerable progress, but Russian security was such that the target was an extremely difficult one. On matters affecting the employment of doubtful persons by the Government, or factories where secret work was going on, we had achieved a good deal.'[53] In reality, there had been little progress. In 1950, some two-and-a-half years previously, Liddell and White had, without bringing vetting into the conversation, told Norman Brook of the difficulties of detecting Soviet intelligence operations. The only significant events since then had been the arrest and conviction of William Marshall on espionage charges, and the expansion of the Registry.[54]

Marshall has been described as a 'naïve' young wireless operator from humble origins who joined the Diplomatic Wireless Service and spent time working in Moscow. Shortly after his return to London in 1951, Marshall was seen in the company of a Soviet diplomat (Pavel Kuznetsov), and although there was no evidence that Marshall had passed on documents or information, at the time of his arrest he had a secret document in his wallet which he had himself transcribed, this forming the basis of a prosecution for 'unlawfully obtaining information for the benefit of a foreign power'. Although Sillitoe was later to claim that MI5 had thus neutralized another attempt by the Soviets to recruit British spies, a more plausible explanation

[51] It appears that it was MI5 that first suggested monitoring schools and universities: TNA, KV 4/472 (Liddell Diary, 1 December 1950).

[52] TNA KV 4/474 (Liddell Diary, 20 October 1952).

[53] TNA KV 4/474 (Liddell Diary, 5 December 1952).

[54] There had been eleven convictions for 'espionage offences' between 1951 and 1963: HC Debs, 11 July 1963, col. 170 WA.

has been provided by Rebecca West, who attended Marshall's trial and is said to have concluded that:

> William Marshall was put on a salver and served up to Special Branch, with love from the Soviet Secret Service . . . It simply cannot be believed that a Soviet diplomat could at meetings with an agent supervised by his own Embassy's police, break rule after rule of security practice, without wishing that this agent should be detected.[55]

That Philby was able to operate undetected for so long was a compelling sign of the failure properly to defend the realm, Philby's association with Guy Burgess and his subsequent questioning by White and Milmo making it very obvious to MI5 that he had been a Soviet agent. The true measure of that failure, however, was the long list of scientists, diplomats, and other intelligence officials who had been turned by the Soviets for a combination of reasons including ideological, blackmail, and greed.[56] That failure was revealed also by the ability of Russian spies to get close to government ministers such as Thomas Galbraith (through Christopher Vassall) and John Profumo (the Secretary of State for War), though it is unclear whether this was part of a deliberate strategy or mere good luck on the part of Soviet intelligence. But whatever the reason, both Galbraith and Profumo were based in defence departments in what were extraordinary examples of 'attempts at espionage' at the highest levels of government. Both incidents revealed the uncomfortable truth that it was the Conservative government, and not the Communist Party, that was the greatest threat to the defence of the realm.[57]

V.

Quite apart from arguments about the legal nature of the mandate, it is quite clear that in the post-war era MI5 exceeded its powers, albeit with the complicity of government, and that in doing so it failed in its overriding duty relating to the defence of the realm. To that extent, there was no Rule of Law, or at least no Rule of Law by which MI5 was governed, in the sense of obedience to defined powers and accountability in the event of failure to comply with these powers, either by

[55] R. West, *The Meaning of Treason* (Harmondsworth, 1965 edn), p. 301.

[56] Indeed, that Guy Liddell's good friends and regular luncheon companions were Blunt, Philby, and Burgess, would be comedic were it not such a serious failure both of procedure and judgement. Consulted by the Head of Security at the Foreign Office in 1950 on the question of Burgess' loyalty, Liddell gave his assessment: 'Carey Foster came to see me about Guy Burgess . . . My own view was that Guy BURGESS was not the sort of person who would deliberately pass confidential information to unauthorized parties': TNA, KV 4/472 (Liddell Diary, 23 January 1950).

[57] Not to mention the equally uncomfortable truth that MI5 was utterly negligent in its assessment of risk and utterly incompetent in the management of its mandate.

over-reach or failure of performance. The next question then relates to the means used by MI5 in pursuit of its objectives under the mandate, an issue also raised by the European Commission of Human Rights in *Hewitt and Harman*, emphasizing that from the perspective of constitutional principle (and specifically the Rule of Law) surveillance powers:

> must be sufficiently clear in its terms to give citizens an adequate indication as to the circumstances in which and the conditions on which public authorities are empowered to resort to this secret and potentially dangerous interference with the right to respect for private life and correspondence.[58]

It could not be said by any stretch of the imagination that the means used by MI5 satisfied this basic requirement, with the lack of clarity about when the means would be used only one of a number of concerns. In regulating (albeit imperfectly) the circumstances in which surveillance may be undertaken, modern legislation proceeds as follows:

- First, it gives power for various forms of surveillance activity to be used (directed surveillance; the use of covert human intelligence sources; intrusive surveillance; and the interception of communications).
- Second, it then determines the circumstances in which these powers may be used (national security, detecting crime, and so on—depending on the nature of the surveillance activity undertaken) and the conditions of their use.
- Third, the use of these powers in any individual case requires prior approval to be given by senior officers within the organization undertaking the surveillance, a judicial officer (justice of the peace or sheriff), or the Home Secretary (or other minister).

Any authorization given would be for the powers in question to be used only to the extent necessary and in a proportionate manner.[59]

Until the Regulation of Investigatory Powers Act 2000 there was no such general authority. So, while Lord Denning could wax lyrically about MI5 officers having no powers of arrest or search, he neglected to say that nor did they have the power to engage in surveillance or to keep files about individuals, or to share information from these files. They did it nevertheless, for in the twisted logic of the British constitution at the time, the government was free to do not only that which was lawful, but also that which was not unlawful.[60] Yet for the most part it seems that MI5 was

[58] *Hewitt and Harman* (n 7), para. 39, citing *Malone v United Kingdom* (n 11), para. 67.

[59] These principles are drawn from the Regulation of Investigatory Powers Act 2000.

[60] This principle is best expressed in *Malone v Metropolitan Police Commissioner* [1979] 1 Ch 344. The closest we got to legal authority was *Thomas v Sawkins* [1935] 2 KB 249, in which it was held that

free to decide who was to be under surveillance and the means to be used for this purpose, with only mail, telegram, and phone intercepts requiring ministerial approval. In the absence of specific regulation of these powers, they were not openly or formally recognized, with the result that there could be no clarity about the circumstances in which they might be used, as the European Commission of Human Rights was later to require.

As it happens, it is now clear that the means used often had only a tenuous connection with MI5's mandate, with surveillance being undertaken not because someone was assessed as a threat to the defence of the realm, but to determine whether they were members of the Communist Party. A good example of this is the case of Kingsley Martin (PF 41,632), encountered in Chapter 4 above. As we saw, Mr Martin was reported by Special Branch for having addressed a meeting in London organized by the London Anarchist Group. The Special Branch report records Martin as having said that:

> There was a creeping plague of injustice and tyranny evident in the world today . . . The Middle Ages were almost kindly in comparison with Europe today, There were however a few patches of freedom left. He spoke of the methods adopted in Spain of making prisoners confess through cruelty . . . and said that such confessions were accepted at the trials. It was the law in Spain that people must adopt themselves to the existing regime . . . . A steady policy is needed of encouraging resistance in Spain, Franco is now sensitive to criticism as he wants to join the Western Community. We must force the Government to say to the Spanish government 'As you are today, the British People will not take you as allies and friends.'[61]

As we also pointed out in Chapter 4, the foregoing was enough to justify surveillance and retention, including surreptitious Special Branch baggage searches at the airport. It seems they were trying to work out whether he was a Communist, disappointed to find out that he was not.

The same is true of phone tapping and the interception of communications generally, often undertaken to discover the political views of the target. Asked in September 1952, to account for the large number of HOWs, Liddell 'reviewed the applications very carefully to see that they were within the four walls of our Charter'.[62] Rather disarmingly, and without embarrassment, Liddell announced

the police had the right to attend public meetings for surveillance purposes where they apprehended a breach of the peace.

[61] TNA, KV 2/2093 (Extract from S. B. report re London Anarchist Group Meeting mentioning Martin). See K. Ewing, J. Mahoney, and A. Moretta 'Surveillance and the Liberal State' UK Const L Blog (16 June 2013) (http://ukconstitutionallaw.org).

[62] TNA, KV 4/474 (Liddell Diary, 17 September 1952).

that the 'large number of checks was partly accountable to the fact that we had so many cases whether it was desirable to clear up one way or another whether an individual serving in a secret department was a [Party] member'.[63] We can only guess at the numbers of interceptions in place and more specifically the number being deployed as part of what was no more than a large-scale fishing exercise. In November 1952, however, Liddell recorded that additional funds had been required from the Treasury 'due to an increase of Registry staff necessitated by a vetting commitment which had now reached 7,000 a week'.[64]

Unlike other forms of surveillance, letter opening and phone tapping required a warrant. This meant that these methods of surveillance were known about, and—at least after the Birkett Report—that the reasons why they might be used would also be known. Like other forms of surveillance, phone tapping had initially taken place on the self-authorization of the head of MI5.[65] The latter would, of course, need the consent of the Director General of the Post Office,[66] but there is no evidence of this having been refused. The rules were changed in 1937, partly because concerns about potential criminal liability under the Telegraph Acts 1868 and 1869, concerns relating inter alia to the liability of Post Office staff who provided the contents of intercepted calls to the police and MI5, liability that carried a mandatory prison sentence.[67] It was in order ostensibly to protect against this risk that HOWs were introduced, though given the confidence about data security, there may have been other factors at work, suggesting the need for closer government supervision.[68]

The warrant procedure was thus not introduced as part of a devotion to civil liberties, nor in response to the need to safeguard the individual whose phone was to be tapped, and as we saw in Chapter 5 there is a sense in which this was something of a formality in most cases rather than a serious interrogation of the grounds for interception in any particular case.[69] Yet although the practice of phone tapping might satisfy the requirement that it should be at least known and acknowledged, it nevertheless failed the hardly demanding test set by the ECtHR that the law must be 'sufficiently clear in its terms to give citizens an adequate indication as

63 ibid.

64 TNA, KV 4/474 (Liddell Diary, 27 November 1952).

65 TNA, HO 144/20619 (Undated and Unsigned Draft Minute, but from 1937).

66 ibid.

67 TNA, HO 144/20619 (Memorandum by CR, 29 April 1937).

68 TNA, HO 144/20619 (Undated and Unsigned Draft Minute, but from 1937).

69 There is little evidence available that applications for HOWs were ever refused, though one example was the refusal by Chuter Ede of an application for the mass surveillance of the London District of the Communist Party. Liddell recorded that a warrant was 'turned down by the Home Secretary on the grounds that "he did not want any general prying into the affairs of the Communist Party"'. On being given the news, Liddell told Newsam that MI5 had been given the task of providing information on Communists in the civil service and engaged in secret work in industry by the Prime Minister, and the Service needed to be able to monitor membership applications. 'In addition', he continued, 'we wished to know about personalities and activities in the Districts which Chief Constables find it difficult, if not impossible to obtain.' Newsam promised to take the matter up with the Home Secretary (TNA KV 4/470, Liddell Diary, 21 December 1948). On Ede and civil liberties, see also pp. 8–9 above.

to the circumstances in which and the conditions' on which the State may use these highly intrusive powers. If that was true of the procedure explained by the Birkett Report,[70] it is difficult to see why it does not continue to be true of the legislation designed inaptly to address these flaws.

The main issue here, of course, is that the reduction of powers and procedures to statute is no guarantee that the Rule of Law is met, except in the most reductionist sense. The point is better made by the Security Service Act 1989, passed post-*Hewitt and Harman* on the one hand, and Peter Wright's revelations on the other. This implicitly acknowledges that MI5 did after all break into people's homes without legal authority, providing that 'No entry on or interference with property shall be unlawful if it is authorised by a warrant issued by the Secretary of State under this section.'[71] But unlike the phone tapping legislation, which gives a wide power to grant warrant for reasons such as national security and the detection of crime, the 1989 Act (and its successor provisions) provides absolutely *no* indication about the circumstances in which a government minister can authorize its own political police force to break the law with impunity.[72]

VI.

Although not expressly addressed in *Hewitt and Harman*, the powers of a secret police force and the circumstances in which they may be used also raise questions about the use of the information collected by these various surveillance means. Here too the same issues arise: (i) the need for formal authority to use the information; (ii) an acknowledgement that the information collected is used in ways that might prejudice the individual; and (iii) the need for clarity as to the circumstances and the conditions in which the information may be used. As we have seen, there were various purge and vetting programmes developed during the Cold War, effectively to exclude Communists from various positions within government and from various forms of private employment. None was the product of legislation, while in some cases they were announced without the full details being made known, and without any opportunity for Parliament to alter the arrangements in question.

If the Rule of Law is about the quality of law as well as its content, it is difficult to see how these arrangements could be said to be 'law'. This would be particularly true of negative vetting, by some way the largest of the programmes to rely on the surveillance harvest. This remained completely secret, never to be published,

[70] Report of the Committee of Privy Councillors Appointed to Inquire into the Interception of Communications, Cmnd 283, 1957.

[71] Security Service Act 1989, s. 3. See now Intelligence Services Act 1994, s. 5.

[72] Nor does it provide any redress where these (remarkably) are unjustifiably used.

ironically for fear of having to meet another Rule of Law obligation, namely provide redress to its victims. And although the other procedures were eventually revealed, it is clear from the files that people were prejudiced by the misuse of information long before the procedures were published. In the case of the private sector, MI5 officials visited workplaces to prevail upon employers to get rid of workers on political grounds, while it is clear from grievances raised by MPs that many were left simply bewildered by what was happening to them.

But these were not the only ways in which surveillance material was used to the prejudice of targets. Cathy Massiter was to reveal that the information collected could be used in other sinister ways, reinforcing the claims made earlier about the surveillance of democracy in order to contain and manage the democratic process. According to Massiter, surveillance files would be used as a basis for the 'assessment' of parliamentary candidates, presumably by MI5. Thereafter:

> Assessments of newly elected MPs are passed on to the Cabinet Office where there is information about the person concerned which might throw doubt upon their security fitness for inclusion on certain parliamentary committees requiring access to highly classified and/or sensitive information.[73]

Ms Harman—who like Ms Hewitt was to have a distinguished record as a minister and a parliamentarian—will no doubt have been consoled by Massiter's evidence that it was unlikely she would have been recommended for exclusion from any activity on the basis of her Security Service record.[74]

As MI5's role as a political police force became more fully developed, so the use of information for anything resembling defence of the realm became ever more tenuous. A Channel 4 '20/20Vision' programme broadcast in 1985 called 'MI5's Official Secrets' made shocking and extremely convincing allegations about MI5's role in industrial disputes and politics.[75] It featured a couple of disenchanted Security Service employees,[76] one being Cathy Massiter, and the other an anonymous MI5 clerk. Massiter had worked for F Division between 1970 and 1984, while the anonymous clerk had been employed transcribing intercepted phone calls and bugged conversations since 1978. Most of what the latter had to reveal concerned the surveillance of trade unionists, it being recalled that:

[73] *Hewitt and Harman* (n 7), para. 15. Note also Alan Clark's encounter with the Cabinet Secretary: having been appointed junior minister in the Department of Employment, Clark was summoned to Cabinet Secretary Sir Robert Armstrong's office. An orange file was produced, and Armstrong questioned Clark on 'certain matters of personal conduct . . . which could quite possibly leave you open to blackmail'. After the interview, Clark 'thought about it for a little while. They *must* have been bugging my phone. There was no other explanation. And for ages' (Alan Clark, *Diaries 1972–1999* (London, 2010)), 24 June 1993.

[74] *Hewitt and Harman* (n 7).

[75] Channel 4 News, *20/20 Vision, MI5's Official Secrets* (1985). The film is available on YouTube.

[76] As well as one Special Branch agent who had infiltrated the National Front and claimed that the Special Branch had encouraged him to join in the violence and general criminality, including burglary.

> After two months training, I went to work in MI5's Industrial Room, with seven other women, transcribing tapes of telephone calls which had been tapped. Each morning I'd collect the actual tapes from a room on the 5th floor which contained banks of recorders operating 24 hours a day.[77]

During a trade dispute at Ford's Dagenham works, Massiter was instructed to listen carefully to the tapes she was transcribing of shop steward Sid Harroway's telephone conversations. There may have been reasons that would have attracted MI5 to Dagenham, though whether these constituted counter-subversion is another matter:

> The other side to Dagenham at the time was on the political Left. And it was extraordinary! It was like a big university of left-wing ideas. There would be an 'Autonomy Group', and Italian Autonomy group. There were anarchists. There were pro-Serbia Communists, Chinese Communists. There were more than one kind of pro-Albanian Communists. There was every kind of Trotskyite movement you could think of. There were all sorts of things. There was a Black Power movement. Indian workers—there were groups that were part of the Indian Workers' Association. There were a lot of political people. The fascists came in later as part of three different kinds of factions. You'd call them the ATA, the National Front. There were different Nazi factions . . . Dagenham was a magnet. If you wanted to work and earn money and also fight for your rights, it was a good place to go.[78]

According to Massiter, however, F Branch had less noble security and intelligence concerns, anxious to find the union's bargaining position, its 'bottom line' in the pay negotiations. Massiter, who was on the F Branch industrial desk at the time, claimed that the information was required by the Department of Employment—not a government department generally considered to be in the front line when it comes to the defence of the realm. By the same token, the anonymous clerk had to transcribe negotiations for a proposed merger between the TASS and the AUEW taking place at the home of Ken Gill, General Secretary of TASS:

> His home had been broken into and a bug placed inside a room to monitor talks between Mr. Gill and other trade unionists prior to or during the merger . . . I found this a sinister intrusion into a person's civil rights and privacy. I think that Parliament should be made aware of interference in and abuse of civil liberties being conducted in this country by the Security Service. This is why I have made this statement.[79]

77 Channel 4 News (n 75).

78 T. Martin Lopez and S. Rowbotham, *The Winter of Discontent: Myth, Memory and History* (Liverpool, 2014), p. 72.

79 Channel 4 News (n 75).

The use of secret information collected in secret ways for secret purposes was, of course, only one of the issues arising even on a low Rule of Law threshold. We can only assume that the information about Sid Harroway and Ken Gill was not collected for the sake of it, and that it was used for the benefit of third parties, including employers in the case of Harroway and possible leadership candidates in the case of Gill.[80] That being likely to be the case, not only was there no legal authority for the use of such information, it was nowhere acknowledged that surveillance information would be used in this way, or indeed any indication of any other purpose for which surveillance information might be used. Similar issues arise in relation to the purge and vetting procedures, which did have the virtue of eventually being made public, in the sense that it was made clear that:

> It is the policy of Her Majesty's Government that no one who is or has recently been a member of the British Communist Party or of a Fascist organisation or who, in such a way as to raise legitimate doubts about his reliability, is or has recently been sympathetic to Communism or Fascism or associated with Communists or Communist sympathisers or is susceptible to Communist pressure, should be employed in connection with work the nature of which is vital to the security of the State.[81]

But clarity of purpose is not the same as clarity of practice, and in no sense could the purge and vetting procedure be said to meet basic obligations about the quality of the law, even to the limited extent that they were made known. The foregoing statement tells us that personal information would be used to the detriment of individuals, but does not tell us how it was obtained or stored, there being no acknowledgement of a database obtained by secret methods and in the case of 'Operation Party Piece' perhaps unlawfully. Equally significant, just as there is no publicity about what information will be used or the manner of its collection and storage, so there is no clarity about the circumstances of its use. The uncertainty of a Communist association of such a kind as would justify exclusion from employment is compounded by the explicit refusal to provide any clarity in a procedure that celebrated its vagueness by providing that no guidance could be given 'as to what constitutes sympathy or association' for these purposes.[82]

[80] But quite how the information obtained on groups such as CND would be used remains a mystery. According to Massiter, 'We were violating our our own rules. It seemed to be getting out of control. This was happening not because CND as such is justified [sic.] for this kind of treatment but simply because [of] political pressure. The heat was on for information on CND and we had to have it.' But to what ends? MI5 used Harry Newton, a lecturer in trade union studies who had previously infiltrated the CPGB, as Massiter's 'eye and ears' in CND headquarters. On being told of Newton's role, in an interview for the Channel 4 programme, Bruce Kent commented that MI5 had only to call: 'They can come in and we'll show them anything they want to see . . . there's no secret.' The High Court nevertheless held that the surveillance of CND was not 'unreasonable' in the peculiar legal sense of that term: *R v Foreign Secretary, ex parte Ruddock* [1987] 1 WLR 1482.

[81] HC Debs, 29 January 1957, col. 152 WA (Mr Enoch Powell).

[82] ibid.

VII.

Returning to the themes of the complacent constitution with principles derived from Dicey and the later Jennings, the lawyer might ask where were the judges when MI5 was strutting its stuff and extending its tentacles as a political police force? It is of course the case that an agency operating in the dark without clear legal authority is hard to see and hard to catch for judges, who can usually only respond to the claims of others. It is nevertheless also the case that rather than defend the Rule of Law and rather than demand clear legal authority for MI5, clearly defined and predictable powers, and proper channels of accountability, judges have been complicit in the absence of legal authority, the existence of arbitrary power, and illegal conduct, and wholly unaccountable procedures. Indeed, as we shall see, even in recent times judges have continued to be safe, supportive, and uncritical friends of MI5, despite the self-serving claims of a new judicial culture.

As we have seen, the judicial role in the post-war era was an administrative one rather than a judicial one, with judges being appointed to review security breaches. These were notably the Conference of Privy Councillors, including the Lord Chancellor and his predecessor (appointed in the wake of Burgess and Maclean),[83] subsequent reviews being conducted or chaired by Lord Justice Romer (Portland),[84] Lord Radcliffe (security procedures in the light of the Blake case),[85] and Lord Denning (the security implications of the Profumo affair).[86] None of these inquiries (to the extent that they have been published—itself an issue of contention) raised any questions about the propriety of the legal framework by which MI5 was governed or the legal powers which it exercised.[87] As pointed out in Part I above, few revealed any concern for civil liberties, the main concern being to tighten security procedures, with no concern being expressed either for the manner in which this might be done.

This is not to deny that judicial tin ears were wholly impenetrable, with Lord Radcliffe resisting pressure that the purge procedure be tilted even more in favour of the State, a step that was in any event unnecessary in view of the fact that the procedure had by now been broken as a result of the combined efforts of MI5 pressure and departmental avoidance strategies.[88] It is also true that Radcliffe proposed better procedures for those refused security clearance under the vetting procedures, though notably this was to be no more than an appeal to a departmental head,

[83] See Chapter 13 above for a full account.
[84] This was referred to in Lord Radcliffe's Report on Security Procedures in the Public Service, Cmnd 1681, 1962. It is also referred to in parliamentary debates, the Prime Minister having issued a summary. See HC Debs, 13 June 1961, col. 211.The report was released to the National Archives in 2017.
[85] Report on Security Procedures in the Public Service (n 84).
[86] Lord Denning's Report, Cmnd 2152, 1963.
[87] Lord Denning revealed the existence of the Maxwell Fyfe Directive for the first time, but did not engage with questions about its provenance or status.
[88] Report on Security Procedures in the Public Service (n 84), para. 56.

with no question of independent scrutiny or review.[89] It is not to be overlooked, however, that while Lord Radcliffe offered little protection for civil liberties, he also played a part in what was one of the most egregious violations of civil liberties during the Cold War, namely the imprisonment of journalists for failing to disclose their sources to his Vassall inquiry.[90]

It was not until the 1980s that judges were to be tested in their judicial capacity in relation to the mandate, powers, and activities of MI5. These cases came in the wake of the revelations by Cathy Massiter and Peter Wright respectively, the first being a direct challenge to the surveillance targets,[91] and the second dealing indirectly with the powers and activities of MI5.[92] In the former, the question before the court was the legality of surveillance of CND on the ground that it was a subversive organization. In a judgment delivered by the Lord Chief Justice in what was for that reason alone clearly an important case, the High Court held that having been assessed as subversive, the surveillance of CND and its personnel was not unlawful. But there was a loud silence as to the legal foundations for the exercise of this power, the court effectively holding that it was lawful for an agency established without legal authority to exercise powers the law had never bestowed.[93]

It was here that the applicants faced the reality of principle in the British constitution, principle that operated in part to serve the interests of the State and its institutions. So while Dicey's Rule of Law might celebrate the freedom of citizens to do anything not unlawful, the same principle applied equally to the State. Under the common law, if not the ECHR, there was no need for MI5 to be a creature of law or exercise powers conferred by law, provided that it did not violate the rights of others in exercising these powers. This had been established in *Malone v Metropolitan Police Commissioner*,[94] where telephone tapping by the police under procedures used also by the Security Service were held not to be unlawful. More worrying, however, were the observations of Lord Donaldson MR in the wake of the allegations made about MI5's illegal activities in terms of breaking into private property for various surveillance and intelligence-gathering purposes.[95]

The *Spycatcher* case was an ultimately unsuccessful attempt by the government to stop the publication of Peter Wright's memoirs,[96] Wright being an unhappily retired MI5 official who had left the jurisdiction.[97] Responding to the claim that MI5 acted illegally, Lord Donaldson dismissed these claims, which he appeared

[89] ibid., para. 67.

[90] Report of the Tribunal Appointed to Inquire into the Vassall Case and Related Matters (Chairman, Viscount Radcliffe), Cmnd 2009, 1963.

[91] *R v Foreign Secretary, ex parte Ruddock* (n 80).

[92] *Attorney General v Guardian Newspapers* (No 2) [1988] 2 WLR 805.

[93] *R v Foreign Secretary, ex parte Ruddock* (n 80).

[94] [1979] 1 Ch 344.

[95] *Attorney General v Guardian Newspapers* (No 2) (n 92).

[96] For details of the litigation in Sydney, London, Edinburgh, and Strasbourg, see K. D. Ewing and C. A. Gearty, *Freedom under Thatcher: Civil Liberties in Modern Britain* (Oxford, 1990).

[97] See *Daily Telegraph*, 28 April 1995 (Peter Wright, Obituary).

to excuse as being equivalent to an ambulance jumping a red light in an emergency.[98] In other words, when all else fails, the courts were willing to extend to MI5 the indulgence of breaking the law, Lord Donaldson turning his back on the great judgment of Lord Camden in *Entick v Carrington*,[99] that the violation of private property rights could not be justified on grounds of expediency: state necessity was no excuse for breaking the law. The complicity was thus complete: judges and lawyers had created the extra-legal framework within which MI5 operated, had stretched principle to allow MI5 to operate with impunity, and where necessary were now prepared to tolerate illegality.

VIII.

At the beginning of this final chapter we suggested that there were a number of reasons for examining the past. These related to the need to understand the aims and values of modern institutions, to better understand the form of modern law, and to help understand current problems within a particular field. Above all, however, the theme underpinning not only this concluding chapter but the book as a whole is that a study of the past is necessary to test claims about the constitutional principles by which the country is governed, and to assess their virtue, vitality, and vibrancy. As such, our main focus has been with the Rule of Law (now elevated to a statutory principle), which the record shows was little more than a figment of the liberal lawyer's imagination, even taking the principle to its lowest level, as expressed by the European Commission of Human Rights in *Hewitt and Harman*.

Scandals of the 1980s led to legislation eventually being introduced.[100] This legislation both acknowledged these failings, and failed adequately to address them. Thus, the Security Service Act 1989 more or less adopted the Maxwell Fyfe Directive, the main provisions of which relating to MI5's mandate were simply transferred from administrative document to statutory text. By virtue of section 1(2), it is thus simply provided that:

> The function of the Service shall be the protection of national security and, in particular, its protection against threats from espionage, terrorism and sabotage, from the activities of agents of foreign powers and from actions intended to overthrow or undermine parliamentary democracy by political, industrial or violent means.

[98] *Attorney General v Guardian Newspapers* (No 2) (n 92).

[99] (1765) 19 St Tr 1029. For an account of the continuing significance of this decision, see K. D. Ewing and C. A. Gearty, 'History of a Dog's Dinner: The Police Bill', *London Review of Books*, 6 February 1997.

[100] Notably the Interception of Communications Act 1985 (post-*Malone*) and the Security Service Act 1989 (post-*Hewitt and Harman*), followed by the Intelligence Services Act 1994 and Regulation of Investigatory Powers Act 2000. The Data Protection Act 2018 is also relevant.

This encapsulates both the terms of the 1952 Directive and aspects of its subsequent elucidation, with additional provisions acknowledging MI5's desire to play a part in the prevention and detection of serious crime.[101]

But although the 1989 Act may have addressed one aspect of legality addressed by *Hewitt and Harman* (legal authority for the existence of MI5), it is difficult to see how it addresses the need to 'provide a framework which indicates with the requisite degree of certainty the scope and manner of the exercise of discretion by the authorities in the carrying out of secret surveillance activities'.[102] Despite the new legal foundations for MI5's activities, the 1989 Act maintained the environment of secrecy and arbitrariness that had produced a Security Service that had in turn metamorphosed from being an agency supposedly concerned with counter-espionage to one concerned principally with 'counter-subversion', a term over-widely defined. In the post-war period, the latter was a term that became a euphemism for the monitoring of the Communist Party, and a range of organizations deemed to be in the same orbit, as well as individuals deemed—as in *Hewitt and Harman*—sympathetic to the aims of the Party.[103]

As we conclude, we are reminded of Wade writing during the Cold War in celebration of the British system underpinned by the Rule of Law, contrasting those regimes in which there were 'secret police and people's courts administering not law, but the orders of those who can dictate what is the people's will'.[104] Yet what we have identified is:

(i) a secret police force;
(ii) established without clear legal authority or legally defined powers;
(iii) unleashed by a revised mandate to determine its own priorities;
(iv) a mandate which expanded in practice in a way only tenuously related to its stated purpose;
(v) in the exercise of which MI5 clearly refused to comply with instructions to confine its activities to the scope of the mandate;
(vi) with authority to exercise some of its powers to pursue its objectives granted by the government department to whom the agency was responsible;
(vii) while in other cases arbitrary powers could be exercised on the authority of the agency itself;
(viii) which at times indulged in unlawful behaviour with impunity;

[101] Security Service Act 1989, s. 1(4). This is a throwback to the war years, when MI5 intruded into criminal investigation on its own volition.

[102] *Hewitt and Harman* (n 7).

[103] The monitoring of the Party, and associated organizations and individuals was, in 1950, estimated to be ninety-five per cent of the work of B1, which employed '29 officers and women assistants'.

[104] E. C. S. Wade and G. G. Phillips, *Constitutional Law* (6th edn, London, 1960), p. 72. We too had secret police, and if not people's courts, then secret courts with decisions by politically vetted juries.

(ix) with no effective accountability for the way in which it conducted its activities, MI5 taking control of the only forum established for this purpose; and
(x) with judges offering no independent voice in different forms of administrative and judicial engagement with MI5.[105]

Although these are not the standards of a constitutional democracy founded on the Rule of Law, they are the standards of the past that continue to haunt the practices of today.

[105] To which we might add that the fruits of its work were consumed in secret trials before politically vetted juries. On political vetting of jurors, K. D. Ewing, 'The Cold War, Civil Liberties and the House of Lords', in T. Campbell, K. D. Ewing, and A. Tomkins (eds), *The Legal Protection of Human Rights: Sceptical Essays* (Oxford, 2011), ch. 8, in relation to *Chandler v DPP* [1964] AC 763.

APPENDIX

Note on the Post-War Structure of MI5

The various roles of the different sections belonging to the divisions, or branches, of MI5 are a source of considerable confusion, and the early Cold War was a time of particular organizational turmoil.[1]

This note gives an overview of the 1945–53 structural changes. These reflected the immediate post-war concern for civil liberties evinced in the Stewart Report and the Attlee Directive, and the subsequent drift back towards political policing which culminated in Dick White's 1953 re-organization of the Service. While we mention some names that will be familiar, such was the frequency with which officers were shifted around within the Service, that for reasons of clarity the focus is on the roles and designations of the various sections rather than on personnel.

I.

We start at the point early in World War Two when the nature of the threat posed by Germany, and the British alliance with the Soviet Union meant that subversion and espionage were for the first time since the end of WWI seen largely as discrete matters. In the autumn of 1941, as part of the reforms instituted by the newly appointed Director General, Sir David Petrie, responsibility for counter-subversion was shifted from B Division (counter-espionage) section B4 to F Division. Petrie, and many of his colleagues regarded only F and B Divisions as the Security Service. A Division, which was the administrative part of the Service; C Division, which handled vetting enquiries in close collaboration with F Division; and the protective security branch, D Division, were seen as parts of the War Office.

F Division was divided into three:

- F3, sub-divided into five sections, F3A–F3E, monitored Fascist organizations and Fascist sympathizers, as well as those connected with pacifist organizations, such as the Peace Pledge Union and the Jehovah's Witnesses.
- F2, under Roger Hollis, was given the responsibility for monitoring the activities of members and sympathizers of the Communist Party and other left-wing organizations.
- F1, identified, monitored, and ultimately oversaw the detention of those ultimate subversives, 'renegade' British citizens who had collaborated with, and sometimes even fought for, the Axis powers during the war.

[1] C. Andrew, *The Defence of the Realm—The Authorized History of MI5* (London, 1995), identifies 'division' as the preferred term between 1931 and 1940, 'branch' between 1940 and 1941, 'division' between 1943 and 1950, and branch after 1953 (p. 127). That said, the terms continued to be used interchangeably by some officers, while others still stuck to one or the other. Tom Bower's book, *The Perfect English Spy: Sir Dick White and the Secret War 1935–90* (London, 1995) suggests that White ordered the shift from division to branch in 1953 (p. 142).

A section designation like F2 was the effective title of the senior officer in that section,[2] cited in almost every note, letter, or memo written by them or presented for their attention.

These broad sections were divided into smaller specialist sections, the designations of which served similarly for each officer working within those sections. F2 comprised of three such sections:

- F2A, under David Clarke, which was tasked with monitoring the activities of the Party.
- F2B, run by Millicent Bagot, MI5's long-serving expert on International Communism.
- F2C, under Hugh Shillito, which had the task of monitoring Soviet espionage.

By 1944, F2A comprised of eleven officers, F2B comprised only of Bagot and three assistants, and F2C comprised just one officer.[3] This allocation of staff reflected both the little that was known about the extent of Soviet espionage operations against the West, and the wartime priorities of the Service.[4]

II.

In 1946 Petrie retired. Percy Sillitoe was appointed as DG, and Guy Liddell, previously head of B Branch, was appointed DDG. The heads of divisions or branches were 'Directors'.

- Dick White, who during the war had charge of those sections of B Division which ran the 'XX' double agents against the Abwehr, took over from Liddell and was often referred to in internal documents as 'DB'.
- Roger Hollis, who by the end of the war had overall charge of F division, had the rank of Assistant Director, and was often referred to as 'ADF' in internal communications. Like White, he too was to become DG in due course.

The post-war re-organization took place at the end of 1946. F Division was absorbed by the counter-espionage B branch, and designated B1. Roger Hollis took control of—and became—B1. B1A covered 'Left Wing Subversive Activities', and B1D. was very briefly the

[2] Lower- or upper-case lettering, and the use of brackets signified nothing and their use or absence appear to have depended on fashion and the practice of the writer or typist.

[3] These staffing arrangements were revealed by Roger Hollis to Harold 'Kim' Philby and sent in a report to Moscow. The first three paragraphs of the report can be seen in the photographic montage in the front and end papers of N. West and O. Tsarov, *The Crown Jewels: The Secrets at the Heart of the KGB Archives* (London, 1998). The full version of the Philby Report has been given the title of 'When Philby Met Hollis' and published in M. Smith (ed.), *The Secret Agent's Bedside Reader: A Compendium of Spy Writing* (London, 2014). Smith tells his readers that the document is held at the SVR Archives in Moscow. The report includes a para on the SF at King St:

> 'Hollis finally turned to his greatest source of information. F Division has derived a great deal of information about the CPGB from the use of "special facilities", ie microphones installed in the telephone apparatus at 16 King Street, and other headquarters of the CPGB. They receive about seventy pages on an average [sic.] every day.'

The report is undated but from the information it contains it is obviously from 1945.

[4] There had been doubts about sidelining Soviet counter-espionage—see, e.g., TNA, CAB 301/25 (Sir David Petrie, 'The Report on the Security Service', 13 February 1941), p. 29. Petrie proposed that the new discrete 'Subversive Movements Division' would include all of B4, but that 'The sub-section dealing with "Soviet Espionage" may require more detailed consideration.' Nevertheless, by the summer of 1942 Soviet Intelligence recorded that they had been informed by Anthony Blunt that Hugh Shillito [F2C], tasked with tackling Soviet espionage, 'practically does not work against us': West and Tsarov (n 3), p. 147.

designation for 'Right Wing Subversive Activities', before it became B1Z (very likely a reflection of the lack of interest in Fascist organizations). Bagot's section was given the title B1D:[5]

MI5 'B' Division (Counter-Espionage)
1947

B1: Overall study of Communist and Fascist Movements: Communism and Fascism in UK

B1A: Left Wing Subversion

B1B: Russian and Communist Espionage Investigation

B1C: Russian and Communist Espionage Information

B1D: International Communism

B1Z: Right Wing Subversive Activities

The absorption of F Division by B Division was the principal change. It reflected the civil liberties concerns raised in the Findlater Stewart Report, and the demands of the subsequent Attlee Directive. It was an attempt at least to appear to draw away from the overt political policing of Communists and fellow travellers, and pass off its long-standing core role as the basis of counter-espionage work.

MI5 'B' Division (Counter-Espionage)
1947

B2: National Groups (other than Russian)

B2A: Finns, Poles, Czechs, Balkans, Italy, Baltic, Ukrainian, White Russian Emigré Groups

B2B: Germany and Austria, France, Scandinavia, Switzerland, Low Countries, Spain, South America, and USA[6]

III.

In a November 1947 re-organization, B1B and B1C were shifted to B2, which now dealt exclusively with 'Russian and Russian Satellite Espionage', and was divided into B2A 'Investigation' and B2B 'Information', the word 'Communist' having been dropped. Bagot's B1D became B1B, and, presumably as the Mosleyites started to enjoy their brief post-war resurgence, B1Z became B1C.

A new B1D was formed, monitoring those foreign subversive groups in the UK formerly undertaken by B2A and B2B, not covered by B1A (left-wing counter subversion) and B1C (right-wing counter subversion), and the investigation of potential espionage cases.

[5] While colleagues were moved from one role to another, in this and in subsequent reshuffles, Bagot's expertise meant that while the designation might change, her duties remained the same.

[6] DG's Circular, 19 December 1946. The USA is not among the States listed as the responsibility of B2B in the formal (redacted) chart of the 1947 structure of B Division. These documents, like much that follows in this appendix that is not specifically attributed to a particular source, are from TNA, KV 4/162 and KV4/166. See also TNA, KV 4/468 (Liddell Diary, 7 November 1946): 'Curry [then head of B2] said that B2A has been divided into B2A and B2B; the former . . . dealing with all satellite countries, and the latter . . . dealing with allied countries.'

Essentially, B1D was required to tackle those cases perceived as presenting less immediate threats to the defence of the realm, and to pass more serious cases on to B2. The section was also given responsibility for housing and controlling defectors.[7]

In July 1948, B1E was established to prepare and submit 'Communist and Fascist cases under the Prime Minister's "purge procedure"', under Graham Mitchell. Its remit was extended beyond the civil service into 'Communism in the Professions' in 1950, following the Fuchs' case. Hollis was promoted to Director of C Division in December 1948, and Mitchell appointed Senior Officer in C3 early 1951,[8] having previously served as B1. In the summer, he was shifted to the same role in C1.[9] C Division was responsible for vetting inquiries. See p. 480 below.

MI5 B1 and B2
1948

B1A: Left Wing Subversion

B1B: International Communism

B1C: Right Wing Subversive Activities

B1D: Residual Counter-Subversive and Counter-Espionage Activities

B1E: Civil Service Purge Cases

B2A: Russian and Russian Satellite Espionage Investigation

B2B: Russian and Russian Satellite Espionage Information

B3 was tasked with supervising the Service's work in certain colonies and ex-colonies: 'Co-ordination of Overseas Intelligence, Liaison with Overseas Stations on Intelligence', and 'Special Subjects as directed':

- B3A covered Security and Intelligence in the Middle East (SIME) and Malta.
- B3B, covered Security and Intelligence in the Far East (SIFE), the Caribbean, and Ireland.
- B3C had responsibility for Africa, the States covered by SIME excepted, and Gibraltar.

On 1 January 1950, B3 became the Overseas Division 'OS'.

B4 co-ordinated technical surveillance—it arranged bugging and phone tapping operations with the GPO, wrote up the reports that were made on the intelligence so gathered, and held the index of HOWs. The section's designation remained the same between 1941 and 1953. In Cabinet Secretary Norman Brook's notes on the Security Service made in the summer of 1950, he describes B4 as the 'support group' for the rest of B Division, providing and maintaining aids to investigation, 'responsible for the operational, administrative and financial aspects' of running agents.

[7] This incarnation of B1D had been established in November 1947 as a section wholly separate from Miss Bagot's B1D—her international communism work continued, as noted above, under the designation B1B—and B1D appears to have been subsequently treated as a dumping ground for roles that other sections would not take. In January 1948, White stated that it should monitor 'foreign espionage activities in the UK other than those studied by B2A. However, having isolated for specialised study by B2A the potentially hostile ones, B1D's responsibilities need not comprise more than the tackling of actual cases as and when they arise.'

[8] An MI5 Directors' meeting had agreed that in order 'to meet our vetting commitment . . . it was essential that Graham Mitchell should take over C1': TNA, KV 4/473 (Liddell Diary, 9 February 1951).

[9] TNA, KV 4/473 (Liddell Diary, 2 July 1951).

The mainstay of the section was Evelyn Grist's B4B team, comprising of both MI5 and GPO staff, who listened to, recorded, and transcribed bugged conversations and telephone interceptions. In November 1947, Malcolm Cumming had taken over from Kenneth Morton Evans to become B4, and through the Liddell Diary, and the publicity he was accorded in Peter Wright's *Spycatcher*, MI5's best-known senior technical surveillance officer. Maxwell Knight's wartime B5B (AKA 'M' Section) was designated B4C 'Agents and Informers'. An MI5 paper sent to Norman Brook in 1950 stated that 'Since 1948 every effort has been made to cover by technical and other intelligence sources the operations of BCP headquarters.'[10] B4 were behind most of these efforts.

MI5 B4
1947

B4A: Co-ordination of Accounts, Source Reports, Technical and Physical Surveillance, Liaison with GCHQ, Contact Index, Analysis Index, and Index of HOWs—'Letter Checks, Telephone Checks and SFs'

B4B: Technical Facilities

B4C: Agents and Informers

B4D: Watchers

B4E: Commercial, Banking and Lloyds Shipping, BOAC and BEA Enquiries, Counter-Sabotage Records

---

Guy Poston was B4E.[11] According to Norman Brook, writing in 1950, his role was to maintain 'certain special confidential contacts with Government Departments, local authorities, private companies, banks etc for the purposes of obtaining information'. Brook did not, however, refer to the reciprocal side to this work—the provision by MI5 of information from the Registry, principally on individuals associated with left-wing politics—of these organizations.

IV.

At the start of 1950, a new counter-subversion section was formed, the Service having become less coy about its obsessive interest in the CPGB:

> As from 1st January 1950 a new section B1F will be formed which will take over from B1A the work in connection with the clandestine activity of the British Communist Party. The subjects covered will include:
>
> Leakages to the Party from Government Departments.
> Investigations of suspected espionage by Party members.
> Secret Party organisation, funds, members and activities.
> Covert relations between the Party and Soviet or Satellite representatives.[12]

[10] TNA, CAB 301/20 (Paper on B Divison sent to Norman Brook by Sillitoe, 3 July 1950).

[11] 'Counter sabotage records' will have comprised lists of those to be detained in a national emergency. Responsibility for those records was shifted later in 1947 to a Major Boddington in C2: see also TNA, KV 4/468 (Liddell Diary, 17 October 1946). Poston was also tasked with providing trustworthy linguists when translators were required.

[12] TNA, KV 4/162 (Memo from Horrocks (Director of A Division), 29 December 1949).

However, B1A was given a more specific brief in July 1950: 'The British Communist Party: Organisation, Policy and Membership'. With sections B1D and B1E covering Communist activity in the civil service, the professions, and in industry,[13] and the role of B1C extended beyond the monitoring of Fascists to the study of 'Subversive and suspect movements other than the Communist Party',[14] much covert activity was thereby addressed.

As a consequence, while senior officer Richard Thistlethwaite remained B1F, he was given the additional responsibility of overseeing B1G, and the study of the 'British Communist Party: Foreign Activities; Communists from Overseas'. By the summer of 1950, the work of B1 was being undertaken, as Norman Brook noted, 'by 29 officers and women assistants'. It was estimated that about ninety-five per cent of that work related to communism,[15] and such was the intensive nature of this political monitoring that it had 'made necessary a campaign to enlist on a wide scale the informed co-operation of the police'.

C Division were said to have had six officers overseeing an administrative team dealing exclusively with 'vetting for Government Departments and for industry'.[16] A chart on the structure of C Division issued at the time indicates that there were at least eight officers, including Hollis, overseeing vetting, although this includes those officers who oversaw travel control. Absent from the chart below, however, is section C3, and also any reference to the vetting of those in, or applying for, other services and industries considered 'sensitive', or with which the Service had close connections, like the BBC, BOAC, and BEA.[17]

MI5 'C' Division
1950

C1: Departmental Security, Vetting and Naturalization

C1A: Civil Departments

C1B: Service Departments

C2A: Industrial Munitions Security

C2B: Security of Economic Industrial Information

C2C: Counter-Sabotage/Security of Premises

C3: Vetting in other Services and Industries

C4A: Port and Travel Control, Liaison with other Departments on Travel Matters

C4B: Exit Permits, Visas, Liaison with Passport Office

---

13 TNA, CAB 301/20 (Brook's notes on B Division). It is notable that following his July 1950 interviews, Norman Brook listed the trade unions as a discrete B1 target, separate from the monitoring Communist influence in the civil service, and 'non-Government establishments, including research establishments and private firms, where secret official work is in progress', and remarkably separate from Communist Party 'participation in industrial disputes'.

14 TNA, KV 4/162 (Note by Horrocks, 8 July 1948). The fortunes of the Fascists had waned after their post-war clashes with Jews and Communists in the East End, and they had been 'thrown in' with the Trotskyites.

15 TNA, CAB 301/20 (Brook's notes on B Division).

16 TNA, CAB 301/20 (Brook's 'Interviews at Leconfield House 14 July, 1950', C Division—Mr Hollis).

17 ibid., chart supplied to Brook. It appears that the chart has not been redacted, but that it was supplied to Brook without any reference to C3.

C1 was a Major Strang, soon to be replaced by Graham Mitchell (made C3 then C1 in 1951), C2 was Martin Furnival Jones, and C4 was Brigadier Hinchley Cooke, who had appalled the head of Special Branch during the war by arresting a suspect in the street.[18]

V.

Such was the increase in vetting that in March 1951 the newly appointed B1, John Marriot,[19] recommended to Dick White that a section of B Division dealing exclusively with vetting enquiries be established.[20] White accepted the recommendation, implementing it as part of yet another re-organization. The new section was designated B1V, but the big change was the establishment of 'a new section which will incorporate that part of B1A at present doing investigation into the underground activities of the CP [Communist Party] to which will be added B4C, *whose agent running activities fit exactly into this context*'.[21]

B4C was, of course, Maxwell Knight's 'M' Section. Previously operating out of Knight's Dolphin Square flat, White's reorganization brought the eccentric ex-Fascist and his spies back under MI5's roof, and into counter-subversion, rather than counter-espionage, an acknowledgement that his roster of agents and informants provided information on those engaged in political rather than espionage activities. A chart laying out the proposals for re-organization for 'summer 1951', has Mr Courtenay Young as B1A, with the additional responsibility of the new agent running section temporarily designated as B1A/INV plus B4C. The latter became B1H

Courtenay Young, and the two other senior officers in B1, were to report to John Marriot, who, as well as having overall responsibility as B1 had personal responsibility for B1H, a section which the chart does not attach a role. Nevertheless, B1H was subsequently responsible for a series of 'source reports' on information supplied both by Knight's agents and agents run by officers who were not part of his coterie, and we can conclude that B1H was the new, if short-lived, designation for B1's agent running section. The files also show that towards the end of 1951 Knight's section once more became a separate entity, known as B1K.[22]

Richard Thistlethwaite relinquished his B1G responsibilities in 1951, but he continued as B1F. While we are not aware of the official role assigned to that section, the files show that following the disappearance of Burgess and Maclean at the end of May 1951, Thistlethwaite became MI5's universities' specialist,[23] and his section was busy monitoring the activities of Party members and suspected fellow travellers working in a variety of professions, including the arts. B1F carried out active investigations, and handled numbers of agents and informants, producing numerous source reports during 1952 and 1953.[24]

18 TNA, CAB 301/11 (Letter to Edward Bridges (then Cabinet Secretary) from the Director of Special Branch, Norman Kendal, 27 July 1943).

19 TNA, KV 4/473 (Liddell Diary, 9 February 1951).

20 TNA, KV 4/162 (Marriot to White, 29 March 1951).

21 TNA, KV 4/162 (White, Minute Sheet Note to MI5 Directors, 1 May 1951).

22 See, e.g., the reports on D. N. Pritt and his wife dated 16 May 1951 and 17 July 1951 in KV 2/1065. These are attributed to B1H, and then later in the file there are a couple of B1K reports, dated 18 December 1951 and 22 January 1952 which have, like the two B1H reports, come from a source very close to the Pritts—very likely the same individual.

23 Thistlethwaite visited Cambridge in October 1951, reporting as B1F on material in college archives on contemporaries of Burgess and Maclean (see Michael Redgrave file, TNA, KV 2/3822).

24 See the file on the MacDonald Discussion Group (TNA, KV 5/80).

MI5 B1
1951–3

B1A: British Communist Party/Organization, Policy, and Membership

B1B: International Communism

B1C: Subversive and Suspect Movements other than the Communist Party

B1D: Communists in Industry

B1E: Communists in the Civil Service and the Professions

B1V: Vetting

B1F: Covert Communist Activity/Investigations Agents and Informers/Communism in the Universities

B1G: Foreign Communists in the UK and CPGB Foreign Activities

B1H: Investigations Agents and Informers (this section was dissolved late in 1951, responsibilities relinquished to B1K and to B1F)

B1K: Maxwell Knight's 'M' Section—Agents and Informers

VI.

In October 1951, Labour lost the general election. Attlee was replaced by Churchill, Chuter Ede by Maxwell Fyfe. In 1952, the Home Secretary took over ministerial responsibility for the Service and allowed it to revise the Attlee Directive, which subsequently became known as the Maxwell Fyfe Directive.

The shuffling of MI5 personnel continued, although the structure remained broadly unchanged until Sillitoe's retirement and White's appointment as DG in 1953. Sillitoe had made it very clear that he did not favour White as his successor. Sir Edward Bridges reported a conversation he had with Sillitoe in 1949:

> I asked him if he saw a successor in the office, and he said he did not. I mentioned the name of White, whose name had been given to me by Petrie as a coming man. Sillitoe said that White did his job well but that he was not a big enough man for the job.[25]

The two had disagreed over many matters, and when White was appointed DG there was a comprehensive overhaul of MI5 in what became known as the 'October Revolution'. White told his biographer that the 'blueprint' for the post-Sillitoe Security Service 'had been repeatedly revised with Liddell's help during the grim Sillitoe years'.[26] Roger Hollis was appointed DDG.

[25] TNA, CAB 301/30 (Note by Bridges on Meeting with Sillitoe, 8 August 1949). Immediately after this memo, two documents have been removed from the file, a letter from Sillitoe, dated 9 September (Letter Ref: SF 205-ME-14(1)/DG), and a letter to Sillitoe dated 28 September (Letter C/1658), both withheld under the Public Records Act 1958, s. 3(4). This 'weeding' is extremely unusual in the Cabinet Office files, which appear to have been released to the National Archive without being subject to the customary, often over-cautious, MI5 censorship.

[26] Bower (n 1), p. 142. White had collaborated with Andrew Boyle, and Bower had been given Boyle's papers after Boyle's death, so these, in addition to the interviews White granted Bower, provided the basis of his book.

The principal change under the new re-organization was the re-establishment of F Division, reversing the 1946 re-organization which had redefined and attempted to restrict political monitoring to that which was required to secure the defence of the realm. Hollis' wartime counter-Communist section, F2, had in effect emerged as the dominant branch in MI5, arguably a frank acknowledgement of a return to pre-war anti-Bolshevism after years of a slow drift away from the idealism of 1945–6.

Peter Wright described the resurrected F Division as 'the domestic surveillance empire, which principally meant keeping tabs on the Communist Party of Great Britain, and especially its links with the trade union movement'.[27] F1 monitored the Party. F2 was the industrial section, which monitored trade unions. Millicent Bagot ran F3 on international communism. Knight's section, B1K, merged with B1F, and Knight, Thistlethwaite, and their colleagues ran their agents as F4 officers. The files show that by 1955 John Bingham had charge of F4.

Tom Bower describes the return of F Division as 'White's major innovation', and there can be little doubt that White had regarded his return to unashamed political policing as a bold move and had talked of it in such terms. In reality, it was a return to the work pioneered by Maxwell Knight in the 1930s, this time bankrolled with many millions of pounds from the Exchequer: 'White expanded MI5's operations to infiltrate every leftist organisation in Britain including the Labour Party . . . long term "sleepers" would, White hoped, mature and progress up the ranks to work alongside other MI5 sources recruited inside the unions.'[28]

We can now see the significance of what White had revealed to his biographers: Attlee had gone, his Directive had been diluted, and now Sillitoe, Attlee's man, had gone. The Findlater Stewart Report was a fading memory. MI5 had been let off the leash.

[27] P. Wright, *Spycatcher—The Candid Autobiography of a Senior Intelligence Officer* (Toronto, 1987), p. 32.

[28] Bower (n 1), pp. 144–5. For completeness, it should be recorded that B Division became the designation for the new personnel division to which John Marriot was promoted as director. B4 became A Division, with Malcolm Cumming still in charge, and it was as an A Division officer that Peter Wright (in A4A with Hugh Winterborn) so famously bugged and burgled his way across London. Evelyn Grist still presided over 'The Gristery', now known as A2A rather than B4B. Martin Furnival Jones was given C Division; D Division (with Graham Mitchell as director) was the new counter-espionage branch; and the Overseas Division became E Division. That the files indicate that E1 had responsibility for monitoring the remains of the British Fascist movement indicates the Service's lack of interest in right-wing politics.

Bibliography

I. Official Publications

1. Command Papers

Report concerning the Disappearance of Two Former Foreign Office Officials, Cmd 9577, 1955

Statement on the Findings of the Conference of Privy Councillors on Security, Cmd 9715, 1956

Report of the Committee of Privy Councillors appointed to inquire into the Interception of Communications (Chair: Lord Birkett), Cmnd 283, 1957

Report of the Tribunal of Inquiry Appointed to Inquire into Allegations of Improper Disclosure of Information Relating to the Raising of the Bank Rate (Chair: Lord Justice Parker), Cmnd 350, 1958

Report on Security Procedures in the Public Service (Chair: Lord Radcliffe), Cmnd 1681, 1962

Report of the Tribunal of Inquiry Appointed to Inquire into the Vassall Case and Related Matters (Chairman: Viscount Radcliffe), Cmnd 2009, 1963

Lord Denning's Report, Cmnd 2152, 1963

Report of the Royal Commission on Trade Unions and Employers' Associations, 1965–68 (Chairman: Lord Donovan), Cmnd 3623, 1968

Report of the Committee on Privacy (Chairman: Sir Kenneth Younger), Cmnd 5012, 1972

Mitrokhin Inquiry Report (Intelligence and Security Committee), Cm 4764, 1999–2000

2. Parliamentary Papers

Select Committee on the Official Secrets Acts, Report, HC 101 (1938–9).

Committee of Privileges, Report (Captain Ramsey), HC 164 (1939–40)

Committee of Privileges, Report (P. Piratin and T. D. Lucy), HC 353 (1946–7)

Home Affairs Committee, *Special Branch*, HC 71 (1984–5)

Lord Hutton, Report of the Inquiry into the Circumstances Surrounding the Death of Dr David Kelly CMG, HC 247 (2003–4).

Public Administration Committee, *Taming the Prerogative: Strengthening Ministerial Responsibility to Parliament*, HC 422 (2003–4)

Lord Leveson, Report of Inquiry into the Culture, Practices and Ethics of the Press, HC 780 (2012–13)

3. Other

Law Commission, Codification of the Criminal Law: Treason, Sedition and Allied Offences (Working Paper 72, 1977)

Ministry of Labour, *Industrial Relations Handbook* (London, 1961 edn)

II. Books and Pamphlets

Aaronovitch, D., *Party Animals: My Family and other Communists* (London, 2015)

Aldrich, R. J., *GCHQ—The Uncensored Story of Britain's Most Secret Intelligence Agency* (London, 2010)

Andrew, C., *Secret Service: The Making of the British Intelligence Community* (London, 1985)
Andrew, C., *The Defence of the Realm: The Authorised History of MI5* (London, 2009)
Andrews, G., Fishman, N., and Morgan, K., *Opening the Books: Essays on the Social and Cultural History of the British Communist Party* (London, 1995)
Anon, *A Year with the Secret Police* (London, 1956)
Anson, Sir W. R., *Law and Custom of the Constitution*, Vol. II (3rd edn, Oxford, 1907)
Bealey, F., *The Post Office Engineering Union—The History of the Post Office Engineers 1870–1970* (London, 1976)
Beckett, F. and Henke, D., *Marching to the Fault Line: The 1984 Miners' Strike and the Death of Industrial Britain* (London, 2009)
Beckett, F. and Murray, J., *Enemy Within—The Rise and Fall of the British Communist Party* (London, 1995)
Beer, S. H., *Modern British Politics* (London, 1965)
Belknap, M. R., *Cold War Political Justice: The Smith Act, The Communist Party and American Civil Liberties* (Westport, CT, 1977)
Blackstone, Sir W., *Commentaries on the Laws of England*, Vol. 1 (Oxford, 1753)
Blake, N. and Rajak, H., *Wigs and Workers: A History of the Haldane Society of Socialist Lawyers* (London, 1980)
Borovik, G. (ed. and intro. P. Knightley), *The Philby Files, The Secret Life of the Master Spy — KGB Archives Revealed* (London, 1994)
Bower, T., *The Perfect English Spy: Sir Dick White and the Secret War 1935–90* (London, 1995)
Boyle, A., *The Climate of Treason: Five Who Spied for Russia* (London, 1979)
Bradley, A. W., Ewing, K. D., and Knight, C. J. S., *Constitutional and Administrative Law* (17th edn, Harlow, 2018)
Bunyan, T., *The History and Practice of the Political Police in Britain* (London, 1977)
Burgmann, M., *Dirty Secrets—Our ASIO Files* (Sydney, NSW, 2014)
Campbell, D., *Phone-Tappers and the Secret State* (Reports from the *New Statesman* first published between February 1979 and July 1980, updated in January 1981)
Campbell, D. and Connor, S., *On the Record: Surveillance, Computers and Privacy—The Inside Story* (London, 1988)
Catterall, P., *The Macmillan Diaries Vol II: Prime Minister and After, 1957–1966* (London, 2011)
Chitty, J., *Treatise on the Law of the Prerogatives of the Crown* (London, 1822)
Clark, A., *Diaries 1972–1999*, (London, 2010)
Close, F., *Half-Life: The Divided Life of Bruno Pontecorvo* (New York, 2015)
Communist Party of Great Britain, *The British Road to Socialism* (London, 1951)
Crawford, I., *The Profumo Affair—A Crisis in Contemporary Society* (London, 1963)
Crown Prosecution Service, *Prosecution Policy and Guidance* (London, 2016)
Darke, B., *The Communist Technique in Britain* (London, 1952)
Davis, C. J., *Waterfront Revolts, New York and London Dock Workers* (Urbana and Chicago, IL, 2003)
Deacon, R., *A History of British Secret Service* (London, 1985 edn)
de Smith, S. A., *Constitutional and Administrative Law* (2nd edn, Harmondsworth, 1973)
Dicey, A. V., *Introduction to the Study of the Law of the Constitution* (London, 1885)
Dicey, A. V., *Introduction to the Study of the Law of the Constitution* (10th edn by E. C. S. Wade, London, 1959)
Dorrill, S. and Ramsey, R., *Smear! Wilson and the Secret State* (London, 1991)
Ewing, K. D., *Britain and the ILO* (2nd edn, London, 1994)
Ewing, K. D., *Ruined Lives: Blacklisting in the UK Construction Industry* (Liverpool, 2010)
Ewing, K. D. and Gearty, C. A., *Freedom under Thatcher: Civil Liberties in Modern Britain* (Oxford, 1990)

Ewing, K. D. and Gearty, C. A., *The Struggle for Civil Liberties: Political Freedom and the Rule of Law in Britain, 1918–1945* (Oxford, 2001)
Felton, M., *That's Why I Went* (London, 1953)
Felton, M., *What I Saw in Korea* (London, [n.d.])
Fishman, N., *The British Communist Party and the Trade Unions 1933–45* (Aldershot, 1995)
Fitzgerald, P. and Leopold, M., *Stranger on the Line: The Secret History of Phone Tapping* (London, 1987)
Foot, P., *Who Framed Colin Wallace?* (London, 1989)
Foote, A., *The Handbook for Spies* (London, 1949)
Fredman, S. and Morris, S., *The State as Employer—Labour Law in the Public Services* (London, 1989)
Furbank, P. N., *E. M. Forster: A Life* (London, 1977, repr. 2008)
Gallacher, W., *The Case for Communism* (Harmondsworth,1949)
Gaster, J., *Korea—I Saw the Truth* (London, 1952)
Goldstein, J., *The Government of British Trade Unions* (London, 1953)
Graham, B., *Break In: Inside the Soviet Trade Delegation* (London, 1987)
Greaves, C. D., *The Life and Times of James Connolly* (London, 1961)
Griffith, J. A. G., *Judicial Politics since 1920* (Oxford, 1993)
Grunfeld, C., *Modern Trade Union Law* (London, 1966)
Heims, P., *Countering Industrial Espionage* (Leatherhead, 1982)
Hemming, H., *Maxwell Knight, MI5's Greatest Spymaster* (London, 2017)
Hennessy, P., *The Secret State: Preparing for the Worst 1945–2010* (London, 2010)
Hepple, B. A. and O'Higgins, P., *Public Employee Trade Unionism in the United Kingdom: The Legal Framework* (Detroit, MI, 1971)
Hinsley, F. H. and Simkins, C. A. G., *British Intelligence in the Second World War: Vol. 4–Security and Counter Intelligence* (London, 1990)
Hinton, J. and Hyman, R., *Trade Unions and Revolution: The Industrial Politics of the Early British Communist Party* (London, 1975)
Hollingsworth, M. and Norton-Taylor, R., *Blacklist, The Inside Story of Political Vetting* (London, 1988)
Hughes, M., *Spies at Work* (London, 2012)
IADL, *Report on US War Crimes in Korea* (London, 1952)
IRIS, *The Communist Solar System* (London, 1957)
Independent Labour Party, *The 100 versus The State* (London, [n.d.])
Jennings, W. I., *The Law and the Constitution* (1st edn, London, 1933)
Jennings, W. I., *The Law and the Constitution* (5th edn, London, 1959)
Jones, M., *The Secret Police and You* (London, 1956)
Kafka, F., *The Trial* (Harmondsworth, 1975 edn)
Kennedy, L. *The Trial of Stephen Ward* (Harmondsworth, 1965 edn)
Kilmuir, Viscount, *Political Adventure, The Memoirs of the Earl of Kilmuir* (London, 1962)
Knightley, P., *Philby, The Spy Who Betrayed a Generation* (London, 1968)
Knightley, P., *Philby: KGB Masterspy* (London, 1985)
Knightley, P. and Kennedy, C., *An Affair of State: The Profumo Case and the Framing of Stephen Ward* (London, 1987)
Labour Party, *Let us Face the Future* (London, 1945)
Leigh, D., *The Wilson Plot: How the Spycatchers and their American Allies Tried to Overthrow the British Government* (New York, 1988)
Lineman, T., *British Fascism 1918–39, Parties, Ideology and Culture* (Manchester, 2000)
Locke, J., *Two Treaties of Government (A Critical Edition with an Introduction by P Laslett)* (Cambridge, 1960 edn)

Lomas, D. W. B., *An Uneasy Relationship? Intelligence, Security and the Attlee Governments, 1945–1951* (Manchester, 2016)
Lustgarten, L. and Leigh, L., *In from the Cold: National Security and Parliamentary Democracy* (Oxford, 1994)
Mackenzie, Sir George, *Observations upon the 18th Act of the 23rd Parliament of King James the Sixth against Dispositions made in Defraud of Creditors etc* (Edinburgh, 1675)
Macmillan, H., *The Macmillan Diaries II: Prime Minister and After 1957–1966* (ed. and intro., P Catterall) (London, 2012 edn)
Maitland, F. W., *The Constitutional History of England* (Cambridge, 1920)
Martin Lopez, T. and Rowbotham, S., *The Winter of Discontent: Myth, Memory and History* (Liverpool, 2014)
Mayhew, C., *A War of Words: A Cold War Witness* (London, 1998)
Miliband, R., *Parliamentary Socialism: A Study in the Politics of Labour* (London, 1961)
Miliband, R., *The State in Capitalist Society* (London, 1969)
Miliband, R., *Capitalist Democracy in Britain* (Oxford, 1982)
Miller, J., *One Girl's War, Personal Exploits in MI5's Most Secret Station* (Kerry, 1986)
Milne, S., *The Enemy Within: The Secret War against the Miners* (London, 1994, pbk edn 1995),
Morgan, K. O., *Labour in Power 1945–1951* (Oxford, 1984)
Morrison of Lambeth, Lord, *Government and Parliament* (3rd edn, London, 1964)
NCCL, *The Strange Case of Major Vernon* (London, 1938)
NCCL, *Political Discrimination in the Civil Service* (London, 1948)
NCCL (Civil Service Branch), *The Purge* (London, 1948)
NCCL, *The Case of Dr Cort* (London, [n.d.])
NCCL (Press Freedom Committee), *The Press and the War* (London, [n.d.])
Newsam, F., *The Home Office* (Oxford, 1954)
O'Higgins, P., *Censorship in Britain* (London, 1972)
O'Higgins, P., *Cases and Materials on Civil Liberties* (London, 1980)
Paige, B., Leitch, D., and Knightley, P. (Intro., J. Le Carré), *Philby the Spy Who Betrayed a Generation* (London, 1968)
Pelling, H., *The British Communist Party: A Historical Profile* (London, 1958)
Penrose, B. and Courtiour, R., *The Pencourt File* (London, 1978)
Philby, K., *My Silent War: The Autobiography of a Spy* (London, 1968)
Philby, R. (with H. Peake and M. Lyubimov), *The Private Life of Kim Philby* (London, 1999)
Pimlott, B., *Harold Wilson* (London, 1992)
Pincher, C., *Inside Story: A Documentary of the Pursuit of Power* (London, 1978)
Pincher, C., *Their Trade is Treachery* (London, 1981)
Pincher, C., *Too Secret Too Long* (London, 1984)
Pincher, C., *The Truth about Dirty Tricks, From Harold Wilson to Margaret Thatcher* (London, 1992)
Pincher, C., *Treachery, Betrayal, Blunders, and Cover Ups: Six Decades of Espionage* (Edinburgh and London, 2011)
Pincher, C., *Dangerous to Know: A Life* (London, 2014)
Pritt, D. N., *Star Spangled Shadow* (London, 1947)
Pritt, D. N., *New Light in Korea* (London, 1951)
Pritt, D. N., *Spies and Informers in the Witness Box* (London, 1958)
Pritt, D. N., *The Labour Government, 1945–51* (London, 1963)
Pritt, D. N., *Autobiography of DN Pritt, Part One, From Right to Left* (London, 1965)
Pritt, D. N., *Autobiography of DN Pritt, Part Two, Brasshats and Bureaucrats* (London, 1966)

Pritt, D. N., *Autobiography of DN Pritt, Part Three, The Defence Accuses* (London, 1966)
Randle, M. and Pottle, P., *The Blake Escape: How We Freed George Blake and Why We Did It* (London, 1989)
Renton, D., *Fascism, Anti-Fascism and Britain in the 1940s* (London, 2000)
Rimington, S., *Open Secret: The Autobiography of the Former Director-General of MI5* (London, 2002 edn)
Roberts, A., *A History of the English-Speaking Peoples since 1900* (London, 2006)
Robertson, G., *Stephen Ward was Innocent, OK: The Case for Overturning His Conviction* (London, 2013)
Robson, W. A., *Justice in Administrative Law* (London, 1947)
Rolph, C. H., *All Those in Favour? The ETU Trial* (London, 1962)
Rusbridger, J., *The Intelligence Game: Illusions and Delusions of International Espionage* (London, 1989)
Rust, W., *The Story of the Daily Worker* (London, 1949)
Rust, W., *The Story of the Daily Worker* (London, 2010 edn)
Samson, A. W., *I Spied Spies* (London, 1965)
Scaffardi, S., *Fire under the Carpet: Working for Civil liberties in the 1930s* (London, 1986)
Schneer, J., *Labour's Conscience: The Labour Left, 1945–51* (London, 1988)
Scott, H., *Scotland Yard* (London, 1954)
Seaman, D. and Mather, J. S., *The Great Spy Scandal: Inside Story of Burgess and Maclean* (London, 1955)
Sherman, T. C., *State Violence and Punishment in India* (London and New York, 2010)
Short, E., *Whip to Wilson: The Crucial Years of Labour Government* (London, 1989)
Sillitoe, P., *Cloak without Dagger* (London, 1955)
Simpson, A. W. B., *In the Highest Degree Odious* (Oxford, 1992)
Smith, D. and Chamberlain, P., *Blacklisted: The Secret War between Big Business and Union Activists* (2nd edn, London, 2016)
Smith, M. (ed.), *The Secret Agent's Bedside Reader: A Compendium of Spy Writing* (London, 2014)
Stammers, N., *Civil Liberties in Britain During the Second World War* (London, 1983)
Street, H., *Freedom, the Individual and the Law* (Harmondsworth, 1963)
Swartz, M., *The Union of Democratic Control in British Politics during the First World War* (Oxford, 1971)
Thompson, E. P, *The Struggle for a Free Press* (London, 1952)
Thompson, E. P., *Writing by Candlelight* (London, 1980)
Trahair, R. C. S. and Miller, R. L., *Encyclopaedia of Cold War Espionage, Spies and Secret Operations* (Westport, CT, 2004)
Wade, E. C. S. and Phillips, G. G., *Constitutional Law* (5th edn, London, 1955)
Wade, E. C. S. and Phillips, G. G., *Constitutional Law* (6th edn, London, by E. C. S. Wade, 1960).
Wade, H. W. R., *Constitutional Fundamentals* (London, 1980)
Walker, M., *The National Front* (2nd edn, Glasgow, 1978)
Walker, S., *In Defense of American Liberties: A History of the ACLU* (New York, 1990)
Weiler, P., *British Labour and the Cold War* (Stanford, 1988)
Werner, R., *Sonya's Report: Fascinating Autobiography of One of Russia's Most Remarkable Secret Agents* (London, 1991)
West, N., *A Matter of Trust* (London, 1982)
West, N., *MI5* (London, 1987 edn)
West, N., *Molehunt* (London, 1987)

West, N. and Tsarev, O., *The Crown Jewels: The Secrets at the Heart of the KGB Archives* (London, 1998)
West, R., *The Meaning of Treason* (various editions, including London, 1952 and Harmondsworth, 1965)
West, R., *A Train of Powder* (London, 1955)
West, R., *The Vassall Affair* (London, 1963)
Wigham, E. L., *From Humble Petition to Militant Action: History of the Civil and Public Services Association* (London, 1980)
Williams, D. G. T., *Not in the Public Interest—The Problem of Security in Democracy* (London, 1965)
Wilson, G., *Cases and Materials on Constitutional and Administrative Law* (Cambridge, 1966)
Winnington, A., *I Saw the Truth in Korea* (London, 1950)
Wolf, M. (with A. McElvoy), *Spymaster: The Man Who Waged a Secret War against the West* (London, 1997)
Wood, N., *Communism and British Intellectuals* (New York, 1959)
Wright, P., *Spycatcher—The Candid Autobiography of a Senior Intelligence Officer* (Toronto, 1987)
Wyatt, W., *The Peril in Our Midst* (London, 1956)
Zuckerman, A. A. S., *Civil Procedure* (London, 2003)

III. Book Chapters and Articles

Anon, 'The Appeal of Aloysius Lincoln Gordon' [1963] *Crim L R* 600
Bingham, Lord, 'The Rule of Law' [2007] 66 *CLJ* 67
Bontecou, E., 'The English Policy as to Communists and Fascists in the Civil Service' (1951) 51 *Columbia Law Review* 564
Cairns, D. A. S., *Hubert Lister Parker, Baron Parker of Waddington, 1900–1972* (Dictionary of National Biography, Oxford).
Carrier, D., 'The Lawyer Who Fought Franco and some Over-Charging Builders' (2007) *Camden New Journal*, 20 July
Clapson, M., 'The Rise and Fall of Monica Felton: British Town Planner and Peace Activist, 1930s to 1950s' (2015) 30 *Planning Perspectives* 211
Creighton, W. B., 'The ILO and Freedom of Association in the UK', in K. D. Ewing, C. A. Gearty, and B. A. Hepple (eds), *Human Rights and Labour Law—Essays for Paul O'Higgins* (London, 1994)
Deery, P., 'The Dove Flies East: Whitehall, Warsaw and the 1950 World Peace Congress' (2002) 48 *Australian Journal of Politics and History* 449
Dorril, S., 'Gone but not Forgotten—Stanley Mayne' (1990) 19 *Lobster Magazine*
Dowd, V., 'The Spies in a Suburban Bungalow', *BBC News*, 14 November 2014
Duxbury, N., 'Lord Radcliffe Out of Time' [2010] 69 *CLJ* 41
Ede, J. Chuter, 'Parliament and the Liberty of the Subject' (1947) 1 *Parliamentary Affairs* 10
Ewing, K. D., 'The State and Industrial Relations—*Collective Laissez Faire* Revisited' (1998) 5 *Historical Studies in Industrial Relations* 1
Ewing, K. D., '*The Law and the Constitution*: Manifesto of the Progressive Party' (2004) 67 *MLR* 716
Ewing, K. D., 'The Cold War, Civil Liberties and the House of Lords', in T. Campbell, K. D. Ewing, and A. Tomkins (eds), *The Legal Protection of Human Rights—Sceptical Essays* (Oxford, 2011)

Ewing, K. D., 'The Resilience of the Political Constitution' (2013) 12 *German Law Journal* 2013

Ewing, K. D. and Gearty, C. A., 'History of a Dog's Dinner: The Police Bill', *London Review of Books*, 6 February 1997

Ewing, K. D., Mahoney, J., and Moretta, A., 'Surveillance and the Liberal State' (2013) UK Const L Blog, 16 June

Ewing, K. D., Mahoney, J., and Moretta, A., 'Tinker, Tailor, Lawyer, Spy?' (2015) 69 *Socialist Lawyer* 18

Ewing, K. D., Mahoney, J., and Moretta, A., 'Civil Liberties and the Korean War' (2018) 81 *MLR* 395

G. L. W., 'The Trial of Dr Ward' [1963] *Crim L R* 597

Goldsworthy, J., 'Legislative Sovereignty and the Rule of Law', in T. Campbell, K. D. Ewing, and A. Tomkins (eds), *Sceptical Essays on Human Rights* (Oxford, 2010)

Goodman, M. S. and Pincher, C., 'Clement Attlee, Percy Sillitoe and the Security Aspects of the Fuchs' Case' (2005) 19 *Contemporary British History* 67

Hennessey, P. and Brownfeld, G., 'Britain's Cold War Security Purge: The Origins of Positive Vetting' (1982) 25 *Historical Journal* 965

Hope, J. G., 'Surveillance or Collusion? Maxwell Knight, MI5 and the British Fascisti' (1994) 9 *Intelligence and National Security* 651

Jackson, D. C., 'Individual Rights and National Security' (1957) 20 *MLR* 364

Khan, S., 'The Left's Favourite Tories: David Maxwell Fyfe', *New Statesman*, 6 October 2011

Laski H. J., 'The Growth of Administrative Discretion' (1923) 1 *Public Administration* 92

Lomas, D. W. B., 'Labour Ministers, Intelligence and Domestic Anti-Communism 1945–1951' (2013) 12 *Journal of Intelligence History* 113

Lomas, D. W. B., '"... the Defence of the Realm and Nothing Else": Sir Findlater Stewart, Labour Ministers and the Security Service' (2015) 30 Intelligence and National Security 793

Maguire, T. J., 'Counter-Subversion in Early Cold War Britain: The Official Committee on Communism (Home), the Information Research Department, and State–Private Networks' (2015) 30 *Intelligence and National Security* 637

Mahoney, J., 'Civil Liberties in Britain during the Cold War' (1989) 33 *American Journal of Legal History* 53

Mahoney, J., 'Constitutionalism, the Rule of Law and the Cold War', in T. Campbell, K. D. Ewing, and A. Tomkins (eds), *The Legal Protection of Human Rights: Sceptical Essays* (Oxford, 2011)

Morrison, H., 'The Phone Talks I Would Tap', *Empire News and Chronicle*, 30 June 1957

Raz, J., 'The Rule of Law and its Virtue' (1977) 93 *LQR* 195

Samuels, A., 'Criminal Law Appeal Act, 1964' (1964) 27 *MLR* 568

Smith, J., 'The MacDonald Discussion Group: A Communist Conspiracy in Britain's Cold War Film and Theatre Industry—or MI5's Honey Pot?' (2015) 35 *History Journal of Film, Radio, and Television* 454

Spencer, M. and Spencer, J., 'The Judge as "Political Advisor": Behind the Scenes at the National Industrial Relations Court' (2006) 33 *JLS* 199

Thompson, D., 'The Committee of 100 and the Official Secrets Act, 1911' [1963] *PL* 20

Wade, E. C. S., 'Seditious Libel and the Press' (1948) 64 *LQR* 203

Wade, H. W. R., 'Procedure and Prerogative in Public Law' (1985) 101 *LQR* 180

West, R., 'The Agent the Soviets Wanted Caught', in A. Dulles (ed.), *Great True Spy Stories* (New York, 1968)

White, L. C., 'Political Discrimination', *Civil Liberty*, May 1948

Wilson, A. N., 'England, his England', *The Spectator*, 17 August 1990

IV. Unpublished Dissertations

Ewing, K. D., *The Legal Regulation of Trade Union Political Activities* (Ph.D. Dissertation, University of Cambridge, 1980, Cambridge University Library)

Mahoney, J., *British Civil Liberties and the Cold War: 1945–1956* (Ph.D. Dissertation, University of Cambridge, 1990, Cambridge University Library)

Moretta, A., *Benchmarking Workplace Rights* (Ph.D. Dissertation, University of Liverpool, 2019, Liverpool University Library)

Index

Note: *For the benefit of digital users, indexed terms that span two pages (e.g., 52–53) may, on occasion, appear on only one of those pages.*